Mount Holyoke College

Quinquennial catalogue of officers and students of Mount Holyoke College

1837-1895

Mount Holyoke College

Quinquennial catalogue of officers and students of Mount Holyoke College
1837-1895

ISBN/EAN: 9783337284114

Printed in Europe, USA, Canada, Australia, Japan

Cover: Foto ©Andreas Hilbeck / pixelio.de

More available books at **www.hansebooks.com**

OF OFFICERS AND STUDENTS OF

MOUNT HOLYOKE COLLEGE,

SOUTH HADLEY, MASS.

1837-1895.

PUBLISHED BY
MOUNT HOLYOKE COLLEGE,
1895.

CONTENTS.

Notes and explanations
Officers, 1837–1895
    Trustees, list of
        Officers of the Board
    Principals of the Seminary
    Presidents of the College
    Teachers
    Superintendents of Domestic Department
    Stewards
    Non-resident Lecturers
Students, class-lists 1837–1895
Index of Married Names
Index of Names of Students
Statistics:—
    Table of attendance by classes
    Table of attendance from States, Territories, etc.
    Summaries of Students from 1837–1895
Addenda:—
    Additions and corrections
    Students not heard from
    Constitution and officers of National Alumnæ Association
    Branch Associations

NOTES AND EXPLANATIONS.

Lists of students' names with home residences when at the Seminary or College are made from the annual catalogues.

Names beginning with M', Mac, Mc, or St., are arranged as if these words were not abbreviated.

When no State is named, Massachusetts is understood.

Non-graduates are classed in the last year of their connection with the Seminary or College.

Present residences are in *italics*. When residence and post-office address are not the same, preference is given to the latter.

The abbreviation "m." denotes *married*; "d.," *died*.

Clergymen, lawyers, and physicians, when reported as such, are indicated by the titles, Rev., Esq., or M.D. A record of other titles is not attempted.

The letter [C.] indicates College Classical Course; [S.]. Scientific Course; [L.], Literary Course.

Items received too late for insertion in their places will be found in the Addenda. Probably many unreported changes have occurred since compilation began.

Notice of any errors will be gladly received. Information is solicited concerning any whose record is not complete.

An early report of changes in any record is desired.

A copy of the annual catalogue will be sent each year to any Holyoke student who will each year report her address.

All communications may be addressed, *Registrar, Mt. Holyoke College, South Hadley, Mass.*

Grateful acknowledgment is made to all who have co-operated in furnishing or obtaining needed information, or contributed in any way to the preparation of this Catalogue.

TRUSTEES.

NOTE.—Of those in office the present residence is given; of others, that at the time of election.

	Elected.	Died or Resigned.
Hon. William Bowdoin, South Hadley Falls	1836	1856
Rev. John Todd, D.D., Northampton	1836	1836
Rev. Joseph D. Condit, South Hadley	1836	d. 1847
Hon. David Choate, Essex	1836	1843
Hon. Samuel Williston, Easthampton	1836	1836
Rev. William Tyler, South Hadley Falls	1836	1856
Rev. Roswell Hawks, Cummington	1836	d. 1870
Hon. Joseph Avery, Conway	1836	d. 1855
Andrew W. Porter, Esq., Monson	1836	d. 1877
Rev. Heman Humphrey, D.D., Amherst	1836	1846
Rev. Edward Hitchcock, D.D., LL.D., Amherst	1836	d. 1864
Hon. Daniel Safford, Boston	1837	d. 1856
Hon. Samuel Williston, Easthampton	1839	1862
Rev. E. Y. Swift, Northampton	1847	1874
Rev. Samuel Harris, D.D., LL.D., Conway	1848	1856
Rev. Edward N. Kirk, D.D., Boston	1856	d. 1874
Hon. Edward Southworth, West Springfield	1856	d. 1869
Abner Kingman, Esq., Boston	1856	d. 1880
Austin Rice, Esq., Conway	1858	d. 1880
Rev. Theron H. Hawks, D.D., Springfield	1858	1861
Rev. Hiram Mead, D.D., South Hadley	1859	1873
Rev. William S. Tyler, D.D., LL.D., Amherst	1862	
Ariel Parish, M.A., Springfield	1864	1865
Sidney E. Bridgman, Esq., Northampton	1865	
Rev. John M. Greene, D.D., Lowell	1866	1875
Henry F. Durant, Esq., Boston	1867	1879
A. Lyman Williston, M.A., Northampton	1867	
Rev. Nathaniel G. Clark, D.D., LL.D., Boston	1868	
Hon. William Claflin, LL.D., Boston	1869	1894
Edward Hitchcock, M.A., M.D., Amherst	1869	
Rev. Julius H. Seelye, D.D., LL.D., Amherst	1872	
Hon. Edmund H. Sawyer, Easthampton	1873	d. 1879
Rev. John R. Herrick, D.D., South Hadley	1875	1879
Francis A. Walker, LL.D., New Haven, Ct.	1876	1886
Rev. John L. R. Trask, Springfield	1879	
Henry D. Hyde, Esq., Boston	1880	1883

OFFICERS.

	Elected.	Died or Resigned.
Charles A. Young, Ph.D., LL.D., Princeton, N. J.	1880	
Rev. William DeLoss Love, D.D., South Hadley	1881	1892
Rev. William M. Taylor, D.D., LL.D., New York	1881	d. 1895
John H. Southworth, Esq., Springfield	1881	1887
G. Henry Whitcomb, M.A., Worcester	1881	
Elizabeth Blanchard, M.A., *ex officio*	1884	1889
Mrs. A. Lyman Williston, Northampton	1884	
Mrs. Helen M. (French) Gulliver, Somerville	1886	1892
Alonzo S. Kimball, Ph.D., Worcester	1888	
Charles E. Garman, M.A., Amherst	1888	
Mrs. Elizabeth S. Mead, M.A., *ex officio*	1890	
Rev. Judson Smith, D.D., Boston	1892	
Pres. Merrill E. Gates, LL.D., Amherst	1892	
Miss Sarah P. Eastman, Wellesley	1892	
Mrs. Michael Burnham, St. Louis, Mo.	1892	
Miss Charlotte Morrill, Brooklyn, N. Y.	1892	
William Skinner, Holyoke	1893	
Rev. Henry A. Stimson, D.D., New York City	1894	
George S. Edgell, New York City	1894	

PRESIDENTS OF THE BOARD.

Rev. John Todd, D.D.	1836	1836
Rev. William Tyler	1837	1858
Rev. Roswell Hawks,	1858	1858
Rev. Edward N. Kirk, D.D.	1858	d. 1874
Rev. William S. Tyler, D.D., LL.D.	1874	1894
Rev. Judson Smith, D.D.	1894	

SECRETARIES.

Rev. Joseph D. Condit	1836	d. 1847
Rev. E. Y. Swift	1848	1850
Rev. Hiram Mead, D.D.	1850	1869
Rev. John M. Greene, D.D.	1869	1874
Edward Hitchcock, M.A., M.D.	1874	1880
Rev. John L. R. Trask, D.D.	1880	1882
Rev. William DeLoss Love, D.D.	1882	1889
Rev. John L. R. Trask, D.D.	1889	

TREASURERS.

Hon. Samuel Williston	1836	1836
Hon. William Bowdoin	1836	1856
Hon. Samuel Williston	1856	1862
Andrew W. Porter, Esq.	1862	1873
A. Lyman Williston, M.A.	1873	

PRINCIPALS OF THE SEMINARY.

	Class.	Term.
Mary Lyon	—	1837–49
Mary C. Whitman	'39	'49–50
Mary W. Chapin, Acting Principal	'43	'50–52
Mary W. Chapin	'43	'52–65

TEACHERS.

	Class.	Term.
Sophia D. (Hazen) Stoddard, Acting Principal	'41	'65-67
Helen M. French	'57	'67-72
Julia E. Ward	'57	'72-83
Elizabeth Blanchard, M.A.	'58	'83-88

ASSOCIATE PRINCIPALS.

Eunice Caldwell	—	'37-38
Abigail Moore	'38	'42-46
Mary C. Whitman	'39	'42-49
Sophia D. Hazen	'41	'49-50
Sophia Spofford	'46	'52-55
Emily Jessup	'47	'55-62
Julia M. Tolman	'48	'58-60
Catharine Hopkins	'54	'60-65
Mary Ellis, M.A.,	'55	'67-72
Julia E. Ward	'57	'67-72
Elizabeth Blanchard, M.A.	'58	'72-83
Anna C. Edwards, M.A.	'59	'72-88

PRESIDENTS OF MOUNT HOLYOKE SEMINARY AND COLLEGE.

Elizabeth Blanchard, M.A., Acting President	'58	'88-89
Mary A. Brigham, elected President, '89; d. '89	'50	
Louise F. Cowles, M.A., Acting President	'66	'89-90
Mrs. Elizabeth S. Mead, M.A.	—	'90-

PRESIDENT OF MOUNT HOLYOKE COLLEGE.

Mrs. Elizabeth S. Mead, M.A.	—	'93-

TEACHERS.

Lucy M. Ainsworth	'49	'49-51
Paulina Avery	'50	'52-53
Laura W. Ayer	'54	'55-56
Hannah O. Bailey	'39	'44-45
Elizabeth D. Ballantine	'57	'60-69
Elisabeth M. Bardwell	'66	'66-
Mary E. Barker	'46	'46-46
H. Augusta Belcher	'60	'60-61
Mary J. Belcher	—	'55-58
Mary A. Berry	'85	'85-92
Elizabeth Blanchard, M.A.	'58	'58-91
Mary E. Blodgett	'70	'75-76
Emily W. S. Bowdoin	'49	'49-50
Sarah Bowen	'64	'70-75
Susan Bowen	'64	'68-75
Ellen P. Bowers	'58	'61-
Martha E. E. Bradford	'69	'71-76
Mary C. Bradford, Ph.B.	'71	'80-
Ella T. Bray	'83	'84-85
Flora Bridges, M.A.,	—	'87-92
Mary A. Brigham	'50	'55-58

TEACHERS.

	Class.	Term.
Sarah Brigham	'38	'38–39
Mary P. Bronson	'58	'58–59
Mary Q. Brown	'49	'49–52
Susan N. Brown	'51	'51–52
Marie F. Browne	'44	'44–45
Laura A. Buckingham	'73	'73–75
Elizabeth Burt	'51	'55–57
Hettie P. Carpenter, B.A.	—	'88–90
Alice Carter, Ph.D.	'87	'88–91
Martha R. Chapin	'42	'42–46
Mary W. Chapin	'43	'43–65
S. Elizabeth Chapin	'54	'54–55
M. Elizabeth Childs	'56	'59–70
Cornelia M. Clapp, Ph.D.	'71	'72–
Caroline W. Clark	'59	'61–66
Martha J. Clark	'86	'86–87
Susan M. Clary	'63	'63–77
Harriet M. Cooley	'53	'53–56
Rebecca Corwin, M.A., S.T.B.	—	'94–
S. Kate Cowan, B.A.	—	'89–90
Lydia G. (Bailey) (Rogers) Cordley	'45	'81–82
Louise F. Cowles, M.A.	'66	'67–
Harriet M. Curtis	—	'91–92
Lucy M. Curtis	'44	'44–49
Mary S. Cutler	'75	'76–78
Annie Dearborn	'65	'66–71
Alice E. Dixon, B.A.	—	'89–91
Martha C. Dole	'41	'43–44
Susan S. Driver	'67	'67–68
Elizabeth Earle	'60	'60–67
Anna C. Edwards, M.A.	'59	'59–92
Lucy J. Ellis	'62	'75–76
Mary Ellis, M.A.	'55	'55–72
Sarah A. Emmons	'53	'55–56
Mary A. Evans	'60	'60–68
Fidelia Fiske	'42	'42–43
Fidelia Fiske	'42	'59–64
Rebecca W. Fiske	'46	'46–49
Helen C. Flint	'80	'81–82
Helen C. Flint, B.A.	'91	'91–93
Mary M. Foote	'47	'58–59
Nancy A. Foote	'44	'44–45
Mary J. Forbes	'65	'65–66
Helen M. French	'57	'57–72
Ann Eliza Fritcher	'57	'59–63
Sarah A. Gilbert	'49	'51–53
Helena F. Giles	'71	'76–77
Anna C. Gilman	'49	'49–50
Martha C. Goldthwaite	'84	'89–90
Julia A. Goodhue	'64	'66–68
Alice W. Gordon, M.A.	'67	'68–70
Mary Graham, Ph.B.	—	'91–92

TEACHERS.

	Class.	Term.
Mary E. Graves	'44	'45-46
Adaline E. Green, Ph.B.	'67	'71-
Harriet A. Hamilton	—	'92-93
Susan F. Hawks	'42	'42-43
Eliza C. Haskell	'56	'59-64
Mary Haynes	'64	'64-68
Frances M. Hazen	'63	'65-
Sophia D Hazen	'41	'41-50
Persis D. Hewitt	'76	'78-79
Martha L. Hills, B.A.	—	'93-
Harriet A. Hinsdale	'44	'55-57
Elizabeth P. Hodgdon	'69	'70-75
Georgiana Hodgkins	'85	'88-91
Amanda A. Hodgman	—	'37-39
Lucy J Holmes	'58	'58-81
Lucy J. Holmes	'58	'86-88
Ann M. Hollister	'45	'45-47
Anna M. Hood	'69	'69-72
Henrietta E. Hooker, Ph.D.	'73	'73-
Catharine Hopkins	'54	'54-65
Ada L. Howard	'53	'58-61
Mary H Humphrey	'43	'44-46
Helen Humphrey	'39	'39-41
Ellen Hunt	'54	'54-55
Marion E. Hurlbut	'89	'93-94
Myra M. Jenkins	'64	'64-66
Sabrina Jennings	'43	'47-48
Emily Jessup	'47	'47-60
Harriet Johnson	'46	'48-52
Mary L. Judd, Ph.B.	'80	'86-91
Marcia A. Keith, B.S.	'83	'85-
C. Belle Kenney, B.S.	—	'88-89
Marietta Kies, M.A.	'81	'81-91
Mary A Kimball	'53	'55-56
Ella A. Knapp, M.A.	—	'90-
Mary F. Leach, B.S.	'80	'93-
Catharine E. Lee	'54	'54-56
Jane E. Lemassena	'57	'57-58
Sarah D. Locke	'50	'50-68
Louisa A. Long	'53	'53-54
Eliza A. Lyon	'56	'56-58
Lucy T. Lyon	'40	'41-46
Isabella G. Mack	'75	'75-86
Margaret Mann	'42	'44-48
Maria E. Mason	'49	'49-50
Catharine McKeen	—	'52-56
Phebe F. McKeen	—	'53-56
Mary L. McMasters, B.S.	—	'91-92
Harriette A. Melvin	'56	'56-58
Helen E. Melvin	'79	'82-83
Sarah H. Melvin	'62	'70-
Caroline H. Merrick	'49	'49-50

TEACHERS.

	Class.	Term.
Mary B. Metcalf	'46	'47-48
Caroline Miles, Ph.D.	—	'92-93
Abigail Moore	'38	'38-46
Vida F. Moore, Ph.B.	—	'93-
Ann R. Mowry	'42	'42-43
Mary A. Munson	'48	'48-57
Mary J. Murdock	'50	'50-51
Martha L. Newcomb	'48	'50-51
Lura E. Newhall	'64	'64-66
Hannah Noble	'58	'61-
Mary O. Nutting	'52	'70-
Olive L. Parmelee	'61	'62-68
Anna A. Parsons	'70	'76-79
Ellen C. Parsons, M.A.	'63	'83-85
Roxana R. Parsons	'41	'41-45
Sarah P. Parsons	'66	'69-71
Sarah G. Patteson	—	'89-93
Elizabeth K. Peabody	—	'66-67
Helen Peabody	'48	'48-53
Mary F. Phinney	'52	'52-55
Clara C. Pond	'57	'58-64
Catharine A. Porter	'44	'44-45
Elizabeth B. Prentiss	'62	'66-
Lucinda T. Prescott	'53	'53-56
Florence Purington	'86	'87-
Louise Fitz-Randolph	'72	'92-
Harriet E. Reed	'64	'65-67
Susan Reed	'39	'39-44
Lois W. Rice	'45	'53-54
Lydia G. (Bailey) Rogers	'45	'50-52
Laura A Rose	—	'89-90
Elizabeth I. Samuel, M.D.	'80	'80-84
Helen M. Savage	'68	'68-70
Emily A. Scott	'52	'52-53
Hannah C. Scott	'43	'48-49
Martha C. Scott	'45	'45-55
Harriet E. Sessions	'56	'57-88
Lydia A. Sessions	'56	'56-59
Lydia W. Shattuck	'51	'51-89
Adelaide Sherman	—	'87-88
Lillie L. Sherman	'80	'80-84
Elizabeth Slater, M.A.	—	'92-
Arma A. Smith, B.A.	'91	'94-
Eliza Smith	'51	'51-52
Mary W. Smith	—	'37-38
Matilda W Smith	'58	'59-60
Minerva Smith	'54	'55-58
S. Effie Smith, B.S.	'86	'86-
Sophie A. Smith	—	'84-86
Sophia Spofford	'46	'51-55
Sophia Spofford	'46	'71-72
M. Ella Spooner	'72	'72-84

TEACHERS.

	Class.	Term.
Sarah A. Start .	'52	'52–58
Mary F. Stearns .	'53	'57–59
Marion H. Sterns .	—	'90–94
Alice P. Stevens, B.A.	'86	'92–
Clara F. Stevens, Ph.M.	'81	'81–
Louise P. Stevens .	'59	'59–61
Mary M. Stevens . . .	'42	'42–48
Sophia D. (Hazen) Stoddard .	'41	'64–67
Sarah D. (Locke) Stow . .	'59	'77–80
Sarah D. (Locke) Stow .	'59	'82–89
Calista A. Streeter .	'57	'57–59
Abbie L. Sweetser .	'74	'75–87
Gertrude Sykes . . .	'53	'53–58
Esther E. (Munsell) Thompson	'59	'69–70
Persis G. Thurston . .	'45	'45–47
Elizabeth Titcomb .	'50	'50–53
Mary Titcomb .	'50	'50–56
Jane C. Tolman .	'51	'58–64
Julia M. Tolman .	'48	'51–60
Susan L. Tolman .	'45	'45–48
Sarah H. Torrey .	'39	'39–43
Mary C. Townsend .	'62	'67–80
Frances V. Turner .	'58	'58–59
Jessie Usher .	'57	'60–61
Susan M. Waite .	'55	'56–58
Adelia C. Walker .	'51	'52–53
Louise B. Wallace .	—	'93–
Julia E. Ward . .	'57	'57–83
Delia H. Warner .	'74	'75–78
Frances E. Washburn .	'69	'70–72
Ann R. Webster .	'42	'43–45
Aurilla P. Wellman .	—	'48–51
Annie M. Wells .	'67	'70–74
Caroline Wentworth .	'53	'53–55
Mary C. Whitman .	'39	'39–50
Caroline L. White .	'71	'72–74
Adeline H. Willcox .	'52	'53–54
Emily S. Wilson .	'61	'61–63
Clara W. Wood .	'73	'73–
Persis C. Woods . .	'38	'38–39
Amelia C. Woodward . .	'58	'59–60
Katherine S. Woodward, B.A.	—	'89–90
Sarah A. Worden . . .	—	'89–
Catharine A. Wright ·	'42	'42–45
Mary E. Yale . . .	'48	'49–50
Caroline R. Yates . .	'51	'51–52

PHYSICIANS AND TEACHERS OF PHYSIOLOGY.

Mary A. B. Homer, M.D.	—	'60–64
Emily N. Belden, M.D. .	—	'64–68
Lucy M. Southmayd, M.D.	—	'68–70
Emma H. Callender, M.D.	—	'69–73

TEACHERS.

	Class.	Term.
Charlotte W. Ford, M.D.	'62	'73-74
Olive J. Emerson, M.D.	'65	'74-76
Adaline D. H. Kelsey, M.D.	'68	'76-78
Adelaide A. Richardson, M.D.	—	'78-82
Fanny G. Heron, M.D.	—	'82-85
Juliet E. Marchant, M.D.	—	'85-86
Elizabeth L. Peck, M.D.	'76	'86-88
Juliet E. Marchant, M.D.	—	'88-89
Mary H. Cotton, M.D.	—	'89-90
Seraph Frissell, M.D.	'69	'90-91
Mary C. Lowell, M.D.	—	'91-

VOCAL MUSIC.

	Class.	Term.
Frances M. Atwood	'30	'38-39
Deborah E. N. Bates	'40	'39-40
Amelia F. Dickinson	'44	'41-44
Harriet Hawes	'48	'44-48
Sarah F. Woodhull	—	'48-49
Emily W. S. Bowdoin	'49	'49-50
Lucy C. Mills	'52	'50-52
Martha A. Bailey	'53	'52-53
Catharine E. Lee	'54	'53-54
Elizabeth W. Shepard	'57	'54-55
Charlotte Morgan	'56	'55-56
Lucinda D Hodge	'60	'57-60
Fanny M. Hidden	'62	'60-62
Eliza Wilder	—	'62-66
Almeda N. Tirrell	'66	'66-69
Mary P. Burgess	'69	'69-71
Abby A. Wilder	—	'71-72
Emma A. Ide	—	'72-73
Annie S. Wilson	—	'73-75

VOCAL AND INSTRUMENTAL MUSIC.

	Class.	Term.
Charlotte M. Steele	—	'75-86
Ada J. Mac Vicar	—	'78-80
Eva F. Pike	—	'81-85
Perry P. Weed	—	'84-85
Edmund Severn, Jr.	—	'85-86
Florence E. Balch	—	'85-92
Florence Grinnell	—	'86-87
Susan M. Moore	—	'87-91
Benjamin C. Blodgett, Mus. Doc., Director	—	'91-94
Laura E. Sawin	—	'91-92
Margarethe Von Mitzlaff	—	'92-94
Olive Van Wagner	—	'92-93
Emma Bates, B.M.	—	'92-93
Marion Gale	—	'93-04
Alfred M. Fletcher	—	'93-04
Alfred M. Fletcher, Director	—	'04-
Harriet L. Ellsworth	—	'04-
Louis Coenen	—	'04-

TEACHERS.

FRENCH.

	Class.	Term.
Abigail Moore	'38	'37-46
J. A. Lucie Robinson	'48	'46-48
Mary A. Munson	'48	'48-50
Eleanor Kevney	—	'50-51
Gertrude de Bruyn Kops	—	'51-52
Sarah J. Gillette	—	'53-54
Mary E. Peabody	'61	'59-61
Lydia Richards	'66	'63-66

FRENCH AND GERMAN.

Caroline de Maupassant	—	'72-73
Valerie Dietz	—	'73-75
Margarethe Vitzthum von Eckstadt	—	'75-85
Marie Gylam	—	'85-86
Anna E. Engelhardt	—	'86-91
Margarethe Vitzthum von Eckstadt	—	'87-
Frau Marie Emilie W. Sommer	—	'92-93
Katherine E. Sihler	—	'92-
Mary E. Hartley	—	'93-

PHYSICAL CULTURE.

Eliza S. Clark	—	'91-93
Frances S. Sanborn	—	'93-94
Nellie A. Spore	—	'94-

ASSISTANT PUPILS.

Abigail Moore	—	'37-38
Persis C. Woods	—	'37-38
Susan Reed	—	'37-39
Martha A. Leach	—	'38-39
Lucy T. Lyon	—	'39-40
Rachel Blanchard	—	'39-40
Maria K. Whitney	—	'39-40
Sarah M. Paine	—	'40-41
Mary M. Stevens	—	'40-42
Julia Hyde	—	'40-42
Lucy M. Curtis	—	'42-43
Caroline Avery	—	'44-46
Caroline H. Merrick	—	'48-49
Mary A. Burt	—	'55-76
Lillie L. Sherman	—	'78-80
Adelaide S. Phillips	—	'80-81
Ella T. Bray	—	'83-84

LABORATORY ASSISTANTS.

Lucy T. Marsh	—	'90-93
Charlotte E. Lee	—	'92-93
Sarah Averill	'93	'93-
Mary Helen Keith, B.S.	'94	'93-
Annie L. Richardson	—	'93-

OFFICERS.

LIBRARIANS.

	Class.	Term.
Mary O. Nutting	'52	'70–
Lucy J. Holmes	'58	'91–92
Abbie R. Knapp, Assistant	—	'93–

REGISTRAR.

| Caroline B. Greene. | '89 | '93– |

SUPERINTENDENTS OF DOMESTIC DEPARTMENT.

Miss Emily Bridge	—	'41–45
Mrs. Mary K. Carroll	—	'59–65
Mrs. Mary A. Foster	—	'64–87
Mrs. Mary K. Carroll	—	'68–73
Miss Sarah A. Thayer	—	'73–74
Mrs. Harriet G. Dutton	—	'74–82
Mrs. R. L. Wright	—	'82–92
Miss Clara E. Lane	—	'87–91
Miss Emily M. Edson	'65	'91–
Mrs. E. L. Purnell	—	'92–
Mrs. C. E. Greene	—	'93–94
Miss A. T. Bemis	—	'94–

STEWARDS.

Ira Hyde			'38–44
Rev. Roswell Hawks			'44–55
John H. P. Chapin			'55–66
Ithiel Lawrence			'66–85
David E. Phillips			'85–86
Lewis H. Porter			'86–92
Joseph S. Wells			'92–

NON-RESIDENT LECTURERS.

GEOLOGY.

Rev. Edward Hitchcock, D.D., LL.D.	'37–62
William D. Gunning	'65–68
Charles H. Hitchcock, Ph.D.	'68–

ARCHITECTURE.

| Ebenezer S. Snell, LL.D. | '37–75 |

HISTORY OF SCULPTURE.

| Rev. Richard H. Mather, D.D. | '74–88 |

HISTORY AND PHILOSOPHY OF ART.

| William Henry Goodyear, M.A. | '77–93 |

NATURAL PHILOSOPHY.

Ebenezer S. Snell, LL.D.	'37–51
Rev. Albert Hopkins, M A., LL.D.	'51–52
Ebenezer S. Snell, LL.D.	'53–68

OFFICERS.

Term.

PHYSICS.
Charles A. Young, Ph.D., LL.D. . '66-65
Alonzo S. Kimball, Ph.D. . '87-

ANATOMY AND PHYSIOLOGY.
Rev. Edward Hitchcock, D.D., LL.D. '44-55

CHEMISTRY.
Edward Lasell, M.A. . . . . '50-51
Charles B. Adams, M A. . . . . '51-52
Rev. Paul A. Chadbourne, M.D., D.D., LL.D. '52-56
W. S. Clark, Ph.D., LL D. . . . . '57-
Rev. Paul A. Chadbourne, M D , D D., LL.D '58-64
William S. Clark, Ph.D., LL.D. . . '64-65
Cyrus F. Brackett, M.D., LL.D. . '66-67
Charles Porter, M.D . . '67-69
Charles O. Thompson . . '72-82
Leverett Mears, Ph.D. . . '83-

ELOCUTION.
Professor Taverner . . . '55-56
Lewis B. Monroe, M.A. . . . '63-64
Rev. John W. Churchill . '68-69
Mark Bailey, M A. . . '70-75
Rev. John W. Churchill . '75-82
Mark Bailey, M.A. . . '82-83

HISTORY.
John Lord, LL.D. . . . '5-61
John Lord, LL.D. . . . '79-85

ASTRONOMY.
Charles A. Young, Ph.D., LL D. . . . '71-

BIOLOGY.
William N. Rice, Ph.D. . . '82-83
Edmund B. Wilson, Ph.D. . '84-85
William T. Sedgwick, Ph.D. . '85-86

POLITICAL ECONOMY.
Edward W. Bemis, Ph.D. . . . . . '86-89
John B. Clark, M.A. . . . . '89-93

STUDENTS.

1838.

GRADUATES.

Abbott, Martha A., Framingham ; m. Rev. N. Shotwell, '41 ; d. West Liberty, Va., '49.
Brigham, Sarah, Grafton ; m. *Rev. C. B. Kittredge, '40 ; d. Westboro, '71.
Moore, Abigail, Fredonia, N. Y. ; m. *Rev. Ebenezer Burgess, '46 ; d. Mahabaleshwar, India, '53.
Woods, Persis C., Enfield ; m, Rev. Geo. C. Curtis, '48 ; 37 S Washington St., Rochester, N. Y.

NON-GRADUATES.

Adams, Sarah B., Franklin ; m. *Rev. E. W. Robinson, '38 ; 1513 Corcoran St., Washington, D. C.
Adams, Julia, Hopkinton ; d. Chicago, '70.
Alden, Mary G., Ashfield ; m. Josiah Parsons, '43 ; d. Northampton, '78.
Allen, Elvira P., Barre ; m. *Henry Chickering, '44 ; d. Pittsfield, '83.
Arms, Theresa T., Deerfield ; m. *George Herbert, '40 ; d. Beloit, Wis., '90.
Bailey, Charlotte, Holden ; m. *Rev. Aldin Grout, '38 ; 20 Florence St., Springfield.
Barnard, Lucy, Woburn ; m. Benjamin Page, '44 ; d. Haverhill, '77.
Bigelow, Abigail, Winchendon ; m. *Rev. Ezra Adams, '39 ; d. Gilsum, N. H., '59.
Bixby, Harriet, West Wrentham ; d. West Wrentham, '43.
Blanchard, Charlotte, S. Weymouth ; m. Albert Tirrell, '38 ; d. S. Weymouth, '65.
Bosworth, Abby M., Bristol, R. I. ; m. *Frederick A. Burgess, '46 ; d. Warren, R. I., '82.
Bosworth, Anna E., Bristol, R. I. ; m. *Henry Wanning, '44 ; 202 W. 103d St., N. Y. City.
Bowdoin, Laura G.. S. Hadley Falls ; d. S. Hadley Falls, '45.
Brigham, Hannah, Grafton ; m. *Rev. Stillman Pratt, '49 ; d. Marlboro, '81.
Bridgman, Mary, Northampton ; m. Horace Wait, '45 ; d. N. Hatfield, '77.
Bucklen, Elizabeth, Ludlow ; d. Mount Holyoke Seminary, '38.
Bull, Ursula, Danbury, Ct. ; d. Danbury, Ct., '78.
Burr, Elmina. Conway ; m. Ephraim C. Jencks, '45 ; d. River Falls, Wis., '76.
Caldwell, Mary A., Ipswich ; m. *Oliver Rice, '46 ; Meriden, Ct.
Cambell, Eliza, Acworth, N. H. ; m. Rev. William S. Lewis, '43; d. Pleasanton, Mich., '75.
Cary, Amelia, Enfield ; m. Loomis Cook, '45 ; Hadley.
Chase, Mary A., Leominster ; d. Worcester, '86.
Clapp, Sophia A., Belchertown ; m. George L. Clapp, '42 ; d. Sabinetown, Tex., '57.
Clarke, Sarah E., Granby ; d. Granby, '38.
Clemens, Emily C., Granby, Ct. ; m. *Rev. Charles H. Pearson, '46 ; 10 Oakdale Sq., Jamaica Plain.
Coggeshall, Joanna M., Bristol, R. I. ; m. Chas. W. Rogers, '42 ; 13 Elm St., Norwalk, Ct.
Day, Eliza M., S. Hadley Falls ; m. *Abel F. Hildreth, '44 ; Auburndale.
Dickinson, Cordelia, Amherst ; m. Rev. H. J. Gaylord, '41 ; d. Plainfield, '47.
Egery, Mary P., Hardwick ; m. Josiah S. Richards, M.D., '50 ; d. Bangor, Me., '53.
Ely, P. Augusta, Lyme, Ct. ; m. *Oscar F. Avery, '42 ; 2239 Michigan Ave., Chicago, Ill.
Everett, Nancy S., Wrentham ; m. John Dwight, '41 ; d. N. Y. City, '82.
Ferry, Emeline, Granby ; m. Edward S. May, '40 ; d. Lee, '76.
Fish, Elizabeth (Farrington), Dedham ; d. Dedham, '74.
Forbes, Eliza S., Westboro ; d. Worcester, '81.
Gillett, Mary A., S. Hadley Falls ; m. Elias P. Butts, '46 ; d. S. Hadley, '59.

1838.

Goodale, Elizabeth H., Marlboro ; m. Rev. Luther Dodd, '59 ; d. Toledo, Io., '61.
Goodwin, Hannah L. B., Norton ; m. *Reuben Tolman, '38 ; *Wythville, Va.*
Gould, Lydia, Rochester, N. Y. ;
Grout, Sarah H., Hawley ; m.*C. F. Crosby, '39; *S. Deerfield.*
Haskell, Mary C., Hardwick ; d. Hardwick, '38.
Hathaway, Rachel, Freetown ; m. *Rev. Frederick Plummer, '51 ; d. Freetown, '83.
Hawkes, Philena N., Charlemont ; m. *Luther Bodman, '39 ; d. Northampton, '94.
Howe, Maria, Marlboro ; m.*Rev. Charles Kendall, '41 ; d. Petersham, '59.
Judd, Eliza, S. Hadley ; m. Jonathan Burnette, '49 ; d. S. Hadley, '60.
McLane, Eliza, Boston ;
Mann, Elizabeth, Boston ; m.*John A. Whipple, '47 ; 11 *Norton St., Cambridge.*
Mather, Sarah A., Northampton ; d. St. Augustine, Fla., '94.
Mather, Huldah, Utica, N. Y. ;
Matson, H. Aurelia, Ithaca, N. Y. ; d. Ithaca, N. Y., '47.
Maynard, Persis F., Princeton, N. J. ;
Miller, Bethiah A., Heath ; m. Rev. W. A. Nichols, '38 ; d. Lake Forest, Ill., '65.
Miller, Hannah B., Heath ; m. Rev. Lemuel Leonard, '39 ; d. Detroit, Mich., '62.
Newell, Elizabeth, Southbridge ; d. Southbridge, '40.
Packard, Louisa F., N. Bridgewater ; m. *Rev. Lewis Towers, '40 ; m. John S. Leverette, '57 ; d. Atlanta, Ga., '84.
Platt, Sarah, Bethel, Ct. ; m. Rev. David Perry, '40 ; d. Barlow, O., '48.
Pomeroy, Jerusha, Stonington, Ct. ; m. Wm. W. Rodman, M.D., '48 ; d. New Haven, Ct., '71.
Rice, Harriet, Charlemont ; m. *Jas. M. Greenlee, '43 ; d. Greenlee, N. C., '94.
Richardson, Louisa (Thayer), Harford, Pa. ; m.*Rev. Edward Allen, '45; d. Harford, Pa.,'86.
Shepard, Wealthy H., Buckland ; m. *Eli Cooley, '49 ; *S. Deerfield.*
Smead, Martha A., Greenfield ; m. *Quintus Allen, '49 ; d. Greenfield, '52.
Smith, Lavinia S., S. Hadley ; m. *Martin W. Burnette, '41 ; *S. Hadley.*
Smith, Martha, Northampton ; d. Northampton, '73.
Smith, Mary E., Amherst ; d. Amherst, '40.
Spaulding, Abigail N., Honesdale, Pa. ; m. *Rev. Calvin Gray, '42 ; *Fort Dodge, Webster Co., Io.*
Stewart, Sarah A., Pittsford, Vt. ; m. *Horace B. Perry, '44 ; *Holly, Orleans Co., N. Y.*
Sutherland, Ann M., Bath, N. H. ; m. Fredrick W. Morrison, '43 ; *Care David Sutherland, Grinnell, Io.*
Sweasey, Emeline A., Newark, N. J.; m.*Rev. Joseph M. Ogden, '49 ; d. Chatham, N. J., '90.
Tirrell, Hannah, S. Weymouth ; d. S. Weymouth, '88.
Torrey, Catherine D., Killingly, Ct. ; m. *F. H. Peckham, M D., '40 ; d. Providence, R. I., '53.
Trask, Rebecca W. (Brooks), Lincoln ; m. Chas. Tidd, '48 ; d. Lexington, '80.
Tyler, Elizabeth S., Attleboro ; m. Atherton Wales, '53 ; d. Attleboro, '63.
Walker, Sarah E., Belchertown ; d. Belchertown, '39.
Wheeler, Harriet, Hardwick ; m. *John Holyoke, '43 ; *Cor. Main and States Sts., Beaver, Mo.*
Wright, Harriet, Templeton ; m. Henry Allen, '60 ; d. W. Brookfield, '80.

1839.

GRADUATES.

Atwood, Frances M., Nashua, N. H. ; m. *E. M. Cowles, '41 ; d. Milledgeville, Ga., '52.
Bailey, Hannah O., Amesbury ; m. *Rev. H. O. Howland, '45 ; *DeMill College, Oshawa, Ont.*
Bass, Lucia L., Colebrook, Ct. ; m. *Wm. L. Mitchell, Esq., '54 ; d. Athens, Ga., '78.

1839.

Breed, Eliza M., Keene, N. H. ; m. *Rev. M. M. Post, '41 ; d. Logansport, Ind., '84.
Brigham, Lucy A., Grafton ; m. *Francis N. Merrifield, '61 ; d. Worcester, '93.
Bruce, Elmira S., Hardwick ; m. J. Rhodes Mayo, '53 ; 23 *Putnam St., Somerville.*
Eastman, Clarissa, Lodi, N. Y. ; m. *William R. Schuyler, '44 ; *Marshall, Mich.*
Humphrey, Helen, Southwick ; m. *Albert A. Palmer, '45 ; m. *William H. Stoddard, '52 ; d. Northampton, '66.
Leach, Martha A., Pittsford, Vt. ; m. *Rev. William S. Curtis, '45 ; 5760 *Woodlawn Ave., Chicago, Ill.*
Reed, Susan, Heath ; m. *Rev. William W. Howland, '45 ; d. Jaffna, Ceylon, '87.
Torrey, Sarah H., N. Bridgewater (Brockton) ; m. Rev. Henry Eddy, '43 ; d. Cincinnati, O., '85.
Whitman, Mary C., East Bridgewater ; m. *Morton Eddy, '51 ; d. Fall River, '75.

NON-GRADUATES.

Arms, Susan E., Brattleboro, Vt. ; m. *Rev. Edward Wright, '43 ; m. Rev. Jason Atwater, '58 ; *Phelps, N. Y.*
Arnold, Harriet T., Somers, Ct. ; m. *Allen H. Griswold, '42 ; 2018 *Garfield Ave., Minneapolis, Minn.*
Avery, Mary, Conway ; m. Rev. R. M. Loughridge, '46 ; d. Tullahasse, Creek Nation, '50.
Baldwin, Elizabeth K., Ashfield ; m. *Rev. Eliphalet Whittlesey, '43 ; *Elwood, N. J.*
Barstow, Margaret F., Kingston, N. H. ; d. Randolph, Vt., '87.
Belden, Chloe B., Amherst ; m. *Rev. Rufus P. Wells, '45 ; 1211 *Judson Ave., Evanston, Ill.*
Betts, Harriet M., Southwick ; m. Thaddeus Foote, '47 ; *Grand Rapids, Mich.*
Bliss, Eliza F., West Springfield ; d. Springfield, '88.
Bliss, Emma L., Springfield ; m. Rev. H. J. Van Lennep, '39 ; d. Smyrna, Turkey, '40.
Booth, Emily, E. Windsor, Ct. ; m. Rev. Henry G. Pendleton, '52 ; d. Chenoa, Ill., '84.
Bowen, Phebe F., Richmond, N. H. ; m. Nahum S. Sisson, '49 ; d. New Orleans, La., '64.
Brooks, Almira, Gloucester ; m. Henry F. Clark, '51 ; d. Rockport, '57.
Bucklin, Mary I., Marlboro ; m. Ezra F. Wood, '40 ; d. Roxbury, '60.
Chamberlain, Emma, Austerlitz, N. Y. ; m. Cyrus Bell, M.D., '41 ; *Tipton, Io.*
Chandler, Abby A., Saxton's River, Vt. ; m. *Rollin W. Keyes, '40 ; *care Mrs. Mary Babcock, Kenilworth, Ill.*
Chandler, Clarissa C., S. Hadley ; d. S. Hadley, '38.
Chandler, Mary A., S. Hadley ; m. Samuel Ware, '43 ; *Garden Grove, Cal.*
Charevoy, Elizabeth, Spencertown, N. Y. ; 221 *W. Park St., Portland, Or.*
Clark, Lovisa, Westhampton ; m. *Elijah Allen, '49 ; 201 *Prospect St., Northampton.*
Clark, Mary, Tewksbury ; m. Rev. William S. Coggin, '40 ; *Boxford.*
Colt, Sarah J., Hinsdale ; m. *Lucius L. Clark, '42 ; *Kalamazoo, Mich.*
Crosby, Elizabeth, Hawley ; d. Hawley, '43.
Dike, Loraine H., Pittsford, Vt. ; m. *George Page, M.D., '44 ; *Pomona, Cal.*
Dimond, Laurinda M., Meriden, N. H. ; m. Rev. John Wood, '40 ; d. Wellesley, '72.
Dinsmore, Elizabeth, Windham, N. H. ; m. Josiah W. Pillsbury, '41 ; *Milford, N. H.*
Dwight, Clara, Belchertown ; m. *Levi Adams, '54 ; m. *Charles Duncan, '76 ; *Belchertown.*
Fox, Angelina H., Fulton, N. Y. ; m. *Daniel Nolton, '41 ; *Holland Patent, N. Y.*
Fuller, Elizabeth, Milford, N. H. ; m. *Calvin McQuesten, M.D., '53 ; *Toronto, Can.*
Gates, Elizabeth S., Ashby ; m. *Rev. J. C. Farwell, '42 ; d. Boston, '76.
Granger, Elizabeth H., Suffield, Ct. ; m. Rev. Samuel Haskell, '43 ; d. Ann Arbor, Mich., '87.
Graves, Cordelia M., S. Deerfield ; d. S. Deerfield, '40.
Graves, Fanny A., Sunderland ; m. J. E. Linnell, M.D., '48 ; d. Norwich, Ct., '90.
Green, Charlotte A., Westmoreland, N. H. ; m. *Dexter Warren, '43 ; d. Westmoreland, N. H., '78.
Green, Harriet C., Westmoreland, N. H. ; 40 *Elm St., Keene, N. H.*

1839.

Harrington, Eliza C., Hoosick Falls, N. Y.; m. *William Fish, '44; m. *Jona. C. Bell, '52; *Waterford, N. Y.*
Hawks, Harriet R., Charlemont; m. William Hallowell, '45; 757 *State St., Waukegan, Ill.*
Hayes, Mary E., Cincinnati, O.; d. Hinsdale, '82.
Henry, Helen A., Amherst; m. H. J. M. Smith, Esq., '59; d. N. Y. City, '87.
Hitchcock, Frances M., Pittsford, Vt.; m. *Jas. M. Chatterton, '44; 67 *N. Grove St., Rutland, Vt.*
Hunt, Charlotte, Attleboro; d. Attleboro, '44.
Hutchinson, Lucy M., Sutton; m. *J. D. Holbrook, '54; d. Sutton, '82.
Jones, Mary W., Spencer; m. Rev. Gideon S. Johnson, '41; d. Pecatonica, Ill., '57.
Lillie, Janett, Coventry, Ct.; m. Andrew J. Batten, '69; d. Chicago, Ill., '75.
Lyman, Theresa, Easthampton; m. *Ahira Lyman, '40; 90 *Buckingham St., Springfield.*
Moore, Julia B., Greenport, N. Y.; d. Greenport, N. Y., '86.
Morton, Electa F., Winchendon; m. *Jonas Minot, '49; *Brockport, N. Y.*
Murdock, Lucy, Rutland; m. Rev. J. G. D. Stearns, '43; d. Zumbrota, Minn., '81.
Nash, Mary S., S. Hadley; m. Dr. Horace S. Nye, '42; d. Zanesville, O., '81.
Nelson, Caroline E., Amherst; d. Amherst, '39.
Page, Nancy J., Acton, Me.; m. *Rev. Chas. Dame, '40; care Prof' S. P. *Dame, Sharon, Pa.*
Penfield, Eleanor B., Pittsford, Vt.; m. *Henry F. Lothrop, Esq., '48; *Pittsford Mills, Vt.*
Pope, Harriet A., Millbury; m. *Rev. Samuel Wolcott, '43; *Longmeadow.*
Randall, Amelia, Stow; d. Mt. Holyoke Seminary, '39.
Richardson, Mary L., Attleboro; m. Henry C. Starkey, '43; d. Chelsea, '89.
Richardson, Sarah W., Chesterfield, N. H.; m. *Chas. Butterfield, '63; *Chesterfield Factory, N. H.*
Robinson, Martha, Hardwick; m. *Rev. W. B. Stone, '85; d. Lawrence, Kansas, '93.
Robinson, Phebe W., Hardwick; m. *Rev. W B. Stone, '42; d. W. Brookfield, '52.
Rogers, Deidameia S., Billerica; d. Tewksbury, '88.
Root, Elizabeth L., Dover, N. H.; m. Dr. —— Potter; (*Plainfield, Ct. ?*)
Sawin, Catharine F., Sherborn; m. Aldus M. Chapin, '40; d. Worcester, '78.
Sawyer, Martha, Heath; m. Rev. Thomas S. Burnell, '47; d. Bellville, Can., '85.
Shumway, Mary H., Oxford; m. Rev. John C. Hurd, '40; d. Beaver Dam, Wis., '54.
Sibley, Sarah A., Rochester, N. Y.; m. Lewis H. Alling, '41; d. Rochester, N. Y., '49.
Smith, Elizabeth P., S. Hadley; m. H. W. Dean, M.D., '42; d. Rochester, N. Y., '77.
Smith, Maria H., S. Hadley; *S. Hadley.*
Smith, Miranda A., Hatfield; d. Madison, Ind., '58.
Spencer, Eliza, Hinsdale; m. *Jas. H. Moseley, '44; d. Brooklyn, N. Y., '89.
Spencer, Julia, Hinsdale; m. Dr. Ashman H. Taylor, '45; d. Charlemont, '61.
Spencer, Lucy, Hinsdale; d. Hinsdale, '40.
Stone, Lucy. W. Brookfield; m. H. B. Blackwell, '55; d. Pope's Hill, Dorchester, '93.
Thompson, Helen M., Heath; m. Jos. W. Miller, '43; d. Colerain, '48.
Thompson, Sarah M., Monson; m. *John R. Lewis, M.D., '44; d. Champaign, Ill., '91.
Tinkham, Anna Eddy, Enfield; m. L. B. Simmonds, '42; d. Athol, '78.
Topping, Sophronia H., Bridgehampton, N. Y.; m. David Burnet, '48; d. Bridgehampton, N. Y., '84.
Tower, Mary E., Lancaster; m. *S. W. Buffum, '42; *Winchester, N. H.*
Tyler, Mary E., Haddam. Ct.; m. Hubbard Ventres, '53; d. Haddam. Ct., '78.
Warner, Harriet M., Sunderland; m. Rev. Nathan F. Tuck, '45; 143 *Walnut St., Knoxville, Tenn.*

1840.

GRADUATES.

Browne. Maria J. B.. Templeton ; 78 *Madison Ave., N. Y. City.*
Browne. Rebekah R.. Templeton ; m. A. S. McClean, M.D.. '49 ; d. Springfield. '80.
Browne. Sarah H.. Templeton ; d. Springfield, '83.
Clarke, Lucy H.. S Deerfield ; d. S. Deerfield, '40.
Leach. Catharine S.. Pittsford. Vt. ; m. *Rev. E. Y. Swift, '43 ; *Pleasant Hill, Lane Co., Or.*
Lothrop. Almira W., Easton ; d. Easton, '41.
Lyon. Lucy T.. Stockton. N. Y. ; m. Rev. Edward C. Lord, '46; d. Fredonia, N. Y., '53.
Morton, Lucretia P., Winchendon ; m. *Rev. Myron W. Safford, '42 ; d. Philadelphia, Pa., '86.
Morton, Mary E.. Whately ; m. *Rev. John A. McKinstry, '43 ; d. Richfield, O., '82.
Ordway, Hannah. Amesbury ; m. *Oliver Cunningham, '43 ; *Gallatin, Mo.*
Richardson. Prudence, Dracut ; m. Rev. Wm. Walker, '41 ; d. Cape Palmas, W. Africa, '42.
Shumway, Zeviah L., Oxford ; m. Rev. Wm. Walker. '45 ; d. Gaboon Station, W. Africa,'48.
Thompson. Harriet N., Heath ; m. John G. Mead, '48 ; *Northwood Center, N. H.*
Tirrell, Eliza A., Boston ; 150 *Henry St.. Brooklyn, N. Y.*
Tufts, Margaret. New Haven. Ct. ; m. Sherman Booth, '42 ; d. Milwaukee, Wis., '49.

NON-GRADUATES.

Adams, Sarah A.. Hopkinton ; m. *Rev. O. W. Cooley, '51 ; 10 *Bryant Ave.. Chicago, Ill.*
Allen, Joann. Lebanon. N. H. ; m. *Rev. Samuel M. Stone, '43 ; d. Lebanon. N. H., '55.
Atkinson. Louisa M.. Natchez, Miss. ; m. *William K. Henry, '46 ; d. Natchez, Miss., '68.
Backus. Harriet, Palmer ; m. Stephen C. Griggs, M.D., '59 ; d. Brooklyn, '89.
Batcheller, Mary D.. Brookfield ; m. Abel Harwood. '41 ; d. Bloomington. Ill., '56.
Bates, Mary E. M.. Wareham ; m. ——— Thomas, '40 ; m. Geo. Vandenhoff, '58 ; d. N. Y.,'85.
Bates, Deborah E. N., Boston ; m. Isaac F. Shepherd, '44.
Bingham, Mary L., Cornwall, Vt. ; m. *Rev. Josiah Lyman, '44 ; d. E. Orange. N. J., '91.
Blanchard, Rachel, S. Weymouth ; m. *Joseph Pool, '40 ; m. Abner P. Nash, '54 ; d. Boston, '59.
Blanchard, Sarah, S. Weymouth ; m. *John W. Thomas, '45 ; *Box 207, Dedham.*
Borden. Mary, New Braintree ; m. John Hill, Esq., '40 ; d. N. Brookfield, '51.
Bridgman, Catharine W.. Belchertown ; m. Capt. Timothy Meigs ; *near Boston.*
Bull. Elizabeth G., Danbury, Ct. ; m. Rev. O. S. St. John, '41 ; d. Easton, Pa., '52.
Bull. Susan T., Danbury. Ct. ; m. *John Abernethy. '45 ; d. Woodbury, Ct., '92.
Cady, Mary W., Somers, Ct. ; m. Spencer Davis, '53 ; *Somers, Ct.*
Clark, Charlotte M.. Whately ; m. *George Sanders, '57 ; m. *Zenas Allen, '70 ; 60 *Central Ave., Hyde Park.*
Colman, Emily P.. Hancock. N. H. ; m. Henry E. Baker, '55 ; 172 *Selden Ave.,Detroit, Mich.*
Dana, Persis C., Pomfret, Vt. ; m. *Elisha Hewitt, '42 ; *N. Pomfret, Vt.*
Douglass, Elizabeth L., Waterford. Ct. ; m. Henry P. Haven, '40 ; d. New London, Ct., '74.
Eaton. Sarah E.. Hardwick ; m. Alfred W. Rose, '60 ; 6 *Tirrell St., Worcester.*
Field, Serena. N. Bridgewater ; m. *C. A. Southworth, '47 ; d. Brockton. '86.
Fuller, Caroline, Somers, Ct. ; m. *Samuel Pomeroy, '43 ; d. Edgar, Neb., '86.
Fuller. Harriet. W. Medway ; m. Alfred B. White, '44 ; d. Chicopee Falls, '74.
Gleason, Welthy A., W. Brookfield ; m. *Chandler Giddings, '42 ; d. W. Brookfield, '91.
Goodale, Lucy T., Marlboro ; d. Marlboro, '40.
Gould, Mary M. C., Gallipolis, O. ; m. *Rev. Matthew Meigs, '42 ; "*The Hill," Pottstown, Pa.*
Gould, Sarah R.. Gallipolis, O. ; m. Rev. William R. Work. '46 ; d. Pottstown, Pa., '54.
Graves. Maria. Hatfield ; d. Hatfield, '40.
Hall, Harriet P., E. Hartford, Ct. ; d. E. Hartford, Ct., '54.
Hall, Lois W., N. Bridgewater ; d. Rehoboth, '61.

1840.

Hall. Louisa A., Northboro; "dismissed from church in Northboro to church in York. Pa. '48."
Hatch, Elizabeth B., Warwick ; m. Rev. John Douglas, '50 ; *Hotel Wakerley, Minneapolis, Minn.*
Haven, Elizabeth B., New London. Ct. ; d. New London, Ct., '42.
Hawks, Adeline S., Charlemont ; d. Mount Holyoke Seminary, '39.
Hodges, Lucy, Sharon ; m. *Asahel Dean, '46 ; *Box 108, Foxboro.*
Hollister, Harriet B., Manchester, Vt. ; d. Manchester. Vt., '40.
Hollister, Julia P., Manchester. Vt. ; m. Rev. Theodore J. Clark, '42 ; *E. Northfield.*
Hyde, Sophronia C., Somers, Ct. ; m. Barney Reybold, '43 ; d. Delaware City, Del., '84.
Jones, Adeline, E. Medway ; m. Abijah R. Wheeler, '41 ; d. E. Medway, '48.
Judd, Dorothy L., Westhampton ; m. *Charles H. Robertson, '49 ; *Wytiesburg, Va.*
Judd, Silence S., Westhampton ; d. Westhampton. '40.
Lewis, Elizabeth F., Falmouth ; m. Moses Rogers. M.D., '49 ; *Falmouth.*
Lyon, Nancy A., Stockton. N. Y. ; m. *Rev. J. M. Purinton, '46 ; *Granville, O.*
McFarland, Clara D., Concord, N. H. ; m. John W. Noyes. Esq., '42 ; d. Concord. N. H., '53.
Mann. Marion A., W. Medway ; m. *Elihu White, '61 ; *W. Medway.*
Marsh, Elizabeth S., Hadley ; m. Lucius Nash, '46 ; d. Hadley, '56.
Miner, Sarah B., Northfield ; m. Rev. E. S. Barnes ; d. Unionville, O., '75.
Packard, Eliza L., Monson ; m. Geo. H. Gates, '46 ; *Monson.*
Paine, Elizabeth. E. Woodstock. Ct. ; d. E. Woodstock, Ct., '40.
Peck, Abigail, N. Greenwich, Ct. ; d. Tuscarora Reservation, '93.
Phelps, Fidelia, Chesterfield ; d. Chesterfield, '40.
Reed, Rhoda A., Westminster, Vt. ; m. Jas. Cooley, '41 ; d. Leroy, N. Y., '50.
Richards. Sarah B., Oxford ; m. Benj. Boynton, '50 ; d. '94.
Richards, Sarah H., Norwich. Vt. ; m. *Rev. Thomas Hall. '58 ; m. *Rev. E. W. Clark, '59 ; d. about '84.
Rowe, Sarah E., E. Kingston. N. H. ; m. Wm. Coggswell, '46 ; d. Derry, N. H., '49.
Savage, Harriot B., Sharon ; m *Rev. Ephraim Chambers, '42 ; d. Marblehead. 84.
Sawyer. Catharine. Heath ; m. *Geo. Donkin, '47 ; *Grenada, Miss.*
Sherman, Jane T., Suffield, Ct. ; m. *Jas. M. Smith. M.D., '45 ; m. Jas. H. Osgood. '56 ; *Tarrytown on Hudson, N. Y.*
Smith, Mary C., Poughkeepsie. N. Y. ; m. Rev. Josiah Leonard. '45 ; d. Malden, N. Y., '53.
Stillman, Lucia M., Colebrook, Ct. ; m. *Samuel Cross, '42 ; m. S. T. Cooke, '57 ; d. Solono, Ill., '71.
Swift. Mary M., Falmouth ; m. Wm. Stetson, '48 ; d. Falmouth. '50.
Swift, Susan M., Falmouth ; m. Wm. H. Price, Esq., '42 ; d. Utica. N. Y., '63.
Tappan, Caroline G., Poughkeepsie, N. Y. ; *S. Hamilton St., Poughkeepsie, N. Y.*
Thompson, Susan. Woburn ; m. Rev. David J. Poor. '40 ; d. Lexington, Ill., '88.
Tufts. Sarah P., New Haven, Ct. ; m. Lucius T. Fitch, '45 ; d. New Haven, Ct., '84.
Vaill, Asenath C., Monson ; m. *Freeman Barrows, Esq., '42 ; *Papinsville, Mo.*
Walker, Martha A., Belchertown ; d. Belchertown, '43.
Ward, Lucy A., Heath ; m. Jas. Love. '46 ; d. Liberty. Mo., '91.
Washburn, Elizabeth S., Putney, Vt. ; m. Rev. M. S. Shirk. '46 ; d. Shreveport, La., '72.
Washburn. Harriet M., Putney, Vt. ; m. *Eben P. Stratton. '46 ; d. Knoxville, Miss., '88.
Webster, Lucy D., Hartford, Ct. ; d. Hartford, Ct., '40.
White, Sarah H., Hinsdale ; m. Chas. T. Huntington. '48 ; *W. Brookfield.*
Whitney, Maria K., Charlestown ; m. *Rev. John F. Pogue. '48 ; *3 Schele Ave., San Jose, Cal.*
Winchell, Amanda F., Norwich ; m. *Wm. H. Burt. '42 ; *52 Sumner Ave., Springfield.*
Wing. Martha C., E. Hartford, Ct. ; m. L. H. Baker. M.D., '46 ; d. Oak Park. Ill., '95.
Young, Lucina S., Orwell. Vt. ; m. *Luther S. Jenison, '45 ; *S. Cedar St., Lansing, Mich.*

1841.

GRADUATES.

Bradstreet, Lydia, N. Danvers ; m. *Stephen White, '47 ; d. Boston, '92.
Burr, Caroline, Norfolk, Ct. ; m. Daniel Grant, '43 ; d. '92.
Chapin, Malvina J., Newport, N. H. ; m. *Rev. Geo. B. Rowell, '42 ; *care George S. Gay, Craftonville, Cal.*
Chenery, Zillah D., Holden ; m. James M. Campbell, '43 ; d. Manchester, N. H., '53.
Dole, Martha C., Georgetown ; d. Georgetown, '92.
Hazen, Sophia D., Berlin, Vt. ; m. *Rev. D. T. Stoddard, '51 ; m. *William H. Stoddard, '67 ; d. Northampton, '91.
Hill Eliza B., New Brunswick, N. J. ; m. Nelson W. Cray, '52 ; d. Flemington, N. J., '84.
Le Conte, Caroline, Ovid, N. Y. ; m. C. V. H. Morris, M. D., '47 ; *Lodi, N. Y.*
Paine, Sarah M., Woodstock, Ct. ; *care Wm. W. Paine, 2d National Bank, Providence, R. I.*
Parsons, Roxana R., Northampton ; m. Caleb Green, M.D., '45 ; d. Homer, N. Y., '85.

NON-GRADUATES.

Arms, Harriet, Conway ; m. Rev. Charles Sylvester, '57 ; d. Feeding Hills, '68.
Arnold, Sophia, Westminster, Vt. ; d. Mount Holyoke Seminary, 1841.
Baker, Malvina, Lebanon, N. H. ; m. Rev. Leonard Tenney, '45 ; *Waterbury, Vt.*
Bassett, Mary E., W. Suffield, Ct. ; m. R. M. Campbell, '48 ; d. Suffield, Ct., '61.
Bates, Mary, Conway ; m. James H. Pratt, '50 ; d. Hillsdale, Mich., '50.
Bissell, Elizabeth A., Suffield, Ct. ; m. Henry C. Lawrence, '43 ; d. Hartford, Vt., '49.
Blair, Catharine L., Blandford ; m. *Thomas S. Chaffee, '43 ; *Fort Collins, Col.*
Browne, Anna A., Somers, N. Y. ; m. George G. Carville, '43 ; d. Faribault, Minn., '77.
Browne. Malvina, Hopkinton, N. H. ; *Hopkinton, N. H.*
Capen, Miranda W., Enfield ; m. Myron H. Crafts, '43 ; d. Dimondale, Mich., '56.
Clarke, Anne M., Richmond ; d. Richmond, '41.
Clarke, Helen M., Richmond ; m. *William Dwight, M.D., '46 ; *N. Amherst.*
Clarke, Sophia. Derry, N. H. ; d. Ypsilanti, Mich., '44.
Crowell, Mary L., Essex ; *Amherst.*
Doane, Abby, Orleans ; m. John W. Atwood, '47 ; *Astoria, N. Y.*
Doane, Keziah S., Orleans; m.*Rev. Geo.W. Cleaveland,'43; 814 *Ninth Ave., Beaver Falls, Pa.*
Dunlap, Mary J., Ovid, N. Y. ; d. Ovid, N. Y., '43.
Eldridge, Sarah C., W. Springfield ; m. John F. Hyde, '45 ; d. W. Springfield, '46.
Fisher, Elizabeth D., Windham, Ct. ; m. —— Anning ; *New Mexico.*
Fiske, Martha E., Weston ; d. Canton, Io., '56.
Grosvenor, Caroline D., Boston ; m. *T. W. Perry, M.D., '47 ; *Pomfret, Ct.*
Harmon, Adeline B., Boston ; 159 *Madison St., Brooklyn, N. Y.*
Hawley, Lucy A., Arlington, Vt. ; m. Justus Harmon, '49 ; d. Chicago, Ill., '51.
Hitchcock, Fanny W., Westminster,Vt.; m. W. F. Guernsey, '42; d. Kalamazoo, Mich., '85.
Hitchcock, Phebe A., Westminster, Vt. ; m. Rev. J. A. Ranney, '41 ; d. Bellville, Ill., '52.
Hume, Lydia C., Windsor ; d. Hinsdale, '70.
Humphrey, Sophia S., Canton, Ct. ; *Middletown, Ct.*
Hyde, Charlotte A., Wayland ; d. Becket, '42.
Jones, Elizabeth W., N. Woodstock, Ct. ; m. *William D. Ware, '55 ; d. W. Medway, '90.
Knight, Eunice B., Brimfield ; d. Honolulu, Oahu, H. I., '95.
Lathrop, Julia A., Dover, N. Y. ; deceased.
Lord, Harriet W., Canaan, N. Y. ; m. *Rev. Sidney Bryant, '41 ; d. W. Haven, Ct., '86.
Lord, Lavinia S., Canaan, N. Y. ; d. Canaan, N. Y., '52.
Merrick, Dorcas N., N. Wilbraham ; d. Wilbraham, '49.
Moody, Irene M., S. Hadley ; m. *Rev. J. W. Tuck, '43 ; d. Ludlow, '44.
Morton, Harriet A., Whately ; d. Whately, '94.

1841.

Newton, Abby T., Colchester. Ct.; m. *Geo. W. Arms, '49; 136 *Court St., Binghamton, N. Y.*
Orcutt, Lucretia F., Cummington; d. Cummington, '42.
Packard, Elizabeth T., N. Bridgewater; m. *James R. Young, '50; 131 *3d St., New Orleans, La.*
Palmer, Caroline, Boston; 98 *Mt. Vernon St., Boston.*
Palmer, Mary S., Boston; m. Samuel Foster, '45; d. Boston, '46.
Park, Harriet S., Orange, N. J.; m. James M. Lincoln, '42; d. Charlestown, Ind., '52.
Parker, Mary J., Boston; m. J. W. Hayes, '48; d. Newtonville, '86.
Pendleton, Lydia E., N. Stonington, Ct.; d. N. Stonington, Ct., '41.
Pendleton, Mary N., N. Stonington, Ct.; d. N. Stonington, Ct., '41.
Phillips, Sarah B., Monson; m. Sidney H. Hall, '45; d. Madison, Wis., '86.
Pratt, Mary J., Tamworth, N. H.; m. Thomas B. Read, '43; d. Florence, Italy, '55.
Putnam, Sarah (Bradstreet), N. Danvers; d. W. Newton, '88.
Rice, Abby C., Wayland; d. '83.
Rice, Charlotte, Charlemont; d. Charlemont, '42.
Sage, Elizabeth A., Colebrook, Ct.; m. Pleasant Valley, Ct., '76.
Sanders, Lucy S., Whately; m. *Asahel W. Sanderson, '61; 50 *West St, Northampton.*
Seymour, Susan S., Hadley; m. James M. Hosford, Esq., '48; d. Geneseo, Ill., '76.
Sheldon, Nancy C., Southampton; m. *Rev Lewis F. Clark, '43; *Whitinsville.*
Smith, Margaret, W. Springfield; m. Addison Day, '47; d. St. Louis, Mo., '71.
Spear, Elizabeth, Hanover, N. H.; m. Jesse P. Bancroft, M.D., '45; d. Concord, N. H., '92.
Starkweather, Jane C., Chesterfield; m. Rev. P. C. Baldwin, '50; d. Maumee, O., '92.
Stillman, Jennette, Wethersfield, Ct.; 231 *E. 12th St., N. Y. City.*
Strong, Abby B., Auburn, N. Y.; m.*Nelson H. Gaston, '50; 802 *Mulberry St., Scranton, Pa.*
Taylor, Lucinda, Canton, Ct.; m. Rev. L. H. Barber, '42; *Ellington, Ct.*
Taylor, Sarah J, Derry, N. H.; m. *C. C Parker, '44; d. Derry, N. H., '80.
Tilton, Eunice A., S. Deerfield; m. Smith Harding, '45; d. S. Deerfield, '67.
Tolman, Elizabeth, Ware; m. Wm. DeWitt, '42; d. Ware, '45.
Tolman, Emily N, Ware; m. John L. Condron, '47; d. Rochester, N. Y., '56.
Tolman, Sarah D., Ware; m. Freeman S. Foster, '43; d. Palmer, '52.
Twombly, Mary L., Dover, N. H.; d. Dover, N. H., '42.
Waldo, Sarah M., Portage, N. Y.; m. Elmon D. Smith, '48; d. Hornellsville, N. Y., '78.
Warner, Mary H., Northampton; m. *D. Worthington Miner, M.D., '45; *Ware.*
White, Mary C., Longmeadow; m. *Rev. Theodore A. Leete, '51; d. Detroit, Mich., '91.

1842.

GRADUATES.

Baldwin, Estimate R. E., Antrim, N. H.; m. *Calvin McQuesten, M D., '44; d. Hamilton, Ont., '51.
Burr, Mary, Norfolk. Ct.; m. Wm. Hill, '49; d. Flemington, N. J., '84.
Chapin, Martha R., Somers, Ct.; m. Rev. Allen Hazen, '46; d. Deerfield, '81.
Fiske, Fidelia, Shelburne; d. Shelburne, '64.
Hawks, Elizabeth S., S. Hadley; m. *Wm. B. Reed, M.D., '43; m. *John Putnam, M D., '50; 1001 *Prairie Ave., Chicago, Ill.*
Hawks, Marion A., S. Hadley; m. C. P. Buckingham, '45; 583 *The Rookery, Chicago, Ill.*
Hawks, Susan F., S. Hadley; m. *Rev. Chas. A. Williams, '55; 747 *Fullerton Ave., Chicago, Ill.*
Hyde, Julia, Becket; m. *Rev. Edward Clarke, '44; 584 *State St., Springfield.*
Mann, Margaret, Boston; m. *Rev. Thomas O. Rice, '50; 1339 *K St., Washington, D. C.*

1842.

Mowry, Ann R., Norwich, Ct. ; m. *Rev. J. W. Tuck, '45 ; 69 *Clarendon St., Springfield*.
Rogers, Martha, Billerica ; m. *R. H. Tupper, '51 ; *Bethel, Vt*.
Savage, Maria, Hartford. Vt. ; m. *Joseph E. Hood, '45 ; *Pacific Grove, Cal*.
Webster, Ann R., Boscawen, N. H. ; m. *Rev. Horace Eaton, D.D , '45 ; *Palmyra, N. Y*.
Wright, Catharine A., Blandford ; m. J. M. Brewster, M.D., '46 ; d. Blandford, '51.
Wright, Laura E., Columbus, Miss. ; m. *Charles Eagar, Esq., '46 ; d. Columbus, Miss., '90.

NON-GRADUATES.

Allen, Martha D., Sterling, Ct.; m. John D. Gallup, '54 ; *Agawam*.
Ames, Mary L., Wayland ; m. *Chas H. Rice, '47 ; *Wayland*.
Baker, Susan M., Bridport, Vt. ; m. Chas. Saxe, '43 ; d. Highgate, Vt., '47.
Baldwin, Sarah A., Antrim, N. H. ; m. Gideon F. Dodge, '48 ; d. Fairfax, Io., '84.
Barker, Susan W., Fredonia, N. Y. ; m. *Stephen P. Mead, '44 ; *Room 45, 205 Washington St., San Francisco, Cal*.
Bassett, Catharine A., W. Suffield, Ct. ; d. W. Suffield, Ct., '46.
Bassett, Mary T., Hawley ; m. *Wm. M. Corner, '45 ; m. Benj. M. Ludden, M.D., '84 ; d. Savannah, Ga., '93.
Bayley, Charlotte P., Boston ; m. *Reuben Stephenson, '45 ; *San Francisco, Cal*.
Belden, Mary, Amherst ; m. *Rev. Josiah H. Temple, '47 ; d. Framingham, '94.
Bierce, Lewey A., Cornwall Bridge, Ct. ; m. *Wait R. Griswold, M.D., '52 ; *Rocky Hill, Ct*.
Bissell, Arabella J., Suffield, Ct. ; m. Wm. L. Loomis, '68 ; *Suffield, Ct*.
Boies, Caroline E., Blandford ; m. *Geo. B. Ely, Esq., '48 ; *Riverside Drive, 85th and 86th Sts., N. Y. City*.
Boies, Jane L., New London, Ct. ; m. Rev. Joel L. Dickinson, '45 ; d. Plainville, Ct., '58.
Booth, Selina, E. Windsor, Ct. ; m. *John W. Newell, '57 ; *Farmington, Ill*.
Bosworth, Minerva A., Fredonia, N. Y. ; m. S. C. Stevenson, '68 ; *Orleans, Ill*.
Boynton, Sarah, Pepperell ; m. Alfred L. Lawrence, '53 ; *Pepperell*.
Bradley, Cornelia, Stockbridge ; d. Stockbridge, '82.
Breed, Eunice, Keene, N. H. ; d. Logansport, Ind., '45.
Browne, Lucia W., Pittsford, Vt. ; m. Chas. H. Bond, '52 ; *25 Caleb Place, Pontiac, Mich*.
Bull, Serina, Danbury, Ct. ; m. Chas. F. Thurston, '47 ; *27 Lawrence St., Boston*.
Burnham, Sarah J., Essex ; m. Francis Cogswell, '50 ; d. Essex, '64.
Bush, Martha A., Whately ; m. B. F. Parsons, '47 ; d. Dayton, Ala., '61.
Buttrick, H. Maria, Pepperell ; m. *Rev. J. K. Bragg, '44 ; d. Brookfield, '59.
Case, Julia M., Canton, Ct. ; m. Jas. L. Smith, '66 ; *Tabor, Io*.
Clapp, Harriette, Chesterfield ; m. David Rice, M.D., '44 ; d. Leverett, '85.
Clizbe, Cecelia, Amsterdam, N. Y. ; m. Chas. Bartlett, '54 ; d. Poughkeepsie, N. Y., '80.
Coan, Martha D., Ovid, N. Y. ; m. *Clement Leach, Esq., '48 ; *Marshall, Mich*.
Coit, Sarah E., Norwich, Ct. ; m. *Thomas Barrows, '49 ; m. Archibald H. Welch, '66 ; d. Morristown, N. J., '92.
Collins, Cornelia W., S. Hadley ; m. Dr. Asa A. Howland, '47 ; d. Barre, '69.
Colman, Abby P., Hancock, N. H. ; m. Wm. Converse, M.D., '54 ; *care Rev. Geo. W. Colman, Lake Forest, Ill*.
Colton, Marcia, Springfield ; *Presbyterian Home, Philadelphia, Pa*.
Comstock, Sarah, Kent, Ct. ; m. *Norman Lathrop ; d. Torrington, Ct., '93.
Cook, Louisa F., Williamstown ; m. Rev. Wm. R. Stevens, '47 ; d. Indiana.
Crosby, Phebe H., Hawley ; m. *Rev. Josiah Crawford, '47 ; *Solon, Ind*.
Danforth, Clarissa M., Williamstown ; m. Rev. Geo. R. Entler ; d. Williamstown.
Daniels, Frances, Worthington ; m. Eli A. Hubbard, '44 ; *26 Essex St., Holyoke*.
Dickinson, Caroline, Conway ; m. Lewis Bissell, '51 ; d. Wheaton, Ill., '76.
Dickinson, Sophronia M., Granby ; m. Spencer A. White, '45 ; d. Granby, '90.

1842.

Dixon, Susan W., Dedham ; m. *Lewis W. Seaver. '44 ; m. Rufus E. Dixon, '50 ; 258 *New-bury St., Boston.*
Eaton. S. Rebecca, Framingham ; *Framingham.*
Edwards, Elizabeth. Andover ; *Andover.*
Fisk, L. Arabella, Shelburne ; m. Rev. Henry Seymour, '44 ; d. Hawley, '50.
Fisk, Sarah S., Shelburne ; m. *Daniel Whitney, '45 ; d. Grafton, '89.
Fitch, Abigail T., Hatfield ; m. Geo. O. Whitney, '47 ; d. San Francisco, Cal., '72.
Fletcher, Lucy, Jamestown, N. Y. ; m. Alpheus F. Hawley, '43 ; d. Arcola, Ill., '78.
Fletcher, S. Maria, Jamestown, N. Y.; m. Edw. A. Dickinson, '42; d. Jamestown, N.Y., '63.
Flint, Lucy, N. Reading ; m. Rev. Daniel Wight, '42 ; d. N. Scituate, '46.
Fox, Prudence V., Dracut; d. Lowell, '93.
Francis, Emily C., Hartford, Ct. ; m. *Hyacinthe Lamarche, '51 ; d. Brooklyn. N. Y., '91.
Fuller, Chloe L., Somers, Ct. ; m. *Chas. Kimball, '50; 479 *Washington Boul., Chicago, Ill.*
Gerould, Deborah D., Keene, N. H ; m. *J. W. Ranney, M.D., '49; 43 *West St., Keene, N. H.*
Gerrish, Martha A. (Smith), Boscawen, N. H. ; m. Enoch G. Wood, '44 ; d. Boscawen, N. H., '89.
Greenough, Ann F., Boscawen, N. H. ; m. *John W. Sullivan, '60; *Boscawen, N. H.*
Hall, Harriet A., Wallingford, Ct. ; m. Horace Austin, '47; *Wallingford, Ct.*
Halsey, Margaret, Westhampton, N. Y.; m. *Philip P. Werlein, '46; d. New Orleans, La., '85.
Hancock, Maria T., Dudley ; m. Cady Webster, '60; d. Pawtucket. R. I., '84.
Haskell, Susan B., Rockport; m. Benj. Giles, '43; *S. Lincoln.*
Haven, Ellen M., Framingham ; m. John Swan; d. Ayer, '84.
Hayden, Mary A., Hartford, Ct. ; m.*Rev. J. O. Stedman. D.D., '55; 438 *Court St. Ext'd, Memphis, Tenn.*
Hazeltine, Susanna, Jamestown, N. Y.; m. Wm. Post, '45; d. Jamestown. N. Y., '70.
Hitchcock, Mary, Amherst; *Hanover. N. H.*
Howe, Caroline S., Princeton ; m. Noah R. Harlow, '48 ; d. Lowell, '73.
Hurd, Mary A., Oxford; m. *Rev. J. P. Foster, '42; d. Whately, '91.
Hyde, Adeline, Becket; m. Jas. Farrar. '45 ; *S. Lincoln.*
Jewell, Sarah C., Durham, N. Y. ; d. Ashland. N. Y., '92.
Leavitt, Sophia S., Vergennes, Vt. ; d. Vergennes, Vt., '44.
Lee, Julia, Salisbury, Ct. ; d. Salisbury, Ct., '50.
Lyman, Elizabeth, Easthampton; m. Edward L. Snow, '42 ; d. Brooklyn. N. Y., '74.
Lyman, Sarah C. (Hannum). Easthampton; m. Noadiah P. Bowler, '44; d. Cleveland. O., '50.
McClure. Nancy H., Boston ; m. Joseph P. Ellicott, '62 ; *Hotel Cluny, Boston.*
Mack, Clarissa L., Plainfield ; m. H. H. Forsyth, '46; d. Maumee City, O., '56.
Mack, Mary H., Plainfield ; m. Rev. H. J. Gaylord. '54 ; *Clyde, Kan.*
McLean, Sarah, Vernon. Ct. ; m. Jas. B. Maynard, '57 ; d. Hartford. Ct., '70.
Moody, Eliza P., S. Hadley ; m. Elisha Bridgman, '45 ; d. Belchertown. ('46?).
Moore, Elizabeth P., Norwich, Ct. ; m. *Uriah A. Pollard, '44 ; d. Norwich, Ct.,'52.
Morehouse, Cynthia. Monroe, Mich.; m. Wm. Vaughn. '43; d. Clinton, Mich., '14.
Newton, Sarah A., Worcester; m. Edward H. Maynard. '47 ; 1828 *Mt. Vernon St, Philadelphia, Pa.*
Nicholson, Selinda T. L., New Haven. Ct.; m. Edgar Sherman. '45; 220 *W. 38th St , N. Y. City.*
Noyes, Harmony A., N. Bridgewater ; m. Simeon L. Whitcomb, '49; 19 *Richardson St., Newton.*
Paige, Caroline L., New Salem; m. John S. Weeks, '62 ; d. S. Athol, '78.
Parkhurst, Sarah E., Jersey City, N. J.; m. *Warren Holt. '46; *Montclair, N. J.*
Pomeroy, Miranda, Somers, Ct. ; m. Cyrus Cole, '45; d. Middletown. Ct., '75.
Potter, Elvira S., Harwinton, Ct. ; m. Alexander Starne ; d. Springfield, Ill., '80.
Potter. Virginia, Washington, D. C. ; m. *William Tate, '42 ; d. New London. Ct., '84.

1842.

Putnam, Harriot O., Middleboro; m. *Chas. F. Peirce, '52; *care S. O. Putnam*, 1020 *Washington St., San Francisco, Cal.*
Ranney, Sarah S., E. Granville; m. J. Austin Scott, '47; d. Ann Arbor, Mich., '83.
Root, Lucy A., Westfield; m. Patrick H. Boise, '49; d. Westfield, '58.
Roys, Rhoda A., Landaff, N. H.; m. *Rev. Almon Benson. '45; *Center Harbor, N. H.*
Seaver, Sarah R., Marlboro; m. Horace Day, '44; 10 *College St., New Haven, Ct.*
Sedgwick, Elizabeth S., Sharon, Ct.; *Aiken, S. C.*
Sellon, Eliza A., Amherst; m. *Samuel Maxwell, '43; d. Marietta, O., '44.
Sherwood, Mary C., Greenfield, Ct.; m. *Rev. Lewis Pennell, '46; *Southport, Ct.*
Spaulding, Sarah J., Norfolk, Ct.; m. Jenison J. Whiting, '42; d. W. Winsted, Ct., '69.
Sprague, Eunice, Abington; d. Abington, '42.
Stearns, Abby M., New Ipswich, N. H.; m. *Rev. Seneca Cummings, '47; *New Ipswich, N. H.*
Stevens, Mary M., Plainfield, N. H.; d. Plainfield, N. H., '88.
Stevens, Sabra A., Plainfield, N. H.; m. *Geo. D. Wotkyns, '48; d. Troy, N. Y., '91.
Swift, Sarah B., S. Dennis; m. *Obed B. Whelden, '49; *S. Dennis.*
Talcott, Elizabeth A., Vernon, Ct.; m. *J. Q. A. Perrin, '44; d. Lafayette, Ind., '89.
Tarbox, Cornelia P., Vernon, Ct.; m. Henry Phelps, '51; d. Wilbraham, '85.
Tarbox, Laura, Vernon, Ct.; m. Myron E. Humphrey, '43; d. Attica, N. Y., '45.
Taylor, Frances H., Westfield; d. Westfield, '47.
Thomas, Susan A., Utica, N. Y.;
Thorpe, Mary C., Southport, Ct.; m. Maurice Wakeman, '45; *Southport, Ct.*
Tufts, Sarah A. B., Dudley; m. *Francis H. Dewey, Esq., '52; 23 *Chestnut St., Worcester.*
Wells, Experience P., Whately; m. Samuel B. White, Esq., '48; d. Whately, '61.
Wilder, Elizabeth J., Keene, N. H.; m I. W. Gates, '55; d. Logansport, Ind., '56.
Wright, Augusta, Easthampton; m. Lewis Clapp, '45; d. Easthampton, '71.
Wright, S. Rebecca, Ludlow, Vt.; m. Col. A. J. Pool, '48; d. Waukesha, Wis., '57.

1843.

GRADUATES.

Blanding, Juliet M., Rehoboth; d. Rehoboth, '53.
Bonney, Sarah A., Nelson, O., m. Rev. W. A. Nichols, '07; *Lake Forest, Ill.*
Chapin, Mary W., Somers, Ct.; m. C. B. Pease, '65; d. Savannah, Ga., '89.
Hayes, Harriet L., S. Hadley; m. Edward Strong, M.D., '46; *Auburndale.*
Humphrey, Mary H., Southwick; m. *Silas Ames, M.D., '56; d. Montgomery, Ala., '59.
Jennings, Sabrina, S. Brookfield; d. Swanton, Vt., '90.
Jewell, Maria, Winchester, N. H.; m. J. E. Coleman, '57; d. Paris, France, '78.
Major, Susanna, Durham Flat, Can.; d. Morris Plains, N. J., '81.
Rockwell, Olivia C., Peru; d. Peru, '45.
Roff, Mary W. (Judd), Newark, N. J.; m. B. F. Stevenson, '46; *Medford, Or.*
Taylor, Mary E., Derry, N. H.; m. *Hon. Horace Fairbanks, '49; *St. Johnsbury, Vt.*
Trumbull, Julia S., Southampton; m. E. L. Miller, Esq., '44; d. S. Hadley Falls, '93.
Wilcox, Melissa R., Sandisfield; d. Mill River, '89.
Williams, Tirzah M., New Haven, Ct.; d. New Haven, Ct., '47.
Woodbridge, Nancy M., Candor, N. Y.; m. *Rev. Edward R. Geary, '45; d. Oregon, '89.
Woodhull, Ann H., Riverhead, N. Y.; m. Rev. A. F. Dickson, '50; d. Orangeburg, S. C., '67.

NON-GRADUATES.

Allen, Phebe H., Conway; m. *Shepherd Leach, '48; d. Rockford, Ill., '94.
Alling, Emeline S., Newark, N. J.; d. Ga., '87.

1843.

Arms, Mary W., Greenfield; d. Greenfield, '46.
Badger, Emily D., Philadelphia, Pa.;
Bardwell, Harriet W., S. Hadley Falls; m. Jas B Benton, '48; d. S. Hadley Falls, '70.
Batchelder, Mary S., Conway; m. Geo. A. Waite, '50; *N. Amherst*.
Blackwell, Adaline. Mapleton, N. J.;
Blinn, Sarah M. S., Spencertown, N. Y.; m. *Wm. C. Niles, '45; *Fergus Falls, Minn*.
Bowen, Annette L., Woodstock, Ct.; m. *Harrison Johnson, Esq., '48; *Putnam, Ct*.
Bowlend, Mary L. W., Lowell; m. W. A. Newton, '54; d. Minneapolis, Minn., '88.
Bradley, Mary E., Meriden, Ct.; m. Chas E. Scott, M.D., '48; d. S. Meriden, Ct., '86.
Bridges, Lucy M., Williamstown; m. *L. H. Graves, '46; d. Williamstown, '65.
Brigham, Cornelia A., Grafton; m. *Calvin Taft, '60; 772 *Main St., Worcester*.
Brigham, Maria C., Grafton; m. Wm. T. Merrifield, '47; d. Worcester, '91.
Burrage, Mary C., Sterling; m. Emory Lyon, M.D., '48; d. Sterling, '52.
Catlin, Laura S., New Marlboro; m. *Marcus D. Bearden, '49; m. *David Richardson, '57; 402 *Vine St., Knoxville, Tenn*.
Chapin, Elizabeth, Great Barrington; d. Great Barrington, '43.
Chapin, Jane E., Cabotville (now Chicopee); d. Chicopee, '42.
Chapin, Mary, W. Springfield; d. Holyoke, '50.
Clark, Elizabeth E., Boston; *Quincy Point*.
Clifford, Amanda E., Milwaukee, Wis.; m. L. F. Jackson, Esq., '45; d. Watertown, Wis., '47.
Cooke, Adah J., New Hartford, Ct.; d. New Hartford, Ct., '92.
Cooley, Amelia S., S. Deerfield; m. David Stewart, '53; d. Oshkosh, Wis., '56.
Corbin, Sylvia Dudley; m. *Samuel H. Davis, '46; *Webster*.
Crane, Sarah M., Newark, N. J.; *Orange, N. J*.
Denison, Augusta M., Sackett's Harbor, N. Y.; m. Samuel Ellis, '59; 833 *S. Olive St., Los Angeles, Cal*.
Dickinson, Sophia C., Hinsdale, N H.; m. Horace T. N. Pierce, '50; 104 *Cross St., Keene, N.H*.
Dowse, Mary B., Oxford; m. *Henry G. Davis, '45; 43 *Appleton Ave., Pittsfield*.
Dwight, Ellen F., Sturbridge; m. Rev. C. R. Hendrickson, '48; d. Memphis, Tenn, '54.
Edwards, Lydia, Andover; *Andover*.
Elliot, Augusta C., Springfield; 789 *Main St., Springfield*.
Elliott, Mary M., Youngstown, N. Y.; m. Chas. Andrews, Esq., '49; d. Armada, Mich., '88.
Ely, Elizabeth. W. Springfield; m. *William Newkirk, '46; d. Holyoke, '92.
Fanning, Glorianna, Greenport, N. Y.; m. C. Halsey Benjamin, '70; *Riverhead, N. Y*.
Field, Caroline, Geneva, N. Y.; 188 *Main St., Geneva, N. Y*.
Field, Lucy A., Geneva, N. Y.; d. Geneva, N. Y., '93.
Fletcher, Mary A., Oberlin, O.; d. Boston, '85.
Foote, Elizabeth J., Jamestown, N. Y.; d. Cincinnati, O., '51.
Francis, Elizabeth S., Hartford, Ct.; m. Edward Lamarche, '50; d. Hartford, Ct., '51.
Gilbert, Mary A., Amherst; m. Samuel J. Learned, '49; d. Grand Haven, Mich., '50.
Hale, Eliza L., Chester, N. H.; m. Lauren Armsby, '49; *Council Grove, Kan*.
Henshaw, Caroline, Leicester; m. *N. W. Metcalf, '50; '81 *Elm St., Worcester*.
Hough, Hannah J., Bozrah, Ct; m. *Isaac Johnson, '46; d. '63.
Howe, L. Eliza, Marlboro; m. *Rev. Archibald F. Gilbert, '50; *Montclair, N. J*.
Howe, Martha N., S. Canaan, Ct.; m. *Peter L. Van Houten, '45; *Matteawan, N. Y*.
Howland, Mary E., Worcester; m. Edward Smith, '67; d. Enfield, '70.
Husted, Mary A., Spencertown, N. Y.; m. Josiah A. Mills, Esq., '58; d. Buffalo, N. Y., '63.
Ives, Mary C., New Haven, Ct.; 169 *Davenport Ave., New Haven, Ct*.
Jerome, Mary J., Springfield; m. Samuel Dale, '45; d. Springfield, '51.
Johnson, Charlotte E., Worcester; d. Worcester, '51
Johnson, Selena L., Fredonia, N. Y.; m. Rev. Almond C. Barrell, '54; *Albion, N. Y*.
Kentfield, Charlotte M., Enfield; m. C. Stratton, M.D., '45; *Amherst*.

1843.

Kingman, Jane J., Pelham ; d. Amherst, '53.
Land, Margaret A., W. Dennis ; m. *Woodbridge Clifford, '47 ; *N. Edgecomb, Me.*
Leonard, Marion H., Meriden, Ct. ; m. *Chas. Pomeroy, '48 ; 68 *Pleasant St., Meriden, Ct.*
McIntyre, Eliza M., Charlton ; m. *Ozias Bowen, '48 ; d. Marion, O., '70.
McLean, Harriet, Vernon, Ct. ; m. *C. D. Talcott, '51 ; d. Talcottville, Ct., '74.
McMonagle, Mary W., Wallkill, N. Y. ; m. Moses B. Green, '51 ; d. Green Oak, Mich., '70.
Marshall, H. Jane, Nashville, N. H. ; m. Lucius Patterson, '44 ; d. Windham, N. H., '52.
Mason, H. Louise, Louisville, Ky. ; m. Reuben L. Post, '47 ; d. Louisville, Ky., '50.
Meeker, Harriet E., Wallingford, Vt. ; m. Wm. B. Green, '45 ; *Lisle, Ill.*
Miller, Nancy B., S. Hadley Falls ; m. *John Miller, '50 ; d. Wakeman, O., '94.
Newbury, Helen M., Brooklyn, Ct. ; d. Brooklyn, Ct., '84.
Nooney, Abigail, Chester ; m. *Stephen N. Elder, '46 ; *Huntington.*
Parkman, H. Sophia, Westboro ; m. Henry C. Taft, '51 ; d. Orange, Cal., '87.
Perkins, Ellen L., Boston ; m. Chas. E. Parker, '47 ; d. Auburndale, '57.
Perry, Martha K., Leominster ; m. Joel W. Fletcher, Esq., '50 ; d. Leominster, '93.
Pettee, Harriet N., N. Y. City ;
Pier, Amelia S., Fredonia, N. Y. ; *Box 609, Fredonia, N. Y.*
Putnam, Mary P., Brooklyn, N. Y. ; m. Henry G. Ely, '51 ; d. Brooklyn, N. Y., '78.
Rice, Lucretia, Charlemont ; d. Charlemont, '43.
Richardson, Martha A., N. Y. City ;
Richmond, Frances T., Hartford, Ct.; *Newport, R. I.*
Richmond, Martha E., Hartford, Ct. ; *Newport, R. I.*
Robbins, Anne E., Geneva, N. Y. ; m. Bartholomew Brown, '53 ; d. '91.
Russell, Catharine, Kingston ; d. Kingston, '59.
Sanders, Mary J., Williamstown ; m. Rev. Edward Lord, '46 ; *Patchogue, N. Y.*
Sandford, Sarah, Lodi, N. Y. ; m. *Rev. H. R. Dunham, '54 ; m. Josiah B. Chapman, '66 ; *Ovid, N. Y.*
Scrugham, Eleanor L., N. Y. City ; m. *Jas. Warner, '43 ; *Palma Sola, Fla.*
Sears, Harriet, Ashfield ; m. Isaac R. Jones, '47 ; 133 *Prospect St., E. Orange, N. J.*
Sears, Lucy A., Ashfield ; d. Ashfield, '52.
Seaver, Elizabeth W., Marlboro ; m. *N. S. Frost, '44 ; m. Rev. John McLeod, '56 ; d. Berwyn, Pa, '82.
Sipp, Mary E., Paterson, N. J. ; m. Thos. G. Orwig, '64 ; 1210 *Pleasant St., Des Moines, Io.*
Smith, Lucy W., S. Hadley ; m. *Albert Chamberlain, '63 ; m. Horace Putnam, '71 ; 48 *Bradford St., Springfield.*
Sumner, Mary H., Hill, N. H. ; d. Hill, N. H., '47.
Taylor, Nancy M., Newark, N. J. ; m. Wm. L. Tinker ; 1072 *Broad St., Newark, N. J.*
Thomas, Nancy B., Hardwick ; m. Geo. J. Newton, M.D., '55 ; d. Gloversville, N. Y., '58.
Udell, Caroline, Alden, N. Y. ; m. A. N. Woolverton, M.D., '45 ; d. Grimsby, Ont., '49.
Van Dyke, Margaret G., Mapleton, N. J. ; m. John G. Van Dyke,'46 ; d. Mapleton, N. J.,'48.
Waldo, Frances, Portage, N Y. ; m. Jas. S. Cowdry, M.D., '48 ; 85 *Hartford St., La Fayette, Ind.*
Walker, Almira G., Fredonia, N. Y. ; d. Lebanon, Ky., '46.
Warren, Hannah L., Grafton ; m. Henry P. Bliss, '45 ; d. Newton Corner, '49.
West, Margaretta A., Newark, N. J. ; m. *Benj. Davison, M.D., '46 ; d. Nyack, N. Y., '84.
Whipple, Mary L., S. Shaftsbury, Vt. ; d. S. Shaftsbury, Vt., '77.
Whipple, Stella C., Shaftsbury, Vt. ; m. Gordon E. Cole, '55 ; d. Faribault, Minn., '72.
Whittlesey, Louisa D., Farmington, Ct. ; 6414 *Lexington Ave., Chicago, Ill.*
Wilcox, Harriet E., Farmington, Ct. ; m. Levi Prosser, '48 ; d. Bloomfield, Ct., '53.
Williams, Clara A., Cummington ; m. Horatio R. Bardwell,'49 ; 62 *N. 3d St., San Jose, Cal.*
Williams, Harriet H., Stonington, Ct. ; *N. Stonington, Ct.*
Woods, Amanda M., Enfield ; d. Enfield, '49.

1843.

Woods, Charlotte E., Enfield ; m. D. B. Gillett, '45 ; d. Enfield, '56.
Wright, Martha A., Blandford ; m. John Young, '53 ; d. Mobile, Ala., '65.
Youngs, Emeline C., Farmington, Ct. ; m. *Rev. J. C. Searle,'50 ; m. Wm. S. Spencer, '58 ; d. Warsaw, Ill., '59.

1844.
GRADUATES.

Bailey, Sarah T., Hopkinton, N. H. ; m. L. S. Crawford. '56 ; d. Rome, N. Y., '56.
Brown, Marie F., Somers, N. Y. ; d. Somers, N. Y., '47.
Chapin, Mary B., Springfield ; m. *Rev. P. B. Day, '52 ; d. Grinnell, Io , '83.
Clark, Elizabeth P., Danbury, Ct. ; m. Rev. G. R. Rossetter, '49 ; d. Marietta, O., '61.
Clarke, Josephine, S. Hadley ; m. *Ephraim A. Chapin, '45 ; d. Brooklyn, N. Y., '88.
Cobine, Rosanna H., Argyle, N. Y. ; m. Rev. —— Parker; '50; d. Austin, Minn., '64.
Cook, Jane A., Hadley ; m. *James Temple, '55 ; 2420 Jay St., Denver, Col.
Cooley, Julietta, Attica, N. Y. ; m. Hon. W. Canfield, '73 ; Bakersfield, Cal.
Curtis, Lucy M., Sturbridge ; d. W. Brookfield, '49.
Dana, Rebecca H., Pomfret, Vt. ; m. *Rev. Edward E. Atwater, '45 ; 29 Trumbull St., New Haven, Ct.
Dickinson, Amelia F., Springfield ; m. *Rev. Edward D. Bangs, '44 ; d. Galesburg, Ill., '91.
Dickinson, Louisa S., Springfield ; 576 Main St., Springfield.
Foote, Nancy A., Cayuga, N. Y. ; m. Rev. Edward Webb, '45 ; Oxford, Pa.
Graves, Mary E., Hatfield ; m. Silvanus Miller, '50; Deerfield.
Hinsdale, Aurelia B., Amherst ; m. *A. W. Davis, '47 ; Amherst.
Hinsdale, Harriet A., Amherst ; m. Rev. Henry L. Hubbell, D.D., '63 ; Lake Charles College, Lake Charles, La.
Hubbell, Eliza A., N. Y. City ; m. Rev. Charles Peabody, '47 ; d. N. Y. City, '51.
Jones, Hannah D. G., Marlboro, N. H. ; m. *D. W. Orbison, '47 ; m. Rev. M. G. Grosvenor, '65 ; d. Troy, O., '78.
Knight, Eliza P., Brimfield ; m. R. S. Wilcox, '53 ; d. Brimfield, '54.
Knowlton, Elizabeth G., Hopkinton, N. H. ; m. Rev. Milton B. Starr, '48 ;
Martin, Emily A. G., Fort Mifflin, Pa. ; d. Fort Mifflin, Pa., '45.
Martin, M. Augusta, Fort Mifflin, Pa. ; m. *H. B. Schreiner,'55 ; Ellsworth Ave., Danbury, Ct.
Merrill, Eliza A., Middlebury, Vt. ; m. *Henry W. Starr, Esq., '57 ; 309 N. 6th St., Burlington, Io.
Montague, Clara S., S. Hadley ; d. Brooklyn, N. Y., '45.
Peabody, Melissa, Boxford ; m. *J. Q. Batchelder, '45 ; Boxford.
Pomeroy, Lucinda, Somers, Ct. ; Somers, Ct.
Porter, Catherine A., Somerville, N. J. ; m. *Rev. F. H. Pitkin, '45 ; m. *Rev. Addison Lyman, '47 ; Lock Box 324, Grinnell, Iowa.
Scales, Sarah M., Cornwall, Vt. ; d. Alexandria, Mo., '55.
Smith, Lucy, Middlefield ; m. *Ambrose Newton, '67 ; Middlefield.
Smith, Sarah, Middlefield ; m. De Witt Gardner, Esq., '56 ; Fulton, N. Y.
Warren, Delia M., Grafton ; m. Henry P. Bliss, '50 ; d. Cambridgeport, '78.
Washburn, Mary C., Pittsfield ; m. *Rev. T. O. Rice, '45 ; d. W. Killingly, Ct., '49.
White, Caroline A., W. Chester, Ct. ; m. *Jas. H. Denison, '57 ; d. Keene Valley, N. Y., '80.
Wood, Mary S., Athol ; m. *Rev. George J. Tillotson, '60 ; Wethersfield, Ct.

NON-GRADUATES.

Adams, Mary E., Amherst ; m. *David Aiken, Esq., '48 ; d. Greenfield, '85.
Adams, Sarah E., Boston ; m. Joseph S. Potter, '46 ; 13 Byron St., Boston.

1844.

Allen, Abby, Oakham ; m. Rev. S. B. Fairbank, '46 ; d. Bombay, India, '52.
Allyn, Mary R., Windsor, Ct. ; m. *Spencer B. Root, '47 ; d. Greenfield, '52.
Arms, Sarah S., Greenfield ; d. Greenfield, '44.
Atwood, Harriet P., Newington, Ct. ; m. John S. Kirkham, '59 ; d. Newington, Ct., '82.
Babcock, Jerusha, Junius, N. Y. ; d. Syracuse, Neb., '77.
Bailey, Elizabeth G., Fairfax Co., Va. ; m. *Geo. W. Francis, '45 ; 233 *Monroe St., Brooklyn, N. Y.*
Beardsley, Mary, Danby, N. Y. ; m. Richard R. Hauley, M.D., '52; *Sidney, Io.*
Boies, Elizabeth T., Blandford ; *Blandford.*
Boudinot, Elinor S., Washington, Ct. ; m. Henry J. Church, '48 ; d. Washington, Ct., '56.
Bouton, Laura A., N. Y. City.
Bowen, Cynthia, Colchester, Ct. ; m. *Wm. R. Potter, '47 ; *Norwich Town, Ct.*
Bowen, Emily J., Woodstock, Ct. ; d. Woodstock, Ct., '90.
Burns, Lydia F., Rockport ; m. Alfred C. Pool, '47 ; d. Chelsea, '85.
Button, Mary A., Wallingford, Vt. ; m. Calvin M. Townsend, '48 ; *Fresno, Cal.*
Buxton, Eliza J., New Boston, N. H. ; m. *Robert M. Gregg, '51 ; *Box 53, Northfield, Vt.*
Chapin, Jane, W. Springfield ; *Plattekill, N. Y.*
Chapman, Julia A., Warehouse Point, Ct. ; *Windsor Locks, Ct.*
Child, Frances S., N. Y. City ; m. Geo. W. Williams, '47 ; 140 *Willow St., Brooklyn, N. Y.*
Clark, Mary S., Hartford, Ct. ; m. Latham Kassick, '49 ; *Cor. Main and Blackstone Sts., Jackson, Mich.*
Comstock, Mary J., Kent, Ct. ; m. *John H. Dimock, '57 ; *Torrington, Ct.*
Cooke, Sarah E., New Haven, Ct. ; m. *Edward Crowell, '55 ; m. Thos. Guyer, '65 ; d. S. Norwalk, Ct., '88.
Currier, Julia M., W. Chester, N. H. : *Washington, D. C.*
Cushman, Eliza F., Orwell, Vt. ; m. Hiland H. Young, '50 ; *Orwell, Vt.*
Cushman, Mary A., Orwell, Vt. ; m. *Wm. More, '49 ; *Lindley, N. Y.*
Dana, Isabella G., Pomfret, Vt. ; m. Oliver C. Woodward, '48 ; *Northfield, Vt.*
Danielson, Charlotte T., W. Killingly, Ct. ; m. *Orville M. Capron, '52 ; *Broad St., Danielsonville, Ct.*
Davison, M. Elizabeth, Norwich, Ct. ; d. Norwich, Ct., '94.
Deuel, Mary M., Pine Plains, N. Y. ; d. Pine Plains, N. Y., '84.
Dewing, Nancy A., Canterbury, Ct. ; m. *Lippett Congdon, '49 ; 15 *Crocker Ave., Providence, R. I.*
Eastman, Hannah, Amherst ; m. Wm. Chapman, '49 ; d. W. Springfield, '80.
Ferguson, Christiana, N. Y. City ; m. *Thos. Wallace, '58 ; 210 *W. 104th St., N. Y. City.*
Fithian, Mary H., Bridgeton, N. J. ; 139 *Commerce St., Bridgeton, N. J.*
Grant, Martha, Colebrook, Ct. ; d. Colebrook, Ct., '47.
Graves, Fanny, Hatfield ; d. Hatfield, '84.
Hathaway, Lydia D., Freetown ; m. *Benj. W. Smith, '48 ; m. *Jas. Dearden, '73 ; *Box 129, Phenix, R. I.*
Hathaway, Olive D., Freetown ; m. Benj. Strowbridge ; care *Mrs. Martha Day, Watertown.*
Hawkes, Elizabeth W., Charlemont ; m. *A. I. Van Vorhes, '49 ; *Circleville, O.*
Hinds, Hannah, Winchester, N. H. ; m. Isaac P. Alexander, '45 ; d. Davenport, Io., '60.
Hitchcock, Laura S., Park Hill, Ind. Ter. ; d. Mt. Holyoke Seminary, '43.
Hobart, Julia, Berlin, Vt. ; m. Rev. P. F. Barnard, '46 ; *Westminster, Vt.*
Huntington, Charlotte S., Norwich, Ct. ; m. *John H. Clark, '46 ; care *Lyman-Eliel Drug Co., Minneapolis, Minn.*
Huse, Charlotte A., Methuen ; m. Edward S. Ryder, M.D., '63 ; 85 *Congress St., Portsmouth, N. H.*
Kilburn Sarah A., Princeton ; m. *Rev. Wm. D. Hitchcock, '52 ; m. *Rev. Randolph Campbell, '61 ; 606 *N. 16th St., Lincoln, Neb.*

1844.

Kingsley, Rhoda, Canterbury. Ct. ; m. *John P. Webb, '50 ; d. Windham, Ct., '93.
Knowlton, Sarah A., Brattleboro, Vt. ; m. *Theodore Brown, '45 ; 116 *Lincoln St., Worcester.*
Lincoln, Emeline, Oakham ; m. C. P. Fitch, M.D., '58 ; 133 *W. 97th St., N. Y. City.*
Lincoln, Sarah A. B., Petersham ; m. N. L. Look, '48 ; d. Broad Ford, Va., '57.
McCray, Caroline, Springfield ; m. John S. Putnam, '46 ; 412 *7th St.,S., Minneapolis, Minn.*
Martindale Jane M., Greenfield ; m. *Whiting Griswold, Esq., '44 ; d. Greenfield, '52.
Merriam, Eleanor M., Grafton ; d. Grafton, '52.
Nickerson, Eleanor, S. Dennis ; m. John Baxter, '50 ; d. S. Dennis, '58.
Ordway, Lucy A., Amesbury ; *Amesbury.*
Paine, Amelia O., Elmira, N. Y. ; m. *John Warner, '45 ; 679 *Broadway, Chelsea.*
Pomeroy, Lydia B., Stonington, Ct. ; m. *Thos. Wheeler, '46 ; d. Southport, Ct., '88.
Poole, Henrietta, Rockport ; m. Thos. T. Tufts, '48 ; d. Rockport, '92.
Russ, Eliza P., N. Y. City ; d. (N. Y. City?) before '63.
Safford, Helen E., Philadelphia, Pa. ;
Sanderson, Lucy W., Ashfield ; d. Ashfield, '64.
Sands, Catharine, N. Y. City ;
Scrugham, Elizabeth, N. Y. City ; m. *Theodore Lyman, M.D., '50 ; d. S. Hadley, '53.
Seaver, Hannah P., Marlboro ; m. *Wilson Homer, '46 ; deceased.
Seymour, Mary A., Hadley ; m. Edwin Bliss, '48 ; *Holly, N. Y.*
Sherman, Sarah P., Woodbury, Ct. ; m. David H. Meloy, '50 ; 44 *Linden St., Waterbury, Ct.*
Smith, Annie, Stonington, Ct. ; d. Stonington, Ct., '89.
Smith, Eliza J., W. Rutland, Vt. ; m. *Rev. Royal G. Wilder, '46 ; d. Kolapur, India.
Smith, Harriet A., W. Springfield ; d. W. Springfield, '49.
Smith, Jane, Enfield ; d. Whitefield, Vt., '79.
Smith, Margaret O., Granby ; m. Jason L. Dwight, '49 ; *Boulder, Col.*
Smith, Mary A., Lee ; m. *Hon. Elizur Smith, '65 ; *Lee.*
Solander, Eliza A., Brimfield ; m. Harrison G. Whitney, '55 ; d. Westminster, '89.
Spaulding, Harriet N., Townsend ; *Townsend.*
Spencer, Ardelia A., Gouverneur, N. Y. ; m. *Rev. Howard Burnside, '50 ; m. James McClurg, '54 ; d. Westfield, N. Y., '78.
Sprague, Lucy D., Colchester, Ct. ; d. Colchester, Ct., '44.
Steele, Emeline M , Washington, Ct. ; m. *Chas. B. Vaill, '51 ; 174 *Hicks St., Brooklyn, N. Y.*
Sweetland, Anne, Hartford, Ct. ; m. E. C. Griswold, '52 ; 110½ *Middle Ave., Elyria, O.*
Tole, Nancy A., W. Brattleboro, Vt. ; d. Charlestown, N. H , '53.
Torrey, Delia C., Millbury ; *Millbury.*
Torrey, Louisa M., Millbury ; m. *Hon. Alphonso Taft, '55 ; *Millbury.*
Weaver, Mary C., Penfield, N. Y.; m. *Rev. S. S. Goss, '49 ; *care Rev. M. W. Stryker, D.D , Clinton, N. Y.*
Weeks, Maria E., Bennington, Vt. ; m. Chas. C. Hinsdale, '47 ; d. Cleveland, O., '61.
Welles, Abby, Newington, Ct. ; m. John D. Seymour, '52 ; *Newington Junction, Ct.*
Wendall, Kate, Brooklyn, N. Y. ; m. Oscar Edwards, '51 ; 41 *Elm St., Northampton.*
Wheeler, Martha J., Burlington, Vt. ; m. *Theodore C. Elliott, '48 ; 946 *West Ave., Buffalo, N. Y.*
Wheelock, Martha S., Warren ; m. *H. M. Matthews, M.D , '48 ; d. St. Louis, Mo., '92.
Whithed, Isabella, Vernon, Vt. ; 105 *Inman St., Cambridgeport.*
Whittlesey, Cornelia, Newington, Ct. ; d. Newington, Ct., '85.

1845.

GRADUATES.

Allen, Harriette, Lebanon, N. H.; m. J. P. Dunlap, M.D., '48; d. Syracuse, N. Y., '84.
Allen, Susan M., Manchester; m. *M. P. Greenleaf. M.D., '46; d. Bradford, '54.
Avery, Caroline. Conway; m N. A. Halbert, Esq., '50; d. Midland Park, N. J., '80.
Bagg, Jane F., W. Springfield; m. Henry A. Marsh, '51; d. Amherst, '76.
Bailey, Lydia G., Hopkinton, N. H.; m. *Rev. N. B. Rogers, '49; m. *Rev. C. M. Cordley, '52; *Ridgewood Ave., Glen Ridge, N. J.*
Baldwin, Lydia R., Southampton; m. *David B. Phelps, '49; d. Southampton, '72.
Bates, Susan F., N. Brookfield; m. Joel A. Jennings, '46; d. N. Y. City, '84.
Bissell, Mary H., Norwalk, Ct.; d. Norwalk, Ct., '45.
Clarke, Sarah D., Chelsea; m. Jonathan A. Lane, '51; *623 Tremont St., Boston.*
Cook, Harriet E., Manchester, Ct.; d. Middletown, Ct., '82.
Ellis, Mary A., Lowell; m. *Richard Emerson, '50; 2215 *Dupont Ave., N., Minneapolis, Minn.*
Everett, Sarah E., Benson, Vt.; *Sutter City, Cal.*
Foote, Sarah E., Cayuga, N. Y.; m. *A. F. Prentiss, '56; d. New London, Ct., '63.
Fowler, Cynthia, Westfield; m. *Rev. L. S. Hobart, '55; *92 Mill St., Springfield.*
Fowler, Susan H., Greenfield, N. H.; 4010 *Girard Ave., Philadelphia, Pa.*
Green, Hannah, Auburn; d. Auburn, '84.
Green, Mary S., Lowell; m. William P. McKay, '50; d. Boston, '50.
Green, Sarah E., Lowell; d. Brooklyn, N. Y., '83.
Hayes, Julia A., S. Hadley; m. Benj. Douglass, '56; d. Santa Barbara, Cal., '94.
Hitchcock, Catharine, Amherst; m. *Rev. H. M. Storrs, D.D., LL.D., '52; d. Orange, N. J., '95.
Hollister, Ann M., Manchester, Vt.; m. *Rev. A. B. Campbell, '51; 72 *Alleghany St., Boston.*
Hooker, Mary, Longmeadow; *Longmeadow.*
Hopkins, Mary, Miller's Place, N. Y.; m. *J. B. Marshall, '49; d. Miller's Place, N. Y., '85.
Humphrey, Mary E., Amherst; m. Rev. David Torrey, '48; d. Ann Arbor, Mich., '67.
King, Elizabeth, Vernon, Ct.; m. S. G Resley, M.D., '49; d. Vernon, Ct., '52.
Lane, R. Augusta, Boston; m. Rev. Elihu Loomis, '51; d. Littleton, '67.
Leach, Frances S., Pittsford, Vt.; m. *Wm Warner, '60; d. Detroit, Mich., '93.
Lee, Diantha C., Northampton; m. *Rev. Wm. Bates, '48; *Abbott St., Wellesley.*
Locke, Clementine M., Hinsdale, N. H.; m. Rev. Wm. Porter, '49; *Tropico, Cal.*
Loomis, Sarah, Bennington, Vt.; m. *Rev. A. M. Beveridge, D.D., '49; 614 *Fifth Ave., Lansingburgh, N. Y.*
McIntyre, Flora P., Charlton; m. *Rev. J. M. Stearns, '47; m. *Chas. Boswell, '61; d. W. Hartford, Ct., '82.
Niles, Harriet S., Spencertown, N. Y.; 805 *Park Ave., Plainfield, N. J.*
Oliphant, Mary P., Haverhill; m. *Rev. L. C. Ford, '50; d Coolville, O., '51.
Olmsted, Anna M, E. Hartford, Ct.; m. H. K. Olmsted, M.D., '55; d. Hartford, Ct., '85.
Osgood, Sarah H., Springfield; m. *A. H. Avery, '54; *3 Lafayette St, Springfield.*
Parsons, Mary E, Newbury; d. Crown Point, Ind., '60.
Pease, Mary C., Blandford; d. Independence, Io., '76.
Perkins, Rhoda K., Braintree; m. J. W. Porter, '51; d. Burlington, Me., '75.
Pitkin, Elizabeth, E. Hartford, Ct.; *Providence, R. I.*
Pond, Mary A., W. Medway; m. *Rev. F. Y. Washburne, '48; *Hancock, Mich.*
Rice, Lois W., Conway; m. Thomas E. Hale, '54; d. Castine, Me., '73.
Schuyler, Julia W., Ovid, N. Y.; m *Edward H. Lawrence, '49; 203 *W. 103d St., N. Y. City.*
Scott, Martha C., N. Hadley; m. *O. Dickinson, '56; 323 *State St., Waukegan, Ill.*
Sherwood, Eveline A., Jamesville, N. Y.; m. R. M. Richardson, Esq., '50; 800 *Mulberry St., Syracuse, N. Y.*
Stevens, Helen M. G., Springfield; *Norwalk, Ct.*

1845.

Taylor, Emma L., Derry. N. H. ; d. St. Johnsbury, Vt , '86.
Tenny, Roxena B , Orwell, Vt. ; m. Daniel Newhall, '57 ; *Waukesha, Wis.*
Thompson, Mary P., Durham. N. H. ; d. Durham, N. H., '94.
Thurston, Persis G , Kailua, H. I. ; m. *Rev. T. E. Taylor, '47 ; *care J. P. Winne, Redwood City, Cal.*
Tolman, Susan L., Ware; m. *Rev. Cyrus T. Mills, '48 ; *Mills College P. O., Cal.*
Youngs, Cornelia. Farmington, Ct.; d. Baton Rouge, La., '47.

NON-GRADUATES.

Allen, Mary H., Enfield. Ct.; m. P. Smith Williams, '47 ; d. Hadley. '72.
Andros. Martha N., Freetown ; m. *John K. Deane, '83; d. Boston. '94.
Archer, Amanda M., Fall River ; 79 *High St., Fall River.*
Bailey, Emily L., Hartford. Vt.; m. *Rollin White, '51; 892 *Elmwood Ave., Buffalo, N. Y.*
Bailey, Sarah. Somers, N. Y.; m. Alonzo B. Thacker, '49; *Somers, N. Y.*
Baird, Abbie E., W. Becket ; m. *H. C. Wilson, '49; 827 *S. W. St., Rockford, Ill.*
Barrett. Ellen C., Rutland, Vt.; 39 *Washington St., Rutland, Vt.*
Belknap, Clara, Sturbridge ; m. Wm. Holbrook, M.D., '50; *Palmer.*
Benedict, Martha, New Preston, Ct. ; d. N. Preston, Ct., '50.
Benton, Maria W., Hartford, Ct.; 159 *Elm St., Northampton.*
Bigelow, Catharine A , Framingham ; m. Job T. Perry, '53; d. Reading, '84.
Bigelow, Martha F., Boston ; m. *Rev. Heman R. Timlow. '54 ; *Nutley, N. J.*
Bodman, Elizabeth B., Williamsburg; m. Rev. Nathan Bosworth. '49; d. Emporium. Pa . '87.
Bogue, Catharine, Chittenden, Vt. ; m. Dr. Ebenezer H. Drury, '50 ; d. Pittsford, Vt., '56.
Booth, Caroline, E. Windsor, Ct. ; m. Albert S. Wells. '51 ; *Granby, Ct.*
Bridgman, Rebecca A., Northampton ; m. Chas. F. Goodwin, '54 ; 35 *Park Ave., Waterbury, Ct.*
Brown. Caroline O., Brownhelm. O. ; d. Elyria. O., '48
Brown, Eliza C. H., Hampton, Ct.; d. Hampton, Ct., '46.
Brown. Mary J , Buffalo, N. Y.; *care Rev. Horatio Brown, Wooster, O.*
Burt, Abbey A., Great Barrington ; m. John Bascom. '52 ; d. Great Barrington. '54.
Carver, Lydia A , Taunton ; d. Newport, R. I., '86.
Chapin, Julia A., Springfield ; m *Rev. J. B Grinnell. '52 ; *Grinnell, Io.*
Chapman, Ann E., E. Haddam, Ct. ; m. Robert S. Cone, '49 ; *Moodus, Ct.*
Chase, Lydia P., Millbury; m. H. D. P. Bigelow, Esq., '54 ; d. Chicago. Ill., '78.
Chase. Martha A., Cabotville (now Chicopee) ; m. Ralph Morgan, '51 ; d. Chicopee, '56.
Clark, Mary, Williamsburg ; m. Benjamin R. Tilton, '48 ; d. S. Deerfield. '86.
Clarke, Sarah E., Montpelier, Vt.; m. Chauncey M. Rubler. M.D.; '49; d. Montpelier, Vt., '55.
Clarke, Wealthy. Williamstown, Vt. ; d. Worcester, '56.
Cowdery, Abby A., E. Haddam, Ct.; m. Ozias E. Palmer, '49 ; *N. Thornington St , Algona, Io.*
Cowles, Abigail F., Norfolk, Ct ; m *Rev. Joel Grant, '45 ; d Chicago. Ill.. '81
Crofut, Florilla H., Arlington, Vt.; m. *Geo. M. Van Vechtend. '48 ; *Manteno, Ill.*
Curtis, Sarah E., Bristol, Ct. ; m. Frank Woodworth, '53; *Thomaston, Ct.*
Dana, Mary J., Lebanon, N. H. ; m. S. J. Mills Wilcox, '63 ; d. Utica. Ill., '79.
Dickinson, Emeline H., Springfield; m. *Thos. Bishop, '51 ; d Springfield. '93.
Dixon, Eliza F., Dedham ; m. Geo. H. Vose. '50; *Castleton Hotel, Brighton Heights, Staten Island, N. Y.*
Dunklee, Ruth C., W. Brattleboro, Vt.; m. Nelson Barbour, '49; d. Wolfboro, N. H., '54.
Dutcher, Henrietta F., Kent, Ct.; m. *Peter W. Badgley. '49; m. John Bradford. '61 ; d. Milwaukee, Wis.. '79.
Eaton, Elizabeth, Framingham ; m. *Rev. Jesse Guernsey. '56; *Framingham.*
Eddy, Maria R., Auburn; m. *Rev. Isaac N. Hobart. '51; *Downer's Grove, Ill.*
Edwards, Julia A., Southampton; m. Rev. C. H. Taylor, '50; d. Alton. Ill., '89.

1845.

Edwards, Rachel C., Southampton; m. *Isaac Parsons, '50; *Southampton.*
Finch, Tamson J., Somers. N. Y.; m. Wm. M. Ambler, '50; *Nyack on the Hudson, N. Y.*
Flagg, Harriet D., Boylston; m. Henry G. Smith, '50; d. Boylston, '64.
Flagg, Sarah E., Boylston; m. Oliver H. Perry, '56; d. Boylston, '57.
Franklin, Charlotte L., Canaan, Ct.; d. Canaan, Ct., '63.
Gridley, Caroline D., Granby; m. O. H. Pratt, '47; d. Englewood, N. J., '86.
Griswold, Ellen A., Newburyport; m. *Wm. S. Phillips, '50; *Box 307, W. Winsted, Ct.*
Hall, Frances A., Ithaca, N. Y.; m. Rev. Timothy Hill, '51; 1613 *Belleview Ave., Kansas City, Mo.*
Hall, H. Rosamond, Ithaca, N. Y.; m. *B. R. Hawley, '51; 35 *Cass St., Chicago, Ill.*
Harding, Eliza M., E. Medway; m. *Rev. Augustus Walker, '52; *Auburndale.*
Harris, Mary S., Southampton, N. Y.; m. Francis W. Cook, '49; d. Southampton, '51.
Hastings, Lois S., Warwick; m. Edward F. Mayo, '48; *Northboro.*
Hayes, Mary, S. Hadley; m. Sumner I. Smith, '46; d. Lyons, Io., '78.
Holbrook, Rachel, Washington, N. Y.; *Lakeville, Ct.*
Howard, Nancy, Townsend; m. Abner Hunt, '52; d. Townsend, '61.
Hunt, Mary A., Columbia, Ct.; m. Samuel Hitchcock, '50; 49 *North St., Bayonne City, N. J.*
Hurd, Harriet C., Newark, N. J.; m. Orrin Blackmar, '47; d. Newark, N. Y., '54.
Jacobs, Mary, Galena, Ill.; m. *H. A. Mix, '49; d. Oregon, Ill., '84.
Janes, Martha A., Northampton; m. *Wm. Truesdell, Esq., '50; d. Iowa City, Io., '59.
Jewell, Caroline, Salisbury, Ct.; m. Jas. Wm. Parks, '46; d. Salisbury, Ct., '50.
Jewell, Maria, Salisbury, Ct.; m. *Jas. Wm. Parks, '51; *Ashley Falls.*
Josselyn, Adeline D., Plainfield; m. Edward W. Noyes, '64; d. Newton Center, '69.
Kellogg, Sarah W., Newington, Ct.; m. *Samuel K. Camp, '54; 257 *Lafayette Ave., Brooklyn, N. Y.*
Leland, Adeliza, Holliston; d. Holliston, '59.
Leland, Rhoda A., Holliston; m. *Alden Leland, '55; *Church Ave., Holliston.*
Lewis, Ellen H., Terryville, Ct.; m. *J. L. Page, '49; 519 *Lake St., Madison, Wis.*
Little, Margaretta C., Bridgeton, N. J.; m. *Isaac A. Sheppard, '50; d. Philadelphia, Pa., '81.
Longley, Henrietta A., Hawley; d. Hawley, '50.
McLean, Hester, Evans Mills, N. Y.; m. Aaron Dexter, '47; d. Black River, N. Y., '88.
Merrill, Sarah P., Stratham, N. H.; m. Rev. O. R. Bachelder, '47; *New Hampton, N. H.*
Miller, Maria A., Newark, N. Y.; m. John S. Cromise, '53; d. Newark, N. Y., '77.
Mobley, Amanda, Gainesville, Ala.; m. *H. F. Eaton, '50; m. Wm. H. Childe, '64; *Gainesville, Ala.*
Mobley, Martha, Gainesville, Ala.; m. Rev. Geo. W. Boggs, '55; *Macon, Tenn.*
Montague, Harriet, S. Hadley; m. *Edward H. Judd, '62; *S. Hadley.*
Morgan, Mary F., Northfield; m. Sullivan L. Ward, '53; d. Lowell, '87.
Nash, Susan L., Middle Haddam, Ct.;
Nickerson, Bethia S., Chatham; m. Milton Gage, '50; d. Chatham, '51.
Norton, Cornelia D., Salisbury, Ct.; m. John O. Niles, M.D., '54; d. Brooklyn, N. Y., '94.
Ordway, Susan S., W. Newbury; m. David Plumer, '54; *Box 400, Newburyport.*
Osgood, Anna, Springfield; d. San Francisco, Cal., '56.
Parker, Margaret A., Philadelphia, Pa.; m. Rev. Sam. W. Crittenden, '55; d. S. Orange, N. J. '59.
Parkinson, Frances C., Nashua, N. H.; m. *Rev. M. G. Wheeler, '48; *N. Woburn.*
Payson, Sarah E., Peterboro, N. H.; d. Milton, '67.
Pease, Elizabeth M., Rochester, N. Y.; m. Geo. Dutton, Jr., '50; d. Utica, N. Y., '56.
Penfield, Catharine J., Pittsford, Vt.; 234 *South St., Bennington, Vt.*
Perkins, Mary D., Marietta, O.; m. Joseph P. Shaw, '49; d. Marietta, O., '53.
Phelps, Martha, Stonington, Ct.; m. Gurdon Gates, '53; d. Mystic Bridge, Ct., '84.
Pier, Eveline H., Fredonia, N. Y.; m. Amzi Morey, '46; *Ness City, Kan.*
Pier, Louisa W., Fredonia, N. Y.; m. *Isaac A. Saxton, Esq., '55; *Box 609, Fredonia, N. Y.*

1845.

Pierpont, Mary J., Rutland, Vt.; d. Rutland, Vt., '45.
Pierpont, Susan S., Rutland, Vt.; d. Rutland, Vt., '90.
Pomeroy, Phebe W., Stonington, Ct.; d. Stonington, Ct., '46.
Powell, Harriet N., Cedarville, N. J.; m. O. B. Gauss, '48; d. Philadelphia, Pa., '56.
Pritchard, Elizabeth A., Waterbury, Ct.; d. Waterbury, Ct., '54.
Proctor, Edna Dean, Henniker, N. H.; *Framingham.*
Putnam, Julia, Hinsdale; m. Phineas L. Page, Esq., '53; d. Pittsfield, '69.
Radford, Elizabeth H., Middlebury, Ct.; m. Chas. Evans, '50; *Gaylordsville, Ct.*
Randall, Lucretia M., Wallingford, Vt.; m. Frank Miller, '56; *Wallingford, Vt.*
Rice, Nancy M., Sturbridge; m. Stanley G. Wight, '57; *Brookfield.*
Robinson, Charlotte L., Oakham; m. John H. G. Mead, '50; d. Cleveland, O., '57.
Savage, Jane W.,Schnectady,N. Y.; m. *Geo. W. Allen,'47; 265 *Martin St., Milwaukee, Wis.*
Seabury, Caroline R., Granby; d. Washington, D. C., '93.
Sears, Mary J., Boston; m. Samuel P. May, '52; d. Boston, '60.
Seaver, Angeline T., Chelsea; m. Wm. E. Bissell, '46; d. Norwalk. Ct., '56.
Simes, Sarah E., Portsmouth, N. H.; d. Stratham, N. H., '80.
Smith, Mary, Chatham, Ct.; d. Colchester, Ct., '47.
Spalding, Martha E., Montpelier, Vt.; d. Montpelier, Vt., '48.
Sparrow, Sarah A., Cambridge; d. Cambridge, '72.
Sperry,Henrietta C., Brooklyn,N. Y.; m. Rev. Robert S. Macloy,'50; d. Yokohama,Jap.,'79.
Swan, Angelina B., Stonington, Ct.; m. Albert Hancox, '47; d. Springfield, '70.
Talcott. Elizabeth K., Coventry, Ct.; 56 *Whalley Ave., New Haven, Ct.*
Taylor, Jane, Sturbridge; d. Fiskdale, '49.
Taylor, Sarah A., Dunstable; m. *Samuel M. Fletcher, '49; d. Westerly, R. I., '67.
Thomas, Sarah E., Stephentown, N. Y.; m. *W. L. Jones, '48; m. *S. C. Vary, Esq., '55;
    m. M. T. Garvey, '69; d. Cassopolis, Mich., '90.
Tolman, Ann, Dorchester; *Arlington.*
Travis, Henrietta, Holliston; m. Wm. Gay, '52; *Norwood.*
Tyler, Elizabeth B., Amherst; *Auburndale.*
Van Deusen, Rebecca P., Newark, N. Y.; m. Edwin E. Rogers. '63; *Palmyra, N. Y.*
Van Vechten, Catharine, Schenectady, N. Y.; m. Rev. E. A. Huntington, '68; 11 *Seminary St., Auburn, N. Y.*
Waldo, Harriette L., Portage, N. Y.; m. *Wm. S. McNair, '48; d. Ottawa, Ill., '93.
Waldo, Margarette, Portage, N.Y.; m. Lorin J. Ames, M. D., '48; d. Mt. Morris, N.Y., '88.
Warren, Mary E., Chesterfield, N. H.; m. Rev. James Tufts, '55; *Monson.*
Wells, Helen, Stockbridge; d. Stockbridge, '51.
Westcott, Mary L., Fairton, N. J.; m. J. A. Parvin, '60; d. Muscatine, Ia., '65.
Wheeler, Martha W., Keene, N. H.; m. Thos. H. Williams, '50; 255 *Nicolet Ave., Minneapolis, Minn.*
Williston, Harriet R., Easthampton; m. *Col. Wm. S. Clark, '53; 19 *Baldwin St., Newton.*
Wilson, Mariette, Milan, N. Y.; m. David Messner,'54; d. New Haven, Ct., '88.
Wolcott, Elizabeth E., Tallmadge, O.; d. Mt. Holyoke Seminary, '45.
Woodward, Lydia M., Concord. N. H.; m. Rev. Jas. Fletcher, '49; d. Groton, '77.
Youngs, Caroline E., Farmington, Ct.; m. Edwin Ayer, '83; *Saybrook, Ct.*

1846.

GRADUATES.

Abbott, Lydia E. M., Gilsum, N. H.; d. Westfield, N. Y., '47.
Ainslie, Abbie M., Onondaga Valley, N. Y.; m. *N. Mickles, '49; *Good Thunder, Minn.*

1846.

Aldrich, Laura, Westmoreland, N. H.; m. Rev. Wm. Cunningham, '67; d. Princeville, Ill., '67.
Barker, Mary E., Amenia, N. Y.; d. Amenia, N. Y., '46.
Bates, Lydia, Springfield, Vt.; m. Rev. Lewis Grout, '46; *W. Brattleboro, Vt.*
Beaman, Mary A., Princeton; m. Rev. Henry Cummings, '51; *Strafford, Vt.*
Brigham, Lucy H., Bridgewater; d. St. Charles, Mo., '53.
Brinsmade, Mary M., Washington, Ct.; m. Geo. L. Brown, '64; d. Washington, Ct., '87.
Charlton, Jane E., Littleton. N. H.; m. Rev. Ebenezer Cutler, '49; d. Worcester, '59.
Condit, Hannah Maria, Oswego, N. Y.; m. Rev. Wm. W. Eddy, '51; *Beirut, Syria.*
Curtis, Mary M., Sturbridge; m. *F. W. Seymour, '55; d. Ravenna, O., '59.
Dewey, Elizabeth, Moriah. N. Y.; *Moriah, N. Y.*
Dutton, Eliza P., Boston; m. Rev. Daniel T. Fiske, '49; d. Newburyport, '62.
Dutton, Lucia E., Boston; m. *Rev. Edwin S. Wright, '48; *Amherst.*
Eastman, Sarah M., Derry, N. H.; m. Frank M. Harris, '55; 8 *W. 130th St., N. Y. City.*
Fiske, Rebecca W., Shelburne; m. Rev. Burdett Hart, '49; d. New Haven, Ct., '92.
Forman, Mary E., Nichols, N. Y.; m. *Edwin S. Woodbridge, '48; 25 *Murray St., Binghamton, N. Y.*
Frissell, Elizabeth S., Peru; m. Henry F. Marsh, '55; d. New York City, '70.
Garfield, Jane E., Lee; m. H. F. Waite, Esq., '53; 7 *Astor St., Chicago, Ill.*
Gilbert, Elizabeth H., North Coventry, Ct.; m. F. T. Chapman, '50; d. *Wethersfield, Ct , '79.*
Hartwell, Melicent J., New Marlboro; d. New Marlboro, '46.
Herrick, Eliza A., Crown Point, N. Y.; m. *C. F. Dike, '51; m. Rev. Joshua M. Chamberlain, '80; *Grinnell, Ia.*
Houghton, Marilla, Dana; m. *J. C. Gallup, M.D., '58; d. Clinton, N. Y., '94.
Howes, Mary W., Buckland; m. P. M. Goddard, '65; 757 *D St., Tacoma, Wash.*
Johnson,Harriet,Sturbridge; m. Rev. R. M. Loughridge,D.D.,'53; 500 *N. 14th St.,Waco,Tex.*
Kellogg, Nancy M., N. Amherst; *Seymour House, Oshkosh, Wis.*
Metcalf, Mary B., Hudson,O.; m. *Rev. Erastus Chester, '54; *Clifton Springs, N. Y.*
Miles, Jane M., Goshen, Ct.; d. Goshen, Ct., '50.
Packard, Sarah D., Spencer; m. James C. Holden, '50; *Madison, N. J.*
Preston, Frances O., S. Hadley; d. S. Hadley, '46.
Rice, Mary S., Lincoln; *Lincoln.*
Smith, Isabella, Enfield; m. *Hon. Rufus D. Woods, '48; *Enfield.*
Spalding, Caroline A., Haverhill, N. H.; d. Haverhill, N. H., '83.
Spofford, Sophia, Thomaston, Me.; *Rockland, Me.*
Stillman, Julia E., Colebrook, Ct.; m. S. D. Crosby, '49; d. Aurora, Ill., '75.
Thompson, Eliza J., Derby, Ct.; m. *J. W. Mitchell, M.D., '50; 58 *E. 86th St., N. Y. City.*
Wheeler, Achsah, New Marlboro; m. *J. P. Perkins, M.D.,'47; m. *Geo. H. Woodruff,'57; 207 *N. Broadway, Joliet, Ill.*
Wheeler, Lydia A., N. Stonington, Ct.; m. *Warren Newton, Esq., '51; *Norwich, N. Y.*
Whittemore, Harriet L, Spencer; m. Phineas Jones, '53; d. Newark, N. J., '66.
Wing, Electa, Ashfield; d. Willoughby, O., '47.
Wright, Celia S., Blandford; m. Rev. John C. Strong, '46; d. Illinois, '50.
Wyman, Lucy G., Fitchburg; m. *A. T. Gibson, '46; m. A. G. Coes, Esq., '56; d. Worcester, '61.

NON-GRADUATES.

Ainslie, Helen A., Onondaga Hollow, N. Y.; m. Daniel W. Hastings, '54; d. Onondaga Valley, N. Y., '80.
Ames, Semantha M., N. Becket; m. Rev. Joshua Barnard, '47; *Delavan, Minn.*
Ball, Semantha W., Leverett; m. *Rev. Chas. Galpin, '50; *Excelsior, Minn.*
Barlow, Lucy, S. Amenia, N. Y.; m. Rev. Samuel F. Bacon, '52; d. Peru, '92.

1846.

Blackler, Ellen L., Marblehead ; m. *Frederick Perkins ; *Florence, Italy.*
Brigham, Angeline, Westboro ; m. *Daniel Mitchell, '50 ; *Prescott, Arizona.*
Browne, Clara, Somers, N. Y.; m. Samuel C. Merritt, Esq., '59 ; *Mt. Kisco, N. Y.*
Browne, Frances L., Bloomfield, Ct.; m. Emerson Johnson,'46 ; *The Jackson Sanatorium, Dansville, N. Y.*
Buck, Mary E., Sturbridge ; m John G. Avery, '49 ; d. Windham, Ct., '54.
Burnham, Mary A., Essex ; m Wm Marshall, '49 ; d. Essex, '72.
Catlin, Frances C., New Marlboro ; m. *Almon P. Ticknor,M D.,'53 ; m. *M. C. Richardson, M.D. '65 ; *New Marlboro.*
Clark, Lucy A., Waterbury, Ct.; m. *J. Edward Smith, '49 ; *Waterbury, Ct.*
Cogswell, Martha P., Woodbury, Ct.; d Woodbury, Ct, '54.
Cook, Elizabeth, Homer, N. Y; m. A. N. Read, M D., '56 ; *Norwalk, O.*
Cooper, Harriet A., Sag Harbor, N. Y.; m. *Dr. Almond D. Teachout, '51 ; d. Sag Harbor, N. Y., '81
Dougherty, Emma, Newark, N. J.; m. *Alfred B. Brittin, '52 ; *New Brunswick, N. J.*
Dowse, Deborah, Sherborn ; m. Jones Leland, '49 ; d. Sherborn, '51.
Dwight, Nancy M , S. Hadley ; m. Byron Smith, '47 ; *S. Hadley.*
Ely, Fanny E., W. Springfield ; m. Sidney Tracy, '55 ; *Newtonville.*
Freeman, Sarah H., Plainfield, N. H.; d Plainfield, N. H., '69.
Goodell, Abbie D , Constantinople, Turkey ; m. *Rev. E. D. G. Prime,'60 ; d. N.Y. City,'91.
Goodell, Eliza, Constantinople, Turkey ; m. Jas. Bird, '55 ; *Great Barrington.*
Gordon, Elizabeth M , Newtown, Pa.; *Cooperstown, N. Y.*
Gorton, Hannah G., S. Hadley Falls ; m *Franklin Crosby, '50 ; *850 Broadway, Chelsea.*
Guild, Mary J., Newark, N. J.; d. Canton, O., '88.
Hapgood, Dorcas W., Boston ; m. *Rufus Scott, '46 ; *Amherst.*
Harvey, Maria A., Penn Yan, N. Y.; d. Penn Yan, N. Y., '48.
Hathaway, Amy J., N. Adams ; d. N. Adams, '46.
Holbrook, Eliza, Sturbridge ; m E. S. Smith, '53 ; d. Derby, Ct., '90.
Holt, Elizabeth, Bloomfield, Me.; m. *Wm. D. Babbitt, '50 ; d. St. Louis, Mo., '94.
Hooker, Sarah D., Longmeadow ; *Longmeadow.*
Howe, Charlotte, S. Brookfield ; m. Samuel F. Miller, '51 ; d. Lake Forest, Ill., '63.
Howe, Susan M., S. Brookfield ; d. Brookfield, '47.
Johnson, Rosa, Rome, N. Y.; m. Henry B. Woodbridge, '57 ; d. Vergennes, Vt., '73.
Kellogg, Keziah C., S. Hadley ; m. Wm. Smith, '52 ; d. S. Hadley, '88.
Kimball, Margaret A , Worcester ; *Southville.*
Landon, Cornelia, Salisbury, Ct.; m Silas B. Moore, '64 ; *Salisbury, Ct.*
Loomis, Harriet, Southwick ; m. *Sidney Birge, '54 ; d. Westfield, '77
Mann, Martha S., Boston ; m. *Geo. F. Harrington, Esq., '50 ; m. *Joseph J. Whiting, '62 ; m. *S. C. Pomeroy, '65 ; *1339 K St., Washington, D. C.*
Manning, Charlotte G., S. Coventry, Ct.; d. Hartford, Ct., '63.
Martin, Cornelia H., Fort Mifflin, Pa.; m. Jacob Schreiner, '47 ; d. Gratz, Pa., '49.
Noble, Eliza R., Canton, N. Y.; m. *Lyman L. Covey, '72 ; m. Delvan De Lance, '75 ; *Canton, N. Y.*
Packard, Lucinda J., Worcester ; m. Lucius Dunbar, '53 ; *W. Bridgewater.*
Parker, Henrietta, Pepperell ; m. *A. Chandler, '54 ; d. Pepperell, '69.
Parkhurst, Emily R., N. Y. City ; d. Montclair, N. J., '94.
Parsons, Mary J., Stanstead, Can.; m. *Thos. Snowden, '57 ; d. Augusta, Ga., '58.
Peabody, Ann Maria, New Boston, N H.; m. Rev. Chas. Seccombe, '50 ; d. St. Anthony, Minn., '53.
Phelps, Anna C., Fort Plain, N. Y.; m. M N. Gulick, '60 ; *Justin City, Cal.*
Pierce, Julia A., Stanstead, Can.; m. Geo. L. Goodwin, '50 ; *Boston.*
Pomeroy, S. Catharine, Somers. Ct.; m. *Henry B. Kirkland, Esq., '54 ; *Box 686, Springfield.*

38   1846.

Putnam, Lucy P., Plaistow, N. H.; d. Haverhill, '49.
Ransom, Sarah A., Owego, N. Y.; m. Francis M. Tower, '52; *Cornwall-on-the-Hudson, N.Y.*
Raymond, Emma A., Chatham, N. Y.; m. J. Braisted, '52; d. Louisville, Ky., '52.
Raymond, P. Jane, Chatham, N. Y.; m. C. C. Waldo, '56; d. Utica, Ind, '65.
Reed, Cornelia A., Montpelier, Vt.; d. Montpelier, Vt., '40.
Robbins, Mary J., Plymouth; *Plymouth.*
Rockwell, Chloe P., Parishville, N. Y.; d. Parishville, N. Y., '46.
Root, Caroline A., Guilford, Ct.; d. New Haven, Ct., '52.
Russell, Susan, Stafford, Ct.;
Scudder, Jane M., Boston; *Linden Place, Brookline.*
Sheldon, Mary, Westfield; m. *Rowse R. Clarke, M.D.,'57; *Box 260, Whitinsville.*
Slocumb, Maria R., Sutton; m. Wm. Terry, M.D., '48; 12 *S. Cliff St., Ansonia, Ct.*
Smith, Anna, S Hadley; d. S. Hadley, '47.
Smith, Emily F., Lincoln; m. Jas. S. Chapin, Esq., '48; *Lincoln.*
Stevens, Eleanor F., Plainfield, N. H.; m. *Horace S. Horton, '58; d. Pomeroy, O., '89.
Stoddard, Mary D., Groton, Ct.; m. Silas Fish, '51; 96 *Fort Greene Place, Brooklyn, N. Y.*
Swan, Mary S., M.D., Rochester, N. Y.; m. Thos. Sutton, '63; 16 *Wallace St., Cambridge.*
Talcott, Mary J., N. Coventry, Ct.; m. M. T. Landfear, '48; 125 *St. John St.,New Haren,Ct.*
Tarbell, Sarah Antoinette, Pepperell; m. E. F. Jones, '50; d. Pepperell, '02.
Taylor, Susan H., Hinsdale, N. H.; m. *Fred'k T. Kemper, '54; *Box 52, Santa Barbara,Cal.*
Todd, Lodema H., Hinsdale, N. H; m. Wm. Ketcham, '56; d. Richland City, Wis., '81.
Torrance, Anna A., Enfield; d. Philadelphia, "about '48."
Turner, P. Jane, Newburgh, N. Y.; m. Chas. H. Goodrich, '51; *Napierville, Ill.*
Walker, Mary A., Cooperstown, N. Y.; m. *Wm. S. Huntington, '50; 32 *Hillside Ave., Montclair, N. J.*
Ward, Eliza J., W. Brookfield; m. Francis A. Houghton, '48; d. Hyde Park, '73.
Wells, Harriette A., New Hartford, N. Y.; m. Julius H Royce,'48; d. Cape May, N.J.,'02.
Wheeler, Laura E., Burlington, Vt.; m. Henry J. Shuttleworth, '54; d. Buffalo, N. Y.,'01.
Whitcomb, Sarah, Berlin; m. *Wm. Lincoln, '56; *W. Boylston.*
Whitmore, Mary A., N. Guilford, Ct.; m. *Walter Stillman, '50; *Closter, N. J*
Wilder, Fidelia A., Waitsfield, Vt.; m. Lucius Parmalee, '51; d. Denver, Col., '81.
Williams, Emily, Stonington, Ct.; d. Stonington, Ct, '53.

1847.

GRADUATES.

Allen, Susan A., Lebanon, N. H.; m. Rev. J. J. Blaisdell, '53; 647 *College Ave., Beloit,Wis.*
Barrett, Elizabeth G, Manchester, Vt.; d. Manchester, Vt., '48.
Bell, Elizabeth M, Cornwall, Ct; m. John H. Welch, M.D., '48; d. Hartford, Ct., '76.
Bissell, Harriet L., Norwalk, Ct; m. Willard S. Pope, Esq., '56; d. Rome, N. Y., '57.
Bliss, Georgiana M., Longmeadow; m. *Rev. Geo. McQueen, '55; *Longmeadow.*
Brainerd, Mary C., S. Hadley; d. S. Hadley, '81.
Carrier, Lucy A., Volney, N. Y.; m. R. K. Sanford, '49; d. Fulton, N. Y., '59.
Church, Ann E., N. Y. City; m. Henry Pease, '56; d. Hartford, Ct., '86.
Dutton, Lucy E., Northfield; m. *Samuel Woodruff, '56; 68 *Main St., Hartford, Ct.*
Dwight, Anne E., S. Hadley; *S. Hadley.*
Fanning, Caroline E., Rushville, N. Y.; m. Rev. M. B. Gelston, '51; *Ann Arbor, Mich.*
Field, Caroline M., Ware; m. John H. Knapp, Esq., '49; d. Fort Madison, Io., '54.
Field, Elmira O., Ware; m. O. D. Cass, M.D., '53; d. Denver City, Col., '70.
Fitch, Susanna, Bedford; m. *J. G. Marchant, '50; 131 *Ogden Ave., Oak Park, Ill.*

1847.

Foote, Mary M., Cayuga, N. Y.; 17 *Penn Ave., Oxford, Pa.*
Goddard, Sarah C., Worcester; m. *Robert E. Ruthven, '52; *Waverly, N. Y.*
Graves, Pamelia A., Kinderhook, N. Y.; 333 *Summer Ave., Newark, N. J.*
Greene, Philomela S., Rushville, N. Y.; m. E. C. Mower, '48; d. Rushville, N. Y., '68.
Guilford, Lucinda T., Lanesboro; 1958 *Euclid Ave., Cleveland, O.*
Harwood, Mary E., Rushville, N. Y.; d. Rushville, N. Y., '49.
Hinsdale, Sarah H., Blandford; d. Blandford, '80.
Howland, Esther A., Worcester; 9 *Adam St., Quincy.*
Jessup, Emily, Norwalk, Ct.; d. Oxford, O., '93.
Kimball, Elizabeth R., Littleton; m. *Geo. Stevens, Esq., '50; d. St. Paul, Minn.
King, Julia A., Homer, N. Y.; m. *Rev. O. B. Stone, '51; 824 *E. Douglass St., Bloomington, Ill.*
Kingsbury, Harriette N., Francestown, N. H.; m. Rev. Sylvanus Jewett, '52; d. Francestown, N. H., '55.
Knowlton, Mary C., Hopkinton, N. H.; m. J. H. Todd, '51; d. Peru, Ind., '55.
Landon, Harriet, Salisbury, Ct.; m. *J. E. Lee, M.D., '57; *Salisbury, Ct.*
Martindale, Lucy A., Greenfield; m. Samuel O. Lamb, Esq., '51; *Greenfield.*
Mattocks, Martha (Porter), Danville, Vt.; m. *Isaac Dyer, '50; d. Danville, Vt., '90.
Niles, Mary E., Spencertown, N. Y.; m. *Rev. H. B. Gardiner, '50; d. Brooklyn, N. Y., '76.
Osgood, Julia H., Middleboro; 25 *Orchard St., N. Cambridge.*
Parker, Lucy A., Plainfield, N. H.; m. *F. H. Chamberlain, '57; *care Mrs. John B. Pike, Lebanon, N. H.*
Phillips, Elizabeth W., N. Y. City; m. *Geo. Keeney, '61; 628 *Market Ave., care George K. Phillips, San Francisco, Cal.*
Rankin, Lucy A., Chester, Vt.; m. *Sumner Albee, Esq., '55; 48 *Lake View Ave., Cambridge.*
Robertson, Mary R., Sherbrooke, P. Q.; m. Rev. Donald Gordon, '51; d. Toronto, Ont., '90.
Robinson, Anna A., Enfield; m. H. W. Taylor, Esq., '54; 730 *N. Church St., Rockford, Ill.*
Sherwood, Marietta, Greenfield, Ct.; m. Rev. D. D. Frost, '48; d. Wabashaw, Minn., '03.
Stone, Atossa F., Harwich; m. *T. W. Whittemore, '51; d. N. Y. City, '93.
Stoughton, Nancy P., Gill; m. Gurley A Phelps, M.D., '58; *Jaffrey, N. H.*
Taylor, Mary J., Newark, N. J.; m. Isaac Pomeroy, Esq., '52; d. Newark, N. J., '80.
Walker, Harriet E., Palmyra, N. Y.; m. Benj. Throop, M.D., '53; d. Palmyra, N. Y., '60.
Wheeler, Augusta, Chatham, N. Y.; d. Stuyvesant, N. Y., '89.
Williams, Mary B., Camden, O.; m. *Chauncey N. Olds, Esq., '52; d. N. Y. City, '89.

NON-GRADUATES.

Allen, Elizabeth C., Northampton; d. Northampton, '48.
Arms, Adelia, Sherbrooke, P. Q.; m. John McNicol, '63; *Sherbrooke, Can., P. Q.*
Baird, Esther C., Grafton, Vt.; *Westminster.*
Barnes, Martha A., Montpelier, Vt.; m. Rev. A. D. Barber, '49; d. Williston, Vt., '52.
Bascom, Philomela O., Newport, N. H.; m. Rev. Glen Wood, '51; d. Chicago, Ill., '66.
Bates, S. Cornelia, N. Brookfield; m. J. N. Smith, M.D., '48; d. Paris, Ky., '49.
Belden, Cornelia J., Newtown, Ct.; m. Dr. Joseph Maddox, '59; d. Newark, N. J., '70.
Blackington, Frances, N. Adams; m. William Pomeroy, '52; d. N. Y. City, '76.
Bliss, Eliza L., Warren; d. Warren, '74.
Bogardus, Ruth, DeWitt, N. Y.; d. De Witt, N. Y., '48.
Boone, Julia M., Waterbury, Ct.; m. *J. H. Gage, '61; 278 *Main St., Winchester.*
Bowdoin, Abby W. A., S. Hadley Falls; d. Brooklyn, N. Y., '87.
Bradley, Ann E., Farmer, N. Y.; m. Gilbert Holmes, '51; d. N. Fairfield, O., '56.
Buel, Lucy H., Worthington; d. Worthington, '48.
Burritt, Anna E., New Britain, Ct.; m. *J. B. Hawkes, '59; m. *Rev. T. W. Lewis, '68; m. *Hon. J. D. Giddings, '79; *Washington St., Pasadena, Cal.*

1847.

Butler, Mary C., Fairfield, Cher. Na.; m. Jas. C. Beach, '50; d. Bloomfield, N. J., '94.
Chaffee, Sarah, Becket; m. *Jona. W. Wheeler, '50; Becket.
Chapin, Julia A., Cabotville (now Chicopee); Hinsdale, Ill.
Chesley, Justina, Bangor, Me.; m. *Rev. J. R. Greenhough, '47; d. Bangor, Me., '56.
Child, Myra B., Lowell; 5 St. James Ave., Boston.
Clemence, Ruth D.,Bethlehem,N.Y.; m. *Ferdinand H. Griggs, '58; Box 1231, Penn Yan, N.Y.
Crane, Harriet, Somers, N. Y.; m. *Wm. Coffin, '54; d. N. Y. City, '57.
Crossman, Julia A., Great Barrington; m. Charles E. Mousseau, '57; 1213 Pearl St., Sioux City, Io.
Dawes, Clara, Cummington; m. *Chandler T. Ford, '48; Red Oak, Io.
Day, Eunice B., W Springfield; m. *Rev. Isaac G. Bliss, '47; W. Springfield.
Denny, Charlotte E., Westboro; d. Westboro, '54.
Driver, Helen E., Salem; m. D. Brainerd Brooks, '50; d. Salem, '82.
Eaton, Mary A., Princeton, Ill.; m. Rev. Ira Case, '49; care J. O. Winsor, Olneyville, R. I.
Estabrook, Ellen A., Holden; 5424 Howe St., Pittsburgh, Pa.
Farrar, Louisa F., Swanton, Vt.; m. Clark S. Jennison, '51; d. Swanton Center, Vt., '58.
Farrington, Abigail A., E. Brewer, Me.; m. Rev. Henry S. Loring, '48; d. Winthrop, Me., '87.
Ferry, Amanda H., Ashfield; m. Henry C. Hall, '55; home address, Ashfield.
Gallagher, Susan B., Orange, N. J.; m. Wm. A. Packard, '62; d. Princeton, N. J., '86.
Goldsbury, Ann Maria, Warwick; Warwick.
Harwood, Marion P., N. Brookfield; m. Thos. A. Bingham, '49; 166 K St., S. Boston.
Hatch, Sarah H, Warwick; Newton.
Hawks, Adaline H., N. Adams; m. *Geo. B. Cook, '54; d. Sheffield, '84.
Hawley, Emily C., Arlington, Vt.; m. *J. J. Reynolds, '58; d. Hartford, N. Y., '90.
Hayes, Alice, W. Granby, Ct.; m. Geo. F. Mellen, '50; d. W. Granby, Ct., '77.
Hinman, Sarah C., Farmer, N. Y.; m. B. F. Coleman, M.D., '51; King's Ferry, N. Y.
Hoadley, Hannah S., Northford, Ct.; m. E. C. Maltby, '51; d. Shelton, Ct., '87.
Hoadley, Lydia S.,Northford, Ct.; m. *Rev. J. Evarts Pond,'74; 59 Elm St., New Haven, Ct.
Hollister, Elizabeth M., Salisbury, Ct.; m. Rev. W. L. Lyons, '56; Grinnell, Io.
Hollister, Sarah H., Manchester, Vt.; d. Brattleboro, Vt., '76.
Holman, Ellen D., Gardiner, Me.; m. *Ebenezer G. Burgess, M.D., '60; Dedham.
Holmes, Harriet S., Sherburne, N. Y.; m. *Henry L. Boies, '58; Sycamore, Ill.
Howland, Elizabeth S., Worcester; m. H. Danforth Perry, '52; d. Cincinnati. O., '55.
Huntting, Margaretta B., Sag Harbor, N. Y.; m. Philos B. Tyler,'62; San Diego, Cal.
Hyde, M. Isabella, Williamsburg; d. S. Hadley, '54.
Jennings, Marcia A., Brookfield; m. *Rev. James Kilbourn,'63; 1228 State St., Racine, Wis.
Knight, Elizabeth, Salisbury, Ct.; 300 Bushkill St., Easton, Pa.
Linsley, N. Ellen, Meriden, Ct.; d. Meriden, Ct., '48
Man,Caroline F.,Westville,N. Y.; m. Marshall Conant,Esq.,'49; 520 King St.,La Crosse,Wis.
Man, Mary A., N. Y. City; m. Rev. A. B. Dilley, '49; Lake Worth, Fla.
Marsh, Jeannie E., Lowell; m. Rev. H. E. Niles, '50; York, Pa.
Martindale, Minerva S., Greenfield; m. Chester A. Bascom, '57; Greenfield.
Mattocks, Martha A., Danville, Vt.; m. Geo. H. Weeks, '49; Lyndonville, Vt.
Morse, Catharine S., Hopkinton; m. Wm. G. Davis, '50; d. Hopkinton, '84.
Noble, Sarah M., Fayetteville, N. Y.; m. *Henry Lord, '56; m. Chas. Richmond, '62; 1810 13th St., Washington, D. C.
Osband, Louisa J., Macedon, N. Y.; m. Hon. John W. Stebbins, '48; 30 Hawthorn St., Rochester, N. Y.
Parkhurst, Caroline M., Fort Covington, N. Y.; m. Rev. Chas. Gillette, '48; d. Quogue, N. Y., '57.
Pellet, Charlotte, N. Brookfield; d. N. Brookfield, '51.
Pixley, Alzina V., Plainfield; m. *Rev. David Rood, '47; Lakewood, N. J.

1847.

Plimpton, Catharine, Sturbridge ; d. Sturbridge, '53.
Price, Helen F., Philadelphia, Pa. ; m. Thos. Yardley, '53 ; d. Philadelphia, Pa., '54.
Reed, Susan W., Rowe ; d. Greenfield, '53.
Richardson, Emily O., E. Alstead, N. H. ; m. Rev. John C. Kimball, '60 ; 282 *Main St., Hartford, Ct.*
Sargeant, Maria, Springfield ; m. Geo. King ; d. Detroit, Mich., '87.
Sears, Eliza H., Williamsburg ; m. *Enos Parsons, Esq., '61 ; *Northampton.*
Seelye, Elizabeth B., Bethel, Ct. ; d. Bethel, Ct., '80.
Selden, Cynthia M., Chatham, Ct. ; m. Geo. S. Hubbard, '49 ; d. Middle Haddam, Ct., '54.
Shaw, Hannah L., New Braintree ; m. Chas. H. Anderson, '49 ; d. St. Luke's Home, Richmond, Va., '89.
Slate, Harriet A., Bernardston ; m. Daniel Snow, '53 ; *Blue Island, Ill.*
Smith, Anna, Middlefield ; m. S. F. Root, '49 ; d. Boston, '74.
Smith, Elizabeth A., Amherst ; m. Rev. Joseph T. Noyes, '48 ; d. Kodikanal, Madura District, S. India, '80.
Spencer, Ann E., Royalston ; d. Gasport, N. Y., '55.
Stearns, Elvira, Hinsdale, N. H. ; m. Dwight L. Sanderson, '49 ; *Hinsdale, N. H.*
Stebbins, Laverna, Vernon, Vt. ; *Vernon, Vt.*
Swan, Ann B., Manlius, N. Y. ; m. *Robert H. Hynds, Esq., '51 ; d. Dandridge, Tenn., '92.
Taylor, Rebecca W., Worcester ; m. Chas. Whittemore, '63 ; d. Worcester, '88.
Weare, Harriet S., Rochester, N. Y. ; m. *Lowell Daniels, '54 ; m. Lawson Daniels ; *Cedar Rapids, Io.*
Whaples, Elizabeth L., New Britain, Ct. ; m. Geo. R. Post, '51 ; d. New Britain, Ct., '86.
White, Martha E., Crawfordsville, Ind. ; d. Crawfordsville, Ind., '50.
Whittemore, Eliza, Fitzwilliam, N. H. ; m. *Rev. A. Jenkins, '52 ; *Fitzwilliam, N. H.*
Wright, Melancia B., Troy, N. H. ; m. L. C. Pratt, '55 ; *Kalamazoo, Mich.*

1848.

GRADUATES.

Ackley, Mary E., New Preston, Ct. ; m. Edwin R. Beeman, '50 ; d. New Preston, Ct., '51.
Anderson, Sarah J., Roxbury ; m. *Abner Kingman, '54 ; d. Boston, '66.
Babbitt, Lydia H., Mendham, N. J. ; m. *Rev. Edward M. Dodd, '48 ; *Boonton, N. J.*
Bigelow, Frances F., Marlboro, Ct. ; m. A. Lord, M.D., '50 ; d. *North Haven, Ct., '68.*
Bissell, Julia A., Norwalk, Ct. ; m. Willard S. Pope, Esq., '61 ; d. *Detroit, Mich., '72.*
Cole, Amanda M., Jackson, N. Y. ; m. Franc M. Paul, '56 ; 635 *Fogg St., Nashville, Tenn.*
Cushing, Sarah W., Woodstock, Vt. ; m. Henry Boynton, M.D., '54 ; *Woodstock, Vt.*
Cushman, Harriet W., Manlius, N. Y. ; m. Rev. J. N. McGiffert, '53 ; 35 *Division St., Ashtabula, Ohio.*
Edmands, Lucy E., Framingham ; m. Harrison W. Latham, '69 ; *Framingham.*
Fenn, Sarah G., Hartford, O. ; m. Wm. P. Clark, '49 ; d. Montville, O., '93.
Gallagher, Frances E., Orange, N. J. ; m. *Rev. Carroll Cutler, '58 ; *Glen Ridge, N. J.*
Graham, Laura, DeWitt, N. Y. ; m. *Wm. S. Boxley, '60 ; d. California, '84.
Greene, Miranda D., Miller's Place, L. I. ; m. Rev. Wm. J. Jennings, '50 ; d. *Redding, Ct., '91.*
Haile, Harriette C., Hinsdale, N. H. ; m. *John M. Stebbins, '53 ; 204 *N. Main St., Springfield.*
Hanmer, Mary, E. Hartford, Ct. ; d. E. Hartford, Ct., '88.
Hawes, Harriet, Boston ; *Wellesley College, Wellesley.*
Higgins, Jennette C., Southington, Ct. ; m. Henry D. Smith, '50 ; d. Plantsville, Ct., '87.

1848.

Higgins, Laura A., Southington, Ct.; m. *Jos. B. Beadle, '50; 554 *Chapel St., New Haven, Ct.*
Hodges, Anna E., Clarendon, Vt. ; m. T. L. Miller, '61 ; *Beecher, Ill.*
Hubbard, Harriet A., Boston ; 112 *Newbury St., Boston.*
Humphrey, Jane, Southwick ; m. Wm. H. Wilkinson, '58 ; *Southwick.*
Humphreys, Sarah M., Derby, Ct. ; m. *Edw. C. Hubbard, '49 ; 131 *Center St, Ashtabula, O.*
Kingsbury, Abby L., Francestown, N. H.; m. J. G. Kerr, M.D., '53; d. Macao, China, '55.
Kirk, Celestia A., Parishville, N. Y. ; m. *Rev. Eliphal Maynard, '48 ; m. Rev. Henry K. Edson, '52 ; d. Grinnell, Io., '89.
Lyon, Rosina, Stockton, N. J. ; m. Rev. P. C. Dayfoot, '50; d. Fentonville, Mich., '69.
Moore, Ellen E., Kensington, Ct. ; d. New York City, '60.
Munson, Mary A., Manchester, Vt. ; m. S. S. Burton, Esq., '57 ; d. Rome, N. Y., '81.
Newcomb, Martha L., Bernardston; 616 *12th St., Oakland, Cal.*
Nichols, Eliza J., Hampstead, N. H. ; m. Sydenham Brooks, '49; d. Skinquarter, Va., '70.
Norcross, Emily L., Monson; d. Monson, '52.
Owen, Clarissa, Granby ; d. Granby, '48.
Peabody, Helen, Newport, N. H. ; 212 *Euclid Ave., Pasadena, Cal.*
Peabody, Matilda F., Reading; m. Dean Peabody, Esq., '52 ; *Lynn.*
Philbrick, Elizabeth A., Boscawen, N. H. ; m. A. C. Partridge, '52 ; d. Oakland, Cal., '81.
Plimpton, H. Louisa, Sturbridge; m. *Rev. Lyman B. Peet, '58 ; m. Rev. Charles Hartwell, '85 ; *Foochow, China.*
Pratt, Jane W., Orwell, O. ; d. Orwell, O., '64.
Rice, Hannah E., Bridport, Vt.; m. W. W. Hibbard, M.D., '52 ; *Poultney, Vt.*
Scott, Hannah C., N. Hadley; m. Hon. Francis E. Clarke, '58 ; 451 *N. State St., Waukegan, Ill.*
Stearns, Mary A., Naples, N. Y. ; m. T. J. Word, '53 ; d. Palestine, Tex., '69
Sweetser, Emily P., Onondaga Valley, N. Y.; m. Winslow B. Barnes, '50; d. Plymouth, '69.
Tolman, Julia M., Ware ; m. *Lucius A. Tolman, '62 ; d. W. Roxbury, '71.
White, Martha L., Hartford, Ct.; m. Charles G. Merriman, '55; *Westville, Ct.*
Whitney, Emily E., Waimea, Kauai, H. I ; m. *Rev. Salmon McCall, '53; *Saybrook, Ct.*
Wolcott, Harriet, Pepperell; d. Pepperell, '48.
Wood, Caroline E., Lebanon, N. H.; m. *A. K. West, '60; d. Sanders, Ky., '92.
Yale, Martha R., New Hartford, Ct.; m. *Rev. E. R. Beadle, '52; *care Rev. Heber Beadle, Bridgeton, N. J.*
Yale, Mary E., New Hartford, Ct. ; d. New Hartford, Ct., '52.

NON-GRADUATES.

Abbott, Lydia R., Frankfort, Me. ; d. Winterport, Me., '76.
Aldrich, Juliana, M.D., Macedon, N. Y.; m. Wm. R. Joscelyn, M.D., '64 ; *Santa Cruz, Cal.*
Allis, Mary E. W., Whately ; d. E. Whately, '88.
Arms, Maria P., Windham, Vt. ; d. Springfield, Vt., '92.
Arnold, Cornelia R., N. Y. City ;
Atkins, Marietta, Bristol, Ct. ; m. Rev. H. S. Stephens, '56 ; d. Cromwell, Vt., '58.
Avery, Anne F., Gilford, N. H. ;
Avery, Elizabeth A., Gilford, N. H. ;
Balcom, Mary A., Mendham, N. J. ;
Bancroft, Caroline T., Grafton, Vt. ; d. Worcester, '52.
Barrows, Caroline B., E. Thomaston (now Rockland), Me. ; m. *L. O. Corey, '60 ; *Box 166, Cromwell, Io.*
Belknap, Beulah M., Sturbridge ; m. *Rev. Salem M. Plimpton, '51 ; m. *Samuel M. Lane, '81 ; P. O address, *Globe Village.*
Bigelow, Isabella H., Walpole; m. Chas. W. Kittredge, '56 ; 1025 *Bush St., San Francisco, Cal.*
Bishop, Elizabeth, Lisbon, Ct. ; d. Lisbon, Ct., '48.

1848.

Bishop, Mary, Lisbon, Ct.; m. Rev. Chas. L. Ayer, '49; *Bethlehem, Ct.*
Bissell, Julia A., Litchfield, Ct.; m. *Wm. M. Ensign, '64; 17 *High St., Waterbury, Ct.*
Booth, Alma, Berlin, Ct.; d. Milwaukee, Wis., '76.
Boudinott, Mary H., Manchester, Vt.; m. L. W. Case. Esq., '49; d. Winchester. Ct., '53.
Burdett, Mary J, Blackstone; m. *D. M. Rowan; *Washington, D. C.* (in 1880).
Bush, Hannah C, Westfield; m *Rev. E. P. Smith, '56; 231 *W. 83d St., N. Y. City.*
Carpenter, Sylvira A., Greenfield; m. Rev. Jas. Averill, '54; d. *Greenfield*, '77.
Catlin, Cornelia L., Litchfield, Ct.; m. G. T. Chamberlain, '51; d. St. Louis, Mo., '63.
Chapin, M. Augusta, St. Louis, Mo.; *Box 175, Upper Alton, Ill.*
Chick, Harriet N., Frankfort, Me.; m. *Chas. Abbott, M.D., '51; *Winterport, Me.*
Comstock, Mary L., Hartford, Ct.; m. Rev. N. P. Bailey, '49; 179 *North St., Massillon, O.*
Cook, Caroline A., Wakefield, N. H.; d. Concord, N. H., '53.
Cummings, Martha, Ware; m. Frank H. Palmer, '56; *Standish House, S. Duxbury.*
Dakin, Harriet, North East, N. Y.; m. *J. W Paine, '65; *Millerton, N. Y.*
Dewell, Elizabeth M., Norfolk, Ct.; m. *Robert C. Peck, '56; 532 *Chapel St., New Haven, Ct.*
Dewey, Eliza M., Hanover, N. H.; m. *Rev. N. H. Pierce, '74; *St. Louis Park, Minn.*
Dickinson, Emily E., Amherst; d. Amherst, '86.
Eastman, Caroline T., Bradford, Me.; m. Calvin C. Bliss, '54; d. Little Rock, Ark, '81.
Elmer, Sarah E., Morristown, N. J.; d. Morristown, N. J., '48.
Ely, Mary P., W. Springfield; m. *Henry A. Pierce, '52; 822 *4th Ave., Lansingburgh, N. Y.*
Fletcher, Abby R. Andover; 8 *Linden St, Everett.*
Foote, Harriet H., Williamstown; m. Henry H. Seys, M.D., '53; d. Oil City, Pa., '76.
Fowler. Harriet M., Washington, Ct.; *Washington, Ct.*
Frost, Hester A, Carmel, N. Y.; d. Peekskill, N. Y, '86.
Gifford, Laura H., Waterville, N. Y.; d. Paducah, Ky., '54.
Gilbert, Margaretta M., Phil., Pa.; m. Rev. Geo. N. McNeill, '49; d. Fayetteville, N. C., '54.
Gilson, Samantha W., Proctorsville, Vt; m. *Rev. C. B. Andrews, '63; m. B. B. Bowman, '87; 813 *N Madison Ave., Peoria, Ill.*
Goodwin. Helen S., Litchfield, Ct.; 8 *E. 40th St., N. Y. City.*
Graves, Harriet S., S. Hadley; m. Albert Goldthwaite, '55; *S. Hadley.*
Gridley, Eliza B., Granby; m. Rev. W. H. Collins, '53; d. Quincy, Ill., '75.
Hall, Almeria S., E. Hartford, Ct.; m. *Henry E. Woodruff, '50; d. Hartford, Ct., '54.
Hand, J. Elizabeth, Bridgehampton, N. Y.; m Rev. Wm. H. Lester, '54; *W. Alexander, Pa.*
Hart, Ellen M., New Britain, Ct.; m. *L. R. Wells, '53; 27 *Walnut St., New Britain, Ct.*
Hartwell, Mary A., Lincoln; m. *Geo. M. Rogers, '68; 53 *Norfolk St., Cambridgeport.*
Harwood, Martha L., Whately; m. *Edward A. Crafts, '51; m. Bliss Sutherland, '82; *Box 613, Huron, S Dak.*
Humiston, Esther S., Waterbury, Ct.; d. Waterbury, Ct., '61.
Huxley, Frances E., New Marlboro; m. *Lewis Emmons, '49; *Box 333, Torrington, Ct.*
Jones, Hannah, Ludlow; m. Quartus Sikes, '51; d. Hatfield, '55.
Kimball, Alice C., E. Thomaston (now Rockland), Me.; m. *John A. Meserve, Esq., '52; m. *Henry Treat, '75; 32 *Beech St., Rockland, Me.*
Kingman, Marietta, Winchester, N. H.; m. H. A. Pratt, '48; d. Hightstown, N. J., '72.
Langè, Wilhelmina H., Quincy, Ill.; m. B. H. Randall, Esq., '54; *Winona, Minn.*
Lawton, Catharine M., Hillsboro, N. H.; d. Hillsboro, N. H., '51.
Lewis, Margaret B., Portland, Ct.; m. *Rev. Wheelock N. Harvey, '52; *Gildersleeve, Ct.*
Linsley, Abby T., Millville, N. Y.; m. *Rev. H. A. Wilder, '49; *care Rev. G. H. Gutterson, Winchester.*
Lord, Mary L., Canaan, N. Y.; m. Henry J. Fahnestock, '53; d. Gettysburgh, Pa., '71.
Lyman, Climene C., Westhampton; m. Gilson Judd, '54; d. Holyoke. '70.
McCabe, Eliza M., Terre Haute, Ind.; d. Topeka, Kan., '74.
Marsh, Elizabeth W., Sandusky, O.; d. Hudson, Wis., '82.

1848.

Martin, Virginia M., Fort Mifflin, Pa. ; m. *James Monroe, '49 ; d. Danbury, Ct., '89.
Martindale, Julia R., Greenfield ; m. Elisha F. Harris, '55 ; d. Greenfield, '60.
Maynard, Lucy A., Potsdam, N. Y. ; m. Rev. C. S. Smith, '54 ; d. N. Walton, N. Y., '57.
Millard, Hannah, Delhi, N. Y. ; m. Wm. C. Coffin, '80 ; *Kelseyville, Lake Co., Cal.
Morrill, Sara, Alexandria, Va. ; *care John E. Graeff, Philadelphia, Pa.*
Newell, Eliza J., Johnstown, Wis. ; m. *Theodore Treat, M.D., '50 ; d. Tokio, Japan, '85.
O'Dwyer, Mary J., Abbotsford, Can. ; m. Alex. W. Wells, '55 ; d. Granby, Can., '57.
Otis, Eliza P., Cleveland, O. ; m. Hon. T. D. Crocker, '53 ; *836 Euclid Ave., Cleveland, O.*
Packard, Clara S., Spencer ; m. *Simeon Newton, '55 ; *Worcester.*
Paine, Eliza, S. Hadley ; m. *N. S. Weeks, '58 ; m. Benj. E. Warner, '73 ; d. Rosemond, Ill., '89.
Parsons, Harriet S., Amherst ; d. Washington, D. C., '94.
Patrick, Madelia A., Warren ; m. Thos. J. Morgan, '53 ; *Brimfield.*
Patrick, Mary R., Granby ; m. Geo. Bliss, '54 ; d. Santa Cruz, Cal., '94.
Phelps, Emma M., Simsbury, Ct. ; m. R. L. Hawley, '50 ; *161 King St., Springfield.*
Phelps, Mary F., Norfolk, Ct. ; m. *Henry M. Knight, M.D., '50 ; *Lakeville, Ct.*
Pitkin, Jerusha C., E. Hartford, Ct. ; m. Auguste D. Schlesinger, '53 ; *College Point, L. I., N. Y.*
Ramsdell, Hannah P., Milford, N. H. ; d. Milford, N. H., '64.
Reed, Eliza S., Montpelier, Vt. ; m. A. C. May, Esq., '53 ; *61 Stockton Ave., San Jose, Cal.*
Reed, Emily D., Montpelier, Vt. ; m. *Chas. W. Willard, Esq., '55 ; d. Boston, '86.
Rice, Elizabeth A., Bridport, Vt. ; d. Bridport, Vt., '94.
Robertson, Margaret M., Sherbrooke, Can. ; *Clark Ave., Côte St. Antoine, Montreal, Can.*
Robinson, J. A. Lucie, New Haven, N. Y. ; m. Rev. Edwin R. Beach, '61 ; *Lexington, Or.*
Rogers, Ann E., Pleasant Mount, Pa. ; m. *Ezra R. Brown, '53 ; *Pleasant Mount, Pa.*
Sanders, Frances C., Williamstown ; m. *Samuel Duncan, '58 ; d. Williamstown, '93
Sanford, Caroline U., Lowell ; m. *Samuel Allen, '55 ; m. Wm. H. Seamans, Esq., '60 ; d. Boston, '84.
Sanford, Emily, New Haven, Ct. ; m. *J. F. Armstrong, '58 ; m. Edward C. Billings, Esq., '75 ; d. N. Y. City, '86.
Sanford, Harriet N., Medway ; m. Eleazer Thompson, '56 ; *Newton Highlands.*
Scovell, Julia R., Essex, Ct. ; d. Essex, Ct., '74.
Smith, Charlotte M., Oxford, Ct. ; m. Wm. C. Baldwin, '55 ; d. New Haven, Ct., '60.
Stetson, Almira B., Brooklyn, Ct. ; m. Rev. Courtland T. DeNormandie, '53 ; *Kingston.*
Stevens, Elizabeth C., Newburyport ; *care Mr. P. K. Hills, Newburyport.*
Thomas, Clara E., Hardwick ; m. *Addison A. Hunt, '52 ; *Barre Plains.*
Thompson, Harriet, Plympton ; m. *Joshua T. Faunce, '56 ; *Sandwich.*
Thompson, Sarah G., Heath ; d. Brooklyn, N. Y., '83.
Thurston, Clara B., Searsport, Me. ; m. *S. W. Blanchard, M.D., '50 ; *3 Monroe Place, Portland, Me.*
Tolman, Harriet M., Atkinson, N. H. ; m. Rev. Chas. Seccombe, '54 ; d. Springfield, S. Dak., '95
Tolman, Lucy D., Atkinson, N. H. ; m. David L. Peabody, '59 ; d. Minneapolis, Minn., '85.
Wadsworth, Mary M., New Marlboro ; m. Oliver F. Clarke, '49 ; d. New Marlboro, '51.
Walker, Frances, Cooperstown, N. Y. ; m. *Rev. J. Addison Priest, '52 ; *Montclair, N. J.*
Walker, Sarah I., Cooperstown, N. Y. ; *Montclair, N. J.*
Ward, Lucy B., N. Brookfield ; m. Prof. Mark Bailey ; *Yale Univ., New Haven, Ct.*
Washburn, Emma G., Suffield, Ct. ; d. Mt. Holyoke Seminary, '48
Washburn, Ruth, Grafton, Vt. ; m. *Wm. G. Bancroft, '49 ; *44 Whitney Place, Buffalo, N. Y.*
Wheeler, Emeline A., Westport, Ct. ; m. Isaac Adams, '49 ; d. Huntington, N. Y., '57.
White, Ann Augusta, N. Adams ; *34 Edgewood Place, Cleveland, O.*
White, Jeannette C., Longmeadow ; d. Longmeadow, '58.

1848.

Williams, Lucinda, Canandaigua, N. Y.; m. *Chas. P. Johnson, '48; *Wisner, Mich.*
Williams, Mary E., Concord, N. H.; m. Chas. W. Harvey; d. Concord, N. H., '83.
Williams, Susan A., Concord, N. H.; m. *Geo. H. Hutchins, '52; 19 *N. State St., Concord, N. H.*
Wood, Olive W., Montpelier, Vt.; m. Theron M. Howard, '53; *St. Johnsbury, Vt.*
Woodruff, Jane T., Catskill, N. Y.; m. Auguste Kursteiner, M.D., '59; *Englewood, N. J.*
Woods, Caroline M., Enfield; d. Enfield, '91.
Woods, Charlotte J., Enfield; m. Edward P. Smith, '55; d. Enfield, '81.
Woods, Harriet E., Enfield; m. Sumner L. Darte, '54; *Enfield.*

1849.

GRADUATES.

Ainsworth, Lucy M., Williamstown, Vt.; m. T. D. Strong, M.D., '52; d. Westfield, N. Y., '91.
Atwood, Mary K., Newington, Ct.; m. John S. Kirkham, '85; *Newington, Ct.*
Bowdoin, Emily W. S., Springfield; m. *James Armour, '55; d. Memphis, Tenn., '94
Brown, Abigail M., Norfolk, Ct.; d. Norfolk, Ct., '73.
Brown, Mary Q., Newburyport; 112 *State St., Newburyport.*
Calvert, Emma H., Bowling Green, Ky.; m. Rev. Wm. L. Tarbet, '54; d. Pisgah, Ill., '85.
Dodge, Martha A., Amherst, N. H.; m. Rev. Allen H. Brown, '52; d. Newark, N. J., '85.
Estabrook, Caroline J., Camden, Me.; m. *Hon. Wm. H. Hunt, '60; *Liberty, Me.*
Fitch, Rachel A., Bedford; m. *David G. Rabb, '56; *Rising Sun, Ind.*
Foster, Lucretia, Fitchburg; m. Wm. A. J. Smith, '56; d. Fayetteville, Ark., '63.
Gilbert, Sarah A., Philadelphia, Pa.; m. Henry Anderson, '53; d. N. Y. City, '56.
Gilman, Anna C., Lowell; m. Rev. Chas. D. Lothrop, '54; d. Norton, '64.
Harwood, Clara J., Rushville, N. Y.; d. Rushville, N. Y., '49.
Harwood, Helen A., Rushville, N. Y.; d. Wauwantosa, Wis., '53
Johnson, Lucy T., N. Brookfield; m. L. Fullam, '53; d. N. Brookfield, '57.
Jones, Amelia D., Hudson, Mich.; m. *Rev. Geo. I. Stearns,'52; 165 *W. Newton St., Boston.*
Mason, Maria E., Palmer; m. Rev. M. K. Cross, '52; d. Moline, Ill., '55.
Merrick, Caroline H., Cortland, N. Y.; d. El Paso, Texas. '93.
Olmsted, Elizabeth S., E. Hartford, Ct.; m. Rev. Lyman Warner, '57; d. Salisbury, Ct.,'92.
Stanton, Malvina, Manchester, N. H.; m. *C. S. Gale, '54; m. Thomas Lang, '59; 202 *Mountain Ave., Malden.*
Stearns, Lucy E., New Ipswich, N. H.; m. Rev. Chas. Hartwell,'52; d. Foochow, China, '89.
Wingate, Ann S., East Weare, N. H.; m. *R. Merrick Rice, '61; *Shrewsbury.*
Wingate, Sarah A., East Weare, N. H.; d. Mt. Holyoke Seminary, '49.

NON-GRADUATES.

Adams, Mary E., Bangor, Me.; m. *Alexander Warfield; *San Diego, Cal.*
Arey, Annie E., Frankfort, Me.; m. *Hon W. G. Frye, '55; 28 *Park St., Dorchester.*
Arey, Susan, Frankfort, Me.; m. *Thos. Frye, M D., '51; 14 *Summer St., Rockland, Me.*
Barker, Catharine K., Wakefield, N H.; d. Wakefield, N. H., '56.
Blanchard, Mary A., Greensboro, Vt.; m. Moses Root, '52; *N. Crafisbury, Vt.*
Bliss, Mary S., Pawtucket, R. I.; m Daniel A. Clark, '54; d. Pawtucket, R. I., '82.
Boies, Sarah E., Northampton; m. *E. P. Cowles, Esq.. '52; *Rye N. Y.*
Bouton, Harriette S., Concord, N. H.; m. Hon. John W. Noyes, '55; *Chester, N. H.*
Briggs, Sarah A., Schaghticoke, N. Y.; 200 *W. 119th St., N. Y. City.*
Brown, Harriet, Norfolk, Ct.; d. Norfolk, Ct. '86.

1849.

Burchard, Harriet M., Vernon, N. Y.; *Winona, Minn.*
Capron, Caroline L., Little Falls. N. Y.; m. Spencer W. Coe, '56; *Murray Hill Hotel, N. Y. City.*
Carpenter, Mary F., Stephentown, N. Y.; m. Joseph Keeney, '51; d. Lebanon, Ill., '58.
Chaffee, Elizabeth, Becket; m. *Wm. A. Messenger, '52; *Windham, O.*
Clancy, Mary L., Belchertown; removed to Charlton, N. Y., '51.
Clark, Catharine L., Rowe; d. Philadelphia, Pa., '56.
Clark, Sarah B., Madison, N. Y.; m. *Henry R. White, M.D., '56; 1636 *Prairie Ave., Chicago, Ill.*
Comstock, Frances J., Essex. Ct.; m. *F. Augustus Tiffany, '62; *Essex, Ct.*
Connell, Mary, Montreal, Can. ; m. *John Elliott, '53; 449 *Ogden St., Denver, Col.*
Converse, Sarah E., Philadelphia, Pa ; *Alderson, West Va.*
Cooke, Harriet P., S. Hadley ; m. *Burritt D. Barnes, '52; *Oswego, N. Y.*
Corbin, Laura M., Lansingburgh, N. Y. ; d. Lansingburgh, N. Y , '50.
Crawford, Mary C., Woodstock, Va.; m. Chas. T. Weston, '54; d. Bethany, Pa., '64.
Crosby, Mary E., Troy, N. H.; m. John G. Penfield, '56 ; 716 *Seminary St., Rockford, Ill.*
Cushing, Lucy E., E. Hartford, Ct.; m. Wm. Faxon, '55; d. Hartford, Ct., '57.
Cushing, Verona K., Woodstock, Vt.; d. Woodstock, Vt., '49.
Damon, Sarah J., Amherst, N. H.; d. Amherst, N. H., '53.
Denniston, Annie, Bethlehem, N. Y.; d. Utica, N. Y., '68.
Dexter, Eliza B., Rochester; m. *Chas. H. Haskell, '54; 528 *Broadway, S. Boston.*
Doane, Cornelia M., Essex, Ct.; m. *Edward W. Pratt, '55; *Essex, Ct.*
Ely, Harriet, Huntington, Ct. ; d. Huntington, Ct., '50.
Eustis, Julia W., Dixfield, Me.; m. Edward Little, '56 ; 16 *Pratt Place, Chicago, Ill.*
Fanning, Julia, Rushville. N. Y.; *Rushville, N. Y.*
Farr, Andelusia, Fulton, N. Y.; m. Dr. Cook. ——. *Mich.*
Farrar, Sarah E., New Ipswich, N. H.; d. New Ipswich, N. H., '67.
Fifield, Sarah J., Sullivan, N. H.; m. Orlando Mason, '51; d. Winchendon, '58.
Fletcher, Susan A., Westford ; m. *Reuben J. Butterfield, '69 ; *Westford.*
Francis, Mary A., Canaan, Ct.; m. *Wm. P. Edwards, '55 ; m. *Christopher C. Allen, '82 ; 80 *College St., Burlington, Vt.*
French, Susan B., New Market, N. H.; m. *Perley W. Tenney, '68; *New Market, N. H.*
Gallagher, Mary C., Orange, N. J.; m. *Philander W. Fobes, '57 ; d. Syracuse, N. Y., '75.
Goodale, Elizabeth D., S. Orrington, Me.; m. Rev. Simeon Waters, '55; d Whitinsville, '84.
Goodspeed, Harriet, Phillipston ; m. Theodore T. Miller, '53; d. Phillipston, '66.
Graves, Jennett L., Easthampton ; m. Chauncy Barbour, '69; d. Denver, Col., '64.
Green, Eliza A., Meriden, Ct.; m. *M. G. Page, '51; m. Isaac Butler, '69; *Lock Box 115, Charlottesville, Va.*
Greenleaf, Elizabeth C., Chester, N. H.; 26 *Winchester St., Springfield.*
Gunn, Sophia C., Montague ; m Chas. S. Ferry, '56; 451 *Chestnut St., Springfield.*
Hall, Amanda P., Concord, N. H.; m. David S. Vittum, '59; d. Baraboo, Wis., '81.
Hall, Elizabeth, Newport, Ind.; m. *Luther T. Woodward, '49; d. Or.
Harris, Mary C., Newark, N. J.; *Montclair, N. J.*
Harrison, Clara C., Westfield; m. J. S. T. Stranahan, '70; *Brooklyn, N. Y.*
Haskell, Harriet R., Rochester; 67 *4th St, New Bedford.*
Hatch, Ellen T., Warwick ; m. *Hon. William Windom, '56 ; *Washington, D. C.*
Haynes, Olive E., Northboro; m. Chas. E. Elliot, '55 ; d. Cambridge, '90.
Hedges, Mary E., Rensselaerville, N. Y.;
Holmes, Sarah, Waterbury, Ct.; m. Rev. J. W. Hough, '58 ; d. Santa Barbara, Cal., '77.
Hosmer, Angelina, Bedford ; m. Rev. John H. Carr, '52 ; d. Warren, Tex., '64.
Howland, Elizabeth, Conway ; d. Conway, '70.
Hubbard, Harriet J., Concord ; *Concord.*

1849.

Isbell, Emily J., W. Meriden, Ct.; m. Erastus L. Ripley, '50; d. Jackson, Mich., '59.
Jones, Mary H., New Scotland, N. Y.; 609 *State St., Hudson, N. Y.*
Kellogg, Sarah P., Shelburne; 83 *Prospect St., Waterbury, Ct.*
Kendall, Alicia, Dunstable; m. Levi Putnam, '68; *Wilton, N. H.*
Kidder, Angeline H., New Alstead. N. H.; m. Rev. Chas. Hutchinson, '51; *New Albany, Ind.*
Kimball, Ariadne L., Frankfort, Me.; m. Dyer D. Bullock, '52; m. Seth Webb, '75; *S. Deer Isle, Me.*
Kingsbury, Emily L., S. Glastonbury, Ct.; m. *Shelton Hollister, '55; m. Thos. B. Cheney, '65; 733 *Asylum Ave., Hartford, Ct.*
Kingsbury, Sarah E., Francestown, N. H.; *Box 132, Francestown, N. H.*
Lane, Hittie P., E Abington; m. Rev. J. W. Harding, '52; *Longmeadow.*
Lawrence, Elizabeth G., Amherst, N. H.; d. Amherst, N. H., '87.
Leathe, Paulina A., Royalston; m. Jas. Willard Thompson, '54; d. Gardner, '59.
Loomis, Frances A., Whately; m. Alfred Starkweather, '57; *Farmington. Cal.*
Loomis, Philomela A., Whately; m.*Evan D. Ashton,'58; 511 *S.42d St., W.Philadelphia,Pa.*
Luce, Martha, Kingsville, O.; m. *Luke Osborn, '51; *Kingsville, O.*
Lupton, Rhoda O., Bridgeton, N. J.; 160 *W. Commerce St., Bridgeton, N. J.*
Marsh, Susan F., Cayuga, N. Y.; m. *Edson Kellogg, Esq., '58; m. Jas. M. Camp, Esq., '84; *Delevan, Wis.*
Means, Emeline W., Hallowell, Me.; d. Augusta, Me., '67.
Mix, Mary H., Oswego, N. Y.; m. Lucien C. Seymour, '52; d. Fulton, N. Y., '94.
Morgan, Arabella C., Lowell; d. Portsmouth, N. H., '94.
Morse, Emeline, Pawtucket, R. I.; m. Zenas M. Lane, Esq., '51; *Rockland.*
Parks, Sarah E., Springfield; m. Dr. Hall; 169 *E. Market St., Galveston, Texas.*
Partridge, Lydia S., W. Medway; m. Addison P. Thayer, Esq., '53; *Great Barrington.*
Patrick, Maria L., Granby; m. Perkins Bass, Esq., '56; d. Chicago. Ill., '58.
Pike, Harriet N., Boston; 1 *Summit St., Roxbury.*
Preble, Louisa, Charlestown;
Preston, Amanda, S. Hadley; m. *Wm. White, '52; *Chicopee.*
Preston, Mary E., Waterville, N. Y.; m. Rev. T. D. Hunt, '62; d. Waterville, N. Y., '63.
Rice, Frances M., Charlemont; *E. Charlemont.*
Rice, Louisa J., Lincoln; 1 *St. James Terrace, Roxbury.*
Rider, Mary F., Watertown, Ct.; m.*Joseph B. Sherwood,'51; 431 *Kan. St., Huron. S. Dak.*
Ruggles, Elizabeth C., Rochester; m. *Daniel J. Robbins. '53; d. Plymouth, '79.
Sanborn, Susan A., New Market, N. H.; *New Market, N. H.*
Sawyer, Ann E., Franklin, N. H.; m. *John Chandler, '59; *Box 415. Harvey, Ill.*
Seabury, Helen F., Granby; d. N. Y. City, '53.
Skinner, Sarah, Williston, Vt.; m. Simeon Lee, '51; 203 *W. 1st St., Los Angeles, Cal.*
Smith, Francese, Granby; d. Granby, '54.
Sperry, Ann O., Waterbury, Ct.; 222 *Hillside Ave., Waterbury, Ct.*
Stow, Elizabeth P., New Haven, Ct.; 49 *Wooster St., New Haven, Ct.*
Stubbs, Helen M., Hallowell, Me.; deceased.
Thompson, Harriet, Montreal, Can.; *care Miss Eastman, Peacham, Vt.*
Walker, Laura. Manchester, Vt.; d. Manchester, Vt., '93.
Warren, Caroline A., Mechanicsville, N. Y.; m. *Chauncey H. Cromwell,'73; *Camden,N.J.*
Wheeler, Ellen C., Warwick; m. *John A. Millard, '65; 64 *Western Ave., Brattleboro. Vt.*
Whittlesey, Helen M., New Preston, Ct.; m. Darius P. Griswold, '54; *Litchfield, Ct.*
Williams, Caroline M., Kingsville,O.; m. Aaron Pickett, '52; 41 *Prospect St., Ashtabula,O.*
Williams, Frances L., Rehoboth; m. Henry G. Read, '52; d. Taunton. '57.
Winans, Mary A., Adrian, Mich.; m. Wm. H. Scott, '52; 2505 *Monroe St., Toledo, O.*
Woodhull, Sarah F., Thomaston, Me.; m. *Edmund R. Webb, '50; m. Philip Coombs, '56; 24 *Maple St., Bangor, Me.*
Wright, Mary M., Lowell; m. *Edward Haire, '52; 8249 *Houston Ave., Chicago, Ill.*

1850.

GRADUATES.

Avery, Paulina, Conway; m. *Rev. O. L. Woodford, '56; d. Grasshopper Falls, Kan., '58.
Bissell, Emily L., Suffield, Ct.; m. N. S. Bouton, '56; d. Chicago, Ill., '57.
Bodge, Caroline A., Rochester, N. H.; d. Fox Lake, Wis., '68.
Boies, Mary P., Blandford; m. *Levi Spiller, '02; *Blandford*.
Burt, Delia B., Longmeadow; 3401 *Powelton Ave., Philadelphia, Pa.*
Chamberlain, Mary E., S. Hadley; m. Warren J. Burgess, M.D., '67; *Du Quoin, Ill.*
Collins, M. Theresa, Cortland, N. Y.; m. Chas. Bishop, Esq., '52; *Cortland, N. Y.*
Dickinson, Nancy H., Amherst; m. Wm. Youmans, Esq., '53; *Delhi, N. Y.*
Eastman, Sarah S., Granby; d. Granby, '51.
Force, Hannah Maria, Hanover, N. J.; m. Rev. Epher Whitaker, '52; *Southold, N. Y.*
Gregg, Frances, Belleville, N. J.; m. *Fred. Smith, M.D.; m. *Geo. W. Bartlett, Esq.; *Box 429, Faribault, Minn.*
Hallock, Eliza, Plainfield; m. Rev. Thos. H. Rouse, '51; *Belleview, Fla.*
Hallock, Fannie, Plainfield; m. Rev. Henry M. Hazeltine, '57; *Jamestown, N. Y.*
Hayes, Adaline H., Washington, Ct.; m. Geo. Churchill, '58; d. Galesburg, Ill., '69.
Hills, Mary E., Amherst; m. Rev. Jay Clizbe, '66; *Mason, Mich.*
Hittell, Mary A., Hamilton, O.; m. Hon. John W. Killinger, '51; *Lebanon, Pa.*
Holmes, Eliza J., Waterbury, Ct.; 174 *Stratford Ave., Bridgeport, Ct.*
Hufnagel, Julia M., Stockbridge; m. Judge Thos. Ewing, '59; 15 *Lincoln Ave., Alleghany City, Pa.*
Lawson, Catharine, Cornwallis, N. S.; m. John Laurie, '52; d. Jacksonville, Ill., '64.
Livingston, Caroline A., Lowell; m. *Paul R. George, Esq., '55; 20 *Chelmsford St., Lowell.*
Mann, Charlotte, N. Wrentham; m. Horace M. Paine, M.D., '52; *West Newton.*
Marsh, Anna, Cayuga, N. Y.; m. *Benj. S. Gregory, Esq., '72; 483 *Shoemard St., Syracuse, N. Y.*
Masters, Anna M. L., Schaghticoke, N. Y.; m. Geo. G. Arnold, '56; 1343 F *St., N. E. Washington, D. C.*
Mathews, Sarah J., Lee, N. H.; m. Alexander McCoy, Esq., '57; d. Peoria, Ill., '63.
Murdock, Mary J., S. Orange; m. Geo R. Gold, Esq., '57; 698 *Harrison St., Flint, Mich.*
Penny, Elizabeth W., Greenport, N. Y.; m. *Rev. Wm. Wood, '65; *Madison, Ct.*
Putnam, Julia M., Middleboro; m. Alfred S. Thayer, '53; d. Middleboro, '59.
Sargeant, Cordelia, Manchester, Vt.; d. N. Y. City, '87.
Stone, Mary E., Danbury, Ct.; 278 *Main St., Danbury, Ct.*
Titcomb, Elizabeth, Farmington, Me.; m. *Benj. V. Abbott, Esq., '53; d. Brooklyn, N. Y., '91.
Titcomb, Mary, Farmington, Me.; 9 *Middagh St., Brooklyn, N. Y.*
Tuthill, Sarah S., Greenport, N. Y.; d. Brooklyn, N. Y., '82.
Ward, Elizabeth D., Rochester, N. Y.; *St. Andrew's Bay, Fla.*
Worcester, Sarah, Park Hill, Cher. Na.; m. Dwight D. Hitchcock, '53; d. Park Hill, Cher. Na., '57.

NON-GRADUATES.

Abbott, Fannie O., Westfield; *Westfield.*
Ainsworth, Emma L., Williamstown, Vt.; *Williamstown, Vt*
Allen, Anna C., Champlain, N. Y.; m. Rev. F. A. Douglass, '54; 484 *Decatur St., Brooklyn, N. Y.*
Allen, Delenda J., Albany, N. Y.; m. *Hiram A. Edmonds, M.D., '54; d. Albany, N. Y., '62.
Allen, Maria, Oakham; m. Wm. Lincoln, '52; d. Oakham, '55.
Atwood, Elizabeth P., Royalton, Vt.; m. Zerah Stetson, '60; d. Champlain, N. Y., '61.
Baldwin, Emily G., Newark, N. J.; m. S. S. Stevens, '53; d. Newton, N. J., '82.
Bailey, Caroline P., Boston; m. Chas. R. Story, '52; 1778 *Green St., San Francisco, Cal.*

1850.

Bartlett, Margaret C., Longmeadow ; m. B. F. Orcar, '58 ; *Box 351, Mexico, Mo.*
Beach, Sarah J., Milford, Ct. ; m. W. C. Willcox, '51 ; d. Stamford, Ct., '71.
Bigelow, Chloe M., Brattleboro, Vt. ; m. Rev. J. K. Harris, '57 ; *Scotia, Neb.*
Bixby, Sarah E., E. Boxford ; m. Chas. S. Foster, '57 ; d. N. Andover, '57.
Blackly, Marion M., Dane, Wis.; " family moved to Iowa."
Blair, Sarah E., Allamuchy, N. J. ; d. Newark, N. J., '62.
Bliss, Mary W , Longmeadow ; m. *Richard S. Chamberlain, '66 ; *22 Vernon St., Springfield.*
Bridges, Julia A., Newton Corner ; m. *Jas. H. Sparrow, '58 ; *62 Auburn St., Cambridgeport.*
Brigham, Mary A., Westboro ; d. '89.
Burrill, Martha J., E. Abington ; m. Alanson A. Holbrook, '52 ; *E. Weymouth.*
Butler, Agnes M., Oxford, Ct. ; m. *Roswell Bronson, M.D., '52 ; m. I. L. Graham, M.D . '61 ; *Muscatine, Io.*
Butler, Helen A., Little Falls, N. Y. ; *291 Webster Ave., Chicago, Ill.*
Chambers, Laura A., Carthage, N. Y. ; m. Irwin W. Johnson, M.D., '56 ; d. Battle Creek, Mich., '83.
Crawford, Mary A., N. Y. City ;
Davidson, Catharine M., Milford,Ct. ; m. Saml. G. White, M.D.,'70; d. Milledgeville, Ga.,'77.
Davis, Elizabeth, Springfield, Vt. ; m. Chas. A. Forbush, '59 ; d. Springfield. Vt., '84.
Davis, Mary F., Westfield ; m. Chas. Peck, '53 ; *34 Pearl St.,New Britain, Ct.*
Day, Harriet N., Lonsdale, R. I. ;
Day, R. Alice, Sauquoit, N. Y. ; m. Dr. John C. Spencer, '60 ; *139 W. 61st St., N. Y. City.*
Dewey, M. Adeline, Hanover, N. H.; m. Augustine McCutchen, '58 ; d. Canton, Ill., '68.
Dewey, S. Jane, Hanover, N. H. ; m. *Caleb C. Foster, '60 ; *Toulon, Ill.*
Dickinson, Mary A., Romeo, Mich. ; *Romeo, Mich.*
Dickinson, Sarah J., Romeo, Mich. ; m. Darwin L. Gillett, '63 ; *41 Broad St , Westfield.*
Dunbar, Martha F., Westmoreland, N. H. ; m. Lewis Webster, '52 ; *Dunlap. Kan.*
Eastman, Mary W., Granby ; d. Granby, '53.
Eaton, Betsey S., Francestown, N. H. ; m Wm. T. Hall, '54 ; d. N. Chelsea, '68.
Felch, Mercy J., Groton ; m. Wm. S. Nutting, '52 ; d. Groton, '56.
Freeman, Sarah W , Guildhall, Vt. ; d. Guildhall, Vt., '53.
Gates, Anne N., Edwardsburg, Can. ; m. Rev. Chas. G. Goddard, '50 ; *W. Hartland, Ct.*
Gilbert, Jane E., Pomfret, Ct. ; m. Nelson Curtis, '56 ; *4 St. Botolph St., Boston.*
Goodale, Mary H., Marlboro ; m. Samuel Holmes, '56 ; *288 Grove St., Montclair, N. J.*
Gorham, Esther M., New Haven, Ct. ; m. Benj. F. Holmes, '57 ; *Belford, N. J.*
Goulding, Agnes S., Phillipston ; *60 Catharine St., Springfield.*
Graves, Myra B., Northampton ; m. H. Hyde, Esq., '59 ; *Oxford, N. Y.*
Hale, M. Elizabeth, Stowe ; m. *Rev. Theodore Cooke, '58 ; *20 William St., Worcester.*
Harlow, Sarah P., Bangor, Me. ; m. Rev. L. G. Marsh, '58 ; *Lewiston, N. Y.*
Hasbrouck, Jane E., Stone Ridge, N. Y. ; m. Alexander S. Clark, '73 ; *Westfield, N. J.*
Hayes, Sarah, S. Hadley ; m. Chas. B. Whiting, '53 ; d. Taylor's Falls, Minn., '57.
Hebard, Eliza S., Attica, N. Y. ; *Alexander, N. Y.*
Hills, Amelia G., Amherst ; m. Henry D. Fearing, '60 ; *Amherst.*
Humphrey, Martha, Southwick ; d. Southwick, '51.
Knight, Elizabeth, Boscawen, N. H. ; m. *Walter L. F. Gage, '50 ; *174 Clinton St., Grand Rapids, Mich.*
Knowlton, Sarah T., Hopkinton, N. H. ; d. Peru, Ind., '50.
Knowlton, Sophia V. W., Watertown, N. Y.; m. C. W. Perkins. Esq.. '52 ; d. Watertown, N. Y., '53.
Ladd, Mary J., Meredith, N. H. ; m. Wm. T. Hatch, '51 ; d. '61.
Lambert, Mary A., Bangor, Me. ; m. *Chas. P. Weld, '53 ; *Box 773, Bangor, Me.*
Lefler, Jane C., Owego, N. Y. ; " m. and lived in Hornellsville, N. J."

1850.

Lyon, Sarah P., Woodstock, Ct. ; m. B. F. Pratt, '52; d. Dryden, N Y., '90.
Maltby, Margaret L. A., Bangor, Me. ; m. Minot S. Crosby, '52 ; 210 *Prospect St., Waterbury, Ct.*
Maltby, S. Elizabeth, Bangor, Me. ; m. *John A. Winn, '54; m. Alwyn Partridge, '84 ; 805 *Cascade Ave., Colorado Springs, Col.*
Marsh, Caroline B., Nottingham, N. H.; m. Dr. Geo. A. Grace, '59; d. Nottingham, N. H., '74.
Marsh, Elizabeth A., Nottingham, N. H. ; *N. Nottingham, N. H.*
Marsh, Lucy A., Guildhall, Vt. ; m. Rev. Geo. Dustan, '55 ; d. Tunbridge, Vt., '62.
Marshall, Eliza A., Derry, N. H. ; m. Alpheus H. Kenney, '60 ; *Broadlands, Ill.*
Miller, Emma S., Constableville, N. Y. ; m. Isaac Burrell, '53 ; *Salisbury, N. Y.*
Mosher, Mary, Racine, Wis. ; m. *Fred B. Norcom, M.D., '58 ; *Box* 1742, *Fernando, Cal.*
Moulton, Emma S., Watertown, N. Y. ; *care Mrs. Rosa Bowie, Leland, Md.*
Murchison, Annie M., Buffalo, N. Y. ; m. Geo. C. Cole, '53 ; *Sheboygan, Wis.*
Murphy, Rose H., Philadelphia, Pa. ; m. Rev. John Edwards, '51 ; d. Oakland, Cal., '81.
Neale, Jane E., Boston ;
Newcomb, Sophia W., Grantville ;
Nichols, Frances E., Enosburgh, Vt. ; d. Enosburgh, Vt., '63.
Norton, Mary R., Racine, Wis. ; m. Augustus R. Gray, '54 ; 2240 *Mich. Ave., Chicago, Ill.*
Owen, Lucia A., Belchertown ; d. Belchertown, '52.
Parke, B. Jane R., Lowell ;
Parsons, S. Elizabeth, Ludlow; m. Henry S. Jones, '52; *Ludlow.*
Patten, Elizabeth, Candia, N. H. ; m. *Chas. Pressey, '58 ; *Winchester.*
Peck, Harriette M., Shelburne ; m. Justin H. Tyler, '61 ; *Napoleon, O.*
Petrie, Ellen A., Little Falls, N. Y. ; m. Joseph W. Helmer, '56 ; d. Lockport, N. Y., '04.
Reed, Mary A., Warwick ; m. Rev. H. P. Osgood, '69; d. Granby, Ct., '75.
Rieman, Elizabeth G., Baltimore, Md.; 9 *W. Mulberry St., Baltimore, Md.*
Schultz, Margaret A., m. Rev. Joseph Mayon, '58 ; *Marysville, Kan.*
Skinner, Jane M., Waitsfield, Vt. ; m. Rev. Lucino Parker, '57 ; m. Rev. Nehemiah Cobb, '75; d. Washington, D. C., '79.
Southwick, Sarah J., Blackstone ; m. Ellis Albee, '53; *Millville.*
Smith, Sarah E., Hartford, Ct. ;
Sparrow, Susan, Cambridgeport ; 32 *Magazine St., Cambridgeport.*
Spencer, Susan B., Waterbury, Ct. ; *Waterbury, Ct.*
Stone, Helen E., Vergennes, Vt. ; m. *Jacob P. Willard, '54 ; d. Chicago, Ill., '63.
Swett, Lucy F., Craftsbury, Vt. ; m. Samuel H. Graham ; *N. Craftsbury, Vt.*
Taplin, Susan P., E. Corinth, Vt. ; m. Samuel Batchelder; d. Pa., '61.
Tower, Julia S., Waterville, N. Y. ; d. Waterville, N. Y., '64.
Tyler, Lucy I., Williamstown ; m. Rev. Geo. W. Counitt, '53 ; d. Woodbourne, N. Y., '64.
Wadsworth, Julia A., New Marlboro ; m. Manning W. Stevens, '54 ; d. Keokuk, Io., '93.
Walker, Anne E., Boston ;
Walker, Arabella, Rockville ; m. *Frederick L. Church, '60 ; *Box* 503, *Andover.*
Walker, Isabella, Rockville ; *Box* 503, *Andover.*
Wall, Helen L., N. Y. City ;
Warner, Rebecca, Boston ; 32 *Dorset Sq., London, England.*
Webster, Anna C., Pembroke, N. H. ; m. Lewis A. Hyde, '51 ; d. Norwich, Ct., '53.
Whitman, Rosina P., Windsor ; m. *Rev. Joseph B. Baldwin, '58 ; d. Peru, '80.
Whitmore, Ellen R., Marlboro ; m. Warren Goodale, '52 ; d. Honolulu, H. I., '61.
Wood, Arabella M. G., Concord, N. H. ; m. James Greeley, M.D.; *Thornton's Ferry, N. H.*
Woodward, Mary W., Taunton ; d. Taunton, '73.
Wright, Mary A., Northampton ; m. Chas. F. Lynn, '59 ; 7432 *Bond Ave., Windsor Park, Chicago, Ill.*
Wright, Sarah E., N. Granville, N.Y.; m. Samuel F. Hance, M.D., '55; 720 *6th Ave., S. Minneapolis, Minn.*

1851.

GRADUATES.

Armstrong, Caroline P., Honolulu, H. I.; m. Rev. Edward G. Beckwith, '53; *Paia, E. Maui, H. I.*
Atwood, Hannah J., Nashua, N. H.; m. *E. M. Cowles, '54; *Decatur, Ga.*
Ayer, E. Josephine, Manchester, N. H.; m. *DeWitt C. Warner, M.D.,'68; *Atkinson Depot, N.H.*
Baker, Hettie E., Wilkesbarre, Pa.; m. Fred. S. Giddings, Esq., '52; *952 Gorham St., Madison, Wis.*
Baker, M. Antoinette, Amherst; m.*Wm.S.Aumock,'55; *30 Lake View Park, Rochester. N. Y.*
Barrett, Lucy A., Manchester, Vt.; *186 Hillside Ave., Waterbury, Ct.*
Bierce, Isabella G., Cornwall Bridge, Ct.; m. Wm. D. Saxton, M.D., '68; *Cohocton. N. Y.*
Bigelow, Sarah W., Northboro; *2 Holmes Place, Cambridge.*
Boynton, Susan P., Lynn; *7 Howard St., Lynn.*
Brown, Susan N., Newburyport; *112 State St., Newburyport.*
Burnham, Martha L.,Concord, N.H.; m.Frank Coburn,Esq.,'64; *260 W. 34th St., N.Y.City.*
Burt, Elizabeth, Schenectady, N. Y.; *411 Union St., Schenectady, N. Y.*
Camp, Nancy E., Bristol, Ct.; d. Bristol, Ct., '54.
Cary, Mary A., Foxboro; m. A. B. Keith, '54; *Braintree.*
Coan, Julia M., Medina, N. Y.; m. *J. M. Plumer, M.D., '56; *759 Tremont St., Boston.*
Crofut, Mary J., Danbury, Ct.; m. Rev. A. B. Morse, '56; d. Danbury, Ct., '90.
Curtis, Martha A., Hazel Green, Wis.; m. *Edward W. Prentiss, '61; *25 W. St., Aurora, Ill.*
Cutler, Almira, Waterford, Vt.; m. A. M. McKinney, M.D., '61; d. Goshen, Ind., '62.
Fairbanks, Sarah, St. Johnsbury, Vt.; m. *Chas. M. Stone, '58; *St. Johnsbury, Vt.*
Farwell, Elizabeth M., Fitchburg; m. Chas. H. Merrill, '57; *3 Cudworth St., Medford.*
Fisher, Sophronia S., Northboro; m. Rev. Philo B. Wilcox, '54; d. Northboro, '92.
Fowler, A. Eugenia, N. Y. City; m. John E. Brown, '59; *44 W. 49th St., N. Y. City.*
Gere, Amelia R., Granville, Ill.; m. Alverin A. Mason, '72; *113 Cass St., Chicago, Ill.*
Gillett, E. Louisa, Colchester, Ct.; m. *Stephen H. Matthews, '52; d. Medina, O., '56.
Goddard, Sarah L., Troy, N. H.; m. *A. M. Caverly, M.D., '54; *Pittsford, Vt.*
Gorham, Helen, Darien, Ct.; m. John J Warren, '59; *Stamford, Ct.*
Green, M. Augusta, Madison, N. J.; m. *D. B. Greene, Esq., '55; *Madison, N. J.*
Greenfield, Sarah E., Norway Plains, N. H.; m. *E. G. Wallace, '53; *Rochester, N. H.*
Hale, Mary E., Derry, N. H.; d. Derry, N. H., '55.
Hedden, Emily, Orange, N. J.; m. B. S. Bryan, '54; *553 E. Oak St., E. Portland, Or.*
Hubbard, Maria L., Concord; m. *Rev. L. C. Ford, '58; *Wellesley Hills.*
Johnson, Frances B., Guilford, Ct.; m. *Rev. Jas. C. Beecher, '64; m. Frederic B. Perkins, '94; *Cos Cob in Greenwich, Ct.*
Leavitt, Frances M., W. Stockbridge; m. Jas. Noyes,'56; *1616 Buchanan Ave.,St. Joseph, Mo.*
Leonard, Hannah B., Stafford, Ct.; m. J. C. Fitch, M.D., '57; d. S. Windham, Ct., '59.
Loomis, Martha A., N. Pownall, Vt.; m. Rev. H. J. Patrick, '60; *Newtonville.*
McCutcheon, Harriet N., Pembroke, N. H.; *209 Normal St., Ypsilanti, Mich.*
Maynard, Frances E., Whitewater, Wis.; d. Whitewater, Wis., '52.
Mead, Maria E., Greenwich, Ct.; m. *V. A. Hilburn, '57; *401 E. 20th St., Baltimore. Md.*
Miller, Sara M., Stamford, Ct.; m. *Henry S. McCall,'56; *324 N. Cedar St., Galesburg. Ill.*
Millett, Laura G., Derry, N. H.; m. Rev. Jas. Laird, '67; d. Hollis, N. H., '87.
Moody, Anna W., S. Hadley; m. *David L. Flack, '82; *Elkhorn, Wis.*
Newcomb, Elizabeth M., Bernardston; d. '90.
North, Harriet M., Berlin, Ct.; m. Rev. Chas. F. Dowd,'52; *Temple Grove Seminary, Saratoga Springs, N. Y.*
Pease, Delia S., Blandford; m. *Chas. G. Woodruff, '61; *Quasqueton, Io.*
Shattuck, Lydia W., E. Landaff. N. H.; d. Mt. Holyoke College, '89.
Smith, Eliza, E. Abington; m. Rev. J. L. Howell, '53; d. Stillwater, Minn., '71.
Somers, Anna M., W. Haven, Ct.; *Knox Seminary, Galesburg, Ill.*

Spaulding, Mary L., S. Reading; d. S. Reading, '64.
Storrs, Harriet M., E. Bloomfield, N. Y.; d. E. Bloomfield, N. Y., '53.
Thorpe, Emily C., Southport, Ct.; m. Samuel S. Rowland, '52; d. Weston, Ct., '75.
Tolman, Jane C.. Ware; *Mills College P. O., Cal.*
Walker, Adelia C., Warsaw, N. Y.; *Warsaw, N. Y.*
Walker, Mary A., Warsaw, N. Y.; m. *Wm. M. Cowgill, '55; *Warsaw, N. Y.*
Watson, Caroline A.. Torringford, Ct.; m. Gaylord B Miller, M.D.,'53; 3 *John St.,Grand Rapids, Mich.*
Whitcomb, Ellen C., Albany, N. Y.; m. *J. P. Haven, '51; m. Peter Naylor, '63; home address, *Boston.*
Whiton,Ann E.,Ridgeway, O.; m. *Geo. W. Chapman,'52; *Clearwater,Los Angeles Co., Cal.*
Woodhull,Josephine.Patchogue,N. Y.; m. *Rev. Robt.Bolton,'54; *P. O. New Rochelle,N.Y.*
Yates, Caroline R., Lonsdale, R. I.; m. Rev. S. B. Goodenow, '53; *Battle Creek, Io.*

NON-GRADUATES.

Adams, Mary H., Ashford, Ct.; *care Dr. Storrs*, 91 *Ann St., Hartford, Ct.*
Adams, Susan P., Ashford. Ct.; m. M. P. White; 371 *Gray St., Elmira, N. Y.*
Allen, Alida. Salem, N. Y.; *Salem, N. Y.*
Allen, Sophia, Ellsworth, O.; d. Mt. Holyoke Seminary, '51.
Anderson, Caroline B., Manchester, Vt.; m. *Wm. I. Price. '56; m. Geo. W. Barrus, '63; 5 *Willow Place, Mt. Vernon, N. Y.*
Arms, Fanny. Springfield, Vt.; m. *Daniel Goddard, '65; *Springfield, Vt.*
Ayrault, Jane, Wethersfield, Ct.; m. *Rev. J. A. Bailey, '51; d. Wethersfield, Ct., '88.
Baldwin, Jane M., Newark,N. J.; m. *Thos. S. Baldwin,'52; *care C. D.Laws,Richmond,Va.*
Barnard, Sarah A., Springfield, Vt.; d. St. Louis, Mo.. '53.
Battis,Harriet L.,N. Leominster;m. *Thos. F. Burrage,'57; 17 *Trowbridge Place, Cambridge.*
Beard, Susan H., Falmouth; m. Wm. A. Carwith, '60; *Bridgehampton, N. Y.*
Becker, Helen, Geneva, N. Y.; m. Geo. Hipple. '53; *Ravenswood, Ill.*
Bingham, Elizabeth K., Honolulu, H. I.; *Honolulu, H. I.*
Blackwell, Sophie S., Princeton, N. J.; m. *Dr. Thos. Blackwell; *Philadelphia, Pa.*
Bowen, Ellen M., Marion, O.; m. John L. Harper, '54; d. Indianapolis, Ind., '65.
Boyd, Ellen W., W. Winsted, Ct.; *St. Agnes Hall, Albany, N. Y.*
Brokaw, Margaret V.. Groton, N. Y.; m. Harvey D. Spencer, '83; *Groton, N. Y.*
Brooks, M. Augusta, Dalton, N. H.; m. Rev. Thos. H. Johnson, '53; 196 *Lander St., Newburgh, N. Y.*
Bushnell. Lavinia A., Saybrook, Ct.; *Saybrook, Ct.*
Byington, Lucy R., Stockbridge; m. *Gustavus Ames, '54; *Stockbridge.*
Carter, Anna A., Bridgewater, Ct.; m. *Marcus E. Merwin, '65; *Delta, O.*
Chamberlain, Sarah A., Hudson, O.; m. Rev. Joseph Scudder, '51; d. Saratoga,N. Y.,'70.
Chase,Annie S.,W. Dennis;m. Rev. Worcester Willey,'54; d. Dwight Station,Ind. Ter.,'62.
Chase, Charlotte, Lyndon, Vt.; m. Chas. S. Cahoon, M.D., '57; d. Lyndon, Vt., '73.
Coe, Adelaide E., Detroit, Mich.; 45 *Alfred St., Detroit, Mich.*
Colegrove, Sarah M., Columbus, Pa.; d. Kansas.
Colton, Nancy E., Longmeadow; *Longmeadow.*
Crocker, Abby H., Boston; m. Rev. Edwin W. Murray, '57; d. Boston, '66.
Cross, Catharine C., W. Boylston; m. Geo. M. Lourie, '79; *W. Boylston.*
Cummins. Julia B., Belvidere,N.J.; m.Dr.Joseph F. Sheppard,'56; d.Phillipsburgh,N.J.'57.
Davis, Julia A., Jackson, Miss.; d. between '52 and '57.
Day, Helen R., Westfield; m. Jesse G. Pitts, '59; *Newark, N.Y.*
Denison, Caroline N., Burke, Vt.; m.Geo.W. Higgins,'53; 108 *W. 81st St., N. Y. City.*
Dibble, Maria C., Clinton, N. Y.; m. *Rev. Jas. Pierpont, '52; d. Murphys, Cal., '62.
Dickinson, Sarah T., N. Amherst; m. Rev. Fred. B. Phelps, '65; *Irasburg, Vt.*

1851.

Dimond, Eliza, Warner, N. H.; m. Rev. Ozro A. Thomas, '57; *Forest Grove, Or.*
Edwards, Esther, Albany, N.Y.; *Albany, N. Y.*
Fairbanks, Emily, St. Johnsbury, Vt.; m. *Rev. C. L. Goodell, '59; *The Rochdale, Boston Highlands.*
Fay, Zilpah E., Berlin; m. Rev. Wm. Grassie, '55; d. Erie, Pa., '59.
Fitch, Ann E., E. Sheffield; m. Henry Dresser, '72; *Great Barrington.*
Follett, Maria B., Temple, N. H.; m. *Denison K. Smith, Esq., '54; d. Barre, Vt., '59.
Fowler, Sarah F., Guilford, Ct.; m. Geo. Cruttenden, '58; d. Guilford, Ct., '62.
Getty, Anna M., W. Hebron, N. Y.; m. Geo. C. Hale, '55; *Catskill, N.Y.*
Goddard, Elizabeth J., Worcester; m. Franklin Hall, '56; *38 Granite St., Nashua, N. H.*
Goodrich, Caroline E., Ware; m. *Rev. John E. Tyler, '55; *Crescent St., Northampton.*
Goodrich, Julia, Middletown, Ct.; m. *Ira Ferguson, '53; m. Chas. H. Young, '69; *Steuben, N.Y.*
Graves, Helen M., Chazy, N. Y.; m. Rev. Eben. Douglass, '55; *18 11th St. S., Minneapolis, Minn.*
Greves, Augusta M., Marshall, Mich.; m.*Hon. Joel McCollum, '58; *Box 421, Marshall, Mich.*
Grover, Helen M., Bennington, Vt.; m. Thos. B. Beach, '74; d. Highgate, Vt., '87.
Hamlen, Laura B., Plainfield; m. Jas. O. Bellman, '53; *1724 Carr St., St. Louis, Mo.*
Harrison, Juliet, Westfield; m. Chas. I. Snow, '52; d. Westfield, '57.
Hawley, Sarah M., Salem, N. Y.; m. Rev. John K. McLean, '61; *520 13th St., Oakland, Cal.*
Hayes, Mary E., M.A., Washington, Ct.; m. *Wm. P. Jones, '57; d. Mt. Morris, Ill., '94.
Hopkins, Frances M., Racine, Wis.; m. *Darwin P. Flinn, '59; *830 Center St., Hannibal, Mo.*
Hudson, Almira C., Allegan, Mich.; *Fennville, Mich.*
Hyde, Eliza R., Brattleboro, Vt.; *Office Compt. Currency, Washington, D. C.*
Jayne, Hannah J., Setauket, N. Y.; m. *Edson Adams; d. San Jose, Cal., '94.
Johnson, Priscilla, Boston; *23 Circuit St., Roxbury.*
Kevney, Eleanor, N. Y. City;
Kidder, Tryphena, Warren, Pa.; m. Rodolphus C. Dyer, '71; *Hickory St., cor. 4th, Warren, Pa.*
King, Charlotte E., Saybrook, Ct.; m. Chas. Tomlinson, '65; d. Old Saybrook, Ct., '66.
Kinney, Happy T., Royalton, Vt.; m. Rev. Lucien W. Chaney, '54; d. Mankato, Minn., '73.
Kinney, Mary N., Bridgewater, Ct.; m. Chas. L. Ford, '71; d. New Milford, Ct., '88.
Lancaster, Sarah S., Durham, N. H.; d. Hyde Park, '79.
Lane, Harriet N., Candia, N. H.; m. *Harrison Eaton, M.D., '68; *Lancaster.*
Lawrence, Susan F., Groton; m. Reuben Lewis, '66; *Groton.*
Lindsey, Harriet F., Prescott; m. *Rev. Geo. H. Newhall, '51; m. A. K. Holmes, M.D., '58; *Canton.*
McMillen, Phebe, Collins, N. Y.; m. Daniel Allen, '53; d. Buffalo, N. Y., '84.
Maitland, Mary, Allegheny, Pa.; *140 Grant Ave., Allegheny, Pa.*
Marks, Arlina C., Blandford; m. *Howard Kendall, '55; *Easthampton.*
Marshall, Louisa, Derry, N. H.; d. Derry, N. H., '55.
Mason, Mary J., Southbridge; d. Southbridge, '52.
Maynard, Laura, Potsdam, N. Y.; m. Franklin Flint, '59; *Box 119, Denmark, Io.*
Mead, Charlotte B., Philadelphia, Pa.; m. Harrison Robbins, '56; *3030 Diamond St., Philadelphia, Pa.*
Merrill, Catharine, Canton Center, Ct.; m. Samuel B. Allyn, '68; d. Holyoke, '74.
Merrill, Jane, Canton Center, Ct.; m. Geo. M. Henderson, '53; m. *G. C. De Rochefort, '08; m. John W. Mitchell, '80; d. Turlock, Cal., '92.
Mersereau, Anna, Newark, N. J.; m. Silas P. Tomkins, '58; *61 Roseville Ave., Newark, N.J.*
Miner, Marion, Allegan, Mich.; m. Moses Hoyt, '52; d. Watson, Mich., '68.
Moore, Martha M., Huntingdon, Pa.; m. *Luke Doe; *Cal.*
Morehouse, Almira, Albion, N. Y.; m. Geo. H. Sickels, '53; *Albion, N. Y.*

1851.

Morgan, Anna, Colchester, Ct.; m. Abraham Bragaw, '57; 11 *N. Main St., New London, Ct.*
Nichols, Harriet S., Huntington, Ct.; m. Wm. H. Fletcher, '53; *Brooklyn Center, Minn.*
North, Helen P., Torrington, Ct.; m. Jas. M. Holmes, '56; d. Detroit, Mich., '66.
Owen, Abby, Belchertown; d. Belchertown, '70.
Pease, Maria E., Blandford; m. Richmond L. Wright. '62; *Quasqueton, Io.*
Plummer, Harriet M., Newburyport; m. Warren Currier, '54; d. Newburyport, '55.
Pomeroy, Candace L., Easthampton; m. *Joseph Sadler, '57; *S. Pittsburg, Tenn.*
Pratt, Elizabeth A., Meriden, Ct.; m. J. C. Hinsdale, Esq., '56; d. Meriden, Ct., '70.
Robinson, Mary M., Rutland, N. Y.; m. Rinaldo M. Bingham, '52; *Box 375, Portland, Or.*
Rogers, Lavinia J., Winchester; m. Sylvanus Elliott, '52; 12 *Chestnut St., Winchester.*
Rogers, Rebecca A., Winchester; m. *Jas. W. McDonald, '53; 54 *Warren St., Woburn.*
Rust, Elizabeth W., Little Falls, N. Y.; m. *Joshua J. Gilbert, '57; 36 *Prospect St., Little Falls, N. Y.*
Skeele, Clara, Chicopee; m. *Rev. Wm. R. Palmer, '52; *Chicopee.*
Solomon, Susan E., Lewistown, Ill.; m. *Chas. Shutter, N. Y. City, '71; *care Mrs. Eveline Delmont, 6 Commerce St., N. Y. City.*
Starkweather, Elizabeth, Northampton; m. *Aaron Breck, '56; *Lawrence, Kan.*
Sylva, Delia, Granby; m. Lucien Warner; d. St. Paul, Minn., '82.
Thomas, Hortensia M., Hotchkissville, Ct.; m. *Elam B. Burton, '69; *Hotchkissville, Ct.*
Thompson, Susan F., Lee, N. H.; m. Matthew J. Harvey, Esq., '56; *Box 173, Epping, N. H.*
Towne, Cornelia, Rutland, N. Y.; m. John F. Peck, '52; *Plessis, N. Y.*
Tufts, Caroline C., Milton; m. Abraham Voorhees, Esq., '67; 110 *Prospect St., N. Y. City.*
Turrill, L. Maria, Meridian, N. Y.; m. *Francis Graham, '57; *Elk Grove, Cal.*
Twining, Sarah J., Tolland; d. Webster, '64.
Van Deusen, Ellen M., Stuyvesant, N. Y.; m. Dr. W. P. Hazelton, '70; *Tarrytown, N. Y.*
Weeks, Mary J., Lyndon, Vt.; *Kenosha, Wis.*
Whiting, Cyrene E., Winsted, Ct.; m. Reuben Hamlin, '54; d. Santa Barbara, Cal., '87.
Wilkins, Mary A., Middleton; m. Jacob Coggin, '51; d. Tewksbury, '67.

1852.

GRADUATES.

Austin, Eliza H., Austinburg, O.; d. Austinburg, O., '75.
Benton, Anna E., Windsor, Ct.; m. Horace King, '53; *Thompsonville, Ct.*
Breed, M. Elizabeth, M.D., Lynn; m. Geo. O. Welch, '69; d. Lynn, '83.
Chamberlain, Jane E., Peacham, Vt.; 454 *Broadway, Cambridge.*
Daniels, Mary T., Plainfield, N. H.; m. P. R. Smith, '67; d. Fayetteville, Ark., '81.
Ellis, Abby W., W. Roxbury; m. *R. B. Smith, '57; *W. Roxbury.*
Everett, Jane L., Rensen, N. Y.; d. Osawatomie, Kan., '91.
Foster, Eliza J., Towanda, Pa.; m. *Rev. James L. Scott, '54; d. Landour, India, '92.
Haskell, Clara W., Weathersfield, Vt.; m. Henry Freeman, '60; 1707 *E. State St., Rockford, Ill.*
Haskell, Sarah J., Weathersfield, Vt.; d. Lansingburgh, N. Y., '84.
Judson, Jane L. B. (name afterwards changed to Jane L. Bolles), Hartford, Ct.; d. Hartford, Ct., '78.
Lloyd, Juliet E., Blandford; d. Blandford, '54.
McLean, Mary, Vernon, Ct.; m. Jacob Hardy, '69; 6030 *Ellis Ave., Chicago, Ill.*
Marshall, Mary A., Milford, Ct.; 83 *Grove St., New Haven, Ct.*
Mills, Lucy C., St. Johnsbury, Vt.; m. S. T. Brooks, M.D., '55; 87 *Main St., St. Johnsbury, Vt.*
Nutting, Mary O., Randolph, Vt.; *Mt. Holyoke College, S. Hadley.*

1852.

Painter, Julia M., W. Haven, Ct.; m. *D. W. Bartlett, '54; 324 *Orange Road, Montclair, N. J.*
Phinney, Mary F., Lee ; m. H. K. Whiton, Esq., '55; d. Janesville, Wis., '65.
Pomeroy, Harriet S., Somers, Ct. ; *Somers, Ct.*
Porter, Catharine M., Prattsburgh, N. Y.; m. Chas. R. St. John, '60; d. Prattsburgh, N. Y., '87.
Scott, Emily A., N. Hadley; m. C. W. Cleveland, '59; d. N. Hadley, '60.
Smead, Maria L., Greenfield; m. J. P. Howard,'57; *Box* 34, *Bay View Station, Milwaukee, Wis.*
Start, Sarah A., Rockton, N. Y.; d. Morristown, N. J., '72.
Thresher, Mary A., Stafford, Ct. ; m. D. S. Carr, '57 ; 23 *William St., East Orange, N. J.*
Tucker, Julia N., Albany, N. Y. ; d. Albany, N. Y., '81.
Twombly, P. Jane, Great Falls, N. H. ; *Framingham.*
Ware, Louisa M., Grantville; m. Rev. E. H. Greeley, '54; 5 *Liberty St., Concord, N. H.*
Ware, Mary E., Grantville; m. Chas. T. Wilder, '56; *Wellesley Hills.*
Wilkinson, Ellen J., Newtown, Pa. ; d. Livingston, Miss., '62.
Willcox, Adeline H., Clinton, Ct.; m. *Chandler Richards, Esq., '59; 111 *W. Vine St., Kalamazoo, Mich.*
Wright, Cynthia A., Chicopee; m. Henry S. Herrick, '54; *Chicopee.*
Wright, Georgiana M., Northampton ; *Box* 321. *Northampton.*

NON-GRADUATES.

Aldrich, Angeline M., Hadley, N. Y.; m. Myron Griffin, '57; d. Glens Falls, N. Y., '91.
Bacon, Nancy J., St. Johnsbury, Vt. ; m. R. C. Vaughn, '56; d. St. Johnsbury, Vt., '68.
Baldwin, Adelaide A., Newark, N. J. ; d. Newark, N. J., '55.
Barton, Josephine H., Orange ; m. Rev. W. D. Herrick, '59 ; *Amherst.*
Bateman, Ellen E., Cedarville, N. J.; m. *John S. M'Gear, '56; m. J. B. Ware, M. D., '80 ; *Pedricktown, N. J.*
Beman, Orrell C., Alden, N. Y.; 166 *W. Jackson St., Chicago, Ill.*
Benthall, Mary L., Lowell; m. Victor Keyes, '55; d. Lawrence, '56.
Bentley, Julia M., Amherst; d. Amherst, '55.
Blaisdell, Harriet M., Boston; m. *Chas. H. Crane, '56; *Haverhill, N. H*
Blaisdell, Sarah, Boston ; m. Wm. Blanchard, '57 ; *Evanston, Ill.*
Bliss, Harriet S., Longmeadow ; m.*S. D. Burbank, '56 ; 1372 *Telegraph Ave., Oakland, Cal.*
Bogue, Adelaide J., St. Albans, Vt.; m. Denison F. Groves, '63 ; 3046 *Ellis St., Chicago, Ill.*
Bosworth, Nancy C., Lee ; m. Augustus Brandegee, '54 ; d. New London, Ct., '81.
Bowles, Mary Amelia, Newark, N. J. ; m. Fred. W. Lockwood, '60 ; *care Mrs. Hannah W. Brown, 346 Belleville Ave., Newark, N. J.*
Boyce, Margaret E., Stanford, N. Y.; m. Henry Van De Water, '54; *Crum Elbow, N. Y.*
Braddock, Emily A., Essex, Ct. ; *Essex, Ct.*
Bradley, Artemisia E., Lee ; m. Chas. B. Nye, '74 ; *Lee.*
Bradley, M. Ophelia, Lancaster ; d. Lancaster, '61.
Bricket, Louisa A., Claremont, N. H. ; d. Claremont, N. H., '53.
Briggs, Henrietta W., Boston ; m. Edward I. Thomas, '57 ; *Harvard Ave., Brookline.*
Brigham, Mary H., Belleville, N. Y. ; d. Hanover, N. J., '52.
Broaders, Rebecca H., Boston ;
Brookings, Susan A., Woolwich, Me. ; m. Rev. Crosby H. Wheeler, '52; *Harpoot, Turkey, via Constantinople.*
Brown, Emeline F., Pewaukee, Wis. ; m. N. S. Goss, '54 ; d. Waverly, Io., '56.
Burgess, Caroline R., Waltham ; m. *Isaac N. Beals,'59; 2214 *Atherton St., Berkeley, Cal.*
Butler, Lucy C., W. Meriden, Ct.; m. Wm. L. Squire, '56; 5 *Washington Heights, Meriden, Ct.*
Butler, Mary S., Reading ; m. Austin H. Wood, '63 ;
Carpenter, Fidelia T., Boston ; m. S. E. Pettee, '54 ; 400 *Sibley St., Cleveland, O.*

1852.

Chamberlain, Maria J., Honolulu, H. I. ; m. *Rev. A. O. Forbes, '58; *Lunalilo Home, Honolulu, H. I.*
Chapin, Clarissa M., Enfield, Ct. ; m. *E. Olcott Allen, '61 ; *Vernon Center, Ct.*
Chapin, Eunice M., Whitinsville ; m. *Samuel M. Capron, '54; 41 *Willard St., Hartford,Ct.*
Child, Anna M., Derby, Ct. ; m. Rev. Chas. T. White, '56 ; d. Cambridge City, Ind., '77.
Clark, Abigail M., S. Hadley ; m. Byron P. Cardwell, '56 ; 395 *4th St., Portland, Or.*
Curtis,Deborah H.,Camden, Me. ; m. *Joseph P. Dyer,'53; 1257 *Jackson St., Oakland,Cal.*
Cutler, Charlotte M., Burlington, Vt. ; m. John Boyd, '58 ; *Elmhurst, Ill.*
Davis, Aurelia, Kingston, N. Y.;
Eames, Harriet C., Rutland, N. Y. ; m. Wm. A. Winslow, '57 ; d. Chicago, Ill., '93.
Eddy, Elizabeth, Hudson, O. ; m. Nelson M. Holbrook, '65 ; *Delavan, Wis.*
Fenton, Fanny L., Bennington, Vt. ; m. Calvin Park, '64 ; d. Bennington, Vt., '82.
Fithian, Harriet N., Greenwich, N. J. ; m. Chas. Miller, '54 ; *Greenwich, N. J.*
Gardner, Sarah, Big Hollow, N. Y. ; m. F. A. Brackett, '57 ; 1003 *Chestnut St., Atlantic,Io.*
Goodsell, Mary E., Greenwood, Ill. ; m. A. T. Barrows, '58 ; d. Northfield, Minn., '71.
Grant, Hannah J., Halifax, Vt. ; m. Rev. Chas. Scott, '53 ; d. Gloucester, R. I., '75.
Gridley,Celia A.,Southampton ; m. C. W. M. Smith,'53 ; 1719 *Clay St., San Francisco,Cal.*
Hallett, Octavia G., Augusta, Me. ; m. Eben Caldwell,'61 ; 90 *W. Grand St.,Elizabeth,N. J.*
Hamilton, Harriet B., Chester ; d. Chester, '53.
Hanmer, Elizabeth, Wethersfield, Ct. ; *Wethersfield, Ct.*
Harback, Frances J., Camden, Me. ; m. Edwin J. Hulbert,'56 ; d. Rome, Italy, '87.
Harris, Hannah O., Cedarville, N. J. ; m. *Wm. L. Cleaver, '54 ; d. Milwaukee, Wis., '73.
Harrison, Nancy J., N. Y. City ; d. N. Y. City ('53 ?).
Henderson, Eliza J., Dover, N. H. ; *Dover, N. H.*
Hill, Louisa M., Danby, Vt. ; m. Wm. Smith, '53; d. Florence, '69.
Hinsdale, Harriet M., Blandford ; *Blandford.*
Hitchcock, Jane E., Amherst ; m. Granville B. Putnam, '64 ; d. '94.
Hitchcock, Sarah A., Big Hollow, N. Y. ; m. *C. P. Holcomb, '52 ; d. '80.
Houghton, Eliza W., Waltham ; 537 *Main St., Waltham.*
Houghton, Mary J., Waltham ; m. *John G. Thayer, '54 ; d. Waltham,'94.
Huntington, Amelia C., Shaftsbury, Vt. ; 40 *Chestnut St., Rochester, N. Y.*
Hutchins, Philenna R., Waterford, Pa. ; m. Wm. L. Haskins, '58 ; *Lake Mills, Wis.*
Ives, Sarah A., Lenox ; m. Rev. Timothy A. Hazen, '53 ; 82 *Princeton St., Springfield.*
Kellogg, Harriet N., Amherst ; m. Jonas H. Winter, '57 ; *Faribault, Minn.*
King, Sarah R., New Haven, Ct. ; d. New Haven, Ct., '81.
Kittredge, A. Katherine, Lowell ; m. *John N. Taylor, '58 ; *Kingston, R. I.*
Kops, Gertrude de Bruyn, Hoorn, Holland ; d. Mt. Holyoke Seminary, '52.
Lennan, Susan H., Richmond, Me. ; m. *J. S. Hathorn, '54 ; m. Abiel Libby, M.D., '65 ; *Richmond, Me.*
Lewis, Anna G., Pulaski, N. Y. ; m. *Rev. W. W. Warner, '58 ; *Clifton Springs, N. Y.*
Lindsley, Alice M., S. Orange, N. J. ; 748 *N. Fairfield Ave., Chicago, Ill.*
Lindsley, Sarah E., Fair Haven, Ct. ; m. Paul Roessler,'59 ; 75 *Wooster St.,New Haven,Ct.*
Litchfield, Adella R., Leominster ; m. *Addison C. Carter, '57 ; *Leominster.*
Maltby, Isabella G., Northfield, Ct. ; m. Carlos Smith,'57 ; 254 *Orchard St.,New Haven, Ct.*
Marquand, Sarah E., N. Y. City ; m. *Henry J. Townsend, '78 ; *Morristown, N. J.*
Meeker, Caroline B., Schnectady, N. Y. ; m. L. C. Marsh, '64 ; *Watseka, Ill.*
Morris, Lucy P., Norwich, Vt. ; d. Norwich, Vt., '70.
Nearing, Ellen E., Catskill, N. Y. ; d. '90.
Newell, Helen M., Johnstown, Wis. ; m. *B. G. Webster, '59 ; 157 *S. Jackson St., Janesville, Wis.*
Newell, Rebecca E., Brookline ; m. Henry P. Cole, '56 ; 51 *Jefferson St., Newton.*
Nickerson, Almira M., S. Dennis ; m. Ephraim Morris, '54 ; *Hartford, Vt.*

1852.

Nims, Abbie, Greenfield ; d. Mt. Holyoke Seminary, '52.
Nims, Esther, Greenfield ; d. Greenfield, '72.
Norton, Louise C., Rome, N. Y. ; m. *Henry S. Browne, '56; d. N. Y. City, '90.
Page, Mary E., Rochester, N. H. ; m. Wm. N. Hastings, '58; d. Lindsborg, Kan., '76.
Page, Olive M., Rochester, N. H. ; m. *Richard T. Rogers, '77 ; *Rochester, N. H.*
Paine, Hannah C., W. Boylston ; m. *G. M. Nichols, M.D., '53; *108 Greenwich St., Milwaukee, Wis.*
Parish, Mary A., Randolph, Vt. ; m. E. L. Browne, Esq., '56; *Waupaca, Wis.*
Parry, Mary A., Athens, Pa. ; m. Mark Thompson, '54 ; d. Athens, Pa., '82.
Peck, Nancy G., Big Hollow, N. Y. ; m. Alfred P. Hayden, '54 ; *505 Vanderbilt Ave., Brooklyn, N. Y.*
Perkins, Mary D., Grantville; m. *Claudius B. Patten,'55 ; *203 Savin Hill Ave., Dorchester.*
Perry, Flora H., Royalton, Vt. ; m. *Joseph L. Perkins, '55 ; *349 Main St., Fitchburg.*
Pollard, Mary A. B., Plymouth, Vt. ; m. *Wm. W. Howard, '53 ; *634 Wabash Ave., Kansas City, Mo.*
Pratt, Frances L., Liberty, Ga. ; m. Rev. J. F. Baker, '55; d. Roswell, Ga., '57.
Pratt, Martha A., Princeton ; d. Princeton, '55.
Purdy, Anna E., N. Y. City ;
Remington, Sarah E., Wheatland, N. Y. ; d. Wheatland, N. Y., '61.
Richards, Helen C., Lahaina, Maui, H. I. ; d. New Haven, Ct. ; '60.
Richards, Julia M., Lahaina, Maui, H. I. ; m. *Prof. Fisk P. Brewer, '59 ; *Grinnell, Io.*
Sargent, Frances M., Belleville, N. Y. ; m. *John B. Clark, '56; *Woodville, N. Y.*
Seward, Fanny H., Guilford, Ct. ; m. *Ripley Baylies, '57 ; *Box 230, Guilford, Ct.*
Smith, Caroline T., W. Springfield ; 48 *West Silver St., Westfield.*
Smith, Maria, E. Abington ; m. Alonzo Lane, '56 ; d. E. Abington, '65.
Stanton, Abby (Willard), St. Johnsbury, Vt. ; d. Concord, N. H., '56.
Stevens, Mary L., Saratoga Springs, N. Y. ;
Strong, Elizabeth A., Schenectady, N. Y. ; m. Henry N. Raymond, '59 ; *591 Euclid Ave., Cleveland, O.*
Tarr, Julia M., Lowell ; m. *Harrison Williams, '61 ; *Bradford.*
Torrey, Miranda, E. Abington ; m. Benj. F. Hastings, M.D., '66 ; *Whitman.*
Tower, Pamella C., Rochester, N. Y. ; m. *Calvin Hale ; *Olympia, Wash.*
Towne, H. Janette, Rutland, N. Y.; m. Wm. G. Pierce, '55 ; *23 Sterling St., Watertown, N. Y.*
Van Slyke, Anna M., Stuyvesant, N. Y. ; *New Baltimore, N. Y.*
Voorhees, Mary E., Morristown, N. J. ; m. Rev. L. J. Stoutenburgh, '74 ; d. Schooley's Mountain, N. J., '76.
Wadsworth, Maria H., New Marlboro ; m. Frank M. Stratton, M.D., '56 ; d. Fort Madison, Io., '59.
Warner, Caroline E., St. Johnsbury, Vt. ; m. Thos. J. Tull, '56 ; d. Baltimore, Md., '63.
Watson, Charlotte E., Bakerville, Ct. ; m. Henry Gay, '57 ; *W. Winsted, Ct.*
Webb, Emma F., Rahway, N. J.; m. David B. Dunham, '57 ; *Milton Ave., Rahway, N. J.*
Wheeler, Cornelia E., Burlington, Vt. ; m. *James Bowman, '54 ; *Oakland, Cal.*
Wheeler, Mary S., Auburndale; m. John C. Abny, '56; *Ashland.*
Wilcox, Fanny R., New Haven, Ct. ; m. Arthur N. Hollister, '63 ; d. Hartford, Ct., '64.
Wilder, Esther F., Chelsea ; 53 *Fairmount Ave., Newton.*
Wilder, Mary J., Chelsea ; m. J. Rockwell Campbell,'56; *St. James Hotel, Jacksonville, Fla.*
Williams, Adaline, M.D., Mansfield; d. Augusta, Me., '89.
Wood, A. Maria W., Cincinnati, O. ;
Worden, Harriet A., Fayetteville, N. Y. ; d. Syracuse, N. Y., '56.
Wright, Celia P., Syracuse, N. Y. ; m. Warren Chamberlain, '54 ; *Box 60, Honolulu, Oahu, H. I.*

1853.

GRADUATES.

Adams, Elizabeth, Berlin; m. *Jas. C. Dean, '63; *Wichita, Kan.*
Bingham, Martha M., Cornwall, Vt.; m. *E. P. Bishop, '55; 227 *S. Jackson St., Athens, Ga.*
Boies, Rebecca D., Blandford; *Blandford.*
Butler, Esther P., Tahlequah, Cher. Na.; m. *Rev. O. L. Woodford, '59; *Middlebury, Ct.*
Chamberlain, Martha A. J., Honolulu, H. I.; *Honolulu, Oahu, H. I.*
Cheesman, Elizabeth, Bridgeton. N. J.; m. John M. Galloway, Esq., '70; *Guthrie, Okl.*
Church, Fanny, N. Y. City; d. Brooklyn, N. Y., '95.
Coe, Emily M., Norwalk, O.; 59 *Barnet St., E. Orange, N. J.*
Cogswell, Frances S., Woodbury, Ct.; m. Asahel W. Mitchell, '59; d. Woodbury, Ct., '61.
Colton, Clara R., Longmeadow; 138 *Montague St., Brooklyn, N. Y.*
Cooley, Harriet M., Palmer; m. Rev. Amos H. Coolidge, '56; 10 *Wyman St., Worcester.*
Darling, Mary E., Warsaw, N. Y.; m. *Henry B. Jenks, '55; *Warsaw, N. Y.*
Eastman, Martha, Peacham, Vt.; m. Jas. M. Haven, Esq., '64; d. San Francisco, Cal., '78.
Emmons, Sarah A., Sturbridge; m. *Thomas Spooner, '56; *Glendale, O.*
Gilfillan, Helen, Rockville, Ct.; m. John F. Collins, M.D., '73; d. Washington, D. C., '92.
Gleason, Mary E., Barnet, Vt.; m. Isaac Bridgman, '60; *King St., Northampton.*
Goulding, Frances R., Watertown, N. Y.; m. *J. P. Lee, '57; 37 *Winslow St., Watertown, N. Y.*
Harris, Mary A., Coventry, Ct.; m. *Walter Loomis, '59; *Makanda, Ill.*
Howard, Ada L., Temple, N. H.; *Methuen.*
Kimball, Mary A., Boxford; m. Jacob P. Palmer, '59; d. Brookline, '82.
Kimball, Sarah E., Boxford; m. Rev. David Bremner, '54; *Boxford.*
Knowles, Mary J., Greenville, N. Y.; m. *Wm. A. Davidson, '68; *Boulder, Col.*
Littlefield, Martha, Gardiner, Me.; m. Thos. P. Hall, '56; 104 *Benton Ave., N. Springfield, Mo.*
Long, Louisa A., Holyoke; m. *J. P. Woodbury, '57; m. Wm. H. Woodbury, '62; *Northampton.*
McArthur, Catharine, Limington, Me.; d. Limington, Me., '64.
Maynard, Mary E., Whitewater, Wis.; m. Wm. J. Jacobs, Esq., '72; d. Lake City, Minn, '76.
Olcott, Ann M., Watertown, Ct.; m. Wm. L. Smith, '57; *Flint, Mich.*
Parker, Fidelia A., Holliston; m. Anthony J. Johnson, M.D., '66; d. Cambridge, Ill., '73.
Pearson, Mary E., Cambridgeport; d. Cambridgeport, '54.
Prescott, Lucinda T., Candia, N. H.; *Boylston Terrace, Jamaica Plain.*
Roberts, Jennette, New Milford, Ct.; d. New Milford, Ct., '54.
Smith, Mary J., Quincy, Ill.; m. *Henry S. Hitchcock, '55; m. Paul Selby, '70; 442 *E. 45th St., Chicago, Ill.*
Stearns, Abbie S., W. Killingly, Ct.; m. *L. B. Austin, '59; 87 *East Canfield Ave., Detroit, Mich.*
Stearns, Mary F., W. Killingly, Ct.; m. Rev. Augustine Root, '60; d. W. Killingly, Ct., '77.
Sykes, Gertrude, Dorset, Vt.; m. *Rev. Quincy Blakely, '58; *Winchendon.*
Talcott, Elizabeth O., Danbury, Ct.; d. Danbury, Ct., '61.
Tupper, Augusta L., Hardwick; m. Theodore Curtiss, '68; *Waverly, Ill.*
Turner, Susan, Quincy, Ill.; m. L. B. Searle, '64; *Claremont, Cal.*
Ufford, Mary G., S. Hadley; m. Truman Dunham, '57; d. New Britain, Ct., '58.
Wadhams, Antoinette D., Richfield, O.; d. Knoxville, Ill., '64.
Warren, Amanda E., W. Killingly, Ct.; m. Publius D. Foster, Esq., '57; *E. Killingly, Ct.*
Wentworth, Caroline, Dover, N. H.; m. Edward M. Morse, '60; d. Paradise, N. S., '89.
Whitaker, Harriet A., Fairton, N. J.; m. *J. P. Clark, '60; *McMinnville, Tenn.*
Whiton, Ellen A., Ridgeway, O.; m. *Chancy P. King, Esq., '57; m. R. C. Spencer, '63; 178 *Prospect St., Milwaukee, Wis.*
Wilde, Amelia B., Newark, N. J.; m. Thos. S. Hayes, '60; d. St. Louis, Mo., '63.

1853.

NON-GRADUATES.

Adams, Mary S., Harford, Pa.; m. Asa C. Marvin, '54; d. Clinton, Mo., '55.
Amidon, Martha E., Essex, N. Y.; m. Geo W. Seaman, '63; *Bolton, N. Y.*
Babbitt, Hettie W., Mendham, N. J.; *Mendham, N. J.*
Bailey, Martha A., Hopkinton, N. H.; m. Jeremiah McLene, '63; *Brighton Terrace, Denver, Col.*
Baldwin, Hannah C., Nashua, N. H.; m. David Stevens, '56; *Box 32, Wilton, N. H.*
Baldwin, Mary A., Nashua, N. H.; m. Chas. D. French, '53; *Woburn.*
Benton, Frances, Windsor, Ct.; m. Samuel A. Wilson, M.D., '56; d. Windsor, Ct.,'73.
Berry, Eliza A., Bennington, N. Y.; m. *Judge Jona. G. Dickerson, '59; m. Rev. Lindley M. Burrington, '84; 23 *Cedar St., Belfast, Me.*
Berry, Phebe L., Dover, N. J.; m. Rev. I. B. Hopwood, '61; d. Newark, N. J., '84.
Billings, Martha D., Hatfield; m. Lucas F. Richards, '66; d. Unionville, Ct., '70.
Billings, Mary C., Hatfield; *Hatfield.*
Bourne, Celia M., Falmouth; d. Falmouth, '58.
Breck, Sarah B., Northampton; d. Northampton, '56.
Buel, Mary A., Colchester, Ct.; m. Rev. Nathaniel Fellows, '59; d. Worcester, '87.
Cargill, Clarissa, Providence, R. I.; m. *Hiram Atwood,'63; *Olneyville, Johnston, R. I.*
Catlin, Ada L., Harwinton, Ct.; m. *Geo. S. Catlin, '56; 218 *Main St., Hartford, Ct.*
Chase, Mary L., Otego, N. Y.; m. Rev. Jas. R. Smith, '53; *Pleasant Valley, Ill.*
Cheesman, Jane P., Bridgeton, N. J.; m. Jas. Horton, '57; 148 *N.Pearl St., Bridgeton,N.J.*
Clark, Ann E., Honolulu, H. I.; m. Rev. Oramel H. Gulick, '55; *Honolulu, Oahu, H. I.*
Clarke, Ellen M., E. Medway; m. Daniel Mundon, '54; d. Medway, '63.
Clarke, Mary P., Windham, Ct.; m. *Anthony Lane, '65; d. Brooklyn, N. Y., '70.
Coffin, Lucy B., Washington, N. Y.; m. *Newton D. Holbrook, '60; *Mabbettsville, N. Y.*
Cogswell, Emma M., Nashua, N. H.; m. Geo. Turner, '72; 4 *Crown St., Nashua, N. H.*
Cooper, Harriet S., Morristown, N. J.; 406 *W. 58th St., N. Y. City.*
Covert, Jane A., Williamsport, Pa.; *Renovo, Pa.*
Crawford, Eleanor F., Woodstock, Va.; m. *Geo. H. Dosh, '56; m. Jas. M. Briceland, M.D., '04; *Shasta, Cal.*
Crossett, Dora F., Goshen; m. *Rev. Chas. D. Curtis, '70; 40 *Shepard St., Cambridge.*
Cushman, Mary A., Fayetteville, Vt.; m. Joel Page, '04; *Groton.*
Cushman, Mary M., Berkley; m. *Harrison Fuller, '62; 442 *N. Main St., Brockton.*
Davenport, Elizabeth A., Chicopee Falls; m.*Rev. Jas. K. Lombard,'57; Norton Heights.Ct.
Dillingham, Elizabeth N., Sandwich; m. David S. Marchant, '57; d. Malden, '72.
Doane, Abby M., N. Brookfield; m. *John P. Worstell, '55; 341 *W. 51st St., N. Y. City.*
Dowling, Cornelia M., Philadelphia, Pa.; m. Robert Rogers, '58; 64 *E. 61st St.,N.Y.City.*
Eaton, Anna M., Framingham; d. Framingham, '90.
Ellms, Clara M., Scituate; m. John H. Skeele, '56; P. O. Address, *Greenbush.*
Everett, Mary H., M.D., Remsen, N. Y.; *Remsen, N. Y.*
Field, Ellen Z., Albion, N. Y.; *Albion, N. Y.*
Gerrish, Martha, Boscawen, N. H.; m. Wm. S. Freed, '62; d. Waterford, Ont., '75.
Gould, Elizabeth P., Northville, Ill.; m. Horace D. Williams, '57; *Northville, Ill.*
Hammond, Susan R., Grafton; m. *John Wheeler, '62; *Westbrook, Me.*
Harriman, Sarah W., Conway, N. H.; m. *Rev. J. J. Hill, '53; 703 *Park St., Des Moines,Io.*
Harrington, Sarah C., Paxton; m. *Edwin D. Pickett,'57; m. Jacob H. Fuller, '74; *Hampton, Ct.*
Harrison, Sarah F., Orange, N. J.; m. B. F. Williams, '58; 97 *Park St., Orange, N. J.*
Hedden, Catharine, Orange, N. J.; m. Edgar Holden, M.D., '61; d. Orange, N. J., '70.
Hill, Margaret McA., Coila, N. Y.; m. John Moneypenny, M.D., '54; *Cambridge, N.Y.*
Hitchcock, Frances A., Southington, Ct.; m. Henry C. Young, '55; *Jewett City, Ct.*

Hitchcock, Josephine L., Southington, Ct. ; m. Rev. Geo. Buck, '77 ; *Poquetanuck, Ct.*
Hitchcock, Julia M., N. Bergen, N. Y. ; m. Rev. Jas. Walker, '61 ;d.Hesperia, Mich., '75.
Holman, Caroline E., Wilbraham ; m. *Chas. B. Kingsley, '58 ; d. Northampton, '84.
Hough, Sarah L. S., Middletown, Ct..; m. Chas. H. Galpin, '59 ; d. Marion, Ct., '83.
Johnston, Ellen R., Washington, N. J. ; deceased.
Jones, Mary A., Templeton ; m. Arthur W. Hoyt, '65 ; *Templeton.*
Kendall, Mary E., Athol ; m. V. W. Leach, '56 ; *Winchester, N. H.*
Lee, Sarah E., Salisbury, Ct. ; *Jacksonville, Ill.*
Long, Cornelia M., Holyoke ; m. *Henry A. Pratt, '71 ; *258 Franklin St., Buffalo, N. Y.*
Lytle, Anna S., Erie, Pa. ; m. *Sidney Booth, '54 ; d. Erie, Pa., '80.
McKenzie, Sarah, Montreal, Can.; d. Montreal, Can., '63.
Mason, Rebecca W., Nashua, N. H.; m. *Jas. Bass, '70 ; *Fond du Lac, Wis.*
Mulford, Maria B., Havana, N. Y.; m. Mortimer G. Lewis ; 105 *Madison Ave., N. Y. City.*
Nash, Clara S., S. Hadley ; m. Ansel B. Lyman, '60 ; *Easthampton.*
Norton, Mary Ellen, Suffield, Ct.; m. Geo. W. Loomis, '60 ; 549 *Orange St., New Haven, Ct.*
Partridge, Eleanor A., Jamestown, N. Y.; m. Samuel Kidder, '54 ; *Jamestown, N. Y.*
Perrin, Anna, Rochester, N. Y., m. Austin S. Tuttle, '59 ; d. Bath, N. Y., '83.
Phillips, Jane Y., Pleasant Valley, N. Y.; m. *Edwin P. Brown, '57 ; *Schultzville, N. Y.*
Pranker, Elizabeth M., Saugus ; m. Edward Prevear, '56 ; 80 *Main St., Leominster.*
Ransom, Susan H., Bennington, N. H.; m Geo. H. Twiss ; d. Columbus, O., '68.
Reid, Elizabeth A., S. Amenia, N. Y.; m. Asher Teachout, '57 ; d. St. Johns, Mich. '61.
Safford, Frances I., Cambridge ; m. Samuel D. Smith, '54 ; deceased.
Samson, Harriet, St. Catharines, Can.; m. *G. C. Lane, '58 ; m. Rev. S. M. Osmond, D.D., '74 ; 742 *N. 43d St., Philadelphia, Pa.*
Schanck, Eleanor H., Holmdel, N. J.; m. John F. Conover, '55 ; m. Foster English, '68 ; 171 *E. 36d St., N. Y. City.*
Scofield, Mary E., Greenville, N. Y.; m. Francis E. Hickok, '56 ; *Kansas City, Mo.*
Sloan, Mary, Philadelphia, Pa.; 1939 *W. Dauphin St., Philadelphia, Pa.*
Smart, Hannah K., Corinth, Vt.; m. J. H. Chamberlain, '73 ; d. E. Corinth, Vt., '86.
Smart, Mary A., Portsmouth, N. H.; m. E. Tenny Taplin, '54 ; *E. Corinth, Vt.*
Snell, Sarah, Amherst ; m. Rev. Hiram L. Howard, '61 ; d. Burlington, '63.
Speer, Nancy J., Greensboro, N. C.; d. Boonton, N. C., '57.
Strong, Elenora H., Bolton, Ct.; m. Henry Strong, '58 ; *Manhattan, Kan.*
Sturges, Clarina B., Wilton, Ct.; m. Henry Supplee, '55 ; *Brookfield, Ct.*
Sturges, Lucretia M., Norwalk, O.; m. Jonah Crowell, '62 ; 375 42d *St., Chicago, Ill.*
Taylor, Henrietta B., Pittsfield ; m. William W. Peck, '61 ; d. Metamora, Ind., '74.
Thurston, Mary H., Kailu, H. I.; m. *Edwin A. Heydon, '59 ; m. Marcus Benfield, '67 ; d. Berkeley, Cal., '88.
Tolles, Frances J., Claremont, N. H.; *Claremont, N. H.*
Tupper, Emily P., Hardwick ; m. *John C. Norris, M.D., '63 ; d. Philadelphia, Pa., '66.
Wakeman, Mary, Kingsboro, N. Y.; m. *Rev. Morgan L. Wood, '57 ; *Marion, Kan.*
Ward, M. Caroline, Newark, N. J.; *Lyons Farms, N. J.*
Werlein, Barbara A., Clinton, Miss.; m. Wm. J. Neal, '55 ; d. Alexandria, La., '73.
Williams, Rebecca P., Northampton ; m. Wm. H. Corwin, '57 ; *Laurens, N. Y.*
Winans, Pamela C., Newark, N. J.; d. Los Angeles, Cal., '53.
Winton, Mary A., Havana, N.Y.; m.Sam.B.Sheardown, M.D., '54 ; d. Winona, Minn., '77.
Wood, Betsey J., Nashua, N.H.; m. Chas. R. Davis, '54 ; 1068 *9th St., Denver, Col.*
Woodin, Eliza J., Hillsdale, N. Y.; m. Richard Bartlett, '57 ; *N. Hillsdale, N. Y.*
Wright, Augusta L., Sheffield ; m. Geo. Bronson, '59 ; d. Brooklyn, N. Y., '61.

1854.

GRADUATES.

Ayer, Laura W., Haverhill, N. H.; d. Haverhill, N. H., '60.
Benton, Charlotte, Lodi, Mich.; m. *W. D. Wiltsie, '57; d. Detroit, Mich., '79.
Bradford, Celestia, Barre, Vt.; m. Rev. Marcus M. Carleton,'54; d. Brooklyn, N.Y., '83.
Chapin, R. Emily, Chicopee; m. *W. L. C. Gerdine, '58; d. '91.
Chapin, S. Elizabeth, Enfield; *Easthampton*.
Clarke, Elizabeth A., Watertown, N. Y.; *Watertown, N. Y.*
Crane, Eliza R., Newton Lower Falls; m. Chas. E. Cruttenden,'60; 613 *Chapel St., New Haven, Ct.*
Cross, Emeline F., Blandford; m. Edward L. Tinker, '56; d. Tolland, '63.
Eldridge, Lorie A., W. Springfield; m. *Hon. P. L. Page, Esq., '69; 591 *Evanston Ave.,Chicago, Ill.*
Fassett, S. Maria W., N. Bennington, Vt.; d. Cambridge, N. Y., '55.
Fitch, Mary J., East Sheffield (now Clayton); 5 *Oxford Terrace, Boston.*
Gale, Ann E. S., Rockport; m. Lyman R. Williston, '57; 15 *Berkeley St., Cambridge.*
Goodsell, Julia J., Greenwood; m. Chas. S. Hulbert, '56; *Minneapolis, Minn.*
Gowan, Amanda M. F., Rochester, N. H.; d. Rochester, N. H., '54.
Graves, Sarah L., S. Hadley; m. *Fred. R. Proehl, '56; d. Chapel Hill, Texas, '71.
Hall, Esther E., Tully, N. Y.; *Beaver Dam, Wis.*
Harrington, Olive E., Paxton; m. Rev. John C. Bonham, '56; *Westport, Mo.*
Hopkins, Catharine, Rutland, N. Y.; d. Mt. Holyoke Seminary, '65.
Hudson, Martha J., Dorset, Vt.; m. Davis G. Moore, '64; *Danville, Ill.*
Humphrey, Frances M., Southwick; d. Montgomery, Ala., '56.
Hunt, Ellen, Tewksbury; m. *Jonathan Bacon, '58; 3245 *Front St., New Whatcom, Wash.*
Hussey, Ann M., Sanford, Me.; m. Rev. Abner Morrill, '55; *Wolcott, N. Y.*
Lee, Catharine E., Northampton; d. Grantville, '74.
Longstreet, Keturah, Honesdale, Pa.; m. Rev. Jas. T. Rodman, '60; *Hawley, Pa.*
Lowe, Emma C., N. Brookfield; m. Chas. M. Nye, '65; *DeWitt, Io.*
McIntyre, Martha M. W., Charlton; m. P. O. Sharpless, '57; *Marion, O.*
Mayo, Ellen A., Leicester; d. Leicester, '58.
Moody, Mary L., Chicopee; m. T. L. Nelson,'56; d. Elyria, O., '63.
Morse, Emily. Triangle, N. Y.; m. Rev. Bela N. Seymour, '55; 804 *I St., N. E., Washington, D. C.*
Morton, Elvira W., Whately; m. *G. J. Shaw, '60; 335 *E. Colfax Ave., Denver, Col.*
Muzzy, Lucy B., Jamaica, Vt.; m. *Wm. Sanborn,'58; d. Ashtabula, O., '88.
Newell, Julia, Johnstown,Wis.; m. *A. Reeves Jackson, M. D.,'71; *The Vermont, 51st St., Chicago, Ill.*
North, Sarah M., E. Berlin, Ct.; m. *J. Hamilton Whitney, '62; *Morris, Ill.*
Porter, Mary A. L., Penn Yan, N. Y.; m. Rev. Jas. F. Taylor,'58; *Douglas, Mich.*
Putnam, Phebe E., Madison, N. Y.; m. *John T. Montross, '60; 71 *50th St.,Chicago, Ill.*
Scribner, Sarah E., Westport, Ct.; m. Rev. Isaac N. Cundall, '55; d. Rosendale,Wis.,'65.
Smith, Minerva, Worthington; m. E. Hazen, '58; d. Springfield, '64.
Spalding, Mary G., Haverhill, N. H.; m. Jas. H. Towle, '55; d. N. Y. City, '89.
Tomblin, Lucretia W., N. Brookfield; m. Rev. D. P. Young, '57; d. McAfee, Ky., '71.
Torrey,Clara H.,Rushville,N. Y.; m.*Pomeroy Fitch,'56; 36 *Gorham St.,Canandaigua,N.Y.*
Torrey, M. Isabel,Woodstock,Va.; m. Chas. W. Cleveland,'62; 77 *S. 9th St.,Brooklyn,N. Y.*
Twining, Pauline M., Tolland; d. Tolland, '54.
Wilson, Cordelia O.,Factory Point,Vt.; m. Albert W. Pettibone,Esq.,'55; *La Crosse, Wis.*

1854.

NON-GRADUATES.

Abbott. Augusta E., Ahmednagar, India ; m. *Rev. Samuel C. Dean, '56 ; *care Dr. F. W. Dean*, 25 *Douglass Block, Omaha, Neb.*
Baldwin, Abigail C., Lahaina, H. I. ; m. Rev. Dewitt Alexander, '58 ; *Honolulu, Oahu, H. I.*
Bassett, Elizabeth P., Birmingham, Ct. ; m. Rev. Chas. F. Bradley, '75 ; *Quincy, Ill.*
Bean, Lucretia A., Bethel, Me. ; m. Alphonso F. Bean, '57 ; *Pekin, Io.*
Bigelow, Mary J., Grafton ; m. *Andrew H. Adams, '56 ; *Box 1738, Boston.*
Billings, Jane M., Hatfield ; m. Augustus D. Cowles, '68 ; d. Hatfield, '84.
Bliss, Caroline F., W. Brookfield ; m. Gurdon A. Jones, '56 ; *Highland Ave., Newtonville.*
Brainard, Lucy A., Westchester, Ct. ; m. 1476 *Broad St., Hartford, Ct.*
Breck, Isabella, Warsaw, N. Y. ; m. Timothy D. Vaill, '58 ; *Bound Brook, N. J.*
Buckingham, Sarah, Norwalk, O. ; m. Cyrus S. Woodworth, '58 ; d. Salem, Or.,'90.
Butler, Abbie S., Fairfield, Cher. Na. ; m. *Jas. H. Sparks, Esq., '59 ; *Columbia, Mo.*
Chase, Mary C., Springfield ; *Convent of Visitation, Hastings, Neb.*
Colton, Susan, Georgia, Vt. ; m. Andrew J. Fuller, '64 ; d. Swan Lake, Io., '87.
Coney, Amanda A., Holliston ; d. Holliston, '57.
Cooke, Nancy F., Little Falls, N. Y. ; m. Walter F. Suiter, M.D., '56 ; *721 Caledonia St., La Crosse, Wis.*
Crie, Jean L., Portland, Me. ; *83 State St., Portland, Me.*
Daniel, Catharine W., Pomeroy, O. ; m. *Wm. P. Rathburn, '55 ; *603 Pine St., Chattanooga, Tenn.*
Diament, Elizabeth, Cedarville, N. J. ; m. Wm. Canaday, '73 ; *Vermillion Grove, Ill.*
Diament, Mary L., Cedarville, N. J. ; m. Rev. J. Ross Ramsay, '75 ; *Wewoka, Ind. Ter.*
Diament, Naomi, Cedarville, N. J. ; d. Kalgan, China, '93.
Dodd, Maria C., Bloomfield, N. J. ; m. Thos. Holt, '66 ; d. Trieste, Austria, '79.
Elliott, Mary A., Jericho, Vt. ; d. Jericho, Vt., '70.
Emerson, Elizabeth F., Chester, N. H. ; m. *Chas. Bell, M.D., '55 ; m. Rev. John D. Emerson, '63 ; d. Biddeford, Me., '69.
Esten, Sarah E., Boonton, N. J. ; d. Boonton, N. J., '87.
Farley, Mary E., Franklin, N. H. ; d. Franklin, N. H., '87.
Foreman, Ermina S., Park Hill, Cher. Na. ; d. Park Hill, Cher. Na., '58.
Fowler, Frances A., Mendon, Ill. ; m. C. B. Garrett, '63 ; *Mendon, Ill.*
Fowler, Mary J., Mendon, Ill.; m. *Chauncey Noyes, '63 ; m. *David C. Bray, '72 ; *Mendon, Ill.*
Francis, L. Emeline, W. Hartford, Ct. ; m. Jas. M. Williams, Esq., '56 ; *610 9th St., Sheboygan, Wis.*
Fuller, Cornelia A., Dorset, Vt. ; m. Jas. K. Pinkham, '55 ; *Belvidere, Ill.*
Gambell, Elizabeth, Springfield ; m. Horace S. Favour, '57 ; *425 Main St., Springfield.*
Gerrish, Mary, Boscawen, N. H. ; m. Joseph A. Little, '59 ; *Lowell, Ind.*
Giles, Frances M., Racine, Wis. ; m. Loren R. Wainwright, '61 ; *3155 Groveland Ave., Chicago, Ill.*
Gillette, Sarah J., W. Springfield ; m. Wyllis Peck, '59 ; *113 College St., New Haven, Ct.*
Gould, Emily, Peacham, Vt. ; d. Kanawha, W. Va., '55.
Goulding, Cynthia K., Phillipston ; *Mills College P. O., Cal.*
Gowen, Adaline, Rochester, N. H. ; m. Lucius L. Mores, '65 ; *2375 W. Erie St., Chicago, Ill.*
Greeley, Sarah L., Franklin, N. H. ; m. Sherman Hodgdon, '61 ; d. Concord, N. H., '63.
Grover, Charlotte L., Somers, Ct. ; m. John H. P. Chapin, '55 ; d. S. Hadley, '60.
Hallock, L. Emily, Franklinville, N. Y. ; m. *L. Monroe Young, '63 ; *30 Woodfin St., Asheville, N. C.*
Higgins, Mary, Plantsville, Ct. ; m. Edwin P. Hotchkiss, '55 ; d. Plantsville, Ct., '94.
Hills, Ann E., Rockland, Me. ; d. Rockland, Me., '55.

1854.

Hinckley, Mary S., S. Mansfield, Ct. ; m. Edwin G. Sumner, M.D., '55 ; d. Farmington, Ct., '59.
Holmes, Emily L., Springfield ; m. Henry M. Miller, '61 ; d. Springfield, '66.
Holmes, Frances E., Orient, N.Y.; m. Rev. Thos. Stephenson, '57 ; d. Bay Shore, N. Y., '88.
Holmes, Margaret W., Ridgefield, Ct. ; m. Linus O. Northrop, '56 ; d. Ridgefield, Ct., '85.
Howard, Mary W., Westminster, Vt. ; m. Ralph S. Safford, '59; d. Westminster, Vt., '83.
Hunter, Mary H., Brooklyn, N. Y.; m. John S. Lamson, '59; 60 W. 92d St., N. Y. City.
Hurd, Clara A., Galesburg, Ill. ; m. Geo. Churchill, '55 ; d. Galesburg, Ill., '57.
Jewell, Charlotte A., Hartford, Ct ; 140 Washington St., Hartford, Ct.
Kellogg, Julia, S. Hadley ; m. David C. Ayers, '60 ; d. S. Hadley, '64.
Kimball, Lucy S., W. Boxford ; W. Boxford.
King, Abby P., Ludlow, Vt. ; m. *Chas. C. Dewey, Esq., '56 ; d. Rutland, Vt.
Law, Annie M., Nashua, N. H. ; d. Boston, '66.
Lindsey, Melissa A., Blandford ;
Lyon, Mary S., Ogdensburg, N. Y. ; m. Wm. Armstrong, '56 ; d. Ogdensburg, N. Y., '90.
McIntire, Abbie E., Phelps, N. Y.; Exeter, N. H.
Marsh, Julia G., New Milford, Ct. ; m. Cyrus A. Todd, '56 ; d. New Milford, Ct., '57.
Miles, Myra E., Elyria, O. ; m. *J. L. Cole, '55; Pasadena, Cal.
Moore, Rosa, Washington, D. C. ;
Moore, Sarah M., Cedarville, N. J.; Clayton, N. J.
Morris, Lois G., Bridgeport, Ct. ; m. D. Dwight Baldwin, '57 ; Haiku, E. Maui, H. I.
Morton, Ruth C., Plymouth ; m. Jas. D. Whitmore, '55 ; d. New Haven, Ct., '91.
Noyes, Emily M., Perry, Ill. ; 1708 Orrington Ave., Evanston, Ill.
Olmstead, M. Cornelia, Ridgefield, Ct. ; m. Horace Hall, '56 ; d. Canton, Miss., '60.
Olmstead, Sarah F., Ridgefield, Ct. ; Box 207, Greenwich, Ct.
Osborne, Frances M., Birmingham, Ct. ; m. I. DeWitt Drew, '58 ; d. Meriden, Ct., '84.
Painter, Elizabeth W., W. Haven, Ct.; m. *Wm. H. W. Campbell, '61 ; N. Haven, Ct.
Parker, Laura E., Greenwood, Ill. ; m. Rev. Aug. G. Hibbard, '55 ; d. Carthage, Mo., '87.
Perry, Mary S., Worcester ; 124 Vernon St., Worcester.
Pomeroy, Maria E., Suffield, Ct.; m. *Chas. S. Bissell, '63 ; m. C. G. Pomeroy, '63; Suffield, Ct.
Pratt, Anna A., Center Brook, Ct. ; d. Washington, D. C., '82.
Putnam, Ellen A., Grafton ; m. *Edward Bemis, '60 ; m. *Wm. H. Harrington, '79 ; 834 Main St., Worcester.
Rice, Charlotte M., Conway ; m. *Zeno Russell, '56 ; 34 Bartlett Ave., Pittsfield.
Robert, Martha A., Portsmouth, O. ; d. Chicago, Ill., '87.
Ross, Kate A., St. Louis, Mo. ;
Rust, Eliza A., Chester, O. ; m. Frank A. Bridgman, '55 ; Westhampton.
Sanford, Jane, Rome, N. Y. ; m. Jas. B. McKinley, '60 ; Champaign, Ill.
Schirmer, Adelle E., Galena, Ill. ; m. *Joseph G. Miller, '54 ; 415 21st St., Denver, Col.
Scofield, Louisa H., Greenville, N. Y. ; m. John Herbert, '57 ; d. Roseburg, Or., '64.
Scribner, Louisa J., Westport, Ct. ; m. *Rev. Isaac N. Cundall, '68 ; Wauwatosa, Wis.
Sears, M. Eliza, Danbury, Ct. ; Danbury, Ct.
Shiland, Jennette, Bedford, N. Y. ; m. Rev. Wm. W. McNair, '63 ; Audenreid, Pa.
Smith, Matilda K., N. Boscawen, N. H.; m. Hon. A. B. Thompson, '63 ; Concord, N. H.
Smith, Ophelia, Saugatuck, Ct. ; care T. C. Coleman, Shepherdsville, Ky.
Taylor, Emeline, Canton Center, Ct. ; m. Jacob Norcross, '61 ; Muscatine, Io.
Tew, Katie A., Collinsville, Ct. ; m. Jas. B. Hubbell, '58 ; 524 Laurel Ave., St. Paul, Minn.
Thompson, Martha, Cedarville, N.J.; m. Rob't T. Whitaker,'56 ; 3127 Norris St., Phila., Pa.
Thompson, Polly C., Holderness, N. H. ; m. Joseph Clark, Esq., '55 ; 231 Fair Oaks St., San Francisco, Cal.
Torrey, Caroline, E. Abington ; m. Henry L. Beal, '56 ; Box 206, Rockland.

1854.

Tower, Jane S., Springfield, Vt. ; 128 *Pembroke St., Boston.*
Vann, Delia A., Fort Gibson, Cher. Na.; m. *O. Perry Brewer, '55 ; *Webbers Falls, Cher. Na., Ind. Ter.*
Voorhees, Sarah A., Morristown, N. J. ; m. *Chas. H. Dalrymple, '58 ; 81 *S. St., Morristown, N. J.*
Ward, Emily T., Newark, N. J. ; *Lyons Farms, N. J.*
Warner, Ellen, Newtown, Ct. ; d. Danbury. Ct.. '55.
Warner, Lucilla B., Aquebogue (now Jamesport), N. Y.; *Jamesport, N. Y.*
Webb, Josephine A., New Haven, Ct. ; m. Geo. S. Lester, '59; d. New Haven, Ct., '81.
Whiting, Mary E., Johnson, Vt. ; d. Johnson, Vt., '55.
Whittemore, Laura, Fitzwilliam, N. H. ; d. Mt. Holyoke Seminary, '54.
Wight, Emily J., Erie, Pa. ; m. *Jas. A. Jones,'64 ; *Lancaster, Wis.*
Wilcox, Laura O., E. Berlin, Ct. ; *E. Berlin, Ct.*
Wilde, Caroline E., Newark, N. J.; m. *Geo. W. Homan, '73 ; d. Omaha, Neb., '86.
Williamson, Hadassa T., Cape May, N. J. ; m. *A. Southard Hand, '72 ; 8 *Lafayette St., Cape May City, N. J.*
Willis, Rosina, Winchester, N. H. ; m. Edward E. Lyman, '58 ; *Warwick.*
Woods, Catharine, Enfield ; m. I. Norman Lacey, '60 ; *Asylum Station.*
Woods, Mary J., Enfield ; *Athol.*
Wright, Henrietta M., Northampton ; *Box 321, Northampton.*
Wright, Margaret P., Northampton ; *Box 321, Northampton.*

1855.

GRADUATES.

Ballantine, Mary, Ahmednagar, India; m. Rev. Samuel B. Fairbank,'56 ; d. Ahmednagar, India, '78.
Burton, Sarah A., E. Cleveland, O.; m. *David H. Pease,'57 ; 167 *N. Front St., Columbus, O.*
Carpenter, Helen E., Sturbridge ; *West Woodstock, Ct.*
Chase, Augusta S., Springfield ; m. *Jas. M. Stickney, M.D., '72; *Pepperell.*
Chase, Emily, Lyndon, Vt.; d. Lyndon, Vt., '85.
Clapp, Virginia, Easthampton ; d. Easthampton, '63.
Croft, Margaret, Waterbury, Ct.; 48 *Holmes Ave., Waterbury, Ct.*
Cunningham, Jane N., La Porte, Ind.; m. H. W. Knickerbocker,'77 ; *Northwestern College, Naperville, Ill.*
Deering, Mary, Augusta. Me.; *State St., Augusta, Me.*
Dickinson, Clara L., Conway ; m. Willard Merrill,Esq., '58 ; 95 *Prospect Ave., Milwaukee, Wis.*
Dickinson, Mary B., Granby ; m. Rev. Jas. P. Kimball, '58 ; d. Haydenville, '73.
Eager, Mary J., Newfane, Vt.; m. Truman Buck, '69 ; *Omaha, Neb.*
Ellis, Mary, M.A., Uxbridge ; *Mills College P. O , Cal.*
Emery,H.Jane, Andover, N.H.; m. Henry H. Barnes,'63 ; 612 *N. Beaumont St.,St. Louis,Mo.*
Field, Anna, Genoa, N. Y.; 726 *W. Park Ave., Waterloo, Ia.*
Fitluan, Cornelia M., Greenwich, N. J.; m. Thos. E. Hunt, '63; d. Greenwich, N. J., '74.
Foster, Sarah J., Jonesboro, Tenn.; m. *Rev. Samuel A. Rhea, '60; *Lake Forest, Ill.*
Frisbie, Felicia A., Waterbury, Ct.; m. *Fred G. Holmes, M.D., '58 ; m. *Bela A. Welton, '80 ; *S. Auburn, Neb.*
Gilfillan, Catharine, Rockville, Ct.; 12 *C St., N. W., Washington, D. C.*
Gilfillan, Jane, Rockville, Ct.; d. Washington, D. C.. '85.
Gilman, Mary E., N. Sandwich, N. H.; m. Rev. Uriah W. Small, '60; d. Oberlin, O., '86.
Goffe, Elizabeth W., Millbury ; m. *Rev. Chas. H. Peirce, '63 ; *Millbury.*

1855.

Goodale, Harriet W., Marlboro; m. George E. Beckwith, '63; *Haiku, Maui, H. I.*
Goulding, Abbie C. D., Phillipston; m. Rev. J. P. E. Kumler, '56; *413 S. Highland Ave., Pittsburg, Pa.*
Hall, Phebe T., Williamsport, Pa.; m. *Abram Trainer, '62; *234 W. 3d St., Williamsport, Pa.*
Harthan, L. Amanda, W. Boylston; m. *Chas. W. Moore, Esq., '59; d. *Minneapolis, Minn.*, '95.
Haskell, Harriet N., Waldoboro, Me.; *President of Monticello Seminary, Godfrey, Ill.*
Hastings, Mary E., S. Hadley; m. *Rev. Abner DeWitt, '58; 6400 *Madison Ave., Chicago, Ill.*
Heacock, Margaret A. E., Kingston, N. Y.; m. *Jas. E. Perkins, '61; d. *Santa Cruz, Cal.*, '91.
Hetzel, Ellen R., N. Y. City; m. *Henry S. Fitch, Esq., '59; *care of Lieut. Graham D. Fitch, Washington, D.C., War Department.*
Hills, Emily A., Amherst; m. Wm. S. Westcott, '66; d. *Amherst*, '70.
Hunt, Mary I., Providence, R. I.; m. *Leonard F. Fuller, '57; *Box 535, Providence, R.I.*
Judkins, Mary J., Claremont, N. H.; m. Mr. Judson, '71; d. *N. Y. City*, '83.
Kelley, Sarah A., Atkinson, N. H.; m. *D. I. Gibson, M.D., '59; *care Rev. Gale, Gensan, Corea.*
Kellogg, Ellen E., N. Amherst; m. Rev. Geo. E. Fisher, '59; *N. Amherst.*
Kent, Frances L., Enosburgh, Vt.; m. Rev. Stephen Knowlton, '58; *Danville, Vt.*
King, Adelaide W., Suffield, Ct.; m. *David W. Humphrey, '57; *38 Franklin St., Northampton.*
King, Jane M., Suffield, Ct.; m. *Rev. Jas. P. Kimball, '74; *Amherst.*
Lane, A. Maria, Franklin, Pa.; d. Franklin, Pa., '66.
Lathrop, Fanny, S. Hadley Falls; m. D. Pierson, M.D., '68; d. Brookhaven, Miss., '78.
Lewis, Elizabeth N., Walpole; m. *Emerson Wight, '62; d. Springfield, '71.
Meacham, Cleantha M., Meridian, N. Y.; *Meridian, N. Y.*
Post, Celestia L., W. Bainbridge, N. Y.; m. *Archibald Coulter, '59; *Tilden, Madison Co., Neb.*
Reed, Harriet S., N. Bergen, N. Y.; m. *J. D. Lewis, M.D., '66; d. Brockport, N. Y., '87.
Staats, Maria A. L., Gowanda, N. Y.; 128 *E. 23d St., N. Y. City.*
Talcott, Sarah G., Vernon, Ct.; d. Rockville, Ct., '62.
Terry, Hannah W., Wading River, L. I.; m. John Hend, '88; *Santa Clara, N. Y.*
Tingley, Ellen D., Windham, Ct.; m. *Henry A. DeWitt, '60; *care Messrs. Kidder, Peabody & Co., Boston.*
Trask, Elizabeth S., Enfield; m. *Ira B. Wright, '56; *Enfield.*
Treat, Mary B., Tallmadge, O.; m. Rev. Edward D. Morris, '67; d. Cincinnati, O., '93.
Waite, Susan M., Portland, Me.; m. *Rev. Edward P. Thwing, '59; d. Canton, China, '93.
Webster, Mary S., Hartford, Ct.; m. *Otto von Schrader, Esq., '56; d. Maquoketa, Io., '82.
Wheaton, Adela M., Fair Haven, Ct.; m. Benj. J. Van Bochove, '74; *Box 267, Kalamazoo, Mich.*
Wilder, Mary E., Keene, N. H.; m. I. W. Gates, '57; *Superior, Wis.*
Willmarth, Mary E., Whitinsville; 110 *Florence St., Springfield.*
Winter, Eliza D., W. Boylston; m. Rev. Chas. F. Morse, '56; 22 *Mt. Pleasant St., St. Johnsbury, Vt.*
Woodruff, Cornelia K., Ashland, O.; m. Rev. E. Bushnell, D.D., '58; *727 Genesee Ave., Cleveland, O.*

NON-GRADUATES.

Adams, Sarah A., Peoria, Ill.; m. *Sextus Wilcox; m. —— Whittemore; *Washington, D. C.*
Alden, Emily G., Cambridge; *Godfrey, Ill.*
Allen, Mary A., Boston; m. Richard J. Monks, '61; d. Boston, '84.
Allen, Mary M., Schoolcraft, Mich.; m. S. Rolla Barney, '55; *Schoolcraft, Mich.*
Avery, Elizabeth, E. Lyme, Ct.; 46 *Gibbs St., Rochester, N. Y.*

1855.

Baldwin, Mary A., Farm Ridge, Ill. ; m. R. Williams, '57 ; 401 *E. Main St., Streator, Ill.*
Barber, Anna S., Woodbury, N. J. ; m. John L. W. Weutz, '04 ; *Elmer, N. J.*
Bardwell, Mabell W., S. Hadley Falls ; m. Henry A. Frink, '58 ; 605 *Boundary Ave., Baltimore, Md.*
Barnard, Alice L., Sycamore, Ill. ; 2018 *Tracy Ave., Chicago, Ill.*
Barney, Agnes E., Dayton, O. ; m. Rev. Edward F. Platt, '60 ; 90 *Pine St., Chicago, Ill.*
Beers, Phebe H., Chicago, Ill. ; m. John F. Weiss, '59 ; d. Brooklyn, N. Y., '79.
Bliss, Catharine L., Longmeadow ; *Longmeadow.*
Boas, Sarah J., Reading, Pa. ; d. Reading, Pa., '64.
Brewster, Caroline S., Waterford, N. Y. ; m. Edward G. Munson, '63 ; *Waterford, N. Y.*
Briggs, Mary B., Concord, N. H. ; *Dedham.*
Brown, Oella, Schoolcraft, Mich. ; m. Wm. H. Schuyler, '58 ; *Benkleman, Neb.*
Brown, Olympia, Schoolcraft, Mich. ; m. John H. Willis, '73 ; *cor. 10th and Lake Ave., Racine, Wis.*
Browning, Mary L., Chelsea ; m. Rev. David Herron, '57 ; d. Dehrah, India, '63.
Buchanan, N. Amanda, Cane Hill, Ark. ; m. Rev. F. R. Earle, D.D., '65 ; d. Boonesboro, Ark., '94.
Butts, Elizabeth K., Chicopee ; m. Geo. W. Ball, '56 ; *Newton Highlands.*
Carey, Sarah J., Mendham, N. J. ; m. Wellington Cass, Esq., '78 ; 1813 *California Ave., St. Louis, Mo.*
Carter, Julia M., Chicopee Falls ; m. Chas. A. Taylor, '70 ; d. Chicopee Falls, '02.
Cary, Lucretia, Enfield ; *Enfield.*
Clapp, Sarah E., Easthampton ; m. Geo. W. Guilford, '80 ; *Swift River.*
Clarke, Sarah J., Sunderland ; m. *Wm. S. Gould, '66 ; *Riverside, R. I.*
Cline, Annie M., S. Amenia, N. Y. ; d. Rochester, N. Y., '59.
Cobb, Lucia D., Sandwich ; m. Rev. Emanuel V. Gerhart, D.D., LL.D., '75 ; *Lancaster, Pa.*
Cooley, Frances M., Springfield ; m. Israel Harmon, '59 ; 64 *Spring St., Springfield.*
Crawford, Susan A., Cane Hill, Ark. ; m. Jacob P. Carnahan, '58 ; d. Cane Hill, Ark., '70.
Critchlow, Maria, Florence ; m. Gaius H. Narramore, '59 ; *Perth Amboy, N. J.*
Cunningham, Catharine M., La Porte, Ind. ; m. Cheney M. Castle, '82 ; 1506 *Clinton Ave., Minneapolis, Minn.*
Davis, Henrietta, Princeton ; *Princeton.*
Day, Lucy A., Ludlow ; m. Joseph S. Perry, '55 ; 166 *Vernon St., Worcester.*
Dodge, Helen A., Bennington, N. H. ; *Santa Fe, N. M.*
Dole, Elizabeth A., New Haven, Ct. ; m. Lucius B. Skinner, '67 ; d. Du Quoin, Ill., '73.
Doolittle, Catharine E., Hudson, O. ; m. W. F. Chamberlain, '65 ; d. Williamstown, Mo., '79.
Dudley, Ellen M., Lowell ; 24 *Marlboro St., Lowell.*
Eastman, Hannah D., Ovid, N. Y. ; m. David W. Birge, '56 ; d. Hector, N. Y., '66.
Everett, Eliza R., Princeton ; m. Holland N. Batcheller, '57 ; d. Mt. Pleasant, S. C., '67.
Fiske, Caroline A., Southbridge ; m. Joseph Hodges, '58 ; d. Southbridge, '83.
Fletcher, Annie B., Concord, N. H. ; *Prattville, Ala.*
Foskett, Samantha, Charlton ; 26 *Chase Ave., Webster.*
Foster, Sarah M., Erie, Pa. ; m. Rev. I. I. St. John, '50 ; *Salem, Ind.*
Giles, Evelyn A., New Market, N. J. ; m. *Geo. W. Calhoun, '71 ; *New Market, N. J.*
Goffe, Hannah F., Millbury ; *Millbury.*
Goodrich, Martha C., Pittsfield ; m. *Henry T. Dunham, '60 ; *Norwich, N. Y.*
Hall, Seraph A., Newfane, Vt. ; m. Abial D. Atkinson, '75 ; *Burlington, O.*
Hancock, Annette, Lowell ;
Hartwell, Annie M., Greenville, N. Y. ; m. Geo. A. Swalm, '77 ; *Middletown, N. Y.*
Hatch, Lucy H., Rockland, Me. ; *Box 2777, Fresno, Cal.*
Hatch, Mentoria V., Dayton, O. ;
Hawks, Julia E., S. Hadley ; m. *Isaac R. Coe, '56 ; 3027 *Mich Ave., Chicago, Ill.*

1855.

Hawks, Mary D., Charlemont; m. Austin LaF. Peck, '71; *Shelburne.*
Hawks, Sarah E., Charlemont; m. Elisha B. Alvord, '59; d. Charlemont, '75.
Healy, Louisa, Northampton; m. Rev. Stephen C. Pixley, '55; *Lindley, Duff's Road, Natal, S. Africa.*
Hoffses, Isabel M., Waldoboro, Me.; *S. Waldoboro, Me.*
Hudson, Margaret A., Manchester, Vt.; m. Geo. B. Dunton, '67; d. Belvidere, Ill., '70.
Knapp, Mary H., Bedford, N. Y.; m. Israel G. Schryver, '59; *Algona, Io.*
Leonard, Mary J., Boston; m. *Chas. E. Norton, '64; 222 *Osborne St., Cleveland, O.*
Linsley, Aurelia L., Millville, N. Y.; m. Lucius Webster, '58; *Oberlin, O.*
Linsley, Eunice F., N. Haven, Ct.; m. *Arthur F. Daniels, '71; d. Bloomington, Ill., '74.
Loveridge, Elizabeth C., Waterloo, N. Y.; m. J. M. Selfridge, M.D., '55; *960 14th St., Oakland, Cal.*
Lyman, Sarah A., Winchester, N. H.; m. *Chas. W. Wilber, '66; *Amboy, Ill.*
Marsh, Arabella, Greenfield; *1065 Josephine St., Denver, Col.*
Martin, Elizabeth D., Peacham, Vt.; m. Rev. Geo. S. Woodhull, D.D., '55; *2303 S. Washington Ave., E. Saginaw, Mich.*
Maxwell, R. Annie, Middletown. Del.; *Middletown, Del.*
Merwin, Margarett, Durham, Ct.; m. *Abner C. Wetmore, '70; *44 Crown St., Meriden, Ct.*
Miller, Elizabeth H., Somerville; m. C. E. Taber, '65; *N. San Juan, Cal.*
Montague, Mary N., S. Hadley; m. Geo. F. Platt, M.D., '63; *24 E. Market St., Chambersburg, Pa.*
Morrill, Mary A., Albany, N. Y.; d. Minneapolis or St. Paul, Minn.
Morris, Marie A., Philadelphia, Pa.;
Mowry, Eliza R., Norwich, Ct.; m. Chas. H. Johnson, Esq., '75; *Flint, Mich.*
Partridge, Harriet H., Brooklyn, N. Y.; m. Henry I. Bliss; *218 N. 8th St., La Crosse, Wis.*
Rankin, Lois A., Chester, Vt.; *513 6th St., Washington, D. C.*
Reed, Anna, Davenport, Io.; m. Henry W. Wilkinson, '61; *92 Bowen St., Providence, R. I.*
Reeve, Maria, Kinsman, O.; m. *J. T. Edwards, '59; *Box 800, Benton Harbor, Mich.*
Reeve, Sarah M., N. Y. City;
Richards, Sarah G., New Canaan, Ct.; d. New Canaan, Ct., '56.
Rush, Amanda, Farmington, N. Y.; m. Geo. W. McLouth, '66; *Manchester, N. Y.*
Scott, Caroline S., Waterford, N. Y.; m. *Chas. Knickerbocker, '59; *Waterford, N. Y.*
Seymour, Mary A., Syracuse, N. Y.; d. Syracuse, N. Y., '70.
Snow, Julia P., Amherst; m. Chas. H. Whitehouse, '62; *Waltham.*
Stevens, Caroline A., Mt. Vernon, N. H.; m. John P. Brown, M.D., '65; *Hospital, Taunton.*
Stocking, Harriet N., Waterbury. Ct.; m. *Henry E. Lathrop, '59; *17 Angell St., Providence, R. I.*
Strong, Emeline, La Porte, Ind.; m. *Jas. Lewis, '56; m. John Sutherland, '79; *care J. F. Church, 1138 O St., Fresno, Cal.*
Sturdevant, C. Jane, Prattsburgh, N. Y.; m. *James J. Swing, '60; m. Wm. A. Farris, '73; *2030 Walnut St., Kansas City, Kansas.*
Tatlock, Jane, Williamstown; *care Rev. Tatlock, D.D., Stamford, Ct.*
Tower, Abbie L., Springfield, Vt.; *2934 Lucas Ave., St. Louis, Mo.*
Tower, Henrietta B., Springfield, Vt.; d. Springfield, Vt., '67.
Utley, Sarah L., Austerlitz, N. Y.; m. Rev. Simeon F. Woodin, '59; *Foochow, China.*
Vedder, Elizabeth M., Northampton; m. John D. Lloyd; d. Jonesville, Tenn. ('86?).
Vose, Anna M., Lancaster; m. *N. J. Bradlee, '81; *65 Highland St., Roxbury.*
Waite, Lucy B., Whately; d. Easthampton, '85.
Weston, Rebecca J., Boston; *29 W. Cedar St., Boston.*
Wheeler, Caroline R., Bangor, Me.; m. Rev. Orson P. Allen, '55; *Harpoot, Turkey. via Constantinople.*
White, Abbie L., Shelburne Falls; m. L. B. Rice, '56; d. Cedar Falls, Io., '58.

1855.

Woodhull, Phebe W., Jamesport, N. Y.; d. Jamesport, N. Y., '94.
Worthington, Clara, Fairview, Pa.; m. 1. N. Wilson; d. Vineland, N. J., '72.
Wright, Mary A., Bridgehampton, N.Y.; m. Hon. Jas. M.Halsey,'56; *Bridgehampton,N. Y.*
Youngblood, Sarah O., Karangan, Borneo; m. *E. S. West, '57; *Supt. Webb's Academy, Fordham Heights, N. Y. City.*

1856.

GRADUATES.

Adams, Nancy L., Townsend; m.*Rev. Charles Brooks, '58; 20 *Dartmouth St., Boston.*
Alexander, Ada J., Winchester, N. H.; d. N. Y. City, '07.
Alexander, Ellen L., Winchester, N. H.; 359 *Central St., Springfield.*
Barrows, Cornelia C., Columbus, N. Y.; m. Rev. Lyman Bartlett, '57; d. Smyrna, Turkey, '92.
Bartlett, Ellen C., Nottingham, N. H.; m. Rev. John P. Haire, '59; 4327 *Lake Ave., Chicago, Ill.*
Beebe, Sarah, S. Wilbraham; m. Edmund White, '70; d. Holbrook, '95.
Childs, M. Elizabeth, Conway; m. *H. Danforth Perry, '71; *Conway.*
Davis, N. Jane, Kishacoquillas, Pa.; *Birmingham, Pa.*
Dennison, Emily C., Deep River, Ct.; m. Joseph A. Smith, '61; *Deep River, Ct.*
Eaton, Caroline, Sutton, N. H.; m. *S. M. Pennock, '68; 100 *Sycamore St., Somerville.*
Ermentrout, Margaretta C., Reading, Pa.; d. Reading, Pa., '94.
Everett, Mary E., Ellsworth, Ct.; m. Chas. R. Swift, '65; *W. Hartford, Ct.*
Ferguson, Abbie P., Whately; *Wellington, Cape of Good Hope, S. Africa.*
Foster, Mary M., Warsaw, N. Y.; m. *Moses Bartlett, '69; m. *Ira J. Nichols, Esq., '79; 303 *Grove St, Rockford, Ill.*
Hall, Mary P., Batavia, N. Y.; d. Hudson, Wis., '56.
Haskell, Eliza C., Amherst; m. Rev. Edw. S. Frisbie, '64; *care J. E. Porter, N.Brookfield.*
Hayes, H. Sophia, Prattsburgh, N. Y.; m. Rev. W. D. Taylor,'60; d. Binghamton,N.Y., '86.
Jones, Margaret W., Templeton; m. Wm. F. Bradbury, '57; 369 *Harvard St., Cambridge.*
Lyon, Eliza A., Fairfield, Ct.; *Fairfield, Ct.*
Marsh, Gracia, Cayuga, N. Y.; m. Robert Williams, '69; *Burlington, Kan.*
Mather, Mary F., Darien, Ct.; m. Prof. Zalmon Richards, '74; 1301 *Corcoran St., Washington, D. C.*
May, Julia H., Strong, Me.; *Strong, Me.*
Melvin, Harriette A., Chester, N. H.; *Chester, N. H.*
Nichols, Laura B., E. Haddam, Ct.; m. Rev. Henry M. Bridgman, '60; *Umzumbe, Umtwalume, Natal, S. Africa.*
Parce, Sarah E., Norwich, N. Y.; m. Henry De Land, '65; *care De Land & Co., Fairport, N. Y.*
Phelps, Mary, Winsted, Ct.; m. Jenison J. Whiting, '70; *W. Winsted, Ct.*
Pratt, Julia L., Centre Brook, Ct.; d. Columbus, O., '88.
Rice, Laura A., Warsaw, N. Y.; m. *Rev. E. J. Rice, '61; m. Hon. Henry L. Pearson, '75; 316 *Baca St., Trinidad, Col.* ;
Seaver, Ellen E., Painted Post, N. Y.; m. *T. P. Herrick, Esq., '58; *Hiawatha, Kan.*
Seavey, Ellen A., Concord, N. H.; d. Concord, N. H., '72.
Sessions, Harriet E., Hampden; *Hampden.*
Sessions, Lydia A., Hampden; m. *Rev. W. W. Woodworth, '66; *Berlin, Ct.*
Sessions, Mary D., West Woodstock, Ct.; m. *Appleton M. Griggs, '62; 41 *Second Ave., Waterbury, Ct.*

1856.

Small, Beulah, Pownal, Me. ; *West Leeds, Me.*
Smead, A. Amelia, Shelburne ; *Manzana, Cal.*
Smith, Anna E., Norwich, Ct. ; *36 4th St., Norwich, Ct.*
Smith, Mary J., Monson ; m. *Frederic W. Seymour, '62 ; *Monson.*
Stowell, Ellen B., Vergennes, Vt. ; m. Walter A. Weed, '60 ; *Shelburne, Vt.*
Strong, Eliza J., Williamsburgh ; m. Rev. E. W. Merritt, '68 ; *Salem, Ct.*
Thompson, Martha A., Deerfield, N. H. ; *Brunswick. Ga.*
Tichenor, Louise J., Newark, N. J. ; m. J. W. Draffen, Esq., '50 ; *Booneville, Mo.*
Usher, Melissa, Higganum, Ct. ; m. A. W. Tyler, '57.; *Tylerville, Ct.*
Ward, Marion M., Rochester, N. Y. ; m. *Hon. Dan. W. Ingersoll, '59 ; *Tallapoosa, Ga.*
Whipple, Maria J., Racine, Wis. ; d. Chicago, Ill.,'88.
Whiting, Amelia, Canton Centre, Ct. ; m. *Franklin E. Darrow, '60 ; *Bristol, Ct.*
Whiting, L. Amanda, Canton Centre, Ct. ; *Bristol, Ct.*
Whitney, C. Amelia, Darien, Ct. ; m. *Benj. W. Card, '65 ; m. Henry C. Packard, '76 ; *Sing Sing, N. Y.*
Williams, Marietta M., Norwich, Ct. ; m. Wm. S. Palmer, '58 ; *Coshocton, O.*

NON-GRADUATES.

Alford, Mary J., Hitchcocksville, Ct. ; m. Rufus P. Seymour, '60 ; *Norfolk, Ct.*
Allen, E. Maria, E. Windsor, Ct. ; m. Eleazer J. Avery, '57 ; *220 E. 19th St., N. Y. City.*
Armstrong, Lucy W., S. Windham, Ct. ; "married several years ago."
Atkins, Frances M., Northampton ; d. *Northampton, '64.*
Baker, Frances A., Quincy, Ill. ; *316 S. Henry St., Madison, Wis.*
Baker, Frances W., Hallowell,Me. ; m. Albert S. Rice,Esq.,'61 ; *26 Middle St.,Rockland,Me.*
Barber, Mary T., Woodbury, N. J. ; m. Aaron M. Wilkins, '58 ; *151 Euclid St., Woodbury, N. J.*
Barnes, Hinda, Middletown, Ct. ; m. Geo. L. Roberts, Esq., '65 ; *81 Mt. Vernon St.,Boston.*
Barnes, Marilla, Middletown, Ct. ; m. Norman H. Bruce, '70 ; *3 and 5 P. O. Arcade, Saratoga Springs, N. Y.*
Bartlett, Laura E., Sunderland ; m. Edward M. Smith, '73 ; *Sunderland.*
Beale, Adelaide S., Spencertown, N. Y. ; d. *Spencertown, N. Y., '89.*
Becker, Eliza M., Natural Bridge, N. Y. ; m. *Alexander Stewart, '62 ; *74 E. Main St., Johnstown, N. Y.*
Blodgett, Parthena H., Middlesex, Vt. ; m. Samuel Hutchinson, '56 ; *Norwich, Vt.*
Boice, Eliza E., Ashfield ; m. Fred. H. Howes, '58 ; d. *Ashfield, '63.*
Boynton, Caroline, Fitchburg ; m. Rev. Chas. A. Kingsbury, '71 ; d. *Marion, '73.*
Bradbury, Anna R., Bangor, Me. ; m. Rev. Chas. F. Holbrook, '63 ; *Danversport.*
Brainerd, N. Helen, Massillon, O. ; m. *M. L. Morrow, '57 ; *85 S Market St., Canton, O.*
Branscomb, Josephine E., Holyoke ; m. John G. Hill, '68 ; d. *Denver, Col., '92.*
Browne, Mary E., Bangor,Me. ; m. Henry C. Goodenow, Esq.,'60 ; *39 Broadway,Bangor,Me.*
Buckingham, Emma W., Canton, O. ; m. *Jas. E. Lewis, '59 ; *Albuquerque, N. M.*
Buckingham, Julia, Northville, Ct. ; m. Watson C. Booth, '66 ; d. *New Haven, Ct., '75.*
Burt, Mary A., Schenectady, N. Y. ; d. *Schenectady, N. Y., '77.*
Cain, A. Elizabeth, Brooklyn, Ct. ; m. *John Wm. Hunt, '66 ; *Brooklyn, Ct.*
Coolidge, Jane H., Fitzwilliam, N. H. ; m. Timothy Blodgett, '61 ; *Fitzwilliam, N. H.*
Coy, Helen E., Mt. Morris, N. Y. ; *Mt. Morris, N. Y.*
Danforth, Etta C., Webster, N. H. ; m. A. Pierce Bennett, '64 ; d. *Concord, N. H., '76.*
Davis, Abbie P., Hubbardston ; m. *Joseph A. Arnold, '64 ; d. '90.
De Wolf, Elizabeth P., Wakefield, R. I. ; *care Dr. Washington. Asylum, Stockton, Cal.*
Dickson, Elizabeth W., Clarksville, Pa. ; *Auburn, Cal.*
Dickson, Mary A. J., Clarksville, Pa. ; d. *Clarksville, Pa., '67.*

1856.

Dutcher, Mary E., St. Albans, Vt. ; d. St. Albans, Vt., '57.
Dutton, Mary T., Northfield; *Northfield*.
Eames, Martha M., Bethel, Me. ; m. Daniel B. Grover, '60 ; d. Boston, '79.
Eames, Nancy, Bethel, Me. ; m. Joshua Ballard, '59 ; *Zumbrota, Minn.*
Easton, Mary Andelucia, Belvidere, N. J. ; m. Rev. Samuel Laird, D.D., '65 ; 1314 *Spring Garden St., Philadelphia, Pa.*
Edwards, Eunice M., Southampton ; m. *Geo. L. Gaylord, '66 ; *Southampton*.
Ensign, Julia K., Sheffield; m. Wm. Verner, '63 ; 3509 *Spring Gar. St., Philadelphia, Pa.*
Erdman, Amelia D., Reading, Pa.; m. *Rev. A.L. Marden, '62 ; 438 *Chew St., Allentown, Pa.*
Fisher, Eliza D., Bath, Me.; d. Riga, Russia, '76.
Fisher, Joanna, Chester, Vt.; m. Rev. Geo. H. White, '56 ; *Grinnell, Io.*
Foster, Louise A., E. Medway ; m. Wm. C. Loring, '65 ; 365 *Columbus Ave., Boston.*
Fuller, Mary L., Trenton, N. J.; m. Rev. Wm. C. Roberts, D.D., LL.D., '58 ; 53 *5th Ave., N. Y. City.*
Garratt, Harriet L., Roxbury ; 7 *Tremont Place, Boston.*
Gordon, Annie V.,N. Y. City ; d. N. Y. City, '58.
Gorham, Eliza B., Stratford, Ct.; d. Stratford, Ct., '62.
Grout, R. Oriana, Natal, S. Africa ; m. *Rev. W. Ireland, '64 ; *Adams, Durban, Natal, S. Africa.*
Hadley, Maria E., Lowell ; m. Jonathan Ames, '69 ; *S. Lincoln.*
Harrison, Maria L.,Westfield ; m. Henry R.Lovell, Esq., '57 ; 803 *Clifford St., Flint, Mich.*
Hawley, Evelyn P., Homer, N. Y.; m. Rev. Edward Hitchcock, '60 ; d. Homer, N. Y., '86.
Hayes, Mary L., Somerville ; m. Rev. Wm. Carruthers, '65; 89 *Suffolk St., Holyoke.*
Henry, Catharine S., N. Bennington, Vt.; m. Chas. E. Harwood, '58 ; *Ontario, Cal.*
Hewett, Caroline, Worcester; d. Grafton, '81.
Hildreth, Phebe H., Bridgehampton, N. Y.; m. Fred. R. Shattuck, '62 ; 30 *Forest St., Roxbury.*
Holmes, Mary A., Jacksonville, Ill.; *Jacksonville, Ill.*
Hooker, Mary A., S. Hadley ; m. *Henry W. Smith, '64 ; *E. Riverside, Cal.*
Howell, Phebe A., N. Y. City ;
Hubbard, Abbie F., Concord ; m. Chas. Stowell, '65 ; 45 *Russell St., Charlestown.*
Hughes, Emma M., Cape May, N. J.; m. Rev. John S. Roberts, '61 ; *Bellefonte, Pa.*
Hutchinson, Josephine M., Gilead, Ct.; m. Chester M. Hills, '69; *E. Hartford Meadows, Ct.*
Johnston, Sarah E., Ovid, N. Y.; m. Rev. Joel J. Hough, D.D., '69 ; *Berkshire, N. Y.*
Keep, H. Eudora, Dana; *Madison, Wis.*
Kendall, Annie A., Worcester ; m. Theo. F. Fisher, '60 ; 20 *Laurel St., Worcester.*
Lambert, Sarah G., Salem, N. Y.; m. *Rev. Geo. W. Martin, '71 ; *Salem, N.Y.*
Lawrence, Harriet A., Pepperell ; m. Henry O. Wilbur, '58 ; *Bryn Mawr, Pa.*
Lawrence, H. Maria, N. Y. City ;
Lawrence, Mary F., N. Y. City ;
Leonard, Emily J., Meriden, Ct.; d. Meriden, Ct., '84.
Lovell, Mary W., Sharon, Ct.; d. Saco, Me., '74.
May, Harriet M., Southbridge ; m. Jas. H. Sternbergh, '62 ; d. Reading, Pa., '86.
Mead, Mary J., Hinesburgh, Vt.; m. *Nelson W. Fairchild, M.D., '57 ; m. *Chas. H. Frisbie, '77; 703 14*th St., Denver, Col.*
Merriam, Lucy E., Sutton ; m. *Cornelius J. Case, '60 ; *Atlanta University, Atlanta, Ga.*
Merritt, Anna T., S. Amenia, N. Y.; m. Henry F. Reynolds, '73 ; d. Mt. Kisco, N.Y., '83.
Montague, Laura M., Belchertown ; m. *Rev. Chester L. Cushman, '57 ; *Belchertown.*
Morgan, Charlotte, Somers, Ct.; m. Julian Pomeroy, '60 ; d. Springfield, '91.
Nichols, Catharine W., St. Paul, Minn.; 230 *E. 9th St., St. Paul, Minn.*
Norton, Catharine, Lockport, N. Y.; m. Don C. Smith, '58 ; d. Lockport, N. Y., '62.
Paine, Sarah L., Royalston ; m. *Amos C. Fisk, '61 ; 1 *Park Place, Ashtabula, O.*

1856.

Parmelee, Lizzie A., Pittsford, Vt.; m. Tobias New, '57 ; 50 *Gates Ave.*, *Brooklyn, N. Y.*
Pelton, Mary A., Great Barrington ; m. Wm. P. Strickland, Esq., '61 ; *83 Round Hill, Northampton.*
Penfield, Cornelia A., Bridgeport, Ct.; m. Geo. M. Penfield, '83 ; *Box 35, Black Rock, Ct.*
Pomeroy, Emily, Somers, Ct.; m. *Edwin C. Bissell, D.D., '59; *Somers, Ct.*
Randall, Sophia W., Norwich, N. Y.; d. Norwich, N. Y., '60.
Rice, Sarah, Warsaw, N. Y.;
Rossiter, Jane, Great Barrington ; d. Great Barrington, '07.
Rundall, Sarah I., Amenia, N. Y.; *P. O. address, Mrs. Sarah I. Rundall, Carpentersville, Ill.*
Russell, Mary M., Petersburg, Va.; 2 *Adams St., Petersburg, Va.*
Scott, Emma, Rome, N. Y.; m. Samuel Aland, '58; 426 *William St., Rome, N. Y.*
Sears, Elizabeth, Providence, R. I. ;
Seavey, Anna M., Chichester, N. H. ; m. Rev. Daniel J. Smith, '65; *Newmarket, N. H.*
Seavey, Mary J., Chichester, N. H. ; m. Hon. Sylvester Dana, '60 ; 20 *Montgomery St., Concord, N. H.*
Sill, Louisa P., Albany, N. Y. ; m. Jas. G. Betts, '60 ; *Box* 688, *San Diego, Cal.*
Sloan, Mary P., Palmyra, Mo. ; m. Fred Smith, '64 ; m. *Wm. Thatcher, '67 ; *care R. H. Sloan, S. New Berlin, N. Y.*
Smith, Ann M., Jacksonville, Ill. ; m, *Jas. Moore, Esq., '61; d. La Porte, Ind., '91.
Smith, Cornelia H., Appleton, Wis. ; m. Wm. D. Reynolds, '59; d. Chicago, Ill., '88.
Smith, Martha M., N. Hadley ; m. Rev. Walter Barton, '61 ; 21 *Pine St., Hyde Park.*
Smith, Mary J., Assabet; m. Addison Keyes, '70 ; *Berlin.*
Snell, Mary K., Bangor, Me. ; m. Wm. H. Harlow, '72 ; 69 *Harlow St., Bangor, Me.*
Snow, Phebe, Orleans ; m. Russell L. Snow, '59 ; 190 *Hamilton St., Cambridgeport.*
Southworth, Lucy M., W. Townsend ; m.Rev. Addison Blanchard, '64; d. Denver, Col.,'85.
Steele, Joanna D., Albany, N. Y. ; m. —— Lee, '57 ; 4020 *Drexel Boul., Chicago, Ill.*
Strong, Mary J., Northampton ; 26 *North St., Northampton.*
Sykes, Jane S., Templeton ; m. Edw. E. Bradbury, '56; 35 *Benevolent St., Providence, R.I.*
Tuttle, Anna E., Nottingham, N. H. ; m. Francis P. Harvey, '63 ; 108 18*th St., E. Oakland, Cal.*
Tuttle, Lenora, Nottingham, N. H. ; d. Sartatia, Miss., '62.
Upham, Frances A., Townshend, Vt.; m. John H.Converse,'68; 193 *Colony St.,Meriden, Ct.*
Ventres, Ellen J., Haddam, Ct. ; m. *John A. Brainerd, '59 ; *Haddam, Ct.*
Walker, Flora M., Saxton's River, Vt. ; d. E. Boston, '92.
Ward, Mary A. H., Lowell ; *Plymouth, N. H.*
Warriner, Daphne S., Monson ; m. Henry L. Narramore, '71 ; *Sharon.*
Wilcox, Catharine B., Orford, N. H.; m. *Homer O. Hitchcock, M.D., '75 ; *Kalamazoo, Mich.*
Willard, Hannah H., Orford, N. H. ; m. *John W. Sanborn, '61; m. Geo. W. Randlett,'94 ; *Lyme, N. H.*
Woolsey, Mary, Mendon, N. Y. ; m. John Davis ; *Plymouth, N. H.*

1857.

GRADUATES.

Atwood, Anna J., New Boston, N. H. ; m. Rev. J. L. A. Fish, '57 ; d. Duluth, Minn., '75.
Ballantine, Elizabeth D., Ahmednagar, India ; m. Rev. Chas. Harding, '69 ; *Sholapur, Western India.*
Beach, Mary P., Rome, N. Y. ; m. Alonzo H. Greene, '61 ; *Little Falls, N. Y.*
Billings, Mary E., West Bloomfield, N. J. ; *Winchester, Va.*
Brackett, Lydia W., Buckland ; m. *J. Wylie Smith, '65 ; 50 *Hurd St., Cleveland, O.*
Cantrell, Anna C., Yonkers, N. Y. ; 53 *Macdonough St., Brooklyn, N. Y.*

1857.

Chapin, Elizabeth L., Chicopee ; d. West Point, Miss., '62.
Chase, Ada H., Lyndon, Vt.; m. Rev. F. M. Dimmick, '88 ; *Box* 394, *Los Angeles, Cal.*
Chase, Rebecca M., Wolfville, N. S.; m. J. E. Wells, '62; d. Woodstock, Can., '79.
Collins, Cornelia, Northampton ; m. Wm. W. Ward, '60; 251 *Maple St., Holyoke.*
Davis, Elizabeth A., Lewiston, Me.; m. Rev. Joseph K. Greene, '57 ; d. Constantinople, Turkey, '94.
Dickinson, Elizabeth M., Heath ; 540 *Washington Ave., Kansas City, Kan.*
Dickinson, Louisa, N. Amherst; m. Rev. John M. Greene, '57; d. Lowell, '81.
Ela, Emily S., Hamden, Kan. ; m. Moses E. Grimes, '58 ; d. Hamden, Kan., '58.
Eveleth, Helen, New Gloucester, Me. ; m. Augustus T. Jones, '60 ; d. Brockton, '75.
Ford, S. Elizabeth, Morristown, N. J. ; *Box* 521, *Morristown, N. J.*
French, Ellen P., Cummington ; *Cummington.*
French, Helen M., Brattleboro, Vt. ; m. *Lemuel Gulliver, '72 ; 111 *Bartlett St., Somerville.*
French, Lydia, Concord, N. H.; m. *Chas. C. Lund, Esq.,'60; 38 *S. Main St., Concord, N.H.*
Fritcher, Ann Eliza, Fulton, N. Y.; *Marsovan, Turkey.*
Gage, Mary E., Waterford, N. Y. ; d. Waterford, N. Y., '58.
Gates, Harriet C., Rome, Pa. ; m. *Rev. Clark Salmon, '64 ; *Canton, Pa.*
Godding, Isabella D., Gardiner, Me. ; 78 *Cambridge Place, Brooklyn, N. Y.*
Grassie, Annie, Bolton ; m. Rev. G. D. B. Pepper, D.D., LL.D., '60 ; *Waterville, Me.*
Greene, Lucretia A., Hadley ; m. *Harvey Bartlett, '60; d. Rockford, Ill., '65.
Haley, Georgiana, Kennebunkport, Me.; m. *Franklin Sparks, '64 ; m. J. L. Burnham, '85 ; 711 *Belmont Ave., Nashville, Tenn.*
Hallock, Margaret E., Plainfield ; m. *Rev. Theodore L. Byington, '58 ; 418 *Henry St., Brooklyn, N. Y.*
Harrington, Eliza B., Paxton ; m. *Rev. Chas. D. Morris, D.D., '68 ; 2411 *Indiana Ave., Chicago, Ill.*
Hills, Laura, Amherst; m. Frank W. Dickey, '60 ; d. Amherst, '66.
Holman, Myra M. F., Millbury ; 106 *Chestnut St., Springfield.*
Houghton, Amanda L.. N. Y. City ; m. Wm. Ferguson, '63 ; 208 *W.* 104*th St.,N. Y. City.*
Hunt, Mary M., Newton, N. J. ; *Tallman Seminary, Paterson, N. J.*
Jones, Sarah F., Bridgewater ; m. *Chas. R. Ford, '57 ; 238 *N. Main St., Brockton.*
Kingsley, Josephine M., Winchester, N. H. ; m. Silas Hardy, '63; d. Keene, N. H., '71.
Lemassena, Jane E., Newark, N. J. ; 40 *Mt. Prospect Place, Newark, N. J.*
Linsley, Mary E., Millville, N. Y. ; m. Rev. A. B. Goodale, '60; *Pomona, Cal.*
McGee, Rebecca A., Colerain ; d. Colerain, '65.
Mason, L. Jane, Warren, R. I. ; m. Fred. B. Goddard, '60 ; *Nutley, N. J.*
Moore, Julia, Peterboro, N. H. ; m. Cyrus Jordan, '66; d. Peterboro, N. H., '74.
Morrison, Sarah P.. Salem, Ind. ; *Spiceland, Ind.*
Nichols, Laura A., Gilead, Ct. ; m. Rev. Andrew Denison, '67 ; d. New Britain, Ct., '68.
Nichols, Martha W., Gilead, Ct. ; d. Mt. Holyoke Seminary, '57.
Parker, Anna E., Berwick, N. S. ; m. Rev. David Freeman, '57 ; d. Citra, Fla., '84.
Parrey, A. Maria, Wethersfield Spa, N. Y.; m. Rev. Jas. F. Merriam, '71; *Santa Ana, Cal.*
Pond, Clara C., Fulton, N. Y. ; m. *Rev. W. F. Williams, '66; d. Auburndale, '95.
Robie, Clara A., Plymouth, N. H. ; m. *H. P. McCoy, '58; m. Wm. G. Scott, '64 ; *Richmond, Ind.*
Sawyer, Flora A.. Medford, Minn. ; m. Isaac N. Sanborn, '58 ; *Pomona, Cal.*
Shaw, Alice T., Berwick, N. S. ; m. Rev. Alfred Chipman,'62; *Alfred, Maine.*
Shepard, Elizabeth W., Rochester, N. Y. ; m. G. W. Neill, '60 ; *Neill's Conservatory of Music, Grand Rapids, Mich.*
Slocum, Rachel, Manchester, Vt. ; m. John. L. Batchelder, '59; 181 *Alexandrine Ave., Detroit, Mich.*
Streeter, Calista A., Fitzwilliam, N. H. ; m. Orlando Mason, '59; *Winchendon.*

1857.

Temple, Emily A., Galena, Ill. ; m. Rev. Wm. L. Bray, '61 ; *Ashland, Wis.*
Terry, Jane M., Lockport, N. Y. ; m. Norman Geddes, Esq., '59 ; d. Adrian, Mich., '82.
Tower, Frances E., Winchester, N. H. ; m. *James Miller, '94 ; *Winchester, N. H.*
Usher, Jessie, Higganum, Ct. ; *Higganum, Ct.*
Ward, Julia E., Lowell ; *Lowell.*
Ware, Sarah C., Fort Covington, N. Y. ; m. *Rev. Chas. Gillette, '58 ; *84 Adams St., Rochester, N. Y.*
Wheeler, Mary W., Fitzwilliam, N. H. ; *Troy, N. H.*
White, Lydia A., Whately ; d. Whately, '86.

NON-GRADUATES.

Adams, Helen J., Wellington, O. ; m. Simeon Windecker, '67 ; *Wellington, O.*
Adams, Susan A., Townsend ; m. Daniel Davis, '71 ; *Box 84, Lakeport, N. H.*
Allen, Emma T., Cleveland, N. Y. ; d. Cleveland, N. Y., '60.
Atwood, Mary F., New Boston, N. H. ; d. New Boston, N. H., '92.
Badger, Sarah E., Springfield ; m. *John B. Johnston, M.D., '62 ; *615 Locust St., Evansville, Ind.*
Baldwin, Margaret S., Montrose, Pa. ; m. Hon. R. B. Stone, '72 ; *Bradford, Pa.*
Barr, Ellen M., N. Y. City ; d. Boston, '95.
Barrows, Mary E., Middlebury, Vt. ; m. *Rev. Alanson S. Barton, '61 ; d. National City, Cal., '92.
Bean, Mary E., Warner, N. H. ; m. Rev. John G. Bailey, '71 ; *Silver Springs, Ark.*
Bently, Allie R., Amherst ; m. Rev. Justin E. Twitchell, D.D., '59 ; *56 Howe St., New Haven, Ct.*
Billings, Cornelia F., W. Bloomfield, N. J. ; *Winchester, Va.*
Burkett, Ellen L., Waldoboro, Me. ; m. Benj. P. King, '80 ; *Shelburne, N. S.*
Caldwell, Elizabeth, Byfield ; m. *Hon. Addison C. Niles, '59 ; d. Byfield, '91.
Chandler, Mary E., Foxcroft, Me. ; m. Chas. W. Lowell, Esq., '60 ; d. Foxcroft, Me., '63.
Chase, Harriet N., Calais, Me. ; m. Hon. Chas. B. Rounds, Esq., '65 ; *Calais, Me.*
Chilson, Caroline, Plainfield, Ill. ; m. Judson E. Hyland, '64 ; *Plainfield, Ill.*
Clark, Elizabeth M., Orange, Ct. ; m. Silas D. Woodruff, '62 ; *Orange, Ct.*
Coates, Annie E., Chester, Pa. ; m. *Chas. J. Morton, M.D., '60 ; *Toughkenamon, Pa.*
Coleman, Mary L., Easthampton ; m. Marcus J. Ross, '71 ; *Pomona, Cal.*
Comstock, Bessie H., Norwich, N. Y. ; m. Griswold T. Jones, '62 ; *13 Fifth St., Muskegon, Mich.*
Cooley, Lucy S., S. Deerfield ; m. *Henry P. Goodsell, '66 ; m. Baylor S. Shackelford, '82 ; *Fairfield, Neb.*
Coombs, L. Jeannette, Longmeadow ; *care Oliver B. Coombs, Queens, N. Y.*
Curtis, Celia J., Meriden, Ct. ; d. Meriden, Ct., '93.
Cutler, Lucia, Windham, N. H. ; m. John K. McQuesten, '68 ; *Manchester, N. H.*
Cutts, Emily C., Portsmouth, N. H. ; m. *Chas. H. Judd, '58 ; *Honolulu, Oahu, H. I.*
Daniels, Florence E., Plainfield, N. H. ; m. *Edgar C. Wells, '64 ; m. Rev. E. D. Taylor, '74 ; *117 Adelbert Ave., Cleveland, O.*
Dickinson, Helen E., N. Hadley ; m. John C. Howe, '62 ; *N. Hadley.*
Dill, Ruth C., N. Y. City ; m. Jas. Browe, '64 ; d. Belleville, N. J., '86.
Ford, Julia B., Morristown, N. J. ; *30 Harris St., Savannah, Ga.*
Foster, Elizabeth L., Charlemont ; m. *Rev. Samuel Fiske, '59 ; m. Rev. Henry S. Kelsey, '68 ; *416 La Salle Ave., Chicago, Ill.*
Freeman, Hannah, Harmony, N. S. ; m. John F. Roche, '58 ; *Clarence, N. S.*
Freeman, Salome P., Harmony, N. S. ; m. Isaac Shaw, '59 ; *Weston, N. S.*
Gleason, L. Maria, N. Adams ; m. Thos. Holbrook, '58 ; *De Land, Fla.*

1857.

Gorton, Fanny, New London, Ct.; *Waterford, Ct.*
Gray, Anna, Monte Bello, Ill.; m. Chas. C. Warren, '70; d. Ida Grove, Io., '94.
Harrington, Mary P., Middlefield; d. Amherst, '67.
Hibbard, Alice M., Milwaukee, Wis.; m. Elisha C. Hibbard, '59; d. Summit, Wis., '76.
Higgins, Rachel, Flemington, N. J.; m. *John C. Reed, '60; m. Asa Snydam, '67; d. Flemington, N. J., '93.
Hinckley, Ellen M., S. Mansfield, Ct.; m.Edwin G. Sumner,M.D.,'60; *Mansfield Center,Ct.*
Hopkins, Martha, Rutland, N. Y.; m. Harlan P. Dunlap, '62; d. Rutland, N. Y., '65.
Hulburd, Delia S., Rochester, Wis.; m. Benj. E. Gallup, Esq., '58; *1710 Ind. Ave., Chicago, Ill.*
Huston, Esther J., Bristol, Me.; *Hotel Huntington, Boston.*
Knowlton, Evelyn C., Phillipston; *60 Catharine St., Springfield.*
Lamb, Sarah, Norwich, N. Y.; *care Dr. S. H. Talcott, Middletown, N. Y.*
Lawrence, Hannah P., Wilmington, Del.; *1611 Summer St., Philadelphia, Pa.*
Linsley, Mary F., N. Haven, Ct.; d. Kenosha, Wis., '67.
Locke, Sarah A. J., Sullivan, N. H.; d. Mt. Holyoke Seminary, '57.
Lord, Georgiana F., Portland, Me.; m. Edward W. Upham, '64; *3 Center Ave.,Dorchester.*
Manning, Mary E., Littleton; d. Littleton, '59.
Marble, Susan A., Seekonk; *Bedford, N. Y.*
May, Ellen, N. Woodstock, Ct.; m. *Rev. Henry F. Hyde, '63; *Rockville, Ct.*
Merriam, Lucy A., Mason Village, N. H.; m. Rev. S. L. Gerould, '60; d. Stoddard, N. H., '67.
Miller, Jane A., Westminster West, Vt.; m. H. Nelson Flint, '58; d. Putney, Vt., '65.
Montague, M. Eugenia, Montgomery, Ala.; m. Geo. I. Hall, '60; d. Montgomery, Ala., '64.
Morris, Harriet N., Montclair, N. J.; m. Rev. J. B. Beaumont,'67; *105 South St., Morristown, N. J.*
Morse, Abbie C., Canterbury, Ct.; *57 Kemble St., Utica, N. Y.*
Morton, Judith W., Whately; m. Augustus Dow, '72; d. '87.
Nettleton, Martha D., Fulton, N. Y.; d. N. Y. City, '92.
Noble, Frances H., Tinmouth, Vt.; m. John T. Ballard, '64; *Tinmouth, Vt.*
O'Farrell, Adaline E., Spafford Hollow, N. Y.; m. Menzies R. Stebbins, '71; *Bromley,N.Y.*
Overlock, Delia A., Waldoboro, Me.; d. Waldoboro, Me., '65.
Overlock, E. Winnefred, Waldoboro, Me.; d.Waldoboro, Me., '62.
Philbrook, Susan N., Bath, Me.; m. Rev. Geo. L. Montgomery, '86; *Bath, Me.*
Pierce, Augusta E., Chesterfield, N. H.; *Chesterfield, N. H.*
Pitcher, Emma E., Forestport, N. Y.; m. Windsor B. French,'67; d.Saratoga, N. Y., '75.
Pond, Lucy G., Westboro; *Westboro.*
Redman, Jane, Paterson, N. J.; *142 Paterson Ave., Paterson, N. J.*
Rex, Frances L., Philadelphia, Pa.; d. Philadelphia, Pa.
Rockwood, Mary L., E. Readville, Me.; m. *Cyrus S. Robbins, '58; *Winthrop, Me.*
Rogers, Augusta A., New London, Ct.; *McPaul, Io.*
Ryder, Annette E., South East, N. Y.; d. South East, N. Y., '63.
Skinner, Ellen M., Winsted, Ct.; *Woodbury, N. J.*
Smith, Antoinette M., Batavia, N. Y.; m. E. W. Sawyer, '69; d. Kokomo,Ind., '79.
Smith, Catharine S., Winchester, N. H.; m. Henry W. Richardson, '60; *322 W. 23d St., N. Y. City.*
Smith, Juliet B., Berkley; *1226 O St., N. W., Washington, D. C.*
Smith, Maria D., Winchester, N. H.; m. Henry H. Pierce, '75; d. Norwalk, Ct., '94.
Snowdon, Susan, Wilkesbarre, Pa.; m. Desha Patton; *Cleveland, Bradley Co.,Tenn.*
Steele, Angeline L., New Hartford, Ct.; *New Hartford, Ct.*
Stewart, Eveline, W. Alexander, Pa.; m. David Armstrong, '60; d. W. Alexander,Pa.,'73.
Strickland, Ellen M., Springfield; d. Springfield, '87.

1857.

Taber, Sarah B., Albion, Me. ; m. Geo. Cozzens, '63 ; d. Newport, R.I., '66.
Talcott, Maria, Coventry, Ct. ; m. *Rev. J. W. Beach, '69 ; 56 *Whalley Ave., New Haven, Ct.*
Thrall, Virginia T., Bloomfield, Ct. ; m. Wm. B. Smith, '58 ; *39 Imlay St., Hartford, Ct.*
Trevett, Susan T., Bath, Me. ; m. Jas. M. Leezer, '65 ; d. Pendleton, Or., '87.
Tufts, Ursula G., Farmington, Me. ; m. Wm. T. Miller, Esq., '58 ; d. Mt. Carroll, Ill., '66.
Tuttle, Lorena, Middlebury, Ct. ; d. Mt. Holyoke Seminary, '57.
Utley, Julia M., Hudson, N. Y. ; m. Wm. C. Bailey, M.D., '59 ; *Chatham, N. Y.*
Wait, Elvira M., Amherst ; m..*Rev. John H. Dodge, '59 ; 84 *S. Eliot Place, Brooklyn, N. Y.*
Wakeman, Irena J., Easton, Ct. ; *Princeton, Mo.*
Walker, Abbie C., Exeter, Me. ; *Exeter, Me.*
Wheeler, Phebe E., N. Stonington, Ct. ; d. Marshall, Mich., '61.
Whipple, Eliza B., Bloomfield, N. J. ; 68 *Park Ave., Bloomfield, N. J.*
Wilcox, C. Louisa, Romulus, N. Y. ; m. Gilbert A. Van Duyn, '60 ; 1417 *S. 6th St., Springfield, Ill.*
Willmarth, Abbie F., Whitinsville ; m.*Francis G. Searles, '64 ; 110 *Florence St., Springfield.*
Winegar, Clara M., Homer, N. Y. ; m. Edward P. Reed, '59 ; d. San Jose, Cal., '82.
Worcester, S. Elizabeth, Hollis, N. H. ; *Hollis, N. H.*

1858.

GRADUATES.

Barber, Mary E., Sherborn ; m. *Louis Carpenter, Esq., '62 ; m. John C. Rankin, '71 ; *Quenemo, Kan.*
Barrows, Harriet A., Wareham ; *Andover.*
Blanchard, Elizabeth, M.A., Center Sandwich, N. H. ; d. Boston, '91.
Bowers, Ellen P., E. St. Johnsbury, Vt. ; *Mt. Holyoke College. S. Hadley, or care Mrs. C. H. Rugg, Cambridgeport.*
Bronson, Mary P., Springfield ; m. T. S. Bridgman, '60 ; d. Springfield, '65.
Brooks, Julia E., Buckland ; d. Northampton, '74.
Bruen, Evaline, Penn Yan, N. Y. ; m. E. G. Folsom, '68 ; *Penn Yan, N. Y.*
Button, Mary J., Waterford, N. Y. ; d. Waterford, N. Y., '58.
Buxton, Elizabeth M., W. Boscawen, N. H. ; 1015 *Park Ave., Minneapolis, Minn.*
Capron, Laura A. W., Uxbridge ; m. Thos. D. Biscoe, '75 ; d. Marietta, O., '78.
Carpenter, Jane E., Warren ; m. *E. Frank Pomeroy, '58 ; 145 *N. Tenth St., Minneapolis, Minn.*
Chamberlain, Helen M., New Salem ; m. Rev. Wm. A. Lloyd, '62 ; *Ravenswood, Ill.*
Clark, Catharine B., La Port, Ind. ; m. Julius Barnes, '58 ; 1222 *Mich. Ave., La Port, Ind.*
Cochran, Charlotte A., W. Boscawen, N. H. ; m. John C. Carroll, '62 ; *Box 998, Jackson, Mich.*
Courtright, Ruth A., Waymart, Pa. ; m. Carlton O. Lee, '71 ; *Wichita, Kan.*
Dewey, Nancy M., Vergennes, Vt. ; m. *Wm. H. Johnson, '66 ; m. Frank S. Doerenbecher, '79 ; 710 *Jackson St., Milwaukee, Wis.*
Dorr, Sarah E., Westmoreland, N. H. ; *N. Cambridge.*
Eagley, Linda M., W. Springfield, Pa. ; m. Wm. A. Hawks, '60 ; d. Baltimore, Md., '81.
Fitch, Lucy M., Amherst ; m. *D. B. Mellish, '62 ; d. Washington, D. C., '80.
Gardiner, Jemima H., W. Greenfield, N. Y. ; *Middle Grove, N. Y.*
Harrington, S. Louise, Bloomfield, N. J. ; 49 *S. Franklin St., Wilkesbarre, Pa.*
Hawley, Lucy E., Putnamville, Ind. ; m. Rev. John Ing, '70 ; d. Salt Springs, Mo., '81.
Hayward, S. Jane, Gilsum, N. H. ; m. *Geo. Learoyd, '83 ; *Gilsum, N. H.*
Hills, Mary J., Nunda, N. Y. ; m. David Allen, '62 ; d. Highland, Kan., '86.

1858.

Holmes, Lucy J., Londonderry, N. H. ; *Igolpuri, Bombay Pres., India.*
Hunt, Hannah M., Tewksbury ; m. G. H. Candee, '84 ; *Box 42, Lowell.*
Johnson, Adeline N., Augusta, Me. ; m. Isaac S. Belcher, Esq., '61 ; *948 Haight St., San Francisco, Cal.*
Johnson, Laura R., Hadley ; m. Alfred T. Richards, '71 ; *13 Townley St., Hartford, Ct.*
Lapham, Cornelia S., Mendon, N. Y. ; m. Hiram Wheeler, Esq., '59; d. Davenport, Io.,'74.
Little, Priscilla, W. Boscawen, N. H. ; *Webster, N. H.*
Lloyd, Mary W., S. Grove, Ill. ; m. A. J. Van Deren, '66 ; *3306 Lawrence St., Denver, Col.*
Merrell, Susan, Westfield ; m. Charles W. Farnham, '63 ; *Fruitland, Cal.*
Metzger, Minerva M., Lewisburg, Pa. ; m. *Rev. Jas. D. Wilson, '65; *348 W. 57th St., N. Y. City.*
Mills, Sarah L., Crawfordsville, Ind. ; m. Rev. Blackford Condit, '62 ; *629 Mulberry St., Terre Haute, Ind.*
Noble, Hannah, Augusta, Me.; *Mt. Holyoke College, S. Hadley.*
North, Julia S., E. Berlin, Ct.; m. *Orrin S. Mildrum, '65; *Temple Grove, Saratoga Springs, N. Y.*
Pease, Mary J., Monson ; m. *Albert S. Beebe, '66 ; d. Boston, '80.
Peck, Anna M., Triangle, N. Y. ; m. *Ammi Doubleday, M.D., '62 ; *122 Court St., Binghamton, N. Y.*
Perry, Sarah A. C., Ashfield ; m. *Wm. P. Porter, Esq., '60; *67 Church St., N. Adams.*
Powis, Emma A., Seneca Falls, N. Y. ; m. Isaiah Randall, '68 ; *72 Cayuga St., Seneca Falls, N. Y.*
Rayner, Charlotte W., Northampton ; *149 Elm St., Northampton.*
Robinson, Sarah B., N. Middleboro ; d. N. Middleboro, '61.
St. John, Mary C., New London, Ct. ; *498 Van Buren St., Brooklyn, N. Y.*
Sargent, Adeline, Auburn, N. Y. ; d. Auburn, N. Y., '78.
Skerry, Mary J., N. Brookfield ; m. Joseph Green, '61; *Barnesville, Ohio.*
Smith, Asenath L., Palmer; m. Alexander Gilchrist, Esq., '62 ; *421 Chandler Ave., Evansville, Ind.*
Smith, Matilda W., Millbury; m. William A. Magill, '60; *Amherst.*
Spencer, Emily A., W. Salisbury, Vt. ; m. Rev. Milton L. Severance,'59; *Bennington, Vt.*
Stetson, Elizabeth T., Maumee City, O. ; m. J. R. Hardenbergh, Esq., '59; d. Lincoln, Neb., '89.
Sweet, Sadelia S., Hoosick, N. Y. ; m. *Levi A. Knight, '64 ; *Plainville, O.*
Swett, Ellen, Staten Island, N. Y. ; *Englewood, N. J.*
Turner, Frances V., Preston, N. Y. ; d. Preston, N. Y., '62.
Vaughn, Rachel, Coventry, R. I. ; m. Geo. H. Rugg,'65 ; *515 Putnam Ave., Cambridgeport.*
Ware, Alice M., Swanzey, N. H. ; m. *Rev. Ezra Adams, '58 ; d. Gilsum, N. H., '93.
Watson, S. Augusta, Bath, Me. ; *School for the Blind, Janesville, Wis.*
White, Emily A., Marengo, Ill.; m. Rev. Moses Smith, '61 ; *The Manse, Glencoe, Ill.*
Woodward, Amelia C., Lowell ; m.*Orran P.Truesdell,'64 ; *711 Jones St., San Francisco, Cal.*

NON-GRADUATES.

Allender, Annie E., New London, Ct.; d. New London, Ct., '67.
Bachelder, Ellen B. F., London, N. H.; m. Rev. Stephen S. Morrill, '59 ; *St. Johnsbury, Vt.*
Barnes, Mary A., Chicopee ; m. Wm. Valentine,'65 ; *122 School St., Springfield.*
Barnette, Marionette A., Peterboro, N. Y.; m. D. C. Smalley,'75 ; *233 Adams St., Bay City, Mich.*
Beach, Anna A., Newark, N. J.; *15 Clinton Ave., Newark, N. J.*
Beebe, Elizabeth, Hampden ; *Hampden.*
Bell, Abbey A., Portland, Ct.; m. Reuben Paine, '63; d. Portland, Ct., '65.

1858.

Boynton. Eliza, E. Hartford, Ct.; m. Rev. Louis E. Charpiot,'59; d. Stratford, Ct., '65.
Brooks, Sophia W., Buckland; m. Henry G. Maynard, '59; d. Northampton, '84.
Butler, Angeline, Alburgh, Vt.; m. John C. French,'61; 654 *Washington Boulevard, Chicago, Ill.*
Button, Eliza, Waterford, N.Y.; m. Geo. H. Page. '81 ; 58 *Saratoga St., Cohoes, N. Y.*
Cheney, Celestia, Glover,Vt.; m. Briggs F. Stevens. '65; *W. Glover, Vt.*
Church, Anna L., S. Hadley Falls; m. *Benj. P. Axtell. '65; *Brooklyn, Wis.*
Coggin, Helen A., Tewksbury; m. Chas. A. B. Pratt, '67; *care Pratt & Pratt, 132 La Salle St., Chicago, Ill.*
Collins, Mary J., Somers, Ct.; d. Somers, Ct., '59.
Converse, Sarah E., Princeton, Ill.; m. Wm.K.Reed. '68 ; *3038 Groveland Ave.,Chicago, Ill.*
Crane,CorneliaA.,Newton Lower Falls; m.Alfred Washburn,'63 ; d.NewtonLowerFalls,'71.
Crosby, Helen E., Brattleboro,Vt.; d. Brattleboro, Vt., '64.
Curtis, Caroline A., Madison, N. Y.; m. Ransom Truesdell,'71; *Rockdale, N. Y.*
Davis, Morgianna E., Warwick; m. John W. Thatcher. '64 ; *Eagle Lake, Tex.*
Draper, Abbie B., W. Dedham; m. *Jas. F. Pond, '00; 104 *Howland St., Roxbury.*
Eager, M. Thane, Fayetteville, Vt.; 101 *W. 8th St., N. Y. City.*
Eastman, Abby M., N. Bradford, Me.; 1220 *17th Ave., Denver, Col.*
Fessenden, Jane R. S., Brattleboro,Vt.; m. Edward F.Wright, '61 ; d. Menasha, Wis.,'66.
Field, Laura E., S. Scituate, R. I.; m. Rev. Alpha Morton, '72 ; *Paxton.*
Floyd, Sarah A., New Market, N. H.; *care Geo. E. Brown, Winslow Ave., W. Somerville.*
Foot, Almira L., Guilford Center, N. Y.; *Unadilla, N. Y.*
Ford, Abbie C., Morristown, N. J.; *Box 521, Morristown, N. J.*
Freeman, Elizabeth, Eastham; d. Eastham, '61.
French, Celia N., Bedford, N. H.; m. *Rev. A. B. Dascomb, '86 ; *Westminster, Vt.*
French. Jane C., Cummington ; m. *Henry L. Welch, '60; 37 *Hillside Ave.,Waterbury,Ct.*
Goss, Abbie M., Kalamazoo, Mich.; m. Wm.A.Sloo. '70; 1233 *Clay St., Topeka, Kan.*
Goss, Catharine F. E., Kalamazoo, Mich.; m. Samuel P. Wheeler, '60 ; 611 *6th North St., Springfield, Ill.*
Gould, Sarah M., W. Springfield, Pa.; d. W. Springfield. Pa., '63.
Hadselle, Adeliza E., Hancock ; m. Rev. A. F. Mowry, '78; *Hancock.*
Hadselle, Lucy M., Hancock ; m. John B. Wood, '72; *Box 17, Greenbush, N. Y.*
Hawley. Emeline A., Putnamville, Ind.; 57 *E. Walnut Lane, Germantown, Philadelphia, Pa.*
Hibbard, Ellen M., Lisbon, N. H.; *Emporia, Kan.*
Hill, Charlotte E., Ware ; m. Oberlin Smith, '76; *Lockwold, Bridgeton, N. J.*
Hill, Henrietta C., Geneseo, N. Y.; m. Rev. Chas. B. Tifft, '62; d. Antrim. Pa., '73.
Hill, J. Sophia, Middlebury, Ct.; m. Chas. C. Wells, '70; d. Stratford, Ct., '76.
Hill, Nancy M., M.D., Belmont ; 1073 *Locust St., Dubuque, Io.*
Humphrey, Leah M., Yarmouth, Me.; m. Melville C. Merrill, '62 ; *Yarmouth, Me.*
Humphrey, Sophia C.,Yarmouth, Me.; m.Albert D. Dill,'61; 116 *Portland St.,Portland, Me.*
Hunter, Mary J., N. Adams ; m. Chas. Howard, Esq., '08; *N. Adams.*
Jenkins, Marcia D., Cummington ; m. Chas. E. French, '59; d. Clarksville, N. J., '61.
Johnson, Laura M., Dover, Me. ; *Glencoe, Ill.*
Lane, Martha, Candia, N. H. ; m. Wm. Henry Blodgett, '62; d. Manchester, N. H., '63.
Littell, Kate, Cuddebackville, N. Y. ; 331 *Franklin Ave., Scranton, Pa.*
Loomis, Collette, W. Springfield ; d. W. Springfield. '61.
Lyman, Mary H., Chicopee ; m. Joseph E. Patrick, '72; *Chicopee.*
McNair, Catharine, Hartsville, Pa. ; m. Joseph F. Hume. '63 ; d. High Point, Mo., '84.
Marcy, Mattie M. K., Wellington, Ct. ; m. Thos. Chaffee, '70 ; 39 *Put. Ave., Brooklyn,N. Y.*
Martindale, Lucy, Kirtland, O. ; m. T. M. Morley, '64 ; *Mentor, O.*
Mather, S. Jane, Suffield, Ct. ; m. John Q. Bradish, '58 ; d. Meriden. Ct., '59.
Metcalf, Ellen E., Medway ; m. John Edwards, '89 ; d. Philadelphia, Pa., '92.

1858.

Miner, Almira P., Le Roy, N. Y. ;
Moody, Catharine R., Chicopee ; m. Wm. L. Smith, '71 ; *Wilbur, Wash.*
Moore, Mary E., Warren, R. I. ; m. John B. Daniels, '63 ; *Hyde Park, Ill.*
Morris, Eliza K., Cuddebackville, N. Y. ; m. Everett P. Freeman, Esq., '61 ; 211 *Locke St., Mankato, Minn.*
Morrison, Adelaide C., Lowell ; m. *Hugh M. Sanborn, '76 ; *Beach St., Ipswich.*
Noyes, Cynthia E., Waltham ; m. A. C. Sherwood, '65 ; d. Minneapolis, Minn., '82.
Olney, Frances E., Central Village, Ct.; m. Albert H. Olney, '64 ; 211 *Friendship St., Providence, R. I.*
Parshley, Maria A., Whately ; m. John W. Brock, '68; 1502 *Smith St., Burlington, N. Y.*
Peck, Mary F., New Haven, Ct. ; m. Geo. T. Thompson, '60 ; *Litchfield, Ct.*
Perkins, Mary F., Mt. Vernon, N. H.; m. Chas. A. Hutchinson, '66; d. Jacksonville, Fla., '72.
Perry, Mary J., Dummerston, Vt. ; m. Chas. B. Morris, '63; d. Montclair, N. J., '78.
Pettee, Bertha E., Clayville, N. Y. ; m. Wm. Ryder, '67 ; d. Fort Scott, Kan., '72.
Pratt, Emily J., E. Randolph ; m. Geo. M. Patten, '66 ; *Box 25, Georgetown.*
Pratt, Sarah M., E. Longmeadow ; m. *Geo. Kibbe, '63; *E. Longmeadow.*
Prince, Henriette M., Thomaston, Me. ; m. Raymond Handford, Esq., '66 ; d. Danville, Ill., '69.
Quick, Sarah W., N. Salem, N. Y. ; m. *Henry D. Sherwood, '73; d. Fishkill, N. Y., '82.
Rea, Harriette, Tewksbury ; 52 *Willow St., Lowell.*
Reed, Anna P., Sharon, Ct. ; d. Sharon, Ct., '70.
Riggs, Ellen, Warrensburgh, N. Y. ; m. W. O. Robson, '70 ; *Wellesley Hills.*
Roberts, Mary J., W. Williamsfield, O.; m. Rev. Jos. W. Pickett, '62 ; d. Mt. Pleasant, Io., '68.
Rogers, Harriet M., New London, Ct. ; m. *Samuel J. M. Kellogg, '58; *Percival, Io.*
Roper, Jane S., Templeton ; d. Templeton, '59.
Saeger, Emma W., Allentown, Pa. ; m. *David O. Saylor, '67 ; *Allentown, Pa.*
Sargent, Cornelia, Auburn, N. Y. ; d. Auburn, N. Y., '75.
Scott, Watie A., Uxbridge ; m. Chas. S. Seagrave, '61 ; 24 *Hubbard Ave., N. Cambridge.*
Seely, Louise M., S. Onondaga, N. Y. ; m. Merritt H. Eddy, M.D., '67 ; 6 *Waybridge St., Middlebury, Vt.*
Sessions, Mary E., Hudson, O. ; m. Frank Neely, '70 ; d. Waterloo, Io., '90.
Shackleton, Lucy M., Jersey City, N. J.; m. Herman C. Evarts, M.D., '75 ; 6 *Lombardy St., Newark, N. J.*
Sheldon, Catharine C., Salisbury, Vt. ; m. *Chas. Merrill, '66; 1723 *Stout St., Denver, Col.*
Snow, Frances A., Elyria, O.; m. Rev. John Q. Hall, '62 ; *Russell, Io.*
Sweetser, Abby L., Millbury ; m. Edwin F. Ward, M.D., '65 ; 29 *W. 36th St., N. Y. City.*
Thayer, Kalista W., Williamsburg ; m. *Dwight Holbrook, '63; *Yonkers, N. Y.*
Titcomb, Rebecca F., W. Boscawen, N. H. ; m. John N. Park, '59 ; *S. Chelmsford.*
Treadway, Ellen J., Southington, Ct. ; m. Jonathan A. Yeckley, '80 ; *Gorham, N. Y.*
Ufford, Elizabeth D., W. Springfield ; m. Edwin Leonard, '66 ; *Feeding Hills.*
Waters, Marion G., S. Hadley Falls ; m. Henry A. Bowdoin, '59 ; 178 *Monroe St., Brooklyn, N. Y.*
Wetmore, Jane S., Lebanon, Ct. ; d. Lebanon, Ct., '60.
Wheeler, Charlotte E., Rochester ; m. Chas. Hutchins, '72 ; d. Arlington Heights, '85.
Whitney, Mary A., Springfield ; *cor. Beacon and Pleasant Sts., Brookline.*
Whiton, Ellen J., Bloomfield, Ct. ; 27 *Mitchell Ave., Waterbury, Ct.*
Wilkins, Harriet A., Middleton ; m. *Alvan A. Hutchinson, '63; *Elk Grove, Cal.*
Williams, Maria L., Sherburne, N. Y. ; 97 *E. 116th St., N. Y. City.*
Williamson, Martha M., Belmont, N. Y. ; d. Saratoga Springs, N. Y., '66.

1859.

GRADUATES.

Beach, Aura J., Madison, N. Y.; d. Ocean Grove, N. J., '84.
Beard, L. Vesta, Jefferson, N. Y.; m. Lewis Marvin, '02; *Walton, N. Y.*
Beard, Lydia G., Jefferson, N. Y.; m. Moses S. Wilcox, Esq., '60; *Jefferson, N. Y.*
Beard, Mary A., Jefferson, N. Y.; m. *Rev. Lewis M. Purington, '72; *S. Hadley.*
Billings, Catharine E., E. Arlington, Vt.; m. Rev. L. M. Pierce, '76; *Blackstone.*
Bishop, Mary,N. Woodstock,Ct.; m. *Horace P. Whitney,'63; 2920 *Monroe St.,Toledo,O.*
Bliss, Julia M., Longmeadow; *Longmeadow.*
Buckingham, Helen, Canton, O.; m. *Benj. F. Colt, '63; *Putnam Sem.,Zanesville, O.*
Carpenter, Anna E., Seekonk; m. M. S. Bebb, '67; 980 *Grant Ave., Rockford, Ill.*
Clark, Lucy W., Franklin, N. H.; m. Enoch Baneker, Esq., '68; 305 *Wilkins St., Jackson, Mich.*
Clark, Lurissa A., S. Hadley; *S. Hadley.*
Clarke, Caroline W., S. Hadley; m. *Harding Woods, '67; *Barre.*
Clarke, L. Jane, Urbana, N. Y.; m. Francis A. Williams, Esq., '62; 216 *Cedar St., Corning, N. Y.*
Corey, Elizabeth S., Hampton, Ct.; m. *Henry C. Corey, '62; d. Milwaukee, Wis., '72.
Cowles, R. Loretta, Otisco, N. Y.; m. Rev. Isaac N. Hurd, '60; *Concord, Cal.*
Crosby, Martha J., Danbury, Ct.; m. Rev. A. L. Frisbie. D.D., '73; 723 *5th St., Des Moines, Io.*
Cutts, Elizabeth P., Portsmouth,N. H.; m. Asa Lyman, '66; d. Providence, R. I., '93.
Dana,Clara B.,South Amherst; m.*John F. Hutchings,'64; m. Asa Adams,'91; *N.Amherst.*
Earle, Frances A., Brunswick, Me.; d. Waterbury, Ct., '84.
Eastman, Julia, S. Hadley; *S. Hadley.*
Eddy, Cornelia, N. Bridgewater (now Brockton); d. 93.
Edwards, Anna C., M. A., Northampton; 197 *Elm St., Northampton.*
Esty, Julia, Warren, Ill.; m. Henry Schreiner, '74; *N. Harvey, Ill.*
Fisher, Jeannette, Weybridge, Vt.; m. *E. S. Moore, '79; *Three Rivers, Mich.*
French, R. Annie, Philadelphia, Pa.; m. J. J. Campbell, '70; d. Warrensburg, Mo., '77.
Galloway, Mary A., Athens, Ga.; m. Guernsey W. Davis, '71; cor. *13th Ave. and Poplar St.,* 1003, *Pine Bluff, Ark.*
Gerould, Sarah A., Canaan, N. H.; m. Judge Isaac N. Blodgett, '61; *Franklin, N. H.*
Gibbs, Lucy A., Berwick, Me.; m. Rev. Alexander R. Plumer, '74; *Tremont, Me.*
Griswold, Emily M., Adams, N. Y.; m. Albert Gabriel,'81; *Grenell Island Park, River St. Lawrence, N. Y.*
Hatch, Ellen A., Ellicott, N. Y.; m. Willard B. Wells, '61; d. Ionia, Mich., '74.
Hawes, A. Maria, Ashland, Me.; 218 *Tremont St., Boston.*
Hawks, Stella F., Honeoye, N. Y.; m. H. F. Hayward,'68; d. Honeoye, N. Y., '78.
Hitchcock, Emily, Amherst; m. *Rev. Cassius M. Terry, '70; *Smith College, Northampton.*
Howard, Alice, E. Bridgewater; m. R. B. Brown, M.D., '65; d. Milwaukee, Wis.,'71.
Howard, Roxellana, Cochesett; m. A. Frank Haradon, Esq., '68; *Marshalltown, Io.*
Hubbard, Lucy M., Middletown, Ct.; d. Middletown, Ct., '78.
Hurd, Mary A., Helena, Tex.; m. Judson B. Hurd, Esq., '69; 1531 *N. Capitol St., Washington, D. C.*
Jones, Augusta L., Winthrop, Ct.; m. E. P. Brainerd, '81; d. '93.
Jones, Maria E., Templeton; d. Templeton, '70.
Kershaw, Mary B., Norwich, N. Y.; d. Norwich, N. Y.,'63.
Leffingwell, Caroline S., Cleveland, O.; 47 *Trumbull St., New Haven, Ct.*
Locke, Sarah D., New Ipswich. N. H.; m. *Rev. John M. Stow, '68; *Ashburnham.*
Noyes, Zoe A. M., Westmoreland, N. H.; m. Rev. Wm. E. Locke, '68; *E. Alstead, N. H.*
Penniman, Sarah T., Bowen's Prairie, Io.; m. *Chauncy C. Perley, '66; *Monticello, Io.*

1859.

Pitts, Helen, Honeoye, N. Y. ; m. *Fred Douglass,'83; *Cedar Hill, Anacostia, D. C.*
Pitts, Jane W., Honeoye, N. Y.; d. Anacostia, D. C., '94.
Poore, Mary, Atkinson,N. H. ; m. *J. G. Kendall, Esq.,'61 ; 553 *St. Paul Ave., Beloit, Wis.*
Pratt, Jane L., Centre Brook, Ct. ; *Albuquerque, N. M.*
Shumway, Catharine A., Sturbridge ; *Marengo, Io.*
Smith, Harriet B., Southport, Ct. ; d. Southport, Ct., '65.
Stevens, Louise P., Norfolk, Ct. ; 160 *Colony St., Meriden, Ct.*
Thompson, L. Hope, Nassau, N. P., Bahamas; d. Nassau, Bahamas, '74.
Thorpe, Emily D., Booth Bay, Me. ; *Booth Bay Harbor, Me.*
Tinker, Martha W., Old Lyme, Ct. ; m. George C. Raynolds, M.D., '69 ; *Van, Turkey, via Constantinople.*
Wadsworth, Caroline S., Franklin,N. H. ; m. Rev. John W. Hayley,'60 ; *Contoocook,N.H.*
Ward, Myra, Middlefield ; m. Solomon Little, '64 ; *Aurora, O.*
Welch, Cora A., New Haven, Ct. ; m. *Truman Tomson, '66; m. Prof. Alexander Van Millingen, '79 ; d. Mediterranean Sea, '92.

NON-GRADUATES.

Abbott, Adelaide S., Andover ; d. Andover, '60.
Abbott, Chloe, Ahmednagar,India ; m. *Samuel H. Evans, M.D.,'85; *Landour, High Park, Ryde, Isle of Wight, England.*
Adams, Caroline, Whitehall, N. Y. ; m. Prof. Stephen O. Spencer, '62 ; *Station G, Cleveland, O.*
Baker, Caroline P., Wiscasset, Me. ; m. N. Payson Smith, '63 ; *Box 86, Pepperell.*
Ballard, Elizabeth W., E. Charlemont ; m. W. H. Burrington, '70; *Belfast, Me.*
Barnes, Anna M., Charlotte, Vt. ; m. Jas E. White, '65 ; d. Shelburne, Vt., '78.
Barrett, Mary P., Springfield, N. Y. ; m. *John M. Mix, '63; *W. Winsted, Ct.*
Battles, Marietta J., Lowell ; m. Dr. Wm. G. Ward, '60; *Box 476, Lowell.*
Baxter, Caroline E., St. Johnsbury, Vt.; m. Norman T. Ayres, '65 ; 205 *W. 52d St., N. Y. City.*
Belcher, Cornelia E., Gaysville, Vt. ; m. John B. Taggart, '62 ; *Gaysville, Vt.*
Berray, Julia M., Walton, N. Y. ; m. *David B. Dewey, M.D., '59 ; *N. Adams.*
Birge, Charlotte, Hudson, O. ; m. Rev. Jacob Chamberlain, '60 ; *Madnapalle, Arcot Mission, India.*
Blodgett, Adeline M., Charlemont ; m. Warren H. Fox, '60 ; 1423 *Pendleton Ave., St. Louis, Mo.*
Bolles, Elizabeth P., Newark, N. J. ; m. Rev. Wm. A. Holbrook, '67.
Briggs, Elizabeth, N. Adams ; m. Oliver Arnold, '74 ; d. N. Adams, '85.
Brown, Rebecca S., Canton, O. ; m. Chas. F. Manderson, Esq. ; *Omaha, Neb.*
Brownell, Julia F.,N. Pownal,Vt. ; m. Daniel J. Barber,'60 ; 13 *Pleasant St., N. Adams.*
Burton, Mary E., Austinburg, O. ; m. Giles W. Shurtleff,'64 ; *Oberlin, O.*
Chandler, Anna L., New Sharon, Me.; m. Rev. Benj. P. Snow, '62 ; *Yarmouth, Me.*
Chapin, Harriet L., Amsterdam, N. Y. ; m. Thomas B. Van Schaack, '65 ; d. Galesburg, Ill., '92.
Cheseldine, Laura E., Winchester, Ill. ; m. Jas. H. White, '69 ; 223 *Westminster St.,Jacksonville, Ill.*
Church, Laura L., Middlefield ; d. Worcester, '90.
Cogswell, Caroline S., Gilmanton, N. H. ; m. John M. Crane, '84 ; *Millis.*
Colton, Elizabeth, Princeton, Ill. ; d. Princeton, Ill., '66.
Crawford, Frances H., Deerfield ; m. *Edward P. Brewster, '69; m. Rev. Thomas A. Emerson, '75; *Clinton, Ct.*
Davis, Mary E., Lebanon, Ct. ; m. Moses Cristy, '76 ; *Canajoharie, N. Y.*

1859.

Deane, Mary A., Chicopee ; m. Abijah Hastings, '70 ; *Chicopee St., Chicopee.*
DeWitt, Harriet S., Elyria, O. ; m. O. N. Gaylord, '66 ; *Asheville, N. C.*
Dickinson, Sarah A., Waukegan, Ill. ; m. David A. Cory, '66 ; d. Helena, Mont., '90.
Dimmock, Caroline E., Alton, Ill. ; m. Wm. R. Dimmock, '60 ; d. Williamsburg, '69.
Dunnell, Celia E., Charlemont ; m. W. H. Leavitt, '59 ; 514 *14th Ave., Minneapolis, Minn.*
Durell, Elizabeth J., Canaan, N. H. ; m. Hiram E. Worth, '62 ; d. E. Canaan, N. H., '63.
Field, Caroline F., Amherst ; m. Geo. E. Fuller, M.D., '77 ; d. Monson, '91.
Fitch, Fanny C., Ashtabula, O. ; m. *Marshall H. Haskell, '72 ; *47 Park St., Ashtabula, O.*
Franklin, Adaline W., S. Hadley ; d. Amherst, '68.
French, Mary J., Brattleboro, Vt. ; m. Geo. D. Moore, '63 ; d. Somerville, '69.
Fuller, Delia J., Hampton, Ct. ; m. *John R. Tweedy, '65 ; *342 Main St., Danbury, Ct.*
Galloway, Martha R., Princeton, N. J. ; m. *A. T. Akerman, Esq., '64 ; *Cartersville, Ga.*
Gates, Frances F., Monson ; m. Rev. E. Frank Howe, '61 ; d. Newtonville, '62.
Griffin, Lucy T., Hampton, Ct. ; m. W. C. Chapman ; *McHenry, Ky.*
Griswold, Harriet L., Orwell, Vt. ; m. Stanley L. Stevens ; *Chicago, Ill.*
Harris, Sarah L., E. Putnam, Ct. ; m. *Andrew J. Morey, '81 ; *Putnam Heights, Ct.*
Hitchcock, Eliza M., Painesville, O. ; m. Geo. W. Morley, '75 ; 1617 *Washington Ave., E. Saginaw, Mich.*
Hubbard Sarah R., Concord; m. Rev. Albert E. Hastings, '65 ; *Box* 931, *Colorado Springs, Col.*
Huston, Loella E., Bristol, Me. ; m. Wm. O. Blaney, '66 ; *Hotel Huntington, Boston.*
Kingsbury, Mary S., Tamworth, N. H. ; m. Thos. P. Carleton, '73 ; *Box* 231, *Middleboro.*
Laird, Marion, Canton, O. ; m. Wilbur F. Goodspeed, '65 ; d. Cleveland, O., '82.
Leland, Susan A., Millbury ; d. Millbury, '63.
McMechan, Sarah L., Cold Water, Mich.; m. Jas. G. Kyle, '69 ; *Riverside, Cal.*
Mathews, Julia E., Painesville. O. ; d. Riverside Park, Ill., '74.
Mayo, Anna M., Bloomfield, Me.; m. *Samuel Whiting, '68 ; *Box* 43, *Clear Water, Minn.*
Merrill, Susan, Oxford, N. Y. ; d. Croton, N. Y., '65.
Millard, Mary L., Troy, N.Y.; m. T. C. Dickinson, '62 ; 1335 *Corcoran St., Washington, D. C.*
Miller, Emma J., Norwich, N. Y. ; m. Alfred P. Allen, '65 ; *Bath, N. Y.*
Mowle, E. Jane, Boston ; m. *Marmaduke Wand, '61 ; m. Martin Sheldon, '67 ; d. N. Y. City, '73.
Munsell, Esther E., Amherst ; m. *Rev. Amherst L. Thompson, '60 ; *Amherst.*
Noyes, Anna, Waltham ; m. F. R. Bunker, '69 ; 204 *Gordon Ave., W. End, Atlanta, Ga.*
Owen, Minerva A., Milo, N. Y. ; m. Rev. Wm. Dunbar, '59 ; *Penn Yan, N. Y.*
Pardee, Julia A., Trumbull, Ct.; m. Frank D. Brinsmade, '70 ; 121 *Cedar St., New Haven, Ct.*
Pelton, Emily O., Prairie du Chien, Wis.; m. M. W. Wilson, M.D., '86 ; *Spokane, Wash.*
Perkins, Lucy M., Painesville, O. ; d. Painesville, O., '68.
Perry, Phebe S., Chicopee ; m. *Henry H. Jewell, '62 ; d. Wabash, Minn., '92.
Phelps, Alice D., Lexington ; m. Chas. C. Goodwin, '62 ; *Merriam St., Lexington.*
Plumer, Elizabeth M., S. Berwick, Me. ; d. S. Berwick, Me., '87.
Poole, Caroline, E. Abington ; m. Jas. F. Claflin, '59 ; d. Grand Island, Neb., '75.
Poole, Sophia A., Rockport ; m. Alonzo Wheeler, Esq., '73 ; *Avalon, Cal.*
Proseus, Mary C., Valatie, N. Y. ; d. Knoxville, Ill., '71.
Robinson, Susan R., N. Amherst ; m. Rev. J. Oramel Peck, '62 ; d. Brooklyn. N. Y., '88.
Rowe, E. Caroline, Pulaski, N. Y. ; m. Elijah N. Clark, M.D., '87 ; *Beloit, Wis.*
Rowe, Eleanor J., Rockport ; *Schaghticoke, N. Y.*
Samson, Mary M., McGrawville, N. Y.; m. J. R. Watrous, '59 ; 26 *Clinton Ave., Cortland, N. Y.*
Seaton, Mary E., Charlotte, Vt.; m. Edmund Whitney, '66 ; 254 *Maple St., Burlington, Vt.*
Seaton, S. Frances, Charlotte, Vt.; 254 *Maple St., Burlington, Vt.*
Sibley, Persis H., Bennington, Vt.; m. John C. Coleman, '70 ; 1820 *Clay St., San Francisco, Cal.*
Smith, Augusta A., Southport, Ct. ; *Southport, Ct.*

1859.

Smith, Lucy M., Buckland; m. Rev. Elijah Harmon, '66; d. Buckland, '71.
Smith, Martha H., E. Alstead, N. H.; d. Boston, '66.
Spear, Julia S., Rockland, Me.; 11 *Maple St., Rockland, Me.*
Stanton, Edna E., Richmond, Ind.; d. Suffolk, Va., '62.
Stanton, M. Annette, Manchester, N. H.; *Manchester, N. H.*
Strickland, Miranda E., E. Longmeadow; m. *Albert F. Allen, '88; *Enfield, Ct.*
Waller, Hannah E., Bloomsburgh, Pa.; m. Col. M. Whitmoyer, '73; d.Columbus,Neb.,'73.
Ward, Charlotte M., Warren; m. *E. Chas. Morgan, '64; 1631 *Locust St., St. Louis, Mo.*
Waters, Oraville H., S. Hadley Falls; 39 *Prospect St., S. Hadley Falls.*
Wilcox, Sarah J., Painesville, O.; m. Peter Hitchcock, '64; 861 *Prospect St., Cleveland, O.*
Wilder, Mary E., Hadley; m. *John T. McDowell, '70; m. Fernando C. Griffin, '76; 1823 *9th St., N. W., Washington, D. C.*
Wilkins, Henrietta, Henniker, N. H.; m. Chas. A. Sayward, '85; *N. Main St., Ipswich.*
Wilkins, Mary C., Henniker, N. H.; d. Henniker, N. H., '59.
Williams, Clarissa B., New Haven, Ct.; m. Frank W. Holmes, '78; d. Salisbury, Ct., '79.
Wheeler, Adelaide M., New Bedford; m. Isaac Farrar, M.D.,'61; 28 *King St.,Dorchester.*
Wood, Caroline A., Upton; *Upton.*

1860.

GRADUATES.

Bates, Elvira C., Griggsville, Ill.; m. *Prof. John T. Dickinson, '64; 207 *E. Washington St., Mt. Pleasant, Io.*
Belcher, H. Augusta, Gaysville, Vt.; m. S. J. S. Rogers, M.D.,'65; d. Marysville,Cal.,'75.
Bishop, Sarah L., N. Woodstock, Ct.; *N. Woodstock, Ct.*
Boltwood, Caroline A., Amherst; m. *Chas. A. Seeley, '63; 30 *Charles St., Grand Rapids, Mich.*
Burt, Caroline, Westhampton; *Westhampton.*
Bush, Mary T., Worcester; *Shrewsbury.*
Clark, Harriet S., Rochester; m. *Samson M. Robbins, '67; m. John W. Atwood, '78; 362 *Cross St., Malden.*
Clark, Mary J., Bristol, Me.; m. J. W. Spaulding, Esq., '64; *Melrose.*
Crissey, Olive E., Norfolk, Ct.; m. Plumb Brown, '61; d. Norfolk, Ct., '84.
Cristy, Elizabeth H., New Boston, N. H.; d. Greenwich, Ct., '80.
Earle, Elizabeth, Brunswick, Me.; m. Rev. Geo. F. Magoun, '70; *Grinnell, Io.*
Eastman, Anna F., Amherst; m. Henry Cook, '71; *Athol.*
Evans, Mary A., Woodbury, N. J.; *Lake Erie Seminary, Painesville, O.*
Ewart, Mary D., Marietta, O.; m. *Edgar P. Pearce,'05; 4547 *Green St.,Germantown,Pa.*
Francis, Sarah J., W. Hartford, Ct.; *W. Hartford, Ct.*
Goldthwait, Catharine, Longmeadow; d. London, Eng., '91.
Grant, Sarah E., Hartford, Ct.; m. E. Morgan, '61; 273 *State St., Springfield.*
Grassie, Jessie D., Bolton; m. Rev. Joseph F. Dudley, D.D., '64; *Cor. 3d Ave. and Broadway, Eau Claire, Wis.*
Hodge, Lucinda D., Germantown, Pa.; d. Stowe, Vt., '61.
Horton, Ellen M., Barrington, R. I.; *Bible House, N. Y. City.*
Hunt, Fanny M., Sunderland; m. Julius F. Washburn, '68; d. Putney, Vt., '78.
Ingham, Sarah, Middlefield; m. *Rev. N. G. Bonney, '65; *Box 92, Norwich Town, Ct.*
Kasson, Dora M., Bethlehem, Ct.; m. *Horace N. Sanford, '67; *Bridgewater, Ct.*
Keeler, Jennet W., Union, N. Y.; m. P. W. Hopkins, Esq., '65; d. Union, N. Y., '67.
Lee, Elizabeth J., Cincinnatus, N. Y.; m. *Ambrose Blunt, '65; 13 *Willow St., Ann Arbor, Mich.*

1860.

Lovell, Laura G., Sharon, Ct. ; 803 *Clifford St., Flint, Mich.*
Miner, Anna J., Winchester, Ill. ; m. Chas. B. Hubbard, '66 ; *Winchester, Ill.*
Paine, Harriet M., E. Woodstock, Ct. ; m. Jos. S. Johnston, '68 ; 1205 *E. 43d St., Chicago, Ill.*
Perry, Nancy, Holden ; *Holden.*
Rea, E. A. Adelaide, Topsfield ; *Blossom St. School, Boston.*
Reeves, Mary A., Gallipolis, O. ; m. Wm. A. Lawrence, '64 ; *Waterville, N. Y.*
Sessions, Laura R., W. Woodstock. Ct. ; m. A. H. Cortelyou, '73 ; d. Brooklyn, N. Y., '83.
Sibley, Mary L., Bennington, Vt. ; m. *Albert W. Harwood, '66 ; *Box 6, Bennington, Vt.*
Smith, Electa M., S. Hadley Falls ; m. Walter B. Rose, '79 ; S. *Amherst.*
Sweetser, Sarah E., Peoria, Ill. ; m. S. M. Fish ; d. Jacksonville, Ill., '94.
Thayer, Sarah A., New Ipswich, N. H.; *cor. South and 22d St., Santiago, Cal.*
Townsend, Margaret J., Great Barrington ; m. Orlando B. Bidwell, '66 ; *Freeport, Ill.*
Tufts, Ellen M., West Newton ; 19 *Brent St., Dorchester.*
Van Wyck, Mary, Fishkill. N. Y.; d. Brooklyn, N. Y., '90.
Warren, Mary C., Coventry, N. Y.; *Coventry, N. Y.*
Waters, Mary J., Bennington Center, Vt.; m. *Rev. Fred Hicks, '69 ; 87 *Monument Ave., Bennington, Vt.*
White, Abbie T., Portland, Ct.; m. John K. Williams, '64 ; d. Hartford, Ct., '94.

NON-GRADUATES.

Abram, Cynthia M., Parishville, N.Y.; m. Cyrus G. Stafford, Esq., '61 ; d. Auburn, Or., '63.
Aldrich, Anna, N. Easton, N. Y.; m. Lewis Potter, '63 ; d. Easton, N. Y., '08.
Anable, Harriet I., Little Falls, N. Y.; m. Geo. W. Requa, '63 ; *Ridgewood, N. J.*
Balch, H. Anna, Kalamazoo, Mich.; m. John den Bleyker, '64 ; *Kalamazoo, Mich.*
Baldwin, Martha A., New Sharon, Me.; d. New Sharon, Me., '66.
Barton, Adeline S., Granby ; m. *Madison Mixter, '64 ; m. Wm. C. Gates, '67 ; *S. Hadley Falls.*
Bass, Emily A., Milton, Me. ; m. Joshua B. Mayhew, '65 ; *Readfield Depot, Me.*
Berger, Elizabeth L., Mellenville, N. Y.; m. Samuel Thompson ; d. San Francisco, Cal.
Bevier, Alice D., Binghamton, N. Y.; 51 *W. 76th St., N. Y. City.*
Breese, S. Madora, Wilmington, Del.; m. Robert S. Pomeroy, '74 ; 127 *W. Sixth St., Covington, Ky.*
Brown, Julia A., Maquoketa, Io.; m. Lewis H. Dunham, '72 ; *Maquoketa, Io.*
Brown, Margaret E., Kalamazoo, Mich.; m. Stephen S. Smith, '68 ; *Warren, O.*
Campbell, Sarah E., Newburyport ; m. Edward P. Hurd, M.D., '65 ; 42 *Fair St., Newburyport.*
Chidsey, Helen L., Avon, Ct.; d. Avon, Ct., '68.
Childs, Mary E., Wilton, N. H.; m. Morris E. Jones ; *Mirror office, Manchester, N. H.*
Clark, Harriet D., E. Hartford, Ct.; m. Edward L. Molineux, '61 ; 117 *Fort Green Place, Brooklyn, N. Y.*
Cleveland, Mary E., Waukegan, Ill.; m. *J. Ferris, '74 ; 1132 *Main St., Peekskill, N. Y.*
Colburn, Ellen A., S. Ryegate, Vt.; *S. Ryegate, Vt.*
Corbin, Elvira, Union, Ct.; m. Rev. Geo. Curtis, '64 ; d. Harwinton, Ct., '75.
Day, Ellen H., Hollis, N. H.; m. *Chas. A. Lovejoy, '69 ; *Hollis, N. H.*
Denison, Jane A., Deep River, Ct.; m. Chas. C. Bushnell, '61 ; d. Meriden, Ct., '68.
Doland, Emma, Manchester, N. H.; m. Albert R. Gage, '63 ; d. Republican City, Neb., '87.
Dolson, Harriet L., Middletown, N. Y.; *care Mrs. Gen. Badeau, Catskill, N. Y.*
Dunning, Antoinette, New Haven, Ct.; m. Alexander D. Anderson, '69 ; 1335 *R St., N. W., Washington, D. C.*
Dwight, Eliza R., Belchertown ; m. *James P. French, '62 ; *Amherst.*
Eames, Julia C., Hopkinton ; m. *Edw. G. Plimpton, '65 ; *Hopkinton.*
Eglin, S. Cornelia, Athens, Pa. ; d. Athens, Pa., '62.
Ely, E. Carolyn, Lancaster, N. Y. ; m. John F. Hitchcock, '64 ; d. Cincinnati, O., '84.

1860.

Emmons, Mary C., Sturbridge; m. Samuel Morgan, '66; *Sharonville, O.*
Ewart, Harriet L., N. Y. City; m. E. F. Ayers, '65; *New Canaan, Ct.*
Fales, Marcia M., Upton; m. Bradford Beals, '61; d. Stoughton, '65.
Farrington, Emma W., Holden, Me.; m. Rev. Francis Southworth, '61; 108 *Newbury St., Portland, Me.*
Farwell, Annie E., Rockland, Me.; m. Edgar A. Burpee, '66; *Rockland, Me.*
Fay, Henrietta M., E. Alstead, N. H.; m. Solon D. Morrison, '66; *Saxton's River, Vt.*
Francis, Charlotte A., W. Hartford, Ct.; m. H. G. Montgomery, '66; 142 *Seymour St., Hartford, Ct.*
French, Frances E., Cummington; d. Cummington, '67.
French, Mary E., Philadelphia, Pa.; m. Oscar E. Boyd, '63; 53 *Fifth Ave., N. Y. City.*
Gibbons, Blanche, Allentown, Pa.; m. C. Newcomb Stevens; *Gainesville, Tex.*
Gibson, Mary H., New Ipswich, N. H.; m. Alfred H. Hersey, '62; *Hingham.*
Goodman, Anne M., Canton, O.; 460 *Fulton St., Chicago, Ill.*
Graves, Caro A., Newton Center; m. *Abner Kingman, '68; *Auburndale.*
Gurney, Sarah M., S. Abington; m. Rev. Geo. A. Litchfield, '61; *Wollaston.*
Gurney, Susan E., S. Abington; m. Wm. E. Vaughn, '78; *Whitman.*
Guthrie, Fannie S., Orange, N. J.; m. H. H. Merriam, '64; *Canton, O.*
Hale, Lemoyne A., New Haven, N. Y.; m. Jas. H. Hoose, '61; d. Cortland, N. Y., '71.
Hales, Harriet H., Westford; m. Gilman J. Wright, '71; d. Westford, '74.
Harries, Elizabeth D., Miller's Place, N. Y.; m. John B. Thomas, '64; 54 *Lee Ave., Brooklyn, N. Y.*
Harries, Mary W., Miller's Place, N. Y.; m.*Daniel H. Young,'64; d. Franklinville,N.Y.,'65.
Hastings, Caroline E., Barre; 160 *Huntington Ave., Boston.*
Henry, Lucy J., Brooksville, Me.; d. W. Brooksville, Me., '83.
Hills, Lucy G., Rockland, Me.; 18 *N. Main St., Rockland, Me.*
Holt, Emma, Lyndeboro, N. H.; m. Edward H. Spalding, '60; d. Nashua, N. H., '61.
Howard, Julia A., Warrensburg, N. Y.; m. Rev. Albert C. Bishop, '70; *Reeseville, N. Y.*
Howe, Annie M., Key West, Fla.; m. Gen. J. P. S. Gobin, '64; *Lebanon, Pa.*
Huntress, Adeline E., Lincoln, Me.; m. Timothy Heald, '70; 54 *Oxford St., Cambridge.*
Hurd, Laura, Rochester, N. Y.; m. Rev. Frank Ellinwood; 117 *E. 70th St., N. Y. City.*
Kendall, Sarah W., Nashua, N. H.; 168 *Main St., Nashua, N. H.*
Kirby, Josephine N., Bainbridge, N. Y.; m. Geo. W. Evans, '64; *Vancouver, Wash.*
Lawrence, Lucy A., Monkton, Vt.; m. Hon. S. D. O'Bryan, '77; *S. Starksboro, Vt.*
Locke, Frances A., Hollis Center, Me.; d. Hollis Center, Me., '60.
McClelland, Mary C., Columbus, O.; d. Columbus, O., '88.
Magranis, Adeline, S. Hadley; m. Edward L. Smith, '62; *S. Hadley.*
Matthewson, Mary, Pomfret, Ct.; d. Pomfret, Ct., '82.
Mead, Charlotte M., Walton, N. Y.; m. George A. Colton, '64; d. Walton, N. Y., '73.
Mead, Emily G., New Haven, Ct.; m. Rev. Chas. H. Babcock, '66; d. Columbus, O., '80.
Merrill, Ida, New Castle, Me.; m. Orin Hawkes, '71; 59 *Union Park, Boston.*
Mills, Martha A., Bedford, N. Y.; d. Bedford, N. Y., '72.
Montague, Emily B., S. Hadley; *Barre.*
Morris, Caroline S., Deer Park, N. Y.; m. Chas. E. King; *Kirkwood, Mo.*
Nelson, Mary E., Coila, N. Y.; *Cambridge, N. Y.*
Osgood, Mary M., Abington, Ct.; *Abington, Ct.*
Pearson, Sarah, Waterville, Me.; 163 *W. Springfield St., Boston.*
Penfield, Frances E., N. Fairfield, O.; m. Theron H. Kellogg, Esq., '62; 47 *Corwin St., Norwalk, O.*
Phinney, Harriet N., Alton, Ill.; m. F. T. Lewis, '65; d. Alton, Ill, '79.
Pillsbury, Emma L., Hampstead, N. H.; m. *Rev. Jas. P. Lane, '61; 25 *Pierce St., Hyde Park.*

1860.

Pratt, Cornelia B., Providence. R. I.;
Proudfit, Elizabeth L., Peekskill, N. Y.; 35 *Mt. Morris Park, W., N. Y. City.*
Randall, Elnora E., Keene, N. H.; *Marlboro, N. H.*
Redington, Sarah E., Waddington, N.Y.; m. Richmond Bicknell, '63; d. N. Y. City, '74.
Reed, Frances G., Ashtabula, O.; m. J. Sumner Blyth, '65; 31 *Park St., Ashtabula, O.*
Rowley, Mary J., Greenfield; m. Judge Franklin G. Fessenden, '78; 155 *Main St., Greenfield.*
Roys, Martha E., Sheffield; m. *Harry H. Scott, '72; *Sheffield.*
Sawyer, Martha M., Chestertown, N. Y.; d. Chestertown, N. Y., '65.
Scudder, Agnes H., Memphis, Tenn.; 435 *6th Ave., N. Y. City.*
Shaw, Helen F., Saratoga, N.Y.; m. Wm. H. Chamberlin, '69; *Pittsfield.*
Shaw, Sarah H., Newburyport; m. *J. O. Mahana, '66; *Des Moines, Io.*
Sherwood, Mary A., Danbury, Ct.; m. *Peter Esselmont, M.P., '76; 34 *Albyn Place, Aberdeen, Scotland.*
Sprague, Catharine A., Andover, Ct.; m. Albert H. Lyman, '71; d. Andover, Ct., '94.
Stephens, Mary S., W. Newton; d. Worcester, '77.
Stuart, Mary, Cleveland, O.; d. Willoughby, O., '93.
Troxell, Ella E., Allentown, Pa.; m. Alfred G. Saegar, '69; 411 *Walnut St., Allentown, Pa.*
Wakefield, Alice, Reading; m. *Rev. Rufus Emerson, '63; 524 *Tremont St., Boston.*
Walker, Elvira, E. Woodstock, Ct.; d. E. Woodstock, Ct., "about '74."
Walker, Josephine, Mashapaug, Ct.; m. *Wm. M. Corbin, '60; 57 *Willard St., Hartford, Ct.*
Watson, Emma, Stockbridge; m. Oliver C. Titus, '88; 40 *W. 34th St., N. Y. City.*
Webster, Luella, Concord, N. H.; m. David Webster, '69; 40 *Center St., Concord, N. H.*
White, Almira P., Exeter, N. H.; m. *Richard C. Parr, M.D., '76; *Dyersburg, Tenn.*
Winn, Elizabeth A., Marietta, Ga.; *Sacramento, Cal.*
Wolcott, M. Antoinette Whitehall, N. Y.; m. Levi J. Fiske, '68; *Cheshire.*

1861.

GRADUATES.

Baker, H. Henrietta, N. Amherst; m. W. Geo. Stevenson, M.D., '67; 10 *Lafayette Place, Poughkeepsie, N. Y.*
Batchelder, Julia E., Peru, Vt.; m. Rev. Earl J. Ward, '67; d. Grafton, Vt., '71.
Bemis, Seraph A., Warren; m. Rev. Daniel J. Bliss, '66; P. O. ad., *Leonard Bridge, Ct.*
Bronson, Aletta M., Toledo, O.; m. W. H. Simmons, '67; d. Toledo, O., '68.
Burgess, Georgiana M., Westboro; *Westville, Ct.*
Burgess, Maria G., Keene, N. H.; m. *Rev. John Thomson, '69; *Whitman.*
Bushnell, Ellen W., Lisbon, Ct.; *Mills College P. O., Cal.*
Clark, Lucia F., Andover; *Wellesley College, Wellesley;* home address, *Andover.*
Clarke, Mary L., Cromwell, Ct.; m. *H. W. Derby, '64; 167 *Clinton Ave., Brooklyn, N. Y.*
Conklin, Elizabeth G., Old Lyme, Ct.; m. J. D. McCauley, M.D., '74; *Glen Moore, N. J.*
Cooley, Sarah J., S. Deerfield; m. Lucius B. Corbin, '66; d. Carlinville, Ill., '73.
Day, Mary E., Bristol, Ct.; 56 *Federal St., Bristol, Ct.*
Denniston, Sarah E., Newburg, N. Y.; m. Clarence H. Bell, '66; 22 *Cobden St., Boston Highlands.*
DeWolf, Sarah A., Chester; m. Harlow Gamwell, M.D., '68; *Westfield.*
Ditto, Margaret E., New York City; *Wellesley.*
Dunning, Katherine A., New Haven, Ct.; m. Morris W. Clark, '67; *Lock Box 18, Danville, Ky.*
Dyer, Mary E., New Haven, N. Y.; P. O. address, *Spencerport, N. Y.*
Eaman, Mary A., Lodi Plains, Mich.; 25 *Henry St., Detroit, Mich.*

1861.

Eastman, Sarah P., Danville, Vt.; *Dana Hall, Wellesley.*
Ells, Fanny, Harpersfield, N. Y.; d. Oswego, N. Y., '64.
Ely, Charlotte E., Cheektowaga, N. Y.; *Bitlis, Turkey in Asia.*
Ely, Mary A. C., Cheektowaga, N. Y.; *Bitlis, Turkey in Asia.*
Ely, Sarah E., Holyoke; 186 *Walnut St., Holyoke.*
Emmons, Frances M., Sturbridge; *Southbridge.*
Fuller, Henrietta A., E. Abington; m. Stephen Grout, '65; *E. Dorset, Vt.*
Gaylord, Elizabeth, S. Hadley Falls; *S. Hadley Falls.*
Gaylord, Martha R., Hadley; m. Isaac O. Ives, '73; 40 *Newton St., Meriden, Ct.*
Goodman, Emily, Canton, O.; m. Chas. F. Vent, '62; 80 *44th St., Chicago, Ill.*
Graves, Emily C., Greenfield; *Greenfield.*
Greenhill, Adelaide, Paris, N. Y.; m. Rev. S. H. Adams, '64; d. Chicago, Ill., '79.
Hall, Emma L., Saratoga Springs, N. Y.; m Rev. Andrew Cather, '61; *Wellington, Va.*
Hill, Laura P., Newark, N. J.; m. Edwin F. Hyatt, '70; 37 *Main St., Ocean Grove, N. J.*
Horton, Mary E., Barrington, R. I.; 1435 *Atlantic Ave., Brooklyn, N. Y.*
Hunt, Sarah A., Sunderland; m. Julius F. Washburn, '80; d. Putney, Vt., '83.
Huntington, Frances, Danbury, Ct.; m. Henry T. Hoyt, '62; 2 *Hillside Place, Danbury, Ct.*
Keniston, Dora D., Plymouth, N. H.; m. *Charles W. Johnson, Esq., '63; m. *Silas W. Davis, M.D., '69; *Tilton, N. H.*
Lamb, Mary C., S. Hadley Falls; care George Lamb, *S. Hadley Falls.*
Ludlam, Anna C., N. Y. City; m. John H. Thompson, M.D., '68; 36 *E. 30th St., N. Y. City.*
McMasters, Frances L., Granby; m. *G. H. Forward, '70; *Box 456, Springfield.*
Mallery, Caroline J., Cleveland, O.; m. Geo. W. Homan, '65; d. Omaha City, Neb., '66.
Miller, Orra E., Woburn; m. Jay F. Parsons, '74; *Grass Valley, Cal.*
Mitchell, Julia P., W. Hartford, Ct.; m. Geo. M. Carrington, '65; *W. Winsted, Ct.*
Montague, Katherine S., Middleport, O.; m. W. S. Marshall, Esq., '73; 131 *E. Terrace, Chattanooga, Tenn.*
Morrill, Charlotte, St. Johnsbury, Vt.; *Adelphi Academy, Brooklyn, N. Y.*
Munsell, Marion E., Amherst; m. Rev. Augustine Breese, '68; *Fort Dodge, Io.*
Nichols, Adelaide E., Milford; m. Wm. B. Phillips, '63; d. Swarthmore, Pa., '71.
Parmelee, Olive L., Toledo, O.; m. Rev. Alpheus N. Andrus,'75; *Mardin, Turkey in Asia.*
Patrick, Ellen M., Milford; *Hughes High School, Cincinnati, O.*
Peabody, Mary E., Eastport, Me.; d. Shushan. N. Y., '70.
Peckham, Katherine F., Providence, R. I.; 2 *Commonwealth Ave, Boston.*
Perry, Martha A., Holden; *Holden.*
Ranlett, Elizabeth F., Thomaston, Me.; m. Sam'l C. Jordan, '62; d. Calcutta, India, '72.
Rice, Emily M., Auburn; d. Auburn, '65.
Rice, Feronia N., Auburn; m. Rev. C. C. Carpenter, '62; *Andover.*
Romig, Hannah L., Allentown, Pa.; m. *Cyrus V. Mays, '63; m. *Joshua Hunt, '80; 1345 *Hamilton St., Allentown, Pa.*
Roper, Ellen E., Templeton; 120 *Houston St., Atlanta, Ga.*
Shumway, Mary E., Sturbridge; m. Albert K. Hostetter, '71; *Marengo, Io.*
Smead, Sarah A., Greenfield; d. Hampton, Va., '64.
Smith,Clara R.,Candia,N. H.; m. Rev. I. Perley Smith,'70; 89 *Hillside Ave., Waterbury,Ct.*
Thayer, Ruth W., St. Johnsbury, Vt.; m. Roswell S. Twombly, '66; *Barton, Vt.*
Van Valkenburgh, Catharine M., Prattsburgh, N. Y.; *Prattsburgh, N. Y.*
Vinton, Sarah A., S. Hadley; 175 *Nassau St., Princeton, N. J.*
Wadsworth,Mary L.,M.D.,Franklin,N. H.; m. John Bassian,M.D.,'73; d. Fresno,Cal.,'04.
Weeks, Amanda, Damariscotta, Me.; m. Nathaniel Bryant, '72; *Newcastle, Me.*
West, Thera, Hadley; m. W. Henry Fairchild, '65; *Manchester, N. H.*
Wilson, Emily S., Marlboro; *Gilroy, Cal.*

1861.

NON-GRADUATES.

Arms, Ella M., Waterbury, Vt.; d. Stowe, Vt., '61.
Ashbey, Hannah A., Mystic River, Ct.; m. J. Alden Rathbun, '63; *Mystic, Ct.*
Bailey, Ellen S., Fairlee, Vt.; m. Simeon S. Johnson, '73; d. Jeffersonville, Ind., '92.
Bassett, Maria E., Watertown, Ct.; *Watertown, Ct.*
Bates, M. Augusta, S. Hadley; m. Tertius C. Cooley, '67; *32 Webster Ave., Springfield.*
Bigelow, Ann Eliza, Boston; m. Richard E. Ashenden, '64; *Auburndale.*
Bingham, Amorette W., Vergennes, Vt.; m. Jacob W. Smith, '71; m. Isaac H. Smith, '76; d. Vergennes, Vt., '78.
Bliss, Mary A., Worcester; d. Worcester, '61.
Boutelle, Caroline A., Leominster; m. Chas. F. Merriam, '62; d. Leominster, '63.
Boyd, Sarah M., Waldoboro, Me.; m. Caleb J. Camp, '83; *W. Winsted, Ct.*
Brainerd, Julia D., Halifax; 1126 *Broad St., Grinnell, Io.*
Brown, Jane H., Enfield; m. Rev. Edward Graham, '71; *Chico, Cal.*
Brown, L. Maria, Wolfboro, N. H.; d. Wolfboro, N. H., '75.
Brown, Mary E., Ashtabula, O.; *Unionville, O.*
Burke, Margaret, Pittsfield; 393 *West St., Pittsfield.*
Burt, Eudora H., Easthampton; m. Horace W. Gaylord, '62; *S. Hadley.*
Campbell, Joanna M., Paris, N. Y.; *New Hartford, N. Y.*
Carpenter, Clara, Barre, Vt.; m. Francis B. Smith, '68; d. St. Paul, Minn., '82.
Case, Emorette, N. Canton, Ct.; m. *Edward Holcomb, '65; m. Erastus E. Case, M.D.,'86; 100 *Ann St., Hartford, Ct.*
Case, Malvina R., N. Canton, Ct.; d. N. Canton, Ct., '79.
Charles, Luvan A., Brimfield; m. Henry D. Hyde, Esq.; 380 *Commonwealth Ave., Boston.*
Chase, Marion S., Newport, N. H.; d. Mt. Holyoke Seminary, '61.
Childs, Julia E., N. Y. City; m. Edwin Bennett, '65; 780 *Park Ave., N. Y. City.*
Church, Caroline, Middlefield; m. Edwin McElwain, '63; 43 *Federal St., Springfield.*
Clapp, Jane B., Northampton; *Northampton.*
Converse, Sarah A., Enfield, Ct.; m. R. Ensign Abbe, '84; *Enfield, Ct.*
Cooley, Harriet N., S. Deerfield; m. Geo. W. Clark, '60; d. Easthampton, '74.
Crosswell, Elizabeth B., Farmington Falls, Me.; *Alhambra, Cal.*
Cudworth, Armenia, Readsboro, Vt.; d. Readsboro, Vt., '62.
Cutter, Caroline E., Warren; d. U. S. steamer "Northerner," near New Berne, N. C., '62.
Danforth, Mary W., N. Y. City;
Davis, F. Louisa, Reading; m. Edward Rice, '63; 324 *Warren St., Hudson, N. Y.*
Denison, Lucy, Royalton, Vt.; d. Royalton, Vt., '66.
Douglass, Sarah E., Gorham, N. Y.; m. Rev. John T. McMahon, '70; *Dwarahat, Kumaon, India.*
Drake, Cornelia A., Waterbury, Ct.; m. *Raymond H. Gladding, '70; m. Asa W. Kenney, '73; *Lakewood, N. J.*
Dwight, Sophie E., Belchertown; *Wellesley Hills.*
Farnsworth, Olive E., E. Smithfield, Pa.; m. *John T. Reineck, '68; 255 *Townsend St., New Brunswick, N. J.*
Fletcher, Ellen M., Westfield; m. Frank E. Merriman, '61; d. New Orleans, La., '74.
Ford, Caroline, N. Abington; m. Sidney Peterson, '91; 165 *Princeton St., E. Boston.*
French, Sara E., Bedford, N. H.; m. Geo. A. Christian, '70; 121 *Pembroke St., Boston.*
Goodrich, Alice B., Barre, Vt.; d. Barre, Vt., '68.
Goss, Victoria M., St. Johnsbury, Vt.; 32 *Hanson St., Boston.*
Green, Anna E., Coila, N. Y.; m. Chas. D. Warner, '64; *Cœur d'Alene City, Idaho.*
Hammond, Mary L., Big Flats, N. Y.; m. S.G.M.Gates,'63; 821 *Monroe St., Bay City, Mich.*
Harwood, Lemira M., Bennington, Vt.; d. Bennington, Vt., '73.

1861.

Hill, Julia A. M., New Haven, Ct.; m. Dr. J. H. Leavenworth, '69; 75 *Howe St., New Haven, Ct.*
Howard, Sarah A., Temple, N. H.; *Methuen.*
Hunt, F. Evelyn, Unadilla, N. Y.; m. John B. Raymond, Esq., '69; *Cornwall, N. Y.*
Kimball, Lucy E., Littleton. N. H.; d. Janesville, Wis., '72.
King, Mary, Morristown, N. J.; m. John T. Harrison, '65; *St. Michaels, Md.*
Knowlton, Abby C., Phillipston; m. *John H. P. Chapin, '61 ; d. Phillipston, '68.
Lawrence, Clara M., Pepperell; m. J. R. Dwight Lockwood, Esq., '64; *54 Cranberry St., Brooklyn, N. Y.*
Lawrence, Mary A., Pepperell; m. *Rev. Richard D. Douglass, '64; *71 Cranberry St., Brooklyn, N. Y.*
Leonard, Lucy A., Canton, N. Y.; m. Jesse Reynolds, M.D., '74 ; d. Potsdam, N. Y., '82.
Leonard, Theresa M., Jewett City, Ct.; m. *Andrew P. Reed, '68; m. J. Alfred Crary, '77 ; *Wilmington, O.*
Locke, Susan C., Langdon, N. H.; m. Horace E. Boardman, M.D., '63; *Parsons, Kan.*
Meldrum, Susan C. (name changed from *Agnes I.*), Brooklyn, N. Y.; m. Geo. W. Linscott, '66; *25 Folsom St., Dorchester.*
Miller, Esther A., Lyme, Ct.; d. Bozrah, Ct., '90.
Mills, Helen S., Norwich, N. Y.; *Rockdale, N. Y.*
Montague, Delia M., Springfield; m. Chas. D. Ripley, '67; *62 Maple St., Waltham.*
Moore, Martha, Holden; m. Rev. Jas. P. Field, '82; *Amity, Mo.*
Nichols, Ruth S., Randolph, Vt.; m. Rev. *Edward P. Wild, '65; d. Brattleboro, Vt., '91.
Norton, Deborah, N. Livermore, Me.; d. Springfield, '68.
Norton, Lucy M., Norridgewock, Me.; m. Emerson T. Crane, '65 ; *San Lorenzo, Cal.*
Nutt, Mary L., Montpelier, Vt.; *Lasell Seminary, Auburndale.*
Olin, Melicent A., Canton, N. Y.; m. Albert Kendrick, M.D., '66 ; d. Vineland, N. J., '89.
Osborne, Helen E., Beloit, Wis.; m. *Edwin B. Thompson, M.D., '64; *283 5th Ave., Ann Arbor, Mich.*
Paine, Mary Elizabeth, Royalston ; *Royalston.*
Potter, Calista V., Mystic River, Ct. ; m. Seneca S. Thresher, Esq., '78 ; *126 Broadway, Norwich, Ct.*
Potter, Maria E., E. Woodstock, Ct. ; d. E. Woodstock, Ct., '80.
Potts, Margaretta S., Trenton, N. J. ; m. Dorsey Gardner, '63 ; d. Madison, N. J., '72.
Potts, Olivia A., Trenton, N. J.; d. Trenton, N. J., '62.
Russell, Charlotte M., Middlebury, Vt. ; m. *Perry Fletcher, '62; m. Albert H. Fisher, '84; *Bellows Falls, Vt.*
Scammell, Amanda C., Milford ; *82 Congress St., Milford.*
Scribner, S. Grace, Raymond, N. H. ; m. Chas. S. Spencer, Esq., '74; *1018 E. 8th St., Columbus, Ind.*
Sisson, Rhoda D., Bozrah, Ct. ; m. Wm. L. Stark, '64 ; d. Lebanon, Ct., '77.
Smith, Eliza T., Granby; m. *Capt. Wm. B. Clark, '62 ; *S. Hadley.*
Stebbins, Ellen C., N. Y. City ;
Stevens, Elizabeth B., Providence, R. I. ;
Stocking, J. Emily, Oroomiah, Persia ; m. Rev. Alfred T. Waterman, '65; *Baldwin, Mich.*
Stone, Sarah A., St. Johnsbury, Vt.; m. Wm. H. Ward, '68; *17 Spring St., St. Johnsbury, Vt.*
Strong, S. Augusta, Rodman, N. Y. ; m. *Pierson Mundy, '73 ; *37 Washington St., Watertown, N. Y.*
Sykes, Ruth A., Suffield, Ct. ; d. Suffield, Ct., '60.
Walsh, Mary E., Newburgh, N. Y. ; m. W. S. Jackson; *Tom's R'ver, N. J.*
Weeks, Mary B., Hermon, N. Y. ; m. *Rev. Henry F. Spencer, '63 ; *424 Crouse Ave., Syracuse, N. Y.*
Whipple, Francena A., Warehouse Point, Ct. ; m. Moses Wyman, '61 ; *Georgetown, Col.*

1861.

White, Harriet A., Springfield ; m. Wm. S. Kingsley, '66 ; *Box E, Chicopee.*
Whitney, Mary R., Waltham ; m. *Florentine W. Pelton, Esq., '62 ; *Dedham.*
Williams, Susan D.,Shelburne Falls; m. Rev. C. E. Dickinson, D.D., '63 ; *300 4th St., Marietta, O.*
Wilson, Lavinia A., Marlboro ; m. Marshall E. Hunter, '64 ; *23 St. James Ave., Boston.*
Woodford,Henrietta M.,W.Avon, Ct. ; m. Rev. P. R. Day,'64 ; P. O. address, *Unionville,Ct.*

1862.

GRADUATES.

Balch, Laura A., Newburyport ; *232 High St., Newburyport.*
Balcom, Ella L., Winchendon ; *Winchendon.*
Ballantine, Julia A., Ahmednagar, India ; m. Rev. Wm. Greenwood, '74 ; *297 Earlham Terrace, Germantown, Philadelphia, Pa.*
Batchelor, Frances A., Whitinsville ; d. Whitinsville, '86.
Blanchard, Louisa M., E. Abington ; d. E. Abington, '63.
Bliss, Anna E., Amherst; *Wellington, Cape Colony, S. Africa.*
Brewster, Ellen D., Wolfboro, N. H. ; d. Indiana, '66.
Buckingham, Elizabeth H., Canton, O. ; m. Rev. Lewis Gregory, '68 ; d. Lincoln,Neb.,'76.
Burt, Achsah L., Westhampton ; m. Henry W. Montague, '67 ; *Westhampton.*
Carner, Lydia M., Athens, Pa. ; m. *D. F. Park, '65 ; *Athens. Pa.*
Chandler, Emma R., La Porte, Ind. ; *Goshen, Ind.*
Crosby, Marietta. Danbury, Ct. ; m. Rev. Henry G. Marshall, '69 ; d. Avon, Ct , '71.
Dickinson, M. Adelia, Waukegan, Ill. ; m. D. A. Corey, '91 ; *Helena, Mont.*
Dutton, Sarah E., Rutland, N. Y. ; m. S. D. Mack, '64 ; *45 Academy St., Watertown,N. Y.*
Ellis, Lucy J., Fitchburg ; *Newton Centre.*
Farwell, Clara M., Rockland, Me. ; *Rockland, Me.*
Ford, Charlotte W., M.D., Morristown, N. J. ; *Box 521, Morristown, N. J.*
Goldsbury, Harriet, Warwick ; d. Warwick, '65.
Hannum, Clara H., Amherst ; d. Amherst, '79.
Haskell, Frances A., Leominster ; m. Solomon Richards, '76 ; *Unionville, Ct.*
Hayward, Sophia M., Hadley ; m. Zenas W. Bliss, '67 ; *Prohibition Park, W.New Brighton, Staten Island, N. Y.*
Hendric, Elizabeth F., Burlington, Io.; m. Robert J. Cory, '68; *1012 Penn. Ave., Denver, Col.*
Henry, Mary H., N. Bennington, Vt. ; *N. Bennington, Vt.*
Hidden, Fanny M., Candia, N. H. ; m. *Rev. B. G. Page, '65 ; d. Greenwood, Mo., '70.
Hilburn, Lucinda, Easton, Pa. ; m. Jas. O'Gorman, '73; *934 Hollins St., Baltimore, Md.*
Hills, Julia L., Rockland, Me. ; *18 N. Main St., Rockland, Me.*
Hyde, Augusta, Cortland, N. Y. ; d. N. Y. City, '94.
Janes, Sarah P., Westhampton ; *Easthampton.*
Kies, Mary A., West Killingly, Ct. ; d. West Killingly, Ct., '08.
Lane, H. Louisa, Franklin, Pa. ; d. about '83.
Latham, Lucy A., Holyoke ; m. Geo. W. D. Upton, '66 ; d. Springfield, '76.
Marcy, Ellen E., Hillsboro Bridge, N. H. ; d. Jersey City, N. J., '79.
Mathewson, Elizabeth, Pomfret, Ct.; m. Chas. W. Grosvenor, Esq., '66 ; *Pomfret Center, Ct.*
Melvin, Sarah H., Chester, N. H. ; *Mt. Holyoke College, S. Hadley.*
Merwin, Lucy S., Durham, Ct. ; *Durham, Ct.*
Mills, Ellen Z., Thompson, Ct. ; m. Waldo Johnson, '66 ; d. Webster, '74.
Noyes, Elizabeth M., Chester, N. H.; m. Wm. S. Greenough, '69 ; *36 Iron St., Wakefield.*
Packer, Minerva E., Preston, N..Y. ; m. Morris D. Brown, Esq., '72 ; *1620 Sanderson Ave., Scranton, Pa.*

1862.

Poland, Mary F., St. Johnsbury, Vt.; d. St. Johnsbury, Vt., '65.
Porter, Hannah M., S. Hadley; d. S. Hadley, '66.
Prentiss, Elizabeth B., Langdon, N. H.; *Mt. Holyoke College, S. Hadley*; home address, *Langdon, N. H.*
Remsen, Eliza W., Middlebury, Vt.; d. Mt. Holyoke Seminary, '62.
Robinson, Emily S., **Willimantic, Ct.**; d. Ormond, Fla., '80.
Sabin, Maria D., Belchertown; m. *Joshua Longley, '71; *Belchertown.*
Sharp, Caroline B., **Fort Wayne, Ind.**; 251 *W. Main St., Fort Wayne, Ind.*
Smith, Elvira. E. Abington; d. E. Abington, '62.
Sturgess, Josephine G., Wilton, Ct.; m. *O. A. G. Todd, Esq., '68; d. Danbury, Ct., '88.
Taggart, Josephine L., Lowell; m. *Albert L. Fiske, '69; 54 *Bartlett St., Lowell.*
Townsend, Mary C., Great Barrington; 503 *N. Church St., Rockford, Ill.*
Townsend, Susan M., Lysander, N. Y.; m. Thompson T. Hart, '67; *Lysander, N. Y.*
Treadwell, Louise E., Jackson, Mich.; d. Jacksonville, Fla., '71.
Walker, Laura W., Mashapaug, Ct.; m. *J. D. Sessions, '63; m. Rev. Samuel I. Curtiss, '70; 395 *W. Monroe St., Chicago, Ill.*
Walker, Louise, Portsmouth, N. H.; m. Rev. Marshall R. Gaines, '68; *Albuquerque, N. M.*
Wilson, Mary A., Salisbury, N. H.; m. *Rev. I. Newton Locke, '72; *Ohio, Mo.*
Wilson, Mary A., Shelburne; m. Rev. Herbert H. Beaman, '72; d. N. Oxford, '81.
Youngs, Harriet W., Pleasant Valley, Ct.; m. Henry W. Barbour, '68; *Farmington, Ct.*

NON-GRADUATES.

Allen, Sabra A., S. Hadley; m. *Albert H. Salisbury, '71; 32 *Linden St., Allston.*
Atherton, Sarah W. (Lyman), Sheldon, Vt.; m. *Rev. Chas. Duren, '64; 2024 *Oakland Ave., Minneapolis, Minn.*
Bailey, Lucy L., Lexington, Va.; m. Andrew E. Heneberger, '68; *Harrisonburg, Va.*
Barrows, Fanny A., S. Glastonbury, Ct.; m. Christopher Seymour, M.D.; *Elm St., Northampton.*
Barrows, Martha J., Middlebury, Vt.; *Girls' School, Kobe, Japan.*
Bartlett, Abby M., Lawrence; d. Lawrence, '64.
Bartlett, Anna M., Fairmount; *W. Hampstead, N. H.*
Beach, Anna L., Lowville, N. Y.; m. *Horace L. Greene, Esq., '63; *Fort Plain, N. Y.*
Brainerd, Mary J., S. Hadley Falls; *S. Hadley Falls.*
Buchanan, Martha A., Cambridge, Pa.; *Honeybrook, Pa.*
Buck, Althea J., Southbridge; m. Orlando B. Pond, '65; d. New Haven, Ct., '84.
Burnap, Jane E., Grafton, Vt.; d. Grafton, Vt., '75.
Carter, Susan, Boston; m. John McCallom, M.D.; 12 *Newbury St., Boston.*
Chase, Eveline P., Henrietta, N. Y.; 165 *Madison St., Brooklyn, N. Y.*
Clary, Martha H., Conway; *Conway.*
Clements, Alice W., Yarmouth, N. S.; d. Yarmouth, N. S., '66.
Cole, Mary F., Jackson, Mich.; m. Milo C. Jones, '70; *Fort Atkinson, Wis.*
Connolly, Clara, Washington, D. C.; m. Phineas Janney, '67; *Lincoln, Va.*
Cook, Sarah C., Westhampton; *Westhampton.*
Denison, Clara, Royalton, Vt.; m. Robert H. McClellan, '79; *Galena, Ill.*
Dickinson, Helen M., S. Hadley; m. Chas. S. Boynton, '68; d. S. Hadley, '82.
Dowd, Delia E., Vergennes, Vt.; m. Sidney A. Smith, '64; *Montour, Io.*
Elliot, Almira F., Jericho Center, Vt.; m. Rev. Austin Hazen, '81; *Richmond, Vt.*
Foster, Ellen F., N. Andover; m. Harrison T. Chandler, '65; *Cleveland, O.*
Gage, Mary A., Boston; m. P. S. Peterson, '65; *Box 383, Chicago, Ill.*
Gardner, Frances E., Fulton, N. Y.; m. Henry O. Silkman, '65; *Maplewood, Pa.*
Haley, Alice, Norwood; m. Edward C. Huxley, '71; *Newton.*

1862.

Hallock, Mary C., New Haven, Ct.; m. Rev. M. Porter Snell, '62; 551 *Harrison St., Anacostia, D. C.*
Hammond, Melinda, Olcott, N. Y.; m. Stephen C. Hoag, '74; *Newfane Station, N. Y.*
Harrington, N. Amelia, W. Springfield; m. S. C. Vance, '62; d. Indianapolis, Ind., '63.
Hayes, Sophia W., Boston; m. Commodore W. H. Dana, U. S. Navy, '66.
Hayward, Esther C., Hadley; m. *Lewis H. Warner, '68; m. John F. Warner, '83; *Box 391, Florence.*
Hibbard, Luella F., Townshend, Vt.; m. Samuel F. Neal, '68; *Gallipolis, O.*
Hibbler, S. Regina, Philadelphia, Pa.; m. Wm. A. James, '68; *2670 Washington Ave., St. Louis, Mo.*
Hicks, Emma M., Tolland, Ct.; m. H. F. Downing, '80; P. O. address, 16 *Lyman St., Springfield.*
Hopkins, Mary A., Rutland, N. Y.; m. Edward H. Thompson, '66; *Watertown, N. Y.*
Keyes, Susan M., Worcester; 12 *Goulding St., Worcester.*
Knowles, Caroline E., Manchester, N. H.; d. Manchester, N. H.,'71.
Lawrence, Meta L., E.Windsor Hill,Ct.; m.*O. M. Pray,M.D., '68; d. Brooklyn,N.Y.,'70.
Lourie, Jeannie M., Greenwich. N. Y.; m. Henry F. Lamb, '68; d. N.Bennington, Vt.,'70.
Mathewson, Mary, Pomfret, Ct.; d. Pomfret, Ct., '82.
Mead, Myrtilla P., N. Greenwich, Ct.; m. Livingston Disbrow, '73; *Box 704, New Rochelle, N. Y.*
Means, Lilla B., Auburndale; *Andover.*
Merrill, Lucy M., W. Amesbury (now Merrimac); m. Wm. H. H. Blodgett, '68; *Box 608, Merrimac.*
Merrill, Mary E., Athens, Pa.; *Bon Accord, Kan.*
Miller, Henrietta D., Newark, N. J.; 42 *Walnut St., Newark, N. J.*
Montague, Abbie L., S. Hadley; m. Wm. R. Kemp, '73; 181 *Chestnut St., Holyoke.*
Morrow, R. Sophia, Paterson, N. J.; d. Paterson, N. J., '90.
Mussey, Amelia J., Coventry, Vt.; m. Edward Speakman, '68; 482 *W. Adams St., Chicago, Ill.*
Nelson, Anna J., Poughkeepsie, N. Y.; d. New York City.
Newton, Harriet N., Rochester,Vt.; m. Hon. Frank G. Clark,'65; d. Cedar Rapids, Io.,'92.
Peck, Mary L., Montpelier, Vt.; d. Montpelier, Vt., '86.
Phipps, Marion J., Paxton; 203 *St. Botolph St., Boston.*
Plotts,Catharine W., Easton, Pa.; m. Edward Welden,'68; 149 *S. Centre St.,Bethlehem,Pa.*
Randall, Anna L., Buffalo, N. Y.; m. N. Osborne,M.D.,'65; 316 *Summer St.,Buffalo,N.Y.*
Ranney, Martha C., W. Townshend, Vt.; m. Russell Fiske, '65; *Fort Collins, Col.*
Reamy, Martha, Hollidaysburg, Pa.; m. L. S. Hoopes, '73; *Hollidaysburg, Pa.*
Reamy. Sidney, Hollidaysburg, Pa.; m. D. Dighton Morrell, '77; *Henrietta, Pa.*
Rumiser, Louisa, Berlin, Pa.; m. Thos. J. Williams, '70; *Jones Mills, Pa.*
Sears, Eleanor W., Winthrop, Me.; m. Eben S. Bonney, '62; 150 *Whitney St., Auburn, Me.*
Seymour, Amelia, S. Norwalk, Ct.; *S. Norwalk, Ct.*
Siegfried, Sarah A., Easton, Pa.; m. Joseph S. Osterstock, '07; *Easton, Pa.*
Smith, Martha L., Buckland; m. Geo. M. Hubbard, '73; d. New York City, '89.
Spier, Sarah A., Ballston Spa, N. Y.; d. Ballston, N. Y., '64.
Stanley, Juliet M., Winthrop, Me.; m. *Rev. Israel P. Warren, D.D., '86; 315 *Brackett St., Portland, Me.*
Stiles, Flora A., Gorham, N. H.; m. John G. Wight, '65; 428 *S. 42d St., Philadelphia, Pa.*
Stiles, Helen E., Gorham, N. H.; m. John Bellows, '77; m. Chas. W. Fisk, '89; *Logansport, Ind.*
Terry, Ellen, Riverhead, N. Y.; *Aquebogue, N. Y.*
Tewksbury, Sarah E., Oxford, Me.; m. Rev. George Michael, '74; *Greeley, Col.*
Thompson, Harriet D., New Braintree; m. L. Kirke Harlow, '74; *Boulder, Col.*

1862.

Thompson, Josephine G., Lambertville, N. Y.; m. Daniel Fisher, '66; 13 *Grover St., Oil City, Pa.*
Troxell,Emma M.,Allentown,Pa. ; m. Frank K. Smith,'64 ; 523 *Church St., Lock Haven,Pa.*
Vannuys, Mary C., Franklin, Ind.; m. R. S. Overstreet, '63; *Franklin, Ind.*
Wakely, Electa J., Homer, N. Y. ; d. Homer, N. Y., '79.
Walker, Mary, N. Gage, N. Y. ; *N. Gage, N. Y.*
Warner, Jane G., Jericho, Vt. ; m. *Hiram S. Hart, '71 ; *Jericho Center, Vt.*
Washburn, Gertrude H., Berlin, Ct. ; m. *Henry F. Norton, '64 ; *East Helena, Mont.*
Weller, Elizabeth W., Paterson, N. J. ; m. Wm. M. Davis, Esq., '66 ; *Phillipsburg, N. J.*
Williams, Clara, Deep River, Ct. ; d. Deep River, Ct., '63.
Williams, Emma B., Raynham ; m. Bradford B. King, '80 ; P. O. address, *Taunton.*
Winter, Adelaide, Niles, N. Y. ; m. Francis M. Hiett, M.D., '63 ; d. Berlin, Wis., '71.

1863.

GRADUATES.

Atwood, Emma J., Watertown, Ct. ; d. Watertown, Ct., '63.
Beaman, Mary E., N. Hadley ; m. S. L. Stockbridge, Esq., '67 ; d. N. Hadley, '71.
Bliss, Flavia S., Longmeadow ; m. Frank E. Garner, '80; *Cornwall, Ct.*
Butler, Emily A., E. Smithfield, Pa. ; d. Lake City, Minn., '88.
Carruth, Kathleen M., Phillipston ; m. Rev. Geo. G. Phipps, '65 ; *Newton Highlands.*
Chappell, Mary E., Gilead, Ct. ; d. W. Hartford, Ct., '69.
Clary, Susan M., Conway ; d. Pretoria, Transvaal, S. Africa, '78.
Cole, Ellen S., Lyons, N. Y. ; m. *A. F. Gillette, M.D., '74 ; *Lyons, N. Y.*
Cowles, Eliza E., Hadley ; m. *Joseph Rideout, '82 ; *Box 57, Amherst.*
Cowles, Harriet H., Hadley ; m. Chas. L. Storrs, '69 ; d. S. Boston, '86.
Cutler, Olive W., Lindenville, O. ; m. Rev. S. D. Peet, '66 ; *Good Hope, Ill.*
Dickinson, Julia E., Granby ; 87 *East St., Chicopee Falls.*
Fish, Ellen P., Jackson, Mich. ; 409 *S. Jackson St., Jackson, Mich.*
Ford, Elizabeth A., Akron, O. ; m. John F. Earl, '69 ; *care of John Tod, Cleveland, O.*
Francis,Nancy D., Newington,Ct. ; m. Rev. Lucien H. Adams,'67 ; d. Antioch,Turkey,'91.
Freeman, H. Maria, Mansfield, Ct. ; m. *Charles D. Talcott, '76; *Talcottville, Ct.*
Hall, Mary E., Otis ; m. Hon. Henry W. Bosworth, Esq., '65 ; *Springfield.*
Hamilton, Anna, Ulsterville, N. Y. ; m. T. Curwen Jones, '69; *C. P. R. Land Dept., Winnipeg, Canada.*
Hazen, Frances M., Norwich, Vt. ; *Mt. Holyoke College* ; home address, *Middletown, Ct.*
Holbrook, Mary E., Barre ; m. Rev. Thos. G. Grassie, '63 ; *Ashland, Wis.*
Kimball, Lucia E. F., Lawrence ; 644 *Monroe St., Chicago, Ill.*
Leach, Laura J., Saxton's River, Vt.; m. J. Newton Voorhees, '78 ; d. '90.
Norton, Frances A., East Elba, N. Y. ; *East Elba, N. Y.*
Norton, Helen S., Howell, Mich. ; *Howell, Mich.*
Nott, Mary P., Essex, Ct. ; *Essex, Ct.*
Paige,Lucy A.,Alexander,N. Y. ; m. E. Ransom Page,'64 ; 51 *Howell St.,Canandaigua,N. Y.*
Palmer, Elizabeth C., Evans' Mills,N. Y. ; m. A. Marvin Shew,M.D., '66 ; d. Middletown, Ct., '74.
Parsons, Ellen, C., M.A., Northampton ; 53 *5th Ave., N. Y. City.*
Payne, Etta, M.D., Boston ; d. Philadelphia, Pa., '86.
Potts, Amelia P., Sterling, Ill. ; m. Mr. Carson, '78 ; *Maiden Rock, Wis.*
Rothrock, Mary M., McVeytown, Pa. ; m. David M. McFarland, '66 ; *W. Chester, Pa.*
Sawyer, Mary N., Ashburnham ; *S. Framingham.*

1863.

Scribner, Abbie, Raymond, N. H.; m. Jas. F. Brown, M.D., '65; 681 *Union St., Manchester, N. H.*
Snell, Tirzah S., Amherst; m. Rev. E. C. Hall, '67; 127 *Forest Ave., Jamestown, N. Y.*
Swett, Frances M., Newport, N. H.; m. Chas. C. Shattuck, '65; 1208 *Jackson St., San Francisco, Cal.*
Thompson, E. Antoinette, New Salem; m. Joseph A. Shaw, '63; *Highland Military Academy, Worcester.*
Todd, S. Amelia, Charlestown; m. Samuel T. Kingsley, '67; 10 *Elm St., Rutland, Vt.*
Whitney, Elizabeth J., Waltham; 308 *Columbus Ave., Boston.*
Wood, Elizabeth W., Worcester; m. Lewis N. Smith, '66; 16 *Melville St., Worcester.*

NON-GRADUATES.

Aldrich, Mary A., Palmyra, N. Y.; *Palmyra, N. Y.*
Allen, Louisa P., Oakham; m. *Hon. Sanford B. Kellogg, Esq., '70; 19 *Lancaster St., N. Cambridge.*
Ayer, Emily D., Danville, Vt.; d. Danville, Vt., '94.
Bailey, Isabel M., Portland, Me.; m. Clarendon Harris, '65; d. La Porte, Ind., '66.
Balch, Alice M., Newburyport; m. Abiel Abbot, '64; 431 *William St., E. Orange, N. J.*
Beede, Eunice M., Center Sandwich, N. H.; m. A. S. Kimball, '66; d. Sandwich, N. H., '66.
Belcher, Lucy G., Farmington, Me.; m. *Nathan C. Goodenow, '74; 10 *Main St., Farmington, Me.*
Birge, Anna A., Hudson, O.; 51 *Franklin Ave., New Rochelle, N. Y.*
Bissell, Mary R., St. Clair, Mich.; *York, Neb.*
Bridgman, Emma A., Middlefield; m. Rev. Roselle T. Cross, '69; 1116 *S. 11th St., Denver, Col.*
Brown, Emma E., Philadelphia, Pa.; m. Wm. A. Maynard, '74; 7 *Brookfield St., Cleveland, O.*
Chollar, Sophia M., Homer, N. Y.; m. Benjamin F. Walter, '66; *Whitney Point, N. Y.*
Clark, Susan E., Northampton; 26 *Maple St., Northampton.*
Clarke, Elizabeth, Hammondsport, N. Y.; m. *Geo. W. Nichols, '77; *Hammondsport, N. Y.*
Cleveland, Julia A., Barre; m. Rev. Freeman P. Tower, '63; d. '93.
Cone, Sarah E., S. Wilbraham; d. S. Wilbraham, '63.
Connolly, Ada, Washington, D. C.; *care Mrs. James, Lincoln, Va.*
Cook, Frances L., Chester; m. Rev. Selah Merrill, '66; d. Chester, '67.
Cotes, Eliza B., Springfield, N. Y.; m. Rev. U. B. Robinson; P. O. address, " *Church at Home and Abroad,*" 1334 *Chestnut St., Philadelphia, Pa.*
Cowles, Jane E., Ryegate, Vt.; *Cowles Art School, 145 Dartmouth St., Boston.*
Cox, Jemima L., Yarmouth, N. S.; m. Chas. H. Sutherland, '63; 206 *Brookline St., Boston.*
Cox, Margaret C., Yarmouth, N. S.; m. Alexander M. Wood, '64; d. Somerville, '89.
Deming, Louise M., Palmyra, N. Y.; m. *W. Clark, '66; m. N. E. Hulbert, '69; 18 *W. 61st St., N. Y. City.*
Dobyns, Julia L., Maysville, Ky.; m. John R. Procter, '69; *Office Civ. Ser. Com., Washington, D. C.*
Dyer, Josephine L., Hartford, Ct.; m. John Lowe, U. S. N., '67; 203 *East Capitol St., Washington, D. C.*
Eames, Emily W., Upton; m. *Hosea B. Harvey, '68; *Box 121, S. Meriden, Ct.*
Emmons, Julia C., Sturbridge; *Oxford.*
Farr, Caroline, Littleton, N. H.; m. Benjamin F. Page, M.D., '70; *Littleton, N. H.*
Ford, Julia P., Morristown, N. J.; m. Nathan M. Thompson, '85; *Thompson Ridge, N. Y.*
Ford, Martha, N. Abington; m. M. N. Arnold, '67; *N. Abington.*
Foster, Josephine A., Detroit, Mich.; m. Richard Macauley, '67; 61 *Edmund Pl., Detroit, Mich.*

1863.

Gardiner, Marian H., Otisco, N. Y. ; m. Wm. Reardon, '81 ; *Chicago. Ill.*
Gilbert, Emily M., Warren ; m. Giles Blodgett, '65 ; *Warren.*
Goodrich, Harriet, E. Windsor Hill, Ct. ; 17 *Union Park, Boston.*
Goodwin, Julia A., Mason, N. H. ; d. Mason. N. H., '94.
Goodwin, Lucy E., Mason, N. H. ; *Mason, N. H.*
Hallock, A. Adelaide, Riverhead, N. Y.; m. Dr. Chas. J. B. Jackson, '77 ; *Winnemissett, Fla.*
Hamilton, Mary, Ulsterville, N.Y.; m. *Wm. G. Stevenson, M.D., '65; d. Montreal, Can., '68.
Hastings, Mary E., Brooklyn, N. Y.; m. Seman A.Swenarton, '70 ; *Union St., Montclair, N. J.*
Hatch, Marcia M. A., Fayetteville, N. Y. ; m. Lester C. Mitchell, M.D., '07 ; 53 *S. 5th St., Minneapolis, Minn.*
Hawes, Ellen, Bridgeton, Me. ; m. Joseph Merrill, '65 ; 2251 *Stout St., Denver, Col.*
Hayden, Catherine J., E. Granby, Ct. ; m. Chas. H. Clark, '64 ; d. E. Granby, Ct., '72.
Hitchcock, Mary O., Troy, Vt. ; m. Oscar S. Greenleaf, '68 ; 147 *Sumner Ave., Springfield.*
Hoffman, Harriet N., Lewistown, Pa. ; d. New Decatur, Ala., '95.
Horton, Sarah W., Barrington, R. I. ; 964 *18th St., Oakland, Cal.*
Hosmer, Mary Frances, Fisherville, N. H. ; m. *John E. Abbott; *Mountain View, Cal.*
Jackson, Luetta G., Winthrop, Me. ; m. B. F. Small, '71 ; *Old Town, Me.*
Kerr, Ellen M., Allegheny, Pa. ; m. Rev. J. E. Wright, D.D., '69; *Lock Haven, Pa.*
Kingsbury, Julia E., Franklin, Ct. ; m. John G. Cooley, Jr., '65 ; 32 *Church St., Norwich, Ct.*
Kneeland, Mary L., Northampton ; m. Geo. W. Harlow, '65 ; 38 *Fruit St., Northampton.*
Leonard, Emma F., Bridgewater ; *Rochester.*
Lovett, Anna, Yarmouth, N. S. ; m. Jacob Bingay, '68 ; *Yarmouth, N. S.*
Mansfield, Elizabeth A., Fryeburg, Me. ; m. John Hamilton ; *Indianapolis, Ind.*
Maxwell, Elizabeth S., Jackson, N. Y. ;
May, Sarah R., Strong, Me.; d. Strong, Me., '88.
Meigs, Mary G., Pottstown, Pa. ; m. John C. DaCosta, M.D., '68 ; 1633 *Arch St., Philadelphia, Pa.*
Millar, Julia A., Utica, N. Y. ; m. Chas. L. Blakeslee, '67 ; *Menand, Albany, N. Y.*
Morley, A. Elizabeth, Williamstown ; m. Howard S. Nichols, '93 ; *Wahu, China.*
Morris, Frances S., Shelbyville, Ind. ; m. Fred. Yeiser, '76 ; d. Shelbyville, Ind., '82.
Morrison, Helen F., Washington, D. C. ; m. Francis W. Edwards, '68 ; 2023 *Washington Ave., Washington, D. C.*
Newell, Marion, Newport, N. H. ; d. Lebanon, N. H., '63.
Norton, Alice L., Alabama, N. Y. ; m. Wm. M. Ingersoll,'70 ; *Montclair, Suburb of Denver, Col.*
Norton, Fannie E., Otis ; m. Judge Silas A. Robinson,'66 ; 189 *College St., Middletown, Ct.*
Norwood, Elizabeth, Phippsburg, Me. ; m. Wm. Burch, '66 ; d. Chicago, Ill., '83.
Palmer, Phebe, Stamford, Ct. ; m. Wm. M. Cubery, '70; 1527 *Minturn Place, Alameda, Cal.*
Parkhurst, Helen M. A., Clinton ; *care W. C. Parkhurst, Clinton.*
Peck, Juliet E., New Haven, Ct. ; 783 *Orange St., New Haven, Ct.*
Platts, H. Ellen, Fitzwilliam, N. H. ; m. Edward Spaulding, '75 ; d. Rochester, N. Y.,'82.
Potter, Mary J., N. Stonington, Ct. ; m. Edwin B. Coolidge,'67 ; 93 *Main St., E. Hartford, Ct.*
Robbins, Annie E., Calais, Me. ; m. Geo. R. Gardner ; *Calais, Me.*
Rose, Margaretta, Brooklyn, N. Y. ; d. Mamaroneck, N. Y., '94.
Royce, Lillian M., Rochester, N. Y. ; 29 *Park Ave., Rochester, N. Y.*
Sawyer, Kathreen A., Dover, Me. ; m. *L. B. Paine, '68 ; 7 *Morrill Ave., Waterville, Me.*
Sawyer, Laura A., M.D., Salisbury, N. H. ; m. *Lindley M. Edwards, '70 ; 3012 *Sherman Ave., Omaha, Neb.*
Seaver, Anna M., Carillon, Can. E. ;
Serfass, Maria J., Allentown, Pa. ; 1021 *Washington St., Easton, Pa.*
Shaw, Priscilla B., S. Weymouth ; m. James H. Bayley, '67 ; *Box 85, Braintree.*
Shipman, Helen E., Hadley ; d. Hadley, '65.
Smith, Ella G., New Haven, Ct. ; m. Wm. F. Green, '70 ; 33 *7th St., Troy, N. Y.*

1863.

Sterling, Hannah M. L., Poughkeepsie, N. Y. ; d. Poughkeepsie, N. Y., '74.
Sturtevant, Rachel B., McGrawville, N. Y. ; d. McGrawville, N. Y., '64.
Sylvester, Mary, Colchester, Ct. ; d. Colchester, Ct., '63.
Tilton, Susan A., Conway ; m. *Lewis W. Miller, '65 ; 630 *Main St., Springfield.*
Tilton, Theresa M., S. Deerfield ; *Glen St. Mary, Fla.*
Truair, Mary A., Syracuse, N. Y. ; m. *F. Walter Jackson, '69 ; m. Prof. Edward M. Dudley, '73 ; 3 *Ida Terrace, Troy, N. Y.*
Warner, Jane S., Williamsburg ; m. Edwin A. Porter, '73 ; *Williamsburg.*
Wells, Sabra M. S., Kingsboro, N. Y. ; m. Remus D. Burr, '67 ; *Gloversville, N. Y.*
Wheeler, Ellen H., Mystic River, Ct. ; m. Geo. N. Wilcox, '65 ; d. Brooklyn, N. Y., '86.
Wilder, Abbie P., Hadley ; m. Wm. C. Dickinson, '77 ; d. Hadley. '88.
Wilder, Abby A., Princeton ; m. Daniel Davis,'72 ; *Phillipsburg, N. J.*
Williams, Emily A., Deep River, Ct. ; m. John Halliday, '73 ; *Essex, Ct.*
Wilson, Mary A., Gardiner, Me. ; d. Gardiner, Me., '66.
Wood, Asenath B., Evans' Mills, N. Y. ; m. Wm. D. Parker, '67 ; *Lowville, N. Y.*
Woodward, Jane G., Franklin, Ct. ; m. Rev. Edward H. Smith, '73 ; *Oshkosh, Wis.*
Worden, Harriet B., Fayetteville, N. Y. ; m. *John C. King, '65 ; m. *Frank M. Byington, M.D., '67 ; *Fayetteville, N. Y.*
Wright, Katharine E., Oroomiah, Persia ; *Middlebury, Vt.*

1864.

GRADUATES.

Allen, Anna W., Walpole ; m. *H. N. Howard, M.D.,'67 ; 918 *Mass. Ave., Washington, D.C.*
Beaman, Emma W., N. Hadley ; *Amherst.*
Billings, H. Louisa, Beaver Dam, Wis. ; m. Allyn A. Avery, '68 ; *Baraboo, Wis.*
Bishop, Anna M., N. Woodstock, Ct. ; d. N. Woodstock, Ct., '94.
Bissell, Cornelia H., St. Clair, Mich. ; 914 *Temple St., Los Angeles, Cal.*
Bowen, Sarah, Peru ; *Hinsdale.*
Bowen, Susan, Peru ; m. David S. Jordan, '75 ; d. Bloomington, Ind., '85.
Carleton, Sarah L., Rockport, Me. ; m. Rev. T. E. Brastow, '69 ; *Rockport, Me.*
Chamberlain, M. Louise, M.D., Madison, N. Y. ; m. Mr. Purington, '66 ; 23 *Allston St., Dorchester.*
Choate, Alice D., Beverly ; 3855 *Washington Ave., St. Louis, Mo.*
Church, Annie V., Bristol, R. I. ; m. Allan Bourn, '66 ; d. N. Y. City, '68.
Church, Mary E., Middlefield ; *Middlefield.*
Clarke, Anna F., Winchendon ; 458 *Milwaukee St., Milwaukee, Wis.*
Clarke, Sarah G., Conway ; d. Conway, '65.
Clarke, Ursula C., Winchendon ; m. Rev. Geo. D. Marsh, '75 ; *Philippopolis, Bulgaria.*
Cleveland, Mary F., Boston ; m. Edwin T. Witherby, '73 ; *Shelby, Ala.*
Clough, Mary E., Canterbury, N. H. ; *Canterbury, N. H.*
Coburn, Sarah E., Rockland, Me. ; m. R. Ogden Dwight, Esq., '69 ; *S. Hadley Falls.*
Crosby, Annabell F., Milford, N. H. ; m. Chas. C. Secombe, '71 ; d. Minneapolis,Minn.,'73.
Curtis, Chiara A., Amherst ; m. Louis F. S. Plimpton, '70 ; *Florence.*
Cushman, Harriet E., Mechanics Falls, Me. ; d. Mechanics Falls, Me., '67.
Eastman, Maria C., N. Conway, N. H. ; m. James M. Durham, Esq., '68 ; *Ashley, Ill.*
Fenn, Mabel B., M.D., Brimfield, O. ; m. *Robert L. King, M.D., '67 ; 607 *Harrison St., Flint, Mich.*
Ferry, Joan, Belchertown ; *Belchertown.*
Fitch, Frances A., Springfield, N. Y. ; m. Rev. Horace H. Allen, '72 ; *Holland Patent, N. Y.*

1864.

Ford, Emma J., Morristown, N. J.; m. *Gordon Piers, '83; m. Chas. A. Newton,'86; *Box 521, Morristown, N. J.*
Goodhue, Julia A., Westminster West, Vt.; m. *Hoyt Trowbridge, '71; *Glasgow, Mo.*
Gowdy, Julia A., Lowville, N. Y.; m. Henry Hareford, '69; *Watertown, N. Y.*
Graves, Sarah L., Newton; *Seorille Place School, Oak Park, Ill.*
Haynes, Mary, Townsend; m. Rev. John W. Lane, '08; *N. Hadley.*
Jenkins, Myra M., Conway; m. Martin L. Mead, M.D., '67; *Highlandlake, Col.*
Newhall, Lura E., Hinsdale, N. H.; m. * Jay Phetteplace, '69; m. *George F. Geer, '79; m. T. H. Leavitt, '86; *837 S. 13th St., Lincoln, Neb.*
Nolton, Clara A., Holland Patent, N. Y.; d. Holland Patent, N. Y., '90.
Parsons, Henrietta D., Ludlow; m. Wm. C. Howell, '69; *Blairstown, N. J.*
Pettibone, M. Louise, Winchester Center, Ct.; m. A. A. Smith, '84; *Ogdensburg, N. Y.*
Pickit, Sarah, Edwards, N. Y.; m. *Albert M. Spalding, '68; *Fergus Falls, Minn.*
Reed, Harriet E., Madison, N. Y.; m. Austin E. Messenger, '76; *DeWittville, N. Y.*
Root, Caroline E., Belchertown; m. Rev. Payson W. Lyman,'73; *22 Hanover St., Fall River.*
Rose, S. Elizabeth, W. Winfield, N.Y.; m. Hon. Myron A McKee,'66; *Richfield Springs, N. Y.*
Snow, Laura J., Rockland, Me.; m. *J. Llewellyn Wood, '67; m. Nelson F. Evans, '71; *1529 Green St., Philadelphia, Pa.*
Sturges, Artemesia E., Wilton, Ct.; m. W. A. White, M.D., '72; *St. Mary's, Ga.*
Taylor, Isabella W., S. Hadley; m. Frank W. Dorman, '70; *Upper Montclair, N. J.*
Tracy, Emily, M.D., E. Smithfield, Pa.; m. *Wm. F. Woodworth, M.D., '74; *114 S. Wood St., Chicago, Ill.*
Twyman, Harriet S., Paris, Mo.; m. *John W. Kelley, '73; *154 Golden Gate Ave., San Francisco, Cal.*
White, Caroline D., Wardsboro, Vt.; *The Western, Oxford, O.*
Wilder, Sara A., Hadley; m. Samuel R. Bell, '68; *Hadley.*
Willett, Emogene F., Waldoboro, Me.; *195 W. Springfield St., Boston.*
Wilson, Mary L. D., Fulton, N. Y.; m. Franklin E. Libby, '87; *215 E. 13th St., N. Y. City.*
Woodward, Abbie J., Plymouth (now Thomaston), Ct.; m. Henry F. Davis, '78; *Watertown, Ct.*
Woodward, Emma C., Franklin, Ct.; m. Wm. R. Lathrop, '73; *Norwich Town, Ct.*
Wurtz, Anna, New Paltz, N. Y.; d. '87.

NON-GRADUATES.

Adams, Elizabeth D., N. Hadley; m. Thos. Winn, '67; m. D. S. White, '93; *Hadley.*
Adams, Helen A., Ulster, Pa.; m. Geo. W. Kilmer, '65; *Towanda, Pa.*
Andruss, Sarah J., Rainbow, Ct.; m. Emory F. Miller, '74; d. Avon, Ct., '77.
Baldwin, Adelaide, Natchez, Miss.;
Beekman, Sarah W., Easthampton; m. Rev. Joseph H. Sawyer, '70; *Easthampton.*
Bell, Laura V., Warren, O.; m. Edward Hatfield, '68; *Spokane, Wash.*
Betts, Mary A., Stamford, Ct.; m. J. Henry Cummings, '71; *Stamford, Ct.*
Blakeslee, Jane M., Plymouth (now Thomaston), Ct.; m. Edward R. Ives, '66; *65 W. Ave., Bridgeport, Ct.*
Blanchard, Maria E., Wheaton, Ill.; m. Ezra A. Cook, '69; *316 Wash. Boul., Chicago, Ill.*
Bracket, Carrie A., Springfield; m. D. D. Smith, '87; *437 State St., Springfield.*
Brackett, Emily A., E. Parsonsfield, Me.; *E. Parsonsfield, Me.*
Brown, Ada B., Oswego, N. Y.; m. Joseph D. Falley, '67; *Chautauqua, N. Y.*
Butler, Dorcas E., Brooklyn, N. Y.; m. *Wm. H. F. Randolph, M.D., '65; *179 Herkimer St., Brooklyn, N. Y.*
Carruth, Ellen M., Phillipston; m. A. A. Knight, '66; *720 Yakima Ave., Tacoma, Wash.*
Caswell, Harriet P., Portland, Ct.; m. *Edward D. Miller, '71; *S. Glastonbury, Ct.*
Choate, Elsie A., Peacham, Vt.; m. *David A. Merrill, M.D., '68; *Peacham, Vt.*

1864.

Claggett, Rebecca B., New Alstead, N. H.; m. *—— French ; 189 *Cambridge St., E. Cambridge.*
Clark, Aurora B., Conway ; m. Chas. H. Arms, '66; 5410 *Washington Ave., Chicago, Ill.*
Condit, Sarah F., Millburn, N. J.; d. Millburn, N. J., '82.
Crocker, Carrie A., Sunderland ; m. Asa A. Spear, '70; 627 *Lafayette Ave., Brooklyn, N. Y.*
Davis, Olive G., Princeton; m. *Frank B. Davidson, '79 ; *Burncoat St., Worcester.*
Day, Henrietta N., S. Wilbraham ; m. M. H. Twitchell, '76 ; *Kingston, Can.*
Denise, L. Anna, Burlington, Io.; m. Rev. E. R. Burkhalter, '70 ; *Cedar Rapids, Io.*
Dickinson, Mary M., Fitchburg; m. Henry Allison, '70 ; 37 *Prospect St., Fitchburg.*
Doughty, Mary O., Boonton, N. J.; m. Oscar S. Wickham, '71 ; *Franklinville, N. Y.*
Dowling, Lilia R., N. Y. City; m. Rev. John Love, '70 ; d. Germantown, Pa., '84.
Dwight, Amelia L., Binghamton, N. Y.; m. Seymour Coleman, '67 ; 2023 *Mich. Ave., Chicago, Ill.*
Dwight, Clara L., Belchertown ; 18 *Amity St., Amherst.*
Easton, Sarah E., Belvidere, N. J.; m. Ira Otterson, '74 ; *Jamesburg, N. J.*
Eaton, Lurintha A., Ludlow ; m. David H. Simons, '73; *Mason City, Io.*
Ecker, Emma L., Fayetteville, N. Y.; m. Loda V. Sanford, '71 ; *Brooklyn, N. Y.*
Ely, Annie R., Freehold, N. J.; m. Jas. L. Abrahams, LL.D., '76; d. San Diego, Cal., '93.
Emerson, Henrietta C., Somerville ;
Essex, Grace, Bennington, Vt. ; *N. Bennington,* 17.
Feen, Ellen J., Milford, Ct. ; m. *Wm. F. Brooks, '67 ; 335 *W. 55th St., N. Y. City.*
Filley, Eunice R., Bloomfield, Ct. ; m. Edmund D. Sturtevant, '79 ; 148 *Kern St., Los Angeles, Cal.*
Fitch, Florence E., East Sheffield (now Clayton); m. Edward L. Cook, '79 ; *Clayton.*
Ford, Charlotte H., Newark, N. J. ; m. Myron E. Tomlinson, '69; *Grand Rapids, Mich.*
Foster, Ellen F., Dummerston, Vt.; m. John A. Bower, '70 ; 116 *Dithridge St., Pittsburgh, Pa.*
Gandolfo, Josephine M., N. Y. City ; m. Fred. M. Smith, '74 ; *Foxboro.*
Garfield, Jane M., Lee ; *Lee.*
Gilbert, Mary E., Newark, N. J. ; m. W. H. White, M.D. ; *Bloomfield, N. J.*
Gilbert, Matilda E., East Boston;
Gilman, Edna M., E. Hartford, Ct. ; m. Geo. A. Spink, '70 ; d. Natick, R. I., '70.
Godfrey, Harriet E., Conway; m. Butler Dennis, '73; m. John C. Lamson, '90; *Waterloo, N. Y.*
Goldsmith, Mary Harriet, Southold, N. Y.; m. Geo. M. Howell, '69; d. Southold, N Y., '83.
Harrison, Mary A., Orange, N. J. ; m. F. K. Howell, Esq., '69 ; d. Newark, N. J., '76.
Hillard, Emma S., Auburndale; *Arlington Heights.*
Hitchcock, Martha A., Newton ; 550 *Center St., Newton.*
Holliday, Eliza J., N. Springfield, Pa.; m. David M. Richardson, '71 ; 409 *Lafayette Ave, Detroit, Mich.*
Hoxie, Isabel L., Paterson, N. J.; m. Rev. Wm. M. Hughes, '76 ; *S. St., Morristown, N. J.*
Hoxsey, Margaret, Paterson, N. J. ; m. Thos. B. Hoxsey, '82 ; d. Paterson, N. J., '87.
Hubbard, Charlotte E., Montclair, N. J. ; m. *Rev. Thornton B. Penfield, '66; m. Rev. John B. Devins, '83 ; *Hope Chapel,* 339 *E. 4th St , N. Y. City.*
Ingham, Diantha, Middlefield; d. Middlefield, '66.
Inglee, Mary E., Machias, Me. ; m. Rev. Fred. E. Sturges, '68 ; d. Machias, Me., '70.
James, Annie S., Millburn, N. J. ; m. J. B. Burling, M.D., '82 ; *Summit, N. J.*
Johnson, Hannah A., Fiskdale ; m. Wilson Hurd, M.D., '66; *The Jackson Sanatorium, Dansville, N. Y.*
Johnson, Josephine C., Milwaukee, Wis. ; m. Edward M. Herrick, '67 ; 2081 *Webster St., Oakland, Cal.*
Kennedy, Fanny E., Stamford, Ct. ; m. Henry C. Gage, '68 ; 17 *Pleasant St., Danbury, Ct.*
King, Amelia T., Enfield, Ct. ; m. Geo. Lorimer, '69 ; *Box* 113, *Thompsonville, Ct.*
Kingsley, Frances E., Le Roy, Pa. ; *Mansfield, Pa.*

1864.

Lee, Aurora M., Brooksville, Ky.; m. Wm. W. Quinn, '66; *Higginsport, Io.*
Leonard, Ellen E., Exeter, N. H.; m. Jos. H. Houghton, '70; 422 *N. G St., Tacoma, Wash.*
Lincoln, Elizabeth B., Longmeadow; m. Walter W. Loomis, '80; *Windsor, Ct.*
McCullough, Nancy J., Franklin, Ind.; m. *Edwin M. Mears, '68; *San Jose, Cal.*
McDonald, Ella K., Augusta, Me.; 25 *Sewall St., Augusta, Me.*
Makinster, Augusta A., Holyoke; m. Paul L. Chandler, '69; *Westbrook, Me.*
Marshall, Jerusha A., Milford, Ct.; 125 *W. 82d St., N. Y. City.*
Mattocks, Eliza B., Peacham, Vt.; m. Dr. Chas. B. Nichols, '72; d. Franklin Falls, N.H., '83.
Maxwell, Victoria C., Shelburne Falls; m. Franklin B. Gamwell, '66; *Holliston.*
Maynard, Wilhelmina D., Knoxville, Tenn.; m. Felix A Reeve, '65; 1742 *N St., Washington, D. C.*
Merrill, Mary E., Andover; m. Sylvester Tryon; 903 *10th St., Sacramento, Cal.*
Monilaws, Isabel, Somers, N. Y.; m. Benj. Hammond, '75; d. '92.
Monyer, Mary A., Reading, Pa.; m. Rev. W. O. Cornman, '67; 207 *S. 3d St., Reading, Pa.*
Morris, Elizabeth J., Montclair, N. J.; *Montclair, N. J.*
Mosman, Fannie E., Chicopee; m. Edward M. Alden, '67; d. Chicopee, '70.
Mott, Mary L., Sing Sing, N. Y.; d. Sing Sing, N. Y., '71.
Nash, Isabella S., Hadley; m. Lemuel C. Adams, '76; 822 *Shotwell St., San Francisco, Cal.*
Orton, Beulah C., Lakeville, Ct.; m. Jas. R. Hicks, '68; 1638 *Ogden St., Denver, Col.*
Osgood, Daphne E., Peterboro, N. H.; m. Andrew J. Hoyt, '68; 20 *Cushing St., Waltham.*
Page, Louise E., Kendall's Mills, Me.; m. *Geo. H. Newhall, '74; *Fairfield, Me.*
Perkins, M. Isabella, Plympton; m. Rev. Henry A. Goodhue, '64; *Westminster West, Vt.*
Perry, Harriet E., Brookfield, Vt.; m. Chas. L. Rice, '65; *Rockland.*
Pierce, Delia M., Royalston; m. Lucien Lord, '68; *Athol.*
Pike, Adaline A., Melrose; m. Joseph W. Simonds, '65; d. Melrose, '82.
Ranney, Stella E., W. Townshend, Vt.; m. Rev. Joseph A. Leach, '65; *Saxton's River, Vt.*
Redman, Abbie S., Ellsworth, Me.; m. E. F. Robinson, '67; *Ellsworth, Me.*
Reed, Amelia C., S. Weymouth; m. John W. Field, '67; 10 *Melville Ave., Dorchester.*
Robinson, Frances C., N. Middleboro; m. *Luke B. Noyes, '66; 84 *Pleasant St., Malden.*
Rockwell, Mary F., Southwick; m. Joseph E. Rowell, '72; *Southwick.*
Rogers, Martha H., Wethersfield, Ct.; m. Prof. Henry E. Sawyer, '85; *Tougaloo, Miss.*
Root, Frances C., Madison, N. Y.; m. Jay Cushman, '72; *Madison, N. Y.*
Ross, Charlotte A., Terre Haute, Ind.; m. Jay Cummings, '72; 1103 *S. 3d St., Terre Haute, Ind.*
Royce, Gertrude M., Greensboro, Vt.; m. Wilbur F. Coe, '69; *W. Winsted, Ct.*
Russell, Sarah N., Gaylordsville, Ct.; m. Albert P. Eastman, '69; *Falls Church, Va.*
Sanborn, Mary E., Lake Village, N. H.; d. Lake Village, N. H., '67.
Sanderson, Maria L., Athol; m. Rev. Joel D. Miller, '65; 11 *Washington St., Leominster.*
Shattuck, Emma E., Corning, N. Y.; m. Chas. H. Verrill, Ph.D., '71; *Franklin, N. Y.*
Shattuck, Mary A., Corning, N. Y.; m.Wm. F. Fox. '65; 342 *Hudson Ave., Albany, N.Y.*
Sleeper, Nancy T., Rockland, Me.; *Rockland, Me.*
Smead, Jane W., Shelburne; m. L. L. Pierce, '78; *Manzana, Cal.*
Smith, Eleanor F., S. Dartmouth; m. Jas. R. Howell, Esq., '69; *Blue Blanket, S. Dak.*
Smith, Helen E., Brooklyn, N. Y.; m. David W. Arline, '84; *Waukeenah, Fla.*
Smith, Myra A., S. Hadley Falls; m. Benj. P. Clarke, '70; *E. Granby, Ct.*
Stone, Mary B., Nashua, N. H.; *Egypt.*
Tarbox, Mary M., Brunswick, Me.; 20 *Garden St., Bath, Me.*
Tincker, Helen, Boston;
Tinkham, Phebe H., Acushnet; d. Acushnet, '67.
Trow, Lucy E., Buckland; m. *Nelson Joy. '89; *Shelburne Falls.*
Tubbs, Ella E., Binghamton, N. Y.; 23 *Stuyvesant St., Binghamton, N. Y.*
Turner, Helen M., S. Hadley; m. Fred H. Cook, '66; d. Springfield, '93.

1864.

Tuttle, Laura E., Whippany, N. J. ; m. Leander B. Ford, '66 ; d. Whippany, N. J., '87.
Upham, Ellen P., Brookfield, Vt. ; m. Wm. C. Hopkins, '65 ; d. Eagan, Dak., '83.
Ware, Ella M., E. Townshend, Vt. ; d. E. Townshend, Vt., '64.
Webster, Mariette E., Fly Creek, Ind. ; m. Geo. H. Fisherdick. '64 ; *Palmer.*
Weigley, Anna I., Shafferstown, Pa. ; m. Theodore D. Griswold, '77 ; *Shafferstown, Pa.*
Wheeler, Mary L., Oswego, N. Y. ; m. Niel Gray, '67 ; d. Oswego, N. Y., '87.
White, Lizzie H., Manchester, N. H. ; m. Luther Perkins, Esq., '64 ; *Coffeyville, Kan.*
Whittlesey, Mary E., Northampton ; 72 *West St., Northampton.*
Wicker, Mary W., Ticonderoga, N. Y. ; d. Ticonderoga, N. Y., '65.
Wilkins, Almira C., Fairfield, Me. ; 17 *Beale St., Dorchester.*
Williams, Eusebia S., Boston ; m. Dwight Tuxbury, '66 ; *Windsor, Vt.*
Williston, Clara B. S., Easthampton ; m. Rev. Joseph Lanman, '71 ; 2525 3d *Ave., S., Minneapolis, Minn.*
Wilson, Isabella H., Clyde, N. Y. ; m. Wm. C. Lobenstine, '81 ; 925 *Farragut Sq., Washington, D. C.*
Witherell, Eliza J., Kendall's Mills, Me. ; m. Geo. W. F. Chamberlain, '67 ; 608 *4th Ave., Detroit, Mich.*
Wright, Lucy M., Oroomiah, Persia ; m. Samuel S. Mitchell, '67 ; d. Berlin, Ger., '88.
Wyman, Abbie L., Fitchburg ; m. Wm. Steele, '68 ; *Box 912, San Jose, Cal.*

1865.

GRADUATES.

Aldrich, Eleanor W., E. Douglass ; *E. Douglass.*
Barnes, Jane F., Bath, N. Y. ; m. *Hiram Crandall, Esq., '68 ; m. D. V. Purington, '86 ; 2141 *Calumet Ave., Chicago, Ill.*
Bell, Sarah C., Feeding Hills ; m. Julius A. Morrill, '66 ; *Springfield.*
Boardman, Cornelia L., M.D., Brooklyn, N. Y. ; m. Wm. H. Pulsifer, '81 ; *Newton Centre.*
Carpenter, Ellen E., Willington,Ct. ; m. Elmer E. Phillips, '70 ; 52 *W. 56th St.,N. Y. City.*
Clark, Emily A., Amherst ; m. Rev. Francis H. Boynton, '66 ; 640 *Haverhill St., Lawrence.*
Clark, Mary F., Northampton ; 207 *South St., Northampton.*
Cooley, S. Isabelle, W. Springfield ; *Springfield.*
Dearborn, Annie, Plymouth, N. H. ; m. Rev. Cyrus Richardson, D.D.,'71 ; 6 *Summer St., Nashua, N. H.*
Dodge,Clara A., Concord,N. H. ; m. Edw R. Warner,'66 ; 706 *W. Main St.,Jackson, Mich.*
Edson, Emily M., N. Brookfield ; *Mt. Holyoke College, S. Hadley.*
Ely, Adaline, Freehold, N. J. ; m. Luther R. Smith, Esq., '71 ; d. Bladen Springs,Ala.,'75.
Emerson, Olive J., M.D., Rochester, Vt. ; m. Rev. Horatio Morrow, '76 ; *Tavoy, British Burma, Asia.*
Fellows, Susan G., Deerfield Center, N. H. ; d. Saugus, '81.
Folwell, Katherine L., Kendaia, N. Y. ; m. Morris B. Foster,'70 ; *Hector,Renville Co.,,Minn.*
Forbes, Mary J., Westboro ; m. Rev. Daniel C. Greene, D.D., '69 ; *Tokyo, Japan.*
Guernsey, Fannie O., Alton, Ill. ; d. Kalamazoo, Mich., '84.
Harris, Anna M., Port Byron, N. Y. ; m. S. A. Reeder, M.D., '67 ; 605 *Union St.,Philadelphia, Pa.*
Hodges,Caroline S., Augusta,Me. ; m. Eugene S. Fogg, Esq.,'71 ; 6 *Summer St.,,Augusta,Me.*
Hume, Sarah J., New Haven, Ct. ; 24 *Home Place, New Haven, Ct.*
Johnson, Abby C., Augusta, Me. ; 58 *Winthrop St., Augusta, Me.*
Kendall, Harriet E., Auburn ; d. Prattsville, N. Y., '66.
King, Elizabeth, Morristown, N. J. ; m. H. M. Stevens, '91 ; *St. Albans. Vt.*

1865.

Lane, Annie L., S. New Market, N. H. (now Newfields, N. H.); m. John C. Hanson, '67; *Newfields, N. H.*
North, Mary A., Alexander, N. Y.; d. Attica, N. Y., '75.
Parsons, Julia T., Ludlow; m. *Sumner H. Bodfish,'72; *58 B St., N. E., Washington, D. C.*
Pillsbury, M. Abbie, Hampstead, N. H.; m. Sylvanus Thurman, '92; *Redlands, Cal.*
Porter, Alice, Higganum, Ct.; *50 Colony St., Meriden, Ct.*
Pratt, Mary C., E. Longmeadow; m. *Sidney Kibbe, '77; *E. Longmeadow.*
Read, Eliza J., Huntsville, Ill.; m. Rev. J. T. Sunderland,'71; *4 N. State St., Ann Arbor, Mich.*
Robinson, Lydia S., North Middleboro; *28 Glenwood St., Brockton.*
Sabin, Abbie D., Belchertown; m. Lewis K. Williams, '69; *Kent, O.*
Sampson, Eliza J., Palmyra, N. Y.; d. Palmyra, N. Y., '85.
Simmons, M. Elizabeth, Beloit, Wis.; *703 Broad St., Beloit, Wis.*
Stone, Margarette D., Montpelier, Vt.; *Montpelier, Vt.*
Wells, Delia M., Sandwich; m. Francis M. Tyler, '66; *Auburndale.*
Whipple, Clara E., Chesterfield, Ill.; m. *Melville W. Rew, '67; *Grinnell, Io.*

NON-GRADUATES.

Alden, Eleanor P., Belchertown; d. Mt. Holyoke Seminary, '65.
Allen, Mary A., E. Jaffrey, N. H.; m. Geo. F. Sylvester, '74; *S. Hanover.*
Ballard, Alice G., Provincetown; *N. Bucksport, Me.*
Barker, Anna E., Honeoye Falls, N. Y.; m. Albert W. Keyes, '66; d. Mendon, N.Y., '80.
Bates, Charlotte D., E. Machias, Me.; m. Justin P. Moore; *Box 681, San Rafael, Cal.*
Beals, Sarah A., Angelica, N. Y.; *Federalsburg, Md.*
Belden, Sarah E., Hatfield; d. Hatfield, '65.
Bidwell, Mary E., Monterey; d. Freeport, Ill., '91.
Birdsey, Mary A., Middlefield, Ct.; d. Middlefield, Ct., '80.
Bisbee, Clara L., Worthington; *Westfield.*
Bishop, Alice L., Alton, Ill.; m. Alfred O. Elliott, '87; *Payson, Ariz.*
Bishop, Nancy B., Sprague, Ct.; m. *Chas. W. Carey, '65; *57 Prospect St., Norwich, Ct.*
Brigham, Helen F., Wendell; *165 W. Newton St., Boston.*
Bull, Eunice W., Deep River, Ct.; m. Orson P. Morse, '82; *Olmsteadville, N. Y.*
Burt, Mary F., Springfield; m. *Chas. A. Burnham, '66; d. Norwich, Ct., '71.
Case, Abbie J., Weatogue, Ct.; m. Geo. M. Phelps, '70; *Simsbury, Ct.*
Caswell, Helena A., Portland, Ct.; m. Walter E. Derby, '74; d. N. Y. City, '89.
Converse, Elizabeth S., Norwich, Vt.; *Norwich, Vt.*
Couch, Sarah E., Monterey; d. N. Salem, N. Y., '66.
Craig, Harriet M., Leicester; m. *Geo. Newell Fuller, '66; *Claremont, Cal.*
Dana, Mary A., Cummington; *163 South St., Morristown, N. J.*
Danforth, Rachel H., Jamestown, N. Y.; m. Samuel P. Hedges, M.D., '67; *890 Evanston Ave., Chicago, Ill.*
Darling, Margaret A., Warsaw, N. Y.; m. Jas. W. Chapman, '67; *17 Washington Ave., Elyria, O.*
Dowd, Sarah E., M.D., N. Huron, N. Y.; *Fairport, N. Y.*
Driver, Mary E., W. Philadelphia, Pa.; *Ridley Park, Pa.*
Dubuar, Frances M., Northville, Mich.; m. Edward S. Horton, '68; *294 Merrick Ave., Detroit, Mich.*
Dubuar, Mary C., Northville, Mich.; m. Chas. E. Williams, Esq., '69; d. '93.
Edgerton, J. Elizabeth, Mittineague; m. Wm. I. Rice, '72; d. Springfield, '93.
Eldred, Helen E., Fairhaven; d. Worcester, '74.
Fuller, Emma L., New Baltimore, N. Y.; *New Baltimore, N. Y.*
Gage, J. Luella, Albany, N. Y.;
Grant, Abbie E., Colebrook, Ct.; m. Rev. Almon W. Burr, '69; *Beloit, Wis.*

1865.

Grant, Mary W., Stafford, Ct.; m. Julius Pinney, '68; *Stafford Springs, Ct.*
Hammond, Ellen F., M.D., Killingly, Ct.; m. Sidney M. Gladwin, '80; *705 Asylum Ave., Hartford, Ct.*
Harlow, Ettie, Bellows Falls, Vt.; m. Chas. H. Richards,'69; *242 Oak St., Holyoke.*
Hayward, Clara A., Milford; m. Henry E. Fales, Esq., '67; d. Milford, '86.
Hodges, Lucy S., Torrington, Ct.; m. Fred Wilcox, '71; *Waterbury, Ct.*
Holmes, Harriet A., Elbridge, N. Y.;
Hubbard, Harriet M., Philadelphia, Pa.; m. Henry Osgood, Capt. U. S. A.; *Hancock.*
Hunter, Annie, Paterson, N. J.; m. *Robt. M. Vermilye,'77; *24 Orange St., Brooklyn,N.Y.*
Hunter, Jennie B., Paterson, N. J.; m. Herbert H. Hazard, '74; d. N. Y. City, '74.
Hurlburt, Rebecca C., Winchester Center, Ct.; m. L. Tudor Platt,'72; *113 Berkely Place, Brooklyn, N. Y.*
Hyde, Mary P., N. Y. City;
Johnston, Dorcas H., Sidney Plains, N. Y.; m. A. M. Turner, '71; *Sidney, N. Y.*
Jones, Mary K., Bowling Green, Ky.; *3220 Washington Ave., St. Louis, Mo.*
Kanouse, Theodora C. P., Deckertown, N. J.; *Milford, Pa.*
Kingsley, Fidelia M., Northampton; *Louisville.*
Lampman, Catharine E., Coxsackie, N. Y.; m. *Wm. Burroughs, '67; *Coxsackie, N. Y.*
Laskey, Ann E. M., Wilmington; d. Newburyport, '77.
Lawrence,Sarah W.,Ballston,N. Y.; m. Wm. H. Sherman,'66; *Box 263,Ballston Spa.,N.Y.*
Lee, Martha E., Triangle, N. Y.; m. M. J. Ward, '79; *Unadilla, N. Y.*
Lyman, Sarah M., Northampton; *310 Bridge St., Northampton.*
McAlpine, Dana, San Francisco. Cal.;
McNear, Josephine G., Wiscasset,Me.; m. Alden C. Chaney, '75; *Box 334, Wiscasset,Me.*
Melvin, Louise G., Chester, N. H.; d. Chester, N. H., '65.
Merriam, Martha J., Mason, N. H.; d. N. Y. City, '74.
Monroe, M. Augusta, Chesterfield, Ill.; m. *Wm. H. H. Ibbetson, '66; *Box 743, Carlinville, Ill.*
Nash, Abby H., Granby; m. *Alfred Spitzli, '68; *Florence.*
Newton, Sarah P., Greenfield; *Newport News, Va.*
Palmer, Rachel E., W. Winfield, N. Y.; m. Edward E. Walker, '66; *66 Sheldon St., Grand Rapids, Mich.*
Partridge, C. Adelaide, W. Medway; *1 Trinity Place, Boston.*
Pearson, Grace, Waterville,Me.; m. Sumner A. Gilman,'68; *Forbes Ave., Jamaica Plain.*
Potwine, Mary E., Amherst; *904 Lexington Ave., N. Y. City.*
Powers, Kate W., Amherst; m. Edmund Boltwood, '66; *Ottawa, Kan.*
Randall, Elizabeth P., Orange, N. J.; m. Jos. L. Munn, Esq.,'66; *Munn Ave., E.Orange,N.J.*
Ranney,Phebe A.,W. Townshend,Vt.; m. Theodore Buckingham,'71; d.S. Dover,N. Y.,'80.
Rice, Selina A., Auburn; m. *Simon A. Perrin, '71; *34 John St., Worcester.*
Rich, Mary L., Greenfield; m. Geo. P. Chandler, '68; *715 Asylum Ave., Hartford, Ct.*
Rogers, Caroline C., New Fairfield, Ct.; m. Levi P. Treadwell, '66; d. Danbury, Ct., '91.
Rogers, Charlotte E., New Fairfield, Ct.; m. *Rev. Daniel D. Frost, D.D., '65; d. Olivet, Mich., '91.
Russell, Harriet H., Washington, D. C.; m. Geo. J. Brewer, '72; d. Washington,D.C.,'73.
Sheffield, Sarah F., Suffern, N. Y.; m. Lewis B. Halsey, Esq., '71; *E. Chester, N. Y.*
Skinner, Emily D., Princeton; m. David J. Gregory, '67; *Princeton.*
Smith, Helen M., Middlefield; m. Hon. Francis E. Warren. '71; *Cheyenne, Wyo.*
Smith, Lottie M., Panama, N. Y.; m. Jas. A. Galbraith, '70; d. Warren, Pa., '80.
Stone, Maria S., Montpelier, Vt.; *Montpelier, Vt.*
Swasey, Annette F., Stowe, Vt.; d. Stowe, Vt., '68.
Thomas, Isabella (Collins), Fairport, N. Y.; m. Walter S. Thomas, '63; *Troy, O.*
Tower, Mary N., Springfield, Vt.; m. Fred K. Arnold, '69; *335 Jefferson St., Portland, Or.*

1865.

Underwood, Ellen I., Tolland, Ct. ; d. Brooklyn, N. Y., '75.
Upham. Susan B., Winchendon ; m. Chas. W. Bowker, '71 ; 114 *Elm St., Worcester.*
Ward, Celestia E., Unadilla. N. Y. ; m. Orville L. Ireland, '68 ; *Unadilla, N. Y.*
Watson, Ellen M., New Hartford, Ct. ; 148 *Humphrey St., New Hartford, Ct.*
Welch, Emma A., Norfolk. Ct. ; m. W. S. Walcott, '67 ; *New York Mills, N. Y.*
White, Ellen M., Racine, Wis. ; m. Waldo Dennis, '81 ; 715 *Lake Ave., Racine. Wis.*
Worrell, Maria E., Perrineville, N. J. ; *Manasquan, N. J.*
Wright, Mary C., Easthampton ; *Easthampton.*

1866.
GRADUATES.

Ashley, Lydia L., Chaplin, Ct. ; m. Cassius S. Campbell, '69 ; *Berry. N. H.*
Bacon, D. Antoinette, Gilead, O. ; m. R. K. Carleton, Esq., '69 ; d. River View, N. C., '71.
Ballantine, Anna M., Amherst ; m. Rev. Chas. W. Park, '70 ; *Birmingham, Ct.*
Bardwell, Elisabeth M., Shelburne ; *Mt. Hol. College, S. Hadley ;* home address, *Greenfield.*
Betts, Harriet C., Stamford, Ct. ; m. Rev. Robert R. Kendall, '75 ; *Weymouth Heights.*
Bidwell, Harriet A., Monterey ; d. Monterey, '66.
Blake, Ellen S., Gilmanton, N. H. ; m. Charles A. Bunker, '69 ; *Peacham, Vt.*
Brown, Love L., Fond du Lac, Wis. ; m. Rev. Warren Cochran, '67 ; *Aukeny, Or.*
Bullard, Caroline, Royalston ; m. Prof. Ferdinand Hoffman, '67 ; *Box 96, Stockbridge.*
Burnett, Mary A., Southampton, N. Y. ; *Bridgman Home, Shanghai, W. Gate, China, care of Dr. Reifsnyder ;* home address, *Southampton, N. Y.*
Butterworth, Ann, Foster's Crossings, O. ; m. Thomas Thatcher, '69 ; *Pueblo, Col.*
Church, Julia M., Middlefield ; m. *Edward P. Smith, Ph.D., '68 ; 34 *Boynton St., Worcester.*
Cook, Elizabeth, W. Greenville, Pa. ; m. *James Van Deusen, '66 ; d. Ashley Falls, '92.
Cooper, Lydia A., Rochester, Vt. ; m. *George G. Tilden, '67 ; *Ames, Io.*
Cowles, Louise F., M.A., Norfolk, Ct. ; *Mt. Holyoke College, S. Hadley.*
Curtis, Emily A., Amherst ; *Amherst.*
Dame, Anna A., Exeter, N. H. ; m. Leartus Conner, M.D., '70 ; *cor. Lafayette Ave. and Cass St., Detroit, Mich.*
Davis, Elizabeth D., Pittsfield ; *Pittsfield.*
Day, Lydia D., W. Springfield ; 32 *W. 40th St., N. Y. City.*
Denio, Elizabeth H., Albion, N. Y. ; *Wellesley College, Wellesley.*
Dickinson, Caroline E., Granby ; m. Wm. E. Lincoln. '68 ; *Warren.*
Downs, P. Jane, Upper Aquebogue, N. Y. ; m. Wm. H. Tuthill, '92 ; *Mattituck, N. Y.*
Dyer, Sarah E., N. Somerville ; m. Rev. Isaac Pierson, '77 ; d. Pao-ting-fu, China, '82.
Emmons, Helen I., Deep River, Ct. ; *Deep River, Ct.*
Farwell, Catharine S., Leominster ; m. Jas. Steele, '69 ; 4520 *Lake Ave., Chicago, Ill.*
Gardner, Harriet L., Troy, N. Y. ; m. Edgar K. Betts, '75 ; *Lansingburgh, N. Y.*
Gass, Mary E., Lockport, Ill.; m. Lemuel D. Norton, '73; 1806 *Sheridan Road, Evanston, Ill.*
Harriman, Harriet M., Haverhill ; m. Hon. Wm. E. Blunt, Esq., '70 ; *Haverhill.*
Harris, Phebe E., Phillipsburg, N. J. ; m. *Rev. W. H. Dinsmore, '68 ; *Phillipsburg, N. J.*
Hazelton, Martha E., Beloit, Wis. ; d. Beloit, Wis., '90.
Hazelton, Martha F., Plymouth, N. H. ; *Plymouth, N. H.*
Hill, Cordelia M., New Haven, Ct. ; 75 *Howe St., New Haven, Ct.*
Holcomb, Hanna E., Newtown, Pa. ; *Newtown, Pa.*
Judd, Margaret B., Hunter, N. Y. ; m. *Stanley Gaines, '70 ; m. Smith T. Palmer, '85 ; *Hawley, Pa.*
Ladd, Caroline K., Smyrna, Turkey ; m. Rev. Geo. N. Webber, '71 ; 130 *N. Elm St., Northampton.*

1866.

Lawrence, Anna M., Ballston. N. Y. ; m. Francis Savage, '73; 253 *Main St.. Amesbury.*
Marr, Harriet A., Winthrop, Me. ; m. John S. Adams, '72; *Harvard Ave., Brookline.*
Mascroft, Imogene W., Rockdale ; *Uxbridge.*
Moulton, Susan A., Wakefield, N. H ; m. A. B. Hanna. M.D., '70; *Sardis, Tenn.*
Norcross, Roseltha A., Baldwinsville ; d. Eskizagra, Turkey. '70.
Parsons, Sarah P., Northampton ; *Northampton.*
Perry, Martha, M.D., New Bedford ; *Taunton.*
Perry, Mary M., Roxbury ; 33 *McLean St., Boston.*
Poor, Annie L., Belfast, Me. ; m. Irvin Ayres, '72 ; 1205 *Oak St., Oakland, Cal.*
Reed, Emma L., Ashtabula, O. ; 345 *N. Pennsylvania St., Indianapolis, Ind.*
Renne, Zelma H., Crown Point, N. Y. ; m. Levi B. Carlisle, '72 ; *Chariton, Io.*
Richards, Lydia, Montrose, Pa.; P. O. address, *Montrose, Pa.*
Sheldon, Clara, Granville, O. ; *Granville, O.*
Smith, Martha E., Fort Covington, N. Y.; m. Rev. Chas. S. Billings, '74 ; d. Fort Covington, N. Y., '86.
Snell, Sabra C., Amherst ; *Amherst.*
Spooner, Eliza D., Enfield ; m. Seymour F. Adams, Esq., '71 ; 236 *Superior St., Cleveland, O.*
Stoddard, Sarah T., Oroomiah, Persia ; d. Northampton, '73.
Stone, Jane E., Lyndon, Vt. ; m. F. M. Swift, '71 ; *Olivet, Mich.*
Sylvester, Ida P., Lyons, N. Y. ; m. M. Stout, '69; 34 *E. Monroe St., Chicago, Ill.*
Talcott, Martha R., Rockville, Ct. ; *Rockville, Ct.*
Terry, Mary C., Wading River, L. I.; m. Samuel C. Trubee, '80 ; 279 *Lafayette St., Bridgeport, Ct.*
Tirrell, Almeda N., Nashua, N. H. ; m. J. Gilman McAllister, M.D., '69; 31 *Jackson St., Lawrence.*
Truair, Harriet N.,Syracuse, N. Y.; m. Wm. Hollands, Esq., '67; 18 14*th St., W. Troy, N. Y.*
Warren, Clara J., Westboro; d. Westboro, '77.
Wilson, Josephine M., Holden ; 1258 *Hallett St., Denver, Col.*

NON-GRADUATES.

Allen, Sarah A., Warehouse Point,Ct.; m. Samuel J. Allen, Jr., '78 ; d. Plantsville, Ct.. '82.
Andrews, Harriet N., Bradford, N. H. ; *Melrose.*
Barber, Ella J., Scotland, Ct. ; *Ellington, Ct.*
Barber. Fanny A., Conway ; 1854 *Wellington Ave., Chicago, Ill.*
Battelle, Mary L., Wheeling, W. Va. ; m. Fred. Attwood. '71 ; *Mt. Vernon, Ill.*
Birdsey, Esther C.. Middlefield, Ct. ; m. Henry E. Wilcox, '68 ; *Middlefield, Ct.*
Blanchard, Emily E., W. Concord, N. H. ; m. Henry O. Coolidge, '80; *Keene, N. H.*
Brown, Emma G., Jewett City, Ct. ; d. Griswold, Ct., '75.
Burr, Eliza G., Westport, Ct. ; m. Rev. Geo. W. Ely, '80; d. Columbia, Pa., '88.
Chandler, Josephine E., Northfield, Vt. ; m. Rev. Stephen F. Drew, '66; *Stowe, Vt.*
Chapman, S. Frances, Palmyra, N. Y. ; *Palmyra, N. Y.*
Clarke, Mary A., S. Hadley ; m. Lucius P. Goddard, '68 ; 90 *Elm St., Worcester.*
Clarke, Sarah E., Malta, O. ; m. Wm. A. Brown, '72 ; *State Center, Io.*
Cogswell, Marietta M., Washington, Ct. ; m. Walter Reeves, '76; 206 *E. Kent St., Streator, Ill.*
Colley, Annie M., Portland, Me. ; m. *Jas. Noyes,'74 ; *care Bailey & Noyes, Portland,Me.*
Collier,Sallie, Fort Dodge,Io. ; m. Dr. Henry W. Roby,'83; 118 *W. 6th Ave., Topeka,Kan.*
Cook, Frances A., Hadley ; m. Samuel C. Webber, '66 ; *Hadley.*
Crouch, Julia, Ledyard, Ct. ; m. Joseph Z. Culver, '71 ; d. Rochester. N. Y.. '87.
Cushman, Mary C., Litchfield, N. H. ; d. Mattoon. Ill., '89.
Davis, Amelia M., Brooklyn, N. Y. ;

1866.

Emerson, Mary S., Stratford,Ct. ; m. Rev. Vernon B. Carroll,'71 ; d. Warwick, N. Y.,'81.
Ferry, Cordelia M., Easthampton ; m. Albert P. Russell, '69 ; *Easthampton.*
Fithian, Martha R., Bridgeton, N. J. ; d. Bridgeton, N. J., '01.
Fletcher, Ellen W., Pontiac, Mich. ; d. Frankfort, Mich., '80.
Forbes, Louise E., Westboro ; *Westboro.*
Foster, Ella L., Palmyra, N. Y. ; m. Hudson Johnson ; (Boston?)
Gerrish, Olive A. F., W. Lebanon, Me. ; m. John E. Moody, '66 ; d. Lebanon, Me., '83.
Goldthwait, Mary, Longmeadow ; d. Springfield, '71.
Gouldy, Mary E., Newburgh, N. Y. ; 160 *Montgomery St., Newburgh, N. Y.*
Griffin, Maria H.,Riverhead,N. Y. ; m. *Jas. H. Young, '71 ; *Riverhead,Long Island,N. Y.*
Griggs, Catherine F., Chaplin, Ct. ; m. Edgar S. Lincoln, '68 ; *Chaplin, Ct.*
Grout, Annie L., W. Brattleboro, Vt. ; *W. Brattleboro, Vt.*
Grover, Mary E., Foxboro ; 113 *Waverly St., Providence, R. I.*
Gustin, Anna J., Newton, N. J. ; m. Henry J. Smith, '84 ; d. Loudoun, Va., '85.
Harris, Anna R., E. Putnam, Ct. ; d. Putnam Heights, Ct., '73.
Haskins, Abbie D., Windsor Locks,Ct. ; m Rev. Jas. S. Turnbull,'74 ; d. Hartford,Ct.,'82.
Hayes, Effie M., Derry, N. H. ; *care Rev. Samuel J. Barrows, Dorchester.*
Hewitt, Lucy M., Pomfret, Vt. ; *The Portland, Washington, D. C.*
Howard, Ella C., Orange ; m. Wesley Ford, '76 ; d. Orange, '94.
Howe, Melvina A., Norfolk, Ct. ; 218 *Main St., Hartford, Ct.*
Hunting, Mary A., Shutesbury ; d. Meriden, Ct., '72.
Hurd, Minnie E., Butternuts, N. Y. ; m. Jas. H. Thorp, '69 ; *Gilbertsville, N. Y.*
Ide,Sarah W.,E. Providence,R. I.; m. Rev. Amos Skeele,'71; 131 *Jeff. Ave.,Rochester,N. Y.*
Kelsey, M. Josephine, W. Camden, N. Y. ; m. Oliver P. Clarke, '69 ; *Mt.MacGregor,N. Y.*
Marshall, Helen R., W. Chester, Pa. ; 131 *S. 18th St., Philadelphia, Pa.*
Merrick, Catherine S., Amherst ; *Box 408. Amherst.*
Merrill,F. Gertrude,Bernardston;*care Rev. Truman A. Merrill,*116 *Glenwood St.,Malden.*
Miller, Elizabeth H., Grafton ; *Worcester.*
Monroe, Eliza R., Lexington ; m. Theodore P. Robinson, '68 ; *Lexington.*
Nash, Elizabeth C., Harrington, Me. ; m. Capt. Russell Glover, '74 ; *Harrington, Me.*
Nash, Louise M., Hadley ; m. *Jas. Whitehead, '75 ; *care Mrs. Geo. M. Barker, Redwood City, Cal.*
Noble, Margaret E., Dearborn, Mich. ; m. Fred. A. Hayes, '69 ; *Holyoke.*
Parsons, Fanny S., Nashua, N. H. ; 240 *E. Ohio St., Chicago, Ill.*
Parsons, Maria F., Augusta, Me. ; 107 *Bridge St., Augusta, Me.*
Peck, Fannie M., Shelburne ; m. Clinton E. Barnard, '69 ; d. Shelburne, '79.
Peet, Jane S., Foochow, China ; m. Rev. John Magowan, '68 ; *Amoy, China.*
Poor, Rebecca J., Belfast, Me. ; m. *Wm. A. Bourne, '70 ; *Reno, Nev.*
Porter, Matenah, N. Brookfield ; 19 *Summer St., Haverhill.*
Rawson, Martha L., New Alstead, N. H. ; m. Rev. Alfred F. Marsh, '67 ; *Fairfield, Io.*
Richmond, Catharine A., Mt. Upton, N. Y. ; m. Wm. S. Moore, '66 ; *Mt. Upton, N. Y.*
Rogers, Caroline G., Brunswick, Me. ; m. Henry C. Storm, '74 ; *Buchanan, Mich.*
Rogers, Mary E., Brooklyn, N. Y. ;
Rose, Laura A., Newtown, Pa. ; *Newtown, Pa.*
Sharp, Abbie J., Fort Wayne, Ind. ; m. Frank R. Morton, '69 ; 2009 *San Jose Ave., Alameda, Cal.*
Simpson, Sarah E., Deerfield Center, N. H. ; d. Mt. Holyoke Seminary, '65.
Skinner, Helen W., Toledo, O. ; m. *Chas. N. Dimick, '75 ; 630 *Walnut St., Toledo, O.*
Smith, Eliza H., Enfield ; m. Samuel W. Raymond, '71 ; *Clinton, N. Y.*
Smith, Eunice M., Jaffna, Ceylon ; m. Rev. Elijah Harmon, '72 ; d. Winchester, N. H., '72.
Smith, Laura P., Jaffna, Ceylon ; d. at sea, off coast of Portugal, '72.
Stiles, Alice L., Deckertown, N. J. ; m. Jas. Bennett, '69 ; *Tri States, N. J.*

1866.

Stiles, Emma B., Deckertown, N. J. ; m. Edmund H. Davey, '74 ; 241 *Tonnele Ave., Jersey City Heights, N. J.*
Swift, Anna W., Williamsburg ; m. Herbert T. Quinton, '71 ; *Edna, Kans.*
Taft, Sarah S., Uxbridge ; m. Eugene A. Wheelock, '68 ; *Putnam, Ct.*
Tuck, Anna M., Norwich, Ct. ; 69 *Clarendon St., Springfield.*
Van Duzer, Alida C., Nashville, Tenn. ; m. Edgar D. Marshall ; *Hamlet, O.*
Ware, Ellen L., E. Townshend, Vt. ; 240 *Union St., Springfield.*
Watts, Alice M., Peacham, Vt. ; m. Chas. A. Choate, '68 ; d. Barnet, Vt., '82.
Weed, Frances M.,Geneva, N.Y.; m.Rev. Chas. S. Richardson, D.D., '75; *Little Falls, N. Y.*
Westfall, Mary G., Stephensburg, N. Y.;
White, Dorcas, S. Hadley ; m. Joseph N. Clark, '70 ; d. S. Hadley, '94.
White, Ellen S., Amherst ; d. Northfield, '68.
White, Julia S., Shelburne Falls ; d. Shelburne Falls, '66.
White, Mary R., Butternuts, N. Y. ; m. Rev. Thos. D. Barclay, '72 ; *Kent, Ct.*
Wilcox, Annie M., Middletown, Ct. ; P. O. address, *Meriden, Ct.*
Williams, Alice A., Uxbridge ; m. Horace A. Hapgood, '68 ; d. Uxbridge, '72.
Wright, Ella R., Beloit, Wis. ; m. Oliver J. Stiles, '66 ; 539 *Broad St., Beloit, Wis.*

1867.

GRADUATES.

Baird, Emily J., Milford, Ct. ; *Milford, Ct.*
Bates, Myra E., N. Brookfield ; m. J. M. Barnard, '71 ; 627 *N. Fayette St., Saginaw, Mich.*
Beebe, Lucy J., S. Wilbraham ; m. Z. Aaron French, '78 ; *Holbrook.*
Bennett, Ellen L., Sturbridge ; m. Harrison J. Conant, '72 ; *St. Johnsbury, Vt.*
Biggam, Carrie P., Charleston, N. Y. ; *Fort Plain, N. Y.*
Bills, Allie R., Marshall, Mich. ; 1105 *Bush St., San Francisco, Cal.*
Buckingham, Ella J., Chicago, Ill. ; 104 *S. Market St., Canton, O.*
Buell, Louise M., Litchfield, Ct. ; m. Augustus Jones, M.D , '78; d. Litchfield, Ct., '80.
Bullard, Harriet M., Royalston ; m. Charles S. Bullock, '70 ; *Kill Buck, N. Y.*
Daniels, Mary E., Enfield ; *Enfield.*
Dickinson, Emma E., M.D , Fairport, N. Y. ; *Fairport, N. Y.*
Douglas, Emma, San Jose, Cal. ; 15 *Brainard St., New London, Ct.*
Driver, Susan S., N. Danvers ; 1 *La Grange St., Salem.*
Ferry, Lucy E., Belchertown ; d. Hempstead, N. Y., '82.
Fiske, Louise M., Shelburne ; m. Abraham R. Perkins, '72 ; d. Germantown, Pa., '84.
Francis, Anna E., Windsor, Ct. ; *Windsor, Ct.*
Freeman, Georgiana B., Rockford, Ill. ; d. Rockford, Ill., '89.
French, Laura C., Pittsfield, N. H. ; m. *George B. Smith, '68 ; *Quincy.*
French, Minnie P., Marcellus, N. Y. ; m. *Henry H. Kellogg, '70 ; 3144 *Indiana Ave., Chicago, Ill.*
Gleason, Elizabeth C., Thomaston, Me. ; m. Edson Sanford, '69 ; 44 *Akron St., Meriden, Ct.*
Goodrich, Mary E., Plainville, Ct. ; m. Geo. D. Clarke, '72 ; *Plainville, Ct.*
Gordon, Alice W., M.A., Auburndale ; m. *Alvah B. Kittredge, '70 ; m. Rev. Wm. H. Gulick, '71 ; *Avenida de la Libertad, 40, S in Sebastian, Spain.*
Green, Adaline E., Philadelphia, Pa. ; *Mt. Holyoke College* ; home address, 402 *N. 38th St., Philadelphia, Pa.*
Hitchcock, Julia F., Fitchburg ; m. J. M. Snook, M.D., '77 ; 614 *S. Burdic St., Kalamazoo, Mich.*
Hollister, Mary G., E. Glastonbury, Ct. ; m. Wm. D. Franklin, '88 ; *Rocky Hill, Ct.*

Ingraham, Louise A., Cortland, N. Y.; d. Cortland, N. Y., '68.
Ives, Ella G., New Haven, Ct.; 23 *Allston St., Dorchester.*
Johnson, Anna M., Northfield; m. Thomas H. Browning, '69; d. Westerly, R. I., '72.
Kendall, Clara L., Chicopee Falls; m. Joseph H. Sperry, '75; d. Clinton, Ct., '79.
Knight, Mary H., Racine, Wis.; m. C. E. Jewett, '69; *Bakersfield, Cal.*
Knowles, Vina S., Riverhead, N. Y.; *Valmount, Col.*
Lyon, Mary E., Waukegan, Ill.; 413 *State St., Waukegan, Ill.*
McLean, Hannah B., Simsbury, Ct.; m. *Wm. H. Greeley, '80; *Lexington.*
Marvin, Caroline E., Winchendon; m. Frederick W. Russell, M.D., '72; 18 *Central St., Winchendon.*
Norton, Delia H., Goshen, Ct.; d. Mt. Holyoke Seminary, '67.
Ober, Louise L., La Crosse, Wis.; m. Rockwell E. Osborne, '70; 1022 *Division St., La Crosse, Wis.*
Peabody, Hontas A., Lacon, Ill.; m. Prof. Wm. W. Daniels, '71; *Madison, Wis.*
Peckham, Ella L. T., Providence, R. I.; m. Chas. C. Baldwin, '68; 11 *Cedar St., Worcester.*
Peckham, S. Grace, M.D., Providence, R. I.; m. Chas. H. Murray, '93; 11 *Cedar St., Worcester.*
Pike, Sarah W., Newburyport; *Upland Road, Brookline.*
Plummer, Mary W., Georgetown; m. J. B. Moore; d. Georgetown, '90.
Rice, Anna E., New Haven, Ct.; m. James H. Knapp, '73; d. Allegheny, Pa., '86.
Smith, Elizabeth A., Chester Center; d. Huntington, '85.
Smith, Frances E., Union, Wis.; m. Thos. J. Alsop, '70; *Brooklyn, Wis.*
Southworth, S. Jane, Wethersfield, Ct.; m. Rev. T. Clayton Welles, '72; 27 *Cedar St., Taunton.*
Stewart, Sarah A., Baraboo, Wis.; 1520 *Chestnut St., Philadelphia, Pa.*
Stoughton, Anna E., Gill; m. George R. Bliss, '71; 10 *Congress St., Worcester.*
Thorndike, Clara I., Belfast, Me.; m. Edward Sibley, '69; 18 *High St., Belfast, Me.*
Washburn, Annette D., Jersey City, N. J.; *Box 116, Atlantic City, N. J.*
Watson, Susan C., Sing Sing, N. Y.; m. A. B. Clarke, '71; *Box 637, Des Moines, Io.*
Wells, Annie M., Lyndon, Vt.; *Huguenot Sem., Wellington, S. Africa.*
Wheeler, Clara E., Peterboro, N. H.; m. Chas. A. S. Troup, '71; 31 *Claremont Park, Boston.*
Whitcomb, Susan A., E. Randolph; 34 *Bible House, N. Y. City.*
Williams, Emily A., Uxbridge; d. Uxbridge, '73.
Williams, Julia S., Windsor, Ct.; *Windsor, Ct.*
Wilson, Jane M., Holden; m. James L. Oakes, '72; d. Denver, Col., '81.
Worrell, Anna M., Perrineville, N. J.; m. Wm. H. Pancoast, '74; 262 *Hodge Ave., Cleveland, O.*

NON-GRADUATES.

Andruss, Lizzie C., Newark, N. J.; m. Benj. R. Hillman, '71; 1612 *Park Ave., Philadelphia, Pa.*
Bassett, M. Louise, W. Cambridge;
Beebe, Clara S., E. Longmeadow; m. Geo. Fred Clark, '71; 115 *William St., Springfield.*
Billings, Hattie E., Arlington, Vt.; 158 *W. 23d St., N. Y. City.*
Blodgett, Susan G., Greenwich; m. *Samuel F. Crowell, '75; 10 *Newbury St., Roslindale.*
Brigham, Elizabeth M., Rindge, N. H.; *Ashburnham.*
Brown, Amelia M., Leicester; m. Henry L. Watson, '67; d. Fitchburg, '74.
Brown, Jane S., Norristown, Pa.; m. Jas. M. Hewett, '70; *Greenbush, Kan.*
Buell, Florence A., Litchfield, Ct.; d. Litchfield, Ct., '77.
Bullard, Lucy A., Royalston; d. Stockbridge, '77.
Callahan, Amelia, Newport, R. I.; m. Wm. Dame, '69; d. Lynn, '92.

1867.

Carpenter, Frances A., E. Providence, R. I.; m. Hon. Geo. N. Bliss, Esq.,'72; 19 *College St., E. Providence, R. I.*
Case, Lucy L., W. Winsted, Ct.; d. W. Winsted, Ct., '67.
Chase, Eleanor F., Boston; 73 *W. 105th St., N. Y. City.*
Clark, Lucy A., Williston, Vt.; m. Edward M. Carey, '72; d. '96.
Cleaveland, Abbie D., Moorheadville, Pa.; m. A. N. Elliott, '73; *Minneapolis, Minn.*
Cobleigh, Lizzie, Littleton, N. H.; m. Rev. Royal M. Cole, '68; *Billis, Turkey in Asia.*
Connor, S. Alice, Scotchtown, N. Y.; *Middletown, N. Y.*
Crosby, Elizabeth M., Rondout, N. Y.; m. Rev. Wm. F. Basten, '68; d. Troy, Pa., '91.
Crossett, Rosetta E., Northampton; m. Geo. H. Troutman, '70; 163 *N. Church St., Hazleton, Pa.*
Cunningham, Lucy O., Richmond, Mo.; m. Joseph A. Wickham, '72; *Gallatin, Mo.*
Davis, Anna E., Brooklyn, N. Y.;
Davis, M. Belle, Roxbury;
Dickinson, Clara E., S. Hadley; m. J. W. Watson, '87; *Melrose.*
Driver, Louise E., Philadelphia, Pa.; m. *Chas. F. Cheney, '77; *Ridley Park, Pa.*
Ellis, M. Abbie, Fitchburg; *Newton Centre.*
Emerson, Eunice E., Rochester, Vt.; *Rochester, Vt.*
Farnham, Annette E., S. Bridgeton, Me.; m. Robert A. Barnard, '72; *S. Bridgeton, Me.*
Fidler, Julia C., Womelsdorf, Pa.; m. Geo. H. Valentine; *Womelsdorf, Pa.*
Fisk, Fidelia J., Waitsfield, Vt.; d. Waitsfield, Vt., '67.
Ford, Mary E., Gallipolis, O.; 294 *State St., Bridgeport, Ct.*
French, Sarah E., New Market, N. H.; m. Wm. P. Reynolds, '74; 28 *Wigglesworth St., Somerville.*
Fritcher, Julia, Syracuse, N. Y.; m. Albert J. Riegel, '73; d. Buffalo, N. Y., '91.
Frost, Maria A., Granby, Canada East; m. Rev. H. Hammond Cole, '74; *San Francisco, Cal.*
Gilbert, Mary L., Warren; m. Joseph Santon, '87; *Warren.*
Goodnow, Martha, Grafton, Vt.; home address, *Springfield, Vt.*
Harris, Delphine M., Phillipsburg, N. J.; m. George K. McMurtrie, '72; *Belvidere, N. J.*
Hayden, Julia B., Windsor Locks, Ct.; m. *Edwin D. Dexter, '58; *Nashua, N. H.*
Hewitt, Mary B. W., Pomfret, Vt.; m. *John J. Myers; 31 *The Portland, Washington, D.C.*
Horton, Lucy W., Barrington, R. I.; m. Richard M. Anthony, '76; 964 *18th St., Oakland, Cal.*
Johnson, Margery R., Fredericton, N. B.; *Ottawa, Ont.*
Keith, Gertrude A., Northfield, Vt.; *All Healing, N. C.*
Kellogg, Mary S., Gatesville, N. C.; m. Wm. Beaman, '84; *Sunbury, Gates Co., N. C.*
King, Fanny A., Morristown, N. J.; 112 *Washington St., Morristown, N. J.*
Kinsman, M. Rosannah, Princeton, Ill.; *Winterset, Io.*
Kirke, Annie M., Booth's Corner, Pa.; *Booth's Corner, Pa.*
Lawrence, Mira B., Castine, Me.; m. *Willard R. Burr, '86; 230 *Kingsbury Av., Gloversville, N. Y.*
McNaughton Elizabeth W., Mercersburg, Pa.; m. O. A. Thurman, '71; *New Wilmington, Pa.*
Merrifield, Orinda, Townshend, Vt.; m. John J. Dale, '73; d. Bethel, Me., '79.
Mills, Frances C., Ulster, Pa.; m. *Carr W. Dayton, '76; 317 *S. 11th St., Philadelphia, Pa.*
Moore, Melvina M., Windham. Vt.; d. Green Spring, O., '70.
Morse, Calista S., Royalston; m. Geo. H. Wood, '73; *Tangerine, Orange Co., Fla.*
Munn, Margaretta B., Chatham, N. J.; m. William H. Lum, '69; d. Chatham, N. J., '82.
Norris, Lucy G., Canso, N. S.; m. Wm. D. McKenzie, M.D., '87; *Inglewood, Cal.*
Page, Flora F., Greenfield; m. Spencer A. Jones, '79; *Federal St., Greenfield.*
Parmelee, Emily S., Toledo, O.; m. Franklin Moore, '73; *St. Clair, Mich.*
Pease, Henrietta M., Somers, Ct.; m. George E. Stackpole, M.D., '71; 118 *Salem St., Malden.*
Pratt, M. Ella, Yarmouth, Me.; m. Henry C. Houghton, M.D., '68; 12 *W. 39th St., N. Y. City.*
Prescott, Helen, Okoboji, Io.; m. E. Branson Cowgill, '69; d. Great Bend, Kans., '74.

1867.

Reid, Ellen E., E. Providence, R. I.; m. Sidney Goldsborough; 2445 *Lincoln Ave., Denver, Col.*
Rice, Mary W., Boston; m. Frank Waterman, '70; 1426 *S. 28th St., Omaha, Neb.*
Root, Mary A., Whitehall, N. Y.; 3554 *Lindell Ave., St. Louis, Mo.*
Rymph, Jane E., Pleasant Plains, N. Y.; d. Hyde Park, Ill., '71.
Sargent, Ellen H., Hopkinton, N. H.; 1105 *Jackson Boul., Chicago, Ill.*
Savage, Ruth F., New Market, N. H.; m. Channing Folsom, '70; 98 *Silver St., Dover, N. H.*
Southworth, Clara B., S. Dartmouth; m. J. Lowell French, '68; 45 *Vernon St., Brockton.*
Swinerton, Alice, Danvers Center; d. Danvers, '72.
Tenbrook, Ellen C., Lockport, N. Y.; m. Rev. M. E. Hayne, '69; *Greenfield, Mich.*
Tidd, Esther M., Lexington; m. *Hayward Barrett, '68; home address, *N. Waterford, Me.*
Trask, Abbie J., Leicester; 40 *Woodland St., Worcester.*
Underhill, Anna F., Stockton, Cal.; m. Rev. John Hart, '73; *Neshanic, N. J.*
Upton, Dora L. F., Shelburne Falls; m. Chas. H. Ballard, '74; *E. Charlemont.*
Walker, Mary E., Fryeburg, Me.; m. John T. Whitehouse, '70; 6748 *Emerald Ave., Chicago, Ill.*
Ware, Belle F., Townshend, Vt.; m. John B. Jopson, '68; 15 *Foster St., New Haven, Ct.*
Washburn, Celia G., Elyria, O.; m. Henry L. Lathrop, '75; *Samuels Ave., Fort Worth, Tex.*
Wear, Martha J., Pittston, Pa.; m. Jacob A. Schoonover, '69; d. *Pocahontas, Ark., '78.*
Wells, Maria T., Deerfield Center, N. H.; m. John L. Stevens, '82; *Deerfield Center, N. H.*
Whitney, Eugelia M., Keene, N. H.; m. Chas. H. Shepley, '81; *Waverly House, Boston.*
Whittlesey, Jane E., Newington, Ct.; m. Geo. S. Deming, '68; 38 *Church St., Middletown, Ct.*
Wilcox, Myrtie S., Deep River, Ct.; *Deep River, Ct.*
Williams, Anna A., Ashfield; d. Ashfield, '68.
Williams, Margaret, Pittsburgh, Pa.; d. Cincinnati, O., '80.
Wood, Harriet S., Ware; m. Charles B. Holton; 36 *Boylston St., Springfield.*

1868.

GRADUATES.

Anderson, Martha A., M.D., Shelburne; *Shelburne.*
Badgley, Jane M., Waterloo, N. Y.; 2930 *Thomas St., St. Louis, Mo.*
Bailey, Louisa M., Wadham's Mills, N. Y.; m. Rev. J. F. Whitney, '71; *Coventryville, N. Y.*
Baker, Isabella C., Wiscasset, Me.; m. Rev. Wm. R. Stocking, '73; d. Williamstown, '90.
Beach, M. Agnes, New Milford, Ct.; m. Joseph B. Merwin, '74; *New Milford, Ct.*
Bedortha, Mary L., Saratoga Springs, N. Y.; m. Albert A. Wright, '74; d. Oberlin, O., '77.
Carrington, E. Justine, Bethany, Ct.; m. *Frank L. Coe, '73; *Bethany, Ct.*
Carrington, H. Josephine, Bethany, Ct.; m. Herbert W. Beecher, '71; m. H. Bogigian, '88; *cor. Park and Beacon Sts., Boston.*
Clark, Cornelia D., Chicopee; d. Chicopee, '85.
Close, Frances H., Croton Falls, N. Y.; *Croton Falls, N. Y.*
Cochrane, Elizabeth, Ripley, N. Y.; m. Milton W. Little, '77; *Eureka, Kan.*
Coffin, Sarah W., Edgartown; m. Thomas Barrows, '69; d. Chicago, Ill., '70.
Conner, Olivia, Scotchtown, N Y.; d. Scotchtown, N. Y., '83.
Curtis, Anna F., Portland, Me.; m. *Roscoe W. Turner, '73; d. Portland, Me., '83.
Davis, Mary G., Pittsfield; m. Hon. Francis W. Rockwell, '73; 75 *Appleton Ave., Pittsfield.*
Dickinson, L. Jane, Amherst; m. Rev. Henry N. Conden, '78; d. Chatham, N. Y., '84.
Durham, Elizabeth, Beloit, Wis.; m. Nehemiah Mead, '71; *Akron, Io.*
Durham, Sophia, Beloit, Wis.; 3614 *Rhodes Ave., Chicago, Ill.*
Ellis, Edith M., S. Hadley Falls; m. Francis M. Tinkham, '78; 63 *School St., Springfield.*
Eno, H. Annette, Simsbury, Ct.; m. Rufus F. Bond, '80; *Sterling, Kan.*
Farnham, Mary F., S. Bridgton, Me.; *S. Bridgton, Me.*

1868.

Fisher, Annah F., Chicago, Ill. ; m. S. R. Ward, M.D., '71 ; 159 *Oakwood Boul., Chicago, Ill.*
Gallup, Sarah B., Collamer, Ct. ; m. Gideon G. Tillinghast, '79 ; *Vernon, Ct.*
Gilson, H. Juliette, Milford, N. H. ; *Walpole, N. H.*
Jefts, Mary P., Drewsville, N. H. ; 6 *William St., Worcester.*
Johnson, Mary C., Augusta, Me. ; m. Hon. Henry S. Webster, '76 ; *Gardiner, Me.*
Kelsey, Adaline D. H., M.D., W. Camden, N. Y. ; *West Camden, N. Y.*
Kent, Ruth A., Leicester ; m. Rev. M. M. Tracy, '76 ; d. Detroit. Minn., '78.
Merrill, Elizabeth F., Norway, Me. ; 97 *Ocean St., Dorchester.*
Moody, Ellen L., Belchertown ; m. Elliott J. Aldrich ; *Granby.*
Mudge, Clara H., Danvers Center ; m. Geo. W. French, '71 ; 36 *Magnolia St., Roxbury.*
Nims, Delia, Greenfield ; *Greenfield.*
Nolton, Julia E., Holland Patent, N. Y. ; m. Myron G. Willard, '70 ; d. Mankato, Minn., '76.
Paige, Cordelia, Bennington Center, Vt. ; *Box 318, Williamstown.*
Peabody, Lavinia, Virden, Ill. ; m. *Rev. Geo. Pearce, '77 ; *Ootacamund, Nilgiri Hills, S. India.*
Porter, Augusta A., Hatfield ; m. Myron C. Graves, '94 ; 44 *Morgan St., Springfield.*
Powers, Harriet G., Antioch, Syria ; *Bardezag, Turkey.*
Reed, Emily W., Camden, N. J. ; 316 *N. 37th St., Philadelphia, Pa.*
Savage, Helen M., Stowe, Vt. ; m Rev. Albert H. Ball, '70 ; *Anderson, Ind.*
Sawyer, Annie E., Boxford ; m. J. F. Black, '80 ; *Russellville, Ala.*
Smith, Julia Sophia, Manlius, N. Y. ; m. John Manier, '75 ; 199 *Main St., Binghamton, N. Y.*
Thompson, Ella J., Pownal Center, Vt. ; m. A. M. Wilmarth, '90 ; *Stamford, Vt.*
Whitaker, Isabelle, Deckertown, N. J. ; m. Theo. F. Margarum, '72 ; *Deckertown, N. J.*
Williams, Mary, Pittsburgh, Pa. ; m. B. H. Williams, '69 ; *Amherst.*
Williams, Sarah J., M.D., Orange, N. J. ; *Becket.*

NON-GRADUATES.

Adams, Irene F., Lynn ; m. Rev. Edwin A. Withey, '70 ; *Dondo, Angola, Africa.*
Andrews, Frances M., St. Stephen, N. B. ; *Fisk University, Nashville, Tenn.*
Arms, Gertrude G., Bellows Falls, Vt. ; m. Stephen T. Searle, '76 ; d. Bellows Falls, Vt., '79.
Baker, Abbie W., Charlestown, N. H. ; d. Charlestown, N. H., '69.
Barber, Florence I., Canton Center, Ct. ; m. Sherman E. Brown, '68 ; *Collinsville, Ct.*
Barron, Frances G., Topsham, Me. ; *Brunswick, Me.*
Barron, Olive M., Topsham, Me. ; *Brunswick, Me.*
Barry, Mary A., Saxton's River, Vt. ; 69 *Atkinson St., Bellows Falls, Vt.*
Barton, Caroline A., N. Sidney, Me. ; m. Edwin H. Robbins, '78 ; *Sanford, Me.*
Beebe, Sarah H., Litchfield, Ct. ; m. Moses Lyman, '73 ; d. Waverley, N. Y., '91.
Benedict, Flora, Sharon, Ct. ; m. *Clark M. Juckett, '68 ; m. Chas. W. Rhynus, '93 ; *Sharon, Ct.*
Benson, Frances H., Beloit, Wis. ; *School for the Blind, Janesville, Wis.*
Berry, Ella A., Gardiner, Me. ; m. Dr. J. S. Burton, '93 ; 879 *Windsor Ave., Hartford, Ct.*
Bertolet, Elizabeth M., Oley, Pa. ; m. Monroe Heilig, '73 ; *Pine Iron Works, Pa.*
Billings, Abbie L., E. Arlington, Vt. ; m. *Prof. Ernest I. W. Mildner, '77 ; *Princeton, N. J.*
Bishop, Charlotte A., Windsor, Vt. ; m. W. T. Nickerson, '85 ; *Melrose.*
Boyd, Caroline B., Marlboro ; 7 *Pleasant St., Marlboro.*
Brigham, Henrietta M., Marlboro ; 70 *Pleasant St., Marlboro.*
Brown, C. Ida, Uxbridge ; m. Herbert E. Crosswell, '84 ; 69 *Beacon Ave., Providence, R. I.*
Campbell, Mary J., N. Harpersfield, N. Y. ; m. *Joseph A. Douglass, '71 ; *Davenport, N. Y.*
Canfield, Ida G., Athens, Pa. ; m. T. P. Simmons Wilson, '83 ; 550 *E. 3d St., Williamsport, Pa.*
Chamberlain, Katharine S., Auburn ; m. Homer E. Pierce, '69 ; *Brooklyn, N. Y.*
Chapman, Emeline E., Deep River, Ct. ; d. Deep River, Ct., '73.

1868.

Childs, Mary A., Henniker, N. H. ; m. Francis E. Prendergast, '73; *Redlands, Cal.*
Chisholm, Margaret E., Chazy, N. Y. ; m. Bradner F. Bean, '71 ; *Sioux Falls, S. Dak.*
Clarke, Elizabeth M , S. Hadley ; d. S. Hadley, '78.
Clarke, Mary L., Wellesley ; 458 *Milwaukee St., Milwaukee. Wis.*
Clifford, Ella P., Lowell ; m. Frank J. Ladd, '69 ; 100 *Fairmount St., Lowell.*
Converse, Rose S., Monson ; m. Henry S. Gould, '74 ; 465 *Vanderbilt Ave., Brooklyn, N. Y.*
Cowles, Elizabeth A., Plainville, Ct. ; *Plainville, Ct.*
Cowles, Phebe A., Plainville, Ct. ; m. Howard Tyler, '72 ; *Plainville, Ct.*
Cross, Annie G., Springfield ; m. Chas. W. Morse, '74 ; 24 *School St., Brookline.*
Cummings, Marietta, Springfield ; m. *Russell S. Root, '71 ; 9 *Mansfield St., Allston.*
Cutter, Isabel P., Peterboro, N. H. ; m. Albert W. Noone, '68 ; d. Peterboro, N. H., '71.
Dean, Anna L., Foxboro ; *Foxboro.*
Dunham, Jennie A., Manlius, N. Y. ; m. Newton H. Curtis, M.D., '80 ; *Manlius. N. Y.*
Dunham, Mary A., Boston ;
Edwards, Ellen M., Chesterfield ; m. Frank P. Searle, '58 ; 18 *Day Ave., Westfield.*
Farrar, Julia C., Lincoln ; m. *A. Prescott Sherman, '72 ; m. H. Winslow Warren, '84 ; 77 *Rockview St., Jamaica Plain.*
Fiske, Hattie A., Shelburne ; *Arlington.*
Fiske, Mary E., Conway ; *Conway.*
Fogle, Mary L., Canton, O. ; *care Bank of D. O. Mills & Co., Sacramento, Cal.*
French, Clara A., Virden, Ill. ; m. Robert W. Vasey. '74 ; 536 *W. Jackson St., Chicago, Ill.*
Fritcher, Ellen, Syracuse, N. Y. ; m. Isaac P. Burr, Jr., '68 ; d. Cedar Rapids, Io., '87.
Frost, Susan T., Belmont ; m. Geo. H. Andruss, '82 ; 1041 *M St., Fresno, Cal.*
Furey, Ellen P., Canton. Pa. ; m. Chas. S. Riley, '70 ; *Belvidere, N. J.*
Garland, Jane P., Franklin, N. H. ; m. Jas. K. Hosmer, '78 ; 3418 *Lucas Ave., St. Louis. Mo.*
Gerst, Sophronia D., Brooklyn, N. Y. ; m. *Geo. B. F. Hinckley, '75 ; *Providence, R. I.*
Goodwin. Annie E., Augusta, Me. ; m. Alden Potter, '69 ; 32 *Oak St., Bath, Me.*
Graves, Ella M., Hatfield ; d. Hatfield, '89.
Gurney, Mary P., New Braintree ; m. Stephen O. Brown, '71 ; *Dover, Me.*
Howe. Annie S., Marlboro ; *Marlboro.*
Kellogg, Ella M., Syracuse, N. Y. ; m. Geo. D. Whedon, M.D., '70 ; 350 *W. Onondaga St., Syracuse, N. Y.*
Kimball, Lucy J., W. Boxford ; *Andover.*
Kingsley, Mary E. ; m. Wm. B. Orcutt, '73 ; d. Northampton, '93.
Kittredge, Maria A., Westboro ; m. Jona. E. Forbes, '70 ; 115 *W. 5th St., Ottawa, Kan.*
Knowlton, H. Orianna, E. Douglass ; m. Patrick Flynn, '81 ; *Independence, Io.*
McKillip, Margaret C., Westminster, Md. ; *Westminster, Md.*
Merrill, Clara F., Athens, Pa. ; m. Edward E. Murray, '69 ; d. Sellwood, Or., '93.
Montague, Alice L., Belchertown ; m. *J. Osmun Kendall, '70 ; *Belchertown.*
Morse, Mary E., E. Douglass ; m. O. D. Aldrich, '72 ; *Woonsocket, R. I.*
Morton, Clara W., Hatfield ; m. Frank W. Wood, '72 ; 179 *23d St., Milwaukee, Wis.*
Oakman, J. Kate, Montague ; *Montague City.*
Otis, Luella A., Kingston, N. Y. ; m. A. T. Beaman, '73 ; d. Princeton, '76.
Palmer, Louise M., Gardiner, Me. ; m. *Hiram Wait, '68 ; d. '94.
Perry, Marion E., Canton ; m. Jas. W. Farwell, '81 ; 20 *Lawrence St., Wakefield.*
Pierce, Anna K., Brooklyn, N. Y. ; m. Geo. M. Mackenzie, '75 ; *Muscatine, Io.*
Pierce, Emma L., Royalston ; m. Marshall V. Stow, '88 ; *Granville Centre.*
Pierce, R. Ellen, Andover, Vt. ; m. Rev. Paul H. Pitkin, '69 ; 620 *Chestnut St., Springfield.*
Pratt, Adaline M., Shrewsbury ; m. *Lyman Mason, '72 ; m. Geo. W. Berriam, '84 ; *Buena Vista, Col.*
Reed, Anna S., Camden, N. J. ; 316 *N. 37th St., Philadelphia, Pa.*
Rule, Selina A., Arlington, Vt. ; *Burlington, N. J.*

1868.

Sabin, Helen A., Bellows Falls, Vt. ; m. Rev. Earl J. Ward, '73; d. Hyde Park, Vt., '89.
Sanders, Ellen F., Derry, N. H. ; d. Boston, '82.
Smith, Emma E., Hadley ; m. G. Frank Smith, '71 ; *Hadley.*
Smith, Harriet E., W. Haven, Ct. ; m. Fredrique R. Lewis, '89 ; *W. Haven. Ct.*
Smith, Virginia A., W. Meriden, Ct. ; m. Marca B. West, '69; 1014 *N. 13th St., Fort Smith, Ark.*
Stanley, Emily E., Bellville, Ala. ; m. R. J. McCreary, '69 ; d. Bellville, Ala., '70.
Stockbridge, S. Estella, Amherst ; *Amherst.*
Sutherland, Ida E., Easthampton ; *Easthampton.*
Sutton, Adelia W., St. George's, Del. ; m. Wm. Weaver, '70; *N. Y. City.*
Taft, Emoretta M., Keene, N. H. ; m. Cadman D. Robertson ; 18 *Summer St., Keene, N. H.*
Thayer, Clara, Peterboro, N. H. ; m. Henry M. Shepard, '75; 134 *Main St., Winchester.*
Thompson, Mary E., Peru ; m. Chas. McFarland, '90 ; 4 *Congress St., Worcester.*
Thurston, Arista, St. Joseph, Mo.; "removed from St. Joseph about 1870."
Tiffany, Rachel A., Barrington, R. I.; *Barrington, R. I.*
Tracy, Jane, E. Smithfield, Pa.; d. E. Smithfield, Pa., '72.
Webster, Sarah P., Chester, N. H.; *Chester, N. H.*
Wells, Ella A., Keene, N. H.; d. Mt. Holyoke Seminary, '68.
Wells, Marie E., Brooklyn, N. Y.; m. Terence Jacobson, '72 ; 99 *Lincoln Place, Brooklyn, N. Y.*
Wiggins, E. Gertrude, Unionville, N. Y.; 9 *Washington St., Middletown, N. Y.*
Woodbury, Emma C., Sweden, Me.; m. Francis F. Chandler, '71; *Bethel, Me.*
Wright, Mary J., S. Hadley ; m. R. Morrison Smith, '75; *S. Hadley.*
Yale, Caroline A., Williston, Vt.; *Clarke Institute, Northampton.*

1869.

GRADUATES.

Alden, Harriet E., Belchertown ; *Belchertown.*
Bradford, Martha E. E., McIndoes Falls, Vt.; m. Oscar Gilchrist, M.D., '76 ; 79 *Center St., Rutland, Vt.*
Bradley, Sarah E., Gardiner, Me.; 13 *Mason St., Gloucester.*
Burgess, Abbie L., Ahmednagar, India ; m. Rev. Robert A. Hume, '74 ; d. Mahabaleshwar, India, '81.
Burgess, Mary P., Ahmednagar, India ; d. Hudson, N. Y., '92.
Cahoon, Jane, Canton, N. Y.; m. F. G. Rosa, '73 ; 103 *N. Front St., Grand Rapids, Mich.*
Campbell, Theresa M., N. Harpersfield, N. Y.; *Wellington, Cape Good Hope, S. Africa.*
Cobbe, Jennie R., Springfield; m. *Henry J. D. Schermerhorn, '89 ; 195 *Walnut St., Springfield.*
Collins, Helen F., Westfield ; m. Austin P. Cary, '81 ; 16 *Day Ave., Westfield.*
Coy, Sarah L., Sandusky, O.; m. Rev. Loren F. Berry, '78 ; *Ottumwa, Io.*
Dame, Celia A., Exeter, N. H.; m. Wm. H. Hoole, '71 ; 77 *A. Monroe St., Brooklyn, N. Y.*
Dickey, Sarah A., Dayton, O.; *Mt. Hermon Sem., Clinton, Miss.*
Everett, Eleanor M., Sturbridge ; m. Alonzo S. Kimball, Ph.D., '71 ; 28 *Boynton St., Worcester.*
Frissell, Seraph, M.D., Peru ; 796 *State St., Springfield.*
Hatch, Frances H., Castine, Me.; m. Chas. Q. Eldredge, '86; *French American College, Springfield.*
Hathaway, Martha N., Skowhegan, Me.; 138 *N. Hill St., Los Angeles, Cal.*
Hitchcock, Mary E., New Haven, Ct.; d. New Haven, Ct., '71.

Hodgdon, P. Elizabeth, Campton, N. H.; m. Rev. Lester H. Elliot, '75; *Waterbury, Vt.*
Hood, Anna M., Springfield; m. Lucius E. Hall, '74; 78 *E. 1st North St., Salt Lake City, Utah.*
Hunt, Ariana L., St. John, N. B.; care *Miss F. E. Washburn, 22 Oakland St., Medford.*
Kuhn, Anna R., Salem, O.; m. Rev. Willis Weaver, '74; *Elm Grove, Mo.*
Leonard, Anne R., Southbridge; 5 *Chestnut St., Boston.*
Lovell, Martha E., Alstead, N. H.; m. *Sumner T. Smith, M.D. '72; *Athol.*
Mudge, Pamelia J., Danvers Center; m. Rev. Daniel H. Colcord, '81; *Claremont, Cal.*
Phelps, Frances L., Norfolk, Ct.; *Collinsville, Ct.*
Robinson, Mary J., Willimantic, Ct.; *Pomona College, Claremont, Cal.*
Rowland, Mary S., Springfield; m. *Henry L. Wilcox, '77; 97 *Catharine St., Springfield.*
Sanborn, Mary J., Newport, N. H.; m. Rev. George H. Ide, '71; d. Hopkinton, '75.
Sears, Sarah E., Ashfield; m. Rev. John F. Smith, '85; *Marsovan, Turkey.*
Smith, Alice E., Granby; m. Edward S. White, Esq., '74; d. Hartford, Ct., '83.
Smith, Charlotte E., Geneva, N. Y.; m. Rev. O. L. Fisher, '81; 2554 *16th St., Denver, Col.*
Thompson, Mary N., Peterboro, N. H.; *Orphan Asylum, Hartford, Ct.*
Warner, Anna E., Jericho Center, Vt.; *Jericho Center, Vt.*
Washburn, Cassandra V., Abington; m. Rev. Michael Burnham, D.D., '71; *3844 Delmar Boul., St. Louis, Mo.*
Washburn, Frances E., Medford; 22 *Oakland St., Medford.*
Wilson, Ellen L., Rockville, Ct.; *Rockville, Ct.*
Wright, Elizabeth P., Northampton; m. Edward S. Niles, '8); 561 *Boylston St., Boston.*

NON-GRADUATES.

Adams. Emma, Amherst; d. Lebanon, Ct., '78.
Allen, Martha B., Oakham; *Great Barrington.*
Babcock, Maria L., Collinsville, Ct.; m. *Myron W. Thompson, '70; *Hillsdale. N. Y.*
Banning, Mary P., Deep River, Ct.; *Deep River, Ct.*
Barton, Mary E., N. Sidney, Me.; m. M. D. Rittgers, '75; *Ridgedale, Io.*
Blaisdell, Doll H., Springfield; m. Caleb C. Buswell, '83; *Salisbury.*
Blake, Harriet F., Exeter, N. H.; m. Edward J. Cram, '87; *Exeter, N. H.*
Blakslee, Amanda H., Sing Sing, N. Y.; m. Hiram H. Post, '74; *Carthage, Mo.*
Brown, M. Agnes, Newark, N. J.; m. Wm. A. Huff, '70; 116 *Miller St., Newark, N. J.*
Buck, Mary H., N. Y. City; d. Lamington, N. J., '86.
Child, Sarah A., McIndoes Falls, Vt.; m. *Daniel M. Elliot, M.D.,'70; m. John Hare,'89; d. Tallahassee, Fla., '93.
Clark, Alice E., Washington, Ct.; m. Clarence B. Logan, '79; 13 *Whittlesey Ave., New Milford, Ct.*
Codding, Thirza M., Waterville, Vt.; m. Chas. A. Cutting, '82; *Middletown, Va.*
Cooke, M. Sophie, Hanover, N. J.; *Hanover, N. J.*
Crosby, Angeline M., Mankato, Minn.; m. Wm. M. Sanders,'74; *Box 162,Pacific Grove,Cal.*
Dearborn, Elizabeth, Plymouth, N. H.; m. Geo. G. Bulfinch, M.D., '78; 72 *Dudley St., Roxbury.*
Dewing, Caroline E., N. Chelsea; *Broadway, Revere.*
Dickerman, Alice A., Mt. Carmel, Ct.; m. Wm. DeF. Cook, '90; *Box 677, Meriden, Ct.*
Dudley, Katharine M., Guilford, Ct.; *Guilford, Ct.*
Dunning, Mary O., New Haven, Ct.; m. Chas. H. Leavy, '79; *Kansas City, Mo.*
Egleston, Zernah E., Pompey, N. Y.; m. *Almanzor Hutchinson, Jr., '72; m. Samuel W. Peterson,'85; *Box 201, Albion, N. Y.*
Fiske, Ella A., N. Y. City; m. Thos. R. McCall, '72; *Harmon, Col.*
Fletcher, Ada L.,Cleveland,E. Tenn.; m. Horace L. Strickland,'75; d. Owensville,Ind.,'87.
French, Mary Ella, E. Randolph; m. —— Clark; d. Jacksonville, Fla., '90.

1869.

Gallup, Emily, Mystic. Ct.; d. Mystic, Ct., '75.
Gaylord, Henrietta, S. Hadley Falls; d. S. Hadley Falls, '73.
Gilchrist, Elizabeth J., McIndoes Falls, Vt.; m. Ames B. Perry, '74; *McIndoes Falls, Vt.*
Hall, Matilda P., Charlton, N. Y.; m. Chas. Flint, '81; *Amenia, N. Y.*
Haynes, S. Elizabeth, Townsend; m. F. W. M. Coffin, '75; d. Atlanta, Ga., '94.
Hitchcock, Martha J., New Haven, Ct.; m. Rev. Joseph W. Hartshorn, '70; *38 Kensington St., New Haven, Ct.*
Hoover, Rachel M., Millville, N. J.; m. *Wm. Reilly, Esq., '81; *142 Carroll St., Paterson, N.J.*
Ide, Hattie E., St. Armand, Quebec, Can.; m. Theodore F. Fuller, '73; d. Worcester, '79.
Ives, Parnellie M., Cornwall, Ct.; *28 Washington St., E. Orange, N. J.*
Jefts, Mira A., Drewsville, N. H.; m L. C. Sprague, '73; *Oak St., Winchendon.*
Johnson, Alice G., Putnam, Ct.; *Putnam, Ct.*
Johnson, Annie G., Ottawa, Ont.; d. Ottawa, Ont., '69.
Johnson, Virginia H., Bangor, Me.; m. Rev. E. P. Lee, '91; *212 Holland St., W. Somerville.*
Kilbourne, Elizabeth H. S., New Britain, Ct.; m. Milton H. Butler, '75; d. Mt. Clemens, Mich., '78.
Lyon, Ida C., Waukegan, Ill.; m. Edwin W. Hutchins, '72; *318 State St., Waukegan Ill.*
Marvin, Julia S., Deep River, Ct.; d. Deep River, Ct., '75.
McGlashan, Laura, San Francisco, Cal.; m. Henry S. Stedman, '78; *Alameda, Cal.*
Mason, Teresa M., New London, Ct.; m. *Frank Ferris, '71; m. *Edward C. Johnson, '89; *New London, Ct.*
Morse, Eunice N., Wayland; *Wayland.*
Mosman, Emma C., Amherst; *Norwalk, Ct.*
Nash, Helen M., Williamsburg; m. Arthur Hinds, '83; *Richmond Hill, N. Y.*
Osborn, Julia A., Mt. Carmel, Ct.; *Mt. Carmel, Ct.*
Parish, Lizzie, Shelbyville, Ind.; m. —— McIntire; *120 C St., N. E., Washington, D. C.*
Parsons, Anna E., Brooklyn, N. Y.; m. Rev. H. M. Tenney, D.D.; *136 West College St., Oberlin, O.*
Paul, Sarah A., Mashapaug, Ct.; d Mashapaug, Ct., '70.
Perkins, Sarah A., Bellows Falls, Vt.; m. Judge Lavant M. Read, '76; *Bellows Falls, Vt.*
Perry, Eunice L., Greenfield Hill. Ct.; *61 W. 10th St., New York City.*
Petrie, Kate M., Manchester, N. J.; *Phillipsburgh, N. J.*
Philbrick, Ariana S., Skowhegan, Me.; *45 Chambers St., Boston.*
Powers, Ellen M., Westminster West, Vt.; m *Francis E. Plumb, '71; *Westminster West, Vt.*
Powers, Mary L., Phillipston; m. P. M. Sanderson, '69; "*Cassels,*" *Chase, Col.*
Powers, Winifred K., Waldoboro, Me.; m. Melville B. Stevens, '80; *N. Warren, Me.*
Pray, Ella P., Lowell; m. Stephen G. Bailey, M.D., '73; *110 6th St., Lowell.*
Putnam, Emma C., Manchester, N. H.;
Rice, Ella M., Meriden, Ct.,; m. Irving L. Holt, '75; *Meriden. Ct.*
Robinson, Ann M., Bath, Me.; *681 Washington St., Bath, Me.*
Sampson, Amelia J., Palmyra, N. Y.; m. Lucien Ellis, M.D., '77; *108 Welch Ave., Detroit, Mich.*
Sheldon, Jennie M., Mill River; *Mill River.*
Shepard, Susan N., La Crosse, Wis.; m. Edwin E. Bentley, '69; d. La Crosse, Wis., '78.
Sleeper, Emma C., Belfast, Me.; m. Lorenzo G. Coombs, '71; *201 W. Washington St., Phœnix, Ariz.*
Sprague, Mary J., Andover, Ct.; m. Avern Pardoe, '76; *52 Park Road, Toronto, Ont.*
Stearns, Flora P., W. Hartford, Ct.; m. Rev. Marcellus Bowen, '71; *Bible House, Constantinople, Turkey.*
Stewart, M. Frances, M.A., Dover, N. H.; m. Geo. F. Mosher, LL.D., '71; *Hillsdale, Mich.*
Stone, Emma A., Winchester; *102 Washington St., Winchester.*

1869.

Sweetser, Katherine A., Worcester; m. —— Smith, '70; 5 *Harris St., Brookline.*
Taylor, Clara S., Great Barrington; m. Rev. Geo. E. MacLean, '74; 828 *10th Ave., S. E., Minneapolis, Minn.*
Taylor, Lucy S., Mystic, Ct.; m. Rev. Joseph K. Wilson, '76; 17 *Beverley St., Melrose.*
Tillotson, Elizabeth L., Putnam, Ct.; *Wethersfield, Ct.*
Underhill, Georgiana T., Rahway, N. J.; *Rahway, N. J.*
Upton, Lilla F., S. Dedham; *Worcester.*
Warner, Fannie L., W. Winfield, N. Y.; m. H. D. Cunningham, '69; 1 *Sprague Place, Albany, N. Y.*
Wells, Mary S., Southampton; m. Edmund Noyes, '86; d. '92.
Wilder, Helen A., Keene, N. H.; m. Chas. H. Beckler, '83; 1120 *Millard Ave., Boston.*
Wilmarth, Sarah J., N. Oxford; 2 *Highland Terrace, Malden.*
Woodruff, Isabella H., Elizabeth, N. J.; m. *Geo. D. Baremore, '73; d. Elizabeth, N. J.,'75.
Woodward, Valina J., New London, Ct.; m. * Edwin Ross, '79; 15 *Hill St., Morristown, N. J.*
Yale, Jane M., Ware; m. *Josiah Shepard, '71; *Beloit, Wis.*

1870.

GRADUATES.

Anderson, Susan E., Shelburne; *Shelburne.*
Baldwin, Sarah D., Rocky Hill, Ct.; *Rocky Hill, Ct.*
Bement, Mary O., Buckland; d. Sioux Falls, S. Dak., '88.
Birge, Clara S., Troy, N. Y.; m. Benjamin C. Wilcox, '73; 24 *School St., Meriden, Ct.*
Blodgett, Mary E., Greenwich; 68 *Warrenton St., Boston.*
Brown, Adelia M., Mauchaug; m. H. B. Lawrence,'74; *W. Sutton.*
Carpenter, Mary L., Monson; m. * Rev. Wm. S. Howland, '73; d. Auburndale, '87.
Cole, Rev. Elvira, Stark, N. H.; m. * Rev. Nelson F. Cobleigh, '70; 116 *Chestnut St., Walla Walla, Wash.*
Cone, Mary C., West Winsted, Ct.; 9 *Beacon St., Hartford, Ct.*
Cristy, Anne, Greenwich, Ct.; 200 *Warburton Ave., Yonkers, N. Y.*
Dame, Mary L. S., Exeter, N. H.; m. * Hon. E. O. Hall, '78; 36 *W. 17th St., N. Y. City.*
Dutton, Mary C., Rutland, N. Y.; m. Harlan P. Dunlap, '72; *Watertown, N. Y.*
Emerson, Margaret A., Canajoharie, N. Y.; 16 *Oak St., Glens Falls, N. Y.*
Fuller, S. Louise, Sturbridge; m. Lem. T. Denison, '73; 233 *Clinton St., Cleveland, O.*
Gale, Emma S., Newtown, N. H.; m. Norman W. Harris,'79; 4520 *Drexel Boul., Chicago, Ill.*
Griggs, Josephine J., Fleming, N. Y.; m. Henry G. Wise,'77; 8 *Lewis St., Auburn, N.Y.*
Hall, Mary E., Charlton, N. Y.; m. *Charles T. Wicks, '83; d. Cohoes, N. Y., '89.
Hoover, Jennie K., Millville, N. J.; 142 *Carroll St., Paterson, N. J.*
Howland, Susan R., Jaffna, Ceylon; *Oodooville, Jaffna, Ceylon.*
Hurlbutt, Fannie I., W. Winsted, Ct.; 1 *Park Place, Stamford, Ct.*
Jennings, Julia F., Wellesley; *Wellesley.*
Kellogg, Adelaide F., Ogdensburg, N. Y.; d. Mansfield, O., '92.
Kittredge, Harriet D., Westboro; *Ottawa, Kan.*
Knowles, Helen M., Nashua, N. H.; *Watertown.*
McNaughton, Mary E., Mercersburg, Pa.; m. William C. Agnew, '73; 701 *Elm St., Youngstown, O.*
Merrill, Mina K., Peacham, Vt.; m. Herbert P. Hooker, '83; *Peacham, Vt.*
Page, Mary L., Haverhill; *Arenida 40, San Sebastian, Spain.*

1870.

Parsons, Anna A., Northampton ; 231 *Bridge St., Northampton.*
Peabody, Mary C., Erzroom, Turkey ; d. *Los Angeles, Cal.,* '87.
Price, Martha E., Gilmanton, N. H. ; *Duff's Road, Quanda, S. Africa.*
Procter, Ella L., Gloucester ; 83 *Middle St., Gloucester.*
Read, Georgiana, Boston ; m. John S. White, LL.D., '71 ; 52 *W. 54th St., New York City.*
Rowe, Ellen W., Montague ; d. *Montague,* '71.
Smith, Frances A., Hartford, Vt. ; m. Geo. P. Cather, '73; *Bladen, Neb.*
Van Doren, Helen M., Griggstown, N. J. ; *Griggstown, N. J.*
Walker, Harriet A., Huntington ; *Wellesley College, Wellesley.*

NON-GRADUATES.

Adams, Ella M., Willimantic, Ct. ; m. J. B. Baldwin, '70 ; 115 *Prospect St., Willimantic, Ct.*
Adams, Emma M., Boston ;
Alden, Mary C., Belchertown ; m. Arthur E. Ferry, '73; 725 *Adams St., Owosso, Mich.*
Bissell, Angeline S., White Plains, N. Y. ; m. *Frank C. Mather, '76 ; 82 *Washington Ave., Northampton.*
Bliss, Harriet M., Cambridgeport ; 260 *Clarendon St., Boston.*
Bliss, Helen E., Essex Center, Vt. ; m. Rev. Chas L. Tomblen, '75 ; *Ashland.*
Booth, Harriet E., Anamosa, Io. ; m. Rev. Geo. F. Le Clere, '75 ; *Chillicothe, Tex.*
Bowers, M. Lizzie, Milford ; m. Jas. O. Bailey, '75 ; 101 *Church St., Marlborough.*
Brown, Martha C., Sheldon, Vt. ; m. Rev. Charles H. Rowley, '72 ; *Townsend.*
Butler, Lydia M., Brooklyn, N.Y. ; m. Henry E. Tuthill, '72; 83 *Monroe St., Brooklyn, N. Y.*
Carr, Florence A., Coffeeville, Miss. ; *Dallas, Tex.*
Case, Elizabeth J., Owego, N. Y. ;
Chamberlain, Alla S., St. Clair, Mich. ; m. Geo. W. Johnston, '87 ; *Hudson, Wis.*
Chapin, Mary E., Whitinsville ; m. Carlton J. McEwen, '82 ; *Lawrenceville, N. Y.*
Chapman, Alice B., New London, Ct. ; m. *Asa F. Inman, '77 ; d. *Milford,* '82.
Clinton, Imogene L., Council Bluffs, Io. ; m. Frank B. Hart, Esq., '70 ; 728 *E. 10th St., Minneapolis, Minn.*
Colvocoresses, Eva F., Litchfield, Ct. ; m. Geo. E. Jones, '74 ; d. *Litchfield, Ct.,* '75.
Cone, Catie A., Hartford, Vt. ; *Hartford, Vt.*
Cotton, Mary G., Pomfret Landing, Ct. ; m. *Joseph Matthewson, '74 ; *Norfolk, Neb.*
Davis, Maria L., Holyoke ; m. Benj. F. Cooley, '72 ; d. *Chico, Cal.,* '78.
Davison, Annie B., Nyack, N. Y. ; m. Charles H. Marsh, '82 ; 434 *22d St., San Diego, Cal.*
Dean, Emily K., Oakham ; *care Dr. Arthur Webster, Worcester.*
Derby, Ida E., Springfield ; m. Joseph B. Jamieson ; *Edgewater, N. J.*
Dickson, Rebecca C., Gettysburg, Pa. ; m. *F. D. Long, '80 ; *Gettysburg, Pa.*
Dougall, Susan G., M.D., Montreal, Can. ; 294 *Drummond St., Montreal, Can.*
Eldredge, Genevieve S., Lima, N. Y. ; m. *Arthur A. Hawley, '75 ; m. John H. Ray, '85 ; 217 *Lincoln St., Mankato, Minn.*
Ellinwood, Eliza M., M.D., Athol ; 313 *N. James St., Rome, N. Y.*
Fales, Ella E., Wrentham ; P. O. address, *Pondville.*
Fletcher, Mary W., Danvers ; *Concord St., Acton.*
Foster, Kate I., M.D., Nebraska City, Neb. ; m. Rev. Jas. T. Graves, '71 ; 5663 *Washington Ave., Chicago, Ill.*
Foster, Maria J., Sweden, Me. ; m. David P. Wells, '71 ; *Whately.*
Freeman, Mary E., Darien, Ct. ; m. Judson Strong ; 99 *North St., Springfield.*
French, Mary F., Nashua, N. H. ; *Provo City, Utah.*
French, Sarah N., Danvers Center ; m. Geo. H. Gray, '83 ; 28 *Jacobson Building, Denver, Col.*
Gilmour, M. Eleanor, Boston ; 252 *Beacon St., Boston.*
Goddard, Alice M., W. Hartland, Ct. ; *Winsted, Ct.*

1870.

Gordon, Elizabeth P., Auburndale ; *Auburndale.*
Hale, Ellen H., Lunenburg, Vt. ; m. Judge Albert R. Savage,'71 ; 52 *High St., Auburn, Me.*
Hall, Louise W., Plymouth, N. H. ; m. Frank W. Russell, '73 ; *Plymouth, N. H.*
Harris, Addie T., Hinsdale, N. H. ; d. Cleveland, O., '88.
Hart, Annie E., Brooklyn, N. Y. ; m. C. H. Osgood, '79 ; deceased.
Hathaway, Annie F., Burrville, Ct. ; m. Corliss J. Pickert, '77 ; *Berlin, Wis.*
Hathaway, Mary, Skowhegan, Me. ; m. Llewellyn Bixby, '70 ; d. Los Angeles, Cal., '82.
Hills, Lizzie G., Lynn ; m. Justin G. Hayes, '75 ; 145 *Smith St., Atlanta, Ga.*
House, Teresa L., Binghamton, N. Y. ; m. Everett D. Prentice,'73 ; d. Brooklyn,N.Y., '80.
Hoyt, Theresa A., Darien Depot, Ct. ; d. Darien, Ct., '74.
Hull, Sarah E., Darien, Ct. ; m. Joseph J. Fairty, '77 ; 66 *Alexander St., Toronto, Canada.*
Huntington, E. Caroline, McGregor, Io. ; *Windom, N. Y.*
Hurlbut, Mary C., Cambridge ; m. *Edward Shaw, '78 ; 425 *Broadway, Cambridge.*
Jennings, Isabella S., Coventry, Ct. ; m. B. F. Hunt, '71 ; d. E. Randolph, Vt., '87.
Kent, Florence, Taunton ; d. Taunton, '78.
Learoyd, Annie, Danvers ; *Danvers.*
Loveland, Sarah J., Hinsdale ; m. *Rev. Henry W. Eldridge, '76 ; *Pasadena, Cal.*
McCall, Mary H., Albany, N. Y. ; 330 *State St., Albany, N. Y.*
Mack, M. Ellen, N. Y. City; m. Charles Sawyer ; *Marshall, Wash.*
Mann, Emily, Franklin ; m. Willard Everett, '75 ; 12 *Belmont St., Lowell.*
Martin, Julia A., Lancaster, Pa. ; m. Thos. B. Holahan, Esq., '75 ; 230 *N. Charlotte St., Lancaster, Pa.*
Miller, Mary R. C., Goshen, N. J. ; *Cold Spring, N. J.*
Montgomery, Fannie, Derry, N. H. ; m. Milton B. Hood, '72 ; 148 *Myrtle St., Melrose.*
Morrill, Sarah M., Peacham, Vt. ; m. Erskine H. Hamilton, '76 ; *Malvern, Io.*
Morris, Abby F., Ellington, Ct. ; m. Chas. S. Hurlbut, '80 ; *Tolland, Rockville P. O., Ct.*
Norton, Martha J., Strong, Me. ; m. Jas. T. Skillings, '73 ; *Strong, Me.*
Noyes, Charlotte E., Abington; m. Henry F. Starbuck, '72 ; 6 *Groveland Park, Chicago,Ill.*
Olmstead, Mary L., Sheldon, Vt.; *Box 85, Arlington.*
Paige, S. Elizabeth, Hardwick ; *Hardwick.*
Peabody, Anna L., N. Stamford, Ct. ; 2415 *E. 1st St., Los Angeles, Cal.*
Perrin, Emily F., Taunton ; 147 *High St., Taunton.*
Richardson, Carrie V., Ware ; m. Edwin H. Baker, '73 ; *Greenwich, Ct.*
Richardson, Lauretta P., Keene, N. H. ; m. Solon W. Stone,'79 ; 183 *Court St., Keene,N.H.*
Robinson, Louise S., Brookline ; m. Edward Sharp, '76 ; *Brookline.*
Ronk, Letitia B., Brooklyn ;
Sargeant, Ellen F., St. Johnsbury, Vt. ; m. Edw. T. Griswold, '78 ; d. St. Johnsbury, Vt., '80.
Sawyer, Emma C., Danvers ; m. Joseph Woodman, '83, *Auburn St., Malden.*
Shattuck, Georgiana E., Pepperell ; m. Fred. E. Belcher, '77 ; 14 *Prospect St., Winchester.*
Smith, M. Elmina, Troy, N. J. ; d. Troy, N. J., '75.
Smith, Mary B., Sunderland ; *care Dr. L. N. Bedford, San Bernardino, Cal.*
Smith, Mary E., Fairfield, Ct. ; 207 *S. 3d St., Reading, Pa.*
Smith, Mary E., Sunderland ; m. Chas. K. Smith, '71 ; *Sunderland.*
Southmayd, Anna, Middletown, Ct. ; m. Chas. K. Osborne, '74 ; d. Southbury, Ct., '81.
Standish, J. Ella, Middleboro ; *Nantasket Beach.*
Stearns, Fannie E., Conway ; m. John R. Holcomb, '73 ; *Conway.*
Styles, Isabella E., Worcester ; *Boston.*
Tappan, Lucia, Providence, R. I. ; 113 *Ellison St., Paterson, N. J.*
Taylor, Caroline S., Hinsdale, N. H. ; m. Geo. T. Winston, LL.D., '76 ; *Chapel Hill, N. C.*
Treadway, Alice M., Rutland, N. Y. ; *E. Watertown, N. Y.*
Van Doren, Kate T., Griggstown, N. J. ; *Griggstown, N. J.*
Waters, Martha O., Millville, N. J. ; d. Bridgeton, N. J., '83.

1870.

Welch, Mary E., Norfolk, Ct.; m. Geo. D. Harrison, '81; *Lakeville, Ct.*
Wheeler, Emily C., Harpoot, Turkey; *Harpoot, Turkey.*
Whiting, Abbie M., Dummerston, Vt.; 514 *N. E. 4th St., Minneapolis, Minn.*
Whitmarsh, Maria D., Abington; m. Francis A. Dunbar. '91; *Box 268, Abington.*
Wilcox, M. Louise, Post Mills, Vt.; m. Thos. W. D. Worthen, '74; d. Post Mills, Vt., '78.
Wood, C. Alice, Middletown, N. Y.; m. Mark H. Dewsnap, '70; d. Brooklyn, N. Y., '79.
Wright, Velma C., Boston; m. Rev. Theo. C. Williams, '83; 150 *W. 59th St., N. Y. City.*

1871.

GRADUATES.

Anderson, Mercy A., Shelburne; 268 *Washington St., Shelburne.*
Angell, Helen J., Northampton; m. Emery A. Goodwin, '73; P. O. address, *Lake View, N. H.*
Baldwin, H. Gertrude, Foochow, China; m. David J. Gerry, '81; 84 *Sussex Ave., E. Orange, N. J.*
Benson, Elizabeth R., Center Harbor, N. H.; home address, *Center Harbor, N. H.*
Black, Frances B., Geneva, N. Y.; m. J. Dwight Judd, '74; *S. Hadley Falls.*
Bradford, Mary C., Ph.B., McIndoes Falls, Vt.; *Mount Holyoke College, S. Hadley.*
Brink, M. Josephine, Lockport, N. Y.; *Girls' High School, Nostrand Ave., Brooklyn, N. Y.*
Brown, Viette I., Shortsville, N. Y.; m. Rev. Wm. Sprague; *Kalgan, China.*
Clapp, Cornelia M., Ph.D., Montague; *Mount Holyoke College, S. Hadley.*
Cowles, Emma L., Amherst; *Box 57, Amherst.*
Dean, Frances A., S. Canaan, Ct.; 1849 *Jackson St., San Francisco, Cal.*
Dodd, Hettie M., Mendham, N. J.; m. *Rev. Thomas Carter, '74; *Boonton, N. J.*
Durant, Elizabeth A., Titusville, Pa.; m. Ernest N. Smith, '74; 414 *4th St., Warren, Pa.*
Estabrook, S. Adelle, Worcester; d. *Worcester, '94.*
Fiske, Mary F., Newburyport; m. Rev. Chas. A. Savage, '82; 48 *Highland Ave., Orange, N.J.*
Giddings, Sophia C., Sherman, Ct.; m. Maltby Gelston, '75; *Sherman, Ct.*
Giles, Helena F., Rockport; 5488 *Ellis Ave., Chicago, Ill.*
Gore, Mary C., La Harpe, Ill.; m. A. N. Richardson, M.D., '72; 6500 *Wentworth Ave., Englewood, Chicago, Ill.*
Hall, Julina O., Ashfield; *Mount Vernon Seminary, 1100 M St., N. W., Washington, D. C.*
Hersey, Martha E., Amherst; *S. Paris, Me.*
Jewett, Nellie C., Chaumont, N. Y.; m. *Hubbard W. Reed, '73; m. Albert Fish, '88; d. Chaumont, N. Y., '90.
Marshall, Ella C., Newark, N. J.; m. David F. Nichols, '72; 62 *Sherman Ave., Newark, N. J.*
Meader, Wilhelmina T., M.D., Chester, Pa.; m. Robert Nelson, '75; 221 *N. High St., W. Chester, Pa.*
Moody, S. Adelaide, Belchertown; m. Edward S. White, Esq., '85; d. Hartford, Ct., '90.
Munro, Mary E., Baldwinsville, N. Y.; m. Alex. Hamill, M.D., '72; *Baldwinsville, N. Y.*
Parsons, Myra E., Northampton; m. Henry G. Moore, '83; *N. Hatfield.*
Peet, Frances R., Foochow, China; d. West Haven, Ct., '72.
Plimpton, C. Idella, Walpole; m. *Rev. Henry L. Kendall, '75; *Walpole.*
Smith, Mary E., Sunderland; m. Rev. M. O. Harrington, '77; 1342 *Mulvane St., Topeka, Kan.*
Thompson, Mary E., Brooklyn, N. Y.; *Boston.*
Tuttle, Mary C., North Haven, Ct.; m. D. B. O. Bourdon, '79; 24 *Carlton St., Newton.*
Watson, Laura S., M.A., Sedgwick, Me.; *Abbot Academy, Andover.*
Welch, Elizabeth B., Hartford, Ct.; m. Ellsworth Ives, '80; *Norfolk, Ct.*

White, Caroline L., Brookline ; *Tappan St., Brookline.*
White, Victoria A., M.D.; Haydenville ; 316 *Throop Ave., Brooklyn, N. Y.*
Williams, Mary E., Chaplin, Ct.; m. Rev. Wm. H. Phipps, '72 ; *Prospect, Ct.*
Willis, Ianthe, White Plains, N. Y.; *White Plains, N. Y.*

NON-GRADUATES.

Arnold, Amelia D. (name changed from Amelia C. Dickinson), McGregor, Io.; m. Julius R. Ball, '74 ; *Box 236, Montague.*
Arnold, Maria A., N. Abington ; m. Philo S. Tyler, '87 ; *495 Mass. Ave., Boston.*
Arnold, Mary J., Sturbridge ; *Fiskdale.*
Augur, Mary E., Middlefield, Ct.; m. Horace F. Dudley, '74 ; *Guilford, Ct.*
Bancroft, Mary N., Montague ; m. Lawrence Kervan, '72 ; *Norwalk, Fla.*
Barnard, Ellen M., Hopkinton. N. H.; d. Hopkinton, N. H., '86.
Barrett, Alice M., E. Cambridge; m. Henshaw B. Chilson; *N. Y. City.*
Barstow, Sallie C., Haverhill, N. H.; *90 High St., Portland, Me.*
Birdsey, Alice A., Middlefield, Ct.; *Middlefield, Ct.*
Blood, Nellie E., Pepperell ; *Y. W. C. A., 40 Berkeley St., Boston.*
Bowles, Kate E., Coventry, Vt.; m. Rev. Geo. H. Ide, D.D., '76 ; *211 17th St., Milwaukee, Wis.*
Carter, Mary S., Lowell ; m. Rev. Edward A. Benner, '74 ; *Wellesley.*
Chaplin, Mary A., Georgetown ; m. Thos. A. Perley, '80 ; *Georgetown.*
Childs, Emma P., Amherst ; m. Adoniram J. White, '77 ; *Braintree.*
Coe, Mary Frances, Norwalk, O.; m. *L. J. Seward, '82 ; *Roseville, N. J.*
Coffin, Mary C., Glens Falls, N. Y.; m. Chas. W. Kimball, '76 ; d. Penn Yan, N. Y., '93.
Corey, Susan E., Tiverton, R. I.; m. Stephen G. Crandall, '78; *Adamsville, R. I.*
Corle, Frances E., N. Y. City ; m. Wm. Livingstone, '85 ; *33 Culver Ave., Jersey City, N. J.*
Crump, Eliza R., New London, Ct.; *30 Washington St., New London, Ct.*
Dickerman, Emma E., Mt. Carmel, Ct.; *Mt. Carmel, Ct.*
Duncan, Harriet A. N., Florence, Pa.; *Pico Heights, Cal.*
Ely, Helen A., Holyoke ; m. Benj. F. Hawley, M.D., '78 ; *417 N. 33d St., Philadelphia, Pa.*
Eno, Sarah C., Simsbury, Ct.; m. Chas. Parker, '75 ; *27 Arch St., New Britain, Ct.*
Flint, Abby A., Montpelier, Vt.; *Concord, N. H.*
Forbes, Harriet E., Millbury ; m. Chas. E. Searles, '78 ; *Millbury.*
Gerrish, Adaline D., Leetonia, O.; *18 East St., Providence, R. I.*
Giles, Alice A., Abington ; m. Geo. L. Richardson, '80 ; *Abington.*
Goodwin, Alice L., Gorham, Me.; *Gorham, Me.*
Grant, Alice D., Bloomfield, Ct.; *Royalton, Vt.*
Grant, Huldah A., Delhi, N. Y.; m. A. G. Carman, '92 ; *Marengo, Ill.*
Haddock, Elizabeth B., Buffalo, N. Y.; m. H. S. Mulligan ; *44 Sidney Court, Chicago, Ill.*
Hallowell, Ella M., W. Charlton, N. Y.; m. Thomas C. Bunyan, '75 ; *Berthoud, Col.*
Hartshorn, A. Agnes, Canaan, Vt.; m. Harry Johnson, '80; *Sharon.*
Harvey, Sarah E., Danbury, Ct.; m. Rev. Henry M. Ladd, '75 ; *820 Logan Ave., Cleveland, O.*
Hibbard, Kate T., Piermont, N. H.; *Haverhill, N. H.*
Hodgdon, Harriet A., Campton Village, N. H.; m. Jason C. Little, '76 ; d. Campton, N. H., '80.
Holmes, Fanny J., Londonderry, N. H. ; m. Waldo Foster, '72 ; *Aberdeen, S. Dakota.*
Holt, Frances E. L., N. Yarmouth, Me. ; d. Denver, Col., '74.
Homer, Agnes M., Shelburne, N. S. ; *care Jos. Watt, Barrington, Shelburne Co., N. S.*
Howard, Eliza J., Hardwick ; m. *Franklin M. Rice, '70 ; m. John Humphrey, '91 ; *Keene, N. H.*
Howell, Mary P., Middletown, N. Y. ; m. *Howard S. Conklin, '75 ; *41 East Ave., Middletown, N. Y.*
Hoyt, Sarah L., Stamford, Ct. ; *17 Henry St., Stamford, Ct.*

1871.

Hubbard, Adelaide, Hartford, Ct. ; m. Henry F. Trask, '82 ; 79 *Court St., Springfield.*
Hulbert, Charlotte S., Sheldon, Vt. ; m. Geo. E. Stebbins, '71 ; *E. Sheldon, Vt.*
Hunt, Lizzie E., Shoreham, Vt. ; m. Sam. W. Ward, '79 ; 404 *Seward St., Waukegan, Ill.*
Jones, Nellie B., Townsend ; m. Wm. A. Russell, '83 ; *Townsend.*
Joy, Harriet A., Ellsworth, Me. ; 301 *S. 4th St., Grand Forks, N. Dak.*
Judkins, Emma A., Kingston, N. H. ; m. Joshua E. G. Lyford, '83 ; *Kingston, N. H.*
Kimball, Emma F., Lowell ; m. Rev. Geo. L. Clark, '76 ; *Box 33, Farmington, Ct.*
Leach, Elizabeth S., Pittsford, Vt. ; m. Frank B. Clark, '71 ; *Hyde Park, Cal.*
Longley, Grace E., W. Chelmsford ; m. Frank B. Phillips, Esq., '75 ; *Littleton, N. H.*
Lincoln, Rebecca M., Brimfield ; *Brimfield.*
Mack, Mary E., N. Y. City ; m. Chas. Sawyer, '81 ; *Spokane, Wash.*
Masta, Ida C., Lowell ; m. Nath'l J. K. Davis, '75 ; 13 *Mt. Vernon St., E. Somerville.*
Moore, Julia A., Chester, Vt. ; m. Harvey G. Kittredge, '75 ; 3 *Fiske St., Waltham.*
Morey, Frances W., W. Brookfield ; m. Walter C. Rose ; *Box 1297, Fitchburg.*
Morris, Delia M., Ellington, Ct. ; m. Fred N. Pease, '77 ; 1204 *3d Ave., Altoona, Pa.*
Morris, Jerusha, Lodi, N. Y. ; m. John M. Bennett, '78 ; *Lodi, Seneca Co., N. Y.*
Moseley, Eveline J., Ellington, Ct. ; m. Fred. E. Allen, '78 ; d. Melrose, Ct., '81.
Munger, Emma L., Madison, Ct. ; m. Wm. T. Foote, '79 ; *Guilford, Ct.*
Nelson, Lucretia C., Elyria, O. ; m. Rev. Edward P. Butler, '76 ; *Sunderland.*
Noyes, Clara M., Georgetown ; m. Ralph C. Huse, M.D., '74 ; d. Georgetown, '83.
Page, Sarah E., Conway ; m. John W. Tilton, '77 ; *Conway.*
Parsons, E. Lillie, Yonkers, N. Y. ; 100 *Woodworth Ave., Yonkers. N. Y.*
Pease, Eunice M., Lawrence, Kan. ; m. John W. Alder, '73 ; *Lawrence, Kan.*
Piper, Marietta, Lynn ; m. Edward L. Pease, '75 ; d. Ashby, '82.
Purinton, Mary L., Newington Junction, Ct. ; 1579 *Lill Ave., Chicago, Ill.*
Ramsdell, Ada E., Gardiner, Me. ; m. *Robert S. Kelton, '75 ; m. Geo. E. Smith, '90 ; 40 *Elm St., Wakefield.*
Raynolds, Mary C., St. Augustine, Fla. ; *St. Augustine, Fla.*
Rice. Anne R., Westfield ; 133 *Florida St., Springfield.*
Rowe, Rachel A., Wallingford, Ct.; m. Hiram M. Seeley, '80 ; 278 *Clinton St., Brooklyn, N. Y.*
Sawin, Cora L., Baldwinsville ; m. C. O. Norcross, '71 ; *Hotel Monteith, Brookline.*
Slack, Elizabeth H., Frenchtown, N. J.; m. Henry V. D. Rogers, '79 ; *Woodbury, N. J.*
Smith, Martha L., Amherst ; m. W. B. Kridler, Jr., '77 ; *Fremont, O.*
Spaulding, Mary, Falls Village, Ct. ; d. Canaan, Ct., '71.
Terry, Annie M., Ansonia, Ct. ; 12 *S. Cliff St., Ansonia, Ct.*
Tewksbury, Mary A., Bangor, Me. ; d. Bangor, Me., '72.
Thompson, Mary E., Chicago, Ill. ; m. Joseph H. Loomis, M.D., '72 ; *Minneapolis, Minn.*
Waite, Susan A., Swanton Center, Vt.; m.Chas. Ellison, '73; 797 *Putnam Ave., Brooklyn, N. Y.*
Wakefield, Jane M., Dedham ; m. Clifton P. Baker, '74 ; *Dedham.*
Wallace, Emma W., Langdon. N. H. ; 918 *King St., Topeka, Kan.*
Welles, Mary E., Shelburne ; *Genoa, Neb.*
Wilkes, Susan P., Buffalo, N.Y.; m. A. B. Bennett, '78 ; 1260 *32d St., W. Washington, D.C.*
Wilkins, Mary E., Brattleboro, Vt. ; *Randolph.*
Willis, Emilie C., White Plains, N. Y. ; *White Plains, N. Y.*
Wooster, Alice D., W. Cornwall, Vt. ; d. W. Cornwall, Vt.
Wooster, Harriet E., W. Cornwall, Vt. ; m. Martin M. Peck, '87 ; *Cornwall, Vt.*
Wright, Frances A., Shoreham, Vt.; m. Chas. M. Wilds, Esq., '80 ; d. Middlebury, Vt., '90.

1872.

GRADUATES.

Abell, Emeline P., Canajoharie, N. Y.; *Canajoharie, N. Y.*
Allen, Clara F., Walpole ; m. Myron H. Piper, '76; *Walpole.*
Bachelder, Annie A., Hallowell, Me. ; d. St. Mark's Home, Augusta, Me., '89.
Bayley, Sarah E., Waupun, Wis. ; d. Waupun, Wis., '75.
Beane, Ednah F., Providence, R. I. ; m. P. Herbert Smith, '83 ; 10 *Hammond St., Providence, R. I.*
Bennett, Mary S., New Market, N. H. ; m. Chas. W. Morse, '75 ; 24 *Park St.,Haverhill.*
Bissell, M. Louise, Ahmednagar, India ; m. Allan H. Bacon, '74 ; 1223 *Whittier St., St. Louis, Mo.*
Brooks, Caroline A., Montpelier, Vt. ; m. Harmon N. Morse, '76 ; d. Amherst, '87.
Brown, Ethie E., Waterbury, Vt. ; m. Geo. T. Buffum, '74; *Winchester, N. H.*
Buffum, Mary E., Winchester, N. H. ; *Winchester, N. H.*
Butler, Cora E., Jamaica, Vt. ; m. *Fred. P. Jones, '91 ; care F. M. Butler, Rutland, Vt.*
Cahill, Anna M., N. Y. City ; m. Prof. Henry S. Bennett, '90 ; *Oberlin, O.*
Cole, Ella R., Middletown, Ct. ; d. Philadelphia, Pa., '80.
Dibble, Ellen S., Westfield ; m. Geo. A. Clark, '84 ; d. Holyoke, '01.
Doty, Mary A., Amoy, China ; m. Geo. B. Smith, '76 ; *Troy Hills, N. J.*
Dwinell, Alice H., Sacramento, Cal. ; m. Rev. Henry E. Jewett, '76 ; *Vacaville, Cal.*
Hall, Emma V., Ware ; *Box 404, Ware.*
Harris, Mary J., E. Putnam, Ct. ; m. Frank T. Benner, Esq., '86 ; *Newtonville.*
Hartshorn, Eleanor A., Webster ; *Webster.*
Hinman, Lydia, W. Charleston, Vt. ; *Waterloo, Io.*
Hitchcock, Annette M., Putney, Vt. ; m. Alfred S. Hall, Esq., '76 ; d. Westminster West, Vt., '87.
Johnston, Dorlissa E., Barryville, N. Y. ; m. Smith M. Lindsley, Esq., '73 ; 31 *Rutger St., Utica, N. Y.*
Keese, Julia E., Lowell ; m. A. F. Drinkwater, Esq., '75 ; *Andover.*
Libbey, Isabelle H., Limington, Me. ; 27 *Worcester St., Boston.*
Metcalf, Dora L., Franklin ; *Orange, N. J.*
Morris, Eliza, Lodi, N. Y. ; m. William A. Cook, '74 ; *Milford, Io.*
Niles, Kate M., Post Mills, Vt. ; m. Edwin F. Gary, '73; d. Columbia, S. C., '87.
Noyes, Ella M., Abington ; m. Wm. A. Higgins, '77 ; 610 *Park Ave., Omaha, Neb.*
Noyes, Mary E., Dansville, N. Y. ; m. *Wm. M. Colvin, '77 ; *Cleveland, O.*
Nutter, Laura F., Barnstead Parade, N. H. ; m. Rev. Wm. O. Carr ; d. Barnstead,N.H.,'83.
Parker, Florence F., Ithaca, N. Y. ; 9 *Parker Place, Ithaca, N. Y.*
Randolph, Louise F., Panama, N. Y. ; *Mt. Holyoke College, S. Hadley.*
Scott, Mary H., North Hadley ; *Amherst.*
Scribner, Julia A. G., Raymond, N. H. ; *Raymond, N. H.*
Sloan, Virginia G., Kittanning, Pa. ; m. W. L. Peart, Esq., '84 ; *Kittanning, Pa.*
Spooner, M. Ella, B. L., Oakham ; m. Julius W. Brown, '94 ; *Northwood Centre, N. H.*
Van Valkenburgh, Harriet T., Chittenango, N. Y. ; m. Ralph E. Webber, '93 ; *Chittenango, N. Y.*
White, Florence M., Portsmouth, O. ; m. Robert Bell, M.D., '84 ; d. New York City, '84.
Williams, Cornelia P., Mardin, Turkey ; m. Rev. Wm. N. Chambers, '84 ; *Erzroom, Turkey, via Constantinople.*
Williamson, Clara G., Lewistown, Pa. ; *care Women's Foreign Missionary So., 1334 Chestnut St., Philadelphia, Pa.*
Wood, Alice A., Upton ; *Upton.*

1872.

NON-GRADUATES.

Bateman, Elizabeth H., Stapleton, N. Y.; m. Fred. E. Partington, '69; *New Brighton, N. Y.*
Beaman, Mina D., N. Hadley; m. *Rev. John D. Willard, '82; *Amherst.*
Beecher, Flora J., Hinesburgh, Vt.; d. Hinesburgh, Vt., '79.
Bennett, Mary E., New Milford, Ct.; m. John E. Bates, '86; *New Milford, Ct.*
Boynton, Emma S., Hinesburgh, Vt.; m. John C. Pierce, '87; *Elwood, Neb.*
Bradford, Alice R., Boston Highlands; m. Robert H. Wiles, '76; *Freeport, Ill.*
Briggs, Minnie, Clarendon, Vt.; m. *Stephen Rounds, '74; *Clarendon, Vt.*
Brown, Lucia S., Underhill, Vt.; m. *Fred. Hadley, '77; *Shelburne St., Burlington, Vt.*
Bryant, Lucy E., Derby, Ct.; *Derby, Ct.*
Bunker, M. Amanda, Barnstead, N. H.; *Barnstead, N. H.*
Carrier, Emma, Albany, N. Y.; m. Wm. Backus, '81; 135 *South St., Pittsfield.*
Clark, Harriet R., Northfield; m. Eugene Adams, '72; 13 *Myrtle St., Brattleboro, Vt.*
Clarkson, Virginia A., Newburyport; m. Rev. Chauncey M. Cady, '86; 255 *Hamilton St., E. Los Angeles, Cal.*
Cooper, Ella M., Worcester; m. Andrew J. Keith, '77; 16 *Cambridge St., Worcester.*
Crandall, Ella L., Ithaca, N. Y.; m. Pedro de Mello, '79; *Caixa,* 206 *São Paulo, Brazil.*
Cross, Ulee P., Toungho, British Burma; m. Rev. A. V. B. Crumb, '78; *Toungho, British Burma.*
Cummings, Layette E., Maplewood; m. Lyman A. Eldred, '76; 326 *20th St., Detroit, Mich.*
Demree, Almira V., Dublin, Ind.; *High School No. 2, Indianapolis, Ind.*
Dimmick, Emma A., W. Stafford, Ct.; m. Frances W. Preston, '78; *W. Stafford, Ct.*
Dow, Isophene K., New Market (now Newfields), N. H.; *Newfields, N. H.*
Dow, M. Ella, Pepperell; m. Elijah Miller, '77; *Pepperell.*
Dunton, Lillian W., Bath, Me.; *Westport, Me.*
Evans, Elma, Pughtown, Pa.; d. Pughtown, Pa., "about '80."
Everett, Jane M., Rowe; m. Albert J. Pierce, '74; 17 *Atlantic St., Amesbury.*
Farrar, Mary B., S. Lincoln; *S. Lincoln.*
Garland, Celia, Nashua, N. H.; d. Nashua, N. H., '89.
Giles, Anna L., Abington; d. Abington, '78.
Gleim, Mary A., Lebanon, Pa.; *Bryn Mawr, Pa.*
Gordon, Anna A., Auburndale; *Auburndale.*
Grant, Catharine, Essex; m. Wm. Hope, '83; *La Alejandra, Santa Fe, Argentine Republic, S. A.*
Gridley, Ella R., Canton Center, Ct.; m. Rev. J. O. Sherburn, '73; d. Plainfield, Vt., '75.
Griffith, Mary F., Bridgeport, Ct.; m. John H. Lowndes, '89; 400 *Iranistan Ave., Bridgeport, Ct.*
Guild, Clara V., Wrentham; d. Wrentham, '73.
Hague, Gertrude M. (now Mary Le Comte), Bloomfield, N. J.; *Glen Ridge Ave., Glen Ridge, N. J.*
Hall, Ella A., Lyndon, Vt.; d. Lyndon, Vt., '87.
Hastings, Theresa A., Watseka, Ill.; m. I. C. Wade, '73; d. Watseka, Ill., '78.
Hill, Alice, Brooklyn, N. Y.; m. J. H. Dougherty, Esq., '76; 258 *Clinton Ave., Brooklyn, N. Y.*
Hood, Florence, Denver, Col.; m. Henry C. Dillon, Esq., '76; *Long Beach, Cal.*
Howard, Ellen M., Providence, R. I.; m. Henry Edmunds, Esq., '82; *Antrom, Upper Tulse Hill, London, S. W., England.*
Howard, Mary A., Providence, R. I.; m. Arthur W. Claflin, '81; 190 *Waterman St., Providence, R. I.*
Jones, Mary E., Putney, Vt.; 3 *Fiske St., Waltham.*
Judd, Jeanette, Port Henry, N. Y.; *N. Y. City.*
Karch, Maria S., Lebanon, Pa.; m. Rev. A. R. Bartholomew, '78; *Pottsville, Pa.*
Lauriat, Anne G., Medford; m. Robert M. Read, M. D., '84; 175 *Tremont St., Boston.*

1872.

Lewis, Emma F., Winterport, Me. ; 65 3d St., Bangor, Me.
Long, Cornelia B., W. Winsted, Ct. ; Amherst.
McNutt, Martha J. F., Paris. Mo. ; m. Frank O. Collins, '80 ; Paris, Mo.
Marshall, Annie C., Essex ; m. Earle J. Ricker, '77 ; 41 Fenwick St., Malden.
Marshall, Julia L., Newark, N J. ; m. Oscar E. Dudley, '78 ; d. N. Y. City, '89.
Mills, Ada, Southwick ; m. Wm. F. Fletcher, '79; Southwick.
Mills, Elizabeth S., W. Hartford, Ct. ; m. Geo. W. Harris, '76 ; Wethersfield, Ct.
Mills, Helen C., Sharon ; 46 Dudley St., Roxbury.
Morrill, Edith, Winterport, Me. ; m. Geo. M. Page, '85 ; Burlington, Me.
Newton, Abbie M., Monson ; m. Jas. C. Wing, '77 ; Palmer.
Newton, Caroline B., S. Orange, N. J.; m. Robert Wallace, '72; care Mrs. Edward D. Shepard, S. Orange, N. J.
Ordway, Annie M., Epping. N. H. ; m. Thos. C. Webber, '75 ; 29 Ashland St., Malden.
Paige, Mary C., Hardwick ; Hardwick.
Parker, Abbie M., Reading ; m. Wm. Bassett, '77 ; Bridgewater.
Porter, Ada M., Keene, N. H. ; m. Edward S. Bodwell, '74 ; Brunswick, Me.
Prescott, Louise S., Westport, N. Y. ; Au Sable, N. Y.
Proctor, Clara E., Tilton, N. H. ; m. Geo. F. Colson, '82; N. Billerica.
Ripley, Louisa W., Unionville, Ct. ; m. Oren T. Burdon, '73 ; Somers, Ct.
Roberts, Mary E., Amherst; m. John W. Clark, '78 ; N. Hadley.
Rollins, Caroline L., Harlem, N. Y. ; 113 E. 25th St., N. Y. City.
Rollins, Kate, Harlem, N. Y. ; m. Wm. A. McBurney, '80 ; Upper Montclair, N. J.
Sawyer, Julia L., Middletown, Ct. ; m. L. Hoyt Pease, '80 ; 28 Court St., New Britain, Ct.
Sickels, Emma C., Newark, N. J. ; Englewood, Ill.
Smith, Mary A., M.D., Westfield ; 33 Newbury St., Boston.
Sparks, Clara L., Provincetown ; m. J. Hersey Dyer, '75 ; Provincetown.
Stedman, Hattie M., Whately ; E. Whately.
Sterling, Jane H., Bridgeport, Ct. ; m. *Nelson Van Tassel, '82; 271 State St., Bridgeport, Ct.
Stilson, Alice M., Franklin, N. Y. ; m. Clement Gould, '75 ; Netherland Hotel, N. Y. City.
Storm, Fannie A., Sing Sing, N. Y. ; m. Geo. W. L. Curtis, '83; Box 230, Catskill, N. Y.
Van Ness, Anna, Hudson, N.Y.; m. Ezra D. DeLamater, Esq.,'77 ; 202 Union St., Hudson, N.Y.
Waldo, Genevieve, Scotland, Ct. ; Scotland, Ct.
Wear, Abbie L., Pittston, Pa. ; m. Anson G. Chester, '74 ; d. Topeka, Kan., '81.
Weeks, Helen L., Lyndon, Vt.; m. Harley H. Streeter, '77 ; General Delivery, P. O., Boston.
White, Charlotte M., W. Brookfield; m. J. Fred Vaile, Esq.,'75; 1610 Emerson Ave., Denver, Col.
Willcox, Ella G., Reading ; Wellesley College, Wellesley.
Williams, E. Isabel, Ashfield ; d. Ashfield, '79.
Woodford, Ida J., Unionville, Ct. ; m. Theron C. Darling, '73 ; W. Hartford, Ct.

1873.

GRADUATES.

Alford, Clara J., N. Canton, Ct. ; Plainville, Ct.
Boomhour, Clara A., Delhi, N. Y.; Institute for Blind, cor. 9th Ave. and 34th St., N.Y. City.
Buckingham, Laura A., Canton, O. ; care Mrs. H. B. Colt, Putnam Sem., Zanesville, O.
Burdon, Sarah E., Oxford ; m. Eugene Wetherell, '88 ; Oxford.
Butler, Abbie J., Southwick ; m. Geo. M. Black, '84 ; 833 17th Ave., Denver, Col.
Chapman, Eva L., New London, Ct.; m. Dr. Erastus Watrous,'79; 17 S.2d St., Wilmington, N.C.
Crocker, Sallie S., Portland, Me. ; Lakewood, N. J.
Dart, Jessie G., New London, Ct. ; d. New London, Ct., '81.

1873.

Dillon, Mary C., Dublin, Ind.; m. J. B. Knipe, '76; *Dublin, Ind.*
Ellis, Gertrude M., Springfield; m. Henry H. Bowman '74; d. Springfield, '93.
Eno, Fannie A., Simsbury, Ct.; *177 Sigourney St., Hartford, Ct.*
Farrar, Lillian, Rindge, N. H.; *E. Rindge, N. H.*
Field, Mary, Wellesley; *Wellesley.*
Glover, Clara F., Camden, Me.; *Hot Springs, N. C.*
Hague, Charlotte DeW., Bloomfield, N. J.; m. W. R. Cochrane, '79; *Maywood, N. J.*
Hammond, Julia F., Hadley; m. J. A. Sullivan, '82; d. Northampton, '83.
Hemingway, Mary A., Harford, N. Y.; m. Byron Wells, '82; 451 *Bryan St., Dallas, Tex.*
Herendeen, Clara N., Falmouth; m. Rev. J. B. Clark,'78; 271 *McDonough St., Brooklyn, N.Y.*
Hitchcock, Julia E., Ware; m. Franklin T. Webber, '82; *Fredonia, Col.*
Hooker, Henrietta E., Ph.D., Gardiner, Me.; *Mt. Holyoke College, S. Hadley.*
Hull, Caroline P., Madison, Ct.; m. Fred. P.Griswold, M.D.,'78; 481 *Broad St., Meriden, Ct.*
Johnston, H. Jane, Lebanon, Pa.; m. Harris Tabor, Esq., '80; *Elizabeth, N. J.*
Leonard, Marie I., Providence, R. I.; m. *Joseph R. Tuttle,'74; 18 *E. St.,Providence,R.I.*
Lyman, Eunice A., Easthampton; 22 *Hanover St., Fall River.*
Metcalf, Helen W., Franklin; 12 *Manchester St., Attleboro.*
Miner, Anna R., Old Lyme, Ct.; *Lyme, Ct.*
Miner, Eliza N., Ware; m. Prof. Charles E. Garman, '82; *Amherst.*
Muzzy, Alice M. M., Madura, India; 100 *East 57th St., New York City.*
Osgood, Ellen E., Abington, Ct.; *Cushing Academy, Ashburnham.*
Page, Josephine M., Rockport, Me.; m. Arthur B. Arey, '76; *Camden, Me.*
Parsons,Alice C.,Easthampton;m. Wm.O. Ballantine,M.D.,'75;d. Ahmednagar,India,'78.
Parsons, Ellen A., Philadelphia, Pa.; m. Robert W. Robins, '80; *Baldwin, N. Y.*
Pitcher, Eliza M., Searsdale, N. Y.; d. Astoria, N. Y., '92.
Pope, Frances E., Ogdensburg, N. Y.; m. W. H. Weston, M.D.; 400 *W. 22d St..N. Y. City.*
Salt, Ellnor M., Bath, N. Y.; *Bath, N. Y.*
Shumway, Emma A., Belchertown; 1904 *Madison St., Seattle, Wash.*
Smith, Abbie W., Granby; m. John H. Chandler, '79; d. Pasadena, Cal., '88.
Smith, Ellen A., Sunderland; *Sunderland.*
Smith, Rebecca F., South Hadley; *South Hadley.*
Sparhawk, Kate W., Boston Highlands; 80 *Vernon St., Boston Highlands.*
Stone, Harriet E., Phillipston; *Phillipston.*
Taylor, F. Lillian, Brookfield, Ct.; 308 *W. Tompkins St., Galesburg, Ill.*
Twitchell, Emma L., Brooklyn, N. Y.; m. Henry H. Hall; d. East Orange, N. J., '92.
Upson,M. Fannie,Westfield; m. Rev. B. W. Lockhart,'83; 104 *Lowell St.,Manchester,N. H.*
VanMeter, Mary L., M.D., Sandoway, British Burma; m. Rev. E. W. Kelly, '86; *Rangoon, British Burma, Asia.*
Van Ness, Abby, Chatham Center, N. Y.; d. Chatham Center, N. Y., '79.
Webb, Elizabeth M., Southwick; m. George Noble; *Anamosa, Io.*
Wood, Clara W., Holbrook; *Mt. Holyoke College, S. Hadley.*

NON-GRADUATES.

Andrew, Elva W., Danvers; m. *Chas. Lane; *Danvers.*
Atwood, Amanda, Shelburne, N. S.; m. Arnold Doane, '73; *Barrington, N. S.*
Baldwin, Carrie, Orange, N. J.; m. Sylvester Y. L'Hommedieu, '75; *S. Orange, N. J.*
Bardwell, Maria H., Shelburne Center; *Box 327, Greenfield.*
Bates, Irene E., Darien, Ct.; *Darien, Ct.*
Benedict, Elizabeth M., Richmond, Vt.; 186 *S. Willard St., Burlington, Vt.*
Bickmore, Hattie A., Tenant's Harbor, Me.; *Tenant's Harbor, Me.*
Bradford, Edith W., Boston Highlands; 375 *Harvard St., Cambridge.*

1873.

Buffum, Jennie G., Winchester, N. H.; m. Wm. H. Jennings, '75; *Winchester, N. H.*
Butler, Alice M., Essex Center, Vt.; m. Frank C. Granger, M.D., '73; *Randolph.*
Carpenter, Kate L., W. Charleston, Vt.; m. Chas. E. Bennett, '80; *W. Charleston, Vt.*
Chapman, Aurelia A., Essex, Ct.; m. Cassius E. Plimpton, '76; d. Bloomfield, Ct., '84.
Clapp, Harriet, Montague; *Montague.*
Clement, Mary E., Franklin, N. H.; *Franklin, N. H.*
Colby, Sarah M., Jonesville, Vt.; m. Harvey G. Dickey, '76; address in 1889, 195 *Front St., Worcester.*
Converse, Charlotte B., Norwich, Vt.; *Norwich, Vt.*
Crandall, Alice T., Bozrah, Ct.; m. Geo. V. Sevin, '78; *Yantic. Ct.*
Davis, Anna E., Northboro; m. Dwight B. Bradley, '78; *Oberlin, O.*
Dodd, Mary W., Bloomfield, N. J.; m. Wm. J. Simpson, Jr.,'88; 619 *Putnam Ave.,Brooklyn, N. Y.*
Dodge, Mary E., Concord, N. H.; m. Fred Reed, '79; *Auburn St., Concord, N. H.*
Dutton, Ellen H., Cambridge; m. Joseph B. Claus, '83; *Glen Rock, Malden.*
Ely, Sarah M., Mamaroneck, N. Y.; *Riverside Drive, 85th and 86th Sts., N. Y. City.*
Emery, Priscilla, Provincetown; d. Boston, '86.
Fairchild, Eliza B., Staten Island, N. Y.;
Faul, Frances I., Darien, Ct.; d. Darien, Ct., '74.
Faxon, Jeannette E., Milton, Vt.; *Oskaloosa, Io.*
Faxon, Laura W., Milton, Vt.; d. Rock Island, Ill., '75.
Felton, Susan W., Peabody; m. Walter W. Howe, '81; d. Marlboro, '89.
Field, Lucie R., Leverett; m. Thaddeus W. Fowler, '85; *Agawam.*
Fox, Flora W., Buffalo, N. Y.; 154 *W. 98th St., N. Y. City.*
Freyermuth, Kate A. (changed from Freeman), Darien, Ct.; m. *David B. Chase, '76; 15 *Forest St., Whitinsville.*
Genung, Adriana B., Blooming Grove, N. Y.; 17 *Little Ave., Middletown, N. Y.*
Goodale, Mary E., Marlboro; *Marlboro.*
Henderson, Margaret S., New Haven, Ct.; m. Rev. Wm. P. Sprague, '73; d. Rochester, N. Y., '91.
Hill, M. Alice, Fort Wayne, Ind.; 419 *9th St., S., Minneapolis, Minn.*
Homer, Harriet R., Brookline; *W. Roxbury.*
Hughitt, Ella A., Auburn, N. Y.; drowned, Onasco Lake, Cayuga Co., N. Y., '75.
Ives, F. Ella, Southwick; m. Jas. Nicholson, '85; *Southwick.*
Jackson, Mary A., Waldoboro, Me.; m. Rev. Chas. W. Longren, '88; *Franklin.*
Jackson, Mary E., Waldoboro, Me.; m. Wm. L. Allen, '60; 23 *Grove St., Rockland, Me.*
Johnson, Nellie S., Cambridge; m. Frank W. Harrington, '85; *N. Amherst.*
Kimball, Emma E., Walpole; m. Walter B. Allen, '83; d. Argentine, Kan., '88.
Ladd, Sarah P., Epping, N. H.; m. Edward W. Smith, '77; *Box 54, Raymond, N. H.*
Lindsley, Maria V., Raritan, N. J.; *Raritan, N. J.*
Mattoon, A. Lucy, Chicopee; *Southington, Ct.*
Millard, Phebe, N. Adams; m. Chas. S. Burton, '87; 326 *Home Ave., Oak Park, Ill.*
Miller, Martha P., S. Hadley; m. C. A. Gridley, '74; *S. Hadley.*
Munger, Martha C., N. Branford, Ct.; m. Hon. Erastus Dudley, '75; *N. Guilford, Ct.*
Newton, Ellen R., S. Orange, N. J.; m. Edward D. Shepard, '79; *S. Orange, N. J.*
Norton, Annie B., Cincinnati, O.; m. Adolf B. Hartdegen, '81; *Cincinnati, O.*
Penfield, Annie F., Rockford, Ill.; m. Calvin R. Mower, '81; *Box 2023, Rockford, Ill.*
Plowman, Mary, Elmira, N.Y.; m. *Lawrence W. Dimmick, '81; 346 *E. 65th St., N.Y. City.*
Pratt, Emily F., Essex, Ct.; *Essex, Ct.*
Ruggles, M. Theolotia, Hardwick; *Hardwick.*
Sawin, Ella F., Townsend; m. *Eliel S. Ball, '75; 507 *Main St., Waltham.*
Smith, Amelia A., Montpelier, Vt.; d. Montpelier, Vt., '73.

1873.

Smith, M. Anna, Brooklyn. N. Y. ; 372 *Halsey St., Brooklyn, N. Y.*
Swezey, Bertha, Port Jefferson, N. Y.; d. Port Jefferson, N. Y.,'74.
Tirrell, Ruth E., E. Abington; m. Elliot F. Denham, '77; *Westboro.*
Tomlinson, Elizabeth B., Bridgeport, Ct.; m. Clarence H. Kelsey, '85; 21 *Clinton St., E. Orange, N. J.*
Tomlinson, Emmeline S., Bridgeport, Ct.; m. C. Howard Daskam, '77; d. Albion, Mich, '84.
Torrey, M. Louise, Providence, R. I.; 182 *Meeting St., Providence, R. I.*
Troxell, Florence A., Allentown, Pa.; m. Thos. W. Saeger, '75; 113 *S. Fourth St., Allentown, Pa.*
Van Pelt, Gertrude, Roselle, N. J.; 297 *Marlborough St., Boston.*
Warner, Carrie E., Port Henry, N.Y.; m. Robert J. Wait, '76; 478 *Lenox Ave., N. Y. City.*
West, Marion W., Brooklyn, N. Y.; 76 *Pierrepont St., Brooklyn, N. Y.*
Wilkins, Helen M., Peabody; m. Frank W. Tucker, '82; *Clover Bend, Ark.*
Willard, Mary, Montpelier, Vt.; 340 *Commonwealth Ave., Boston.*
Williams, H. Blanche, Vineland, N. J.;
Williams, Minnie A., Brooklyn. N. Y.; *Brooklyn, N. Y.*
Willis, Ida J., Boonton, N. J.; m. Theo. F. Hunter, '83; *care Florida Citizen, Jacksonville, Fla.*
Wright, Sarah E., Oroomiah, Persia; 160 *and* 162 *W. 74th St., N. Y. City.*

1874.

GRADUATES.

Averill, Helen W., Danvers; *Danvers.*
Bailey, Minnie F., Boston; m. C. J. Bragdon, '79; *Excelsior, Minn.*
Bennett, Gazella, S. Wilbraham; 554 *Fourth St., S. Boston.*
Bottum, Caroline E., New Haven, Vt.; m. Edwin H. Hall; *Gorham St., Cambridge.*
Crane, Flora M., Bridport, Vt.; *care J. B. Johnson, Howard Univ., Washington, D. C.*
Davis, Anna Y., Milford, Del.; *Milford, Del.*
Dole, Amelia S., Shelburne; m. W. E. Ford, '76; *Ashfield.*
Ferrin, Ella L., Hinesburgh, Vt.; *Randolph, Vt.*
Ferrin, Emma I., Hinesburgh, Vt.; m. Rev. John Cowan; *S. Deerfield.*
Freeman, Elnora F., Provincetown; m. Henry M. Walradt, '83; *Marblehead.*
Hadlock, Margaret J., Monroe, N. H.; m. Arthur P. Martin, '81; *Iowa Falls, Io.*
Hall, H. Frances (Milligin), S. Hadley; 341 *Central St., Springfield.*
Harvey, Anna M., New Market, N. H.; *New Market, N. H.*
Humphrey, Maria B., Jericho Center, Vt.; m. Lucius R. Hazen, '75; 276 *College St., Middletown, Ct.*
Jennison, Abbie R., E. Templeton; *Greendale.*
Jones, Isabella L., Spencer; m. Chas. L. Kingsbury, M.D.,'81; 688 *Tremont St., Boston.*
Lee, Caroline M., Wayland; m. Chas. Hartwell, '89; 500 *Greene Ave., Brooklyn, N. Y.*
Lord, Sarah A., Montpelier, Vt.; m. Rev. Martin D. Kneeland, '75; 20 *Wyoming St., Roxbury.*
Loveland, Mary A., Norwich, Vt.; *Norwich, Vt.*
Manchester, Emily F., Bristol, R. I.; d. Bristol, R. I., '75.
Merrill, Mary H., Washington, D. C.; m. Edward M. Bentley, '88; 180 *Summer St., Boston.*
Palmer, Celia L., N. Stamford, Ct.; m. Abijah Merritt, '79; *Mt. Kisco, N. Y.*
Parker, Ida F., Winchendon; m. Fred. J. Hill, '81; 3 *Forest St., Cambridge.*
Peckham, Mary D., Providence, R. I.; *Putnam Heights, Ct.*

1874.

Pond, Kate C., New York City; m. Alva Stimis; *Hackensack, N. J.*
Porter, Ada L., Stowe,Vt.; m. Howard Thomas, '81; 1616 *Belknap Ave., W. Superior, Wis.*
Pratt, Helen M., Springfield; 45 *W. 20th St., N. Y. City.*
Scarborough, Mary F., Payson, Ill.; m. Rev. S. A. Wallace, '77; *Faribault, Minn.*
Smith, Charlotte E., Addison, Vt.; m. Everett C. Willard, '86; *Stamford, Ct.*
Smith, Julia R., S. Hadley; m. John A. Bennett, Esq., '77; d. Boston, '86.
Stearns, Mary S., Belchertown; m. *Edward H. Ingram, '78; d. N. Amherst, '82.
Sweetser, Abbie L., Worcester; *Greendale.*
Todd, Helena L., Golden's Bridge, N. Y.; *Golden's Bridge, N. Y.*
Tufts, Mary C., Rockport; m. Wilmot R. Griffin; *Box 182, Rockport.*
Warner, Delia H., Cummington; d. Cummington, '79.

NON-GRADUATES.

Aldrich, Alice L., Conway; m. Peter Hart. '75; *Conway.*
Allen, Abby W., S. Hadley; m. Prof. Clarence A. Waldo, '81; *Greencastle, Ind.*
Allen, Mary E., New Haven, Ct.; m. Wm. E. Gard,'80; 206 *Washington Ave.,Brooklyn, N. Y.*
Alvord, L. Hope, Florence; 221 *W. 44th St., N. Y. City.*
Andrews, L. Caroline, Winona, Minn.; *Albion View, Tenn.*
Avery, Mary E., Brandon, Vt.; d. Wallingford, Vt., '85.
Bannister, Ida C., Northampton; 45 *Prospect St., Northampton.*
Barber, Eva R., Troy, N. Y.;
Batchelder, Annie D., Boxford; m. Eugene C. Hussey, '82; *Topsfield.*
Blackman, Abbie B.,New Haven,Ct.; m.Robert T. Spencer,'79; 52 *Hart St.,Brooklyn,N. Y.*
Blanchard, Henrietta F., St. Johnsbury, Vt.; m. Chas. H. Farnsworth, '80; 61 *Dana St., Cambridge.*
Boynton, Mary H., Biddeford, Me.; m. Allen S. Skillings, '82; *Biddeford, Me.*
Branning, S. Elizabeth, Lee; m. Chas. A. Royce; 29 *Edwards St., Springfield.*
Bridgman, Mary S., Westhampton; m. Edwin B. Bridgman, '83; *Westhampton.*
Brown,Cora I., Minneapolis, Minn.; m. H. W. Brownson, '80; 1802 *E. Lake St. Minneapolis, Minn.*
Buffum, Louise A., N. Berwick, Me.; d. N. Berwick, Me.,'75.
Bushee, Clara F., S. Hadley Falls; *S. Hadley Falls.*
Caldwell, Alice, Waldoboro, Me.; *Waldoboro, Me.*
Campbell, Lillie, Westfield; m. *Frank R. Avery, '77; *Westfield.*
Case, Emma L., Cambridgeport; m. Rev. Chas. A. Marsh, '80; d. Woodfords, Me., '86.
Cheney, Ellen E., Orange; m. Chas. H. French, '78; 11 *Bacon St., Orange.*
Chittenden, Sarah W., Madison, Ct.; m. *Burton A. Hull, '77; *E. River, Ct.*
Clark, Lilian E., Bridgeport, Ct.; 67 *West Ave., Bridgeport, Ct.*
Conklin, Amanda, Rochester, N. Y.; m. —— Watson; deceased
Dann, Mary Emma, Greenville, Ill.; m. *Rev. Brabison B. Dundas, '77; m. Bruce B. Lockard, '90; *Plattville, Col.*
Davis, Mary C., W. Stafford, Ct.; m. John R. Gilbert, '76; *Gilead, Ct.*
Deering,Ella E., Portland, Me.; m. Washington J.Orr,'79; 152 *Cumberland St.,Portland,Me.*
Delano, Maria W., Waterbury, Vt.; d. Waterbury, Vt., '79.
Eaton, Ella M., Bristol, Vt.; m. J. Otis Wardwell, Esq., '77; 44 *Park St., Haverhill.*
Ely, Margaret D., N. Y. City; m. Prof. Anson D. Morse, '78; *Amherst.*
Emerson,Lizzie E., Stratford, Ct.; m. Rev. Hervey Gulick, '81; *Charlotte, Vt.*
England, Abbie H., Newburyport; m. Thos. F. Dodge, '75; 51 *Bloomingdale St., Chelsea.*
Farrar, Abbie C., S. Lincoln; d. S. Lincoln, '76.
Farrar, Jennie, Rindge, N. H.; m. Edward P. Johnson, '76; *E. Rindge, N. H.*
Foresman, Sarah M., Johnsonburg, N. J.; m. Rev. Jas. A.Menaul, '75; *Albuquerque,'N. M.*

1874.

French, Mary W., Danvers Center; *Tapleyville.*
Gulick, Harriet M., Florence, Italy ; m. Cyrus A. Clark, '87 ; *Miyazaki, Japan.*
Hager, Julia A., Proctorsville, Vt. ; m. David F. Rugg, M.D., '81 ; *Hartland, Vt.*
Hager, Sarah E., Proctorsville, Vt. ; m. Chas. W. Goddard, '83 ; *Ludlow, Vt.*
Hersey, S. Elizabeth, S. Abington ; m. *Horace R. Reed, '79 ; *Whitman.*
Hitchcock, Frances E., S. Hadley Falls ; m. Seldon E. McGeehon, '92; *Bangor, Me.*
Holmes, Abbie M., Beaufort, S. C. ; m. Niels Christensen, '75; *Beaufort, S. C.*
Hotchkiss, Emma L., Plantsville, Ct. ; m. Lucius B. Tuttle, '76 ; *217 Mansfield St., New Haven, Ct.*
Howe, Cora W., Brattleboro, Vt. ; m. Hiram W. Moore, '76; *La Fayette, Ind.*
Hurlburt, Mary L., E. Hartford, Ct.; m. Benj. F. Gould, '83; *Wethersfield, Ct.*
Hyde, Hattie E., Milford, N. H. ; m. Albert A. Gilson, '74 ; d. Milford, N. H., '76.
Jenkins, Maria, E. Abington; 15 *Union St., Rockland.*
Jennison, Lucia N., E. Templeton ; 45 *Cottage St., Cambridge.*
Keese, Mary J., Lowell ; m. Otto H. L. Schwartzky, '80; *Fitchburg.*
Kendall, Alice E., Chicopee ; m. Edward E. Gaylord, M. D., '81 ; *Pasadena, Cal.*
Kennedy, Fannie L., Waldoboro, Me. ; *Waldoboro, Me.*
Landfear, Sarah S., New Haven, Ct. ; 125 *St. John St., New Haven, Ct.*
Lindsley, Margaret V., Raritan, N. J. ; *Raritan, N. J.*
Lucas, Jennie M., Marion, O. ; m. Robert W. Harrington, '81 ; *Cuyahoga Falls, O.*
Lyman, Sarah G., Easthampton ; 155 *Catharine St., Springfield.*
Lyon Lenna I., Newark, N. J. ; m. Chas. A. Wharton, '81 ; 134 *W. Kinney St., Newark, N.J.*
McLean, Sarah P., Simsbury, Ct. ; m. *F. L. Green, '88; *Simsbury, Ct.*
Magill, Helen A., Manistee, Mich.; m. *Walter Goff, '83 ; m. Y. H. Brown, '92; d. '93.
Mosman, Bessie G., Waterbury, Ct. ; m. Eugene Fancher, '80 ; d. Waterbury, Ct., '89.
Nettleton, Elnora C., Norfolk, Ct. ; m. Geo. Holt, '77; *Norfolk, Ct.*
Nichols, Jane E., Essex, Vt. ; m. Chas. E. Greene, '76 ; *Essex, Vt.*
Osborne, Alice M., Jackson, Mich.; m. Arthur D. Lathrop, '74; 125 *Stewart Ave., Jackson, Mich.*
Phillips, Mary O., Council Bluffs, Io. ; 2203 *4th St., Seattle, Wash.*
Poor, Clara A., Reno, Nev. ; m. C. C. Powning, '75 ; *Reno, Nev.*
Post, Lucy E., Logansport, Ind.; m. Prof. Stanley Coulter, '77; 273 *Main St., La Fayette, Ind.*
Reamer, Cassie A., Leavenworth, Kan. ; m. Willard S. Terry, '90 ; *Hilo, Hawaii, H. I.*
Reed, Anna G., S. Abington; m. Geo. E. Keith, '77; *Campello.*
Rogers, Belle A., Essex, Ct. ; m. Francis A. Shailer, '77; *Essex, Ct.*
Rogers, Celia A., Falmouth ; *Falmouth.*
Roper, Isabelle M., Boston; m. Hon. Frank L. Coombs, '79; *Coombs St., Napa City, Cal.*
Shattuck, Helen W., Bethlehem, N. H. ; m. W. C. Bartlett, '75; *Wing Road, N. H.*
Shattuck, Ida E., Pepperell; *Pepperell.*
Shattuck, Loella V., Pepperell; *Pepperell.*
Smith, Ida A., Philadelphia, Pa. ; m. Edward M. Alden, '74 ; d. Williamsett, '91.
Snow, Carrie L., Chicopee ; d. Chicopee, '74.
Spaulding, Harriet L., Bristol, Me. ; m. Isaac Allen; 24 *Lorett Place, Lynn.*
Stearns, Margaret E., Springfield, Vt. ; m. Halsted Burnett, '77 ; *St. Louis, Mo.*
Stowe, Harriette B., Suffield, Ct. ; m. Rev. Robert C. Bell, '84 ; *Granby.*
Strong, Ellen S., Colerain ; d. Glencoe, Ill., '80.
Taylor, Abbie W., Granby ; m. Arthur W. Fiske, '84 ; *Granby.*
Taylor, Sarah H., Kennett Square, Pa.; m. Caleb H. Jackson, '76; *Brownrille, N. Y.*
Tuckerman, Corinne E., Austinburg, O.; m. C. Emir Allen, '77 ; 234 *10th East St., Salt Lake City, Utah.*
Turner, Julia A., Killingworth, Ct. ; m. Courtland P. Davis, '80 ; 34 *Ashley St., Hartford, Ct.*
Warfel, Ila, Lancaster City, Pa. ; m. W. F. Beyer, Esq., '80 ; 433 *W. Orange St., Lancaster, Pa.*

Wetmore, Frances M., M.D., Hilo, Hawaii, H. I.; *Hilo, Hawaii, H. I.*
Whallon, Lillian M., Port Henry, N. Y.; m. Chas. S. Judd, '78; *Port Henry, N. Y.*
White, Mary A., Brookline; *Tappan St., Brookline.*
Wilkes, J. Victoria, Buffalo, N. Y.; m. Henry Wright, '77; *Harbor Springs, Mich.*

1875.

GRADUATES.

Adams, Abbie A., Medway; *Northboro.*
Barton, Frances H., Orange; d. Orange, '77.
Bissell, Fannie E., E. Windsor, Ct.; m. Geo. S. Phelps, '78; *Warehouse Point, Ct.*
Brown, Mary E., Winchendon; m. Rev. Fred. H. Rowse,'81; *Plymouth.*
Burrill, M. Letitia, Rockland; m. A. H. Fenn, M.D., '89; 30 *Capitol Ave., Meriden, Ct.*
Campbell, Mary A., Montreal, Can.; 51 *Belmont Park, Montreal, Can.*
Clark, Lucy C., Onondaga Valley, N. Y.; m. Byron Wells, '76; d. Onondaga Valley, N.Y.,'81.
Cutler, Mary S., Florence; *State Library, Albany, N. Y.*
Dickerman, Amelia S., Whitneyville, Ct.; *Whitneyville, Ct.*
Dyer, Caroline E., Spencer; 6 *W. 21st St., N. Y. City.*
Gifford, M. Caroline, New Haven, Vt.; m. Rev. Rufus B. Tobey, '82; d. Boston, '90.
Goldthwait, Elizabeth S., Longmeadow; m. Chas. S. Allen, '77; *Longmeadow.*
Hart, Mary A., New Haven, Ct.; m. Abraham R. Perkins,'83; *W. Upsal St., Germantown, Philadelphia, Pa.*
Hazen, Frances A., Ahmednagar, India; m. Rev. Loren S. Gates, '75; *Sholapur, W.India.*
Huntington, Eliza M., Fairfield, Ct.; m. Wm. H. Burr, '80; *Westport, Ct.*
Ingraham, Carrie E., N. Adams; m. Prof. Friedrich W. Jannasch, '86; *Stellenbosch, Cape of Good Hope, S. Africa.*
Jennings, Eleanor B., Easton, Pa.; m. Rev. John R. Henderson; *Mifflintown, Pa.*
Johnson, Hannah N., Upton; *Upton.*
Kingman, Ella, Bridgeport, Ct.; m. Horace L. Eames, '79; *Seaside Park, Bridgeport, Ct.*
Kneeland, Stella, S. Onondaga, N. Y.; m. F. C. Eddy,'86; 507 *Univ. Ave., Syracuse, N.Y.*
Lamson, Martha E., N. Hadley; m. Stanley A. Phillips, '80; d. Amherst, '92.
Mack, Isabella G., Manchester, N. H.; 128 *S. Main St., Manchester, N. H.*
Newton, Martha C., Southboro; m. L. Hoyt North, '89; *Oklahoma City, Ok.*
Paine, M. Evangeline, E. Putnam, Ct.; m. Newton T. Kitchell, Esq.; *Boonton, N. J.*
Richards, Nellie C., Unionville, Ct.; m. Forbes B. Woodruff, '78; *Southington, Ct.*
Richardson, Orrilla D., Columbia, Ct.; m. Elford C. Russell, '90; *Orange, Ct.*
Rowell, Mary A., Waimea, Kauai, H. I.; m. *Louis H. Stolz, '80; 778 *Putnam Av., Brooklyn, N. Y.*
Sperry, Ruth T., E. Windsor Hill, Ct.; *E. Windsor Hill, Ct.*
Wilkes, Ellen M., Buffalo, N. Y.; 186 *Gordon St., Kingston, Ont., Can.*

NON-GRADUATES.

Allen, Lizzie E., Florence; *Box 5, Florence.*
Baldwin, Helen E., Watertown, Ct.; m. David Woodward, '77; 190 *Forest Ave., Atlanta, Ga.*
Baldwin, Lizzie G., Fair Haven, Ct.; m. Wm. A. Rowe, '79; 79 *Quinnipiac St., New Haven, Ct.*
Beals, L. Dora, Florence; m. E. A. Hannum, '75; *Easthampton.*
Beckley, Annie J., New Haven, Ct.; m. Chas. C. Brewster, '77; *New Haven, Ct.*
Benner, S. Frances, Lowell; m. Louis Morey, '80; 474 *Beacon St., Lowell.*
Bent, Mary E., Winchendon; m. Horace Sanderson, '76; 1710 16*th Ave., Denver, Col.*

1875.

Bigelow, Carrie F., Jaffrey, N. H. ; *Winchendon Springs.*
Blodgett, Estelle M., Stafford, Ct. ; m. Lucius D. Smith, '78 ; *New London, Ct.*
Bosworth, Mary A., Westboro ; m. Joseph E. Tidd, '80 ; *225 Chandler St., Worcester.*
Boyden, Cornelia F., Washington, D. C. ; *22 3d St. S. E., Washington, D. C.*
Brown, Esther M., Wells River, Vt. ; *Escondido, Cal.*
Buck, Eliza H., Fall River ; *20 Prospect St., Fall River.*
Burdic, Louise A., Syracuse, N. Y. ; *356 W. Onondaga St., Syracuse, N. Y.*
Burnette, Delia S., S. Hadley ; m. *J. Edward Miller, '75 ; *S. Hadley.*
Butters, Mary A., Burlington ; m. Thos. A. Green, '80 ; *Carlisle.*
Carpenter, Lilla A., W. Charleston, Vt.; m. Harding A. Clark, '79; *Wallace, Kan.*
Casper, Irena, N. Chatham, N. Y. ; m. Refine L. Rossman, '77 ; *Hudson, N. Y.*
Chamberlain, Mary E., Bath, N. H. ; m. Samuel Ross, '76 ; *Bath, N. H.*
Clapp, Ellen L., Westhampton ; m. *E. Augustus Allen, '82 ; *19 Pleasant St., Holyoke.*
Clark, Clara B., Spencerport, N. Y. ; m. Rev. Theo. B. Williams, '77 ; *Martinsburg, N. Y.*
Clark, Emily W., Amherst ; m. F. W. Stearns, '80 ; *185 Highland St., Boston.*
Coffin, Chloe M., Edgartown ; *Edgartown.*
Cogswell, Mary E., Chicopee ; m. Henry W. Wood, '87 ; *598 Third Ave., Lansingsburg, N. Y.*
Colby, Florence M., Jonesville, Vt. ; *Jonesville, Vt.*
Cook, Mary E., Keene, N. H. ; *202 W. Newton St., Boston.*
Davis, Ada C., Acton ; *Berwick, Io.*
Dudley, Lizzie, Westfield ; m. Henry E. Cushing, M.D., '84 ; *119 W. Hill St., Champaign, Ill.*
Edmands, Anna M., Boston Highlands ; *61 Quincy St., Roxbury.*
Erickson, Carrie L., Kendallville, Ind. ; m. *Marquis De Caskey, '78 ; *6461 Myrtle Ave., Chicago, Ill.*
Ferguson, Mary, New Haven, Ct.; m. Rev. Geo. P. Torrence, '79 ; *Catherton Ave., Zanesville, O.*
Galbraith, Annie M., M.D., Carlisle, Pa. ; *Carlisle, Pa.*
Galbraith, Lois Carrie, Carlisle, Pa. ; *Carlisle, Pa.*
Grace, Emma L., Portsmouth, N. H. ; *8 Richards Ave., Portsmouth, N. H.*
Granger, Elizabeth J., Spencer ; m. *G. H. Sedgwick, '78 ; m. Fred. Arnold Bemis, '83 ; *Littleton, Col.*
Graves, Ella M., Saco, Me. ; m. Chas. Nickerson, '81 ; *Garden City, Minn.*
Hale, Annie M., Foxcroft, Me. ; *Manchester, N. H.*
Harkness, Margaret, Brooklyn, N.Y.; m. *LeGrand B.Smith,'77; *48 N.Y.Ave., Brooklyn, N.Y.*
Harris, Almira M., Phillipsburg, N. J. ; m. Abraham McMurtrie, '85 ; *Belvidere, N. J.*
Harrison, Anna W., N. Adams ; d. N. Adams, '76.
Harrison, Sarah F., N. Adams ; m. Wm. E. Demond, '82 ; *Stafford Springs, Ct.*
Hinks, Jennie I., Bridgeport, Ct.; *care Maj. W. B. Hinks, 181 Broom St., Bridgeport, Ct.*
Hitchcock, H. Catherine, Ashby ; m. Albert H. Rand, '83 ; *181 Brown St., Waltham.*
Hubbard, Frances I. (name changed to Whitaker), Wakefield ; d. Denver, Col., '80.
Hurlbut, Jessie L., Bennington, Vt.; m. Edward H. Scott, '78 ; *150 North St., Bennington, Vt.*
Janes, Jennette C., Easthampton ; m. Frank P. Newkirk, '77 ; *Easthampton.*
Johnson, Mary C., Oberlin, O.; m. Chas. E. Smith, '81 ; *Helena, Ark.*
Jones, Mary R., Falmouth ; m. L. F. Doane, '77 ; *3319 E. Ninth St., Kansas City, Mo.*
Kelley, Mary A., Cambridgeport ; m. Rev. Horace H. Leavitt, '76 ; *342 Harvard St., Cambridge.*
Landfear, M. Emma, New Haven, Ct.; *125 St. John St., New Haven, Ct.*
Laurie, Annie, Providence, R. I.; m. Lawton S. Brooks, M.D., '78 ; *126 Chestnut St., Springfield.*
Leonard, Jane R., Clear Creek, Io.; m. *Geo. Washington Leonard, '74 ; d. Springville, Utah, '94.
Lord, Jane A., Montpelier, Vt.; m. Dr. Geo. W. Sargent ; *Seneca Castle, N. Y.*
McFarland, Lizzie, Worcester ; *117 Thomas St., Worcester.*

1875.

Mellish, Florence, N. Scituate, R. I.; *Killingly, Ct.*
Mendall, Mary E. S., Brooklyn, N. Y.; m. Chas. T. White, '88; 636 *Hancock St., Brooklyn, N. Y.*
Miller, Mary G., N. Y. City; m. Adelbert H. Stephenson, '78; *S. Bend, Ind.*
Moore, Sarah A., Newton, N. J.; *Newton, N. J.*
Newcomb, Elizabeth, M.D., Blissfield, Mich.; *Tewksbury.*
Nichols, Charlotte C., Freetown; *Assonet Village, Freetown.*
Page, Delisa T., Brimfield; m. Allen H. Warner, '78; 31 *Clarendon St., Springfield.*
Pearce, Elizabeth, Boston; *Roslindale.*
Perkins, Blanche, Becket; m. Rev. R. F. Algier; *Readsboro, Vt.*
Phillips, Mary I., W. Winsted, Ct.; m. Henry L. Mallory, '78; 648 *St. Mark's Ave., Brooklyn, N. Y.*
Plumer, Mary F., Biddeford, Me.; m. Edwin C. Neal, '04; *Newburyport.*
Pond, Ida E., N. Y. City; m. I. Waters Sylvester, '84; *Passaic, N. J.*
Ramsey, Loretta A., Stevens Point, Wis.; m. Geo. H. Patch, '75; 824 *Wisconsin Ave., Stevens Point, Wis.*
Rice, Fannie L., Fair Haven, Ct.; m. Prof. E. C. Norton, '84; *Claremont, Cal.*
Roberts, Mary C., Greenfield; *Greenfield.*
Rogers, Annie V., Frenchtown, N. J.; m. Henry N. Van Dyke, '80; *Princeton, N. J.*
Rundell, Emma A., Hunter, N. Y.; m. Roswell S. Harris, '82; *Hunter, N. Y.*
Sabeu, Mary, Winchester, N. H.; m. *Rev. Timothy Lyman, '79; *W. Brookfield.*
Sawyer, S. Emma, E. Templeton; *East Templeton.*
Scrogy, Mary A., Woodstock, Ct.; m. Norman O. Chapin, '76; *East Amherst.*
Shumway, Leila S., Belchertown; m. Herbert F. Curtis, '81; *Belchertown.*
Simpson, Helen L., Hudson, N. Y.; m. *M. G. Emery, Esq.,'82; m. Lieut. Chas. P.Shaw, U. S. N., '91; *Esmont, Va.*
Smith, Harriet E., Bricksburg, N. J.; *Lakewood, N. J.*
Storrs, Sara A., S. Coventry, Ct.; m. Frank R. Jewett, '80; *Woodstock, Vt.*
Strong, Mary E., Northampton; m. O. Leroy Woodward, '80; *Northampton.*
Tirrell, Mary B., S. Weymouth; m. Clarence W. Fearing, '83; *Provincetown.*
Todd, Julia A., Golden's Bridge, N. Y.; m. Theron J. Horton, '78; *Golden's Bridge, N. Y.*
Trow, Elizabeth F., Brockton; 69 *Wyman St., Brockton.*
Turner, Mary S., Bricksburg, N. J.; 333 *Harvard St., Cambridge.*
Warren, Elizabeth H., Berlin, Vt.; d. Berlin, Vt., '79.
Wheaton,Ida B., Detroit, Mich.; m. Wm. E. Riddle,'79; 811 *N. Tejon St.,Col.Springs,Col.*
Whipple, Mary E., Worcester; 16 *Oread St., Worcester.*
Whitaker, Frances I. (see Frances I. Hubbard, above).
Whitcomb,Alice M.,Keene,N. H.; m. Marshall W. Sims,'86; 16 *Rumford St., Concord,N.H.*
White, Kate H., Worcester; m. Harley Stone, '76; 303 *W. 118th St., N. Y. City.*
Wilson, Annie S., Goshen, N. Y.; d. Shrewsbury, N. J., '81.
Wyman, Mary F., Keene, N. H.; *Box 503, Keene, N. H.*
Yale, Mary A., Ware; m. *Wm. N. Shepard, '82; *Box 695, Beloit, Kan.*

1876.

GRADUATES.

Allen, Emma M., West Springfield; *Springville, Utah.*
Avery, Julia S., Columbia, Ct.; 147 *Walcott St., Pawtucket, R. I.*
Barbour, Amie L., Lewiston, Me.; m. Treby Johnson, '80; 58 *Winthrop St., Augusta, Me.*
Chamberlain, Laura M., Southboro; m. Leonard L. Conant; 974 *Main St., Worcester.*

1876.

Chapin, Delia L., M.D., Granby ; 427 *State St., Springfield.*
Cummings, Mary E., Strafford, Vt.; m. Rev. Thos. Gamble,'87; *Heidleberg, Cape Colony, S. A.*
Davis, Alice M., Hubbardston ; m. Amos Armsby, '77 ; *Millbury.*
Doty, E. Marcia, Troy, N. J. ; m. Alfred C. N. Johnson ; 145 *Trenchard St., Yonkers, N. Y.*
Eaton, Mary S., Palmyra, N. Y. ; *Palmyra, N. Y.*
Edwards, Mary H., Raritan, N. J. ; d. Denver, Col., '85.
Farman, Mary F., Ellington, N. Y.; m. J. R. Swigart, M. D. ; *Beloit, Kan.*
Farwell, Julia H., Wells River, Vt. ; *Wells River, Vt.*
Fuller, Eleanor L., N. Ferrisburgh, Vt.; m. Capt. M. C. Martin, '78 ; 1462 *Washington Ave., Denver, Col.*
Gooding, Gertrude, M. D., Bristol, R. I. ; *Bristol, R. I.*
Gottschalk, Mary H. von, Providence, R. I. ; 190 *Bucklin St., Providence, R. I.*
Guild, Fanny C., Milford, N. H.; *Dana Hall, Wellesley.*
Hale, Jennie N., Chester, Vt. ; 141 *E. 19th St., N. Y. City.*
Hewitt, Persis D., North Pomfret, Vt. ; *North Pomfret, Vt.*
Hinman, Harriet A., New Haven, Vt. ; m. John C. Wilder, Jr., '85 ; *New Haven, Vt.*
Hollister, Jane R., Sharon, Ct. (name changed to Jane E. Reed ; see below).
Howland, Abbie B., Chatham, N. Y. ; 3 *Linden St., Cambridge.*
Jones, Martha A., Fort Wayne, Ind. ; m. J. M. Moderwell, '86; 53 *W. Superior St., Fort Wayne, Ind.*
Kimball, Alice S., Chicago. Ill. ; m. Samuel F. Smith, M.D., '77 ; d. Indian Orchard, '90.
Lester, Sarah J., Woodstock, Ct. ; *care Y. W. C. A., Brooklyn, N. Y.*
Littlefield, Helen E., Kennebunk Depot, Me. ; m. Ambrose Littlefield, '80 ; d. Kennebunk Depot, Me., '87.
Lord, Alice F., N. Haven, Ct. ; m. H. W. Painter, M.D., '92; *W. Haven, Ct.*
Loveland, Elizabeth M., Norwich, Vt. ; m. Thomas A. Hazen, '78 ; *Norwich, Vt.*
Peck, Elizabeth L., M.D., Stratford, Ct. ; 819 *N. 40th St., Philadelphia, Pa.*
Reed, Jane E. (see Hollister, above), Sharon, Ct. ; m. Rev. C. Willard Bird, '84 ; *Portland, Mich.*
Root, Susan B., Belchertown ; *Norwalk, Ct.*
Sawyer, Mary L., Boxford ; *Boxford.*
Searle, Minnie F., Onondaga Valley, N. Y. ; m. Wm. H. Fisher, '77 ; 518 *S. Salina St., Syracuse, N. Y.*
Sloan, Emma J., New Haven, Ct. ; 1494 *Chapel St., New Haven, Ct.*
Stevenson, Emma M., Cayuga, N. Y. ; *Cayuga, N. Y.*
Towle, Ellen J., Kingston, N. H. ; m. Henry L. Sweeny, M.D., '84 ; *Kingston, N. H.*
Wheeler, Caroline I., Pigeon Cove; m. David C. Babson, '80; *Pigeon Cove.*
Whitaker, Sara, Southold, N. Y. ; d. Southold, N. Y., '87.
Whitney, Clara S., Winchendon ; *Winchendon.*
Wright, Alvinia S., Central College, O. ; d. Central College, O., '81.

NON-GRADUATES.

Alter, Josephine B., Plainfield, Pa. ; *Plainfield, Pa.*
Babbitt, Emma L., Mendham, N. J. ; 56 *Mills St., Morristown, N. J.*
Barker, Susan E., Boston ; m. W. R. Ray, M.D., '84 ; 26 *Collins St., Melbourne, Victoria, Australia.*
Barnes, Ella S., Chimney Point, Vt. ; m. Winslow C. Watson, Esq., '79 ; *Plattsburg, N. Y.*
Barrows, Annie G., Newark, O. ; m. Chas. A. Hatch, M.D., '78 ; 64 *N. 5th St., Newark, O.*
Bean, M. Ella, Stillwater, Minn. ; m. Jerry C. Brown, '81 ; *N. 12th St., San Jose, Cal.*
Broughton, Fanny H., Kingston, Md. ; m. Edwin D. Long, Esq., '83 ; *Westover, Md.*

Brown, Abbie A., Wells River, Vt. ; m. Henry K. White, '80; 1804 *Vermont Ave., Washington, D. C.*
Bruner, Lizzie P., Albion, N. Y. ; m. John E. Sutton, M. D., '91; *Albion, N. Y.*
Burnette, Mary E., S. Hadley; m. Alden L. Graves, '77 ; *S. Hadley.*
Chaffee, Mary S., Westford, Ct. ; m. E. F. Farrar, '83 ; *683 Main St., Springfield.*
Clapp, Laura H., Westhampton ; m. Fred. A. Dayton, '85 ; *287 King St., Northampton.*
Clark, Anna B., Groton, Ct. ; *148 Spring St., Portland, Me.*
Clark, Mary C., Wilton, Ct. ; m. James T. Hubbell ; *Greenwich, S. C.*
Cleveland, Dora P., Skowhegan, Me. ; *Skowhegan, Me.*
Clough, Mary E., West Amesbury ; *54 Sparhawk St., Amesbury.*
Cole, Lottie R., Middletown, Ct. ; *175 State St., Springfield.*
Converse, Orissa W., Hinsdale ; m. Heman C. Mitchell, '81 ; *Dalton.*
Cooper, Annie F., Lebanon, Pa. ; m. Chas. E. Buell, '77 ; *Plainfield, N. J.*
Cutler, Helen E., Ware ; d. Ware, '76.
Deering, Myra E., Saco, Me. ; m. Dormer Chapin, '88 ; *Box 744, Saco, Me.*
Delano, Alice L., Waterbury, Vt. ; *252 Marlborough St., Boston.*
Duncan, Elizabeth C., Poquonnock, Ct. ; m. J. D. Eggleston, M.D., '81 ; *132 W. Main St., Meriden, Ct.*
Dunham, S. Rosa, Southington, Ct. ; m. Prof. Fred. B. Barnes, '84 ; *Garden Grove, Orange Co., Cal.*
Ellis, Hattie L., Manistee, Mich. ; m. A. C. Lee, '81 ; *Oriska, N. Dakota.*
Farmar, Mary L., Westfield; m. Rev. Egbert N. Munroe, '81 ; *Deerfield.*
Giffin, Emma L., Otter River ; m. Chas. H. Wright, '81 ; *care Edgemoor Bridge Works, Wilmington, Del.*
Gill, Clara E., Brockton ; m. Rev. R. H. Kennedy, '92 ; *Pepperell.*
Gillette, Mary S., Old Lyme. Ct. ; *Lyme, Ct.*
Goodwin, Ellen R., Waterbury, Ct. ; m. Fred. M. Berry, '81 ; d. Waterbury, Ct., '84.
Hale, Lucy E., Castine, Me. ; m. Edward H. Fiske, '90 ; *Shelburne.*
Haley, Etta, Fryeburg, Me. ; m. Edward S. Osgood, '77 ; *48 Winter St., Portland, Me.*
Hartwell, Emily S., Foochow, China ; *701 Laurel Ave., St. Paul, Minn.*
Hemenway, Lizzie V., Hopkinton ; *Hopkinton.*
Herron, Anna B., Dehra, Northern India ; *Saharanpur, Northern India.*
Hilburn, Laura, Easton, Pa. ; *507 and 509 Market St., Philadelphia, Pa.*
Holt, Alice A., Blue Hill. Me. ; *68 Clarendon St., Boston.*
Houk, Mariana P., Dayton, O. ; m. Col. Harry E. Mead, '76 ; *Oakwood, Dayton, O.*
Jaques, Mary E., Washingtonville, N. Y. ; *464 California St., Denver, Col.*
Jenkins, Mary E., Brookside, N. J. ; *Newark, N. J.*
Jones, Mary W., N. Y. City ; m. John Kiernan, '84 ; d. Yonkers, N. Y., '85.
Kendall, Leila, Cambridgeport ; m. Rev. John K. Browne, '76 ; *Harpoot, Turkey, Asia ;* home address, 50 *Chestnut St., Cambridgeport.*
Kilner, Grace E., Templeton ; m. John McIlvene, Esq., '76 ; *Templeton.*
Kilner, Jennie B. H., Templeton ; m. Edward R. Gould ; *37 Highland Ave., Minneapolis, Minn.*
Kimball, Mary W., Plainfield, N. J. ; *110 E. 29th St., N. Y. City.*
King, Emilie F., New Haven, Ct. ; *Talladega College, Talladega, Ala.*
King, Hattie E., Ravenna, O. ; m. Arthur Mosley, '80 ; *541 Greenwood Ave., Detroit, Mich.*
Kingsbury, Frances E., Glastonbury, Ct. ; m. Thos. H. Gordon, '80 ; *Gloucester City, N. J.*
Lyman, Sarah W., Springfield ; m. Joel B. Sexton, '78 ; *11 S. Forest St., Hartford, Ct.*
McLellan, Alice J., Marietta, Ga. ; m. Alonzo J. White, '79 ; *10 W. Ellis St., Atlanta, Ga.*
MacMath, Elizabeth V., New Castle, Pa. ; m. B. C. Young, '81 ; *New Castle, Pa.*
McQuitty, Mary S., Mansfield, Pa. ; m. Robert Moore, '77 ; *Carnegie, Pa.*
Metcalf, Mary E., Medway ; m. Leonard E. Taylor, '81 ; *Woonsocket, R. I.*
Miller, Lucy A., S. Hadley ; *S. Hadley.*

1876.

Miner, Ellen M., Salem, Ct.; d. Salem, Ct., '85.
Montague, Myra A.. S. Hadley; m. Alfred E. Thornton, '84; 28 *Fifth St., New Bedford.*
Munger, Isabel A., N. Branford, Ct.; m. C. A. Harrison, Esq., '76; *Box 634, Wallingford, Ct.*
Murch, Margie J., Carmel, Me.; m. Isaac Hutchinson, '88; *Box 46, Castine, Me.*
Paine, Dollie E., Boston; m. Rev. W. W. Everts, '78; 20 *Newcomb St., Haverhill.*
Payne, Harriet B., Knoxville, Tenn.; d. Dunbar, Neb., '82.
Pease, Clara A., Springfield; 277 *Central St., Springfield.*
Peck, Susan A., Southington, Ct.; *Plainfield, Ct.*
Perkins, Sarah E., Gloucester; m. *Thos. M. Stimpson, Esq., '83; 15 *Main St., Peabody.*
Platts, Lizzie F., N. Abington; *N. Abington.*
Pond, Annie W., N. Y. City; m. Burton J. McGrew, '80; *Los Angeles, Cal.*
Posten, Mary M., Navesink, N. J.; m. Adelbert T. S. Clark, '79; *Metuchen, N. J.*
Pratt, Harriette J., W. Cornwall, Ct.; *W. Cornwall, Ct.*
Randall, Harriette D., Bayonne City, N. J.; m. B. W. Reynolds, '79; *Troy, N. Y.*
Raymond, Fanny E., W. Hartford, Ct.; *Sidney, Neb.*
Rogers, Marcia P., Falmouth; m. W. C. Davis, '91; d. Falmouth, '92.
Rood, Martha A., Westfield; m. Rev. Dwight M. Pratt, '82; 27 *Pine St., Portland, Me.*
Sharp, Katherine A., S. Onondaga, N. Y.; m. D. H. Pinckney, '77; *S. Onondaga, N. Y.*
Shaylor, Emma A., Lee; m. Frank Belding, '80; 72 *William St., Bridgeport, Ct.*
Smith, J. Belle, S. Hadley Falls; m. E. D. Newcomb, '82; *S. Hadley Falls.*
Stannard, Lillie S., New Haven, Ct.; m. Chas. H. Park, '76; *Mystic, Ct.*
Studley, Elma L., Stafford Springs, Ct.; 11 *Flag St., Worcester.*
Sweetser, Martha Z., Worcester; m. Walter F. Gleason, '77; *Greendale.*
Taft, Theo, Whitinsville; m. Edward S. Clark, '80; 40 *Stimson Ave., Providence, R. I.*
Taylor, Agnes, Rockford, Ill.; m. Jas. R. Crocker, '81; *Evanston, Ill.*
Thomas, Georgia, Salisbury, Vt.; m. Cyrus A. Bump, '78; d. Salisbury, Vt., '91.
Thompson, Abbie H., Marshall, Tex.; m. Orlon H. Boies, '87; d. N. Y. City.
Thompson, Anna A., Niagara Falls, N. Y.; *Niagara Falls, N. Y.*
Thompson, Winnie S., Niagara Falls, N. Y.; m. Horace D. Taft, '92; *Watertown.*
Towle, Lilla B., Kingston, N. H.; m. J. H. Dearborn, M.D., '78; 38 *Colon St., Beverly.*
Vaille, Madora C., Springfield; m. Andrew B. Wallace, '83; *Locust Hill, Springfield.*
Van Ness, Lucinda, Hudson, N. Y.; m. Claudius Rockfeller, Esq., '79; *Willard Block, Hudson, N. Y.*
Van Voorhes, Kate, Stratford, Ct.; *Stratford, Ct.*
Waite, M. Ella, Baldwinsville; m. Chas. A. Perley, Jr., '81; *Baldwinsville.*
Wales, Jennie E., N. Abington; *N. Abington.*
Walker, Adelia S., Fryeburg, Me.; m. Tobias L. Eastman, '84; *Fryeburg, Me.*
Warner, Fidelia C., Williamsburg; 416 *E. 26th St., N. Y. City.*
Warren, Lizzie M., Florence; *Florence.*
Washington, Mary A., Oak Grove, Va.; m. Dr. Andrew C. Fisher, '81; *Emmerton, Va.*
Way, Cornelia H., Manchester, Vt.; m. John Leal, '79; d. Plainfield, N. J., '90.
Wight, Ella L., Springfield; m. J. E. Waite, '81; 23 *Grosvenor St., Springfield.*

1877.

GRADUATES.

Ainsworth, S. Elizabeth, Wading River, L. I.; *Hyde Park.*
Austin, Flora L., Dunstable; 1921 *Carroll St., Merriam Park, Minn.*
Bird, Alice E., Bethlehem, Ct.; *Bethlehem, Ct.*
Bouton, Sarah M., South Norwalk, Ct.; 77 *West St., S. Norwalk, Ct.*

Burroughs, Mary H., Trumbull, Ct.; *Long Hill, Trumbull, Ct.*
Cairns, Susan H., Waterbury, Ct.; *1078 W. Main St., Waterbury, Ct.*
Childs, Annie E., Ellenville, N. Y.; m. Arthur B. Ord, '86; *Traders' Bank, Ingersoll, Ontario, Can.*
Cooke, Lydia M., Bristol, R. I.; *904 Lexington Ave., N. Y. City.*
Cope, Lucy, Toughkenamon, Pa.; m. Wm. H. Shelmire, Jr.,'82; *740 N. 2d St., Reading, Pa*
Cristy, Martha W., Greenwich, Ct.; *Greenwich, Ct.*
Dunham, Isabella B., Unionville, Ct.; *121 Main St., Hartford, Ct.*
Dunning, Clara C., S. Norwalk, Ct.; m. Rev. John B. Lawrence, '85; *Claremont, N. H.*
Farnsworth, Carrie P., Cesarea, Turkey; m. Rev. Jas. L. Fowle, '78; *Cesarea, Turkey, Asia.*
Gates, Adelia F., Wales; m. James H. Hensley, '86; *1003 H St., N. W., Washington, D. C.*
Harmon, Harriet B., Lawrence; *89 N. Common St., Lynn.*
Hawley, Emily C., Brookfield, Ct.; *Danbury, Ct.*
Hazen, Mary S., Ahmednagar, India; *Box 427, Washington, D. C.*
Herrick, Anna C., N. Woodstock, Ct.; m. Rev. J. T. Nichols, '01; *Fremont, Seattle, Wash.*
Hodges, Roxa J., Rochester, N. Y.; m. W. F. Clapp, M.D., '79; *Fairport, N. Y.*
Holmes, Emma F., Walpole, N. H.; d. Walpole, N. H., '80.
Hosmer, Mary S., Marshfield, Mo.; m. J. R. Brown, '87; *2 Ellsworth St., Everett.*
Houston, Jennie B., Thompsonville, Ct.; m. A. J. Nelson; *176 W. 75th St., New York City.*
Jay, Mary L., Carbondale, Pa.; *38 W. Wayne St., Fort Wayne, Ind.*
Jennings, Ellen M., Wellesley; *Wellesley.*
Jones, Mary E., Fort Wayne, Ind.; *147 Ashland Boul., Chicago, Ill.*
Kelley, Julia A., Ashfield; *High School, Rutland, Vt.*
Keyes, Amy A., Pomfret, Ct.; m. Rev. Chas. E. Gordon, '78; *Lyme, N. H.*
Kimball, Anna J., Wells River, Vt.; d. '90.
Mayher, Elizabeth M., Easthampton; m. Erastus G. Smith, Ph.D., '83; *649 Harrison Ave., Beloit, Wis.*
Merrill, L. Bell, Washington, D. C.; m. Amos G. Draper, '79; *Kendall Green, Washington, D. C.*
Moorehouse, Jennie L., Shelburne, Vt.; m. Geo. G. Edwards, '80; *55 Sedgwick St., Jamaica Plain.*
Norton, Cornelia A., S. Norwalk, Ct.; d. S. Norwalk, Ct., '80.
Phelps, Mary A., Southampton; *14 S. Hayne Ave., Chicago, Ill.*
Pratt, Augusta C., Deep River, Ct.; m. Geo. S. Marvin, '79; *174 McDonough St., Brooklyn, N. Y.*
Richards, Clara H., Keene, N. H.; d. Keene, N. H., '80.
Richardson, Harriet G., Ware; m. O. M. Billings; *Union Ave. cor. Claybrooke, Memphis, Tenn.*
Robbins, Anne M., Rocky Hill, Ct.; *37 Pemberton Sq., Boston.*
Smith, Emma C., Granby; m. John H. Chandler; *Box 794, San Jose, Cal.*
Straughan, Caroline W., Fort Wayne, Ind.; *Fort Wayne, Ind.*
Tuttle, Eliza W., Cheshire, Ct.; *care C. Simpson, 163 E. 49th St., N. Y. City.*
Waite, Mary F., Holyoke; *100 Bowers St., Holyoke.*
Whitney, Rosabelle, Wadham's Mills, N. Y.; m. Rev. Wm. H. Wolcott, '77; *Moreno, Cal.*
Wilcox, Mary E., Northboro; m. Rev. Geo. R. Freeman, '86; *537 Chestnut St., Meadville, Pa.*

SPECIAL COURSE GRADUATES.

GREEK.—Cooke, Lydia M., Bristol, R. I.; *204 Lexington Ave., N. Y. City.*
" Sweetser, Abbie L., Worcester; *Greendale.*
GERMAN.—Merrill, L. Bell, Washington, D. C.; m. Amos G. Draper, '79; *Washington, D. C.*
" Wilcox, Mary E., Northboro; m. Rev. Geo. R. Freeman, '86; *537 Chestnut St., Meadville, Pa.*

1877.

NON-GRADUATES.

Abbe, Mary P., Westfield; m. Walter A. Smith, M.D., '81; 159 *State St., Springfield.*
Ainsworth, Eva V., Wading River, N. Y.; *Winter Park, Fla.*
Allen, Ina, Florence; m. Morgan L. Rider, '79; *Box 240, Berkeley, Cal.*
Avery, Jerusha P., Groton, Ct.; m. Rev. Wm. A. Farren, '80; *New London, N. H.*
Ayres, Keziah, Ithaca, N. Y.; m. Malcolm Leal, '82; 222 *W. 52d St., N. Y. City.*
Bachelder, Grace D., New Hampton, N. H.; *New Hampton, N. H.*
Barnes, Mary L., Stowe, Vt.; *Alice, Lovedale, S. Africa.*
Barnes, Nellie H., Oshkosh, Wis.; m. H. L. Buxton; d. Milwaukee, Wis.
Bartlett, Cornelia S., Cesarea, Turkey; *care Rev. Lyman Bartlett, Smyrna, Syria.*
Bisbee, Julia E., Charlemont; m. Clinton A. Hawkes, '79; d. Charlemont, '81.
Blanchard, Elizabeth G., Palmer; m. Samuel H. Hellyar, '78; *Palmer.*
Bottom, Mary L., New Haven, Vt.; *New Haven, Vt.*
Brainerd, Mary V., St. Albans, Vt.; m. Leverett Mears, Ph.D., '78; *Williamstown.*
Bridgman, Hannah C., Northampton; *Northampton.*
Broughton, Grace A., Kingston, Md.; m. L. Wesley Beauchamp, '80; *Westover, Md.*
Bumstead, N. Viola, Springfield; m. Robert Johnson, '81; 41 *Smith St., Atlanta, Ga.*
Burrell, Ellen L., Lockport, N. Y.; 101 *Cottage St., Lockport, N. Y.*
Clark, Mary L., Sheffield; *care David Y. Clark, Bristol, Ct.*
Clarke, M. Elizabeth, New Haven, Ct.; m. Frank W. Marsh, Esq., '82; d. '93.
Conklin, Mary H., Brooklyn, N. Y.; *Brooklyn, N. Y.*
Cornelison, Elizabeth F., Washington, Ill.; *Washington, Ill.*
Coyle, Margaret M., Port Royal, Pa.; m. Rev. Geo. W. Plack, '82; 130 *Church St., Hoosick Falls, N. Y.*
Cross, Esther H., Greenfield; m. Chas. F. Dow, '84; d. Auburndale, '94.
Darrow, Julia M., S. Framingham; d. Butte City, Mont., '94.
Day, M. Stella, Norwich, Ct.; *Shetucket St., Norwich, Ct.*
Demarest, S. Emma, N. Y. City; *Office of Century Co., 33 E. 17th St., N. Y. City.*
Dickinson, Emma L., N. Hadley; 521 *W. 5th St., Chattanooga, Tenn.*
Disbrow, Ella P., New Rochelle, N. Y.; m. Howard R. Ware, '83; 51 *Franklin Ave., New Rochelle, N. Y.*
Eastman, L. Carolyn, Middlebury, Vt.; m. Rev. Geo. W. Brooks, '78; *Englewood St., Dorchester.*
Fairbank, Katie, Ahmednagar, India; m. Rev. Robert A. Hume, '87; *Ahmednagar, Bombay Presidency, India.*
Fraser, Frances, Low Point, Ill.; m. Frank M. Eddy, '86; *Glenwood, Minn.*
Gates, Celia J., Kennebunkport, Me.; m. Rev. Edward P. Allen, '86; *Portland, Me.*
Hastings, Alice D. W., S. Hadley; m. Henry Colvin, '82; *Locust Ave., Troy, N. Y.*
Hedden, Harriet E., Verona, N. J.; m. Thos. E. Gore, '81; 78 *N. Y. Ave., Newark, N. Y.*
Hewitt, Alice D., Pomfret, Vt.; *N. Pomfret, Vt.*
Hitchcock, Caroline J., Amherst; *Amherst.*
Hoover, Carrie C., Paterson, N. J.; m. Rev. Walter Bushell, '78; *care Mission Press, Rangoon, Burma, Asia.*
Kemble, Anna E., Vincentown, N. J.; m. Chas. A. Jackson, '86; *Hampton, Va.*
Keyes, Ellen L., Pomfret, Ct.; *Pomfret, Ct.*
Kimball, Helen L., Wells River, Vt.; m. S. L. Hibbard, '81; d. Cherryvale, Kan., '87.
Kittredge, Mary C., Westboro; *Ottawa, Kan.*
Larrabee, Hannah M., Gale's Ferry, Ct.; m. Lucius Brown, Esq., '78; *Norwich, Ct.*
Lyman, S. Arabella, E. Brookfield; m. Elmer R. Taylor, '81; *Chicopee Falls.*
McGill, Susan, Philadelphia, Pa.; m. Irvin Shupp, '78; "*Woodside,*" *W. Philadelphia, Pa.*
Mack, Mary L., Gilead, Ct.; m. Prof. Chas. A. Smith, '82; *Lake Forest, Ill.*

1877.

McQueen, Ella J., Longmeadow; care Geo. McQueen, 2108 Pine St., St. Louis, Mo.
Mann, Elizabeth, Arcola, La.; m. Rev. John Gordon, '86; Arcola, La.
Mayher, Eleanor J., Easthampton; Easthampton.
Meily, Frances J., Lima, O.; m. Wm. P. Orr, '84; Piqua, O.
Miller, Addie E., S. Hadley; S. Hadley.
Miller, Adele S., Webster Groves, Mo.; m. Thos. H. Gist, '89; Denver, Col.
Munson, Lillian G., Chicago, Ill.; m. W. W. Brimm; d. Chicago, Ill., '94.
Owen, Emily, Lebanon, N. H.; m. Wilbur H. Powers, Esq., '80; 23 Childs St., Hyde Park.
Parker, Mary E., Pownal, Vt.; Pownal, Vt.
Pelkey, Mary L., N. Hadley; 30 Mt. Pleasant St., N. Cambridge.
Perry, Elizabeth H., Conway; m. Henry M. Howland, '82; Fruitland, N. M.
Price, Harriet, Wayland; m. E. L. Mowry, '79; d. Kansas City, Mo., '89.
Robbins, Grace G., Rocky Hill, Ct.; m. *Oliver Stanley, '82; m. A. J. P. Moore; Albuquerque, N. M.
Rolfe, Grace I., Newburyport; m. Chas. Cole, '85; Box 32, Salisbury.
Safford, Louise S., Westminster, Vt.; m. John D. Wiley,'77; 56 Brigham St., Detroit, Mich.
Seymour, Mary C., Ridgefield, Ct.; m. David L. Jones, '80; Ridgefield, Ct.
Slayton, Mary L., Woodstock, Vt.; 1 Fifth Ave., N. Y. City.
Smith, Adelaide K., W. Meriden, Ct.; Grand Rapids, Mich.
Smith, Esther R., Virginia City, Nev.; m. Henry L. Harris,'81; 95 Church Lane, Brooklyn, N. Y.
Spilman, Sallie, Bryantsville, Ky.; m. —— Bolton; care C. J. Spilman, Bergin, Ky.
Staples, Mary E., S. Bridgton, Me.; m. *Benj. W. Stevens, '80; S. Bridgton, Me.
Strong, Mary K., Walpole; d. Walpole,'77.
Swain, Gabriella, Stillwater, Minn.; m. Roscoe H. Bronson; Stillwater, Minn.
Taylor, Helen I., Loudonville, O.; m. Hezekiah J. Rowe, M.D., '80; Casselton, N. Dak.
Taylor, I. Hoyland, Loudonville, O.; m. Benj. W. Martin, '80; Harriman, Tenn.
Wallace, Matilda G., Newark, O.; 74 Buena Vista St., Newark, O.
Webber, Elvira F., Richmond, Quebec; m. Allan R. Oughtred, '85; 28 Lincoln Ave., Montreal, Can.
Weeks, Mary E., Lyndon, Vt.; m. Rev. Rowland E. Cross, '79; care J.M. Weeks, Lyndon, Vt.
Wiesing, Bertha A., Enfield, Ct.; Thompsonville, Ct.
Wever, Mary C., Watertown, N. Y.; Watertown, N. Y.
Wilson, Mary M., New Milford, Ct.; m. Henry P. Atwood, '82; Watertown, Ct.
Winter, H. Louise, Brockton; d. Brockton, '83.

1878.

GRADUATES.

Adams, Sarah W., Castine, Me.; m. Francis W. Conrad, '84; Rialto, Cal.
Armstrong, Elizabeth I., New Haven, Ct.; 104 Howe St., New Haven, Ct.
Atwater, Lucy, N. Y. City; m. *Matthew D. Field, M.D.,'85; 115 E. 40th St., N. Y. City.
Bacon, Imogene, South Glastonbury, Ct.; South Glastonbury, Ct.
Beane, Flora S., Littleton, N. H.; Littleton, N. H.
Bell, Emma C., Feeding Hills; m. Rev. Geo. D. Gurley, '88; Leon, Io.
Brown, Louisa M., South Orange, N. J.; P. O. address, Millburne, N. J.
Dudley, Mary C., Easton, Ct.; m. Rev. Chas. H. Willcox, '82; Lawrenceville, N. J.
Dwight, Ada C., Brooklyn, N. Y.; 141 6th Ave., Brooklyn, N. Y.
Eaton, Elizabeth W., Palmyra, N. Y.; Portland Acad., Portland, Or.
Evans, Elizabeth, Newark, N. J.; m. Silas B. Brown, '81; 718 Nostrand Ave., Brooklyn, N. Y.
Fobes, Mary A., Syracuse, N. Y.; d. Syracuse, N. Y., '80.

1878.

Gleason, Laura A., McIndoes Falls, Vt.; *McIndoes Falls, Vt.*
Harris, Ellen E., Putnam Heights, Ct.; d. Denver, Col., '87.
Isham, Christine A., New Haven, Ct.; m. Rufus Waples, Jr., '84; 7211 *Boyer St., Philadelphia, Pa.*
Johnson, Orpha E., Orford, N. H.; *Orford, N. H.*
Lee, Mary, Delaware, O.; m. Frank W. Thomas, M.D., '81; *Marion, O.*
Lockwood, Augusta H., Fordham, N. Y. City; 205 *Phila. St., Saratoga Springs, N. Y.*
Martin, M. Alida, Upper Red Hook, N.Y.; m. M.F. Johnson, '88; 461 *Halsey St., Brooklyn, N. Y.*
Mead, Hannah M., Greenwich, Ct.; m. Judson I. Wood, '85; *Ilion, N. Y.*
Miller, Anna E., S. Hadley Falls; *S. Hadley Falls.*
Murdock, Carrie H., W. Boylston; 11 *Whitman St., Dorchester.*
Ransom, Emma, Hartford, Ct.; m. John Ransom; 44 *Sidney Ave., Chicago, Ill.*
Reed, Addie L., Brattleboro, Vt.; 11 *Green St., Brattleboro, Vt.*
Smith, Clara N., S. Hadley; m. *Rev. Fred A. Gaylord, '85; *S. Hadley.*
Ulrich, Mathilde, Greenfield; m. Robt. Abercrombie, '93; *Greenfield.*
Woodman, Elizabeth C., Danvers; 5 *Prospect St., Fitchburg.*

NON-GRADUATES.

Allen, Emily A., Enfield, Ct.; m. Henry B. Patten, '82; 208 *W. 22d St., Cheyenne, Wyo.*
Angell, Metta E., Brooklyn, N. Y.;
Baker, Minnie F., St. Johnsbury, Vt.; m. Perley F. Hazen, '81; *St. Johnsbury, Vt.*
Baldwin, Sarah C., M.D., Winchester; m. Willett B. Stickney, Esq., '82; d. Savanna, I. T., '83.
Beach, Anna L., Goshen, Ct.; care *Mrs. Chas. B. Strong, W. Suffield, Ct.*
Beach, Ella M., Goshen, Ct.; m. Rev. Chas. B. Strong, '82; *W. Suffield, Ct.*
Bouldrey, Emma D., Raynham; m. Bradley W. Pulling, Esq., '84; *Marshfield.*
Byington, Caroline M., Constantinople, Turkey; m. Rev. Orville D. Reed, '84; 64 *Church St., Montclair, N. J.*
Cavan, Ellen, Waverly, N. Y.; m. Oliver Gilbert, '86; *Montrose, Pa.*
Chapman, Minerva J., Chicago, Ill.; post office address, *Poste Restante, Paris, France.*
Chase, Mary D., Blue Hill, Me.; m. Hon. Addison E. Herrick, Esq., '82; *Bethel, Me.*
Clapp, Hattie M., Southampton; m. Rev. Arthur W. Spooner, '80; 315 *N. 5th St., Camden, N. J.*
Clark, Martha A. W., Somerville; 82 *Heath St., Somerville.*
Davidson, Jane M., Oxford, N. Y.; m. P. B. Andrew, M.D., '80; *Dansville, N. Y.*
Derrin, Lizzie C., West Avon, Ct.; *Avon, Ct.*
Dewar, Isabella H., Easthampton; m. J. W. Prouty, '94; 195 *Walnut St., Holyoke.*
Dews, Nellie L., Woodbury, Ct.; m. Chas. M. Harvey, '83; *Woodbury, Ct.*
Dickinson, Grace K., Benson, Vt.; *Benson, Vt.*
Dudley, Lillie, Salem; 142 *W. 11th St., N. Y. City.*
Dunning, Annie K., Thompson, Ct.; *Thompson, Ct.*
Eaton, Delia M., Chaplin, Ct.; m. Rev. Chas. H. Dalrymple, '84; *Rising City, Neb.*
Ely, Elizabeth L., Brooklyn, N. Y.; *Riverside Drive, 85th and 86th Sts., N. Y. City.*
Ely, Mary B., Brooklyn, N. Y.; *Riverside Drive, 85th and 86th Sts., N. Y. City.*
Ford, Sarah, Geneseo, Ill.; *Northfield, Minn.*
Forward, Elizabeth S., Granby; m. Lewis M. Gaylord, '78; *S. Hadley.*
Foster, Etta M., Middletown, Ct.; m. Joel N. Eno, '83; *Moore Meadows, Willington, Ct.*
Gilbert, Anna F., Coventry, Ct.; m. Edgar F. Storrs, '78; *Spring Hill, Ct.*
Gould, Frances D., Chicago, Ill.; 2310 *Calumet Ave., Chicago, Ill.*
Green, Louise J., Philadelphia, Pa.; 402 *N. 38th St., Philadelphia, Pa.*
Greenwood, Gertrude I., N. Y. City; d. N. Y. City, '79.

1878.

Hall, Lydia M., Milford, Del.; m. Robert D. Grier, '80; *Salisbury, Md.*
Hayden, Gertrude E., Haydenville; *364 Marlboro St., Boston.*
Herrick, Mary B., S. Hadley; *care Rev. J. R. Herrick, Dundee, Ill.*
Holbrook, Mary Anna, M.D., Rockland; *Kobe College, 60 Hill, Kobe, Japan.*
Holt, Marie F., Indianapolis, Ind.; m. David G. Wiley, '82; *221 N. East St., Indianapolis, Ind.*
Homan, Agnes E., Boonton, N. J.; m. Frank P. Cook, '82; d. Hanover, N. J., '84.
Hughitt, Emma M., Auburn, N. Y.; m. Jas. B. Houston, '83; *Thompsonville, Ct.*
Lawrence, Annie M., Ashby; m. Frank D. Rogers, '79; *Natick.*
Lees, Elsie E., Westport, Ct.; m. E. Sterne Wheeler, '82; *Saugatuck, Ct.*
Lyman, Sarah E., Easthampton; m. Rev. Chas. W. Holbrook, '83; *Easthampton.*
McPherson, Jennie, Cambridge, O.; m. John M. Ogier, '87; *Cambridge, O.*
Mateer, Lillian E., Shippensburg, Pa.; m. Rev. Wm. S. Walker, '83; *Monroe, Ga.*
Mattison, M. Elizabeth, Augusta, N. J.; d. Paterson, N. J., '88.
Moody, Sarah M., Methuen; *Ballardvale.*
Morgan, Mary J., Ilion, N. Y.; *229 Columbus Ave., N. Y. City.*
Pease, Annie, Oxford; m. Chas. E. Eddy,'82; d. Kansas City, Mo., '82.
Perry, Meta D., Geneseo, Ill.; m. Rev. S. C. Davis; *Alma, Mich.*
Peters, M. Ella, Blue Hill, Me.; m. Eugene F. Hinckley, '80; *Readfield, Me.*
Pettibone, Mary C., Hannibal, Mo.; m. Jas. F. Barber, '84; d. St. Louis, Mo., '86.
Phelps, Katherine L., Orford, N. H.; *20 E. 28th St., N. Y. City.*
Pope, Jessie D., Coldwater, Mich.; m. C. Burdette Sawyer, '79; *Beaver City, Neb.*
Rand, Ella A., Keene, N. H.; m. Geo. E. Lee, '82; d. Keene, N. H., '83.
Richards, Emma W., Keene, N. H.; *151 West St., Keene, N. H.*
Rogers, Mary P., Tom's River, N. J.; *Tom's River, N. J.*
Rousseau, Mary L. H., Newburyport; m. Louis De La Croix, '81; *Oxford, N. C.*
Sanderson, Lucia, Phillipston; m. Frank P. McGregor, '84; *26 Arlington St., Haverhill.*
Sanford, Elizabeth E., Albion, N. Y.; d. Gaines, N. Y., '85.
Savage, Harriet E., Stowe, Vt.; *Stowe, Vt.*
Scott, Frances M., Bennington, Vt.; m. Arthur G. Sherry, '81; *186 8th St., Troy, N. Y.*
Sigourney, Myrtis S., Oxford; m. Gilbert H. Harrington, '86; *1014 Main St., Worcester.*
Simpson, L. Ida, Hudson, N. Y.; d. Montreal, Can., '80.
Smith, Flora E., Birmingham, Ct.; m. Dr. John Trumbull, '83; *Montecito, Cal.*
Smith, Mary E., Panditeripo, Jaffna, Ceylon; *Winchester, N. H.*
Street, Luella A., Easthampton; *94 Main St., Easthampton.*
Taylor, Ada M., Jefferson, N. Y.; m. Perry E. Field, '82; *8 Porter St., Providence, R. I.*
Tolman, Mary M., Manchester, N. H.; *142 Lowell St., Manchester, N. H.*
Weeden, Maria H., Providence, R. I.; *597 Branch Ave., Providence, R. I.*
West, Carrie P., Worcester; m. Jay E. Phillips, '85; *345 W. 14th St., N. Y. City.*
Wilson, Isabel, Reedsville, Pa.; *Reedsville, Pa.*
Winter, Hattie K., Faribault, Minn.; m. Kendall Greene, '84; d. Morristown, Minn., '92.
Woodard, Mary B., Ashfield; m. Clarence D. Hall, '84; *Belding, Mich.*
Yates, Clementine R., Plainfield, N. J.; *128 E. 7th St., Plainfield, N. J.*

1879.

GRADUATES.

Alexander, M. Jeanette, Springfield; m. Wm. G. Chapin, '82; *204 Macon St., Brooklyn, N. J.*
Andrews, Fanny P., M.D., Makawao, H. I.; m. Fred D. Shepard, M.D., '82; *Aintab, Turkey in Asia.*

1879.

Bardwell, Emma C., N. Hadley; m. Francis J. Heavens, '86; *Willis St., New Bedford.*
Bell, S. Louise, Amsterdam, N. Y.; *Amsterdam, N. Y.*
Boynton, S. Ella, Durham, N. Y.; *East Aurora, N. Y.*
Brown, Stella C., Groton, Ct.; m. Chas. B. Allyn, '90; *Stamford, Ct.*
Brownback, E. Louise, Philadelphia, Pa.; *Tarrytown, N. Y.*
Buxton, Elizabeth N., Springfield, O.; m. John D. Gill, '80; *Ogden, Utah.*
Cairns, Mary F., Waterbury, Ct.; m. Wm. F. Chatfield, '90; 12 *Vine St., Waterbury, Ct.*
Clark, Sarah A., New Haven, Ct.; *452 Orange St., New Haven, Ct.*
Conklin, Stella, Fultonville, N. Y.; *Mt. Carmel, Ct.*
Cowls, S. Jeanette, N. Amherst; m. Francis L. Frary, '82; 3108 *Garfield Ave., Minneapolis, Minn.*
Fairbank, Anna, Ahmednagar, India; m. Rev. Robert M. Woods, '79; *Hatfield.*
Gaylord, Marion I., Gaylordsville, Ct.; m. Edwin Atwell, '84; 1088 *Deane St., Brooklyn, N. Y.*
Hodges, Amy M., Rochester, N. Y.; *Box 216, Rochester, N. Y.*
Jennings, Susan M., M.D., Coventry, Ct.; m. Chas. A. Peterson, M.D.,'84; *Honolulu, H. I.*
Kelsey, Ida B., Killingworth, Ct.; m. Rev. Ira C. Billman, '85; *Yale, Mich.*
Kimball, Kate J., Bath, N. H.; *6 North Div. St., Ann Arbor, Mich.*
McKennan, Effie, Albion, N. Y.; d. Albion, N. Y., '82.
Melvin, Helen E., Chester, N. H.; *Chester, N. H.*
Metcalf, Evelyn A., Providence, R. I.; m. Chas. W. Clapp, '94; *Farren House, Turner's Falls.*
Mosman, Carrie L., Chicopee; d. Chicopee, '81.
Preston, Mary O., S. Hadley; m. Wm. Spafford, '90; *S. Hadley.*
Sawyer, Mary A., Chester, Vt.; *The Western College, Oxford, O.*
Scott, Hettie E., Landour, India; 1311 *Conn. Ave., N. W., Washington, D. C.*
Smith, Helen M., Hadley; m. Henry Stockbridge, Esq.,'82; *N. Calhoun St., Baltimore, Md.*
Todd, Sophie P., Paterson, N. J.; m. J. Douglass Walton, '83; 277 *W. 84th St., N. Y. City.*
Walker, Anna B., Chicopee; m. Wm. H. Snow, '82; 338 *Maple St., Holyoke.*
Warner, Mary L., Hardwick; m. Rev. Arthur B. Wilkes, '82; 212 *Albert St., Kingston, Ont.*
Webb, Mary T., Southwick; m. Wm. C. Pluncy, '85; *W. Winsted, Ct.*
Whitaker, Martha, Southold, N. Y.; *Southold, N. Y.*

SPECIAL COURSE GRADUATES.

FRENCH.—Agard, Sarah J., Staffordville, Ct.; *Staffordville, Ct.*
" Cooke, Rowena P., Belpre, O.; m. Samuel M. Cherrington, '85; *Gallipolis, O.*
" Lathrop, Mary E., Danielsonville, Ct.; *Derby, Ct.*
GERMAN.—Lathrop, Mary E., Danielsonville, Ct.; *Derby, Ct.*

NON-GRADUATES.

Alvord, Susan G., Nashua, N. H.; m. Rev. Willis D. Leland, '82; 113 *Varnum Ave., Lowell.*
Ayers, Elizabeth A., Ithaca, N. Y.; m. Dr. Robert P. Knight, '85; *Amenia, N. Y.*
Beach, Ella C., Cheshire, Ct.; m. Chas. M. Bryant, '89; *Pittsfield.*
Beebe, A. Adelaide, Forreston, Ill.; *Ashland, Or.*
Bell, Mary E., Howell, Mich.; m. Bryan D. Smalley, Esq., '82; *P. O. Box 106, Seattle, Wash.*
Bessé, Hattie C., New Bedford; m. F. Jarvis Patten, '84; 5 *E. 27th St., N. Y. City.*
Bissell, Julia, M.D., Ahmednagar, India; *Ahmednagar, India.*
Blunt, Kate, Bridgeport, Ct.; (*Boston?*).
Brooks, Elizabeth, Franconia, N. H.; m. Elwyn C. Nelson; *Franconia, N. H.*

1879.

Buckingham, Agnes M., Bloomsburg, Pa.; m. J. C. Biddle, M.D., '81; *State Hospital, Fountain Springs, Pa.*
Burgess, Cora J., W. Winfield, N. Y.; m. Rush Bartlett, '81; *Winfield, N. Y.*
Burrall, Jennie D., Lakeville, Ct.; m. Thomas Martin, '87; *Lakeville, Ct.*
Cahoon, Caroline E., Lyndon, Vt.; m. Harry H. McIntire, '80; 1012 4*th Ave., South, Minneapolis, Minn.*
Chase, Lillian E., W. Killingly, Ct.; m. Arthur G. Bill, '80; *Danielsonville, Ct.*
Clapp, Mary E., Montague; *Montague.*
Clark, Elizabeth R., Plainfield; m. Wm. H. Gardiner, '80; 1245 72*d St., Chicago, Ill.*
Clark, Louisa M., Hartford, Ct. ;
Clark, S. Lizzie, Putnam, Ct.; *Putnam, Ct.*
Cole, Hattie E., Northampton; m. Freeman Baker, '79; d. '86 or '87.
Cooke, Rowena P., Belpre, O.; m. Samuel M. Cherrington, '85; *Gallipolis, O.*
Dickinson, Clara A., Conway; m. Frank Sikes, '80; *Conway.*
Dort, Mary E., Keene, N. H.; m. Frank H. Wright, '85; 26 *Water St., Keene, N. H.*
Fifield, Emily W., M.D., Kearney, Neb.; 1919 *Nicollet Ave., Minneapolis, Minn.*
Forsman, Lucinda O., Chicago, Ill.; m. Junius N. Love, '88; *Newcomb Hotel, Quincy, Ill.*
Fortesque, Grace, Philadelphia, Pa.; d. Germantown, Philadelphia, Pa., '92.
Goodhue, Lettie W., Hancock, N. H.; *Hancock, N. H.*
Gorham, Jennie L., Westminster West, Vt.; d. Westminster West, Vt., '86.
Hanor, Florence M., Hudson, N. Y.; m. Fred. M. Haviland; 247 *W. 139th St., N. Y. City.*
Herbert, Georgiana E., Lambertville, N. J.; m. *Jarvis B. Brown, '82; *Beverly, N. J.*
Hinsdale, Anna P., Meriden, Ct.; 80 *Bowles St., Springfield.*
Hodges, Helen R., Torrington, Ct.; m. Edward Norton, '87; *W. Torrington, Ct.*
Hotchkiss, Hattie F., Sharon Valley, Ct.; m. Sidney A. McKelvey, '81; d. Sparta, Ill., '90.
Hovey, Helen C., Fair Haven, Ct.; m. Henry F. Ellinwood; *Pembroke, N. Y.*
Hulbert, Mary E., Middlebury, Vt.; m. Rev. Edwin F. Rogers, '81 ; *Zanesville, O.*
Johnson, Amelia G., Malden; m. Edw. O. Holmes, '90; 136 *Summer St., Malden.*
Johnson, Lizzie L., Cambridge; m. Herbert B. Knight, '82; *Shaffner St., Adams Sq., Worcester.*
Keeler, Laura F., Newburyport; m. Robert Canfield, '90; *care Manville Covering Co., Providence, R. I.*
Kennedy, Elizabeth C., Lowell; 42 18*th St., Lowell.*
Lathrop, Mary E., Danielsonville, Ct.; *Derby, Ct.*
Lincoln, Laura B., Millbury; m. Frank E. Powers, '82; 18 *Maynard St., Worcester.*
Lockwood, Anna L., Cleveland, O.; m. Thos. B. Wilkinson, '88; 365 *Metcalf St., Los Angeles, Cal.*
Ludden, Gertrude V., Pittsburgh, Pa.; m. Chas. D. Armstrong, '85; *Wilkinsburg, Pa.*
Mason, Alice M., S. Coventry, Ct.; m. Frank E. Hall, '84; *Asheville, N. C.*
McKeown, Mary L., Palmyra, N. Y.; m. Justin B. Perkins, '90; *Springfield.*
Merriman, Eliza A., New Windsor, Ill.; m. Wm. C. Henry, '79; *Box 49, Denver, Col.*
Miller, Mary A., Bird-in-Hand, Pa.; d. Bird-in-Hand, Pa., '83.
Nash, Emily E., Williamsburg; m. M. Wilbur Smith, '80; 77 *Garfield St., Springfield.*
Newlin, Annie, Pottstown, Pa.; m. Thos. W. Entwistle, '83 ; *Chester, Pa.*
Palmer, Nettie M., W. Winfield, N. Y.; m. Jas. A. Moors, '83; *W. Winfield, N. Y.*
Payn, Mary L., Chatham Village, N. Y.; m. Azro C. Hanor, M.D., '82; 4 *Payn Ave., Chatham, N. Y.*
Peabody, Annie C., Eastport, Me.; m. Rev. A. Bailey, '91; *Goffstown Center, N. H.*
Perry, M. Stella, Agawam; m. Frederick Dudley, '93; 102 *Norton St., New Haven, Ct.*
Platt, Ella M., Sandusky, O.; *Sandusky, O.*
Porter, Kittie H., Durham, N. Y.; m. Addison O. Hull, '81; 25 *Clinton St., Amsterdam, N. Y.*
Preston, Ellen M., Easthampton; m. Geo. E. Austin, '90; *Montgomery, Ala.*

1879.

Probasco, Lydia C., Longwood, Md.; m. Wm. L. Bailey, '86; *Huron, Kan.*
Probasco, Sarah A., Longwood, Md.; m. W. R. Patterson, '80; *Richards, Mo.*
Pyne, Mary S., Agawam; m. Fred. N. Clark, '81; d. *Agawam, '86.*
Rice, Mary A., Meriden, Ct.; m. John D. Avery, '84; *N. Stonington, Ct.*
Rossiter, Mary, N. Guilford, Ct.; m. Arthur S. Newton, '89; *Durham, Ct.*
Schradi, Charlotte H., N. Y. City; m. *Henry J. Young, '82; 55 *W. 42d St., N. Y. City.*
Silkman, Katherine A., Vineland, N. J.; *Vineland, N. J.*
Stetson, Clara, Leverett; m. Allen G. Clark, '89; *W. Brattleboro, Vt.*
Stobaugh, Lizzie M., Honey Grove, Tex.; m. Harry M. Hill, '92; *Honey Grove, Tex.*
Stobaugh, Nannie E., Honey Grove, Tex.; m. R. J. Thomas, '85; *Honey Grove, Tex.*
Stratton, Nellie M., Melrose; m. Rev. Geo. Allchin; *Osaka, Japan.*
Thayer, Harriet F., Quincy; m. Geo. E. Kinney; *3 Arcadia St., Roxbury.*
Tillotson, Sarah M., Rocky Hill, Ct.; m. L. W. H. Giese, '86; 851 *Corinthian Ave., Philadelphia, Pa.*
Tryon, Anna P., S. Glastonbury, Ct.; *S. Glastonbury, Ct.*
Van Sickle, Anna, Cayuga, N. Y.; *Cayuga, N. Y.*
Van Sickle, Eliza, Cayuga, N. Y.; d. Cayuga, N. Y., '88.
Vosburgh, Sarah J., Lyons, N. Y.; m. James E. Ludlow, '89; 1307 *Jones St., Omaha, Neb.*
Wake, Florence S., Marion, N. Y.; m. Rev. Jared S. Nasmith, '80; *Newton, Io.*
Walker, Mary N., Orange, Ct.; m. John C. Puetz, '85; 1410 *M St., Lincoln, Neb.*
Warner, Elizabeth B., Salisbury, Ct.; d. Salisbury, Ct., '81.
Way, Lucy, Suffield, Ct.; 22 *Niles St., Hartford, Ct.*
Willard, Jennie J., Orford, N. H.; *Orford, N. H.*
Williams, Jessie, Honey Grove, Tex.; m. B. M. Burgher, '82; 326 *Masten St., Dallas, Tex.*
Wilson, Agnes B., Reedsville, Pa.; m. Andrew C. Strode, '82; *Lewistown, Pa.*
Wing, Electa M., Ashfield; *Ashfield.*
Worstell, Fannie F., N. Y. City; m. Clifton G. Marshall, '88; *care Century Co., N. Y. City.*

1880.

GRADUATES.

Agard, Sarah J., Staffordville, Ct.; *Staffordville, Ct.*
Allen, Zella B., Zanesville, O.; m. *Joseph E. Dixson, '81; *Univ. of Chicago Library, Chicago, Ill.*
Baldwin, Julia C., New Haven, Ct.; m. Rev. Edward D. Kelsey, '81; d. *S. Amenia, N. Y., '94.*
Blanchard, Elizabeth D., Des Moines, Io.; *Umatilla, Fla.*
Brown, Sybel G., Whately; *Whately.*
Clark, Clara P., Chatham Village, N. Y.; m. R. B. Arnold, '83; 751 *W. Adams St., Chicago, Ill.*
Coleman, Lucia A., Norwich, Vt.; 339 *Front St., Chicopee.*
Crosby, Samuella, Churchville, N. Y.; 213 42d *Place, Chicago, Ill.*
Flagler, Elizabeth R., New Hackensack, N. Y.; *Steele, Mont.*
Flint, Helen C., B.A., Concord, N. H.; *Concord, N. H.*
French, Carrie E., Boston; m. Irving J. Scoville, '84; *Plainville, Ct.*
Gibson, Emily J., S. Ryegate, Vt.; m. John W. Anderson, '81; *Box 207, Orlando, Fla.*
Graves, Mary S., S. Hadley; m. Elmer D. Severance, '87; *Turner's Falls.*
Hammond, A. Rosalie, Vernon Center, Ct.; m. Gen. Howard L. Porter, '83; 80 *School St., Concord, N. H.*
Hedrick, Alice, Georgetown, D. C.; m. W. Harry Olcott, '84; *Carlins, Va.*
Ingalls, Ellen E., Pomfret, Ct.; 14 *Myrtle St., Jamaica Plain.*
Jennings, C. Elizabeth, Wellesley; d. Washington, D. C., '85.

Judd, Mary I.., Ph.B., S. Hadley ; S. *Hadley.*
Kelsey, Gertrude E., Killingworth, Ct.; m. A. Beverly Stevens, '86; 69 *Dickerman St., New Haven, Ct.*
Kimball, Mary E., Jamaica Plain ; m. Rev. George H. Cummings, '86; *Thompson. Ct.*
Leach, Mary F., B.S., Sedalia, Mo.; *Mt. Holyoke College, S. Hadley;* home address, 74 *Pitcher St., Detroit, Mich.*
Leavenworth, Margaret P., Wallingford, Ct.; m. Chas. E. Moody, '86 ; *West Medford.*
Marean, Valetta C., Hubbardston; *Hubbardston.*
Minor, Emily T., Woodbury, Ct.; *Ratuagiri, Bombay Presidency, India.*
Morse, Carrie E., Adrianople, Turkey ; m. Harry W. Blake, '85; 7028 *Wentworth Ave., Englewood, Ill.*
Parsons, Katherine E., Southampton ; m. Frederick E. Judd, '89 ; *Southampton.*
Samuel, Elizabeth I., M D., Brewster ; *Brewster.*
Seymour, M. Oretha, Stillwater, Minn.; m. Franklyn H. Lemon, '83 ; *Stillwater, Minn.*
Sherman, Lillie L., Newtonville ; *P. O., Newtonville.*
Smith, Annis A., West Camden, N. Y.; *West Camden, N. Y.*
Stimson, Juliet W., Norwich, Vt.; *Norwich, Vt.*
Taylor, Estelle, East Hamburg, N. Y.; 572 *Niagara St., Buffalo, N. Y.*
Wadsworth, Kittie L., Boyntonville, N. Y.; m. Beroth L. Crapo, '84 ; d. Blue Mountain Lake, N. Y., '94.

SPECIAL COURSE GRADUATES.

GREEK. — Minor, Emily T., Woodbury, Ct.; *Ratuagiri. Bombay Presidency, India.*
GERMAN.— Cummings, Anna M., Strafford, Vt.; *Wellington. Cape Colony, S. Africa.*
" Spalding, Isabel, Nashua, N. H.; *care Josiah Spalding. Nashua, N. H.*

NON-GRADUATES.

Allen, Eva E., Maysville, Me.; m. Wm. A. Purington, Esq., '82 ; 248 *E. 7th St., Riverside, Cal.*
Avery, Annie H., Groton, Ct.; *N. Stonington, Ct.*
Ayer, Elizabeth M., Farmington, Ct.; d. Hartford, Ct., '85.
Bilderback, M. Virginia, Salem, N. J.; m. *Rev. Edward H. Bronson, '81 ; 241 *E. Broadway, Salem, N. J.*
Burlingame, Esther A., Danielsonville, Ct.; m. *Wm. O. Jacobs, '84 ; *Danielsonville, Ct.*
Cadmon, Libbie M., Hudson, N. Y.; m. Aurelius M. Tracy, M.D., '83 ; *Hudson. N. Y.*
Church, Edith A., Chaplin, Ct.; m. Chas. B. Smith, '91 ; d. North Haven, Ct., '92.
Cole, E. Viola, Middletown, Ct.; m. Chas. B. Smith, '01 ; d. North Haven, Ct., '92.
Cole, E. Viola, Middletown, Ct.; m. Hubbard St., Middletown, Ct.
Cunningham, Mary, Cadiz, O.; m. John M. Sharon, '83 ; *Cadiz, O.*
Dickinson, O. Adelia, Amherst; m. Walter S. Vanderwater, '83 ; 357 *Merchant St., Kankakee, Ill.*
Everson, Lila D., Buffalo, N. Y.; m. Kirke D. Bishop, '81 ; 779 *Genesee Ave., Cleveland, O.*
Fowler, Alice J., Southwick ; m. Frank W. Noble, '83 ; *Southwick.*
Griggs, Sarah B., Brooklyn, N. Y.; *Lefferts Place, Brooklyn, N. Y.*
Haire, Anna D., Janesville, Wis.; *Box 513, Duluth, Minn.*
Hannahs, Mary E., Utica, N. Y.; 27 *Cottage St., Utica, N. Y.*
Harwood, Isabel H., N. Springfield, Mo. ; m. *Walter E. Scott, M.D., '83 ; 523 *W. 21st St., Los Angeles, Cal.*
Hill, Laura J., E. Douglass ; m. Ralph H. Bowles, Jr., 81 ; *E. Douglass.*
Horton, Flora M., Windsor, Vt.; m. Chas. S. Rounsevel, M.D., '82 ; d. Nashua, N. H., '89.
Hovey, Harriette R., Jericho Center, Vt. ; m. Chas. F. Higgins, '92 ; *Salem.*
Jenks, Ida M., Boston ; m. Edwin P. Jaquith, '81 ; 20 *Hanson St., Boston.*

1880.

Keeler, Lucy H., Newburyport; m. Geo. A. Ives, '88; *Bainbridge, N. Y.*
Knight, Camilla J., Southwick; 174 *College Ave., St. Paul, Minn.*
Leh, Sallie, Allentown, Pa.; m. Horatio Koch, '87; 1204 *Hamilton St., Allentown, Pa.*
McClenahan, Nannie, Fairview, O.; m. Rev. T. J. Finney; *Monsoura, Egypt.*
Makepeace, Susie J., S. Hadley Falls; 306 *Union St., Springfield.*
Martin, Alice B., Danvers; m. B. L. Tibbits, '87; *Danvers.*
Meech, Annie D., Vineland, N. J.; m. John F. McMahan, '85; *8th and Cherry Sts., Vineland, N. J.*
Meech, Ann W., Groton, Ct.; *Groton, Ct.*
Meech, Susan B., Groton, Ct.; *Groton, Ct.*
Minor, Mary R., Woodbury, Ct.; *Kensington, Ct.*
Morrison, Mary M., Montclair, N. J.; *Montclair, N. J.*
Nichols, Emma J., Easthampton; m. Wm. B. Sawyer, M.D., '80; *Riverside, Cal.*
Orr, Mary B., Steubenville, O.; 616 *4th St., Steubenville, O.*
Platt, Eva C., Sandusky, O.; *Sandusky, O.*
Ramsey, Callie E., Reedsburg, Wis.; d. Colorado Springs, Col., '86.
Rice, Minnie J., New Bloomfield, Pa.; m. Chas. Rhinesmith; *Harlan, Io.*
Shaw, Caroline M., Bridgeport, Ct.; m. Chas. M. Suckley, '91; 539 *E. Main St., Bridgeport, Ct.*
Shaw, Mary J., Geneseo, Ill.; m. Alfred Jacques, Esq., '85; 1205 *E. 3d St., Duluth, Minn.*
Sisson, Phebe E., Hamilton, N. Y.; m. Rev. Andrew K. Fuller, '82; 151 *Chamber St., Newburgh, N. Y.*
Smith, Ada K., Winchendon; *Winchendon.*
Smith, Jennie M., W. Springfield; m. Edward W. Newton, '91; *Lenox St., W. Newton.*
Todd, Charlotte E., N. Y. City; m. Geo. T. Wilson, '84; 128 *W. 59th St., N. Y. City.*
Walworth, Clara E., Cambridgeport; m. Louis B. Griffin, '82; *Clarion, Io.*

1881.

GRADUATES.

Baker, L. Jennie, Phillipston; m. Arthur R. Hall, '94; 2444 *Marion St., Denver, Col.*
Bartlett, Lizzie A., Passaic, N. J.; m. Wm. I. Barry, '81; *Passaic, N. J.*
Benedict, Ursula E., Bethel, Ct.; *Bethel, Ct.*
Blakely, Ellen M., Campton, N. H.; *Marash, Turkey*; home address, *Winchendon.*
Clapp, Emily M., Easthampton; *Easthampton.*
Clark, Mary A., Sodus, N. Y.; *Sodus, N. Y.*
Devereux, Harriet L., Castine, Me.; m. Burton D. Stone, M.D., '93; *Berne, N. Y.*
Dickinson, Julia C., Amherst; m. Rev. Chas. S. Nickerson, '86; 22 *Arthur St., Somerville.*
Downer, Mary E., Chittenango, N. Y.; m. Thaddeus Ivey, '83; *Cary, N. C.*
Elliot, Elizabeth M., Guilford, Ct.; *Guilford, Ct.*
Fitch, Clara M., Canandaigua, N.Y.; m. Maynard N. Clement, Esq., '83; *Canandaigua, N. Y.*
Gabrielson, M. Christine, Andover, Ill.; m. John E. Hansen, '83; *Concord, Neb.*
Goss, Adah, Marshfield, Mo.; m. J. L. Briggs, '81; 730 *Wall St., Joplin, Mo.*
Haire, Mary B., Janesville, Wis.; m. Chas. W. Miflin, '89; 4125 *Lake Ave., Chicago, Ill.*
Hewitt, Emily H., N. Pomfret, Vt.; *N. Pomfret, Vt.*
Hodges, M. Louise, Rochester, N. Y.; *Box 216, Rochester, N. Y.*
Houston, Harriet A., Thompsonville, Ct.; m. F. B. Mitchell, Esq., '85; d. Saranac Lake, N.Y.
Hoyt, E. Kate, Danbury, Ct.; m. Geo. D. Northrop, '93; 79 *Deer Hill Ave., Danbury, Ct.*
Johnson, Olive M., Upton; *Upton.*
Jones, Annie L., Auburn, N. Y.; m. Wm. R. Vosburgh, '84; 321 *S. Grove Ave., Oak Park, Ill.*

1881.

Kendall, Agnes M., Stamford, N. Y.; d. Minneapolis, Minn., '83.
Kies, Marietta, Ph.D., Danielsonville, Ct.; *Plymouth.*
Kingsley, Ella S., Marion, N. Y.; 41 *Vick Park, Rochester, N. Y.*
McElwain, Hattie A., Becket; *State College, Center Co., Pa.*
Mudge, Mary B., Danvers; m. Christopher A. Sanborn, M.D., '85; *Redlands, Cal.*
Newhall, Edith F., Sturgis, Mich.; *Lincoln, Ill.*
Norton, Belle M., Wales Center, N. Y.; *Aurora, N. Y.*
Norwood, N. Louise, Richmond, N. H.; m. J. Will Sparhawk, '85; *W. Swanzey, N. H.*
Penfield, Esther J., Danbury, Ct.; m. Ernest L. Staples, Esq., '85; *Shelton, Ct.*
Pennock, Emma R., Chesterville, Pa.; *Chesterville, Pa.*
Pettee, Adaline F., Sharon; *Northfield Seminary, E. Northfield.*
Post, Elizabeth F., S. Hadley; 308 *Clinton Place, Oak Park, Ill.*
Rauch, Marion B., Howard City, Kan.; m. R. F. Glenn, '84; *Howard, Kan.*
Ray, Amelia S., N. Y. City; m. Sidney W. Clark; 130 *Sigourney St., Hartford, Ct.*
Relyea, Grace H., Green's Farms, Ct.; *Secretary's Office, Treasury Dept., Washington, D. C.*
Rexford, Mary E., Stamford, N. Y.; m. A. J. Champion, '83; *Delhi, N. Y.*
Smith, Carrie A., Boonton, N. J.; *Boonton, N. J.*
Smith, S. Bertha, Kennebunkport, Me.; *Kennebunkport, Me.*
Stevens, Clara F., Ph.M., Newburyport; *Mt. Holyoke College, S. Hadley;* home address, 207 *High St., Newburyport.*
Taylor, Bessie R., Green's Farms, Ct.; P. O. address, *Southport, Ct.*
Votey, Martha L., Charlotte, Vt.; m. Rev. Clifford H. Smith, '87; *Pittsford, Vt.*
Walker, Julia S., Groton, Ct.; m. John L. Ruhl, '90; *Clarksburg, W. Va.*
Watson, Ida L., St. Albans, Vt.; m. C. Sandusky, '87; *Raton, New Mexico.*
Welsh, Ida F., Danbury, Ct.; 81 *Deer Hill Ave., Danbury, Ct.*
West, Harriet H., E. Orange, N. J.; m. Wm. E. Doty; 50 *Beech St., E. Orange, N. J.*
Woodward, Helen M., Albion, N. Y.; m. Wm. Deed, Jr., '88; *Albion, N. Y.*

SPECIAL COURSE GRADUATES.

GREEK.—Flint, Helen C., B.A., Concord, N. H.; *Concord, N. H.*
FRENCH.—Spalding, Isabel, Nashua, N. H.; 68 *Concord St., Nashua, N. H.*
GERMAN.—Fogg, Ada M., Norwood; m. Geo. E. Ring, '85; *Mt. Desert, Me.*
" Post, Elizabeth F., S. Hadley; 308 *Clinton Place, Oak Park, Ill.*
" Shively, Flora L., S. Bend, Ind.; m. Geo. B. Beitner, '88; 311 *W. Navarre St., S. Bend, Ind.*

NON-GRADUATES.

Atwater, Lucy F., Westfield; 82 *Broad St., Westfield.*
Benham, Mary P., W. Haven, Ct.; d. Mt. Holyoke Seminary, '81.
Bissell, Emily R., Ahmednagar, India; *Ahmednagar, India.*
Bodurtha, Fannie M., Agawam; *Agawam.*
Bradford, Elizabeth J., Northampton; 159 *Elm St., Northampton.*
Bradley, Florence L., Westport, Ct.; *Westport, Ct.*
Brown, Clara, Chittenango, N. Y.; *Sullivan, N. Y.*
Challon, Winona, Cincinnati, O.; m. Geo. Hughes, '86; *Riverside, Jacksonville, Fla.*
Chase, Alice M., Amherst, Va.; 81 *Seelye Ave., Chicago, Ill.*
Chasmar, Coralie E., Darien, Ct.; m. Simon W. Cooper, '92; *Babylon, N. Y.*
Chellis, Lora E., Claremont, N. H.; m. Walter H. Story, '91; *Claremont, N. H.*
Coolidge, Sarah B., Leicester; m. Franklin E. Brooks, '91; 1324 *N. Nevada Ave., Col. Springs, Col.*
Cutting, Martha P., Templeton; m. Prof. Chas. A. Buffum, '82; *Easthampton.*

1881.

Everett, Ella A., S. Hampton, N. H.; m. D. Emery Eaton, Esq., '80; *Meredith, N. H.*
Ferguson, Mary, Malden Bridge, N. Y.; *Malden Bridge, N. Y.*
Gardner, Seraphine L., Sublette, Ill.; *Wesley Hospital, Chicago, Ill.*
Garrigus, Alice B., Waterbury, Ct.; 108 *Warren St., Bridgeport, Ct.*
Gerould, Mary C., Goffstown, N. H.; *Hollis, N. H.*
Hamilton, Lillian E., Sturgis, Mich.; m. Henry K. Warren, '83; 3d S. cor. 32d E., *Salt Lake City, Utah.*
Harris, Helen, Lowell; d. Lowell, '81.
Haseltine, M. Edna, Haverhill; *Ayers Village, Haverhill.*
Hawthorne, Florence J., New Haven, Vt.; m. Wm. H. Partch, '93; *New Haven, Vt.*
Heidenreich, Katherine, Marlboro; m. Geo. O. Cole, '81; 4 *Union St., Marlboro.*
Hendy, Satie D., Tobyhanna, Pa.; d. Hoboken, Pa., '89.
Hermance, Emma J., Half Moon, N. Y.; m. Henry J. Richmond, '85; 121 *Cannon St., Poughkeepsie, N. Y.*
House, Annie I., S. Manchester, Ct.; 111½ *Ann St., Hartford, Ct.*
Isham, Edith H., Cheshire, Ct.; m. *Marcus M. Mason, '85; 1521 *Spruce St., Philadelphia, Pa.*
Jackson, Josephine A., Goshen, Ind.; *Elkhart, Ind.*
Jones, Allie M., Chatham Village, N. Y.; m. Samuel E. Montague, '86; d. Holyoke, '90.
Jones, Edith S., Bridgeport, Ct.; m. C. Lester Buckingham, '84; 66 *Grove St., Cambridgeport, Ct.*
Joy, Ina A., Easthampton; d. Easthampton, '93.
Joy, Stella F., Easthampton; *Easthampton.*
Lane, Alice B., Waterloo, N. Y.; m. Jas. S. Dennison, '88; *Waterloo, N. Y.*
Lord, Fannie A., Fredonia, N. Y.; m. Wm. H. Bausum, '85; *Harold, S. Dak.*
Lowell, Annie A., W. Springfield; m. Cyrus H. Taber, '86; 61 *Pleasant St., Holyoke.*
McCord, Mary, Brooklyn, N. Y.; m. Geo. H. Redfield, '84; 68 *Evergreen Place, E. Orange, N. J.*
Miles, Harriet J., Cornwall Hollow, Ct.; d. Goshen, Ct., '81.
Peck, Marianna, Stratford, Ct.; 819 *N. 40th St., Philadelphia, Pa.*
Peck, Sarah N., Stratford, Ct.; *Stratford, Ct.*
Phillips, Adelaide S., Harmony, R. I.; m. Warren H. Steere, '83; 1097 *N. Main St., Providence, R. I.*
Pierce, Minnie H., Gardner, m. Edward A. Sawyer, M.D., '83; d. Gardner, '83.
Salmon, Anna F., Westport, Ct.; m. Wm. L. Taylor, '87; d. Westport, Ct., '90.
Sargent, Sarah L., Methuen; m. Wm. A. McGonagle, '87; 1130 *E. 2d St., Duluth, Minn.*
Schuyler, Mabel E., Ann Arbor, Mich; m. Frank Toy, '81; *Benkleman, Neb.*
Shively, Flora L., S. Bend, Ind.; m. Geo. B. Beitner, '88; 311 *W. Navarre St., S. Bend, Ind.*
Smith, Anna M., McKeesport, Pa.; m. Alexander A. Nimmo, '83; *McKeesport, Pa.*
Spalding, Isabel, Nashua, N. H.; 68 *Concord St., Nashua, N. H.*
Taylor, May E., Burlington, Vt.; 353 *Quincy St., Brooklyn, N. Y.*
Tracy, Hattie R., S. Manchester, Ct.; m. H. H. G. Ingalls, '85; *Castleton, N. Y.*
Whitney, A. Minnie, Chicago, Ill.; m. Chas. B. Pelton, '85; *Lake Helen, Fla.*
Widmer, Fannie, Pittsfield; m. Rev. Walter S. Eaton, '88; *Revere.*
Wilcox, L. Augusta, Jefferson, N. Y.; m. Herschell V. Jones, '85; 1816 *Colfax Ave., S., Minneapolis, Minn.*
Willett, Louise A., Bryan, O.; m. Geo. F. Solier, '83; *Pioneer, O.*
Wolverton, Mary E., Easton, Pa.; *College Hill, Easton, Pa.*
Yale, Martha, Ware; m. I. J. Gray; *Beloit, Kan.*

1882.

GRADUATES.

Alexander, Florence H., Toledo, O.; m. J. A. Russell; *Chicago, Ill.*
Bailey, Rebecca, Tom's River, N. J.; m. Halsey Jennings, '88; *Tom's River, N. J.*
Beckwith, Emily H., Norwich, Ct.; *Norwich, Ct.*
Clapp, Harriet E., Easthampton; m. Fred E. Gates, '89; *Woodland Heights,Springfield,Mo.*
Clark, Carrie A., Easthampton; *Easthampton.*
Davis, Sallie M., Milford, Del.; m. Geo. W. Halliwell, '93; *308 Broad St., Bethlehem, Pa.*
Derrickson, Elizabeth M., Warren, Ct.; *222 E. 14th St., N. Y. City.*
Doolittle, Jane E., Wallingford, Ct.; *Wallingford, Ct.*
Durkes, Ida E., Franklin Grove, Ill., m. Henry M. Hewitt, M.D., '83; d. Riverside, Cal., '02.
Edwards, Mary E., Westhampton; *Westhampton.*
Goodnough, Elizabeth, Oneida, Wis.; m. Henry A. Simonds, '84; *Farmington, Mo.*
Gould, Sallie H., Cincinnati, O.; m. Wm. G. Williams, '87; *16 St. James Ave., Walnut Hill, Cincinnati, O.*
Halbert, Pauline W., Midland Park, N. J.; m. Isaac Ford, '94; *Redlands, Cal.*
Hall, Mary A., New Haven, Vt.; m. C. G. Sprague, '84; *New Haven, Vt.*
Harris, Alice B., Athol Center; m. Rev. George B. Smyth, '84; *Foochow, China.*
Hill, Mary E., Kennebunk, Me.; *Kennebunk, Me.*
Hungerford, Antoinette L., Chester, Ct.; m. Trumbull W. Cleaveland, M.D., '86; *45 W. 50th St., N. Y. City.*
Ihling, Annie J., Philadelphia, Pa.; *W. Chester, Pa.*
Jewett, Mary E., Chaumont, N. Y.; m. John F. George, '90; d. Chaumont, N. Y., '95.
Lewis, Carrie E., Waterbury, Ct.; *Box 425, Waterbury, Ct.*
Loring, Mary E., N. Y. City; m. Chas. W. Warner; *150 College St., Middletown, Ct.*
Magee, Harriet C., Fredericton, N. B.; *384 Jackson St., Oshkosh, Wis.*
McIlvaine, Flora B., New Philadelphia, O.; m. Walter G. Shotwell, Esq., '84; *Cadiz, O.*
Miner, Ellen R., Cornwall, Ct.; m. Frank C. Dowd, '84; *Madison, Ct.*
Nichols, C. Adelle, Easthampton; m. Rev. W. S. Young, '89; *122 N. Chicago St., Los Angeles, Cal.*
Ostrom, Florence V., Brooklyn, N. Y.; m. L. P. Woodbury,'82; *22 Bright St., Northampton.*
Pease, Mary E., Oxford; m. Rev. W. S. Hawks, '89; *135 6th St., Salt Lake City, Utah.*
Peck, Jenny, Monson; m. N. W. Rand, M.D., '83; d. Monson, '86.
Twombly, Carrie H., Franklin Grove, Ill.; m. Wm. R. Reed, '85; *Concordia, Kan.*
Walsworth, Mary A., Lake Mahopac, N. Y.; m. James R. Honeywell; *Delhi, N. Y.*

SPECIAL COURSE GRADUATE.

GERMAN.—Ford, Georgiana B., Morristown, N. J.; *Morristown, N. J.*

NON-GRADUATES.

Abbott, Cora E., Chester; *Chester.*
Allen, Constance E., N. Woodstock, Ct.; *Wellesley.*
Ayer, Gertrude, Concord, N. H.; *6 Franklin St., Concord, N. H.*
Barnes, Mary G., Canton, Ill.; m. Chas. I. Colwell; *1421 S. 13th St., Denver, Col.*
Barnum, Susan E., Bethel, Ct.; m. Geo. A. Brown, M.D., '87; *Barre.*
Brown, Mary S., Holliday's Cove, W. Va.; *Holliday's Cove, W. Va.*
Browne, Emily B., Northwood, N. H.; m. Geo. H. Davis, '82; *41 Park St., Dover, N. H.*
Byorth, Emily C., Andover, Ill.; *Fremont, Neb.*
Chapin, Charlotte L., Phillipston; m. V. P. Gibney, M.D., '83; d. N. Y. City, '89.
Chapman, Elva M., Peterboro, N. H.; m. Geo. P. Dustan, '85; *Peterboro, N. H.*
Cordley, Annie M., Lawrence; *Glen Ridge, N. J.*

1882.

Corwin, Euphemia K., Millstone, N. J.; 20 *Chestnut St., Albany, N. Y.*
Corwin, Ida E., Catasauqua, Pa.; m. John A. Williams, '85; *Catasauqua, Pa.*
Cowles, Mary S., Wallingford, Ct.; 407 *Main St., Bridgeport, Ct.*
Dages, Amelia C., Gallipolis, O.; m. Frank R. Thrall, '88; *Muncie, Ind.*
Dana, Minnie L., S. Amherst; *S. Amherst.*
Dodge, Jennie H., Concord, N. H.; m. Oliver E. Williams, '86; d. '93.
Duncan, Margaretta, Paterson, N. J.; 61 *Main St., Paterson, N. J.*
Fanning, Agnes M., Worcester; m. John E. Lancaster; *Salisbury St., Worcester.*
Felician, Anna, Marsovan, Turkey; *Marsovan, Turkey, Asia.*
Ford, Georgiana B., B.A., Morristown, N. J.; *Palo Alto, Cal.*
Foskett, Clara G., New Haven, Ct.; m. Prof. Chas. S. Brown, '91; 915 *Maple Ave., Terre Haute, Ind.*
Fuller, Marie L., Brattleboro, Vt.; m. Josiah Graves, '86; *Walpole, N. H.*
Glines, Emma O., Ware; m. Andrew J. Davis, '87; *Ware.*
Goodale, Ellen C., Marlboro; m. Albert S. Howard, '88; *Townsend.*
Hitchcock, Mary L., Yarmouth, Me.; m. Geo. W. Merrill, '85; 908 *T St., N. W., Washington, D. C.*
Holmes, Mary G., Montclair, N. J.; 288 *Grove St., Montclair, N. J.*
Jennings, Hattie D., E. Orange, N. J.; m. Frank E. Heywood, '94; 60 *William St., Worcester.*
King, Ella, Bradford, Vt.; m. Marshall W. Brigham, '84; d. Worcester, Vt., '90.
Kleefisch, Helena, New Windsor, Md.; m. W. A. Dameron, '89; *Weems, Va.*
Lacey, Eva T., Waterloo, Ind.; m. Wm S. Silver, '86; d. Kingfisher, Okla., '91.
Lawrence, Eudora F. C., Stanley, N. Y.; *Willard, N. Y.*
McCurdy, Elizabeth, Dansville, N. Y.; *Dansville, N. Y.*
McKean, Fanny, Mercer, Pa.; m. Hollis Dean, M.D., '88; *Franklin, Pa.*
Miller, Bertha A., St. Petersburg, Pa.; 10061 *Ave. J, S. Chicago, Ill.*
Miller, H. Adele, Syracuse, N. Y.; m. Rev. John W. Cowan, '83; *Oregon City, Or.*
Miller, Lizana E., Syracuse, N. Y.; m. Fred L. Reed, '83; *Minerville, N. Y.*
Mitchell, Caroline, Des Moines, Io.; m. *Dr. M. J. Drabelle, '86; 1912 *Pleasant St., Des Moines, Io.*
Morgan, Hattie L., Worcester; m. Winthrop D. Mitchell, M.D., '89; 23 *S. Grove St., E. Orange, N. J.*
Neale, Fanny C., Farmington, Ct.; *Miss Carter's School, Catonsville, Md.*
Norton, Ida E., Lewiston, Me.; m. Augustus E. Small, '84; *Boston.*
Parker, N. Gertrude, Worcester; m. Elmer W. Lewis, '86; *Cohasset.*
Patch, Martha A., Stevens Point, Wis.; m. Daniel Campbell, M.D., '90; *Canfield, O.*
Penfield, Edith, Willoughby, O.; m. D. H. McBride, '86; 160 *Eugenie St., Chicago, Ill.*
Pingle, Grace, Jersey City, N. J.; 22 *E. Husatonic St., Pittsfield.*
Porter, Ella V., San Paulo, Brazil; m. Rev. E. A. Tilly; *Rio de Janeiro, Brazil, S. A.*
Prentice, E. Helen, Worcester; m. Roscoe W. Swan, M.D., '91; 41 *Pleasant St., Worcester.*
Sanborn, Alice C., Ashtabula, O.; m. Stephen F. Selby, '89; 63 *Prospect St., Ashtabula, O.*
Sanderson, Mary E., Northampton; m. Geo. B. McClellan, '84; *Whately.*
Sayre, Anna P., Morristown, N. J.; m. Eugene Pierson, '89; *Washington St., Morristown, N. J.*
Shafer, Helen M., Findlay, O.; m. Wm. F. Hosler, '85; 1006 *Main St., Findlay, O.*
Smith, Jennie E., Huntington; *Huntington.*
Staats, N. Louisa, Millstone, N. J.; d. Millstone, N. J., '85.
Tallman, Emily A., Castile, N. Y.; m. Almon B. Lane, '84; *Bloomingdale, Mich.*
Taylor, D. Eloise, E. Hamburg, N. Y.; m. Wm. H. Thornton, M.D., '86; 572 *Niagara St., Buffalo, N. Y.*
Thomas, Blanche, Catasauqua, Pa.; m. Chas. R. Horn, '86; *Box 388, Catasauqua, Pa.*
Townley, Mary B., Watertown, N. Y.; 49 *Howell St., Canandaigua, N. Y.*
Wales, W. Josephine, Brockton; m.;

Walker, J. Maria, Delaware, O. ; *Delaware, O.*
Warner, Mary J., Essex, Vt. ; m. J. Fred Brown, '89 ; *S. Lancaster.*
Whistler, Julia F., Mercer, Pa. ; *Mercer, Pa.*
Whitehill, Mary J., Peacham, Vt. ; m. Lewis A. Bigelow, '87 ; *8 Forest Ave., Everett.*
Wilcox, E. Elizabeth, Portland, Ct. ; m. Franklin Payne, '84 ; *Portland, Ct.*
Witter, M. Agnes, Putnam, Ct. ; m. *John S. Lindsey ; *Brookline.*
Wyckoff, Gertrude A., Brooklyn, N. Y. ; *942 Park Ave., Plainfield, N. J.*
Young, F. Della, Atlantic, Io. ; m. Edward J. Dickerson, '88 ; *Oskaloosa, Mo.*

1883.

GRADUATES.

Barnum, Mary F., Bethel, Ct. ; m. Edward H. Gumbart ; *E. Norwalk, Ct.*
Benedict, Elizabeth, Billings, N. Y. ; m. James W. Story,'90 ; *3 Elmcrest Terrace, Norwalk, Ct.*
Bond, Mary E., Ware ; m. Henry W. Cleveland. '85 ; d. Ware, '91.
Bray, Ella T., Clinton, Io. ; m. Harris Graham, M.D., '85 ; *Beirut, Syria.*
Brockway, Martha S., Lyme, Ct. ; *532 Howard Ave., New Haven, Ct.*
Burnette, Annie J., S. Hadley ; m. J. N. Hubbard, '89 ; *233 Elm St., Holyoke.*
Campbell, Nellie E., Agawam ; *Agawam.*
Croft, Margaret, Waterbury, Ct. ; m. George P. Curtis, '84 ; d. Waterbury, Ct., '88.
Crookham, Elizabeth E., Oskaloosa, Io. ; *Portland, Or.*
Cummings, Anna M., Strafford, Vt. ; Wellington, Cape Colony, S. Africa ; home address, *Strafford, Vt.*
Dickinson, H. Fanny, Amherst ; m. Joseph B. Lindsey, Ph.D., '88 ; *Box 53, Amherst.*
English, Agnes J., New York City ; m. *Edward Simmons ; *1010 Madison Ave., N. Y. City.*
Ferris, Charlotte E., St. Paul, Minn. ; m. Arthur C. Anderson, '85 ; d. St. Paul, Minn., '88.
Fitch, Frances L., Greenfield, N. H. ; m. Bernhard C. Schroeder, '90 ; *Box 197, Wollaston Heights.*
Gates, Grace E., Kennebunkport, Me. ; m. John P. Freese, '89 ; *112 Union Ave., S. Framingham.*
Guernsey, Sarah E., Cornwall, Vt. ; *Summerdale, Chicago, Ill.*
Hall, Mary A., Perth Amboy, N. J. ; *Fishkill-on-the-Hudson, N. Y.*
Hay, Ida W., Easton, Pa. ; m. Wm. C. Atwater, '89 ; *15 Prospect St., Fall River.*
Haynes, Helen E., Townsend ; *Townsend Harbor.*
Holbrook, Annie M., Holbrook ; *151 Wabash Ave., Chicago, Ill.*
Humphrey, Emma H., Collinsville, Ct. ; m. Stanley Neale, '85 ; *Collinsville, Ct.*
Jackson, May, Weston, W. Va. ; m. Blain W. Taylor, '89 ; *652 Acker St., N. E., Washington, D. C.*
Jones, Carrie E., Chatham, N.Y. ; m. Geo. E. Montague, '87 ; *438 N. 33d St., Philadelphia, Pa.*
Keith, Marcia A., B.S.. Braintree ; *Mt. Holyoke College. S. Hadley;* home address, *Braintree.*
McKeown, E. Louise. Palmyra, N. Y. ; m. Herman E. Sweezy ; *164 John St., New Haven, Ct.*
Magness, E. Frances, Waterloo, Io. ; *Porter Flats, Helena, Mont.*
Marvin. Katharine M., Lancaster ; *Lancaster.*
Meader, Ellen L., West Chester, Pa. ; d. West Chester, Pa., '83.
Parker, Hortense, Ripley, O. ; m. O. M. Wood, '86 ; *3016 Caroline St., St. Louis, Mo.*
Patch, Mary H.. Stevens' Point, Wis. ; *284 Wisconsin Ave., Stevens' Point, Wis.*
Peet, Ellen L., West Haven, Ct. ; m. Rev. Geo. H. Hubbard, '84 ; *Foochow, China.*
Pratt. Mary J., Holbrook ; m. Charles B. Whitcomb, '85 ; *Holbrook.*
Smith, Ida V.. Winchendon ; *20 Chelsea St.. E. Boston.*
Stout, Bertha B.. Clarksburg, W. Va. ; *Clarksburg, W. Va.*

1883.

Temple, Anna O., Atlantic. Io. ; *Atlantic, Io.*
Thomas, Ermina L., Tinmouth. Vt. ; m. Jas. M. Mott ; *3249 Troost Ave., Kansas City, Mo.*
Thomas, Margarette B., Shohola, Pa. ; *1319 W. 8th St., Des Moines, Io.*
Walter, Helen. Milton, N. Y. ; *9 West 124th St., N. Y. City.*
Warner, Mary A., Westminster ; d. Westminster, '95.
West, Fanny E., Worcester ; *W. Sutton.*
Wilder, Grace E., Princeton, N. J. ; *Kolapur, Western India.*
Wright. Laura B., Paris, Tex. ; *Paris, Tex.*

SPECIAL COURSE GRADUATES.

GREEK.—MacLeod. Martha A., Poultney, Vt. ; m. Frank W. French, '88 ; *318 Orange St., Manchester, N. H.*
FRENCH.—Cummings, Anna M., Strafford, Vt. ; *Wellington, Cape Colony, S. Africa* ; home address, *Strafford, Vt.*
FRENCH.—Derby, Mary E., Springfield ; m. Starr W. Cutting, Ph.D., '89; *Chicago University, Chicago, Ill.*

NON-GRADUATES.

Aiken, Elizabeth R., Woonsocket, R. I. ; m. Frank E. McFee, '87 ; *65 Park Ave., Woonsocket, R. I.*
Allen, Caro G., New Haven, Ct. ; m. Chas. L. Lyon, '92 ; *41 Lincoln St., Meriden, Ct.*
Armstrong. Mary A., Albert Lea, Minn. ; m. Rev. Henry J. Petran. '94 ; *Wells, Minn.*
Arnold, Belle A. Ballston Spa, N. Y. ; m. H. F. M. Smith, M.D., '87 ; *Orange.*
Arthurs, Julia B., Mendham, N. J. ; m. John Games, '87 ; *St. Andrews Bay, Fla.*
Barkdoll. Anna G., Smithsburg, Md. ; m. L. H. Dielman, '90 ; *New Windsor, Md.*
Barnes, Helen A., St. Albans, Vt. ; m. Wm. T. Roberts ; *St. Albans, Vt.*
Bartlett, Jennie H., Chillicothe, O. ; m. Harry C. Beaman, '87 ; *Princeton.*
Beckwith, Mary E., Westminster, Md. ; *1109 Madison Ave., Baltimore. Md.*
Bickford, Flora M., Peacham. Vt. ; *Peacham, Vt.*
Billings, Mary A., Conway ; *Conway.*
Bronson, Alice P., New Britain, Ct. ; m. Chas. T. Weed, '94 ; *Mechanicsburg, O.*
Chellis, May Belle, Meriden, N. H. ; *Meriden, N. H.*
Clark. Blanche M., Clarksdale. Miss. ; m. Hon. John W. Cutrer, '87 ; *Clarksdale, Miss.*
Clark. Mary R., Amherst ; *Baldwin St., Newton.*
Coleman, Charlotte, Hartford, Ct. ; m. Geo. F. Cary, '89 ; *E. Machias. Me.*
Comstock, Carrie, Ballston, N. Y. ; *Ballston Spa, N. Y.*
Cooke, Frances A., Hadley ; *Hadley.*
Cooke, Lillian R., Boston ; *78 Magnolia St., Roxbury.*
Cooke, Minnie L., Waukegan, Ill. ; m. Leland B. Werden, '86 ; *409 Water St., Waukegan, Ill.*
Danforth, Mattie S., Hamburg, Io. ; m. Louis A. Webb ; *Norden, Neb.*
Dexter. Frances S., Black River, N. Y. ; d. Black River, N. Y., '84.
Dickinson, Maud M., Rico, Col. ;
Douglass. Abbie M., Pittsford, Vt. ; m. Geo. E. Stacey, '88 ; *Yakima. Wash.*
Ellis. Jennie M., Medfield ; m. S. N. Bentley, M.D., '85 ; *Ravenna, Neb.*
Fehrmann, Cornelia S., Orange, N. J. ; m. Wm. M. Patterson, '85 ; *Box 1041, Penn Yan, N. Y.*
Fuller, M. Addie, Bellefontaine, O. ; m. Fernando T. Bell, '85 ; *14 Cross St., Aurora, Ill.*
Gardner, Addie L., Stillwater, Minn. ; m. Frank P. Sullivan, '83 ; *889 Fuller St., St. Paul, Minn.*
Grassie. Jessie D., Cambridgeboro, Pa. ; *Winter Park, Fla.*
Hale, Harriet I., Castine, Me. ; *Bible Institute, 230 La Salle Ave., Chicago, Ill.*

1883.

Hallock, Margaret S., Rocky Point, N. Y.; 490 *Pearl St., Buffalo, N. Y.*
Harmount, Isabel N., New Philadelphia, O. ; *Children's Home, Canal Dover, O.*
Hayes, Stella E , Barkhamsted, Ct.; *Barkhamsted, Ct.*
Holmes, Susan B., W. Winsted, Ct.; m.Robert A. Holmes, '85 ; *35 West St., S. Norwalk, Ct.*
Hooker, Eva F., Carthage, N. Y. ; *24 Selye Terrace, Rochester, N. Y.*
Leach, Mabel E., Westminster, Vt. ; m. Wm. F. Wright; *Holyoke.*
Lee, Fanny S., Falmouth, Ky.; *Falmouth, Ky.*
Leonard, Mary M., Marion, O. ; *377 S. Prospect St., Marion, O.*
Lewis, Agnes M., Westport, Ct. ; m. Neil R. Mitchell ; *Darien, Ct.*
Lowell, Mary C., M.D., Foxcroft, Me. ; *Mt. Holyoke College, S. Hadley.*
McClelland, Annie H., Newark, N. J.; *163 Fairmount Ave., Newark, N. J.*
MacLeod, Martha A., Poultney, Vt. ; m. Frank W. French, '88 ; *318 Orange St., Manchester, N. H.*
Manson, Alice L., Lowell ; *Room 33, 87 Milk St., Boston.*
Martin, Mary L., Peacham, Vt. ; *90 Main St., St. Johnsbury, Vt.*
Mason, Mabel M., Winchendon ; *Winchendon.*
Matthews, Mary L., Millville, N. Y. ; *Millville, N. Y.*
Mellen, Emily K., Worcester ; *153 E. College St., Oberlin, O.*
Norton, Emma S., Bennington, Vt.; m. Clarke H. Emmons, '94 ; *1022 Hawthorne Ave., Minneapolis, Minn.*
Ormsby, Helen M., Xenia, O. ; m. Isaac L. Amberg, '88 ; *Beech Knoll, E. Walnut Hills, Cincinnati, O.*
Parsons, Edith, Rochester, Vt. ; m. Edward L. Greene, '85; *14 Prescott St., Clinton.*
Phelps, Fidelia, S. Deerfield ; *Inanda, via Duff's Road, Natal, S. Africa.*
Rogers, Alice E., Albion, N. Y. ; *Albion, N. Y.*
Shaw, Lucy A., Geneseo, Ill. ; m. Gustav A. F. Meyer, '86; *Joplin, Mo.*
Sheldon, Jessie H., Oxford, N. Y. ; m. Myron E. Powers, '86 ; *Plainville, Ct.*
Strobridge, Ellen L., Peacham, Vt. ; m. N. J. Whitehill, '84 ; *W. Randolph, Vt.*
Townley,Grace,Watertown, N. Y. ; m. Alvin H. Dewey,'86 ; *47 Rowley St., Rochester, N. Y.*
Travis, Josephine E., Holliston ; *Holliston.*
Trusler, N. Salome, Washington, D. C. ; m. Jere Johnson, Esq., '85 ; *Brookland, D. C.*
Tuttle, Theodora A., New Haven, Ct. ; m. Ralph M. Hooker, '83 ; *257 Warren St., Boston.*
Walker, Laura A., Groton, Ct. ; *Clarksburg, W. Va.*
Warner, Mary M., Florence ; m. John P. Eustis, '91 ; *Newtonville.*
Wetmore, Martha S., Meriden, Ct. ; *44 Crown St., Meriden, Ct.*
Whitaker, Corinne, Irvington, N. Y. ; *522 Penn St., Camden, N. J.*
Whitman, Iola E., Enfield; m. Edward B. Downing, '86 ; *Enfield.*
Williams, Alberta K., Washington, D. C.; m. Francis Kempton, '83 ; *N. Y. City.*
Williams, H. Louise, Passaic, N. J. ; *780 Green Ave., Brooklyn, N. Y.*
Wiswell, Lillian A., Worcester ; P. O. address, *Atlantic.*
Woodford, Abbie M., W. Avon, Ct.; *Redlands, Cal.*
Wooster, Elizabeth D., Cuylerville, N. Y.; m. Thos. A. Dodge, '91 ; *Hanford, Cal.*

1884.

GRADUATES.

Annock, Carrie L., Newark, N. Y. ; m. Henry L. Bruner, '90; d. Col. Springs, Col., '94.
Averill, Mary A., Northampton ; *Brattleboro, Vt.*
Avery, Mary A., Ledyard, Ct. ; *44 Oneco St., Norwich, Ct.*

1884.

Bachelder, Carrie W., Wellesley Hills; *Wellesley Hills.*
Bailey, Mary E., Peacham, Vt. ; *Mainpuri, India.*
Ballard, Winifred P., Easton, Pa.; m. *Francis C. Blake, '85; *Box* 181, *Williamstown.*
Bates, Lizzie E., Essex, Vt. ; m. Dr. A. F. Peck, '89; 7 *Winn St., Woburn.*
Bisbee, Nettie M., Delhi, N. Y. ; m. John E. Fanning, '86; *Preston, Norwich, Ct.*
Blakely, Annie G., Campton, N. H. ; *Winchendon.*
Boice, Josephine, Philadelphia, Pa. ; 102 *N. 19th St., Philadelphia, Pa.*
Brundage, Gertrude M., M.D., Hazelton, Pa. ; m. *John S. Streeper,'86 ; 1214 *Locust St., Philadelphia, Pa.*
Carpenter, Frances A., M.D., Wickham, N. B.;*Woman's Medical College, Philadelphia, Pa.*
Chandler, Lucia A., Strafford, Vt. ; m. Edward W. Newell,'85; 203 *Savannah Ave., Wilkinsburg, Pa.*
Clark, Ellen K., Sodus, N. Y. ; *Sodus, N. Y.*
Cohn, Leah, Cobleskill, N. Y. ; m. Ralph S. Everest, *Lansingburg, N. Y.*
Cooper, Mary D., S. Centerville, N. Y. ; m. Frank M. Cummins, M.D., '87 ; d. Warwick, N. Y., '94.
Derby, Mary E., Springfield ; m. Starr W. Cutting, Ph.D., '89 ; address, *Chicago University, Chicago, Ill.*
Duncan, Leslie G., Poquonnock, Ct. ; d. Poquonnock, Ct., '86.
Epler, Blanch N., Jacksonville, Ill. ; 1106 *W. State St., Jacksonville, Ill.*
Giddings, Clara C., W. Brookfield ; *Woodstock School, Landour, N. W. P., India.*
Goldthwait, Martha C., Longmeadow; *Longmeadow.*
Griggs, Nellie M., Chaplin, Ct. ; *Chaplin, Ct.*
Harvey, Julia B., West Barnet, Vt. ; m. Jesse Gale, '90 ; d. Greeley, Col., '91.
Hodges, Fanny L., Rochester, N. Y. ; *Box* 216, *Rochester, N. Y.*
Jack, Mary M., Media, Pa.; m. Owen Shoemaker, '85 ; 109 *S. 20th St., Philadelphia, Pa.*
Judd, Mirah L., Westhampton ; m. W. R. Jones, '90; 60 *North St., Stamford, Ct.*
Kirk, Eleanor H., Boston; 760 *Dudley St., Dorchester.*
Lane, Laura M., Waterloo, N. Y. ; m. Harvey Shoemaker, M.D.; 109 *S. 20th St., Philadelphia, Pa.*
McIlvane, Carrie R., New Philadelphia, O.; m. Stuart B. Shotwell, Jr., '91 ; 509 *Holly Ave., St. Paul, Minn.*
Miner, Ida L., Rochester. Minn. ; 3022 *Dupont Ave., S., Minneapolis, Minn.*
Nichols, A. Frances, Chicago, Ill. ; *Briarwood, Bellevue, Wash.*
Olmstead, Caroline W., Enfield, Ct.; m. Norman F. Allen, '87 ; 520 *Farmington Ave., Hartford, Ct.*
Phelps, Mary E., Jaffrey. N. H. ; *Jaffrey, N. H.*
Pratt, Ettie E., Litchfield,Ct.; m.Wm. Simmons,M.D.,'83; 189 *Prospect Place,Brooklyn,N.Y.*
Robbins, Gertrude, Robbins' Station, Pa.; m. W. M. Carruthers, M.D.; 513 2d *St., Braddock, Pa.*
Sagar, Sarah, W. Hampstead, N. H.; m. Walter J. Richardson, M.D.. '86 ; *Fairmont. Minn.*
Smith, Alice T., N. Hadley ; m. Thomas Gerry. '88 ; *N. Hadley.*
Smith, Lucy M., W. Roxbury ; *Mount Vernon St., W. Roxbury.*
Stockwell, Emma, Windsor Locks, Ct. ; d. Windsor Locks, Ct., '85.
Strickland, Helen L., Enfield, Ct. ; m. F. H. Abbe, '84 ; *Enfield, Ct.*
Thwing, Grace, Brooklyn, N. Y. ; *Port Chester, N. Y.*
Tirrell, M. Alice, S. Weymouth ; m. Warren Tirrell, '90 ; 23 *Brett St., Brockton.*
Tuttle, Lizzie E., Holyoke ; m. Robert M. Ferguson, '85 ; 158 *Elm St., Holyoke.*
Walker, Mary E., Groton, Ct.; m. Robert F. Raymond, Esq., '86 ; 138 *4th St., New Bedford.*
Werkheiser, Rosa A., Easton. Pa.; m. Wm. A. Seibert, M.D.,'85 ; 65 *N. 8th St., Easton, Pa.*
Wilbur, Helena G., Bryn Mawr. Pa.; m. *Robert A. Elliott, '90 ; *Box* 93. *Bryn Mawr, Pa.*

1884.

SPECIAL COURSE GRADUATES.

GERMAN.—Cohn, Leah, Cobleskill, N. Y. ; m. Ralph S. Everest ; *Lansingsburg, N. Y.*
" Giddings, Caroline L., Housatonic ; *Housatonic.*

NON-GRADUATES.

Avery, Jeannette M., Jackson, Mich ; m. ——; *Boston* (?).
Baker, Ada C., Chadd's Ford, Pa. ; *Chadd's Ford, Pa.*
Baldwin, Charlotte E., S. Britain, Ct.; care *Mrs. E. Baldwin*, 141 *Dwight St., New Haven, Ct.*
Bickford, Mary M., Peacham, Vt. ; *Peacham, Vt.*
Bird, Emily F. J., Brooklyn, N. Y. ; 1714 *Preston St., Louisville, Ky.*
Brockway, Emily E., S. Hadley ; m. John E. Lyman, '85 ; *S. Hadley.*
Bronson, Carrie M., Winchester, Ct. ; *Winchester, Ct.*
Chapman, Ethel, Bethel, Ct. ; *Bethel, Ct.*
Chapman, Mary E., Chico, Cal. ; m. Harry J. McKim, '88 ; d. Chico, Cal., '91.
Cooke, Caroline G., Stow ; 103 *Hammond St., Cambridge.*
Cowles, Anna L., Norfolk, Ct. ; *Norfolk, Ct.*
Cowles, Carrie L., Woodbury, Ct. ; m. Arthur Wight, '95 ; care *Art Students' League*, 215 *W. 57th St., N. Y. City.*
Cumiskey, Mary E., S. Dartmouth (see Mary E. McKenzie, '87).
Dailey, Minnie M., N. Y. City ; 1220 *Walnut St., Philadelphia, Pa.*
Davidson, Isabella J., St. Louis, Mo. ; *Box 181, Bunker Hill, Ill.*
Duff, Susie T., Pittsburgh, Pa. ; *Pittsburgh, Pa.*
Earl, Anna M., Elizabeth, N. J. ; *Lock Box 42, Elizabeth, N. J.*
Field, M. Elizabeth, Ticonderoga, N. Y. ; m. *Geo. C. Adams, '85 ; m. G. P. Harley, '94 ; care Stevenson, Blackader & Co., Montreal, Can.*
Fitch, Helen N., Logansport, Ind. ; 584 *Marshall St., Milwaukee, Wis.*
Fogg, Ada M., Norwood ; m. Geo. E. Ring, '85 ; *Mt. Desert, Me.*
George, Elizabeth W., Concord, N. H. ; 88 *School St., Concord, N. H.*
Giddings, Caroline M., Housatonic ; *Housatonic.*
Hall, Emma C., Wallingford, Ct. ; m. Chas. E. Lyman, '86 ; *Middlefield, Ct.*
Harries, Imogen, Ruckawa, O. ; *E. Dayton, Dayton, O.*
Harris, H. Fronia, Nichols, N. Y. ; m. Geo. M. Cady, M.D., '87 ; *Nichols, N. Y.*
Hearne, Margaret J., Cincinnati, O. ; m. Wm. F. Ross ; *Box 625, Cincinnati, O.*
Hill, Sarah M., Redding, Ct. ; m. Prof. A. M. Neadwell, '92 ; *Oxford, O.*
Hinchman, Marie L., Summit, N. J. ; *Summit, N. J.*
Hitchcock, J. Elizabeth, Amherst ; *Amherst.*
Jackson, Sarah E., Ansonia, Ct. ; *Ansonia, Ct.*
Johnson, Eleanor A., St. Peter, Minn. ; d. St. Peter, Minn., '85.
Johnson, Martha E., W. Winsted, Ct. ; m. Miron J. Case, '87 ; 27 *Imlay St., Hartford, Ct.,*
Keith, Flora M. H., E. Machias, Me. ; m. Elwood Holmes, '88 ; *Los Angeles, Cal.*
Kibbe, Julia E., Longmeadow ; m. Frank B. Allen, '86 ; *Longmeadow.*
Kingsley, Mabel D., Northampton ; care *C. B. Kingsley, Elm St., Northampton.*
Littlefield, Ethel A., Malden ; m. Arthur B. Norton ; *Boston Highlands, Boston.*
McCallister, Nancy B., Shippensburgh, Pa. ; d. Shippensburgh, Pa., '84.
Merwin, Agnes D., Durham, Ct. ; *Durham, Ct.*
Oldham, Marie A. (Mulligan),Poona, India ; m. Rev. Wm. F. Oldham, '75 ; 238 *Main St., Pittsburgh, Pa.*
Page, Clara E., Ayer ; m. Edward A. Richardson ; *Box 263, Ayer.*
Pettengill, Annie G., E. Salisbury ; *Salisbury.*
Pierce, Helen A., Franklin Furnace, N. J. ; *Newton, N. J.*

1884.

Pusey, Sophie S., Wilmington, Del.; m. Rev. Thos. R. McDowell; '88 *Parkesburgh, Pa.*
Richardson, Mary E., Becket ; *Becket.*
Ross, Lillian A., S. Hadley ; m. Chas. H. Gordon, '92; *Wabuska, Nev.*
Rumsey, Emma V., Redding, Ct.; *Redding, Ct.*
Sabin, Emily O., Bellows Falls, Vt. ; m. Fred H. Kimball, '86; d. Bellows Falls, Vt., '89.
Safford, Annette, Middlefield, Ct. ; m. Geo. J. Francis, '85; d. Rockfall, Ct., '88.
Saunders, Lucy B., E. Pepperell ; *E. Pepperell.*
Savage, Charlotte E., Rahway, N. J. ; 468 *Ellison St., Paterson, N. J.*
Sherwood, Harriet A., Southport, Ct. ; m. Willis K. Fracker, '86 ; *Berea, O.*
Simonton, Martha S., Emmitsburgh, Md. ; *Emmitsburgh, Md.*
Somers, Maude E., Deansville, N. Y. ; 178 *Bergen St., Brooklyn, N. Y.*
Smith, Florence N., N. Y. City ; *N. Y. City.*
Smith, Jennie A., Shoreham, Vt. ; *Shoreham, Vt.*
Smith, Stella R., N. Hadley ; d. N. Hadley, '86.
Stockbridge, Anna, S. Deerfield ; *Northampton.*
Stockwell, Lula, Windsor Locks, Ct.; *Windsor Locks, Ct.*
Stout, Calore V., Clarksburgh, W. Va. ; m. J. Philip Clifford, '86; *Clarksburgh, W. Va.*
Sturtevant, Florence E., Ware ; m. Franklin H. Upham, '93 ; *Florence, N. J.*
Switzer, Marie A., Philadelphia, Pa. ; 359 *Lexington Ave., N. Y. City.*
Taylor, Harriet P., Green's Farms, Ct. ; m. Alfred J. Wakeman, Ph.D., '92; 72 *Clark St., New Haven, Ct.*
Van Doren, M. Ella, Middlebush, N. J. ; m. Thos. Monie, '94 ; *Archbald, Pa.*
Van Wie, Margaret S., Fultonville, N. Y. ; m. John R. Blood ; '89 ; *Amsterdam, N. Y.*
Vaughan, Grace A., Laconia, N. H. ; m. Chas. F. Pitman ; '90 ; *Laconia, N. H.*
Vining, F. Louise, Southwick ; 2437 *Brooklyn Ave., Kansas City, Mo.*
Walton, Sarah, Alexandria Bay, N. Y. ; *Alexandria Bay, N. Y.*
Ward, Sarah E., St. Helena Island, S. C.; *Frogmore, S. C.*
Wells, Julia E., Claremont, N. H. ; m. Horace B. Humphrey,'92; *Oak Park, Ill.*
Wells, M. Bonita, Tyler, Tex. ; *care E. H. Wells, President Baylor College, Belton, Tex.*
Whitaker, Cora, Camden, N. J. ; 550 *York St., Camden, N. J.*
Wight, Ruth E., Springfield ; m. Nathan D. Bill, '85; 284 *Maple St., Springfield.*
Williams, Clara E., Essex Junction, Vt. ; m. Homer D. Drury, '92 ; *Essex Junction, Vt.*
Wood, Amy U., Atlantic, Io. ; m. Ernest N. Bagg, '88 ; 7 *Grafton St., Dorchester.*
Woodward, Alice L., Concord, N. H. ; m. Wm. J. Drew ; 19 *S. Spring St., Concord, N. H.*

1885.

GRADUATES.

Ayer, Fy, Rochester, Minn. ; *Pomona, Cal.*
Berry, Mary A., Brunswick, Me. ; d. Mt. Holyoke College, '92.
Bowen, Frances C., Chili, N. Y.; *Chili Station, N. Y.*
Carson, Julia A. M., Catasauqua, Pa. ; m. Gen. Richard W. Johnson, '95 ; 550 *Dayton Ave., St. Paul, Minn.*
Chellis, Marcia B., Claremont, N. H. ; *Redlands, Cal.*
Cochrane, Josephine G., Philadelphia, Pa. ; *Morristown, N. J.*
Coley, Carrie E., Westport, Ct. ; m. Dr. Frank Gorham ; d. '92.
Dibblee, Mary D., Moore's Mills, N. B. ; m. Jno. McGibbon, '92 ; *St. Stephen, N. B.*
Hill, Elizabeth G., Red Wing, Minn. ; *Red Wing, Minn.*
Hodgkins, Georgiana, Ames, Io. ; *Ames, Io.*

1885.

Hunt, May, Knoxboro, N. Y.; *Knoxboro, N. Y.*
Körner, Caroline, N. Y. City; m. Rev. Lyman P. Peet, '88; *Foochow, China.*
Lyman, Mary A., Chester Center; *Huntington.*
Miller, C. Irene, S. Hadley; m. Fred H. Cook, '88; *Holyoke.*
Miller, Laura M., N. Brookfield; *N. Brookfield.*
Pettibone. Emily F., Winchester, Ct.; m. Eliot B. Bronson, '86; *Winchester, Ct.*
Phillips, Zoe L., Monson; m. Linus Hall, '88; *Wallingford, Ct.*
Robb, Julia L., Cohoes, N. Y.; *Phœnix, N. Y.*
Semans, Ida E., Naples, N. Y.; m. G. M. W. Bills, '91; *Exchange Building, Rochester, N. Y.*
Smith, Clara E., Northford, Ct.; *Northford, Ct.*
Tirrell, Sarah B., S. Weymouth; *S. Weymouth.*
Tuttle, Alice J., Decatur, Ill.; m. Frank Curtis, '92; 510 *E. Eldorado St., Decatur, Ill.*
Upham, Lucy C., Brookfield, Vt.; m. Frank J. Partridge, M.D., '89; *Uxbridge.*
Upham, Mary C., Brookfield, Vt.; *Brookfield, Vt.*
Whitmore, Lucy M., New Haven, Ct.; 147 *Beadley St., New Haven, Ct.*
Wilbraham, Josephine, Philadelphia, Pa.; *Box 325, Palmyra, N. Y.*
Williams, Mary G., Corning, N. Y.; *Lake Erie Sem., Painesville, O.*

NON-GRADUATES.

Anewalt, Anna E., Allentown, Pa.; m. Dr. Howard S. Seip; *cor. Walnut and 5th Sts., Allentown, Pa.*
Anewalt, Kate R., Allentown, Pa.; m. Edward M. Young, '90; *Allentown, Pa.*
Ashby, May S., Washington, D. C.; m. —— Bacon; d. Dorchester, '92.
Bates, Alice E., Springfield, Vt.; m. Rush Chellis, '87; *Claremont, N. H.*
Beardsley, Katharine A., Roxbury, Ct.; *Roxbury, Ct.*
Bradford, Mary A., Taunton; 24 *Quincy St., Somerville.*
Bray, Alice P., Kenosha, Wis.; *State Normal School, Whitewater, Wis.*
Byington, S. Lillian, Fayetteville, N. Y.; 615 18*th St., Moline, Ill.*
Cobleigh, Nellie F., Bernardston; m. Homer C. Chapin, '89; *Florence.*
Church, Edith T., Phillips, Me.; *Phillips, Me.*
Church, Lena R., Chaplin, Ct.; d. Mt. Holyoke Seminary, '85.
Coleman, Anna M., Goshen, N. Y.; *Goshen, N. Y.*
Coulter, Anna L., Afton, N. Y.; m. Anthony J. Dunlevy, '88; *Tilden, Neb.*
Cowls, Nellie G., N. Amherst; m. Edwin H. Dickinson, '92; *N. Amherst.*
Davis, Mary L., Sioux City, Io.; m. Henry M. Bailey, '88; 1021 *Jones St., Sioux City, Io.,*
Dixon, Roxanna, Snow Camp, N. C.; m. Wm. A. White, '86; *Brunswick, N. C.*
Duley, Lizzie J., Unadilla, N. Y.; m. Frederick H. Meeker, '90; *Unadilla, N. Y.*
Everitt, N. Augusta, Brandville, N. J.; *Lakewood, N. J.*
Fairbank, Grace, Ahmednagar, India; 55 *Chestnut St., Springfield.*
Ferguson, Margaret E., Wellington, S. Africa; *Wellington, Cape Colony, S. Africa.*
Ferry, K. Elizabeth, Westfield; m. Wm. H. Savery, '86; *Summer St., Westfield.*
French, Dora D., Amherst; m. James F. Page, '91; *Amherst.*
George, Clara D., Concord, N. H.; m. Henry C. Brewer, '91; 11 *Pond St., Jamaica Plain.*
Green, Eliza C., Cambridge, N. Y.; *Cambridge, N. Y.*
Hall, Mary, Ashtabula, O.; m. John C. Faulkner, '90; *cor. Bedford Ave. and Pacific St., Brooklyn, N. Y.*
Hallock, Effie V., Steubenville, O.; m. *Rev. Wm. Paxton Braddock, '86; *Dehra Dun, N. W. Province, India.*
Hallock, Kate, Somers, N. Y.; m. Hugh R. Smith, '88; *Somers, N. Y.*
Hatheway, Lissa I., Suffield, Ct.; m. Henry Keigwin, '87; *cor. Williams and Lafayette Sts., Norwich, Ct.*

1885.

Holmes, Edith M., Stroudsburg, Pa.; *Stroudsburg, Pa.*
Hulse, Susan, Goshen, N. Y.; m. Sidney D. Evans, '86; 461 *E. First South St., Salt Lake City.*
Hunter, L. Annie, Machias, Me.; *Machias, Me.*
Hunter, Sarah L., Machias, Me.; *Machias, Me.*
Hutchings, Harriet E., Amherst; d. Mt. Holyoke Seminary, Nov. 20, '84.
Jack, Anna C., Media, Pa.; 1533 *Locust St., Philadelphia, Pa.*
Jennings, Mary R., E. Orange, N. J.; 96 *N. Grove St., E. Orange, N. J.*
Laubach, Annie B., Easton, Pa.; m. John W. Nute, '87; 47 *Nicholson Place, St. Louis, Mo.*
Lewis, Gertrude E., Ketchum, Idaho; m. Peter G. Gates, '87; *Eagle Mills, Ark.*
Linville, Florence M., Fernandina, Fla.; m. Wm. Le Fills, '87; 517 *E. Bay St., Jacksonville, Fla.*
Ludden, Martha A., Easthampton; *Easthampton.*
Lyman, Luella M., Granby; m. Henry Moody, '87; d. *Granby, '93.*
Magill, Maud H., Amherst; *Amherst.*
Mosser, Lucy E., Allentown, Pa.; *Allentown, Pa.*
Newell, Minnie S., Westport, N. Y.; m. Dr. O. H. Mott, '89; d. Fort Ann, N. Y., '90.
Patten, Mary E., Ripton, Vt.; *Winchester.*
Pettengill, Ellen S., E. Salisbury; *Salisbury.*
Pierce, Emma E., Rutland, Vt.; m. Clarence H. Murdick, '93; *Nichols St., Rutland, Vt.*
Rathburn, Maud E., Sweet Air, Md.; *Falls Church, Va.*
Reimer, Fanny, Mt. Bethel, Pa.; *Easton, Pa.*
Sargent, Mary E., Methuen; d. Methuen, '88.
Scoville, Elizabeth W., Brooklyn, N. Y.; 96 *Lafayette Ave., Brooklyn, N. Y.*
Scudder, Harriet, Vellore, India; 414 *Sewall Ave., Asbury Park, N. J.*
Seymour, Mary E., Ashtabula, O.; m. Geo. C. Hubbard, '87; 39 *Prospect St., Ashtabula, O.*
Shumway, Mary F., Seattle, Wash.; 1905 *Madison St., Seattle, Wash.*
Smith, Emma M., Stillwater, N. Y.; d. Stillwater, N. Y., '86.
Smith, Kate L., Manchester, N. H.; 57 *Harrison St., Manchester, N. H.*
Smith, Kittie L., Chicopee; *Chicopee.*
Smith, Nellie L., Albion, N. Y.; m. L. Frank Gates, '94; *Oshkosh, Wis.*
Stout, Anna R., Easton, Pa.; m. Daniel D. Bickham, '87; 319 *W. Monument Ave., Dayton, O.*
Sweeney, Florence D., Hanover; *S. Hanover.*
Tanner, Carolyn C., Chicago, Ill.; m. *Joseph M. Bailey, Jr., '85; m. John K. Mumford, '95; 161 *W. End Ave., N. Y. City.*
Troxell, Marion E., Allentown, Pa.; home address, 838 *Hamilton St., Allentown, Pa.*
Waples, Anna R., Northumberland, Pa.; m.*A. Oakley Van Allen, '88; *Northumberland, Pa.*
Wheeler, Hannah R., Salem, N. J.; m. Samuel Gilmore; *Merchantville, N. J.*
Whittlesey, Margaret B., Oxford; *Nathan Hale St., New London, Ct.*

1886.

GRADUATES.

Abbott, Nora, Albert Lea, Minn.; m. J. M. Todd, M.D., '87; *Albert Lea, Minn.*
Avery, Elizabeth D., Clinton, N. Y.; m. H. N. Newland, '88; *Temple, Texas.*
Barney, Mary E., S. Hadley Falls; m. Rev. Herbert E. Thayer, '88; *Warren, Me.*
Blocher, Flora B., Chicago, Ill.; P. O. address, *Franklin Grove, Ill.*
Boyd, Annie M., Brooklyn, N. Y.; 53 *Fifth Ave., N. Y. City.*
Bridgman, Minnie H., Westhampton; *Westhampton.*

1886.

Clark, Martha J., Peacham, Vt.; m. Rev. Hilton Pedley, '92; *Niigata, Japan.*
Coryell, Mary, Nichols, N. Y.; m. F. C. Lowman, '92; *Nichols, N. Y.*
Cummings, Sarah R., Strafford, Vt.; *Strafford, Vt.*
Cutler, Louisa S., Florence; *Public Library, Utica, N. Y.*
Davis, Florence J., Sioux City, Io.; m. Wm. C. Hutchins, '87; *Sioux City, Io.*
Dole, Mary P., M.D., Ashfield; *Greenfield.*
Dresser, Eunice K., Stockbridge; m. J. R. Edsall, '89; *Nichols, N. Y.*
Engelman, Emma A., Cherryville, Pa.; m. Elwood M. Kuntz, '87; *E. Mauch Chunk, Pa.*
Fisherdick, Anna L., Palmer; *Palmer.*
Fitch, Orianna P., Greenfield, N. H.; *Concord.*
Freeland, Marietta H., Feeding Hills; *Feeding Hills.*
Goldthwait, Carrie M., Marblehead; m. Lafayette Gregory, '90; *Marblehead.*
Goodenough, Mary A., Winchester, Ct.; *Winchester, Ct.*
Hall, Adelle H., Westfield, N. Y.; m. H. W. Thompson, '94; *Westfield, N. Y.*
Hall, Phebe P., Fishkill Landing, N. Y.; *Fishkill-on-Hudson, N. Y.*
Haynes, Emma H., Townsend; *Townsend Harbor.*
Hughes, Mary A., Orange, N. J.; m. Rev. D. O. Ernsberger, '91; *Gulbarga, Deccan, India.*
Hunt, A. May, Mingo, O.; *876 Warren Ave., Chicago, Ill.*
Hunt, Anna J., Barre; m. Rev. George P. Knapp, '90; *Bitlis, Turkey in Asia.*
Johnson, Nellie M., Saxonville; m. S. Frank Danforth, '91; *Saxonville.*
Kimball, Julia F., Amherst; m. Henry N. Dickinson, '92; *38 Rockview St., Jamaica Plain.*
Knowles, Mary E., Westfield; *100 Court St., Westfield.*
Lancraft, Ettie A., New Haven, Ct.; m. Edmund O. Hovey, Ph.D., '88; *210 W. 84th St., New York City.*
Marsh, Emily R., Hadley, *Hadley.*
Montague, Jennie L., Holyoke; m. Frank T. Terry, '89; *40 State St., Ansonia, Ct.*
Munson, Mary J., Chicago, Ill.; d. Chicago, Ill., '91.
Paine, Emily F., Albany, N. Y.; *care Dr. N. E. Paine, W. Newton.*
Patrick, Sarah L., West Newton; *Newtonville.*
Pease, Harriet R., Somers, Ct.; *Monson*; home address, *Somers, Ct.*
Pixley, Martha H., Lindley, Natal; *Durban, Amanzimtote, S. Africa.*
Prescott, Harriet B., Derry, N. H.; *Boylston Terrace, Jamaica Plain.*
Purington, Florence, Waterford, Ct.; *Mt. Holyoke College, S. Hadley.*
Scofield, Jane, Sandy Spring, Md.; *West End, San Antonio, Texas.*
Scofield, Sarah C., Sandy Spring, Md.; *West End, San Antonio, Texas.*
Scudder, Sarah W., Vellore, India; m. S. Downer Scudder, '86; *West End, San Antonio, Texas.*
Smith, Fannie N., Brentwood, N. H.; m. John Whitmore, '92; *147 Bradley St., New Haven, Ct.*
Smith, M. Belle, Rockfall, Ct.; *22 Church St., Marlboro.*
Smith, S. Effie, B. S., Newburyport; *Mt. Holyoke College, S. Hadley*, home address, *19 Walnut St., Newburyport.*
Stevens, Alice P., B. A., Newburyport; *Mt. Holyoke College, S. Hadley*; home address, *207 High St., Newburyport.*
Stevens, Julia W., S. Framingham; m. Henry B. Day, '87; *W. Newton.*
Sweet, Rena E., Jewett City, Ct.; m. Alfred N. H. Vaughn, '90; *36 Oak St., Norwich, Ct.*
Taylor, Ellen S., Granby; m. Rev. Albert D. Smith, '88; *E. Longmeadow.*
Thayer, Emma S., W. Medway; m. Sanford L. Cutler, '88; *Great Barrington.*
Warner, Adelaide S., Westminster; *Westminster.*
Wentworth, Caroline S., Haverhill; m. Adolf J. A. Fredholm, '92; *648 Lombard St., Baltimore, Md.*
Wheeler, Eleanor S., Salem, N. J.; *Salem, N. J.*

1886.

SPECIAL COURSE GRADUATES.

GREEK.—Kimball, Julia F., Amherst; m. Henry N. Dickinson,38 *Rockview St., Jamaica Plain.*
FRENCH.—Comey, Annie F., Quincy; m. Geo. E. Conway, 20 *Mechanic St., Fitchburg.*
" Hyde, Isabella. Ware ; *Ware.*
" Warner, Mary A., Westminster ; d. Westminster, '95.
GERMAN.—Dresser, Eunice K., Stockbridge ; m. J. R. Edsall, '89 ; *Nichols, N. Y.*
" Hommell, Mina L., Southold, N. Y. ; *Southold, N. Y.*
" Stevens, Alice P., Newburyport ; *Mt. Holyoke College, S. Hadley;* home address, 207 *High St., Newburyport;*
" Warner, Mary A., Westminster ; d. Westminster, '95.

NON-GRADUATES.

Ayer, Louise, Saybrook, Ct. ; *Olympia, Wash.*
Baker, Lucretia, W. Chester, Pa. ; *37 S. High St., W. Chester, Pa.*
Bishop, Annette E., Meriden. Ct. ; m. Harvey M. Ives, '92 ; *Meriden, Ct.*
Blasdale, Laura M., Jericho, N. Y. ; m. Rev. Morris W. Morse, '90 ; *Hollister, Cal.*
Chamberlain, Carrie B., Sharon, Vt. ; *care Prof. Randall, San Jose, Cal.*
Chamberlain, Grace M., Sharon, Vt. ; m. Rev. Samuel Rose, '86 ; *Box 223, Provo, Utah.*
Clapp, Emma L., Newton, N. C. ; m. Wm. H. Thompson, '92 ; *Newton, N. C.*
Coleman, Sarah W., Goshen, N. Y. ; *Goshen, N. Y.*
Comey, Annie F., Quincy ; m. Geo. E. Conway ; *20 Mechanic St., Fitchburg.*
Cooley, Nellie D., Sunderland ; *Sunderland;* P. O. address, *N. Amherst.*
Dowd, Ella M., Huron, N, Y. ; *44 Wardell St., Long Island City, N. Y.*
Dupée, June M., Boston ; *44 N. 16th St., Philadelphia, Pa.*
Ely, Kitty M., Chicopee ; m. Thos. E. Coar, '89 ; *46 Carver St, Cambridge.*
Emory, Helen C., Unadilla, N. Y. ; m. Chas. J. Wills ; *1801 9th Ave., S.,Minneapolis, Minn.*
Faddis, Prudence P., Mankato, Minn. ; *716 4th Ave. N., Minneapolis, Minn.*
Farrar, R. Dora, S. Lincoln ; *S. Lincoln.*
Freeman, Annie H., S. Coventry, Ct. ; *181 Lewiston Ave., Willimantic. Ct.*
Ford, Inez H., M.D., Piermont, N. H. ; *Dover, N. H.*
Gallup. Jennie H., D.D. S., Providence, R. I. ; *Lock Box 169, Bristol, R. I.*
Gardiner, Harriet C., Plainfield, N. J. ; *805 Park Ave., Plainfield, N. J.*
Gates, Alice V., Lincoln, Cal. ; m. *David A. Hall, '87 ; *Lincoln, Cal.*
George, Helen, Concord, N. H. ; d. Concord, N. H., '86.
Graham, Anna D., Carleton Place, Ont. ; *680 Wellington St., Ottawa, Can.*
Graves, Mary L., Williamsburg ; m. Edward T. Barrus, '87 ; *Williamsburg.*
Green, Jennie M., Cambridge, N. Y. ; *Cambridge, N. Y.*
Greene, Mary D., Albany, N. Y. ; *2 High St., Albany, N. Y.*
Harwood, Helen L., Brookfield, Mo. ; *San Bernardino, Cal.*
Hooker, Annie J., Carthage, N. Y. ; *Oneida, N. Y.*
Jeudevine, Hatty, Canandaigua, N. Y. ; m. A. J. Nash, '89 ; *Box 60, Minneapolis, Minn.*
Jewett, Annie M., Pelham ; m. Chas. R. Allison '93 ; *73 Beekman St., N. Y. City.*
Kies, Juliette, Danielsonville, Ct.; m. Wm. N. Arnold,'95; *50 Reynolds St.,Danielsonville,Ct.*
Laubach, Jennie, Easton, Pa. ; m. Lieut. Edgar Jadwin, *Willets Point, L. I.*
Leeds, Mary L., Rutherford Park, N. J. ; m. Ralph B. Hooper, '87 ; *315 California St., San Francisco, Cal.*
Little, Alice M., Haverhill ; *Dustin Sq., Haverhill.*
Longfellow, Annie H., Machias, Me. ; *Pasadena, Cal.*
Lyford, Annie M., Foxcroft, Me. ; m. Geo. W. Parker, '89 ; *Foxcroft, Me.*
McLain, Mary B.. N. Y. City ; *N. Y. City.*

1886.

Montague, Jennie A., Granby ; *Granby.*
Morris, Sarah L., Ellington, Ct.; *Ellington, Ct.*
Morse, Annie L., Chester, N. H. ; d. '94.
Palmer, Bertha, Brookline ; 222 *W. 23d St., N. Y. City.*
Partridge, Mary L., N. Bennington, Vt. ; *Taiku, Shansi. China.*
Patterson, Mary S., Oxford, Pa. ; *Oxford, Pa.*
Pease, Katharine F., Oxford; m. Rev. Arthur H. Proffitt, '86 ; *S. Orange, N. J.*
Perry, Esther M., Greenfield Hill, Ct. ; m. Prof. Wm. E. Gardner, '90; *New Canaan, Ct.*
Persons, Mary S., E. Aurora, N. Y. ; m. A. C. Van Deren, '88 ; *Oberlin, O.*
Pilling, Mary E., New Haven. Ct. ; 20 *Maple Ave., Danbury, Ct.*
Pingrey, Mary E., Springville. N. Y. ; m. Fred W. Leland, '90; *Springville, N. Y.*
Rawles, Mary W., Lima, Ind.; m. Frank Robertson, '91 ; *592 2d St., Portland, Or.*
Rogers, May H., Chicago, Ill. ; *2575 Ashland Ave., Ravenswood, Ill.*
Ruggles, Ellen L., Milton; *School St., Milton.*
Severy, Nellie M, Westboro ; m. Rev. Edwin N. Hardy, '90; *Holliston.*
Sherman, Marion L., Camden, N. J. ; *Providence, R. I.*
Smith, K. Maude, Mahanoy City, Pa. ; 21 *E. Mahanoy Ave., Mahanoy City. Pa.*
Soule, Mary C., Hampton. Ct. ; *Naugatuck. Ct.*
Sweet, Clara A., Jewett City, Ct. ; m. John J. Crawford, '91 ; *Jewett City, Ct.*
Talbot, Esther B., E. Machias, Me. ; *E. Machias, Me.*
Tarbet, Emma H., Pisgah, Ill. ; 6122 *Oglesby Ave., Chicago, Ill.*
Tuttle, Ellen J., Manchester, Vt.; *Box 118, Manchester, Vt.*
Voorhees, Mary E., Blawenburg, N. J.; m. Jas. Menzies, '89 ; 404 *W. Beaver St., Jacksonville, Fla.*
Washburn, Elizabeth M., Lowell; m. Chester F. Smith, '89 ; 270 *Gibson St., Lowell.*
West, Kate R., E. Orange, N. J. ; *E. Orange, N. J.*
White, Jessie B., Hannibal, Mo. ; d. Hannibal, Mo., '89.
Wilson, Mary C., Windsor, Ct.; m. Arthur S. Carleton, '93; 117 *Ten Broeck St., Albany, N. Y.*
Wood, Eleanor, Washington, D. C. ; m. Albert Relyea, Esq., '91 ; *Green's Farms, Ct.*
Woods, Helen F., Boalsburgh, Pa. ; *Boalsburgh, Pa.*
Yates, Katharine Y., Plainfield, N. J. ; 128 *E. 7th St., Plainfield, N. J.*
Yeomans, Ellen L., Walworth, N. Y. ; m. Chas. W. Hamilton, '91 ; *Perrysburgh, O.*

1887.

GRADUATES.

Adams, Kate L., Brookline ; *Harvard Ave., Brookline.*
Anderson, Harriet M., Monson; m. Dr. John P. Rand, '89 ; d. Worcester, '92.
Barbour, Catharine H., Canton Center, Ct. ; *Avenida 40, San Sebastian, Spain.*
Brainerd, Helen E., Enfield, Ct. ; *Columbia College Library, N. Y. City.*
Brockway, Alice C., S. Hadley ; *S. Hadley.*
Bruce, Harriet L., Satara, India ; *Satara, Western India.*
Budd, Avarene L., Mt. Holly, N. J.; *Mt. Holly, N. J.*
Butler, Alice, Boston ; m. Herbert H. Cushing, '93 ; 45 *W. Newton St., Boston.*
Carter, Alice, Ph.D., Huntington, N. Y.; m. O. F. Cook, '92; *Huntington, N. Y.*
Church, M. Evelyn, Phillips, Me.; m. Frank H. Wilbur, '87 ; *Phillips, Me.*
Cobb, Helen L., Palmer; m. Luther B. Goldthwaite, '93 ; 867 *Cedar St., Alameda, Cal.*
Coleman, Katharine D., Goshen, N. Y.; m. Harry E. Colwell, '95; 284 *Main St., New Rochelle, N. Y.*

1887.

Crane, Ellen D. M., Dexter, Io.; m. Prof. Homer R. Miller; *Elk Point, S. Dak.*
Crane, Mary P., Dexter, Io.; m. *Rev. J. Ross Lee, '90 ; d. Rockville, Io., '91.
Crowther, Elizabeth, Enfield ; *Smith's.*
De Witt, Katharine, Troy, N. Y.; 6400 *Madison Ave., Chicago, Ill.*
Dutton, Susie A., Tyngsborough ; *Wakefield.*
Eaton, Grace M., Wakefield ; 606 *Main St., Wakefield.*
Edwards, Carrie M., Chesterfield ; *Chesterfield.*
Edwards, Julia M., Westhampton ; *Berea College, Berea, Ky.*
Fowler, Caroline D., Passaic, N. J.; 21 *Bloomfield Ave., Passaic, N. J.*
Goding, Sarah E., Alfred, Me.; 819 *N. 40th St., W. Philadelphia, Pa.*
Griggs, Annie M., Chaplin, Ct.; m. J. V. Reed, '89; 41 *2d Ave., Waterbury, Ct.*
Griswold, Fannie E., Southport, N. Y.; *Kobe, Japan.*
Hommel, Mina L., Southold, N. Y.; *Southold, N. Y.*
Horton, Nettie, Seattle, Wash.; m. Rev. W. G. Jones, '90 ; 16 *Wyman St., Boston.*
Hosack, Isabel, Mercer, Pa.; *Mercer, Pa.*
Hyde, Isabella, Ware ; *Ware.*
King, Anna S., Thompsonville, Ct.; *Thompsonville, Ct.*
Lantz, Augusta W., Newton, N. C.; *Woman's College, Frederick, Md.*
McCalister, Jean P., Shippensburg, Pa.; care *J. R. McCalister, East End, Pittsburgh, Pa.*
McKenzie, Mary E. (name changed from Cumiskey, see '84), S. Dartmouth; *S. Dartmouth.*
Mellish, A. May, Worcester ; d. Brooklyn, N. Y., '94.
Montague, Aurelia L., Westhampton ; m. Henry M. Clapp, '89; *Westhampton.*
Nutting, Mary H., Randolph, Vt.; *Randolph, Vt.*
Parsons, Emma L., Thompsonville, Ct.; 48 *Pearl St., Thompsonville, Ct.*
Phillips, Mary L., Poughkeepsie, N. Y.; 113 *Grove St., E. Orange, N. J.*
Plumer, Catharine M., New Salem; 20 *Tirrell St., Worcester.*
Sanford, May E., Avoca, Io.; *Avoca, Io.*
Schwartz, Jennie E., Bethlehem, Pa.; m. Harry C. Cope, Esq., '94 ; 131 *Broad St., W. Bethlehem, Pa.*
Shepperd, Marion, Fordham, N. Y. City ; m. Rev. John A. Trimmer, '88; *Helmetta, N. J.*
Stevenson, Elizabeth E., Andes, N. Y.; *Andes, N. Y.*
Sykes, E. Louise, Dorset, Vt.; *Dorset, Vt.*
Schrader, Bertha von, Maquoketa, Io.; m. Harry J. Fletcher, Esq., '92 ; 75 *Dell Place, Minneapolis, Minn.*
Walton, Georgiana C., Alexandria Bay, N. Y.; *Waverly, N. Y.*
Wills, Mary E., Pottstown, Pa.; *Pottstown, Pa.*
Wooster, Annie T., Seymour, Ct.; m. Geo. E. Matthies, '00 ; *Box 606, Seymour, Ct.*

NON-GRADUATES.

Baker, Lizzie M., Salem, N. Y. ; *Salem, N. Y.*
Bassett, Grace L., Youngstown, O. ; d. Youngstown, O., '93.
Bassett, Rebecca A., Norfolk, Ct. ; m. Plumb Brown, M.D., '92 ; *S. Manchester, Ct.*
Blair, Grace R., W. Brookfield ; *W. Brookfield.*
Bonar, Mabel S., Marquette, Mich. ; d. Marquette, Mich., '87.
Boice, May, E. Orange, N. J. ; 67 *Grove St., E. Orange, N. J.*
Briscoe, Alice, Thompsonville, Ct. ; m. Rev. John F. George, '90 ; 627 *Holley Ave., Winston, N. C.*
Bronson, Gertrude E., Winchester, Ct. ; m. Frank L. Stephens, '88 ; *Riverton, Ct.*
Buckland, Sarah M., St. Louis, Mo. ; *Marshall, Mo.*
Bushnell, Anna I., Watertown, N.Y.; m. Fred. George, '88 ; 19 *Sterling St., Watertown, N.Y.*
Clark, Alice H., Northampton ; *Univ. Hill, Washington, D. C.*

1887.

Cooke, Althea M., Meriden, Ct. ; m. William M. Quested, '92 ; 629 *Broad St., Meriden, Ct.*
Dunlap, Mary E., Watertown, N. Y. ; 162 *State St., Watertown, N. Y.*
Elmore, Susan M., Arlington, Vt. ; 4 *Porter St., N. Adams.*
Farrar, Anna H., S. Lincoln ; *S. Lincoln.*
Farrar, Grace, S. Lincoln ; *S. Lincoln.*
Fuller, Genie C., Topsfield ; *Topsfield.*
Gardner, Stella M., Laton, Kans. ; *Homewood, Kans.*
Gilbert, Mary A., Warren ; m. Wm. Hallows, '91 ; *Warren.*
Godman, Inez A., Baldwin, La. ; 337 *S. Twelfth St., Philadelphia, Pa.*
Grassie, Annie G., Milwaukee, Wis. ; m. Edward W. Stickney, '87 ; 2818 *Cedar St., Milwaukee, Wis.*
Hawkes, Mary E., S. Hadley Falls ; m. Chas. L. Crockwell, '04 ; 858 *E. 2d S. St., Salt Lake City, Utah.*
Hettinger, Eva F., Freeport, Ill. ; 325 *Stephenson St., Freeport, Ill.*
Hill, Elizabeth C., Auburndale ; *Auburndale.*
Hilton, Louise A., Wells, Me. ; *Colorado Springs, Col.*
Hunt, Gwenllian, Avondale, Pa. ; m. Wm. Vollmer, '91 ; 480 *Trinity Place, W. Philadelphia, Pa.*
Hurlbert, Florence A., Forestville, N. Y. ; *S. Orange, N. J.*
Hurlbert, Sylvia W., Forestville, N. Y. ; m. Geo. J. McAndrew, Ph.D., '88 ; *Bowers Place, S. Orange, N. J.*
Jansen, Katherine E., Quincy, Ill. ; 1662 *Jersey St., Quincy, Ill.*
Jones, Etta E., N. Lebanon, Me. ; d. '02.
Kingsley, Nelly H., Southampton ; m. Edwin B. Clapp ; *Westhampton.*
Kirby, May P., Brooklyn, N. Y. ; m. Chas. S. Sherman, '04 ; 73 *Gates Ave., Brooklyn, N. Y.*
McIntyre, Elsie D., Catasauqua, Pa. ; *Catasauqua, Pa.*
McKean, Eva C., Mercer, Pa. ; m. Rev. G. E. Hawes, '90 ; 386 *Sixth St., Portland, Or.*
Merriam, Lena S., Meriden, Ct. ; m. Lewis A. Miller, '02 ; 68 *Wilcox Ave., Meriden, Ct.*
Milliken, Carrie T., Plainfield, N. J. ; m. Jas. W. DeGraff, '00 ; " *Lone Oak," Central Ave., Plainfield, N. J.*
Mills, Sarah M., Northampton ; m. Willis L. Pond, '02 ; *Torrington, Ct.*
Morgan, Luette J., Cornish, N. H. ; m. Geo. R. Weston, '04 ; *Bellows Falls, Vt.*
Morris, Alice A., Monson ; *Monson.*
Munson, Cora E., Chicago, Ill. ; 1276 *Washington Boul., Chicago, Ill.*
Nye, Helen H., New Bedford ; 45 *Walnut St., Somerville.*
Patrick, Mary L., W. Newton ; *Newtonville.*
Phillips, Elizabeth R., N. Chelmsford ; *Guilford, Ct.*
Phillips, Lenore H., California, Pa. ; m. Rev. John L. McCutcheon, '87 ; *Franklin, Va.*
Reid, Alice B., Greenearth, Pa. ; *Belmont, N. Y.*
Rhody, Margaret A., Freeport, Ill. ; m. Dr. Orville O. Witherbee, '04 ; *Alhambra, Cal.*
Robbins, Elizabeth M., McKeesport, Pa. ; m. James W. Downer, Jr., '02 ; 11 *Clifton Place, Brooklyn, N. Y.*
Rounds, Pauline, Calais, Me. ; *Calais, Me.*
Smythe, Anna M., Freeport, Ill. ; m. Manley H. Crawford, '91 ; d. Freeport, Ill., '94.
Strong, Harriet M., W. Hartford, Ct. ; *W. Hartford, Ct.*
Taintor, Ella E., Lee ; *Box* 317, *Wellesley.*
Wickham, Julia M., Cutchogue, L. I. ; *Cutchogue, N. Y.*
Williams, Jessie M., Jones Mills, Pa. ; m. Rev. Albert Freeman, '03 ; *Iowa Park, Texas.*
Wilson, Anne B., Windsor, Ct. ; *Woodford, Me.*

1888.

GRADUATES.

Allen, Elizabeth S., Belchertown ; m. J. B. Ellis, '95 ; *Crockett, Texas.*
Bailey, Mary F., E. Jaffrey, N. H. ; *E. Jaffrey, N. H.*
Banks, Lizzie C., Greenfield Hill, Ct. ; *Greenfield Hill, Ct.*
Barrett, S. Eliza, Worcester ; *8 Boynton St., Worcester.*
Bassett, Mary, Brooklyn, N. Y. ; m. Chas. M. Harrington,'91 ; *180 Mass. Ave., Buffalo, N. Y.*
Bidwell, Margaret, Freeport, Ill. ; m. Hazen S. Capron, '93 ; *Champaign, Ill.*
Bliss, Clara A., Newburyport ; *10 Allen St., Newburyport.*
Blodgett, Emma M., Warren ; *Warren.*
Boardman, Alice I., Sheffield ; *Sheffield.*
Brown, Nellie E., Enfield ; *Enfield.*
Chandler, Sadie K., Worcester ; m. Rev. Frank L. Garfield, '92 ; *Feeding Hills.*
Chapell, Harriet, Flemington, N. J. ; *118 Pembroke St., Boston.*
Clapp, Lena L., Boston ; *Alpine St., W. Newton.*
Cole, Anna M., Hampton, N. H. ; *Hampton, N. H.*
Fellows, Mary E., Shelburne ; *94 Grove St., Worcester.*
Fiske, Mary P., Greenfield ; *Arlington.*
Hillebrand, Mary E., Honolulu, H. I. ; m. Arthur C. Alexander ; *90 Whalley Ave., New Haven, Ct.*
Hubbard, Nan K., Sunderland ; *N. Amherst.*
Hyde, Susan C.. Norwich, Ct. ; *Adabazar, Turkey, Asia.*
Livingston, Rebecca, Jaffrey, N. H. ; d. Chattanooga, Tenn., '89.
Loomis, Mary S., Albany, N. Y. ; m. Wm. A. Hutchinson, '94 ; *Pennington Sem., Pennington, N. J.*
Mitchell, Anna, E. Orange, N. J. ; *50 Monroe Place, Brooklyn, N. Y.*
Morse, Etta L., Canton ; *Canton.*
Paden, Lulu R., Vanceville, Pa. ; *Vanceville, Pa.*
Paden, M. Frances. Vanceville, Pa. ; *Vanceville. Pa.*
Page, Julia B., Rochester, N. Y. ; *12 Waverly Place, Rochester, N. Y.*
Parker, Orra A., S. Coventry. Ct. ; m. Prof. Chas. S. Phelps, '91 ; *Storrs, Ct.*
Pettee, Emma L., Sharon ; *Sharon.*
Pomeroy, Hattie T., Springfield ; *198 Carew St., Springfield.*
Rhyne, Loula M., Paw Creek, N. C. ; m. Dr. M. R. Adams, '91 ; *Statesville. N. C.*
Rice, Harriet W., Devon, Io. ; *521 Boston Block, Denver, Col.*
Rider, Addie M.. Plainville, Ct. ; *Plainville, Ct.*
Smith, Sarah M., Exeter. N. H. ; *Exeter, N. H.*
Sparks, Alice C., Nashville. Tenn. ; *711 Belmont Ave., Nashville, Tenn.*
Stearns, Lucy A., Saco, Me. ; m. Lory Prentiss, '91 ; *Newark Acad., Newark, N. J.*
Stone, Fairene M., Troy, N. Y. ; m. Howard M. Wilson,'89 ; *204 N. Craig St., Pittsburgh, Pa.*
Swift, Kate B., Springfield ; *177 State St., Springfield.*
Van Wagenen, Loraine M. N., Dedham ; *28 Pearl St., Holyoke.*
Wiswall, Sarah E., Chicago, Ill. ; m. Wm. L. Baker, '90 ; *313 Summit Ave., S. Sioux Falls, S. Dak.*
Wolcott, Emily P., Tallmadge, O. ; *Tallmadge, O.*

NON-GRADUATES.

Atwood, Annie L., Cambridgeport ; m. Chas. W. Henderson, Jr., '92 ; *65 Chestnut St., Cambridgeport.*
Babcock, Cara J., Troy, N. Y. ; d. Troy, N. Y., '89.
Baker, Mabel L., Hyannis ; *Hyannis.*
Bartlett, Annie L., Portland, Ct. ; *Portland, Ct.*

1888.

Blanchard, Ada L., Boston ;
Boyer, Emily M., Catasauqua, Pa. ; *Catasauqua, Pa.*
Buck, Mary H., Foxcroft, Me. ; d. Foxcroft, Me., '89.
Chapman, Harriet C., Saybrook, Ct. ; *Saybrook, Ct.*
Chatterton, Almyra S., Acworth, N. H. ; *Acworth, N. H.*
Church, Isadore L., Chaplin, Ct. ; m. Dr. C. E. Harvey, '91 ; *Chaplin, Ct.*
Clark, Edith, Amherst ; *Newton.*
Clark, Eliza S., Amherst ; m."Wm. B. Greenough,'93 ; 61 *Westminster St., Providence, R.I.*
Clark, Elizabeth C., Samokov, Bulgaria ; *Samokov, Bulgaria.*
Crawford, Clara E., N. Brookfield ; *N. Brookfield.*
Deans, Harriet E., Medway ; m. George C. Conn, '93 ; 9 *Cleveland Ave., Woburn.*
Dutton, Charlotte R., Burlingame, Kan. ; *Meadville, Pa.*
Fiske, Alice B., Shelburne ; *E. Shelburne.*
Fuller, Marian L., Catasauqua, Pa. ; *Catasauqua, Pa.*
Gilbert, Bertha L., N. Brookfield ; m. Herbert W. Bemis, '89 ; *N. Brookfield.*
Graves, Clara L., Hatfield ; m. Wm. C. Dickinson, '91 ; *Hatfield.*
Harmon, Clara, Girard, O. ; m. Wm. A. Smith, '93 ; 33 *Scott St., Youngstown, O.*
Harvey, Nellie, W. Barnet, Vt. ; 50 *Spring St., St. Johnsbury, Vt.*
Hills, Mary J., Buckingham, Ct. ; *Buckingham, Ct.*
Hosmer, Mary R., Freeport, Ill. ; 40 *Grove St., Freeport, Ill.*
Huntoon, Bertha M., Washington, D. C. ; m. Samuel P. Johnson, '94 ; 307 *T St., N. W., Washington, D. C.*
King, Margaret A., Lowell, Vt. ; *Cairo, N. Y.*
Kirby, Mary A., Goldsboro,N C.; m. Rev.Edward Mack,'93; 916 *Garrison Ave., St. Louis,Mo.*
Lambert, A. Louise, Quincy, Ill. ; m. Alton R. Weeks, '89 ; 205 *York St., Quincy, Ill.*
Leonard, Mary A., Reidville, S. C. ; *Reidville, S. C.*
Lippincott, Mary E., Pemberton, N. J. ; *Pemberton, N. J.*
Marcy, Lucretia, Fairfield, Io. ; m. P. S. Junkin, '93 ; *Orange City, Io.*
Montague, Mary N., S. Hadley ; *Barre.*
Newhall, Anna B., Conway ; m. Francis W. Boyden, '94 ; 133 *34th St., Berwyn, Ill.*
Perry, Mary J., Southbury, Ct. ; *Southbury, Ct.*
Pratt, Lizzie J., Princeton ; *Princeton, P. O. address, Brooks Station.*
Pritchett, Sadie B., Glasgow, Mo. ; *Glasgow, Mo.*
Riggs, Cora L., Santee Agency, Neb. ; m. Frank A. Waples, M.D., '92 ; *Kalgan, China.*
Riggs, Grace T., Palmyra, N. Y. ; *Palmyra, N. Y.*
Roberts, Minnie E., Feeding Hills ; m. Reuben J. Rice, '89 ; 95 *Wilcox Ave., Meriden, Ct.*
Robinson, Anna G., Ishpeming, Mich. ; *Ishpeming, Mich.*
Robinson, Rosabel T., Ishpeming, Mich. ; *Ishpeming, Mich.*
Rowley, Clara, N. Brookfield ; *N. Brookfield.*
Sage, L. Belle, Norwich, N. Y. ; *Norwich, N. Y.*
Sanborn, Amy G., Kensington, N. H. ; *Exeter, N. H.*
Sanborn, Frances S., Kensington, N. H. ; *Exeter, N. H.*
Seymour, Charlotte M., Norfolk, Ct. ; *Norfolk, Ct.*
Seymour, May, Meriden, Ct. ; m. Madison B. Huffman, '91 ; *Neligh, Neb.*
Shepard, Ellen F., Mason City, Io. ; *Mason City, Io.*
Shuey, Elizabeth M., Chicago, Ill. ; 321 *Erie St., Oak Park, Ill.*
Simmons, Mary E., Lake Geneva, Wis. ; *Lake Geneva, Wis.*
Smith,Marion S., Brooklyn, N.Y ; m.Henry J., Bristow,'93; 255 *President St.,Brooklyn, N.Y.*
Smock, Carrie M., Hightstown, N. J. ; m. E. E. Wolfe, '90 ; *Ft. Edward, N. Y.*
Stoddard, Alice J., Naples, N. Y. ; *Abilene, Kan.*
Stowell, Ida G., Claremont, N. H. ; m. Wm. H. Ellsworth ; *Redlands, Cal.*
Sturdevant, Bertha L., Norwich, N. Y. ; *Norwich, N. Y.*

Sykes, Anna G., Dorset, Vt. ; m. Edwin B. Child, '94 ; *312 W. 54th St., N. Y. City.*
Tandy, Mabel L., Freeport, Ill. ; m. M. T. Hettinger, '90; *Freeport, Ill.*
Treat, Fanny P., Tallmadge, O.; *Tallmadge, O.*
Walker, Fanny E., Warsaw, N. Y. ; *Warsaw, N. Y.*
Warner, Mary S., Port Henry, N. Y. ; m. Rockwell P. Holden, '94 ; *Port Henry, N. Y.*
Watkins, Grace L., S. Manchester, Ct. ; *S. Manchester, Ct.*
Whitcomb, Jessie, Chicago, Ill. ; *cor. Calumet and 24th Sts., Chicago, Ill.*
Whittlesey, Maude, Erie, Pa. ; *518 Sassafras St., Erie, Pa.*
Wild, Laura H., Charlotte, Vt. ; *Elizabethtown, N. Y.*
Willey, Rose M., Brunswick, Me. ; d. Old Town, Me., '91.
Williams, Lena, Mendon; m. Herbert J. George, '94 ; *522 Lebanon St., Melrose.*
Williamson, Anna A., Mt. Vernon, N. Y. ; *Mt. Vernon, N. Y.*

MOUNT HOLYOKE SEMINARY AND COLLEGE.

1889.

GRADUATES.

Abbott, Alice B., E. Orange, N. J.; 431 *William St.*, *E. Orange, N. J.*
Anderson, Mary, E. Berkshire, Vt.; *E. Berkshire, Vt.*
Brastow, Frances C., Rockport, Me.; m. Capt. Stanley Amesbury, '92; *Rockport, Me.*
Brown, Clara L., B. S., Raymond, N. H.; *Niigata, Japan.*
Cheever, Bertha A., Ware; *Ware.*
Cook, Grace H., Albany, N. Y.; *Loudonville, Albany, N. Y.*
Crowell, Mary W., Amherst; *Amherst.*
Dole, Mary P., M.D., B. S., Ashfield; *Ashfield.*
Dowe, Harriet H., Brooklyn, N. Y.; 334 *Franklin St., Melrose Highlands.*
Eaton, Etta M., Wells, Me.; *Wells, Me.*
Freeman, A. Jean, Scranton, Pa.; m. Frank von Schrader,'94; 413 *N. Market St., Ottumwa, Io.*
Galloway, Ida G., Freeport, Ill.; 198 *Walnut St.. Freeport, Ill.*
Gallup, Annie C., Bristol, R. I.; *Bristol, R. I.*
Grant. Eva A., Westville, N. Y.; *Westville, N. Y.*
Greathead, Frances S., McGregor, Io.; *McGregor, Io.*
Greeley, Estelle E., Foxcroft, Me.; m. J. Walter Jones, '94 ; *N. Lebanon, Me.*
Greene, Annie L., Sterling, Kan.; m. Rev. Clarence W. Rouse, '91; *S. Sudbury.*
Greene, Caroline B., S. Hadley ; *Mt. Holyoke College, S. Hadley.*
Griggs, Hattie A., Chaplin, Ct.; *Chaplin, Ct.*
Griggs, Jennie E., Chaplin, Ct.; *Chaplin, Ct.*
Grout, Edith L. F., E. Dorset, Vt.; *E. Dorset, Vt.*
Hollands, Edith, W. Troy, N. Y.; 18 *14th St.. W. Troy, N. Y.*
Houston, Martha A., Thompsonville, Ct.; m. Walter R. Dyer, '89; 40 *Hancock St., Dorchester Dist., Boston.*
Hubbard, Marion E., B. S., McGregor, Io.; 6128 *Lexington Ave.. Chicago. Ill*
Hubbard, Mary L., McGregor, Io.; 6128 *Lexington Ave., Chicago, Ill.*
Hulsizer, Rachel W.. Sidney, N. J.; *Sidney, N. J.*
Hurlbut, Marion E., Springfield ; 233 *Carew St., Springfield.*
Hussey, Clara A., Brooklyn, N. Y.; m. Stanton K. Davis, '94; *care J. W. Hussey,* 38 *Park Row, N. Y. City.*
Kolb, Theodora M., Easton, Pa; m. Alfred W. Wilmarth, M.D.; *Norristown, Pa.*
Lake, Sadie M., Rockville, Ct.; *Rockville, Ct.*
Landfear, Elizabeth M., New Haven, Ct.; 125 *St. John St.. New Haven, Ct.*
Marchant, Agnes, W. Yarmouth; *W. Yarmouth.*
Miller, Marian R., Mercer, Pa.; m. Lyle W. Orr, '93; *Mercer, Pa.*
Pattangall, Kate H., Pembroke, Me.; *Pembroke, Me.*
Pettengill, Grace F., Brooklyn, N. Y.; m. James M. Wilson, '89; 417 *Hancock St., Brooklyn, N. Y.*
Pitkin, Grace C., Schenectady, N. Y.; m. Rev. Edwin Tasker, '95 ;

1889.

Pyle, Belle H., Youngstown, O.; *Youngstown, O.*
Rogers, Mary A., Marysville, Cal.; *Bennington, N. H.*
Ross, Mary E., Springfield; 72 *Carew St., Springfield.*
Silkman, Emilie C., Yonkers, N. Y.; *Yonkers, N. Y.*
Stokes, Jeanie W., East Hampton, L. I.; *East Hampton, L. I.*
Stokes, Mayne A., East Hampton, L. I.; *East Hampton, L. I.*
Stone, Cora A., Palmyra, N. Y.; *Newark, N. Y.*
Stone, Ida, Windsor, Vt.; m. F. B. Tracy, '92; *Bellows Falls, Vt.*
Tenney, Annie M., Worcester; 111 *York St., New Haven, Ct.*
Warner, Mary W., Evanston, Ill.; care *W. C. Warner, 34 and 36 Canal St., Chicago, Ill.*
Westcott, Maria P., Hopedale; *Hopedale.*
Williams, Grace, Catasauqua, Pa.; *Catasauqua, Pa.*
Williamson, T. Gertrude, Mt. Vernon, N. Y.; 44 *Jackson St., Mt. Vernon, N. Y.*
Wilson, Elizabeth Van Valzah, N. Y. City; 348 *W. 57th St., N. Y. City.*

SPECIAL COURSE GRADUATE.

GREEK.—Love, Harriette N., S. Hadley; m. Rev. Geo. B. Penny, '92; 232 *Third St., Marietta, O.*

NON-GRADUATES.

Ames, Alice W., S. Lincoln; m. Harlan F. Eveleth, '94; *S. Lincoln.*
Barnum, Grace E., Bethel, Ct.; *Barre.*
Boughton, Ellsworth A., Schenectady, N. Y.; m. Albert F. Demers, '93; 16 *Seventh St., Troy, N. Y.*
Burroughs, Alice, Coxsackie, N. Y.; *Coxsackie, N. Y.*
Cook, Harriet S., Kansas City, Mo.; *Kansas City, Mo.*
Davis, Ella M., Watertown, Ct.; *Watertown, Ct.*
Dayton, Clara E., Watertown, Ct.; m. Lucien R. Hitchcock, '92; *Watertown, Ct.*
Dayton, H. Gertrude, Watertown, Ct.; m. James B. Woolson, '90; *Watertown, Ct.*
Dickerson, Frances M., Atlantic, Io.; *Atlantic, Io.*
Dodge, Addie L., Buckland; m. F. Edgar Brown, '93; *Brimfield.*
Fairley, Annie L., Amherst; *Roseland, N. J.*
Francis, Jennie R., New Haven, Ct.; m. Burton R. Dudley, 95; 148 *Whalley Ave., New Haven, Ct.*
Green, Mary E., Shrewsbury; *Shrewsbury.*
Gregg, Marietta, Athens, Pa.; *Athens, Pa.*
Gregory, Mary L., Fredericton, N. B.; *Rothesay Church School for Girls, Rothesay, N. B.*
Hall, Alice K., Cambridge; m. Fred A. Crossman, '93; 20 *Forest St., Cambridge.*
Hall, Mary E., Norwich, N. Y.; *Norwich, N. Y.*
Hamman, Anna B., Little Falls, N. Y.; 10 *Arnold Park, Rochester, N. Y.*
Hayes, Helen A., Malone, N. Y.; *Malone, N. Y.*
Herring, Ida P., Bloomsburg, Pa.; *Bloomsburg, Pa.*
Hobbs, Emily A., W. Medford; m. J. Willis Conant, '94; 331 *Quincy Ave., Scranton, Pa.*
Horton, Luella, Boston; 207 *Savin Hill Ave., Boston.*
Jewett, Jessie E., N. Yarmouth, Me.; m. Wm. H. Huse, '91; *Manchester, N. H.*
Judd, Annie B., S. Hadley; *S. Hadley.*
Love, Harriette N., S. Hadley; m. Rev. Geo. B. Penny, '92; 232 *Third St., Marietta O.*
Lyman, Emma M., S. Hadley; 352 *W. Grove St., Waterbury, Ct.*
Maltby, Mary J., Northford, Ct.; *Northford, Ct.*
Marsh, Grace L., Springfield; 108 *Marion St., Springfield.*
May, Eva L., Higganum, Ct.; m. Earle M. Pease, '92; *Richland Center, Wis.*

1889.

Mayher, Mary S., Easthampton; m. Walter L. Boyden, '89; 66 *Allerton St., Plymouth.*
Mays, Edith R., Allentown, Pa.; 1345 *Hamilton St., Allentown, Pa.*
McElwain, Caroline M., Chicopee; *Chicopee.*
Mead, Mary A., Bridgton, Me.; *Bridgton, Me.*
Millard, Edith H., Milwaukee, Wis.; m. Rev. Frank F. Barrett, '89; d. Prairie Du Sac, Wis. '95.
Montague, Mary L., S. Hadley; m. Frank Church, '93; 2232 *Ogden St., Denver, Col.*
Ottman, Grace M., Carbondale, Pa.; m. Archibald W. Burdick; 1313 *Green St., Philadelphia, Pa.*
Roscoe, Kate M., New Haven, Vt.; m. Weston O. Smith, M.D.,'91; 743 *Santa Clara Ave., Alameda, Cal.*
Russell, Martha M., Amherst; *Amherst.*
Shedd, Jessie, Windsor, Vt.; m. Frederick W. Cady,'91; 11 *Woodruff Place, Indianapolis, Ind.*
Sheldon, Nellie D., Willsboro, N. Y.; *Thomasville, Ga.*
Sherman, Sara L., San Francisco, Cal.; care Sherman, Clay & Co., cor. Sutter and Kearny Sts., *San Francisco, Cal.*
Skavlem, Caroline, Beloit, Wis.; m. E. A. Thompson, '90; 903 *Park Ave., Beloit, Wis.*
Smith, Helena A., Chateaugay, N. Y.; *Chateaugay, N. Y.*
Somes, E. Gertrude, Danielsonville, Ct.; *Danielsonville, Ct.*
Stockwell, Julia S., Aurora, Ill.; *Downer Place, Aurora, Ill.*
Strong, Mary R., Durham, Ct.; *Durham, Ct.*
Swezey, May G., Batavia, N. Y.; *Batavia, N. Y.*
Taylor, Jennie M., Granby; *Granby.*
Taylor, Mary I., Granby; *Granby.*
Telford, Caroline M., Port Byron, N. Y.; *Port Byron, N. Y.*
Voorhes, Helen G., Blawenburgh, N. J.; 140 *Hamilton St., New Brunswick, N. J.*
Walker, Lucretia H., Monson; *Monson.*
West, Thera F., Hadley; *L. Box 104, Northampton.*
Wheeler, Lucy S., York, Neb.; m. Wm. S. Wright, '91; *Box 781, San Diego, Cal.*
Whiting, Ellen L., Norfolk, Ct.; *Norfolk, Ct.*
Williams, Jessica, Catasauqua, Pa.; m. Geo. E. Holton, '94; *Catasauqua, Pa.*
Wood, Fannie, Woodville, N. Y.; *Woodville, N. Y.*

1890.

GRADUATES.

Alger, Florence H., Becket; *Readsboro, Vt.*
Allen, Annie T., Harpoot, Turkey; *Harpoot, Turkey, Asia.*
Allen, Mary L., Hannibal, Mo.; 109 *S. 5th St., Hannibal, Mo.*
Anderson, Mary E., B. S., E. Berkshire, Vt.; *E. Berkshire, Vt.*
Andrews, Katherine, Massena, N. Y.; *Massena, N. Y.*
Baker, Grace B., Worcester; *Salisbury St. and Park Ave., Worcester.*
Barstow, Mabel, Camden, Me.; *Camden, Me.*
Barton, Charlotte, Mercer, Pa.; *Mercer, Pa.*
Benedict, Anna M., Billings, N. Y.; m. Rev. Geo. B. Mead, '93; *La Grangeville, N. Y.*
Boutwell, Sarah K., Medford; *Payson.*
Burgess, C. Idella, Rockport, Me.; m. Lester C. Miller, M.D., '95; 34 *Irving St., Worcester.*
Carter, Emily A., Warren, Ct.; *Warren, Ct.*
Childs, Frances M., Worcester; 64 *Cedar St., Worcester.*

Clapp, Carrie T., Easthampton; *Easthampton.*
Clark, Marion W., Saybrook, Ct.; *Saybrook, Ct.*
Edwards, Emily A., Westhampton; *Westhampton.*
Fenn, Isabelle H., W. Pittston, Pa.; 132 *Susquehanna Ave., Pittston, Pa.*
Gile, Lydia A., N. Andover; m. Prof. Stephen Panaretoff, '92; *Robert College, Constantinople, Turkey.*
Gordon, Margaret, Portland, Ct.; *Portland, Ct.*
Green, Rachel, Sayville, L. I.; m. Prof. Francis E. Lloyd, '93; *Forest Grove, Or.*
Humphrey, Mary H., Simsbury, Ct.; *Simsbury, Ct.*
Ives, Bertha J., New Haven, Ct.; 147 *Quinnipiac St., New Haven, Ct.*
Jewett, Julia L., Westhampton; *Westhampton.*
Kimball, Mary W., Newburyport; m. Nathan W. Goldsmith, '93; *Box 105, Chester, N. H.*
Lindsey, Amy B., Marblehead; *Marblehead.*
Lord, Nettie L., Thompsonville, Ct.; m. John K. Bissland, '94; *Thompsonville, Ct.*
Mayher, Carrie B., Greeley, Col.; *Greeley, Col.*
McDanolds, Charlotte, Passaic, N. J.; *Van Houten Ave., Passaic, N. J.*
Miller, Edith R., N. Brookfield; m. Rev. Wm. Clark Gordon, '94; 215 *W. Sixth St., Michigan City, Ind.*
Noyes, Cora J., Mendon, Ill.; m. Dudley H. Myers, '94; *Mendon, Ill.*
Pierson, Eliza D., Florida, N. Y.; *Florida, N. Y.*
Reynolds, Edith M., Maquoketa, Io.; *Maquoketa, Io.*
Rogers, Ella A., Quincy, Ill.; 2203 *Spring St., Quincy, Ill.*
Sampson, Bessie S., Bedford; *Box 456. W. Newton.*
Schrader, Laura von, Ottumwa, Io.; 413 *N. Market St., Ottumwa, Io.*
Seely, Caroline M., Spencer, N. Y.; *Spencer, N. Y.*
Smith, Arma A., W. Camden, N. Y.; *W. Camden, N. Y.*
Stone, Florence G., Kennebunkport, Me.; m. Rev. Stephen G. Emerson, '90; *Moreno, Cal.*
Taylor, Caroline P., Sharon, Ct.; *Sharon, Ct.*
Van Deusen, Mary E., Ashley Falls; *City Point, Va.*
Waddingham, Nellie A., Watertown, N. Y.; 10 *Paddock St., Watertown, N. Y.*
White, Mabel A., Portland, Ct.; 726 *Warren Ave., Chicago, Ill.*
Wilkinson, Elizabeth, Lawrence; m. Chas. H. Kitchin, '95; 70 *Saunders St., Lawrence.*
Wright, Bessie F., Freeport, Ill.; m. John Burrell, '91; d. *Freeport, Ill., '93.*

SPECIAL COURSE GRADUATES.

GERMAN.—Moore, Susan M., Morgantown, W. Va.; *Granville, O.*
" Rogers, Mary. Peoria, Ill.; 930 *Moss Ave., Peoria, Ill.*
FRENCH.—Bragaw, Annie, New London, Ct.; 11 *N. Main St., New London, Ct.*
" Carter, Julia, Huntington, L. I.; *Huntington, L. I.*
" Grant, Jean, Waterbury, Ct.; 2036 *Wells St., Milwaukee, Wis.*
" Griffin, M. Louise, Danielsonville, Ct.; 9 *Rue le Verrier, Paris, France.*

NON-GRADUATES.

[C] indicates Classical Course; [S] Scientific; [L.] Literary.

Armington, Alice H., Worcester; 140 *Beacon St., Worcester.*
Atkins, Mabel M., S. Amherst; d. *Saluda, N. C., '92.*
Barnard, Rhoda F, Hopkinton, N. H.; *Hopkinton, N. H.*
Barney, Harriet E. [C.], S. Hadley Falls; *S. Hadley Falls.*
Bearse, Lucy J., Hyannis; m. Lopez L. Johnson, '93; *Easton, Ga.*
Bradford, Elfleda J., Hyannis; *Box 416, Hyannis.*
Bragaw, Annie, New London, Ct.; 11 *N. Main St., New London, Ct.*

1890.

Burnham, Emma J., Hillsboro Bridge, N. H.; *Hillsboro Bridge, N. H.*
Butler, Annie, W. Point, N. Y.; *Highland Falls, N. Y.*
Campbell, Emily B., Waverly; *Waverly.*
Carter, Annie, Boonton, N. J.; *Boonton, N. J.*
Carter, Julia, Huntington, L. I.; *Huntington, L. I.*
Chamberlain, E. Louise, Westboro; m. Frederick C. Taylor, '92; *Hyde Park, Vt.*
Chatterton, Minnie, Acworth, N. H.; *Acworth, N. H.*
Chollar, Marion D., Danielsonville, Ct.; *Danielsonville, Ct.*
Clark, Jennie G., Boonton, N. J.; *Boonton, N. J.*
Coe, Virginia M., Middlefield, Ct.; m. Frank A. Coe, '91; *Middlefield, Ct.*
Davis, Elizabeth W., S. Dartmouth; d. S. Dartmouth, '94.
Doty, Agnes J., Stonington, Ct.; m. Harmon J. Kelsey, '91; 237 *Westminster St., Providence, R. I.*
Dudley, Gertrude G., New Haven, Ct.; 505 *Chapel St., New Haven, Ct.*
Estabrook, Susan I. [C.], Olivet, Mich.; *Olivet, Mich.*
Finch, Carolyn L. [S.], Anna, Ill.; *Anna, Ill.*
Fiske, Mary P. [C.], Greenfield; *Arlington.*
Gage, Alice M., Boxford; *Boxford.*
Gage, Bessie M., Concord, N. H.; 1618 *Thomas Place, Minneapolis, Minn.*
Grant, Jean, Waterbury, Ct.; 2636 *Wells St., Milwaukee, Wis.*
Griffin, M. Louise, Danielsonville, Ct.; 9 *Rue le Verrier, Paris, France.*
Harlowe, Abbie F., Shrewsbury; m. H. S. Shepard, '94; *W. Boylston.*
Hill, Sarah E., Worcester; m. Chas. E. Hildreth, '94; 856 *Main St., Worcester.*
Howard, Marion M., Beloit, Wis.; 631 *Church St., Beloit, Wis.*
Humphrey, Mary H. [S.], Simsbury, Ct.; *Simsbury, Ct.*
Hutchinson, Annie P., Danvers Centre; m. James P. Carleton, '94; *Reading.*
Jansen, Amelia P., Quincy, Ill.; 1002 *Jersey St., Quincy, Ill.*
Johnson, Adeline S., New Haven, Ct.; 516 *Howard Ave., New Haven, Ct.*
Leonard, Bessie N., Jewett City, Ct.; *Jewett City, Ct.*
Mackie, Ellen B., Boston; 675 *Tremont St., Boston.*
Marsh, Lucy T., Springfield; 168 *Marion St., Springfield.*
McWilliams, Rose, New Lebanon, N. Y.; *New Lebanon, N. Y.*
Merritt, Lucy S., Andover, Ct.; *Salem, Ct.*
Miller, Belle P., Lowell; 42 *Seventh St., Lowell.*
Perkins, Izzetta B. [S.], N. Brooksville, Me.; d. N. Brooksville, Me., '92.
Roberts, Ethel A., N. Y. City; 61 *E. 73d St., N. Y. City.*
Rogers, Mary, Peoria, Ill.; 930 *Moss Ave., Peoria, Ill.*
Sears, Eugenia C., Plymouth; 221 *Sandwich St., Plymouth.*
Stearns, Ida A. [S.], Danielsonville, Ct.; m. E. Herbert Corttis, '94; *N. Grosvenor Dale, Ct.*
Stockbridge, Mina K., Baltimore, Md.; m. Edward H. Waldo, '93; 4018 *Baring St., Philadelphia, Pa.*
Storrs, Mabel O., Ware; m. George W. Dunham, '92; 11 *High St., Ware.*
Stuart, Mary O. [S.], Independence, Io.; *Cedar Falls, Io.*
Terry, Elvira N., Norwich, N. Y.; *Norwich, N. Y.*
Thayer, Caroline V., Enfield; m. Rev. Charles S. Nightingale, '95; *S. Yarmouth.*
Topping, Leila L., Chester, N. J.; *Chester, N. J.*
Towne, Harriet B. [C.], Williamstown; m. John C. Weeter, '92; *Park City, Utah.*
Waite, Mabel, Chicago, Ill.; m. Edward T. Merrell, '93; *Box 12, La Grange, Ill.*
Watkins, Lucy B., New Brighton, Pa.; *Beaver, Pa.*
White, Maud E., Portland, Ct.; *Portland, Ct.*
Woodmansee, Edith L. [C.], Salt Lake City, Utah; 839 *Lincoln Ave., Salt Lake City, Utah.*
Wright, Isabel [S.], Freeport, Ill.; *Freeport, Ill.*

1891.

GRADUATES.

Ames, Josephine S., Holden; d. Holden, '91.
Banks, Annie C., Guilford, Ct.; *Guilford, Ct.*
Barton, Mellie W., Granby; m. E. D. Burnham, '94; 196 *Sargeant St., Holyoke.*
Beare, Julia T., N. Y. City; 330 *W. 51st St., N. Y. City.*
Bigelow, Fannie L., Framingham; *Framingham.*
Bliss, Lulu F., N. Y. City; *Wellington, Cape Colony, S. Africa.*
Bragg, Louise H., Canaan, Ct.; *Canaan, Ct.*
Bushée, Alice H., Newbury, Vt.; *Avenida 40, San Sebastian, Spain.*
Candler, Eleanor S., Detroit, Mich.; 636 *Woodward Ave., Detroit, Mich.*
Coe, Gertrude W., Middlefield, Ct.; *Middlefield, Ct.*
Crookham, Sara, Oskaloosa, Io.; *Oskaloosa, Io.*
Dillenbeck, Eva, Lyons, N. Y.; *Lyons, N. Y.*
Dustan, Gertrude L., Hartford, Ct.; 87 *Russ St., Hartford. Ct.*
Dutton, Emily H., B. A., S. Framingham; *S. Framingham.*
Dyer, Alice G., Cape Elizabeth, Me.; *Cape Elizabeth, Me.*
Fanning, Helen J., Worcester; 92 *Woodland St., Worcester.*
Feustel, Sarah E., S. Hadley Falls; *S. Hadley Falls.*
Flint, Helen C., B. A., Concord, N. H.; *Concord, N. H.*
Forehand, Annie J., Worcester; 12 *Valley St., Worcester.*
Freeman, Catharine M., Lima, O.; 528 *W. High St., Lima. O.*
Goodenough, Helen E., Winchester, Ct.; *Winchester, Ct.*
Griffith, Lucy F., Buffalo, N. Y.; m. Chas. J. Clark, '92; 504 *W. Fourth St., Marion, Ind.*
Griswold, Florence E., Guilford, Ct.; *Broasa, Turkey, Asia.*
Hadsell, Mary C., Plainville, Ct.; m. Harry A. Castle, '95; *Plainville, Ct.*
Hill, Grace L., Worcester; 32 *May St., Worcester.*
Hodgkins, I. Marion, E. Brookfield; *E. Brookfield.*
Hutchinson, Harriet M., B. S., Norwich, Vt.; *Norwich, Vt.*
Hyde, Mary E., Andover, Ct.; *Andover, Ct.*
Kellogg, Mary' E., Granby; *Granby.*
Kellogg, Laura M., S. Hadley; *S. Hadley.*
Kingsbury, Lucie E., Glastonbury, Ct.; *Glastonbury, Ct.*
Lamprey, Lunette, B. L., Concord, N. H.; 920 *French St., N. W., Washington, D. C.*
Le Maistre, Lida R., Wilmington, Del.; 1410 *Delaware Ave., Wilmington, Del.*
McCampbell, Jennie, Marysville, O.; *Marysville, O.*
McConnel, Lillian A., Beaver, Pa.; *Beaver, Pa.*
Merrick, Mabel E., Springfield; *Park Ave., Springfield.*
Miner, Fannie M., Noank, Ct.; *Noank, Ct.*
Park, Mary I., Huntington, Ct., *Huntington, Ct.*
Parsons, Lillian G., Westhampton; *Westhampton.*
Patten, Lillian W., N. Haven, Ct.; *N. Haven, Ct.*
Patten, Marion T., N. Haven, Ct.; *N. Haven, Ct.*
Pierce, Bertha A., Claremont, N. H.; *Amherst.*
Quick, Leila C., S. Coventry, Ct.; *Ludlow.*
Randolph, Helen C. F., Fredericton, N. B.; *Frogmore, Fredericton, N. B.*
Rice, Corinne L., Sullivan, O.; *Sullivan, O.*
Robinson, Mary D., Goldsboro, N. C.; *Goldsboro, N. C.*
Rogers, Mary I., Albion, N. Y.; *Albion, N. Y.*
Sedgwick, Mabel J., Palmer; *Palmer.*
Smith, Arma A., B. A., W. Camden, N. Y.; *W. Camden, N. Y.*
Smith, Jennie W., S. Hadley; *S. Hadley.*

1891.

Tremper, Edith, Clyde, N. Y.; m. Rev. Jacob Dyk,'92; 18 Church St., Newark, N. Y.
Thompson, E. May, Marysville, O.; Marysville, O.
Walker, Isabel F., Groton, Ct.; 138 Fourth St., New Bedford.
Watrous, Harriet, Berkshire, N. Y.; Berkshire, N. Y.

SPECIAL COURSE GRADUATES.

GERMAN.—Bushée, Alice H., Newbury, Vt.; Arenida 40, San Sebastian, Spain.
" Lee, Charlotte E., Huntington, N. Y.; Huntington, N. Y.
" Le Maistre, Lida R., Wilmington, Del.; 1410 Delaware Ave., Wilmington,Del.
" Stair, Lilian E., Fort Atkinson, Wis.; m. Joseph F. Schreiner, '93; Fort Atkinson, Wis.
FRENCH.—Morrill, Thena, St. Johnsbury, Vt.; d. St. Johnsbury, Vt., '92.
" Stair, Lilian E., Fort Atkinson, Wis.; m. Joseph F. Schreiner, '93; Fort Atkinson, Wis.
" Turner, Lilian M., Great Barrington; Great Barrington.

NON-GRADUATES.

Albee, Ellen L. [S.], Winchester, N. H.; Winchester, N. H.
Benedict, Susan, Billings, N. Y.; 3 Elmcrest Terrace, Norwalk, Ct.
Best, Nellie D., Freeport, Ill.; 383 Stephenson St., Freeport, Ill.
Coleman, Clatina [S.], King's Ferry, N. Y.; Troy Fem. Sem., Troy, N. Y.
Coney, Harriette M. [L.], Ware; Ware.
Cook, Mary A., Chicago, Ill.; 316 Washington Boul., Chicago, Ill.
Crowell, Annie L., Amherst; Amherst.
Danielson, Caroline F. [S.], Danielsonville, Ct.; Danielsonville, Ct.
Emerson, Adaline, Beloit, Wis.; 754 Tuttle Ave., Chicago, Ill.
Evans, Mary, Circleville, O.; Circleville, O.
Grant, Mabel E., Goldsboro, N. C.; Goldsboro, N. C.
Grosvenor, Mary M., Pomfret, Ct.; Pomfret, Ct.
Hall, Julia E., Westford; 82 Morton St., Dorchester.
Hanson, Myra H. [S.], Perrysburg, O.; Wellman and East Sts., Massillon, O.
Harding, Mary B., Sholapur, India; 151 N. Professor St., Oberlin, O.
Lougee, Maud A., Somerville; 9 Lexington St., Everett.
Lyle, Hattie B. [C.], Gloucester; 281 E. Main St., Gloucester.
Lyman, Alice S., Cincinnati, O.; cor. Franklin and 4th Aves., Des Moines, Io.
Meredith, Charlotte R. [S.], Austin, Ill.; 311 S. Pine Ave., Austin, Ill.
Miller, Mae, Lowell; d. Lowell, '95.
Morrill, Thena, St. Johnsbury, Vt.; d. St. Johnsbury, Vt., '92.
Nichols, Etta S., Natick; 40 Summer St., Natick.
Norton, Effie J., Thomaston, Ct.; m. Stanley A. Mallette, '92; 120 Clerk St., Jersey City, N. J.
Orr, Matilda K., Amherst; Amherst.
Osborn, Mary E., Lisle, N. Y.; 59 S. Aurora St., Ithaca, N. Y.
Partrie, Mary F., Norwalk, Ct.; Norwalk, Ct.
Platt, Jeannette E. [L.], Rockdale Mills; Gt. Barrington.
Scott, Rachel T., Oak Hill, Pa.; Lansdowne, Pa.
Smith, May A. [C.], Albion, N. Y.; Albion, N. Y.
Smith, Winnifred B., Cambridge; 41 Dana St., Cambridge.
Stair, Lillian E. [S.], Fort Atkinson, Wis.; m. Joseph F. Schreiner,'93; Fort Atkinson, Wis.
Sterrett, S. Lulu, New Concord, O.; m. W. J. Machwart, '90; Fredericksburgh, O.

1891.

Thayer, Elsie P., Enfield ; *Enfield.*
Wetzell, Annie A., Knoxville, Tenn.; m. Leonard T. Waldron, Esq., '92; 306 *Highland Ave., W. Knoxville, Tenn.*
Whitcomb, Gertrude F. [C.], Yarmouth, Me.; *Yarmouth, Me.*
White, Annie E., Warwick, N. Y.; *Warwick, N. Y.*
Whiting, Sara, Norfolk, Ct.; m. Irving F. Barnes, M.D., '91 ; *Oyster Bay, N. Y.*
Whitmore, Amy G., New Haven, Ct.; m. James L. Stevens, '93; *Box 124, Exeter, N. H.*

SPECIAL STUDENTS.

Capron, Jessie C., Lansingburgh, N. Y.; 518 *Second Ave., Lansingburgh, N. Y.*
Gilt, Anna C., Lysander, N. Y.; m. Rev. J. A. Curtis, '91 ;
Simpson, Margaret F., Christiansburg, Va.; *Christiansburg, Va.*
Smith, Abbie M., Lawrence ; 9 *Cherry St., St. Johnsbury, Vt.*
Smith, Josephine A., Lawrence ; 54 *Butler St., Lawrence.*
Tilton, Mary B., Andover ; *Andover.*
Wilson, Minnie, Brooklyn, N. Y.; 348 *W. 57th St., N. Y. City.*

1892.

GRADUATES.

Allen, Carrie M., Spencer ; *Spencer.*
Berry, Grace E., W. Boylston ; *W. Boylston.*
Bidwell, Clara L., Monterey ; *Monterey.*
Bliss, Maria W., Newburyport ; 10 *Allen St., Newburyport.*
Bloomfield, E. Evangeline, Meriden, Ct. ; 18 *Chestnut St., Meriden, Ct.*
Bockée, Anna B., B. S., Orange City, Fla. ; *Orange City, Fla.*
Brown, Annie L., Middleboro ; 33 *Pearl St., Middleboro.*
Burt, Grace M., Springfield ; 134 *Princeton St., Springfield.*
Bushnell, Lottie, B. S., Watertown, N. Y. ; 20 *Sterling St., Watertown, N. Y.*
Carrier, Florence L., Beloit, Wis. ; m. Rev. James A. Blaisdell, '92 ; *Waukesha, Wis.*
Cobleigh, Katrina A., B. L., S. Gardner ; *S. Gardner.*
Davis, Mary B., Nashua, N. H. ; 8 *Locust St., Nashua, N. H.*
Fletcher, Martha L., Lowell ; 1808 *Spruce St., Philadelphia, Pa.*
Gray, Miriam. B. L., Worcester; m. Edward S. Eichelberger, '94 ; *Frederick, Md.*
Gould, Annie A., B. S., Portland,Me ; *Pao-ting-fu, China, Port of Entry, Tientsin.*
Grassie, Mary K., Milwaukee, Wis. ; *Ashland, Wis.*
Hall, Mabel B., B. A., Mexico, N. Y.; *Mexico, N. Y.*
Hicks, Clara K., B. S., Wyoming, Pa. ; 620 *E. Market St., Scranton, Pa.*
Holmes, Elizabeth W., Ayer; *care Daniel Davis, Phillipsburg, N. J.*
Hyde, Sara G., Ware ; *Ware.*
Keith, Lucy E., Braintree ; *The Western, Oxford, O.*
Keith, Mary H., Braintree ; *Mt. Holyoke College, S. Hadley* ; home address. *Braintree.*
Lake, Sadie M., B. S., Rockville, Ct. ; *Rockville, Ct.*
Locke, Addie L., B. A., Philippopolis, Bulgaria; *Westmoreland, N. H.*
Lufkin, Virginia, Anna, Ill. ; *Anna, Ill.*
Olin, Jenny, Höganäs, Sweden ; *Thomaston, Ct.*
Patrick, Augusta L., W. Newton ; *Newtonville.*
Quick, Marian J., Ludlow ; 500 *Mauch Chunk St., Pottsville, Pa.*

Richards, Mary A., Newark, N. Y.; *Newark, N. Y.*
Sanford, Emma D., Geneva, N. Y.; *469 Main St., Geneva, N. Y.*
Schrader, Rosamund S. von, Ottumwa, Io.; *Ottumwa, Io.*
Smith, Annis A., B. L., W. Camden, N. Y.; *W. Camden, N. Y.*
Snell, Ada L., Geneva, N. Y.; *Geneva, N. Y.*
Stanley, Eva M., Goldsboro, N. C.; *Goldsboro, N. C.*
Stratton, Anna R., Milford, N. H.; *Commercial Gazette, Fifth Ave., Pittsburgh, Pa.*
Turner, Bessie M., Northfield, Ct.; *Northfield, Ct.*
Turner, Lillian M., Great Barrington; *Great Barrington.*
Wenner, Bertha E., Allentown, Pa.; *411 Walnut St., Allentown, Pa.*
Wiggin, Annie P., Stratham, N. H.; *Box 85, Stratham, N. H.*
Woods, Edith B., Barre; *Barre.*

NON-GRADUATES.

Archbald, Jessie, Hopkinton; *Hopkinton.*
Bassett, Emily M. [S.], Bristol, Ct.; *Bristol, Ct.*
Beach, Dorothy B., Columbus, O.; m. Edward Grafstrom, '94; *892 Dennison Ave., Columbus, O.*
Budd, Bernice M. [C.], Geneva, N. Y.; m. Frank E. Rupert, '93; *Seneca, N. Y.*
Caskey, Mary A. [S.], Morristown, N. J.; m. Edward Fairbank, '93; *Ahmednagar, India.*
Clapsadel, Katherine E., Jamestown, N. Y.; *128 Forest Ave., Jamestown, N. Y.*
Collings, Laura W., Albuquerque, N. M.; *500 S. Walter St., Albuquerque, N. M.*
Cook, Julia E., Chicago, Ill.; *316 Washington Boul., Chicago, Ill.*
Cook, Margaret H., Bellefonte, Pa.; *Bellefonte, Pa.*
Daniels, Caroline E., Blackstone; *Box 90, Blackstone.*
Davis, Neva O. [L.], Troy, O.; *133 S. Oxford St., Troy, O.*
Dean, Elizabeth [C.], Wichita, Kan.; m. Edward Maynard, '92; *Wichita, Kan.*
Dean, Margaret W., Wichita, Kan.; *Fletcher Block, Wichita, Kan.*
Dill, Lenora A., Conway; *Conway.*
Durgin, Martha L. [L.], Portland, Me.; m. Rev. Andrew L. Chase, '93; *Foxcroft, Me.*
Ellsworth, Julia, Braintree; *Braintree.*
Ferrin, Bertha L., Essex Junction, Vt.; *Essex Junction, Vt.*
French, Sarah A. [C.], Foxcroft, Me.; *Foxcroft, Me.*
Gates, Sarah F., Brandt, Pa.; *E. Canton, Pa.*
Gile, Almira H., N. Stephentown, N. Y.; *N. Stephentown, N. Y.*
Grosvenor, Julia E., Pomfret, Ct.; *Pomfret, Ct.*
Hallock, Harriet P. [C.], Catskill, N. Y.; *Catskill, N. Y.*
Hayward, Lena G. [S.], Beloit, Wis.; *911 School St., Beloit, Wis.*
Hendershott, Delia A., Chatham, N. J.; *Box 103, Chatham, N. J.*
Hubbard, Anna M. [L.], Winchester, Ill.; *Winchester, Ill.*
Hubbard, Lucy M. [L.], Winchester, Ill.; *Winchester, Ill.*
Jewett, Bessie M., Pepperell; *Pepperell.*
Kosboth, Kittie W., Schenectady, N. Y.; m. Rev. Wm. Landon, '92; d. Chicago, Ill., '93.
Leavitt, Chloe M., E. Charlemont; *E. Charlemont.*
Lewis, Carolyn M., Plainville, Ct.; *Plainville, Ct.*
McConnel, Mary E. [C.], Washington, D. C.; *W. Bridgewater, Pa.*
Miller, Carrie S. [L.], Alexandria, Minn.; *Alexandria, Minn.*
Murray, Elizabeth R. [L.], Clearfield, Pa.; *Clearfield, Pa.*
Pinkham, Georgia A. [C.], Cumberland Center, Me.; d. '92.
Rollins, Maud M., Brooklyn, N. Y.;
Rouillard, Gertrude, Cambridge; *Mountainside Farm, Hinsdale, N. H.*

Sears, Amelia N., Chicago, Ill. ; 71 *Park Ave., Chicago, Ill.*
Smith, Eva M., Newburyport ; 19 *Walnut St., Newburyport.*
Sollenberger, Marion J. [L.], Newville, Pa.; m. Rev. Robert H. Sharpe, '93 ; *Oak Ridge, N.J.*
St. John, Julia E., Norwalk, Ct. ; 27 *Cannon St., Norwalk, Ct.*
Stevenson, Emily G., Philadelphia, Pa. ;
Sweet, Nellie J., Blue Hill, Me. ; *Blue Hill, Me.*
Waldron, Ada [L.], Binghamton, N. Y. ; 28 *Front St., Binghamton, N. Y.*
Waters, Mary J. [C.], New Britain, Ct. ; 90 *Winthrop St., New Britain, Ct.*
Williams, Maud, New Milford, Pa. ; *New Milford, Pa.*
Wright, Anne F., Coharie, N. C. ; m. Dr. Alfred A. Kent, '93 ; *Lenoir, N. C.*

SPECIAL STUDENTS.

Burritt, Jessie M., Rockford, Ill. ; *Box 1734, Rockford, Ill.*
Cleveland, Rose C., Milwaukee, Wis.; m. Edward E. Browne, LL.D., '93 ; *Waupaca, Wis.*
Craig, Alice L., Rochdale ; *Rochdale.*
Fisherdick, Anna L.., Palmer ; *Palmer.*
Fuller, Frances E., Rockford, Ill. ; *Box 2194, Rockford, Ill.*
Hollister, Mary A., Granville, N. Y. ; m. Charles H. Barnard, '93 ; *Granville, N. Y.*
Pierson, Fannie L., Florida, N. Y. ; *Echo Bank Farm, Florida, N. Y.*
Prentiss, Mary J., Chicago, Ill.; m. John D. Couffer, '93 ; 292 *Ashland Boul., Chicago, Ill.*
Ruggles, Eleanor M., Ware ; *Ware.*
Sears, Bertha M., Bucyrus, O. ; *Honolulu, H. I.*
Sedgwick, Mabel J., Palmer ; *Palmer.*
Wallace, Louise B., Bellevue, Pa. ; *Mount Holyoke College, S. Hadley* ; home address, *Sewickley, Pa.*
Whitaker, Jennie E., W. Springfield ; *Chicopee.*

MOUNT HOLYOKE COLLEGE.

1893.

GRADUATES.

Adams, Florence L., B. L., Shirley ; *Shirley.*
Annett, Sarah E., B. L., E. Jaffrey, N. H. ; *E. Jaffrey, N. H.*
Averill, Sarah, Pomfret, Ct. ; *Mount Holyoke College, S. Hadley ;* home address, *Pomfret, Ct.*
Beach, Emily K., B. A., New Haven, Ct. ; *56 Whalley Ave., New Haven, Ct.*
Beckwith, Martha W., B. S., Haiku, Maui, Hawaiian Islands ; *Haiku, Maui, H. I.*
Berry, Grace E., B. S., W. Boylston ; *W. Boylston.*
Blakely, Bertha E., B. L., Winchendon ; *Winchendon.*
Bloomfield, Evangeline, B. S., Meriden, Ct. ; *18 Chestnut St., Meriden, Ct.*
Bull, Caroline A. G., B. A., Woodstock, N. B. ; m. Willard Carr, '94 ; *Woodstock, N. B.*
Burt, Grace M., B. S., Springfield ; *134 Princeton St., Springfield.*
Cleveland, Mary, B. A., Brooklyn, N. Y. ; *77 S. 9th St., Brooklyn, N. Y.*
Cooper, Gertrude M., B. A., Syracuse, N. Y. ; *44 W. Buffalo St., Ithaca, N. Y.*
Dickinson, Laura A., Amherst ; *N. Amherst.*
Dickinson, Louise, B. S., Amherst ; *N. Amherst.*
Dollinger, Anna W., B. A., Wheaton, Ill. ; *Wheaton, Ill.*
Everett, Ida J., B. L., Norwood ; *Norwood.*
Fairbank, Elizabeth, B. L., Ahmednagar, India ; *Box 463, Shelburne Falls.*
Faunce, Sara E., B. S., Plymouth ; *375 Court St., Plymouth.*
Graham, Mertie L., B. L., Richford, Vt. ; *E. St. Johnsbury, Vt.*
Holmes, Elizabeth W., B. L., Ayer ; *care Mrs. Daniel Davis, Phillipsburg, N. J.*
Johnson, Annie A., B. S., Morristown, N. J. ; *17 Early St., Morristown, N. J.*
Kellogg, Cora H., B. S., Granby ; *Granby.*
Kingsley, Charissa A., B. A., Taunton ; *28 Pearl St., Norwich, Ct.*
Knapp, Grace H., B. L., Bitlis, Turkey ; *Bitlis, Turkey, Asia.*
Locke, Marinda A., Philippopolis, Bulgaria ; *E. Alstead, N. H.*
MacNulty, Gertrude A., B. L., Washington, D. C. ; *917 N. Carolina Ave., S. E., Washington, D. C.*
McDonald, Alice M., Bath, Me. ; *958 Washington St., Bath, Me.*
Moody, Julia E., Chicago, Ill. ; *1085 Millard Ave., Chicago, Ill.*
Miyagawa, Toshi, B. L., Osaka, Japan ; *Kobe College, Kobe, Japan.*
Mott, Sarah F., B. L., Yonkers, N. Y. ; m. H. Lansing Quick, '93 ; *207 Woodworth Ave., Yonkers, N. Y.*
Park, Mary I., B. A., Huntington, Ct. ; *Huntington, Ct.*
Rice, Caroline K., B. L., New Haven, Ct. ; *82 Grand Ave., New Haven, Ct.*
Rich, Hattie S., B. S., Morrisville, Vt. ; *Morrisville, Vt.*
Richardson, Abby M., Francestown, N. H. ; *Francestown, N. H.*
Rowland, Tace F., B. S., Lee ; *43 W. 47th St., N. Y. City.*
Smith, Carrie L., B. L., Granby ; *Granby.*
Sprague, Olive A., B. A., Jersey City, N. J. ; *283 Grove St., Jersey City, N. J.*

Stevens, Alice P., B. A., Newburyport; *Mt. Holyoke College, S. Hadley;* home address, 207 High St., *Newburyport.*
Stevens, Grace, B. L., S. Framingham; *S. Framingham.*
Stewart, Helen A., B. A., Rutland, Vt.; 1 *Harrington Ave., Rutland, Vt.*
Stockwell, Adeline R., Williamsville, Vt.; *Williamsville, Vt.*
Ward, E. Lena, B. A., Johnson, Vt.; *City Hospital, Hartford, Ct.*
Wemple, Jeanne E., Schenectady, N. Y.; 12 *Mynderse St., Schenectady, N. Y.*
Yeomans, Frances A., B. S., Danville, Ill.; 212 *W. Harrison St., Danville, Ill.*

NON-GRADUATES.

Barron, Dorothy H. [L.], Kenwood, N. Y.; *Kenwood, N. Y.*
Beeman, Alberta L. [S.], St. Albans, Vt.; 3 *Brown Ave., St. Albans, Vt.*
Bevin, Pernella [C.], S. Hadley Falls; m. William H. Gleason, '94; 20 *Corey St., Braddock, Pa.*
Borden, Sallie [L.], Goldsboro, N. C.; *Goldsboro, N. C.*
Bradford, Flora L. [L.], Wakefield; *S. Billerica.*
Brainard, Nellie J. [L.], Devil's Lake, N. Dak.; *Devil's Lake, N. Dak.*
Bray, Mary C. [L.], Mendon, Ill.; *Mendon, Ill.*
Brown, Helen C. [C.], S. Hadley Falls; *Housatonic.*
Burr, Jean M. [L.], Monroe, Ct.; *Monroe, Ct.*
Chapell, Evalena [L.], Boston; 118 *Pembroke St., Boston.*
Chapin, Florence E. [L.], Southbridge; *Southbridge.*
Colton, Elizabeth [C.], Burksville, Ky.; *Burksville, Ky.*
Comstock, Elizabeth [S.], Ballston, N. Y.; *Ballston Spa, N. Y.*
Comstock, Jennie [S.], Ballston, N. Y.; *Ballston Spa, N. Y.*
Duncan, Elsie [L.], Northfield; *Northfield.*
French, Frances W. [C.], S. Chesterville, Me.; *S. Chesterville, Me.*
Grant, Emelyn [L.], Goldsboro, N. C.; m. Daniel F. Gay, '94; 21 *Lancaster St., Worcester.*
Griffeth, Sara J. [L.], Penn Yan, N. Y.; *Penn Yan, N. Y.*
Gund, Elizabeth [C.], Freeport, Ill.; m. John H. Dow, '95; 120 *Fourteenth St., Lockport, Ill.*
Gund, Emma [L.], Freeport, Ill.; m. Frederick Wagner, '94; 57 *High St., Freeport, Ill.*
Hazel, Frances D. [L.], New Haven, Ct.; 56 *Whalley Ave., New Haven, Ct.*
Hazen, Ella M. [S.], Hartford, Vt.; *White River Junction, Vt.*
Henney, Christine [S.], Hiawatha, Kan.; *Hiawatha, Kan.*
Hettinger, Alice [L.], Freeport, Ill.; 325 *Stephenson St., Freeport, Ill.*
Hicks, Grace [L.], Wyoming, Pa.; 629 *E. Market St., Scranton, Pa.*
Ives, Julia I. [C.], Auburn, N. Y.; 111 *South St., Auburn, N. Y.*
Jobes, Anna B. [L.], Menomonie, Wis.; *Menomonie, Wis.*
Johnson, Ruth I. [S.], Easton, Pa.; *College Hill, Easton, Pa.*
Jones, Nellie L. [L.], Peoria, Ill.; 5417 *Cottage Grove Ave., Chicago, Ill.*
Kimball, Marian [L.], Newport, N. H.; *Newport, N. H.*
Lee, Charlotte E. [S.], Huntington, N. Y.; *Huntington, N. Y.*
Lufkin, Arizona [S.], Anna, Ill.; *Anna, Ill.*
McConnel, Jessie [L.], Beaver, Pa.; *Beaver, Pa.*
Musgrove, Carolyn G. [L.], Pittsfield; 75 *Maplewood Ave., Pittsfield.*
Near, Grace [C.], S. Hadley; *Brooks' Arcade, Salt Lake City, Utah.*
Newell, Annie M. [C.], Southbridge; *Southbridge.*
Pettee, Julia L. [S.], Lakeville, Ct.; *Lakeville, Ct.*
Prentice, Helen [L.], Mystic, Ct.; *Mystic, Ct.*
Purington, Emily [S.], Waterford, Ct.; *S. Hadley.*

1893.

Reed, Elizabeth F. [L.], Boothbay Harbor. Me.; *Boothbay Harbor, Me.*
Reed, Kate L. [C.]. Boothbay Harbor. Me.; *Boothbay Harbor, Me.*
Richardson. Frances C. [L.], Salem. Or. ; m.
Richmond, Anna [L.], Armstrong, Io.; *Armstrong. Io.*
Shaw, M. Agnes [C.], Portland, Pa.; *Portland. Pa.*
Smith. Adeline [L.], Troy, O.; 210 *W. Franklin St., Troy, O.*
Smith, Maud E. [L.], Chester. Ill.; *Claremont, Cal.*
Usher, Jessie H. [L.], Plainville, Ct.; m. Chas. R. Clark, '94 ; *Plainville, Ct.*
Walsworth. Luella M. [L.], Delhi, N. Y.; *Delhi. N. Y.*
Walter, Mary E. [L.], Whitney's Point, N. Y.; *Whitney's Point. N. Y.*
Watkins, Ella M. [S.], Beaver, Pa.; *Beaver, Pa.*
Worth. Marion W. [L.], Oxford, Pa.. *Oxford, Pa.*

SPECIAL STUDENTS.

Bailey, Mary F., E. Jaffrey, N. H. ; *E. Jaffrey, N. H.*
Bell, Jessie M., Granby ; m. Horace S. Taylor, '93 ; *Granby.*
Bemis, Agnes T., Shrewsbury ; *Mt. Holyoke College, S. Hadley* : home address, *Shrewsbury.*
Bliss, Lulu F., Prohibition Park, Staten Island, N. Y. ; *Wellington, Cape Colony, S. Africa.*
Genthner, Nellie E., Foxcroft, Me. ; *Foxcroft, Me.*
Grier, Eva M., Hulton, Pa. ; *Hulton, Pa.*
Hosack, Isabel, Mercer, Pa. ; *Mercer, Pa.*
McCaine, Adelaide M., St. Paul, Minn. ; 609 *Canada St., St. Paul, Minn.*
Reid, Martha M., Monmouth, Ill. ; *Monmouth, Ill.*
Scism, Josephine, Scranton Pa. ; *Scranton, Pa.*
Viets, Clara B., Granby, Ct. ; *Copper Hill, Ct.*
Walker, Mary W., Danville, Va. ; *Danville, Va.*
Wilson, Emma W., Worcester, N. Y. ; *Worcester, N. Y.*

1894.

GRADUATES.

Abbot, Fanny H., B. A., E. Orange, N. J. ; 431 *William St., E. Orange, N. J.*
Allyn, Eleanor, B. A., Lyme, Ct. ; *Black Hall, Ct.*
Ayres, Frances C., B. S., Peoria, Ill. ; 906 *N. Main St., Bloomington, Ill.*
Bacon, Imogene, B. S., S. Glastonbury, Ct. ; *S. Glastonbury, Ct.*
Barber, Harriet A., B. A., Seymour, Ct. ; *Seymour, Ct.*
Beare, Cornelia, B. L., N. Y. City ; 330 *W. 51st St., N. Y. City.*
Bemis, Leigh J., B. A., Shrewsbury ; m. Rev. Frank B. Doane, '94 ; *Dayton, Wash.*
Blake, Clara L., B. A., Nashua, N. H. ; *Nashua, N. H.*
Brierly, Addie O., B. L., New Brighton, Pa. ; *New Brighton, Pa.*
Brierly, Ella T., B. L., New Brighton. Pa. ; *New Brighton, Pa.*
Budd, Sarah R., B. A., Mount Holly, N. J. ; *Mount Holly, N. J.*
Bunnell, Elizabeth H., B. A., Tunkhannock, Pa. ; *Tunkhannock, Pa.*
Denns, Gertrude A., B. L., West Medway ; *West Medway.*
Dickinson, Laura A.. B. A., Amherst ; *N. Amherst.*
Durgin, Cora A., B. S., Worcester ; 156 *Pleasant St., Worcester.*
Ferrin, Ella L.. B. L., S. Deerfield ; *Randolph, Vt.*
Foster, Annie G., B. L., Westerly, R. I.; *Westerly, R. I.*

1894.

Fowler, Elizabeth B., B. L., Biddeford, Me.; *Biddeford, Me.*
Frost, Caroline E., B. A., Methuen; *Methuen.*
Gifford, Grace, B. S., Jamestown, N. Y.; 19 W. 7th St., Jamestown, N. Y.
Glen, Catherine Y., B. L., Elizabeth, N. J.; 808 Salem Ave., *Elizabeth, N. J.*
Goodale, Sophia B., B. L., N. Y. City; 200 W. 99th St., *N. Y. City.*
Gordon, Mary, B. L., Portland, Ct.; *Portland, Ct.*
Gund, Minnie C., B. L., Marcus, Io.; *Marcus, Io.*
Hayes, Edith P., B. A., Holyoke; 26 *Beacon St., Holyoke.*
Holbrook, Bertha E., B. L., Morrisville, Vt.; *Morrisville, Vt.*
Houghton, Bertha R., B. L., Worcester; 6 *Marston Way, Worcester.*
Howe, Grace B., B. L., N. Hadley; *N. Hadley.*
Howell, Elizabeth M., B. L., Blairstown, N. J.; *Blairstown, N. J.*
Jones, Bessie L., B. L., Chatham, N. Y.; *Chatham, N. Y.*
Kane, Elizabeth G., B. A., Waterbury, Ct.; 155 *Cherry St., Waterbury, Ct.*
Keith, Mary H., B. S., Braintree; *Mt. Holyoke College, S. Hadley;* home address, *Braintree.*
Knowles, Ruth M., B. S., E. Orleans; *E. Orleans.*
Lyon, Martha, B. S., Morrisville, Vt.; *Morrisville, Vt.*
McGill, Margaret, B. A., Dover; *Dover.*
Moody, Julia E., B. S., Chicago, Ill.; 1085 *Millard Ave., Chicago, Ill.*
Morse, Emma D., B. A., St. Johnsbury, Vt.; *St. Johnsbury, Vt.*
Mosher, Rhena E., B. S., Westfield, N. Y.; *Westfield, N. Y.*
Osgood, Lucy R., B. A., Ellsworth, Me.; *Ellsworth, Me.*
Pattangall, Kate H., B. A., Pembroke, Me.; *Pembroke, Me.*
Smith, Kate W., B. A., Middlefield; *Middlefield.*
Smith, Mabel E., B. A., Palmer; *Palmer.*
Stanley, Irene, B. L., Goldsboro, N. C.; *Goldsboro, N. C.*
Stowe, Mabel E., B. L., W. Brattleboro, Vt.; *W. Brattleboro, Vt.*
Strong, Mabel D., B. L., Philadelphia, Pa.; 109 *W. Main St., Amsterdam, N. Y.*
Stryker, Minnie, B. A., Flemington, N. J.; *Flemington, N. J.*
Tenney, Charlotte L., B. L., Morrisville, Vt.; *Morrisville, Vt.*
Weeks, Angelina L., B. A., Gorham, Me.; *Gorham, Me.*
White, Caroline L., B. A., Brookline; *Tappan St., Brookline.*
Wilcox, Alice M., B. S., Meriden, Ct.; *Meriden, Ct.*
Wright, Alice C., B. L., Bridge Hampton, N. Y.; *Bridge Hampton, N. Y.*

NON-GRADUATES.

Alcott, Mary H. [S.], Boxford; *Boxford.*
Allen, Elsie A. [L.], La Porte, Tex.; *La Porte, Tex.*
Aten, Edna B. [S.], Hiawatha, Kan.; *Hiawatha, Kan.*
Brown, Alice E. [L.], Groton, Ct.; *Groton, Ct.*
Bruce, Sara S. [C.], Beaver, Pa.; *Beaver, Pa.*
Chatterton, Gertrude M. [C.], Acworth, N. H.; *Acworth, N. H.*
Cobleigh, Grace N. [L.], Walla Walla, Wash.; 116 *Chestnut St., Walla Walla, Wash.*
Deyo, Ella M. [C.], Honeoye, N. Y.; *Honeoye, N. Y.*
Eastman, Margaret [C.], Albany, N. Y.; 198 *Lancaster St., Albany, N. Y.*
Fallows, Sarah H. [C.], Southbridge; *Southbridge.*
Fenno, Amanda D. [L.], Portland, Me.; 258 *Spring St., Portland, Me.*
Franchois, Henrietta M. [S.], Binghamton, N. Y.; 268 *Front St., Binghamton, N. Y.*
Gaylord, Cassie E. [C.], S. Hadley; *S. Hadley.*
Glen, Mary A. [L.], Elizabeth, N. J.; 808 *Salem Ave., Elizabeth, N. J.*
Gossler, Ella M. [L.], Philadelphia, Pa.; 2022 *N. Broad St., Philadelphia, Pa.*

1894.

Grassie, Effie D. [L.], Ashland, Wis.; *Ashland, Wis.*
Grier, Jean B. [S.]. Hulton, Pa.; *Hulton, Pa.*
Harlow, Persis B. [S.], Red Beach, Me.; *Robbinston, Me.*
High, Anna P. [L.], Pittsburgh, Pa.; 117 *Kelly St., Pittsburgh, Pa.*
Ingalls, Henrietta E. [L.], Abington, Ct.; *Abington, Ct.*
Johnson, Maude A. [L.], Verona, N. J.; *Verona, N. J.*
Ladd, Grace E. [L.], Northfield, Vt.; *Northfield, Vt.*
Lombard, Maud E. [C.], W. Randolph, Vt.; *W. Randolph, Vt.*
Lyon, Florence [L.], Amsterdam, N. Y.; *Rockton, N. Y.*
Nichols, Susie P. [C.], Phippsburg, Me.; *Phippsburg, Me.*
Northrop, Helen [L.], Tunkhannock, Pa.; *Tunkhannock, Pa.*
Pierson, Harriet W. [L.], Florida, N. Y.; *Florida, N. Y.*
Pilsbury, Annie K. [C.], Biddeford, Me.; 18 *Birch St., Biddeford, Me.*
Runnette, Grace [L.], Pittsburgh, Pa.; 4410 *Butler St., Pittsburgh, Pa.*
Savage, Marietta I. [L.], New Haven, Ct.; 64 *Whalley Ave., New Haven, Ct.*
Spence, Adele P. [C.], Snow Hill, Md.; *Snow Hill, Md.*
Van Winkle, Edla M. [C.], Detroit, Mich.; *Williamsburg, Va.*
Yeomans, Edith M. [S.], Danville, Ill.; 212 *Harrison St., Danville, Ill.*

SPECIAL STUDENTS.

Cole, Clara S., Tolland, Ct.; *Tolland, Ct.*
Deuel, Josephine, Millbrook, N. Y.; *Millbrook, N. Y.*
Gleason, Amy E., Hannibal, Mo.; *Hannibal, Mo.*
Glover, Ida M., New Britain, Ct.; 96 *Maple St., New Britain, Ct.*
Hill, Adella C., Phelps, N. Y.; *Phelps, N. Y.*
Lord, Anna B., Rutland, Vt.; 32 *Church St., Rutland, Vt.*
McClure, Elizabeth M., Nashua, N. H.; 58 *Abbott St., Nashua, N. H.*
Morrow, Margaret G., Lexington, Va.; *Lexington, Va.*
Schumacher, Rosalie, Millington, N. J.; *Millington, N. J.*
Takahashi, Chika, Tokio, Japan; *Tokio, Japan.*

1895.

SENIOR CLASS.

Averill, Sarah [S.], Pomfret, Ct.; home address, *Pomfret, Ct.*
Barbour, Catharine H. [S.], San Sebastian, Spain; 40 *Avenida de la Libertad, San Sebastian, Spain.*
Bartholomew Ellen E. [S.], Ansonia, Ct.; 106 *S. Cliff St., Ansonia, Ct.*
Beede, Alice G. [C.], Centre Sandwich, N. H.; *Centre Sandwich, N. H.*
Blake, Ethel W. [L.], Westfield; 80 *Broad St., Westfield.*
Bliss, Seraph A. [S.], Lebanon, Ct.; P. O. address, *Leonard Bridge, Ct.*
Blunt, Kate M. [L.], Haverhill; 122 *Water St., Haverhill.*
Bond, Violet R. [L.], Monastir, Macedonia; 249 *E. Front St., Plainfield, N. J.*
Briggs, Ella M. [S.], Shelton, Ct.; *Shelton, Ct.*
Brown, Alice W. [L.], Palmer; *School St., Palmer.*
Bryant, Florence M. [L.], Morrisville, Vt.; *Morrisville, Vt.*
Caskey, M. Olivia [L.], Morristown, N. J.; 143 *Speedwell Ave., Morristown, N. J.*
Clark, Mary L. [C.], Worcester; 155 *Geore St., Worcester.*

1895.

Davis, Evelyn H. [S.], Gardiner, Me. ; 41 *Washington Ave., Gardiner, Me.*
Dresser, Annie S. [C.]. Richmond Furnace ; *Richmond Furnace.*
Goodrich, Mary A. [L.], Delhi, N. Y. ; 19 *High St., Delhi, N. Y.*
Greeley, Florence P. [L.], Lowville, N. Y. ; 15 *Trinity Ave., Lowville, N. Y.*
Hall, Alice C. [S.], Chicago, Ill. ; *Yarmouth.*
Hall, Martha S. [C.], Jamestown, N. Y. ; 127 *Forest Ave., Jamestown, N. Y.*
Halsey, Annie S. [S.], N. Paterson, N. J. ; *N. Paterson, N. J.*
Haynes, Frances E. [L.], Fitchburg ; 59 *Highland Ave., Fitchburg.*
Herrick, Minnie T. [S.], Constantinople, Turkey ; *American Bible House, Constantinople, Turkey.*
Hinchman, Lesbia R. [S.], Denville, N. J. ; *Denville, N. J.*
Holmes, Alice M. [S.], Eastport, Me. ; *Water St., Eastport, Me.*
Hyde, Elizabeth H. [C.], Ware ; *Ware.*
Jones, Cassina M. [L.], Hanover, N. H. ; 5 *College St., Hanover, N. H.*
Keith, S. Emma [S.], Braintree ; *Braintree.*
Kellogg, Ellie L. [C.], Granby ; *Granby.*
Leavitt, Marian F. [C.], Melrose ; 137 *Greene St., Melrose.*
Meserve, Elizabeth E. [S.], Vassalboro, Me. ; *Vassalboro, Me.*
North, Eva M. [L.], Chicago, Ill. ; 425 *Claremont Ave., Chicago, Ill.*
Nye, Grace [S.], Hiawatha, Kan. ; *Hiawatha, Kan.*
Osborne, Ella L. [L.], La Crosse, Wis. ; 1022 *Division St., La Crosse, Wis.*
Parsons, Angie E. [C.], S. Hadley Falls ; *S. Hadley Falls.*
Post, M. Agnes [C.], Clinton, N. Y. ; *Clinton, N. Y.*
Robinson, Alice M. [C.], New Castle, Me. ; *New Castle, Me.*
Root, Helena C. [L.], Thomaston, Ct. ; 42 *Elm St., Thomaston, Ct.*
Sanderson, Lydia E. [C.], Cleveland, O. ; 166 *Sawtelle Ave., Cleveland, O.*
Sargent, Martha A. [C.], W. Boylston ; 1 *Fletcher St., W. Boylston.*
Schwendler, Sadie [C.], Rochester, N. Y. ; 28 *Oak St., Rochester, N. Y.*
Searle, Clara P. [C.], Westfield ; 18 *Day Ave., Westfield.*
Smith, Elsie F. [L.], Brooklyn, N. Y. ; 255 *President St., Brooklyn, N. Y.*
Swartz, E Pauline [L.], Chicago, Ill. ; 17 *Park Ave., Chicago, Ill.*
Syvret, Florence [L.], Worcester ; 48 *King St., Worcester.*
Terrill, Bertha M. [L.], Morrisville, Vt. ; *Morrisville, Vt.*
Thomas, Letitia E. [L.], Troy, O. ; 328 *Grant St., Troy, O.*
Walton, Edith M. [C.], N. Cambridge ; 26 *Russell St, N. Cambridge.*
Welles, Graycc S. [C.], Taunton ; 27 *Cedar St., Taunton.*
Wright, Mary H. [C.]. Bridge Hampton, N. Y. ; *Bridge Hampton, N. Y.*
Yamawaki, Hana [S.], Okayama, Japan ; *Kobe College, 60 Hill, Kobe, Japan.*

NON-GRADUATES.

Adams, Kate E. [L.], Wethersfield, Ct. ; *Wethersfield, Ct.*
Agard, Katherine M. [C.], Tolland, Ct. ; *Tolland, Ct.*
Aldrich, Lena M. [C.], E. Douglass ; *E. Douglass.*
Allen, Luella M. [L.], Winchendon ; *Winchendon.*
Allen, Mabel L. [L.], W. Hartford, Ct. ; *W. Hartford, Ct.*
Allen, May W. [L.], Hartford, Ct. ; 520 *Farmington Ave., Hartford, Ct.*
Andrea, Elizabeth R. [C.], New Haven, Ct. ; 60 *Sylvan Ave., New Haven, Ct.*
Andrews, Florence M. [S.], Lynn ; 83 *Franklyn St., Lynn.*
Andrews, Harriet E. [S.], Rochester, N. Y. ; 262 *Allen St., Rochester, N. Y.*
Babb, Emily A. [C.], Holden ; *Holden.*
Baker, Lucy F. [C.], Jamestown, N. Y. ; 20 *W. 4th St., Jamestown, N. Y.*

Baldwin, Jessie M. [C.], Willimantic, Ct.; 115 Prospect St., Willimantic, Ct.
Balkam, Susanne L. [L.], Haverhill; Haverhill.
Barber, Harriet S. [C.], Warsaw, N. Y.; 56 S. Main St., Warsaw, N. Y.
Bass, Mary E. [L.], Boston; 524 Tremont St., Boston.
Bates, Emeline C. [C.], Willimantic, Ct.; 191 High St., Willimantic, Ct.
Beach, Martha [L.], Franklin, N. Y.; Franklin, N. Y.
Beaman, Harriet E. [L.], Princeton; Princeton.
Beers, Florence E. [C.], Huntington, N. Y.; Huntington, N. Y.
Belcher, Ida M. [L.], Newark Valley, N. Y.; Newark Valley, N. Y.
Benedict, Mary [C.], Riverhead, N. Y.; Riverhead, N. Y.
Benner, Caroline F. [L.], Wellesley; Wellesley.
Bidwell, Bertha C. [L.], Freeport, Ill.; Freeport, Ill.
Billam, Flora E. [L.], Ansonia, Ct.; Ansonia, Ct.
Bishop, Elizabeth A. [C.], Warsaw, N. Y.; Warsaw, N. Y.
Bissell, Alma W. [C.], Holland; Holland.
Blackstock, Mary I. [C.], Auburn, N. Y.; 22½ Jefferson St., Auburn, N. Y.
Bliss, M. Alice [S.], Lebanon, Ct.; Lebanon, Ct.
Blunt, Florence T. [L.], Haverhill; 122 Water St., Haverhill.
Bradbury, Emilie G. [C.], Machias, Me.; Machias, Me.
Brown, Adeline S. [C.], New Haven, Ct.; 150 Shelton Ave., New Haven, Ct.
Budd, Mary W. [S.], Mt. Holly, N. J.; Mt. Holly, N. J.
Burleigh, Nettie C. [L.], Vassalboro, Me.; Vassalboro, Me.
Burroughs, Grace [C.], Coxsackie, N. Y.; Coxsackie-on-Hudson, N. Y.
Burtt, Gertrude A. [C.], Andover; Andover.
Butler, Mabel L. [C.], W. Boylston; W. Boylston.
Byington, Martha D. [C.], E. Hardwick, Vt.; E. Hardwick, Vt.
Calder, Helen B. [S.], Hartford, Ct.; 288 Sigourney St., Hartford, Ct.
Calder, Matilda S. [S.], Hartford, Ct.; 288 Sigourney St., Hartford, Ct.
Campbell, Francena L. [C.], Derry, N. H.; Derry, N. H.
Campbell, Harriet [C.], Auburn, N. Y.; 121 Wall St., Auburn, N. Y.
Campbell, Mary F. [C.], W. Suffield, Ct.; W. Suffield, Ct.
Carpenter, Jane B. [L.], Andover; Andover.
Carr, Bertha G. [L.], Ashby; Ashby.
Carter, Emma D. [L.], Huntington, N. Y.; Huntington, N. Y.
Cheney, Alice M. [L.], Beloit, Wis.; Beloit, Wis.
Clark, Elizabeth [S.], E. Peacham, Vt.; E. Peacham, Vt.
Clark, Florence R. [C.], W. Brattleboro, Vt.; W. Brattleboro, Vt.
Clary, Losanna M. [L.], Hallowell, Me.; Hallowell, Me.
Converse, Anna B. [C.], Somerville, Ct.; Somerville, Ct.
Cotton, Ethel H. [S.], Portsmouth, O.; Portsmouth, O.
Coolidge, Nettie E. [C.], Framingham; Framingham.
Copeland, Sara F. [C.], Columbus, O.; 946 Madison Ave., Columbus, O.
Coulter, Bertha [S.], Danville, Pa.; Danville, Pa.
Crafts, Sue G. [L.], Wolcott, N. Y.; Wolcott, N. Y.
Crosby, Georgina [L.], Somerville; 17 Madison St., Somerville.
Curtiss, Adele L. [L.], Meriden, Ct.; 21 Linsley Ave., Meriden, Ct.
Davis, Annie L. C. [L.], N. Y. City; 263 W. 130th St., N. Y. City.
Davis, Myrtie I. [C.], Granby; Granby.
Day, Alice R. [L.], New Haven, Ct.; 270 Ferry St., New Haven, Ct.
Davidson, Eva F. [S.], Beaver, Pa.; Beaver, Pa.
Deacon, Mamie E. [L.], Bridgeport, Ct.; Bridgeport, Ct.
Dickinson, Ella S. [C], Rockville, Ct.; 36 Prospect St., Rockville, Ct.

1895.

Dolley, Grace L. [L], Gorham, Me. ; *Gorham, Me.*
Donaldson, Jessie B. [L.], Ellenville, N. Y. ; *Ellenville, N. Y.*
DuBois, Clara A. [L.], W. Randolph, Vt. ; *Randolph, Vt.*
Eaton, Mabel L. [C.], Collinsville, Ct. ; *Collinsville, Ct.*
Ellison, Gertrude H. [C.], N. Andover ; *N. Andover.*
Emery, Mary L. [C.], Warsaw, N. Y. ; *Warsaw, N. Y.*
Estabrook, Lula B. [L.], Saratoga Springs,N. Y. ; *179 S. Broadway,Saratoga Springs,N. Y.*
Galloway, Jennie G. [L.], Freeport, Ill. ; *198 Walnut St., Freeport, Ill.*
Gay, Maude C. [S.], Terryville, Ct. ; *Terryville, Ct.*
Geddes, Margaret S. [L.], Williamsport, Pa. ; *331 High St., Williamsport, Pa.*
Gibbons, Dora B. [L.], Franklin, N. Y. ; *Franklin, N. Y.*
Gibbons, Vernette L. [S.], Franklin, N. Y. ; *Franklin, N. Y.*
Glazier, Hattie E. [C.], Lisbon, N. H. ; *Lisbon, N. H.*
Gleason, Margaret A. [L.], Hannibal, Mo. ; *Hannibal, Mo.*
Goddard, Agnes L. [C.], Ashtabula, O. ; *250 Main St., Ashtabula, O.*
Gould, Hattie L. [C.], W. Hingham ; *W. Hingham.*
Grady, Florence J. [C.], Trenton, N. J. ; *40 Wall St., Trenton, N. J.*
Grant, Annie E. [C.], Winsted, Ct. ; *Winsted, Ct.*
Hall, Annie [C.], Wallingford, Vt. ; *Wallingford, Vt.*
Hall, Margaret R. [L.], Catskill, N. Y. ; *Catskill, N. Y.*
Hall, Mary E. [S.], Salt Lake City, Utah ; *78 E. 1st North St., Salt Lake City, Utah.*
Hallock, Mary E. [C.], Steubenville, O. ; *511 N. 5th St., Steubenville, O.*
Hamilton, Christine H. [L.], Kenwood, N. Y. ; *Kenwood, N. Y.*
Harmon, Winnifred L. [L.], Somersworth, N. H. ; *Somersworth, N. H.*
Hathaway, Bertha F. [C.], Stoughton ; *Stoughton.*
Hay, Fanny A. [S.], New Brighton, Pa. ; *New Brighton, Pa.*
Hayden, Celia M. [L.], Columbus, O. ; *46 Lexington Ave., Columbus, O.*
Hayes, Alma L. [C.], Holyoke ; *26 Beacon St., Holyoke.*
Haynes, Harriet T. [L.], Fitchburg ; *59 Highland Ave., Fitchburg.*
Hazen, Lucia W. [C.], Middletown, Ct. ; *Middletown, Ct.*
Hazen, Martha M. [C.], Northfield, Vt. ; *Northfield, Vt.*
Heath, Adeline F. [C.], Manchester, N. H. ; *73 Liberty St., Manchester, N. H.*
Hill, Myra A. [C.], Williamsburg ; *Williamsburg.*
Hill, Nellie L. [L.], Northwood, N. H. ; *Northwood, N. H.*
Hirst, Emma A. [S.], Paola, Kan. ; *Paola, Kan.*
Hirst, Sara J. [S.], Paola, Kan. ; *Paola, Kan.*
Holton, Grace B. [L.], S. Framingham ; *159 Irving St., S. Framingham.*
Hooker, Bessie M. [C.], Amherst ; *Amherst.*
Hoyt, Olive S. [S.], Augusta, Me. ; *15 Capitol St., Augusta, Me.*
Hutchins, Mary L. [L.], Waukegan, Ill. ; *Waukegan, Ill.*
Hyde, Bertha C. [S.], Rockville, Ct. ; *N. Park St., Rockville, Ct.*
Hyde, Gertrude S. [C.], Norwich, Ct. ; *268 Washington St., Norwich, Ct.*
Ives, Sue B. [L.], New Haven, Ct. ; *147 Quinnipiac St., New Haven, Ct.*
Jay, Carrie B. [L.], Saint Mary's, O ; *St. Mary's. O.*
Johnson, Edina M. [S.], Winsted, Ct. ; *104 Main St., Winsted, Ct.*
Johnson, Louise B. [L.], Enfield, Ct. ; *Enfield, Ct.*
Johnston, May J. [C.], Chicago, Ill. ; *359 E. 43d St., Chicago, Ill.*
Joy, Katherine D. [C.], Ellsworth, Me. ; *12 Pleasant St., Ellsworth, Me.*
Kajiro, Yoshi [S.], Osaka, Japan ; *Baikwa Girls' School, Osaka, Japan.*
Kathan, Florence A. [C.], Putney, Vt. ; *Putney, Vt.*
Keith, Cora F. [C.], Braintree ; *Braintree.*
Kenyon, Elizabeth W. [S.], Point Judith, R. I. ; *Point Judith, R. I.*

1895.

Knott, A. Lois [L.], Beaver Falls, Pa. ; 619 *Sixth St., Beaver Falls, Pa.*
Knowles, Wilhelmina C. [L.], Washington, Ct. ; *Washington, Ct.*
Koehler, Margaret B. [L.], Penn Yan, N. Y. ; *Penn Yan, N. Y.*
Lake, Margaret B. [L.], Rockville, Ct. ; *Rockville, Ct.*
Lasell, Gail, [C.], Orange, N. J. ; 121 *Day St., Orange, N. J.*
Latimer, Anna C. [L.], New Britain, Ct. ; *New Britain, Ct.*
Leavitt, Edith W. [C.], Melrose ; 137 *Greene St., Melrose.*
Long, Sue G. [L.], Rutland, Vt. ; 32 *West St., Rutland, Vt.*
Lovejoy, Sara C. [L.], Haverhill ; 9 *Williams St., Haverhill.*
Loveland, Mary H. [L.], Newark Valley, N. Y. ; *Newark Valley, N. Y.*
Low, Grace E. [S.], Whitinsville ; *Whitinsville.*
Lyman, Annie A. [S.], Fall River ; 22 *Hanover St., Fall River.*
Lyon, Karleen S. [S.], Morrisville, Vt.; *Morrisville, Vt.*
Mansfield, Mary P. [C.], W. Hartford, Ct. ; *W. Hartford, Ct.*
McKissick, Elizabeth F. [C.], Oxford, Pa. ; *Oxford, Pa.*
McWilliams, Martha E. [S.], New Haven, Ct. ; 51 *Avon St., New Haven, Ct.*
Mead, Clara B. [S.], Greenwich, Ct. ; *Greenwich, Ct.*
Mellor, Eva T. [L.], Auburn, N. Y.; 9 *Jefferson St., Auburn, N. Y.*
Merriam, Grace L. [C.], Mount Vernon, N. Y. ; 130 *S. 3d Ave., Mt. Vernon, N. Y.*
Merriam, Helen S. [C.], Mount Vernon, N. Y. ; 130 *S. 3d Ave., Mt. Vernon, N. Y.*
Merrill, May [L.], Quincy ; 18 *Canal St., Quincy.*
Mildrum, Clara E. [L.], E. Berlin, Ct. ; *E. Berlin, Ct.*
Miller, Frances [S.], New Britain, Ct. ; 110 *Camp St., New Britain, Ct.*
Minchew, Annie A. [L.], Taunton ; *Norton.*
Mitchell, Bessie A. [C.], Acworth, N. H. ; *Acworth, N. H.*
Morse, Kate N. [C.], Haverhill ; 24 *Park St., Haverhill.*
Mowry, Florence P. [L.], Woonsocket, R. I. ; *Woonsocket, R. I.*
Munson, Maude E. [S.], Huntington ; *Huntington.*
Neal, Lotta E. [L.], Auburn, Me. ; *Auburn, Me.*
Nell, Cora [C.], Rochester, N. Y. ; 175 *N. Union St., Rochester, N. Y.*
Nettleton, Amy A. [C.], Washington, Ct. ; *Washington, Ct.*
Northrop, Evelyn H. [C.], Tunkhannock, Pa. ; *Tunkhannock, Pa.*
Noyes, Nellie M. [C.], Hingham ; *Hingham.*
Orcutt, Mary C. [C.], Northfield, Vt. ; *Northfield, Vt.*
Packard, Edith M. [L.], Syracuse, N. Y. ; 303 *University Place, Syracuse, N. Y.*
Park, Jennie A. [S.], Huntington, Ct. ; *Huntington, Ct.*
Pearson, Florence I. [L.], Beloit, Wis. ; *Beloit, Wis.*
Pease, Jennie E. [L.], Thompsonville, Ct.; 95 *Westminster St., Springfield.*
Peck, Margaret [C.], Madison, N. J.; *Madison, N. J.*
Percival, Mary [L.], Auburn, Me.; *Auburn, Me.*
Pettengill, Agnes E. [L.], Holley, N. Y.; *Holley, N. Y.*
Pettengill, Lillian [L.], Haverhill ; 22 *Bartlett St., Haverhill.*
Pierce, Marion [C.], Gardiner, Me.; 36 *Maple St., Gardiner, Me.*
Plumb, Mary L. [S.], Townshend, Vt.; *Westminster West, Vt.*
Pomeroy, Annie L. [L.], Springfield ; 198 *Carew St., Springfield.*
Post, Estelle L. [S.], New York City ; 107 *West 74th St., New York City.*
Ransom, Caroline L. [C.], Toledo, O.; *Toledo, O.*
Redman, Edith [L.], Lexington ; *Lexington.*
Reed, Cora P. [L.], Wolcott, N. Y.; *Wolcott, N. Y.*
Reynolds, Agnes R. [L.], Richmond, Ind.; 30 *S. 12th St., Richmond, Ind.*
Richard, Dorothy M. [C.], Newport, Vt.; *Newport, Vt.*
Richards, Mae L. [C.], Unionville, Ct.; *Unionville, Ct.*

1895.

Ridlon, Sarah E. [L.], Gorham, Me.; *Gorham, Me.*
Robinson, Mabel S. [C.], N. Andover Depot; *N. Andover.*
Robinson, Mary B. [L.], Bangor. Me.; *Essex St., Bangor, Me.*
Roeth. Natalie S. [S.], Meriden, Ct.; 102 *Liberty St., Meriden, Ct.*
Rogers, E. Gertrude [L.]. New Britain, Ct.; 29 *Camp St., New Britain, Ct.*
Rolston, Martha B. [L.], Worcester; 8 *Burncoat St., Worcester.*
Sanger, Abbie M. [L.], Franklin Falls, N. H.; *Franklin Falls, N. H.*
Saxton, Mary L. [L.], W. Randolph, Vt.; *Randolph, Vt.*
Seymour, Mary C. [S.], Norfolk, Ct., *Norfolk, Ct.*
Seymour, Mary F. [C.], W. Winsted, Ct.; *W. Winsted. Ct.*
Shank, Jessie L. [C.], Millington, Tenn.; *Millington, Tenn.*
Shearer, Elizabeth E. [C.], N. Y. City; 117 *E. 54th St., N. Y. City.*
Sheldon, Lena [S.], New Britain, Ct.; *Bassett St., New Britain, Ct.*
Sherman, Anna P. [S.], Jamaica Plain; 77 *Rockview St., Jamaica Plain.*
Small, Vivian B. [C.], Augusta, Me.; *Augusta, Me.*
Smith, Emily L. [L.], Worcester; 34 *Boynton St., Worcester.*
Smith, Eva F. [C], Huntington, N. Y.; *Huntington, N. Y.*
Smith, M. Helena [L.], E. Orange, N. J.; 246 *Dodd St., E. Orange, N. J.*
Smith, Laura E. [L.], Montpelier, Vt.; 20 *Bailey Ave., Montpelier, Vt.*
Smith, Nellie L. [C.], Palmer; *Palmer.*
Smith, Stella E. [L.], Wakefield; *Wakefield.*
Soule, Theresa H. [C.], S. Freeport, Me.; *S. Freeport, Me.*
Stebbins, Jessie W. [L.], Fishkill-on-Hudson, N. Y.; *Fishkill-on-Hudson, N. Y.*
Stevens, Carolyn C. [C.], Cincinnati, O.; *Station C, Cincinnati, O.*
Stevens, Louise D. [L.], Newington Junction, Ct.; *Newington Junction, Ct.*
Stevens, Mary A. [L.], Cincinnati, O.; *Station C, Cincinnati, O.*
Stickney, Julia H. [C.], Washington, D. C.; 607 *M St., N. W., Washington, D. C.*
Stodder, Elizabeth T. [C.], Hingham; *Hingham.*
Stone, Henrietta [C.], Kittanning, Pa.; *Kittanning, Pa.*
Stowe, Mary E. [C.], Scitico, Ct.; *Scitico, Ct.*
Stowell, Elizabeth D. [L.], Boston; 45 *Russell St., Charlestown.*
Strong, Carolyn A. [L.], E. Orange, N. J.; *E. Orange, N. J.*
Stubbs, Helen G., Foxcroft, Me.; *Foxcroft, Me.*
Sutphen, Minnie C. [C.], Palmyra, N. Y.; *Palmyra, N. Y.*
Swift, Nellie H. [L.], Middleborough; 28 *Oak St., Middleborough.*
Syvret, Clara M. [L.], Worcester; 48 *King St., Worcester.*
Taylor, Martha J. [L.], Westford; *Westford.*
Thomas, Lucinda C. [C.], Troy, O.; 328 *Grant St., Troy, O.*
Tiffany, Jessie W. [C.], S. Hadley; *S. Hadley.*
Tombes, Edyth H. [L.], Ashtabula, O.; *Ashtabula, O.*
Treadwell, Alice [L.], Danbury, Ct.; 50 *W. Wooster St., Danbury, Ct.*
Tucker, Emma C. [C.], Swansea Center; *Swansea.*
Turner, Abbie H. [C.], Nashua, N. H.; 4 *Crown St., Nashua, N. H.*
Usher, Maude P. [L.], Plainville, Ct.; *Plainville, Ct.*
Van Nostrand, Harriet L. [C.], Little Neck, N. Y.; *Little Neck, N. Y.*
Vickery, Myra F. [L.], Bangor, Me.; 100 *Center St., Bangor, Me.*
Voorhees, Grace M. [L.], Woodbridge, N. J.; *Woodbridge, N. J.*
Walker, Alice J. [C.]. Stafford Springs, Ct.; 14 *Grove St., Stafford Springs, Ct.*
Ward, Mary I. [C.], Newton Centre; *Homer St., Newton Centre.*
Warren, Harriet R. [L.], Lawrence; 12 *Winslow Place, Lawrence.*
Watson, Evelyn H. [L.], Woonsocket, R. I.; *Woonsocket, R. I.*
Watson, Lena L. [L.], Northwood Narrows, N. H.; *Northwood Narrows, N. H.*

Watson, Mabel A. [C.], Everett; 67 *A Hancock St., Everett.*
Watts, Faustina E. [S.], Haverhill ; 28 *Kent St., Haverhill.*
Wheldon, Elizabeth K. [L.], Williamstown; *Williamstown.*
White, Lucy M. [S.], Mansfield ; *Mansfield.*
Wiard, Bertha L. [L.], New Britain, Ct.; 150 *W. Main St., New Britain, Ct.*
Wiggin, Mary P. [L.], Auburn, Me. ; 90 *High St., Auburn, Me.*
Williams, Winifred M. [C.], N. Craftsbury, Vt. ; *N. Craftsbury, Vt.*
Wills, Rebekah B. [S.], Rancocas, N. J. ; *Rancocas, N. J.*
Wilson, Carolyn E. [L.], Haverhill ; 12 *Union St., Haverhill.*
Wilson, Mary F. [C.], Hollis, N. H. ; *Hollis. N. H.*
Wood, Edith H. [S.], E. Boston; 51 *Eutaw St., E. Boston.*
Woodbury, Mary H. [S.], Salem ; *Northey St., Salem.*
Woodward, Elizabeth W. [S.], Jamaica Plain ; 38 *Greenough Ave., Jamaica Plain.*
Worthley, Evelyn M. [C.], Brunswick, Me. ; *Brunswick, Me.*
Wright, Mary L. [C.], Plainville, Ct. ; *Main St., Plainville, Ct.*
Wyckoff, Harriet J. [C.], New Brunswick, N. J. ; *New Brunswick, N. J.*
Wyckoff, Julia [C.], Brooklyn, N. Y. ; 58 *Hanson Place, Brooklyn, N. Y.*

SPECIAL STUDENTS.

Baker, S. Marinda, Lancaster ; *Lancaster.*
Bird, Mabel E., Chicago, Ill. ; m. John A. Burnette, '95 ; *S. Hadley.*
Boardman, Elizabeth W., Sheffield ; *Sheffield.*
Chambers, Martha, Jacksonville, Ill. ; 839 *W. State St., Jacksonville, Ill.*
Clark, Grace L., Mount Vernon, N. Y. ; 102 *South St., Mt. Vernon, N. Y.*
Clauson, Jessie L., Rutland, Vt. ; *Rutland, Vt.*
Colegrove, Lottie M., Clinton, N. Y. ; *Clinton, N. Y.*
Davis, Isabella H., Windsor, Vt. ; *Windsor, Vt.*
Feustel, Mary E., S. Hadley Falls ; *S. Hadley Falls.*
Fitch, Mabel I., Kansas City, Mo. ; 589 *Forest Ave., Kansas City, Mo.*
Hall, Bessie M., Portsmouth, O. ; *Portsmouth, O.*
Harmon, Aurelia P., Warren, O. ; *Warren. O.*
Kellogg, Cora, Granby ; *Granby.*
Lawson, Susie M., Union, Ct. ; *Union, Ct.*
Lewis, Grace, Brockport, N. Y. ; *Brockport, N. Y.*
Mckeel, Gertrude, Yorktown Heights, N. Y. ; *Yorktown Heights, N. Y.*
Montgomery, May (Forbush), Gilman, Io. ; *Gilman, Io.*
Nichols, Edith, Aurora, Ill. ; 198 *Walnut St., Aurora, Ill.*
Noyes, Eva J., Haverhill ; 378 *Washington St., Haverhill.*
Ortman, A. Elizabeth, Sterling, N. J. ; *Sterling, N. J.*
Parks, Greta, Springfield ; 2 *Lincoln St., Springfield.*
Perrine, Elizabeth S., Upper Red Hook, N. Y. ; *Upper Red Hook, N. Y.*
Phipps, Harriet, New Castle, Pa. ; 133 *N. Jefferson St., New Castle, Pa.*
Pulsifer, Mary H., Auburn, Me. ; *Auburn, Me.*
Rankin, Mary H., Saybrook Point, Ct. ; *Saybrook Point, Ct.*
Richardson, Annie L., Cornish, Me. ; *Cornish, Me.*
Scudder, Isabelle, Asbury Park, N. J. ; *Asbury Park, N. J.*
Stearns, Harriet N., W. Lebanon, N. H. ; *W. Lebanon, N. H.*
Stoerlein, Mary, Spirit Lake, Io. ; *Spirit Lake, Io.*
Taylor, Jacobina W., Southbridge ; *Orchard St., Southbridge.*
Trask, Elizabeth, Springfield ; 495 *Chestnut St., Springfield.*

1895.

Verrill, Ina B., Alexandria, N. H. ; *Alexandria, N. H.*
Warden, Frances I.., Hanover, N. H. ; *Hanover, N. H.*
Winslow, Clara F., Amherst ; *Amherst.*
Woodside, Grace O., Brunswick, Me. ; *Brunswick, Me.*

1837-1895.

TEACHERS

WHO WERE NOT HOLYOKE STUDENTS.

MARY LYON, founder of the Seminary, and Principal '37-'49; d. Mt. Holyoke Seminary, March 5, '49.
Eunice Caldwell, Associate Principal, '37-'38 ; m. *Rev. J. P. Cowles, '38; *Ipswich.*
Mrs. Elizabeth S. Mead, M.A., President, '90— ; *Mount Holyoke College, S. Hadley.*

Balch, Florence E., '85-'92 ; m. E. C. Kinney, '93; *care Benjamin Balch, Topsfield.*
Belcher, Mary J., '55-'58 ; d. Del Monte, Cal., '92.
Belden, Emily N., M.D., '64-'68 ; m. *Albert Taylor, '69 ; m. J. W. McCabe, '74 ; d. De Funiak Springs, Fla., '86.
Bridges, Flora, B.A., '87-'92; *Mattoon, Ill.*
Callender, Emma H., M.D., '69-'73; d. Middlebury, Vt., '78.
Carpenter, Hettie P., B.A., '89-'90; m. Frank L. Morse, '91 ; 1543 *Fulton St., Chicago, Ill.*
Corwin, Rebecca, M.A., S.T.B., '94— ; *Mount Holyoke College, S. Hadley;* home address, 1280 *Willson Ave., Cleveland, O.*
Cotton, Mary H., M.D., '89-'90; *Portsmouth, O.*
Cowan, S. Kate, B.A., '89-'90; m. Hamilton L. James, '93; 1327 *Clayton Ave., Denver, Col.*
Curtis, Harriet M., '91-'92 ; *Vermontville, Mich.*
Dietz, Valerie, '73-'75 ; *care Miss F. L. Richey, Bay Ridge, King's Co., N. Y.*
Dixon, Alice E., B.A., '89-'91 ; 1507 *Walnut St., Philadelphia, Pa.*
Engelhardt, Anna E., '86-'91 ; d. Orange, N. J., '91.
Graham, Mary, Ph.B., '91-'92 ; *Middletown, Ct.*
Grinnell, Florence, '86-'87 ; *East Saginaw, Mich.*
Gylam, Marie, '85-'86 ; d. New York City, '88.
Hamilton, Harriet, '92-'93; *care Dr. Winslow, Ithaca, N. Y.*
Hartley, Mary E., '93— ; *Mount Holyoke College, S. Hadley ;* home address, *care G. G. Hartley, Duluth, Minn.*
Heron, Fannie G., M.D., '82-'85 ; m. William Guthrie, '89 ; 237 *W. George St., Glasgow, Scotland.*
Hills, Martha L., B.A., '93— ; *Mount Holyoke College, S. Hadley ;* home address, 64 *Church St., Middletown, Ct.*
Hodgman, Amanda A., '37-'39; m. —— Nourse, '52 ; d. Cincinnati, O., '54.
Homer, Mary, A. B., M.D., '60-'64 ; m. *Samuel D. Arnold, '64 ; 9 *Lincoln Flats, 6th St., Milwaukee, Wis.*
Ide, Emma A., '72-'73 ; m. Rev. John A. Cruzan ; *Santa Cruz, Cal.*
Kenney, C. Belle, B.S., '88-'89 ; 111 *Saratoga St., E. Boston.*
Knapp, Ella A., M.A., '90— ; *Mount Holyoke College, S. Hadley.*
MacVicar, Ada J., '78-'80 ; m. George N. Carmen, '83 ; *Morgan Park, Ill.*
Marchant, Julia E., M.D., '85-'86, '88-'89 ; *La Porte, Tex.*
Maupassant, Caroline de, '72-'73 ; m. —— Cripps ;

1837-1895.

McKeen, Catherine, '52–'56 ; d. Elm Grove, W. Va., '58.
McKeen, Phœbe F., '53–'56; d. on a journey from Baltimore to Boston, '80.
McMaster, Mary L., B.S., '91–'92; *Greenwich, N. Y.*
Miles, Caroline, Ph.D., '92–'93; m. William Hill, '95; *Chicago University, Chicago, Ill.*
Moore, Susan M., '87–'91 ; *Granville, O.*
Moore, Vida F., Ph.B., '93—; *Mount Holyoke College, S. Hadley;* home address, *Steuben, Me.*
Patteson, Sarah G., '89–'93 ; *Farmville, Va.*
Peabody, Elizabeth K., '66–'67 ; m. Rev. William Wilmer, '75 ; *Attica, Ind.*
Pike, Eva F., '81–'85 ; *Wesleyan Academy, Wilbraham.*
Richardson, Adelaide A., M.D., '78–'82 ; d. Mount Holyoke College, '85.
Sherman, Adelaide, '87–'88 ; *4 Crawford St., Roxbury.*
Sihler, Katherine E., '92— ; *Mount Holyoke College, S. Hadley;* home address, *McDonogh, Md.*
Slater, Elizabeth, M.A., '92— ; *Mount Holyoke College, S. Hadley.*
Smith, Mary W., '37–'38 ; m. R. A. Severance, M.D., '38; d. Saxton's River, Vt., '44.
Smith, Sophie A., '84–'86 ; m. Rev. Arthur W. Burt, '87 ; *Pomona, Cal.*
Sommer, Frau Marie E. W., '92–'93; *care Gustavus Sommer, 743 Broad St., Newark, N. J.*
Southmayd, Lucy M., M.D., '68–'70 ; m. Lucius Garvin, M.D.; *Lonsdale, R. I.*
Spore, Nellie A., '94— ; *Mount Holyoke College, S. Hadley;* home address, *Florence, O.*
Steele, Charlotte M., '75–'86 ; *59 N. Main St., Oberlin, O.*
Sterns, Marion H., '90–'94 ; *23 Main St., Springfield.*
Vitzthum von Eckstadt, Margarethe, '75–'85 ; '87——; *Mount Holyoke College, S. Hadley.*
Wellman, Aurilla P., '48–'51 ; m. Alfred F. Hitchcock, M.D., '51; d. Fitchburg, '62.
Wilder, Eliza, '62–'66 ; m. Rev. Henry M. Holmes, '67 ; *care Daniel Davis, Phillipsburg, N.J.*
Woodward, Katherine S., B.A., '89–'90; *138 Montague St., Brooklyn, N. Y.*
Worden, Sara A., '83— ; *Mount Holyoke College, S. Hadley;* home address, *Xenia, O.*

1837-1895.

SUPERINTENDENTS DOMESTIC DEPARTMENT

WHO WERE NOT HOLYOKE STUDENTS.

Bridge, Emily, '41–'45; m. John Smith, Esq., '47 ; d. Boscawen, N. H., '87.
Carroll, Mrs. Mary K., '59–'65, '68–'73 ; d. Lowell, '87.
Dutton, Mrs. Harriet G., '74–'82 ; m. Chas. Dutton, '82 ; *Holland, Mich.*
Greene, Mrs. Clara E., '93–'94 ; *Barre.*
Lane, Clara E., '87–'91 ; m. Eugene E. Whitaker, M.D., '91 ; *Newport, Vt.*
Purnell, Mrs. E. L., '92— ; *Mount Holyoke College, S. Hadley;* home address, *Gardiner, Me.*
Wright, Mrs. R. L., '82–'92 ; *Newport, Vt.*

INDEX OF MARRIED NAMES.

Names of graduates are indicated by the letter *g* prefixed.

		Page
Abbe, Frank H.	*g* Helen L. Strickland,	151
R. Ensign	Sarah A. Converse,	87
Abbot, Abiel	Alice M. Baleh,	93
Abbott, Benj. V., Esq.	*g* Elizabeth Titcomb,	48
Charles, M.D.	Harriet N. Chick,	43
John E.	Mary Frances Hosmer,	94
Abercrombie, Robert	*g* Mathilde Ulrich,	137
Abernethy, John	Susan T. Bull,	20
Abrahams, Jas. L.	Annie R. Ely,	97
Adams, Andrew H.	Mary J. Bigelow,	62
Asa	Clara (Dana) Hutchings,	79
Edson	Hannah J. Jayne,	53
Eugene	Harriet R. Clark,	121
Rev. Ezra	{ Abigail Bigelow,	16
	{ *g* Alice M. Ware,	76
George C.	M. Elizabeth Field,	152
Isaac	Emeline A. Wheeler,	44
John S.	*g* Harriet A. Marr,	103
Lemuel C.	Isabella S. Nash,	98
Levi	Clara Dwight,	18
Rev. Lucien H.	*g* Nancy D. Francis,	92
Dr. M. R.	*g* Loula Rhyne,	161
Rev. S. H.	*g* Adelaide Greenhill,	86
Seymour F., Esq.	*g* Eliza D. Spooner,	103
Agnew, William C.	*g* Mary E. McNaughton,	114
Aiken, David, Esq.	Mary E. Adams,	29
Akerman, A. T., Esq.	Martha R. Galloway,	81
Aland, Samuel	Emma Scott,	71
Albee, Ellis	Sarah J. Southwick,	50
Sumner, Esq.	*g* Lucy A. Rankin,	39
Alden, Edward M.	{ Fannie E. Mosman,	98
	{ Ida A. Smith,	127
Alder, John W.	Eunice M. Pease,	119
Aldrich, Elliot J.	*g* Ellen L. Moody,	109
O. D.	Mary E. Morse,	110
Alexander, Arthur C.	*g* Mary E. Hillebrand,	161
Rev. DeWitt	Abigail O. Baldwin,	62
Isaac P.	Hannah Hinds,	30
Algier, Rev. R. F.	Blanch Perkins,	130
Allchin, Rev. Geo.	Nellie M. Stratton,	141
Allen, Albert F.	M. E. Strickland,	82
Alfred P.	Emma J. Miller,	81
C. Emir	Corinne E. Tuckerman,	127
Chas. S.	*g* E. S. Goldthwait,	128
Christopher C.	Mary A. (Francis) Edwards,	46
Daniel	Phebe McMillen,	53

		Page
Allen, David	*g* Mary J. Hills,	75
E. Augustus	Ellen L. Clapp,	129
E. Olcott.	Clarissa M. Chapin,	56
Rev. Edward	Louisa T. Richardson,	17
Rev. Edward P.	Celia J. Gates,	135
Elijah	Lovisa Clark,	18
Frank B.	Julia E. Kibbe,	152
Frederick E.	Eveline J. Mosely,	119
George W.	Jane W. Savage,	35
Henry	Harriet Wright,	17
Rev. Horace H.	*g* Frances A. Fitch,	95
Isaac	Harriet L. Spaulding,	127
Norman F.	*g* Caroline W. Olmstead,	151
Rev. Orson P.	Caroline R. Wheeler,	67
Quintus	Martha A. Smead,	17
Samuel	Caroline C. Sanford,	44
Samuel J., Jr.	Sarah A. Allen,	103
Walter B.	Emma E. Kimball,	124
William L.	Mary E. Jackson	124
Zenas	Charlotte M. (Clark) Sanders,	20
Alling, Lewis H.	Sarah A. Sibley,	19
Allison, Chas. R.	Annie M. Jewett,	157
Henry,	Mary M. Dickinson,	97
Allyn, Chas. B.	*g* Stella C. Brown,	139
Samuel B.	Catharine Merrell,	53
Almy, John C.	Mary S. Wheeler,	57
Alsop, Thomas J.	*g* Frances E. Smith,	106
Alvord, Elisha B.	Sarah E. Hawks,	67
Amberg, Isaac L.	Helen M. Ormsby,	150
Ambler, Wm. M.	Tamson J. Finch,	34
Ames, Gustavus	Lucy R. Byington,	52
Jonathan	Maria E. Hadley,	70
Lorin, J., M. D.	Margarette Waldo,	35
Silas, M.D.	*g* Mary H. Humphrey,	26
Amesbury, Capt. Stanley	*g* Frances Brastow,	164
Anderson, Alexander D.	Antoinette Dunning,	83
Arthur C.	*g* Charlotte E. Ferris,	148
Charles H.	Hannah L. Shaw,	11
Henry, Esq.	*g* Sarah A. Gilbert,	15
John W.	*g* Emily J. Gibson,	141
Andrew, B. P., M.D.	Jane M. Davidson,	137
Andrews, Rev. C. B.	Samantha W. Gilson,	43
Charles,	Mary M. Elliott,	27
Andrus, Rev. A. N.	*g* Olive L. Parmelee,	86
Andruss, Geo. H.	Susan T. Frost,	110
Anning, ——	Elizabeth D. Fisher,	22
Anthony, Richard M.	Lucy W. Horton,	107

INDEX.

		Page			Page
Arey, Arthur B.	g Josephine M. Page,	123	Badgley, Peter W.	Henrietta F. Dutcher,33	
Arline, David W.	Helen E. Smith,	98	Bagg, Ernest N.	Amy U. Wood,	153
Armour, James	g Emily W. S. Bowdoin,	45	Bail, George W.	Elizabeth K. Butts,	66
Arms, Charles H.	Aurora B. Clark,	97	Bailey, Rev. A.	Annie C. Peabody,	140
George W.	Abby T. Newton,	23	Henry M.	Mary L. Davis,	154
Armsby, Amos	g Alice M. Davis,	131	Rev. J. A.	Jane Ayrault,	52
Lauren,	Eliza L. Hale,	27	James O.	M. Lizzie Bowers,	115
Armstrong, Charles D.	Gertrude V. Ludden,140		Rev. John G.	Mary E. Bean,	73
David	Eveline Stewart,	74	Joseph M., Jr.	Carolyn C. Tanner,	155
J. F.	Emily Sanford,	44	Mark	Lucy B. Ward,	44
William	Mary S. Lyon,	63	Rev. N. P.	Mary L. Comstock,	43
Arnold, Fred K.	Mary N. Tower,	101	Stephen G., M.D.	Ella P. Pray,	113
George G.	g Anna M. L. Masters,	48	William C., M.D.	Julia M. Utley,	75
Joseph A.	Abbie P. Davis,	69	William L.	Lydia C. Probasco.	141
M. N.	Martha Ford,	93	Baker, Clifton P.	Jane M. Wakefield,	119
Oliver	Elizabeth Briggs,	80	Edwin H.	Carrie V. Richardson,116	
R. B.	g Clara P. Clark,	141	Freeman	Hattie E. Cole,	140
Samuel D.	Mary A. B. Homer,		Henry E.	Emily P. Colman,	20
	M. D.,	185	Rev. J. F.	Frances L. Pratt,	57
Wm. N.	Juliette Kies,	157	L. H., M.D.	Martha C. Wing,	21
Ashenden, Richard E.	Ann Eliza Bigelow,	87	Wm. L.	g Sarah E. Wiswall,	161
Ashton, Evan D.	Philomela A. Loomis,	47	Baldwin, Charles C.	g Ella L. T. Peckham,	106
Atkinson, Abial D.	Seraph A. Hall,	66	D. Dwight	Lois G. Morris.	63
Attwood, Frederick	Mary L. Battelle,	103	Joseph B.	Ella M. Adams.	115
Atwater, Rev. Edw. E.	g Rebecca H. Dana,	29	Rev. Joseph B.	Rosina P. Whitman,	50
Rev. Jason	Susan E. (Arms)		Rev. P. C.	Jane C. Starkweather,23	
	Wright,	18	Thomas S.	Jane M. Baldwin.	52
Wm. C.	g Ida W. Hay,	148	William C.	Charlotte M. Smith,	44
Atwell, Edwin	g Marion I. Gaylord,	139	Ball, Rev. Albert H.	g Helen M. Savage,	109
Atwood, Henry P.	Mary M. Wilson,	136	Eliel S.	Ella F. Sawin,	124
Hiram	Clarissa Cargill,	59		Amelia C. Dickinson,	
John W.	Abby Deane,	22	Julius R.	name changed to	
John W.	g Harriet S. (Clark)			Amelia D. Arnold,	118
	Robbins,	82	Ballantine, W.O.,M.D.	g Alice C. Parsons,	123
Aumock, Wm. S.	g M. Antoinette Baker,	51	Ballard, Charles H.	Dora L. F. Upton.	108
Austin, Geo. E.	Ellen M. Preston,	140	John T.	Frances H. Noble,	74
Horace	Harriet A. Hall,	25	Joshua	Nancy Eames	70
L. B.	g Abbie S. Stearns,	58	Bancker, Enoch, Esq.	g Lucy W. Clark,	79
Averill, Rev. James	Sylvira A. Carpenter,	43	Bancroft, Jesse P., M.D.	Elizabeth Spear,	23
Avery, Alexander H.	g Sarah H. Osgood,	32	William G.	Ruth Washburn,	44
Allyn A.	g H. Louisa Billings,	95	Bangs, Edward D.	g Amelia F. Dickinson, 29	
Eleazer J.	E. Maria Allen,	69	Barber, Rev. A. D.	Martha A. Barnes,	39
Frank R.	Lillie Campbell,	126	Daniel J.	Julia F. Brownell,	80
John D.	Mary A. Rice,	141	James F.	Mary C. Pettibone,	138
John G.	Mary E. Buck,	37	Rev. L. H.	Lucinda Taylor,	23
Oscar F.	P. Augusta Ely,	16	Barbour, Chauncy	Jennett L. Graves,	46
Axtell, Benjamin P.	Anna L. Church,	77	Henry W.	g Harriet W. Youngs,	90
Ayer, Rev. Chas. L.	Mary Bishop,	43	Nelson	Ruth C. Dunklee,	33
Edwin	Caroline E. Youngs,	35	Barclay, Rev. Thomas D.Mary R. White,		105
Ayers, David C.	Julia Kellogg,	63	Bardwell, Horatio N.	Clara A. Williams.	28
Ayres, E. F.	Harriet L. Ewart,	84	Baremore, Geo. D.	Isabella H. Woodruff.114	
Irvin	g Annie L. Poor,	103	Barnard, Chas. H.	Mary A. Hollister,	173
Norman T.	Caroline E. Baxter,	80	Clinton E.	Fannie M. Peck,	104
Babbitt, William D.	Elizabeth Holt,	37	J. M.	g Myra E. Bates,	105
Babcock, Rev. C. H.	Emily G. Mead,	84	Rev. Joshua	Semantha M. Ames,	36
Babson, David C.	g Caroline L. Wheeler,	131	Rev. Pliny F.	Julia Hobart,	23
Bachelder, Rev. O. R.	Sarah P. Merrill,	34	Robert A.	Annette E. Farnham,107	
Backus, William	Emma Carrier,	121	Barnes, Burritt B.	Harriett P. Cooke,	46
Bacon, ———	May S. Ashby,	154	Rev. E. S.	Sarah B. Miner.	21
Allen H.	g M. Louise Bissell,	120	Fred B.	S. Rosa Dunham,	132
Jonathan	g Ellen Hunt,	61	Henry H.	g H. Jane Emery,	64
Rev. Samuel F.	Lucy Barlow,	36	Irving F., M. D.	Sara Whiting.	171

MARRIED NAMES.

		Page
Barnes, Julius	g Catharine B. Clark,	75
Winslow B.	g Emily P. Sweetser,	42
Barney, S. Rolla	Mary M. Allen,	65
Barrell, Rev. Almond C.	Selena L. Johnson,	27
Barrett, Rev. Frank F.	Edith H. Millard,	106
Hayward	Esther M. Tidd,	108
Barrows, A. T.	Mary E. Goodsell,	56
Freeman, Esq.	Asenath C. Vaill,	21
Thomas	Sarah E. Colt,	24
Thomas	g Sarah W. Coffin,	108
Barrus, Edward T.	Mary L. Graves,	157
George W.	C.B.(Anderson) Price,	52
Barry, William I.	g Lizzie A. Bartlett,	143
Bartholomew,Rev.A.R.	Maria S. Karch,	121
Bartlett, Charles,	Cecelia Clizbe,	24
D. W.	g Julia M. Painter,	55
George W., Esq.	g Frances (Gregg) Smith,	48
Harvey	g Lucretia A. Greene,	72
Rev. Lyman	g Cornelia C. Barrows,	68
Moses	g Mary M. Foster,	68
Richard	Eliza J. Woodin,	60
Rush	Cora J. Burgess,	140
W. C.	Helen W. Shattuck,	127
Barton, Rev. Alanson S.	Mary E. Barrows,	73
Rev. Walter	Martha M. Smith,	71
Bascom, Chester A.	Minerva S.Martindale,	40
John	Abbey A. Burt,	33
Bass, James	Rebecca W. Mason,	60
Perkins, Esq.	Maria L. Patrick,	47
Bassett, William	Abbie M. Parker,	122
Bassian, John, M.D.	g Mary M. Wadsworth, M.D.,	86
Basten, Rev. Wm. F.	Elizabeth M. Crosby,	107
Batcheller, John L.	g Rachel Slocum,	72
John Q.	g Melissa Peabody,	29
Samuel	Susan P. Taplin,	50
Batcheller, Holland N.	Eliza R. Everett,	66
Bates, John E.	Mary E. Bennett,	121
Rev. William	g Diantha C. Lee,	32
Batten, Andrew J.	Janett Lillie,	19
Bausum, Wm. H.	Fannie A. Lord,	145
Baxter, John	Eleanor Nickerson,	31
Bayley, James H.	Priscilla B. Shaw,	94
Baylies, Ripley	Fanny H. Seward,	44
Beach, Rev. Edwin R.	J. A. Lucie Robinson,	44
Rev. J. W.	Maria Talcott,	75
James C.	Mary C. Butler,	40
Thomas B.	Helen M. Grover,	53
Beadle, Rev. E. R.	g Martha R. Yale,	42
Joseph B.	g Laura A. Higgins,	42
Beal, Henry L.	Caroline Torrey,	63
Beals, Bradford	Marcia M. Fales,	84
Isaac N.	Caroline R. Burgess,	55
Beaman, A. T.	Luella A. Otis,	110
Harry C.	Jennie H. Bartlett,	149
Rev. Herbert H.	g Mary A. Wilson,	90
William	Mary S. Kellogg,	107
Bean, Alphonso F.	Lucretia A. Bean,	62
Bradner F.	MargaretE.Chisholm,	110
Bearden, Marcus D.	Laura S. Catlin,	27
Beauchamp, L. Wesley	Grace A. Broughton,	135

		Page
Beaumont, Rev. J. B.	Harriet N. Morris,	74
Bebb, M. S.	g Anna E. Carpenter,	79
Beckler, Chas. H.	Helen A. Wilder,	114
Beckwith, Rev. E. G.	g CarolineP.Armstrong,	51
George E.	g Harriet W. Goodale,	65
Beebe, Albert S.	g Mary J. Pease,	76
Beecher, Herbert W.	g H. Josephine Carrington,	108
Rev. James C.	g Frances B. Johnson,	51
Beeman, Edwin R.	g Mary E. Ackley,	41
Beitner, George B.	Flora L. Shively,	144, 145
Belcher, Fred E.	Georgiana E. Shattuck,	116
Isaac S., Esq.	g Adeline N. Johnson,	76
Belding, Frank	Emma A. Shaylor,	133
Bell, Charles, M.D.	Elizabeth F.Emerson,	62
Clarence H.	g Sarah E. Denniston,	85
Cyrus, M.D.	Emma Chamberlain,	18
Fernando T.	M. Addie Fuller,	140
Jonathan C.	Eliza C. Harrington,	19
Robert, M.D.	g Florence M. White,	120
Rev. Robert C.	Harriette B. Stowe,	127
Samuel R.	g Sarah A. Wilder,	96
Bellman, James C.	Laura B. Hamlen,	53
Bellows, John	Helen E. Stiles,	91
Bemis, Edward	Ellen A. Putnam,	63
Fred Arnold	Elizabeth (Granger) Sedgwick,	129
Herbert W.	Bertha Gilbert,	102
Benfield, Marcus	Mary H. Thurston) Heydon,	60
Benjamin, C. Halsey	Glorianna Fanning,	27
Benner, Rev. Edward A.	Mary S. Carter,	118
Frank T., Esq.	g Mary J. Harris,	120
Bennet, James	Alice L. Stiles,	104
Bennett, A. B.	Susan P. Wilkes,	119
A. Pierce	Etta C. Danforth,	69
Charles E.	Kate L. Carpenter,	124
Edwin	Julia E. Childs,	87
Henry S.	g Anna M. Cahill,	120
John A., Esq.	g Julia R. Smith,	126
John M.	Jerusha Morris,	119
Benson, Rev. Almon	Rhoda A. Roys,	26
Bentley, Edward M.	g Mary H. Merrill,	125
Edwin E.	Susan N. Shepard,	113
S. N., M.D.	Jennie M. Ellis,	149
Benton, James B.	Harriet W. Bardwell,	27
Berriam, George W.	Adaline M. (Pratt) Mason,	110
Berry, Frederick M.	Ellen R. Goodwin,	132
Rev. Loren F.	g Sarah L. Coy,	111
Betts, Edgar K.	g Harriet L. Gardner,	102
James G.	Louisa P. Sill,	71
Beveridge, Rev. A. M.	g Sarah Loomis,	32
Beyer, W. F., Esq.	Ila Warfel,	127
Bickham, Daniel D.	Anna R. Stout,	155
Bicknell, Richmond	Sarah E. Redington,	85
Biddle, J. C., M.D.	Agnes M. Buckingham,	140
Bidwell, Orlando B.	g MargaretJ.Townsend,	83
Bigelow, H. D. P., Esq.	Lydia P. Chase,	33
Lewis A.	Mary J. Whitehill,	148

		Page			Page
Bill, Arthur G.	Lillian E. Chase,	140	Blunt, Ambrose	g Elizabeth J. Lee,	82
Nathan D.	Ruth E. Wight,	153	William E., Esq.	g Harriet M.Harriman,102	
Billings, Rev. Chas. S.	g Martha E. Smith,	103	Blyth, J. Sumner	Frances G. Reed,	85
Edward C., Esq.	Emily (Sanford) Armstrong,	44	Boardman, H. E., M.D.	Susan C. Locke,	88
O. M.	g Harriet G. Richardson,	134	Bodfish, Sumner H.	g Julia T. Parsons,	100
			Bodman, Luther	Philena N. Hawkes,	17
Billman, Rev. Ira C.	g Ida B. Kelsey,	139	Bodwell, Edward S.	Ada M. Porter,	122
Bills, G. M. W.	g Ida E. Semans,	154	Boggs, Rev. Geo. W.	Martha Mobley,	34
Bingay, Jacob	Anna Lovett,	94	Bogigian, W. H.	g H. Josephine Carrington,	108
Bingham, Rinaldo M.	Mary M. Robinson,	54	Boies, Henry L.	Harriet S. Holmes,	40
Thomas A.	Marion P. Harwood,	40	Orion H.	Abby H. Thompson,	133
Bird, Rev. C. Willard,	g Jane E. Reed,	131	Patrick H.	Lucy A. Root,	26
James	Eliza Goodell,	37	Bolton, ———	Sallie Spilman,	136
Birge, David W., M.D.	Hannah D. Eastman	66	Rev. Robert	g Josephine Woodhull,	52
Sidney	Harriet Loomis,	37	Boltwood, Edmund	Kate W. Powers,	101
Biscoe, Thomas D.	g Laura A. W. Capron,	75	Bond, Chas. H.	Lucia W. Browne,	24
Bishop, Rev. Albert C.	Julia A. Howard,	84	Rufus F.	g H. Annette Eno,	108
Charles, Esq.	g M. Theresa Collins,	48	Bonham, Rev. John C.	g Olive E. Harrington,	61
E. P.	g Martha M. Bingham,	58	Bonney, Eben S.	Eleanor W. Sears,	91
Kirke D.	Lila D. Everson,	142	Rev. Nath'l G.	g Sarah Ingham,	82
Thomas	Emeline H. Dickinson,	33	Booth, Sherman	g Margaret Tufts,	20
			Sidney	Anna S. Lytle,	60
Bissell, Charles S.	Maria E. Pomeroy,	63	Watson C.	Julia Buckingham,	69
Edwin C.	Emily Pomeroy,	71	Boswell, Charles	g Flora P. (McIntyre) Stearns,	32
Lewis	Caroline Dickinson,	24			
William E.	Angeline T. Seaver,	35	Bosworth, H. W., Esq.	g Mary E. Hall,	92
Bissland, John K.	g Nettie L. Lord,	167	Rev. Nathan	Elizabeth B. Bodman,	33
Bixby, Llewellyn	Mary Hathaway,	116	Bourdon, D. B. O.	g Mary C. Tuttle,	117
Black, George M.	g Abbie J. Butler,	122	Bourn, Allan	g Annie V. Church,	95
J. F.	g Annie E. Sawyer,	109	Bourne, William A.	Rebecca J. Poor,	104
Blackmar, Orrin	Harriet C. Hurd,	34	Bonton, N. S.	g Emily L. Bissell,	48
Blackwell, H. B.	Lucy Stone,	19	Bowdoin, Henry A.	Marion G. Waters,	78
Thomas	Sophie S. Blackwell,	52	Bowen, Rev. Marcellus	Flora P. Stearns,	113
Blaisdell,Rev.James A.	g Florence L. Carrier,	171	Ozias	Eliza M. McIntyre,	28
Rev. J. J.	g Susan A. Allen,	38	Bower, John A.	Ellen F. Foster,	97
Blake, Francis C.	g Winifred P. Ballard,	154	Bowker, Charles W.	Susan B. Upham,	102
Harry W.	g Carrie E. Morse,	142	Bowler, Noadiah P.	Sarah C. (H.) Lyman,	25
Blakely, Rev. Quincy,	g Gertrude Sykes,	58	Bowles, Ralph H., Jr.	Laura J. Hill,	142
Blakeslee, Chas. L.	Julia A. Millar,	94	Bowman, B. B.	Samantha (Gilson) Andrews,	43
Blanchard,Rev.Addison.	LucyM.Southworth,	71			
S. W., M.D.	Clara B. Thurston,	44	Henry H.	g Gertrude M. Ellis,	123
William	Sarah Blaisdell,	55	James	Cornelia E. Wheeler,	57
Blaney, Wm. O.	Luella E. Huston,	81	Boxley, William S.	g Laura Graham,	41
den Bleyker, John	H. Amna Balch.	83	Boyd, John	Charlotte M. Cutler,	56
Bliss, Calvin C.	Caroline T. Eastman,	43	Oscar E.	Mary E. French,	84
Rev. Daniel J.	g Seraph A. Bemis,	85	Boyden, Francis W.	Anna B. Newhall,	162
Edwin	Mary A. Seymour,	51	Walter L.	Mary S. Mayher,	166
George	Mary B. Patrick,	44	Boynton, Benjamin	Sarah B. Richards,	21
George N., Esq.	Frances A. Carpenter,107		Charles S.	Helen M. Dickinson,	90
George R.	g Anna E. Stoughton,	106	Rev. Francis H.	g Emily A. Clark,	99
Henry I.	Harriet H. Partridge,	67	Henry, M. D.	g Sarah W. Cushing,	41
Henry P.	{ Hannah L. Warren,	28	Brackett, F. A.	Sarah Gardner,	56
	{ g Delia M. Warren,	29	Bradbury, Edward E.	Jane S. Sykes,	71
Rev. Isaac G.	Eunice B. Day,	40	William F.	g Margaret W. Jones,	68
Zenas W.	g Sophia M. Hayward,	89	Braddock, Rev. Wm. Paxton,	Ellie V. Hallock,	154
Blodgett, Giles	Emily M. Gilbert,	94			
Isaac N., Esq.	g Sarah A. Gerould,	79	Bradford, John	Henrietta F.(Dutcher) Badgley,	33
Timothy	Jane H. Coolidge,	69			
Wm. H. H.	Lucy M. Merrill,	91	Bradish, John Q.	S. Jane Mather,	77
Wm. Henry	Martha Lane,	77	Bradlee, N. J.	Anna M. Vose,	67
Blood, John R.	Margaret S. Van Wie,153		Bradley, Rev. Chas. F.	Elizabeth P. Bassett,	62

MARRIED NAMES.

		Page
Bradley, Dwight B.	Anna E. Davis,	124
Bragaw, Abraham	Anna Morgan,	54
Bragdon, C. J.	*g* Minnie F. Bailey,	125
Bragg, Rev. J. K.	H. Maria Buttrick,	24
Brainerd, E. P.	*g* Augusta L. Jones,	79
John A.	Ellen J. Ventres,	71
Braisted, J., Jr.	Emma A. Raymond,	38
Brandegee, Augustus	Nancy C. Bosworth,	55
Brastow, Rev. T. E.	*g* Sarah L. Carleton,	95
Bray, David C.	Mary J.(Fowler)Noyes,92	
Rev. William L.	*g* Emily A. Temple,	73
Breck, Aaron	Elizabeth Starkweather,	54
Breese,Rev.Augustine	*g*Marion E. Munsell,	86
Bremner, Rev. David	*g* Sarah E. Kimball,	58
Brewer, Fisk P.	Julia M. Richards,	57
George J.	Harriet H. Russell,	101
Henry C.	Clara D. George,	154
O. Perry	Delia A. Vann,	64
Brewster, Chas. C.	Anna J. Beckley,	128
Edward P.	Frances H. Crawford,	80
John M., M. D.	*g* Catharine A. Wright,	24
Briceland, J. M., M. D.	E. F.(Crawford)Dosh,	59
Bridgman, Edwin B.	Mary S. Bridgman,	126
Elisha,	Eliza P. Moody,	25
Frank A.	Eliza A. Rust,	63
Rev Henry M.	*g* Laura B. Nichols,	68
Isaac,	*g* Mary E. Gleason,	58
Thomas S.	*g* Mary P. Bronson,	75
Briggs, J. L.	*g* Adah Goss,	143
Brigham, Marshall W.	Ella King,	147
Brinsmade, Frank D.	Julia A. Pardee,	81
Brimm, Willard W.	Lillian G. Munson,	136
Bristow, Henry J.	Marion S. Smith,	162
Brittin, Alfred B.	Emma Dougherty,	37
Brock, John W.	Maria A. Parshley,	78
Bronson, Rev. E. H.	M. Virginia Bilderback,	142
Eliot B.	*g* Emily F. Pettibone,	154
George	Augusta L. Wright,	60
Roscoe H.	Gabriella Swain,	136
Roswell, M. D.	Agnes M. Butler,	49
Brooks, Rev. Charles	*g* Nancy L. Adams,	68
D. Brainerd	Helen E. Driver,	40
Franklin E.	Sarah B. Coolidge,	144
Rev. Geo. W.	L. Carolyn Eastman,	135
Lawton S., M. D.	Annie Laurie,	129
S. T., M. D.	*g* Lucy C. Mills,	54
Sydenham	*g* Eliza J. Nichols,	42
William F.	Ellen J. Fenn,	97
Browe, James	Ruth C. Dill,	73
Brown, Rev Allen H.	*g* Martha A. Dodge,	45
Bartholomew,	Anne E. Robbins,	28
Prof. Chas. S.	Clara G. Foskett,	147
Edwin P.	Jane Y. Phillips,	60
Ezra R.	Ann E. Rogers,	44
F. Edgar	Addie L. Dodge,	165
George A., M. D.	Susan E. Barnum,	146
George L.	*g* Mary M. Brinsmade,	36
J. Fred	Mary J. Warner,	148
J. Randolph	*g* Mary S. Hosmer,	134
James F., M. D.	*g* Abbie Scribner,	93

		Page
Brown, Jarvis B.	Georgiana E. Herbert,	140
Jerry C.	M. Ella Bean,	131
John E.	*g* A. Eugenia Fowler,	51
John P., M. D.	Caroline A. Stevens,	67
Julius W.	*g* M. Ella Spooner,	120
Lucius, Esq.	Hannah M. Larrabee,	135
Morris, D., Esq.	*g* Minerva E. Packer,	89
Plumb	*g* Olive E. Crissy,	82
Plumb, M. D.	Rebecca A. Bassett,	170
R. B., M. D.	*g* Alice Howard,	79
Silas B.	*g* Elizabeth Evans,	136
Sherman E.	Florence I. Barber,	109
Stephen O.	Mary P. Gurney,	110
Theodore	Sarah A. Knowlton,	31
William A.	Sarah E. Clarke,	163
Y. H.	Helen A. Magill,	127
Browne, E. L., Esq.	Mary A. Parish,	57
Edward E.,LL.D.	Rose C. Cleveland,	173
Henry S.	Louise C. Norton,	57
Rev. John K.	Leila Kendall,	132
Browning, Thomas H.	*g* Anna M. Johnson,	106
Brownson, H. W.	Cora I. Brown,	126
Bruce, Norman H.	Marilla Barnes,	69
Bruner, Henry L.	*g* Carrie L. Aunock,	150
Bryan, B. S.	*g* Emily Hedden,	51
Bryant, Chas. M.	Ella C. Beach,	139
Nathaniel	*g* Amanda Weeks,	86
Rev. Sidney	Harriet W. Lord,	22
Buck, Rev. George	Josephine L. Hitchcock,	60
Truman	*g* Mary J. Eager,	
Buckingham, C. Lester	Edith S. Jones,	145
C. P.	*g* Marion A. Hawks,	23
Theodore	Phebe A. Ranney,	101
Buell, Charles E.	Annie F. Cooper,	132
Buffum, Charles A.	Martha P. Cutting,	144
George T.	*g* Ethie E. Brown,	120
S. W.	Mary E. Tower,	19
Bulfinch, Geo. G., M. D.	Elizabeth Dearborn,	112
Bullock, Chas. S.	*g* Harriet M. Bullard,	105
Dyer D	Ariadne L. Kimball,	47
Bump, Cyrus A.	Georgia Thomas,	133
Bunker, Chas. A.	*g* Ellen S. Blake,	102
F. R.	Anna Noyes,	81
Bunyan, Thomas C.	Ella M. Hallowell,	118
Burbank, S. D.	Harriet S. Bliss,	55
Burch, William,	Elizabeth Norwood,	94
Burdick, Archibald W.	Grace M. Ottman,	166
Burdon, Oren T.	Louisa W. Ripley,	122
Burgess, Rev. Eben.	*g* Abigail Moore,	16
Ebenezer G.,M.D.	Ellen D. Holman,	40
Frederick A.	Abby M. Bosworth,	16
Warren J.,M.D.	*g* Mary E. Chamberlain,	48
Burgher, B. M.	Jessie Williams,	141
Burkhalter, Rev. E. R.	L. Anna Denise,	97
Burling, J. D., M. D.	Annie S. James,	97
Burnell, Rev. Thos. S.	Martha Sawyer,	19
Burnet, Henry	Sophronia H. Topping,19	
Burnett, Halstead	Margaret E. Stearns,	127
Burnette, Jonathan	Eliza Judd,	17
John A.	Mabel E. Bird,	184

INDEX.

Name		Page
Burnette, Martin W.	Lavinia Smith,	17
Burnham, Chas. A.	Mary F. Burt,	100
E. D.	Mellie W. Barton,	169
J. L.	*g* Georgiana (Haley) Sparks,	72
Rev. Michael	*g* Cassandra V. Washburn,	112
Burnside, Rev. Howard	Ardelia A. Spencer,	31
Burpee, Edgar A.	Annie E. Farwell,	84
Burr, Rev. Almon W.	Abbie E. Grant,	100
Isaac P., Jr.	Ellen Fritcher,	110
Remus D.	Sabra M. S. Wells,	95
Willard R.	Mira B. Lawrence,	107
William H.	*g* Eliza M. Huntington,	128
Burrage, Thomas F.	Harriet L. Battis,	92
Burrell Isaac	Emma S. Miller,	50
John	*g* Bessie F. Wright,	167
Burrington,Rev.Lindley M.	Eliza A Berry,	59
W. H.	Elizabeth W. Ballard,	80
Burroughs, Wm.	Catharine E. Lampman,	101
Burt, Rev. Arthur W.	Sophie A. Smith,	186
William H.	Amanda F. Winchell,	21
Burton, Charles S.	Phebe Millard,	124
Elam B.	Hortensia M. Thomas,	54
J. S., M. D.	Ella A. Berry,	109
S. S., Esq.	*g* Mary A. Munson,	42
Bushell, Rev. Walter	Carrie C. Hoover,	135
Bushnell, Charles C.	Jane A. Denison,	83
Rev. E.	*g* Cornelia K. Woodruff,	65
Buswell, Caleb C.	Doll H. Blaisdell,	112
Butler, Rev. Edward P.	Lucretia C. Nelson,	119
Isaac	Eliza A.(Green) Page,	46
Milton H.	Elizabeth H. S. Kilbourne,	113
Butterfield, Charles	Sarah W. Richardson,	19
Reuben J.	Susan A. Fletcher,	46
Butts, Elias P.	Mary Ann Gillett,	16
Buxton, H. L.	Nellie H. Barnes,	135
Byington, F. M., M. D.	Harriet B. (Worden) King,	95
Rev.Theodore L.	*g* Margaret E. Hallock,	72
Cady, Rev.Chauncey M.	Virginia A. Clarkson,	121
Frederick W.	Jessie Shedd,	166
Geo. M., M.D.	H. Fronia Harris,	152
Cahoon, Chas. S., M. D.	Charlotte Chase,	52
Caldwell, Eben	Octavia G. Hallett,	56
Calhoun, George W.	Evelyn A. Giles,	66
Camp, Caleb J.	Sarah M. Boyd,	87
James M.	Susan F. (Marsh) Kellogg,	47
Samuel K.	Sarah W. Kellogg,	34
Campbell, Rev. A. B.	*g* Ann M. Hollister,	32
Cassius S.	*g* Lydia L. Ashley,	102
Daniel, M. D.	Martha A. Patch,	147
J. J.	*g* R. Annie French,	79
James M.	*g* Zillah D. Chenery,	22
J. Rockwell	Mary J. Wilder,	57
R. M.	Mary E. Bassett,	22
Rev. Randolph	S. A. (Kilburn) Hitchcock,	30
Campbell, Wm. H. W.	Elizabeth W. Painter,	63
Canaday, William	Elizabeth Diament,	62
Candee, G. H.	*g* Hannah M. Hunt,	76
Canfield, Robert M.	Laura F. Keeler,	140
Wellington	*g* Julietta Cooley,	29
Capron, Hazen S.	*g* Margaret Bidwell,	161
Orville M.	Charlotte T. Danielson,	30
Samuel M.	Eunice M. Chapin,	56
Card, Benjamin W.	*g* C. Amelia Whitney,	69
Cardwell, Byron P.	Abigail M. Clark,	56
Carey, Chas. W.	Nancy B. Bishop,	100
Edward M.	Lucy A. Clark,	107
Carleton, Arthur S.	Mary C. Wilson,	158
James P.	Annie P. Hutchinson,	168
Rev. M. M.	*g* Celestia Bradford,	61
R. K., Esq.	*g* D. Antoinette Iacom,	102
Thomas P.	Mary S. Kingsbury,	81
Carlisle, Levi B.	*g* Zelma H. Renne,	103
Carman, A. G.	Huldah A. Grant,	118
Carmen,Geo,H.	Ada J. McVicar,	185
Carnahan, Jacob P.	Susan A. Crawford,	66
Carothers, W.M.,M.D.	*g* Gertrude Robbins,	151
Carpenter, Rev. C. C.	*g* Feronia N. Rice,	86
Louis, Esq.	*g* Mary E. Barber,	75
Carr, D. S.	*g* Mary A. Thresher,	55
Rev. John H.	Angelina Hosmer,	46
Willard	*g* Caroline A. G. Bull,	174
Rev. William O.	*g* Laura F. Nutter,	120
Carrington, Geo. M.	*g* Julia P. Mitchell,	86
Carroll, John C.	*g* Charlotte A. Cochran,	75
Rev. Vernon B.	Mary S. Emerson,	104
Carruthers, Rev. Wm.	Mary L. Hayes,	70
Carson,————	*g* Amelia P. Potts,	92
Carter, Addison C.	Adelia B. Litchfield,	56
Rev. Thomas	*g* Hettie M. Dodd,	117
Carville, George G.	Anna A. Browne,	22
Carwith, William A.	Susan H. Beard,	52
Cary, Austin P.	*g* Helen F. Collins,	111
Geo. F.	Charlotte Coleman,	149
Case, Cornelius J.	Lucy E. Merriam,	70
Erastus E., M. D.	Emorette (Case) Holcomb,	87
Rev. Ira	Mary A. Eaton,	40
Lyman W., Esq.	Mary H. Boudinott,	43
Miron J.	Martha E. Johnson,	152
Cass, O. D., M. D.	*g* Elmira O. Field,	38
Wellington, Esq.	Sarah J. Carey,	66
Castle, Cheney M.	Catharine M. Cunningham,	66
Harry A.	*g* Mary C. Hadsell,	160
Cather,Rev. Andrew	*g* Emma L. Hall,	86
George F.	*g* Frances A. Smith,	115
Catlin, George S.	Ada L. Catlin,	59
Caverly, A. M., M. D.	*g* Sarah L. Goddard,	51
Chaffee, Thomas	Mattie M. K. Marcy,	77
Thomas S., Esq.	Catharine L. Blair,	22
Chamberlain, Albert	Lucy W. Smith,	28
Francis H.	*g* Lucy A. Parker,	39
Geo. W. F.	Eliza J. Witherell,	99
Guilford T.	Cornelia L. Catlin,	43
J. H.	Hannah K. Smart,	60

MARRIED NAMES. 193

		Page
Chamberlain,Rev.Jacob	Charlotte Birge,	80
Rev. Joshua M.	g Eliza A. (Herrick) Dyke,	36
Richard S.	Mary W. Bliss,	49
W. F.	Catharine, E. Doolittle,	66
Warren	Celia P. Wright,	57
Wm. H.	Helen F. Shaw,	85
Chambers, Rev. E.	Harriot B. Savage,	21
Rev. Wm. N.	g Cornelia P. Williams,120	
Champion, A. J.	g Mary E. Rexford,	144
Chandler, A.	Henrietta Parker,	37
Francis F.	Emma C. Woodbury,	111
George P.	Mary L. Rich,	101
Harrison T.	Ellen F. Foster,	90
John	Ann E. Sawyer,	47
John H.	g Abbie W. Smith,	123
	g Emma C. Smith,	134
Paul L.	Augusta A. Makinster.	98
Chaney, Alden C.	Josephine G. McNear101	
Rev. Lucien W.	Happy T. Kinney,	53
Chapin, Aldus M.	Catharine F. Sawin,	19
Dormer	Myra E. Deering,	132
Ephraim A.	g Josephine Clarke,	29
Homer C.	Nellie F. Cobleigh,	154
James S., Esq.	Emily F. Smith,	38
John H. P.	Charlotte L. Grover,	62
	Abby C. Knowlton,	88
Norman O.	Mary A. Scroggy,	150
William G.	g M. Jeanette Alexander,	138
Chapman, Fred T.	g Elizabeth H. Gilbert,	36
Geo. W.	g Ann E. Whiton	52
James W.	Margaret A. Darling,100	
Josiah B.	S. (Sanford) Dunham,	28
W. C.	Lucy T. Griffin,	81
William	Hannah Eastman,	30
Charpiot, Rev. Louis E.	Eliza Boynton,	77
Chase, Rev. Andrew L.	Martha L. Durgin,	172
David B.	Kate A. Freyermuth	124
Chatfield, Wm. F.	g Mary F. Cairns,	139
Chatterton, James M.	Frances M.Hitchcock	19
Chellis, Rush	Alice E. Bates,	154
Cheney, Chas. F.	Louise E. Driver,	107
Thomas B.	Emily L. (Kingsbury) Hollister,	47
Cherrington,Samuel M.	Rowena P. Cooke,	139,140
Chester, Anson G.	Abbie L. Wear,	122
Rev. Erastus,	g Mary B. Metcalf,	36
Chickering, Henry	Elvira P. Allen.	16
Child, Edwin B.	Anna G. Sykes,	163
Childe, Wm. H.	Amanda (Mobley) Eaton.	34
Chilson, Henshaw B.	Alice M. Barrett,	118
Chipman, Rev. Alfred	g Alice T. Shaw,	72
Choate, Charles A.	Alice M. Watts,	105
Christenson, Niels	Abbie M. Holmes,	127
Christian, Geo. A.	Sara E. French,	87
Church, Frank	Mary L. Montague,	166
Frederick L.	Arabella Walker,	50
Henry J.	Elinor S. Houdinot,	30

		Page
Churchill, Geo.	Clara A. Hurd,	63
	g Adaline H. Hayes,	48
Claflin, Arthur W.	Alice Howard,	121
James F.	Caroline Poole,	81
Clapp, Chas. W.	g Evelyn Metcalf,	139
Edwin B.	Nellie H. Kingsley,	160
George L.	Sophia A. Clapp,	16
Henry M.	g Aurelia L. Montague,150	
Lewis	Augusta Wright,	26
W. F., M. D.	g Roxa J. Hodges,	134
Clark,———	Mary Ella French,	112
Adelbert, T. S.	Mary M. Posten,	133
Alexander S.	Jane E. Hasbrouck,	49
Allen G.	Clara Stetson,	141
Charles H.	Catherine J. Hayden,	94
Charles J.	g Lucy F. Griffith,	169
Charles R.	Jessie H. Usher,	176
Cyrus A.	Harriet M. Gulick,	127
Daniel A.	Mary S. Bliss,	45
Rev. E. W.	Sarah H. (Richards) Hall,	21
Elijah N., M. D.	E. Caroline Rowe,	81
Edward S.	Theo Taft,	133
Frank B.	Elizabeth S. Leach,	119
Frank G. Esq.	Harriet N. Newton,	91
Fred, N.	Mary S. Pyne,	141
George A,	g Ellen S. Dibble,	120
George Fred.	Clara S. Beebe,	106
Rev. George L.	Emma F. Kimball,	119
George W.	Harriet N. Cooley,	87
Harding A.	Lilla A. Carpenter,	129
Henry F.	Almira Brooks,	18
Rev. J. B.	g Clara N. Herendeen,	123
J. P.	g Harriet A. Whitaker.	58
John B.	Frances M. Sargent,	57
John H.	Charlotte S. Huntington,	30
John W.	Mary E. Roberts,	122
Joseph, Esq.	Polly C. Thompson,	63
Joseph N.	Dorcas White,	105
Rev. Lewis F.	Nancy C. Sheldon,	23
Lucius L.	Sarah J. Colt,	18
Morris W.	g Katherine A.Dunning,85	
Sidney W.	g Amelia S. Ray,	144
Rev. Theodore J.	Julia P. Hollister,	21
W.	Louise M. Deming,	93
William B.	Eliza T. Smith,	88
William P.	g Sarah G. Fenn,	41
William S.	Harriet R. Williston,	35
Clarke, A. B.	g Susan C. Watson,	106
Benjamin P.	Myra A. Smith,	98
Rev. Edward	g Julia Hyde,	23
Francis E.,Esq.	g Hannah C. Scott,	42
George Dwight,	g Mary E. Goodrich,	105
Oliver F.	Mary M. Wadsworth,	44
Oliver P.	M. Josephine Kelsey,104	
Rowse E., M. D.	Mary Sheldon,	38
Claus, Joseph B.	Ellen H. Dutton,	124
Cleaveland, Rev. G. W.	Keziah S. Doane,	22
T. W., M. D.	g Antoinette L. Hungerford,	146

INDEX.

		Page			Page
Cleaver, Wm. L.	Hannah O. Harris,	56	Conden, Rev. Henry N.	y L. Jane Dickinson,	108
Clement, M. N., Esq.	y Clara M. Fitch,	143	Condit, Rev. Blackford	y Sarah L. Mills,	76
Cleveland, Chas. W.	y Emily A. Scott,	55	Condron, John L.,	Emily N. Tolman,	23
	y Isabel M. Torrey,	64	Cone, Robert S.,	Ann E. Chapman,	33
Henry W.	y Mary E. Bond,	148	Congdon, Lippitt,	Nancy A. Dewing,	30
Clifford, J. Philip, Esq.	Calore V. Stout,	153	Conklin, Howard S.	Mary P. Howell,	118
Woodbridge	Margaret A. Land,	28	Conn, George C.	Harriet E. Deans,	162
Clizbe Rev. J.	y Mary E. Mills,	48	Conner, Leartus, M.D.	y Anna A. Dame,	102
Coar, Thomas E.	Kitty M. Ely,	157	Conover, John F.	Eleanor H. Schanck,	60
Cobb, Rev. Nehemiah	Jane M. (Skinner) Parker,	50	Conrad, Francis W.	y Sarah W. Adams,	136
Cobleigh, Rev. N. F.	y Elvira Cole,	114	Converse, John H.	Frances A. Upham,	71
Coburn, Frank Esq.	y Martha L. Burnham,	51		William, M.D.	Abby P. Colman,	24
Cochran, Rev. Warren	y Love L. Brown,	102	Conway, Geo. E.	y Annie F. Coney,	157
Cochrane, Wm. R.	y Charlotte D. Hague,	123	Cook, ——, M.D.	Andalusia Farr,	46
Coe, Frank A.	Virginia Coe,	108	Edward L.	Florence E. Fitch,	97
Frank L.	y E. Justine Carrington,	108	Ezra A.	Maria E. Blanchard,	96
			Francis W.	Mary S. Harris,	34
Isaac R.	Julia E. Hawks,	66	Frank P.	Agnes E. Homan,	138
Spencer W.	Caroline L. Capron,	46	Fred. H.	Helen M. Turner,	108
Wilbur F.	Gertrude M. Royce,	98	Fred H.	y C. Irene Miller,	154
Coes, A. G. Esq.	y Lucy G. (Wyman) Gibson,	36	George B.	Adaline H. Hawks,	40
			Henry	y Anna F. Eastman,	82
Coffin, Wm. C.	Hannah Millard	44	Loomis	Amelia Carey,	16
F. W. M.	S. Elizabeth Haynes	143	O. F.	y Alice Carter,	158
William	Harriet Crane,	40	William A.	y Eliza Morris,	120
Coggin, Jacob	Mary A. Wilkins,	54	William De F.	Alice A. Dickerman,	112
Rev. Wm. S.	Mary Clark,	18	Cooke, Sherman T.	Lucia M. (Stillman) Cross,	21
Coggswell, Wm.	Sarah E. Rowe,	24	Rev. Theodore	M. Elizabeth Hale,	49
Coggswell, Francis	Sarah J. Burnham,	24	Cooley, Benjamin F.	Maria L. Davis,	115
Colcord, Rev. D. H.	y Pamelia J. Mudge,	112	Eli	Wealthy H. Shepard,	17
Cole, Charles	Grace L. Rolfe,	136	James	Rhoda A. Reed,	21
Cyrus	Miranda Pomeroy,	25	John G., Jr.	Julia E. Kingsbury,	94
George C.	Annie M. Murchison,	50	Rev. O. W.	Sarah A. Adams,	20
George O.	Katherine Heidenreich,	145	Tertius C.	M. Augusta Bates,	87
Gordon E.	Stella C. Whipple,	28	Coolidge, Rev. A. H.	y Harriet M. Cooley,	58
Rev. H. Hammond	Maria A. Frost,	107	Edwin B.	Mary J. Potter,	94
Henry P.	Rebecca E. Newell,	56	Henry O.	Emily E. Blanchard,	103
J. L.	Myra E. Miles,	63	Coombs, Frank L.	Isabelle M. Roper,	127
Rev. Royal M.	Lizzie Cobleigh,	107	Lorenzo G.	Emma C. Sleeper,	113
Coleman, B. F., M. D.	Sarah C. Hinman,	40	Philip	Sarah F. (Woodhull) Webb,	47
J. E.	Maria Jewell,	26	Cooper, Simon W.	Coralie E. Chasmar,	144
John C.	Persis H. Sibley,	81	Cope, Harry C., Esq.	y Jennie E. Schwartz,	159
Seymour, Jr.	Amelia L. Dwight,	97	Corbin, Lucius B.	y Sarah J. Cooley,	85
Collins, Frank O.	Martha J. F. McNutt,	122	Wm. M.	Josephine Walker,	85
John F. M. D.	y Helen Gilfillan,	58	Cordley, Rev. C. M.	y Lydia G. (Bailey) Rogers,	32
Rev. W. H.	Eliza B. Gridley,	43			
Colson, Geo. F.	Clara E. Proctor,	122	Corey, D. A.	y M. Adelia Dickinson,	89
Colt, Benjamin F.	y Helen Buckingham,	79	Henry C.	y Elizabeth S. Corey,	79
Colton, George A.	Charlotte M. Mead,	84	L. O.	Caroline B. Barrows,	42
Colvin, Henry	Alice D. W. Hastings,	135	Corner, Wm. M.	Mary T. Bassett,	24
William M.	y Mary E. Noyes,	120	Cornman, Rev. W. O.	Mary A. Monyer,	98
Colwell, Charles J.	Mary G. Barnes,	146	Cortelyon, A. H.	y Laura R. Sessions,	83
Harry E.	y Katharine D. Coleman	158	Corttis, Herbert E.	Ada A. Sterns,	108
Comstock, Richard W. (See addenda)	Cornelia B. Pratt,	85	Corwin, Wm. H.	Rebecca P. Williams,	60
			Cory, David A.	Sarah A. Dickinson,	81
Conant, Harrison J.	y Ellen L. Bennett,	105	Robert J.	y Elizabeth F. Hendrie,	89
J. Willis	Emily A. Hobbs,	165	Coulfer, John D.	Mary J. Prentiss,	173
Leonard L.	y Laura M. Chamberlain,	130	Coulter, Archibald Stanley	y Celestia L. Post,	65
Marshall, Esq.	Caroline F. Mann,	40		Lucy E. Post,	127
			Connitt, Rev. Geo. W.	Lucy L. Tyler,	50

MARRIED NAMES.

		Page
Covey, Lyman L.,	Eliza R. Nolde,	37
Cowan, Rev. John	*g* Emma I. Ferrin,	125
Rev. John W.	H. Adele Miller,	147
Cowdry, James S., M.D.	Frances Waldo,	28
Cowgill, William M.	*g* Mary A. Walker,	52
E. Branson	Helen Prescott,	107
Cowles, Augustus D.	Jane M. Billings,	62
E. M.	{ *g* Frances M. Atwood,	17
	{ *g* Hannah J. Atwood,	51
E. P., Esq.	Sarah E. Boies,	45
Rev. John P.	Eunice Caldwell,	185
Cozzens, George	Sarah B. Taber,	75
Crafts, Edward A.	Martha L. Harwood,	43
Myron H.	Miranda W. Capen,	22
Cram, Edward J.	Harriet F. Blake,	112
Crandall, Hiram, Esq.	*g* Jane F. Barnes,	80
Stephen G.	Susan E. Corey,	118
Crane, Charles H.	Harriet M. Blaisdell,	55
Emerson T.	Lucy M. Norton,	88
John M.	Caroline S. Coggswell,	80
Crapo, Beroth L.	*g* Kittie L. Wadsworth,	142
Crary, J. Alfred	Theresa M. (Leonard) Reed,	88
Crawford, Rev. Josiah	Phebe H. Crosby,	24
L. S.	*g* Sarah T. Bailey,	29
John J.	Clara A. Sweet,	158
Manley H.	*g* Anna M. Smythe,	160
Cray, Nelson W.	*g* Eliza B. Hill,	22
Cripps, ——	C. de Maupassant,	185
Cristy, Moses	Mary E. Davis,	80
Crittenden, Rev. S. W.	Margaret A. Parker,	34
Crocker, James R.	Agnes Taylor,	133
T. D.	Eliza P. Otis,	44
Crockwell, Charles L.	Mary E. Hawkes,	160
Cromwell, Chauncey H.	Caroline A. Warren,	47
Cronise, Johu S.	Maria A. Miller,	34
Crosby, C. F.	Sarah B. Grout,	17
. Franklin	Hannah G. Gorton,	37
Minot S.	Marg. L. A. Maltby,	50
Samuel D.	*g* Julia E. Stillman,	36
Cross, Rev. M. K.	*g* Maria E. Mason,	45
Rev. Roselle T.	Emma A. Bridgman,	93
Rev. Rowland E.	Mary E. Weeks,	136
Samuel	Lucia M. Stillman,	21
Crossman, Fred A.	Alice K. Hall,	165
Crosswell, Herbert E.	C. Ida Brown,	109
Crowell, Jonah	Lucretia M. Sturges,	60
Edward	Sarah E. Cooke,	30
Samuel F.	Susan G. Blodgett,	106
Crumb, Rev. A. V. B.	Ulee P. Cross,	121
Cruttenden, Chas. E.	*g* Eliza R. Crane,	61
George	Sarah F. Fowler,	53
Cruzan, Rev. John A.	Emma A. Ide,	185
Cubery, Wm. M.	Phebe Palmer,	94
Culver, Joseph Z.	Julia Crouch,	103
Cummings, Rev. G. H.	*g* Mary E. Kimball,	142
Rev. Henry	*g* Mary A. Beaman,	36
J. Henry	Mary A. Petts,	96
Jay	Charlotte A. Ross,	98
Rev. Seneca	Abby M. Stearns,	26
Cummins, Frank M., M.D.	*g* Mary D. Cooper,	151

		Page
Cundall, Rev. I. N.	{ *g* Sarah E. Scribner,	61
	{ Louisa J. Scribner,	63
Cunningham, H. D.	Fannie L. Warner,	114
Oliver	*g* Hannah Ordway,	20
Rev. William	*g* Laura Aldrich,	36
Currier, Warren	Harriet M. Plummer,	54
Curtis, Rev. Chas. D.	Dora F. Crossett,	59
Frank	*g* Alice J. Tuttle,	154
Rev. George	Elvira Corbin,	83
Rev. George C.	*g* Persis G. Woods,	16
George P.	*g* Margaret Croft,	148
George W. L.	Fannie A. Storm,	122
Herbert F.	Leila S. Shumway,	130
Rev. J. A.	Anna C. Gilt,	171
Nelson	Jane E. Gilbert,	49
Newton H., M.D.	Jennie A. Dunham,	110
Rev. William S.	*g* Martha A. Leach,	18
Curtiss, Rev. S. I.	*g* Laura W. (Walker) Sessions,	90
Theodore	*g* Augusta L. Tupper,	58
Cushing, Henry E., M.D.	Lizzie Dudley,	129
H. H.	*g* Alice Butler,	158
Cushman, Rev. C. L.	Laura A. Montague,	70
Jay	Frances C. Root,	98
Cutler, Rev. Carroll	*g* Frances T. Gallagher,	41
Rev. Ebenezer	*g* Jane E. Charlton,	36
Sanford L.	*g* Emma S. Thayer,	156
Cutrer, John W.	Blanche M. Clark,	149
Cutting, Charles A.	Thirza M. Codding,	112
Prof. Starr W.	*g* Mary E. Derby,	149, 151
Da Costa, John C., M.D.	Mary G. Meigs,	94
Dale, John J.	Orinda Merrifield,	107
Samuel	Mary J. Jerome,	27
Dalrymple, Chas. H.	Sarah A. Voorhees,	64
Rev. Chas. H.	Delia M. Eaton,	137
Dame, Rev. Chas.	Nancy J. Page,	19
William	Amelia Callahan,	106
Dameron, W. A.	Helena Fleefsch,	147
Dana, Sylvester, Esq.	Mary J. Seavey,	71
W. H.	Sophia W. Hayes,	91
Danforth, S. Frank	*g* Nellie M. Johnson,	156
Daniels, Arthur F.	Eunice F. Linsley,	67
John B.	Mary E. Moore,	78
Lawson	Harriet S. (Weare) Daniels,	41
Lowell	Harriet S. Weare,	41
Wm. W.	*g* Hontas A. Peabody,	106
Darling, Theron C.	Ida J. Woodford,	122
Darrow, Franklin E.	*g* Amelia Whiting,	69
Darte, Sumner L.	Harriet E. Woods,	45
Dascomb, Rev. A. B.	Celia N. French,	77
Daskam, C. Howard	Emmeline S. Tomlinson,	125
Davey, Edmund H.	Emma B. Stiles,	105
Davidson, Frank B.	Olive G. Davis,	97
William A.	*g* Mary J. Knowles,	58
Davis, Andrew J.	Emma O. Glines,	147
Armon W.	*g* Aurelia B. Hinsdale,	29
Charles B.	Betsey J. Wood,	60
Courtland, P.	Julia A. Turner,	127
Daniel	Abby A. Wilder,	95

INDEX.

			Page
Davis, Daniel	Susan A. Adams,		73
George H.	Emily B. Browne,		146
Guernsey W.	g Mary A. Galloway,		79
Henry F.	g Abby J. Woodward,		96
Henry G.	Mary B. Dowse,		27
John	Mary Woolsey,		71
Nathaniel J. K.	Ida C. Masta,		119
Rev. S. C.	Meta C. Perry,		138
Samuel H.	Sylvia Corbin,		27
Stanton K.	g Clara Hussey,		164
Silas W., M.D.	g Dora D. (Keniston) Johnston,		86
Spencer	Mary W. Cady,		20
W. C.	Marcia P. Rogers,		133
William G.	Catharine S. Morse,		40
Wm. M., Esq.	Elizabeth W. Weller,		92
Davison, Benj., M.D.	Margaretta A. West,		28
Day, Addison	Margaret Smith,		23
Henry B.	g Julia W. Stevens,		156
Horace	Sarah R. Seaver,		26
Rev P. B.	g Mary B. Chapin,		29
Rev. P. R.	Henrietta M. Woodford,		80
Dayfoot, Rev. P. C.	g Rosina Lyon,		42
Dayton, Carr W.	Frances C. Mills,		107
Frederick A.	Laura H. Clapp,		132
Dean, Asahel	Lucy Hodges,		21
H. W., M.D.	Elizabeth P. Smith,		19
Hollis, M.D.	Fannie McKean,		714
James C.	g Elizabeth Adams,		58
Rev. Samuel C.	Augusta E. Abbott,		62
Deane, John K.	Martha N. Andros,		33
Dearborn, J. H., M. D.	Lilla B. Towle,		133
Dearden, James	L. (Hathaway) Smith,		30
DeCaskey, Marquis	Carrie L. Erickson,		129
Deed, William, Jr.	g Helen M. Woodward,		144
DeGraff, James W.	Carrie S. Milliken,		160
De La Croix, Louis	Mary L. H. Rousseau,		138
Delamater, E. D., Esq.	Anna Van Ness,		122
DeLance, Delevan	Eliza R. (Noble) Covey,		37
DeLand, Henry	g Sarah A. Parce,		68
Demers, Albert F.	Ellsworth A. Boughton,		165
Deming, Geo. S.	Jane E. Whittlesey,		108
Demond, Wm. E.	Sarah F. Harrison,		129
Denham, Elliot F.	Ruth E. Tirrell,		125
Denison, Rev. Andrew	g Laura A. Nichols,		72
James H.	g Caroline A. White,		29
Lem. T.	g S. Louise Fuller,		114
Dennis, Butler Waldo	Harriet E. Godfrey,		97
	Ellen M. White,		102
Dennison, James S.	Alice B. Lane,		145
DeNormandie, Rev.C.T.	Almira B. Stetson,		44
Derby, H. W.	g Mary L. Clark,		85
Walter E.	Helena A. Caswell,		100
DeRochefort, G. C.	Jane (Merrill) Henderson,		53
Devins, Rev. John, B.	C. E. (Hubbard) Penfield,		97
Dewey, Alvin H.	Grace Townley,		150
Charles C., Esq.	Abby P. King,		63
Dewey, David B., M. D.	Julia M. Berray,		80
Francis H., Esq.	Sarah A. B. Tufts,		26
DeWitt, Rev. Abner	g Mary E. Hastings,		65
Henry A.	g Ellen D. Tingley,		65
William	Elizabeth Tolman,		23
Dewsnap, Mark H.	C. Alice Wood,		117
Dexter, Aaron,	Hester McLean,		34
Edwin D.	Julia B. Hayden,		107
Dickerson, Edward	F. Della Young,		148
Judge, Jona. G.	Eliza A. Berry,		59
Dickey, Frank. W.	g Laura Hills,		72
	'Sarah M. Colby,		124
Dickinson, Rev. C. E.	Susan D. Williams,		89
D. O.	g Martha C. Scott,		32
Edward A.	S. Maria Fletcher,		25
Edwin H.	Nellie G. Cowls,		154
Henry N.	g Julia F. Kimball,		156,157
Rev. Joel L.	Jane L. Boles,		24
John T.	g Elvira C. Bates,		82
T. C.	Mary L. Millard,		81
William C.	Clara L. Graves,		162
William C.	Abbie P. Wilder,		95
Dickson, Rev. A. F.	g Ann H. Woodhull,		26
Diehman, L. H.	Anna G. Barkdoll,		149
Dike, C. F.	g Eliza A. Herrick,		36
Dill, Albert D.	Sophia C. Humphrey,		77
Dilley, Rev. A. B.	Mary A. Man,		40
Dillon, Henry C., Esq.	Florence Hood,		121
Dimick, Charles N.	Helen W. Skinner,		104
Dimmick, Rev. F. M.	g Ada H. Chase,		72
Lawrence W.	Mary Plowman,		124
Dimmock, William R.	Caroline E. Dimmock,		81
Dimock, John H.	Mary J. Comstock,		30
Dinsmore, Rev. W. H.	g Phebe E. Harris,		102
Disbrow, Livingston	Myrtilla P. Mead,		91
Dixon, Rufus E.	Susan W. (Dixon) Seaver,		25
Dixson, Joseph E.	g Zella B. Allen,		141
Doane, Arnold	Amanda Atwood,		123
Rev. Frank B.	g Leigh L. Bemis,		176
L. F.	Mary R. Jones,		129
Doe, Luke	Martha M. Moore,		53
Dodd,Rev.Edward M.	g Lydia H. Babbitt,		41
Rev. Luther	Elizabeth H. Goodale,		17
Dodge, Gideon F.	Sarah A. Baldwin,		24
Rev. John H.	Elvira M. Wait,		75
Thomas A.	Elizabeth D. Wooster,		150
Thomas F.	Abbie H. England,		126
Doerenbecher, F. S.	g Nancy M. (Dewey) Johnson,		75
Donkin, George	Catharine Sawyer,		21
Dorman, Frank W.	g Isabella W. Taylor,		96
Dosh, S. H.	Eleanor F. Crawford,		59
Doty, William E.	g Harriet H. West,		144
Doubleday, A., M. D.	g Anna M. Peck,		76
Dougherty, J. H., Esq.	Alice Hill,		121
Douglas, Rev. John	Elizabeth B. Hatch,		21
Douglass, Benjamin	g Julia A. Hayes,		32
Rev. Ebenezer	Helen M. Graves,		53
Rev. F. A.	Anna C. Allen,		48
Frederick	g Helen Pitts,		80
Joseph A.	Mary J. Campbell,		109

MARRIED NAMES.

		Page
Douglass, Rev. Rich'd D.	Mary A. Lawrence,	88
Dow, Augustus	Judith W. Morton,	74
Charles F.	Esther H. Cross,	135
John H.	Elizabeth Gund,	175
Dowd, Frank C.	g Ellen R. Miner,	146
Rev. Charles F.	g Harriet M. North,	51
Downer, Jas. W., Jr.	Elizabeth M. Robbins,	160
Downing, Edward B.	Iola E. Whitman,	150
H. F.	Emma M. Hicks,	91
Drabelle, M. J.	Caroline Mitchell,	147
Draffen, J. W., Esq.	g Louise J. Tichenor,	69
Draper, Amos G.	g L. Bell Merrill,	134
Dresser, Henry	Ann E. Fitch,	53
Drew, I. DeWitt	Frances M. Osborne,	63
Rev. Stephen F.	Josephine E. Chandler,	103
Rev. William J.	Alice L. Woodward,	153
Drinkwater, A.F., Esq.	g Julia R. Keese,	120
Drury, E. H., M. D.	Catharine Rogue,	33
Homer, D.	Clara E. Williams,	153
Dudley, Burton R.	Jennie R. Francis,	165
Edward M.	Mary A (Truair) Jackson,	95
Erastus	Martha C. Munger,	124
Frederick A.	M. Stella Perry,	140
Horace F.	Mary E. Augur,	118
Rev. Joseph F.	g Jessie D. Grassie,	82
Oscar E.	Julia L. Marshall,	122
Dunbar, Francis A.	Maria D. Whitmarsh,	117
Lucius	Lucinda J. Packard,	37
Rev. William	Minerva A. Owen,	81
Duncan, Charles	Clara (Dwight) Adams,	18
Samuel	Frances C. Sanders,	44
Dundas, Rev. Brabison B.	Mary Emma Dann,	126
Dunham, David B.	Emma F. Webb,	57
George W.	Mabel O. Storrs,	168
Rev. H. R.	Sarah Sandford,	28
Henry T.	Martha C. Goodrich,	66
Lewis H.	Julia A. Brown,	83
Truman	g Mary G. Ufford,	58
Dunlap, Harlan P.	{ Martha Hopkins,	74
	{ g Mary C. Dutton,	114
J. P., M. D.	g Harriette Allen,	32
Dunlevy, Anthony J.	Anna L. Coulter,	154
Dunton, Geo. B.	Margaret A. Hudson,	67
Duren, Rev. Chas.	Sarah W. L. Atherton,	90
Durham, J. M., Esq.	g Maria C. Eastman,	95
Dustan, Rev. George	Lucy A. Marsh,	50
George P.	Elva M. Chapman,	146
Dutton, Charles	Mrs. H. G. Dutton,	186
George, Jr.	Elizabeth M. Pease,	34
Dwight, Jason L.	Margaret O. Smith,	31
John	Nancy S. Everett,	16
R. Ogden, Esq.	g Sarah E. Coburn,	95
William, M. D.	Helen M. Clarke,	22
Dyer, Isaac	Martha P. Mattocks,	39
J. Hersey	Clara L. Sparks,	122
Joseph P.	Deborah H. Curtis,	56
Rodolphus, C.	Tryphena Kidder,	53
Walter R.	g Martha A. Houston,	164
Dyk, Rev. Jacob,	g Edith Tremper,	170

		Page
Eager, Charles Esq.	g Laura E. Wright,	24
Eames, Horace L.	g Ella Kingman,	128
Earl, John F.	g Elizabeth A. Ford,	92
Earle, Rev. F. R.	N. Amanda Buchanan,	66
Eastman, Albert P.	Sarah N. Russell,	98
Tobias L.	Adelia S. Walker,	133
Eaton, D. Emery Esq.	Ella A. Everett,	145
H. F.	Amanda Mobley,	34
Harrison, M. D.	Harriet N. Lane,	53
Rev. Horace	g Ann R. Webster,	24
Rev. Walter S.	Fannie Widmer,	145
Eddy, Charles E.	Annie Pease,	138
F. C.	g Stella Kneeland,	128
Frank M.	Frances Fraser,	135
Rev. Henry	g Sarah H. Torrey,	18
Merritt H., M. D.	Louise M. Seely,	78
Morton	g Mary C. Whitman,	18
Rev. Wm. W.	g Hannah Maria Condit,	36
Edmands, John	Ellen E. Metcalf,	77
Edmonds, H. A., M. D.	Delenda J. Allen,	48
Edmunds, Henry, Esq.	Ellen M. Howard,	121
Edsall J. R.	g Eunice K. Dresser,	156,157
Edson, Rev. Henry K.	g Celestia A. (Kirk) Maynard,	42
Edwards, Francis W.	Helen F. Morrison,	94
George G.	g Jennie L. Morehouse,	134
J. T.	Maria Reeve,	67
Rev. John	Rose H. Murphy,	50
Lindley, M.	Laura A. Sawyer, M.D.,	94
Oscar	Kate Wendall,	31
William P.	Mary A. Francis,	46
Eggleston, J. D., M.D.	Elizabeth C. Duncan,	132
Eichelberger, Edward S.	g Miriam Gray,	171
Elder, Stephen N.	Abigail Nooney,	28
Eldred, Lyman A.	Layette E. Cummings,	121
Eldredge, Charles Q.	g Frances M. Hatch,	111
Rev. Henry W.	Sarah J. Loveland,	116
Ellicott, Joseph P.	Nancy H. McClure,	25
Ellinwood, Rev. Frank	Laura Hurd,	84
Henry F.	Helen C. Hovey,	140
Elliot, Charles E.	Olive E. Haynes,	46
Daniel M., M.D.	Sarah A. Child,	112
Rev. Lester H.	g Elizabeth Hodgdon,	112
Elliott, A. N.	Abbie D. Cleaveland,	107
Alfred O.	Alice L. Bishop,	100
John	Mary Connell,	46
Robert A.	g Helen G. Wilbur,	151
Sylvanus	Lavinia J. Rogers,	54
Theodore C.	Martha J. Wheeler,	31
Ellis, J. B.	g Elizabeth S. Allen,	161
Lucien, M.D.	Amelia J. Sampson,	113
Samuel	Augusta M. Denison,	27
Ellison, Charles	Susan A. Waite,	119
Ellsworth, Wm. H.	Ida G. Stowell,	162
Ely, George B., Esq.	Caroline E. Boies,	24
Rev. George Wells	Eliza G. Burr,	103
Henry G.	Mary P. Putnam,	28
Emerson, Rev. John D.	Elizabeth F. (Emerson) Bell,	62
Richard	g Mary A. Ellis,	32

INDEX.

		Page			Page
Emerson, Rev. Rufus	Alice Wakefield,	85	Ferris, J.	Mary E. Cleveland,	83
Rev. Stephen G.	g Florence G. Stone,	167	Ferry, Arthur E.	Mary C. Alden,	115
Rev. Thomas A.	Frances H. (Crawford) Brewster,	80	Charles S.	Sophia C. Gunn,	46
Emery, M. G., Esq.	Helen L. Simpson,	130	Fessenden, F. G. Esq.	Mary J. Rowley,	85
Emmons, Clarke H.	Emma S. Norton,	150	Field, Rev. James P.	Martha Moore,	88
Lewis	Frances E. Huxley,	43	John W.	Amelia C. Reed,	98
English, Foster	Eleanor H. (Schanck) Conover,	60	Matt. D., M. D.	g Lucy Atwater,	136
Eno, Joel N.	Etta M. Foster,	137	Perry E.	Ada M. Taylor,	138
Ensign, Wm. M.	Julia A. Bissell,	43	Finney, Rev. T. J.	Nannie McClenahan,	143
Entler, Rev. Geo. R.	Clarissa M. Danforth,	24	Fish, Albert	g Nellie C. (Jewett) Reed,	117
Entwistle, Thomas W.	Annie Newlin,	140	Rev. J. L. A.	g Anna J. Atwood,	71
Ernsberger, Rev. D. O.	g Mary A. Hughes,	156	S. M.	g Sarah E. Sweetser,	83
Esselmont, Peter	Mary A. Sherwood,	85	Silas	Mary D. Stoddard,	38
Eustis, John P.	Mary M. Warner,	150	Wm.	Eliza C. Harrington,	19
Evans, Charles	Elizabeth Radford,	35	Fisher, Albert H.	C.M.(Russell)Fletcher,	88
George W.	Josephine N. Kirby,	84	Andrew C.	Mary A. Washington,	133
Nelson F.	g Laura J.(Snow)Wood,	96	Daniel	Josephine G.Thomson,	92
S. H., M. D.	Chloe Abbott,	80	Rev. Geo. E.	g Ellen E. Kellogg,	65
Sidney D.	Susan Hulse,	155	Rev. O. L.	g Charlotte E. Smith,	112
Evarts, H. C., M. D.	Lucy M. Shackleton,	78	Theodore F.	Annie A. Kendall,	70
Eveleth, Harlan F.	Alice W. Ames,	165	William H.	g Minnie F. Searle,	131
Everest, Ralph S.	g Leah Cohn,	151, 152	Fisherdick, Geo. H.	Mariette E. Webster,	99
Everett, Willard	Emily Mann,	116	Fisk, Amos C.	Sarah L. Payne,	70
Everts, Rev. W. W.	Dolly E. Paine,	132	Charles W.	Helen (Stiles) Bellows,	91
Ewing, Thomas, Esq.	g Julia M. Hufnagel,	48	Fiske, Albert L.	g Josephine L. Taggart,	30
Fahnestock, Henry J.	Mary L. Lord,	43	Arthur W.	Abbie W. Taylor,	127
Fairbank, Edward	Mary A. Caskey,	127	Rev. Daniel T.	g Eliza P. Dutton,	36
Rev. S. B.	{ Abby Allen,	30	Edward H.	Lucy E. Hale,	132
	{ g Mary Ballantine,	64	Levi J.	M. Antoinette Wolcott,	85
Fairbanks, Horace	g Mary E. Taylor,	26	Russell	Martha C. Ranney,	91
Fairchild, N. W., M. D.	Mary J. Mead,	70	Rev. Samuel	Elizabeth L. Foster,	73
W. Henry	g Thera West,	86	Fitch, C. P., M. D.	Emeline Lincoln,	51
Fairty, Joseph J.	Sarah E. Hull,	116	Henry S. Esq.	g Ellen R. Hetzel,	65
Fales, Henry E. Esq.	Clara A. Hayward,	101	J. C., M. D.	g Hannah B. Leonard,	51
Falley, Joseph D.	Ada B. Brown,	96	Lucius T.	Sarah P. Tufts,	21
Fancher, Eugene	Bessie G. Mosman,	127	Pomeroy	g Clara L. Torrey,	61
Fanning, John E.	g Nettie M. Bisbee,	151	Flack, David L.	g Anna W. Moody,	51
Farnham, Chas. W.	g Susan Merrell,	76	Fletcher, Rev. James	Lydia M. Woodward,	35
Farnsworth, Chas. H.	Henrietta F. Blanchard,	126	Henry J.	g Bertha von Schrader,	159
Farrar, E. F.	Mary S. Chaffee,	132	Joel W., Esq.	Martha K. Perry,	28
Isaac, M. D.	Adelaide M. Wheeler,	82	Perry	Charlotte M. Russell,	88
James	Adeline Hyde,	25	Samuel M.	Sarah A. Taylor,	35
Farren, Rev. Wm. A.	Jerusha P. Avery,	135	William F.	Ada Mills,	122
Farris, Wm. A.	C. Jane (Sturdevant) Swing,	67	William H.	Harriet S. Nichols,	54
Faulkner, John C.	Mary Hall,	154	Flinn, Darwin P.	Frances M. Hopkins,	53
Faunce, Joshua T.	Harriet Thompson,	44	Flint, Charles	Matilda P. Hall,	113
Farwell, Rev. J. C.	Elizabeth S. Gates,	18	Franklin	Laura Maynard,	53
James W.	Marian E. Perry,	110	H. Nelson	Jane A. Miller,	74
Favour, Horace S.	Elizabeth Gambell,	62	Flynn, Patrick	H. Orianna Knowlton,	110
Faxon, William	Lucy E. Cushing,	46	Fobes, Philander W.	Mary C. Gallagher,	46
Fearing, Clarence W.	Mary B. Tirrell,	130	Fogg, Eugene S. Esq.	g Caroline S. Hodges,	90
Henry D.	Amelia G. Hills,	49	Folsom, Channing	Ruth F. Savage,	108
Fellows, Rev. Nathaniel	Mary A. Buel,	50	E. G.	Evaline Bruen,	75
Fenn, Ava H., M. D.	g M. Letitia Burrill,	128	Foote, Thaddeus, Esq.	Harriette M. Betts,	18
Ferguson, Ira	Julia Goodrich,	53	Wm. T.	Emma L. Munger,	119
Robert M.	g Lizzie E. Tuttle,	151	Forbes, Rev. A. O.	Maria J.Chamberlain,	56
William	g Amanda L. Houghton,	72	Jona. E.	Maria A. Kittredge,	119
Ferris, Frank	Teresa M. Mason,	113	Forbush, Charles A.	Elizabeth Davis,	49
			Ford, Chandler T.	Clara Dawes,	40

MARRIED NAMES.

Name	Spouse	Page
Ford, Charles L.	Mary N. Kinney,	33
Charles R.	g Sarah F. Jones,	72
Isaac	g Pauline W. Halbert,	146
Rev. L. C.	{ g Mary P. Oliphant,	32
	{ g Maria L. Hubbard,	51
Leander B.	Laura E. Tuttle,	99
W. E.	g Amelia S. Dole,	125
Wesley	Ella C. Howard,	104
Forsyth, H. H.	Clarissa L. Mack,	25
Forward, G. H.	g Frances L. M'Masters.	86
Foster, Caleb C.	S. Jane Dewey,	49
Charles S.	Sarah E. Bixby,	49
Freeman S.	Sarah D. Tolman,	23
Rev. John P.	Mary A. Hurd,	25
Morris B.	g Katherine L. Folwell,	90
Publius D., Esq.	g Amanda E. Warren,	58
Samuel	Mary S. Palmer,	23
Waldo	Fanny J. Holmes,	118
Fowle, Rev. James L.	g Carrie P. Farnsworth.	134
Fowler, Thaddeus W.	Lucie R. Field,	124
Fox, Warren H.	Adeline M. Blodgett,	80
Wm. F.	Mary A. Shattuck,	98
Fracker, Willis K.	Harriet A. Sherwood,	133
Francis, Geo. J.	Annette Safford,	153
Geo. W.	Elizabeth G. Bailey,	30
Franklin, Wm. D.	g Mary G. Hollister,	105
Frary, Francis L.	g S. Jeanette Cowls,	139
Fredholm, Adolf J. A.	g Caroline S. Wentworth,	156
Freed, Wm. S.	Martha Gerrish,	59
Freeman, Rev. Albert	Jessie M. Williams,	160
Rev. David	g Anna E. Parker,	72
Everett P., Esq.	Eliza K. Morris,	78
Rev. Geo. R.	g Mary E. Wilcox,	134
Henry	g Clara W. Haskell,	54
Freese, John P.	g Grace E. Gates,	148
French,——	Rebecca B. Claggett,	97
Chas. D.	Mary A. Baldwin,	59
Chas. E.	Marcia D. Jenkins,	77
Chas. H.	Ellen E. Cheney,	126
Frank W.	Martha MacLeod,	149, 150
George W.	g Clara H. Mudge,	109
J. Lowell	Clara B. Southworth,	108
John C.	Angeline Butler,	77
James P.	Eliza R. Dwight,	83
Windsor B.	Emma E. Pitcher,	74
Z. Aaron	g Lucy J. Beebe,	105
Frink, Henry A.	Mabell W. Bardwell,	66
Frisbie, Rev. A. L.	g Martha J. Crosby,	79
Chas. H.	Mary J. (Mead) Fairchild,	70
Rev. Edward S.	g Eliza C. Haskell,	68
Frost, Rev. Daniel D.	{ g Marietta Sherwood,	39
	{ Charlotte E. Rogers,	101
Norman S.	Elizabeth W. Seaver,	28
Frye, Thomas, M. D.	Susan M. Arey,	45
W. G.	Annie E. Arey,	45
Fullam, L.	g Lucy T. Johnson,	45
Fuller, Andrew J.	Susan Colton,	62
Rev. Andrew K.	Phebe E. Sisson,	143
Fuller, Geo. E., M. D.	Caroline F. Field,	81
Geo. Newell	Harriet M. Craig,	100
Harrison	Mary M. Cushman,	59
Jacob H.	Sarah C. (Harrington) Pickett.	59
Leonard F.	g Mary I. Hunt,	65
Theodore F.	Hattie E. Ide,	113
Gabriel, Albert	g Emily M. Griswold,	79
Gage, Albert R.	Emma Doland,	83
Henry C.	Fanny E. Kennedy,	97
John H.	Julia M. Boone,	39
Milton	Bethia S. Nickerson,	34
Walter L. F.	Elizabeth Knight,	49
Gaines, Rev. M. R.	g Louise Walker,	90
Stanley	g Margaret B. Judd,	102
Galbraith, James A.	Lottie M. Smith,	101
Gale, C. S.	g Malvina Stanton,	45
Jesse	g Julia B. Harvey,	151
Galloway, J. M. Esq.	g Elizabeth Cheesman,	58
Gallup, Benj. E., Esq.	Delia S. Hubbard,	74
J. C., M. D.	g Marilla Houghton,	36
John D.	Martha D. Allen,	24
Galpin, Rev. Chas.	Semantha W. Ball,	36
Charles H.	Sarah L. S. Hough,	60
Gamble, Rev. Thomas	g Mary E. Cummings,	131
Games, John	Julia B. Arthurs,	149
Gamwell, Franklin B.	Victoria C. Maxwell,	98
Harlow, M. D.	g Sarah A. DeWolf,	85
Gard, William E.	May E. Allen,	126
Gardiner, Rev. H. B.	g Mary E. Niles,	39
William H.	Elizabeth R. Clark,	140
Gardner, DeWitt, Esq.	g Sarah Smith,	29
Geo. R.	Annie E. Robbins,	94
Prof. Wm. E.	Esther M. Perry,	158
Dorsey	Margaretta S. Potts,	88
Garfield, Rev. Frank L.	Sadie K. Chandler,	161
Garman, Charles E.	g Eliza N. Miner,	123
Garner, Frank E.	g Flavia S. Bliss,	92
Garrett, C. B.	Frances A. Fowler,	62
Garvey, M. T.	g Sarah E. (Thomas) (Jones) Vary,	35
Garvin, Lucius, M. D.	Lucy M. Southmayd, M. D.	186
Gaston, Nelson H.	Abby B. Strong,	23
Gary, Edwin F.	g Kate M. Niles,	120
Gates, Fred E.	g Harriet E. Clapp,	146
Geo. H.	Eliza L. Packard,	21
Gurdon	Martha Phelps,	34
I. W.	{ Elizabeth J. Wilder,	26
	{ g Mary E. Wilder,	65
L. Frank	Nellie L. Smith,	155
Rev. Loren S.	g Frances A. Hazen,	128
Peter G.	Gertrude E. Lewis,	155
S. G. M.	Mary L. Hammond,	87
Wm. C.	Adaline S. (Barton) Mixter,	83
Gauss, O. B.	Harriet N. Powell,	85
Gay, Daniel F.	Emelyn Grant,	175
Henry	Charlotte E. Watson,	57
William	Henrietta Travis,	35
Gaylord, E. E., M. D.	Alice E. Kendall,	127
Rev. Fred A.	g Clara N. Smith,	137

	Page		Page
Gaylord, George L.	Eunice M. Edwards, 70	Goddard, Lucius P.	Mary A. Clarke, 103
Rev. H. J.	Cordelia Dickinson, 16	Peter M.	*y* Mary W. Howes, 36
Rev H. J.	Mary H. Mack, 25	Goff, Walter	Ellen A. Magill, 127
Horace W.	Eudora H. Burt, 87	Gold, Geo. R., Esq.	*g* Mary J. Murdock, 48
Lewis M.	Elizabeth S. For-	Goldsborough, Sidney	Ellen E. Reid, 108
	ward, 137	Goldsmith,Nathan W.	*g* Mary W. Kimball, 167
O. N.	Harriet S. DeWitt, 81	Goldthwaite, Albert W.	Harriet S. Graves, 43
Geary, Rev. Edw'd R.	*g* Nancy M.Woodbridge,26	Luther B.	*g* Helen L. Cobb, 158
Geddes, Norman,Esq.	*g* Jane M. Terry, 73	Goodale, Rev.A.B.,	
Geer, George F.	*g* Laura E. (Newhall)	M.D.	*g* Mary E. Linsley, 72
	Phetteplace. 96	Warren	Ellen R. Whitmore, 50
Gelston, Maltby	*g* Sophia C. Giddings, 117	Goodell, Rev. C. L.	Emily Fairbanks, 53
Rev. Mills B.	*g* Caroline E. Fanning, 38	Goodenow, H. C., Esq.	Mary E. Browne, 89
George, Frederick,	Anna I. Bushnell, 159	Nathan C.	Lucy G. Belcher, 83
Herbert J.	Lena Williams, 163	Rev. Smith B.	*g* Caroline R. Yates, 52
Rev. John F.	Alice Briscoe, 159	Goodhue, Rev.HenryA.	M. Isabella Perkins, 98
John F.	*g* Mary E. Jewett, 146	Goodrich, Chas. H.	P. Jane Turner, 38
Paul R., Esq.	*g* Caroline A. Livings-	Goodsell, Henry P.	Lucy S. Cooley, 73
	ton, 48	Goodspeed, Wilbur F.	Marion Laird, 81
Gerdine, W. L. C.	*g* R. Emma Chapin, 61	Goodwin, Chas. C.	Alice D. Phelps, 81
Gerhart, Rev. E. V.	Lucia D. Cobb, 66	Chas. F.	Rebecca A.Bridgman,33
Gerould, Rev. Sam'l L.	Lucy A. Merriam, 74	Emery A.	*g* Helen J. Angell, 117
Gerry, David J.	*g* H.Gertrude Baldwin,117	George L.	Julia A. Pierce, 37
Thomas	*g* Alice T. Smith, 151	Gordon, Rev. Chas. E.	*g* Amy A. Keyes, 134
Gibney, V. P., M. D.	Charlotte L. Chapin, 146	Chas. H.	Lillian A. Ross, 153
Gibson, Alden T.	*g* Lucy G. Wyman, 36	Rev. Donald	*g* Mary R. Robertson, 39
D. L., M. D.	*g* Sarah A. Kelly, 65	Rev. John	Elizabeth Mann, 136
Giddings, Chandler	Welthy A. Gleason, 20	Thomas H.	Frances E. Kings-
FrederickS.,Esq.	*g* Hettie E. Baker, 51		bury, 132
J. D.	Anna E. (Burritt)	Rev. Wm. Clark	Edith R. Miller, 167
	(Hawks) Lewis, 39	Gore, Thomas E.	Harriet E. Hedden, 135
Giese, L. W. H.	Sarah M. Tillotson, 141	Gorham, Dr. Frank	*g* Carrie E. Coley, 153
Gilbert, Rev. A. F.	L. Eliza Howe, 27	Goss, Nath'l S.	Emeline F. Brown, 55
John R.	Mary C. Davis, 126	Rev. S. S.	Mary C. Weaver, 31
Joshua J.	Elizabeth W. Rust, 54	Gould, Benj. F.	Mary L. Hurlburt, 127
Oliver	Ellen Cavan, 137	Clement	Alice M. Stilson, 122
Gilchrist, Alex. Esq.	*g* Asenath L. Smith, 76	Edward R.	Jennie B. H. Kilner, 132
Oscar, M. D.	*g* Martha E. E. Brad-	Henry S.	Rose S. Converse, 110
	ford, 111	William S.	Sarah J. Clarke, 66
Giles, Benjamin	Susan B. Haskell, 25	Grace, Geo. A.	Caroline B. Marsh, 50
Gill, John D.	*g* Elizabeth N. Buxton,139	Grafstrom, Edward	Dorothy B. Beach, 172
Gillett, D. B.	Charlotte E. Woods, 29	Graham, Rev. Edward	Jane H. Brown, 87
Darwin L.	Sarah J. Dickinson, 49	Francis,	L. Maria Turrill, 54
Gillette, A. F., M. D.	*g* Ellen S. Cole, 92	Harris, M.D.	*g* Ella T. Bray, 148
Rev. Chas.	*g* Sarah C. Ware, 73	I. L., M.D.	Agnes M. (Butler)
	CarolineM.Parkhurst, 40		Bronson, 49
Gilman, Sumner A.	Grace Pearson, 101	Samuel H.	Lucy F. Swett, 50
Gilmore, Samuel,	Hannah R. Wheeler, 155	Granger,Frank C., M.D.	Alice M. Butler, 124
Gibson, Albert A.	Hattie E. Hyde, 127	Grant, Daniel	*g* Caroline Burr, 22
Gist, Thomas H.	Adele S. Miller, 136	Rev. Joel	Abigail F. Cowles, 33
Gladding, Raymond H.	Cornelia A. Drake, 87	Grassie, Rev. T. G.	*g* Mary E. Holbrook, 92
Gladwin, Sidney M.	Ellen F. Hammond,	Rev. William	Zilpah E. Fay, 53
	M. D., 101	Graves, Alden L.	Mary E. Burnette, 132
Gleason, Walter F.	Martha Z. Sweetser, 133	Rev. James T.	Kate I. Foster, M.D.,115
William H.	Pernella Bevin, 175	Josiah	Marie L. Fuller, 147
Glenn, R. F.	Marion B. Rauch, 144	L. H.	Lucy M. Bridges, 56
Glover, Capt. Russell	Elizabeth C. Nash, 104	Myron C.	*g* Augusta A. Porter, 109
Gobin, J. P. S.	Annie M. Howe, 84	Gray, Augustus R.	Mary R. Norton, 50
Goddard, Rev. Chas. G.	Anne N. Gates, 49	Rev. Calvin	Abigail N. Spaulding, 17
Charles W.	Sarah E. Hager, 127	Geo. H.	Sarah N. French, 115
Frederick B.	*g* L. Jane Mason, 72	I. J.	Martha Vale, 145
Daniel	Fanny Arms, 52	Niel	Mary L. Wheeler, 99

MARRIED NAMES.

		Page
Greeley, Rev. E. H.	g Louise M. Ware,	55
James, M.D.	Arabella M. G. Wood,	50
William H.	g Hannah B. McLean,	106
Green, Caleb, M.D.	g Roxana R. Parsons,	22
Joseph	g Mary J. Skerry,	76
Moses B.	Mary W. McMonagle,	28
F. L.	Sarah P. McLean,	127
Thomas A.	Mary A. Butters,	129
William B.	Harriet E. Meeker,	28
Wm. F.	Ella G. Smith,	94
Greene, Alonzo H.	g Mary P. Beach,	71
Charles E.	Jane E. Nichols,	127
Rev. Daniel C.	g Mary J. Forbes,	99
David B., Esq.	g M. Augusta Green,	51
Edward L.	Edith Parsons,	150
Horace L., Esq.	Anna L. Beach,	90
Rev. John M.	g Louisa Dickinson,	72
Rev. Joseph K.	g Elizabeth A. Davis,	72
Kendall	Harriet K. Winter,	138
Greenhough, Rev. J. R.	Justina Chesley,	40
Greenleaf, M. P.,M.D.	g Susan M. Allen,	32
Oscar S.	Mary O. Hitchcock,	94
Greenlee, James M.	Harriet Rice,	17
Greenough, Wm. B.	Eliza S. Clark,	162
William S.	g Elizabeth M. Noyes,	89
Greenwood, Rev.Wm.	g Julia A. Ballantine,	89
Gregg, Robert M.	Eliza J. Buxton,	30
Gregory, Benj.S.,Esq.	g Anna Marsh,	48
David J.	Emily D. Skinner,	101
Lafayette	g Carrie M. Goldthwait,	156
Rev. Lewis,	g Elizabeth H. Buckingham,	89
Gridley, C. A.	Martha P. Miller,	124
Grier, Robert D.	Lydia M. Hall,	138
Griffin, Fernando C.	Mary E. (Wilder) McDowell,	82
Louis B.	Clara E. Walworth,	143
Myron	Angeline M. Aldrich,	55
Wilmot R.	g Mary C. Tufts,	126
Griggs, Appleton M.	g Mary D. Sessions,	68
Ferdinand H.	Ruth D. Clemence,	40
Stephen C., M.D.	Harriet Backus,	20
Grimes, Moses E.	g Emily S. Ela,	72
Grinnell, Rev. J. B.	Julia A. Chapin,	33
Griswold, Allen H.	Harriet T. Arnold,	18
Darius P.	Helen M. Whittlesey,	47
E. C.	Anne Sweetland,	31
Edward T.	Ellen F. Sargent,	116
Fred P., M.D.	g Caroline P. Hull,	123
Theodore D.	Anna I. Weigley,	99
Wait R., M.D.	Lewey A. Bierce,	24
Whiting, Esq.	Jane M. Martindale,	31
Grosvenor,C.W.,Esq.	g Elizabeth Mathewson,	89
Rev. Moses G.	g H. G. (Jones) Orbison,	29
Grout, Rev. Aldin	Charlotte Bailey,	16
Rev. Lewis	g Lydia Bates,	36
Stephen,	g Henrietta A. Fuller,	86
Grover, Daniel B.	Martha M. Eames,	70
Groves, Denison F.	Adelaide J. Bogue,	55
Guernsey, Rev. Jesse W. F.	Elizabeth Eaton,	33
	Fanny W. Hitchcock,	22
Guilford, George W.	Sarah E. Clapp,	66

		Page
Gulick, Rev. Hervey.	Lizzie E. Emerson,	126
M. N.	Anna C. Phelps,	37
Rev. Oramel H.	Ann E. Clark,	59
Rev. Wm. H.	g Alice W. (Gordon) Kittredge,	105
Gulliver, Lemuel	g Helen M. French,	72
Gundkart, Edward H.	g Mary F. Barnum,	148
Gurley, Rev.George D.	g Emma C. Bell,	136
Guyer, Thomas	Sarah E. (Cooke) Crowell,	30
Hadley, Frederick	Lucia S. Brown,	121
Haire, Edward	Mary M. Wright,	47
Rev. John P.	g Ellen C. Bartlett,	68
Halbert, N. A., Esq.	g Caroline Avery,	32
Hale, Calvin	Pamelia C. Tower,	57
George C.	Anna M. Getty,	53
Thomas E.	g Lois W. Rice,	32
Haley, Rev. John W.	g Caroline S. Wadsworth,	80
Hall, Dr.	Sarah E. Parks,	47
Alfred S., Esq.	g Annette M. Hitchcock,	120
Arthur R.	g L. Jennie Baker,	143
Clarence D.	Mary B. Woodard,	138
David A.	Alice V. Gates,	157
Rev. E. C.	g Tirzah S. Snell,	163
E. O.	g Mary L. S. Dame,	114
Edwin H.	g Caroline E. Bottum,	125
Frank E.	Alice M. Mason,	140
Franklin	Elizabeth J. Goddard,	53
George I.	M. Eugenia Montague,	74
Hall, Henry C.	Amanda H. Ferry,	40
Henry H.	g Emma L. Twitchell,	123
Horace	M. Cornelia Olmstead,	63
Rev. John Q.	Frances A. Snow,	78
Linus	g Zoe L. Phillips,	154
Lucius E.	g Anna M. Hood,	112
Sidney H.	Sarah B. Phillips,	23
Rev. Thomas	Sarah H. Richards,	21
Thomas P.	g Martha Littlefield,	58
William T.	Betsey S. Eaton,	49
Halliday, John	Emily A. Williams,	95
Halliwell, George W.	g Sallie Davis,	146
Hallowell, William	Harriet R. Hawks,	19
Hallows, Wm.	Mary A. Gilbert,	160
Halsey, Jas. M.	Mary A. Wright,	68
Lewis B., Esq.	Sarah F. Sheffield,	101
Hamill, Alex., M.D.	g Mary E. Munro,	117
Hamilton, Chas. W.	Ellen L. Yeomans,	158
Erskine H.	Sarah M. Morrill,	116
John	Elizabeth A. Mansfield,	94
Hamlin, Reuben	Cyrene E. Whiting	54
Hammond, Benj.	Isabel Monilaws,	98
Hance, Samuel F., M.D.	Sarah E. Wright,	50
Hancox, Albert	Angelina B. Swan,	35
Hand, A. Southard	Hadassa T. Williamson,	64
Handford, R., Esq.	Henriette M. Prince,	78
Hanley, R. R., M.D.	Mary Beardsley,	30
Hanna,Alex. B., M.D.	g Susan A. Moulton,	163
Hannum, E. A.	L. Dora Beals,	128

INDEX.

Name	Page
Hanor, Azro C., M.D., Mary L. Payn,	140
Hansen, John E. g M. Christine Gabrielson,	143
Hanson, John C. g Annie L. Lane,	100
Hapgood, Horace A. Alice A. Williams,	105
Haradon, A. F., Esq. g Roxellana Howard,	79
Hardenberg, J. R. g Elizabeth T. Stetson,	76
Harding, Rev. Chas. g Elizabeth D. Ballantine,	71
Rev. J. W. Hittie P. Lane,	47
Smith Eunice A. Tilton,	23
Hardy, Rev. Edwin N. Nellie M. Severy,	158
Jacob g Mary McLean,	54
Silas, Esq. g Josephine M. Kingsley.	72
Hare, John Sarah A. Child,	112
Hareford, Henry g Julia A. Gowdy,	96
Harley, G. P. M. Elizabeth Field,	152
Harlow, Geo. W. Mary L. Kneeland,	94
L. Kirke Harriet D. Thompson,	91
Noah R. Caroline S. Howe,	25
William H. Mary K. Snell,	71
Harmon, Rev. Elijah { Lucy M. Smith,	82
{ Eunice M. Smith,	104
Israel Frances M. Cooley,	66
Justus Lucy A. Hawley,	22
Harper, John L. Ellen M. Bowen,	52
Harrington, Chas. M. g Mary Bassett.	161
Frank W. Nellie S. Johnson.	124
George F., Esq. Martha S. Mann,	37
Gilbert H. Myrtis S. Sigourney,	138
Rev. Myron O. g Mary E. Smith.	117
Robert W. Jennie M. Lucas,	127
William H. Ellen A. (Putnam) Bemis,	63
Harris, Clarendon Isabel M. Bailey,	93
Elisha F. Julia R. Martindale,	44
Frank M. g Sarah M. Eastman,	36
George W. Elizabeth S. Mills,	122
Henry L. Esther R. Smith,	136
Rev. J. K. Chloe M. Bigelow,	49
Norman W. g Emma S. Gale,	114
Roswell S. Emma A. Rundell,	130
Harrison, C. A., Esq. Isabel A. Munger,	123
George D. Mary E. Welch,	117
John T. Mary King,	88
Hart, Rev. Burdett g Rebecca W. Fiske,	36
Frank B., Esq. Imogene L. Clinton,	115
Hiram S. Jane G. Warner,	92
Rev. John Anna F. Underhill,	108
Peter Alice L. Aldrich,	126
Thompson T. g Susan M. Townsend,	90
Hartdegen, Adolf B. Annie B. Norton,	124
Hartshorn, Rev. Jos. W. Martha J. Hitchcock.	113
Hartwell, Rev. Chas. { g Lucy E. Stearns,	45
{ g H. Louisa (Plimpton) Peet,	42
Chas. g Caroline M. Lee,	125
Harvey, Dr. C. E. Isadore I. Church,	162
Chas. M. Nellie L. Dews	157
Chas. W. Mary E. Williams,	45
Francis P. Anna E. Tuttle,	71
Hosea B. Emily W. Eames,	96
Harvey, Matthew J., Esq. Susan F. Thompson,	54
Rev. Wheelock N. Margaret B. Lewis,	43
Harwood, Abel Mary D. Batcheller,	20
Albert W. g Mary L. Sibley,	83
Chas. E. Catharine S. Henry,	70
Haskell, Chas. H. Eliza B. Dexter,	46
Marshall H. Fannie C. Fitch,	81
Rev. Samuel Elizabeth H. Granger,	18
Haskins, Wm. L. Philenna R. Hutchins,	56
Hastings, Abijah Mary A. Deane,	81
Rev. Albert E. Sarah R. Hubbard,	81
Benj. F., M.D. Miranda Torrey,	57
Daniel W. Helen A. Ainslie,	36
William N. Mary E. Page,	57
Hatch, Chas. A., M. D. Annie G. Barrows,	131
Wm. T. Mary J. Ladd,	49
Hatfield, Edward Laura V. Bell,	96
Hathorn, J. S. Susan H. Lennan,	56
Haven, Henry P. Elizabeth L. Douglass,	20
J. P. g Ellen C. Whitcomb,	52
Jas. M., Esq. g Martha Eastman,	58
Haviland, Fred'k M. Florence M. Hanor,	140
Hawes, Rev. G. E. Eva C. McKean,	160
Hawkes, Clinton A. Julia E. Bishee,	135
Joseph B. Anna E. Burritt,	39
Orin Ida Merrill,	84
Hawks, William A. g Linda M. Eagley,	75
Rev. Winfield S. g Mary E. Pease,	146
Hawley, Alpheus F. Lucy Fletcher,	25
Arthur A. Genevieve S. Eldridge,	115
B. R. H. Rosamond Hall,	34
Benj. F., M.D. Helen A. Ely,	118
R. L. Emma M. Phelps,	44
Hayden, Alfred P. Nancy G. Peck,	57
Hayes, Fred A. Margaret E. Noble,	104
Jonathan W. Mary J. Parker,	23
Justin G., M.D. Lizzie G. Hills,	116
Thomas S. g Amelia B. Wilde,	58
Hayne, Rev. M. C. Ellen C. Tenbrook,	108
Hayward, H. F. g Stella F. Hawks,	79
Hazard, Herbert H. Jennie B. Hunter,	101
Hazeltine, Rev. H. M. g Fannie Hallock,	48
Hazen, Rev. Allen g Martha R. Chapin,	23
Rev. Austin Almira F. Elliot,	90
E. Minerva Smith,	93
Lucius R. g Maria B. Humphrey,	125
Perley F. Minnie F. Baker,	137
Rev. Timothy A. Sarah A. Ives,	56
Hazelton, A. g Elizabeth M. Loveland,	131
Hazleton, W. P. Ellen M. Van Deusen,	54
Heald, Timothy Adeline E. Huntress,	84
Heavens, Francis J. g Emma C. Bardwell,	139
Hedges, Samuel P., M.D. Rachel H. Danforth,	100
Hellyar, Samuel H. Elizabeth G. Blanchard,	135
Heilig, Monroe Elizabeth M. Bertolet,	103
Helmer, Joseph W. Ellen A. Petrie,	50
Hend, John Hannah W. Terry,	65
Henderson, Chas. W., Jr. Annie L. Atwood,	161
Geo. M. Jane Merrill,	53
Rev. John R. g Eleanor B. Jennings,	128
Hendrickson, Rev. C. R. Ellen F. Dwight,	27

MARRIED NAMES.

Name	Spouse	Page
Heneberger, Andrew	E. Lucy L. Bailey	90
Henry, William C.	Eliza A. Merriman,	140
William K.	Louisa M. Atkinson,	20
Hensley, James H.	g Adelia F. Gates	134
Herbert, George	Theresa T. Arms,	16
John	Louisa H. Scofield,	63
Herrick, A. E., Esq.	Mary D. Chase,	137
Edward M.	Josephine C. Johnson,	97
Henry S.	g Cynthia A. Wright,	55
T. P., Esq.	g Ellen E. Seaver,	68
Rev. Wm. D.	Josephine H. Barton,	55
Herron, Rev. David	Mary L. Browning,	66
Hersey, Alfred H.	Mary H. Gibson,	84
Hettinger, M. T.	Mabel L. Tandy,	163
Hewett, James M.	Jane S. Brown,	106
Hewitt, Elisha,	Persis C. Dana,	20
Henry M., M.D.	g Ida E. Durkes,	146
Heydon, Edwin A.	Mary H. Thurston,	60
Heywood, Frank E.	Hattie D. Jennings,	147
Hibbard, Rev. A. G.	Laura E. Parker,	63
Elisha C.	Alice M. Hibbard,	74
S. L.	Helen L. Kimball,	135
W. W., M.D.	g Hannah E. Rice,	42
Hickok, Francis E.	Mary E. Scofield,	60
Hicks, Rev. Fred	g Mary J. Waters,	83
James R.	Beulah C. Orton,	98
Hiett, Francis M., M.D.	Adelaide Winter,	92
Higgins, Chas. F.	Harriette R. Hovey,	142
Geo. W.	Caroline N. Denison,	52
William A.	g Ella M. Noyes,	120
Hilburn, V. A.	g Maria E. Mead,	51
Hildreth, Abel F.	Eliza M. Day,	16
Chas. E.	Sarah E. Hill,	168
Hill, Frederick J.	g Ida F. Parker,	125
Harry M.	Lizzie M. Stobaugh,	141
Rev. J. J.	Sarah W. Harriman,	59
John, Esq.	Mary Borden,	20
John G.	Josephine E. Branscomb,	60
Rev. Timothy	Frances A. Hall,	34
William	g Mary Burr,	23
Hillman, Benj. R.	Lizzie C. Andruss,	106
Hills, Chester M.	Josephine M. Hutchinson,	70
Hinckley, Eugene F.	M. Ella Peters,	138
George B. F.	Sophronia D. Gerst,	110
Hinds, Arthur	Helen M. Nash,	113
Hinsdale, Chas. C.	Maria E. Weeks,	31
James C., Esq.	Elizabeth A. Pratt,	54
Hipple Geo.	Helen Becker,	52
Hitchcock, A. F., M.D.	Aurilla P. Wellman,	186
D. D., M. D.	g Sarah Worcester,	48
Rev. Edward	Evelyn P. Hawley,	70
H. O., M.D.	g Caroline B. Wilcox,	71
Henry S.	g Mary J. Smith,	58
John F.	E. Carolyn Ely,	83
Lucien R.	Clara E. Dayton,	165
Peter	Sarah J. Wilcox,	82
Samuel	Mary A. Hunt,	34
Rev. Wm. D.	Sarah A. Kilburn,	30
Hoag, Stephen C.	Melinda Hammond,	91
Hobart, Rev. I. N.	Maria R. Eddy,	33
Rev. L. Smith,	g Cynthia Fowler,	32
Hodgdon, Sherman	Sarah L. Greeley,	62
Hodges, Joseph,	Caroline A. Fiske,	66
Hoffman, Ferdinand	g Caroline Bullard,	102
Holahan, Thos. B., Esq.	Julia A. Martin,	116
Holbrook, Alanson A.	Martha J. Burrill,	49
Rev. Chas. F.	Anna R. Bradbury,	69
Rev. Chas. W.	Sarah E. Lyman,	138
Dwight	Kalista W. Thayer,	78
J. D.	Lucy M. Hutchinson,	19
Nelson M.	Elizabeth Eddy,	56
Newton D.	Lucy B. Coffin,	59
Thomas	L. Maria Gleason,	73
Wm., M.D.	Clara Belknap,	33
Rev. Wm. A.	Elizabeth P. Bolles,	80
Holcomb, Carlos P.	Sarah A. Hitchcock,	56
Edward	Emorette Case,	87
John R.	Fannie E. Stearns,	116
Holden, Edgar, M.D.	Catharine Hedden,	59
James C.	g Sarah D. Packard,	36
Rockwell P.	Mary S. Warner,	163
Hollands, Wm., Esq.	g Harriet N. Truair,	163
Hollister, Arthur N.	Fanny R. Wilcox,	57
Shelton	Emily L. Kingsbury,	47
Holmes, A. K., M.D.	Harriet F. (Lindsey) Newhall,	53
Benj. F.	Esther M. Gorham,	49
Edward O.	Amelia G. Johnson,	140
Elwood,	Flora M. H. Keith,	152
Frank W.	Clarissa B. Williams,	82
Fred G., M.D.	g Felicia A. Frisbie,	64
Gilbert	Ann E. Bradley,	39
Rev. Henry M.	Eliza Wilder,	186
Jas. M.	Helen P. North,	54
Robert A.	Susan B. Holmes,	150
Samuel	Mary H. Goodale,	49
Holt, George	Elnora C. Nettleton,	127
Irving L.	Ella M. Rice,	113
Thomas	Maria C. Dodd,	62
Warren	Sarah E. Parkhurst,	25
Holton, Chas. B.	Harriet S. Mould,	108
Geo. E.	Jessica Williams,	166
Holyoke, John	Harriet Wheeler,	17
Homan, Geo. W.	{ Caroline J. Mallery, / Caroline E. Wilde	86 / 64
Homer, Wilson	Hannah P. Seaver,	31
Honeywell, James R.	g Mary Walsworth,	146
Hood, Joseph E.	g Maria Savage,	24
Milton B.	Fannie Montgomery,	116
Hooker, Herbert P.	g Mina K. Merrill,	114
Ralph M.	Theodora A. Tuttle,	150
Hoole, William H.	g Celia A. Dame,	111
Hooper, Ralph B.	Mary L. Leeds,	157
Hoopes, L. S.	Martha Reamy,	91
Hoose, Jas. H.	Lemoyne A. Hale,	84
Hope, William,	Catharine Grant,	121
Hopkins, P. W., Esq.	g Jennet W. Keeler,	82
William C.	Ellen P. Upham,	99
Hopwood, Rev. I. B.	Phebe L. Berry,	59
Horn, Chas. R.	Blanche Thomas,	147
Horton, Edward S.	Frances M. Dulmar	100

		Page			Page
Horton, Horace S.	Eleanor F. Stevens,	38	Hume, Joseph F.	Catharine McNair,	77
James	Jane P. Cheesman,	50	Rev. Robert A.	Katie Fairbank,	135
Theron J.	Julia A. Todd,	130		g Abbie L. Burgess,	111
Hosford, Jas. M., Esq.	Susan S. Seymour,	23	Humphrey, David W.	g Adelaide W. King,	65
Hosler, Wm. F.	Helen M. Shafer,	147	Horace B.	Julia E. Wells,	153
Hosmer, Jas. K.	Jane P. Garland,	110	John	Eliza J. Howard,	118
Hostetter, Albert K.	g Mary E. Shumway,	86	Myron E.	Laura Tarbox,	26
Hotchkiss, Edwin P.	Mary Higgins,	62	Hunt, Abner	Nancy Howard,	34
Hough, Rev. J. W.	Sarah Holmes,	46	Addison A.	Clara E. Thomas,	44
Rev. Joel J.	Sarah E. Johnston,	70	B. F.	Isabella S. Jennings,	116
Houghton, Francis A.	Eliza J. Ward,	38	John Wm.	A. Elizabeth Cain,	69
Henry C., M.D.	M. Ella Pratt,	107	Joshua	g Hannah L. (Romig)	
Joseph H.	Ellen E. Leonard,	98		Mays,	86
Houston, Jas. B.	Emma M. Hughitt,	138	Rev. T. Dwight	Mary E. Preston,	47
Hovey, Edmund O.	g Ettie A. Lancraft,	156	Thomas E.	g Cornelia M. Fithian,	64
Howard, Albert S.	Ellen E. Goodale,	147	Wm. H.	g Caroline J. Estabrook,	45
Charles, Esq.	Mary J. Hunter,	77			
H. N., M.D.	g Anna W. Allen,	95	Hunter, Marshall E.	Lavinia A. Wilson,	89
Rev. Hiram L.	Sarah Snell,	60	Theodore F.	Ida J. Willis,	125
James P.	g Maria L. Smead,	55	Huntington, Chas. T.	Sarah H. White,	21
Theron M.	Olive W. Wood,	45	Rev. E. A.	Catharine Van Vechten,	35
Wm. W.	Mary A. B. Pollard,	57			
Howe, Rev. E. Frank,	Frances F. Gates,	81	William S.	Mary A. Walker,	38
John C.	Helen E. Dickinson,	73	Hurd, Edward P., M.D.	Sarah E. Campbell,	83
Walter W.	Susan W. Felton,	124	Rev. Isaac N.	g R. Loretta Cowles,	79
Howell, F. K., Esq.	Mary A. Harrison,	97	Rev. John C.	Mary H. Shumway,	19
Geo. M.	Mary H. Goldsmith,	97	Judson B., Esq.	g Mary A. Hurd,	79
Jas. R., Esq.	Eleanor F. Smith,	98	Wilson, M.D.	Hannah A. Johnson,	97
Rev. Jesse L.	g Eliza Smith,	51	Hurlbut, Chas. S.	Abby F. Morris,	116
Wm. C.	g Henrietta D. Parsons,	96	Huse, Ralph C., M.D.	Clara M. Noyes,	119
Howes, Fred H.	Eliza E. Boice,	69	Wm. H.	Jessie E. Jewett,	165
Howland, Asa A.	Cornelia W. Collins,	24	Hussey, Eugene C.	Annie D. Batchelder,	126
Rev. H. O.	g Hannah O. Bailey,	17	Hutchins, Chas.	Charlotte E. Wheeler,	78
Henry M.	Elizabeth H. Perry,	136	Edwin W.	Ida C. Lyon,	113
Rev. Wm. S.	g Mary L. Carpenter,	114	Geo. H.	Susan A. Williams,	45
Rev. Wm. W.	g Susan Reed,	18	William C.	g Florence J. Davis,	156
Hoxsey, Thos. B.	Margaret Hoxsey,	97	Hutchings, John F.	g Clara B. Dana,	79
Hoyt, Andrew J.	Daphne E. Osgood,	98	Hutchinson, A. Jr.	Zeruah E. Eggleston,	112
Arthur W.	Mary A. Jones,	60	Alvan A.	Harriet A. Wilkins,	78
Henry T.	g Frances Huntington,	86	Rev. Chas.	Angeline H. Kidder,	47
Moses	Marion Miner,	53	Chas. A.	Mary F. Perkins,	78
Hubbard, Chas. B.	g Anna J. Miner,	83	Isaac	Margie J. Murch,	133
Edward C.	g Sarah M. Humphreys	42	Samuel	Parthena H. Blodgett,	69
Eli A.	Frances Daniels,	24	Wm. A.	Mary S. Loomis,	161
George C.	Mary E. Seymour,	135	Huxley, Edward C.	Alice Haley,	90
Rev. George H.	g Ellen L. Peet,	148	Hyatt, Edwin F.	g Laura P. Hill,	86
George M.	Martha L. Smith,	91	Hyde, Henry D., Esq.	Lavan A. Charles,	87
George S.	Cynthia M. Selden,	41	Rev. Henry F.	Ellen May,	74
J. N.	g Annie J. Burnette,	148	John F.	Sarah C. Eldridge,	22
Hubbell, Rev. H. L.	g Harriet A. Hinsdale	29	Lewis A.	Anna C. Webster,	50
James B.	Katie A. Tew,	63	Wm. H., Esq.	Myra B. Graves,	49
James T.	Mary C. Clark,	132	Hyland, Judson E.	Caroline Chilson,	73
Huff, Wm. A.	M. Agnes Brown,	112	Hynds, Robert H., Esq.	Ann B. Swan,	41
Huffman, Madison B.	May Seymour,	102	Ibbetson, William H. H.	M. Augusta Monroe,	101
Hughes, George	Winona Challen,	144	Ide, Rev. Geo. H.	g Mary J. Sanborn,	112
Rev. Wm. M.	Isabel L. Hoxie,	97		Kate E. Bowles,	118
Hulbert, Chas. S.	g Julia J. Goodsell,	61	Ing, Rev. John	g Lucy E. Hawley,	75
Edwin J.	Frances J. Harback,	56	Ingalls, H. H. G.	Hattie R. Tracy,	145
N. E.	Louise M. (Deming) Clark,	93	Ingersoll, Daniel W.	g Marion M. Ward,	69
			William M.	Alice L. Norton,	94
Hull, Addison O.	Kittie H. Porter,	140	Ingram, Edward H.	g Mary S. Stearns,	126
Burton A.	Sarah W. Chittenden,	126	Inman, Asa F.	Alice B. Chapman,	115

MARRIED NAMES.

		Page
Ireland, Orville L.	Celestia E. Ward,	102
Rev. William	R. Oriana Grout,	70
Ives, Edward R.	Jane M. Blakeslee,	96
Ellsworth	g Elizabeth B. Welch,	117
George A.	Lucy H. Keeler,	143
Harvey M.	Annette E. Bishop,	157
Isaac O.	g Martha R. Gaylord,	86
Ivey, Thaddeus,	g Mary E. Downer,	143
Jackson, A. R., M.D.	g Julia Newell,	61
Caleb H.	Sarah H. Taylor,	127
Chas. A.	Anna E. Kemble,	135
Chas. J. B.	A. Adelaide Hallock,	94
F. Walter	Mary A. Truair,	95
L. F., Esq.	Amanda E. Clifford,	27
W. S.	Mary E. Walsh,	88
Jacobs, Wm. J., Esq.	g Mary E. Maynard,	58
William O.	Esther A. Burlingame,	142
Jacobson, Terence	Marie E. Wells,	111
Jacques, Alfred, Esq.	Mary J. Shaw,	143
Jadwin, Lieut. Edgar	Jennie Laubach,	157
James, Wm. A.	S. Regina Hibbler,	91
Jamieson, Joseph B.	Ida E. Derby,	115
Jannasch, Freid. W.	g Carrie E. Ingraham,	128
Janney, Phineas	Clara Connolly,	90
Jaquith, Edwin P.	Ida M. Jenks,	142
Jencks, Ephraim C.	Elmina Burr,	16
Jenison, Luther S.	Lucina S. Young,	21
Jenkins, Rev. Abraham	Eliza Whittemore,	41
Jenks, Henry B.	g Mary E. Darling,	58
Jennings, Joel A.	g Susan F. Bates,	32
Halsey	g Rebecca Bailey,	146
William H.	Jennie G. Buffum,	124
Rev. Wm. J.	g Miranda D. Greene,	41
Jennison, Clark S.	Louisa F. Farrar,	40
Jewell, Henry H.	Phebe S. Perry,	81
Jewett, Chas. E.	g Mary H. Knight,	106
Frank R.	Sara A. Storrs,	130
Rev. Henry E.	g Alice H. Dwinell,	120
Rev. Sylvanus	g Harriette N. Kingsbury,	39
Johnson, Alfred C.V.	g E. Marcia Doty,	131
Anthony J., M.D.	g Fidelia A. Parker	58
Chas. H., Esq.	Eliza R. Mowry,	67
Chas. P.	Lucinda Williams,	45
Chas. W., Esq.	g Dora D. Keniston,	86
Edward C.	Teresa M. Mason,	113
Edward P.	Jennie Farrar,	126
Emerson	Frances L. Browne,	37
Rev. Gideon S.	Mary W. Jones,	19
Harrison, Esq.	Annette L. Bowen,	27
Harry	A. Agnes Hartshorn,	118
Hudson	Ella L. Foster,	104
Irwin W., M.D.	Laura A. Chambers,	49
Isaac	Hannah J. Hough,	27
Jere., Esq.	N. Salome Trusler,	150
Lopez L.	Lucy J. Bearse,	167
Millard F.	g Alida Martin,	137
Gen. Richard W.	g Julia A. M. Carson,	153
Robert	N. Viola Bumstead,	135
Samuel P.	Bertha M. Huntoon,	162
Simeon S., Esq.	Ellen S. Bailey,	87
Johnson, Rev. Thomas H. M.	Augusta Brooks,	52
Treby	g Amie L. Barbour,	130
Waldo	g Ellen Z. Mills,	89
William H.	g Nancy M. Dewey,	75
Johnston, Geo. W.	Alla S. Chamberlain,	115
John B., M.D.	Sarah E. Badger,	73
Joseph S.	g Harriet M. Paine,	83
Jones, Augustus. M.D.	g Louise M. Buell,	105
Augustus T.	g Helen Eveleth,	72
David L.	Mary C. Seymour,	136
E. F.	Sarah Antoinette Tarbell,	38
Fred P.	g Cora E. Butler,	120
George E.	Eva F. Colvocoresses,	115
Griswold, T.	Bessie H. Comstock,	73
Gurdon A., Jr.	Caroline F. Bliss,	62
Henry S.	S. Elizabeth Parsons,	50
Herschel V.	L. Augusta Wilcox,	145
Isaac R.	Harriet Sears,	28
J. Walter	g Estelle E. Greeley,	164
James A.	Emily J. Wight,	64
Milo C.	Mary F. Cole,	90
Morris E.	Mary E. Childs,	83
Phineas	g Harriet L. Whittemore,	36
Spencer A.	Flora F. Page,	107
T. Curwen,	g Anna Hamilton,	92
Rev. W. G.	g Nettie Horton,	159
W. L.	Sarah E. Thomas,	35
W. R.	g Mirah L. Judd,	151
Wm. P.	Mary E. Hayes, M.A.	53
Jopson, John B.	Belle F. Ware,	108
Jordan, Cyrus	g Julia Moore,	72
David S., M.D.	g Susan Bowen,	95
Samuel C.	g Elizabeth F. Ramlett,	86
Joscelyn, Wm. R., M.D.	Juliana Aldrich, M.D.	42
Joy, Nelson	Lucy E. Trow,	98
Juckett, Clark M.	Flora Benedict,	109
Judd, Chas. H.	Emily C. Cutts,	73
Chas. S.	Lillian M. Whallon,	128
Edward H.	Harriet Montague,	34
Frederick E.	g Kath. E. Parsons,	142
Gilson	Clinene C. Lyman,	43
J. Dwight	g Frances B. Black,	117
Judson, ——	g Mary J. Judkins,	65
Junkin, P. S.	Lucretia Marcy,	162
Kassick, Latham	Mary S. Clark,	30
Keeney, George	g Elizabeth W. Phillips,	39
Joseph	Mary F. Carpenter,	46
Keigwin, Henry	Lissa Hatheway,	154
Keith, Andrew J.	Ella M. Cooper,	121
Arza, B.	g Mary A. Cary,	51
George E.	Anna G. Reed,	127
Kelley, John W.	g Harriet S. Twyman,	96
Kellogg, Edson, Esq.	Susan F. Marsh,	47
Henry H.	g Minnie P. French,	105
Samuel, J. M.	Harriet M. Rogers,	78
Sanford B., Esq.	Louisa P. Allen,	93
Theron H., Esq.	Frances E. Penfield,	84
Kelly, Rev. E. W.	g Mary L. Van Meter, M.D.	123

INDEX.

	Page
Kelsey, Clarence H.	Elizabeth B. Tomlinson, 125
Rev. Edward D.	g Julia C. Baldwin, 141
Harmon J.	Agnes J. Doty, 168
Rev. Henry S.	g Elizabeth L. (Foster) Fiske, 73
Kelton, Robert S.	g Ada E. Ramsdell, 119
Kemp, William R.	Abbie L. Montague, 91
Kemper, Frederick T.	Susan H. Taylor, 38
Kempton, Francis	Alberta K. Williams,150
Kendall, Rev. Charles	Maria Howe, 17
Rev. Henry L.	g C. Idella Plimpton, 117
Howard	Arlina C. Marks, 53
J. G., Esq.	g Mary Poor, 80
J. Osmun	Alice L. Montague, 110
Rev. Robert R.	g Harriet C. Betts, 102
Kendrick, Albert, M.D.	Mellicent A. Olin, 88
Kennedy, Rev. R. H.	Clara E. Gill, 132
Kenney, Alpheus H.	Eliza A. Marshall, 50
Rev. Asa W.	Cornelia A. (Drake) Gladding, 87
Kent, Dr. Alfred A.	Anne F. Wright, 173
Kerr, Jona. G., M.D.	g Abbie L. Kingsbury, 42
Kervan, Lawrence	Mary N. Bancroft, 118
Ketcham, William	Lodema H. Todd, 38
Keyes, Addison	Mary J. Smith, 71
Albert W.	Anna E. Barker, 100
Rollin W.	Abby A. Chandler, 18
Victor	Mary L. Benthall, 55
Kibbe, George	Sarah M. Pratt, 78
Sidney	g Mary C. Pratt, 100
Kidder, Samuel	Eleanor M. Partridge, 60
Kiernan, John	Mary W. Jones, 132
Kilbourn, Rev. James	Marcia A. Jennings, 40
Killinger, J. W., Esq.	g Mary A. Hittell, 48
Kilmer, George W.	Helen A. Adams, 96
	Eunice M. Beede, 93
Kimball, Alonzo S.	{ g Eleanor M. Everett. 111
Chas.	Chloe L. Fuller, 25
Chas. W.	Mary C. Coffin, 118
Fred H.	Emily O. Sabin, 153
Rev. Jas. P.	{ g Mary B. Dickinson, 64 / Jane M. King, 65
Rev. John C.	Emily O. Richardson, 41
King, Benj. P.	Ellen L. Burkett, 73
Bradford B.	Emma B. Williams, 92
Chancy P., Esq.	g Ellen A. Whiton, 58
Chas. E.	Caroline S. Morris, 84
George	Maria Sargeant, 41
Horace	g Anna E. Benton, 54
John C.	Harriet B. Worden, 95
Robert L., M.D.	g Mabel B. Fenn, M.D. 95
Kingman, Abner	{ Sarah J. Anderson, 41 / Caro A. Graves, 84
Kingsbury, Rev. C. A.	Caroline Boynton, 63
Chas. L., M.D.	g Isabella L. Jones, 125
Kingsley, Chas. B.	Caroline E. Holman, 60
Samuel T.	g S. Amelia Todd, 93
William S.	Harriet A. White, 89
Kinney, George E. S.	Harriet F. Thayer, 141
E. C.	Florence E. Balch, 185

	Page
Kirkham, John S.	{ Harriet P. Atwood, 30 / g Mary K. Atwood, 45
Kirkland, H. B., Esq.	S. Catharine Pomeroy,37
Kitchell, N. T., Esq.	g M. Evangeline Paine,128
Kitchin, Chas. H.	g Elizabeth Wilkinson,167
Kittredge, Alvah B.	g Alice W. Gordon, 105
Rev. Chas. B.	g Sarah Brigham, 16
Chas. W.	Isabella H. Bigelow, 42
Harvey G.	Julia A. Moore, 119
Knapp, Rev. Geo. P.	g Anna J. Hunt, 156
Jas. H.	g Anna E. Rice, 106
John H., Esq.	g Caroline M. Field, 38
Kneeland, Rev., M.D.	g Sarah A. Lord, 125
Knickerlocker, Chas.	Caroline S. Scott, 67
H. W.	g Jane N. Cunningham,64
Knight, A. A.	Ellen M. Carruth, 96
Henry M., M. D.	Mary F. Phelps, 44
Herbert B.	Lizzie L. Johnson, 140
Levi A., Esq.	g Sadelia S. Sweet, 76
Robert P.	Elizabeth A. Ayers, 139
Knipe, J. H.	g Mary C. Dillon, 123
Knowlton, Rev. S.	g Frances L. Kent, 85
Koch, Horatio	Sallie Leh, 143
Kridler, Wm. B.	Martha L. Smith, 119
Krumler, Rev., J. P. E.	g Abbie C. D. Goulding, 65
Kuntz, Elwood M.	g Emma A. Engelman, 156
Kürsteiner, A., M.D.	Jane T. Woodruff, 45
Kyle, Jas. G.	Sarah L. McMechan, 81
Lacey, Norman	Catharine Woods, 64
Ladd, Frank J.	Ella P. Clifford, 110
Rev. Henry M.	Sarah E. Harvey, 118
Laird, Rev. Jas.	g Laura G. Millett, 51
Rev. Samuel	M. Andelucia Easton, 70
Lamarche, Edward	Elizabeth S. Francis, 27
Hyacinthe	Emily C. Francis, 25
Lamb, Henry F.	Jeannie M. Lourie, 91
Samuel O., Esq.	g Lucy A. Martindale, 39
Lamson, John C.	Harriet E. Godfrey, 97
John S.	Mary H. Hunter, 63
Lancaster,Lieut.JohnE.	Agnes Fanning, 147
Landfear, M. T.	Mary J. Talcott, 38
Landon, Rev. William	Kittie Kosboth, 172
Lane, Chas.	Elva W. Andrew, 123
Almon B.	Emily A. Tallman, 147
Alonzo	Maria Smith, 57
Anthony	Mary P. Clarke, 50
G. C.	Harriet Sampson, 60
Rev. Jas. P.	Emma L. Pillsbury, 84
Rev. John W.	g Mary Haynes, 96
Jonathan A.	g Sarah D. Clarke, 32
Samuel M.	Beulah (Belknap) Plimpton, 42
Zenas M., Esq.	Emeline Morse, 47
Lang, Thomas	g Malvina(Stanton)Gale,45
Lanman, Rev. Joseph	Clara B. S. Williston, 93
Latham, Harrison W.	g Lucy E. Edmands, 41
Lathrop, Arthur D.	Alice M. Osborne, 127
Henry E.	Harriet N. Stocking, 67
Henry L.	Celia G. Washburn, 108
Norman	Sarah Comstock, 24
William R.	g Emma C. Woodward, 96
Laurie, John	g Catharine Lawson, 48

MARRIED NAMES.

		Page
Lawrence, Alfred L.,	Sarah Boynton,	24
Edward H.	*g* Julia W. Schuyler,	32
H. B.	*g* Adelia M. Brown,	114
Henry C.	Elizabeth A. Bissell,	22
Rev. John B.	*g* Clara C. Dunning,	134
Rev. Wm. A.	*g* Mary A. Reeves,	83
Leach, Clement, Esq.	Martha D. Coan,	24
Rev. Joseph A.	Stella E. Ranney,	98
Shepherd	Phebe H. Allen,	26
V. W.	Mary E. Kendall,	60
Leal, John	Cornelia H. Way,	133
Malcolm	Keziah Ayres,	135
Learned, Samuel J.	Mary A. Gilbert,	27
Learoyd, George	*g* S. Jane Hayward,	75
Leavenworth,J.H.,M.D.	Julia A. M. Hill,	88
Leavitt, Rev. Horace H.	Mary A. Kelley,	129
T. H.	*g* Laura E. (Newhall) (Phetteplace) Geer,	86
W. H.	Celia E. Dunnell,	81
Leavy, Chas. H.	Mary O. Dunning,	112
Le Clerc, Rev. Geo. F.	Harriet E. Booth,	115
Lee, ———	Joanna D. Steele,	71
A. C.	Hattie L. Ellis,	132
Carlton, O.	*g* Ruth A. Courtright,	75
Rev. E. P.	Virginia H. Johnson,	113
George E.	Ella A. Rand,	138
J. E., M.D.	*g* Harriet Landon,	30
James P.	*g* Frances R. Goulding,	58
Rev. J. Ross	*g* Mary P. Crane,	139
Simeon	Sarah Skinner,	47
Leete, Rev. Theodore A.	Mary C. White,	23
Leezer, James M.	Susan T. Trevett,	75
Le Fills, ———	Florence M. Lineville,	155
Leland, Alden	Rhoda A. Leland,	34
Fred W.	Mary E. Pingrey,	158
Jones	Deborah Dowse,	37
Rev. Willis D.	Susan G. Alvord,	139
Lemon, Franklyn H.	*g* M. Oretha Seymour,	142
Leonard, Edwin	Elizabeth D. Ufford,	78
George W.	Jane R. Leonard,	129
Rev. Josiah	Mary C. Smith,	21
Rev. Lemuel	Hannah B. Miller,	17
Lester, George S.	Josephine A. Webb,	64
Rev. Wm. H.	J. Elizabeth Hand,	43
Leverette, John S.	Louisa F. (Packard) Towers,	17
Lewis, Mortimore G.	Maria B. Mulford,	60
Elmer W.	N. Gertrude Parker,	147
Fredrique R.	Harriet E. Smith,	111
F. T.	Harriet N. Phinney,	84
J. D., M.D.	*g* Harriet S. Reed,	65
James	Emeline Strong,	67
James E.	Emma W. Buckingham,	69
John R., M.D.	Sarah M. Thompson,	19
Reuben	Susan F. Lawrence,	53
Rev. T. Willard	Anna E. (Burritt) Hawkes,	39
Rev. Wm. S.	Eliza Cambell,	16
L'Hommedieu, S. Y.	Carrie Baldwin,	123
Libby, Abiel, M.D.	Susan H. (Lennan) Hathorn,	56

		Page
Libby, Franklin E.	*g* Mary L. D. Wilson,	36
Lincoln, Edgar S.	Catharine F. Griggs,	104
James M.	Harriet S. Park,	23
William	Maria Allen,	48
William	Sarah Whitcomb,	38
Wm. E.	*g* Caroline E. Dickinson,	102
Lindsey, John S.	M. Agnes Witter,	148
Joseph B.	*g* H. Fanny Dickinson,	148
Lindsley, S. M., Esq.	*g* Dorlissa E. Johnston,	129
Linnell, J. E., M.D.	Fanny A. Graves,	18
Linscott, Geo. W.	Susan C. Meldrum,	88
Litchfield, Rev. Geo.	A. Sarah M. Gurney,	84
Little, Edward M.	Julia W. Eustis,	46
Jason C.	Harriet C. Hodgdon,	118
Joseph A.	Mary Gerrish,	62
Milton N.	*g* Elizabeth Cochrane,	108
Solomon	*g* Myra Ward,	80
Littlefield, Ambrose	*g* Helen E. Littlefield,	131
Livingstone, William	Frances E. Corle,	118
Lloyd, Prof. Francis E.	Rachel Green,	167
John D.	Elizabeth M. Vedder,	67
Rev. Wm. A	*g* Helen M. Chamberlain,	75
Lobenstine, Wm. C.	*g* Isabella H. Wilson,	139
Lockard, Bruce B.	Mary E. Dann,	126
Locke, Rev. L. Newton	*g* Mary A. Wilson,	30
Rev. Wm. Edwin	*g* Zoe A. M. Noyes,	79
Lockhart, Rev. B. W.	*g* M. Fannie Upson,	123
Lockwood, Fred W.	Mary Amelia Bowles,	55
J. R. Dwight, Esq.	Clara M. Lawrence,	88
Logan, Clarence B.	Alice E. Clark,	112
Lombard, Rev. Jas. K.	Eliz. A. Davenport,	59
Long, Edwin D.	Fanny H. Broughton,	131
F. D.	Rebecca C. Dickson,	115
Longley, Joshua	*g* Maria D. Sabin,	90
Longren, Rev. Chas. W.	Mary A. Jackson,	124
Look, N. L.	Sarah A. B. Lincoln,	31
Loomis, Rev. Elihu	*g* R. Augusta Lane,	32
George W.	Mary E. Norton,	60
Joseph H., M. D.	Mary E. Thompson,	119
Walter	*g* Mary A. Harris,	58
Walter W.	Elizabeth B. Lincoln,	98
William L.	Arabella J. Bissell,	24
Lord, A., M.D.	*g* Frances F. Bigelow,	41
Rev. Edward	Mary J. Sanders,	28
Rev Edward C.	*g* Lucy T. Lyon,	20
Henry	Sarah M. Noble,	40
Lucien	Delia M. Pierce,	98
Lorimer, George	Amelia T. King,	97
Loring, Rev. Henry S.	Abigail A. Farrington,	40
Wm. Claflin.	Louise A. Foster,	70
Lothrop, Rev. C. D.	*g* Anna C. Gilman,	45
Henry F., Esq.	Eleanor B. Penfield,	19
Longbridge, Rev. R. M.	{ Mary Avery, / *g* Harriet Johnson,	18 / 36
Lourie, Geo. M.	Catharine C. Cross,	52
Love, James	Lucy A. Ward,	21
Rev. John	Lilia R. Dowling,	97
Junius N.	Lucinda O. Forsman,	140
Lovejoy, Charles A.	Ellen H. Day,	83
Lovell, Henry R., Esq.	Maria L. Harrison,	70
Lowe, John	Josephine L. Dyer,	93
Lowell, C. W., Esq.	Mary E. Chandler,	73

INDEX.

Name	Spouse	Page
Lowman, F. C.	g Mary Coryell,	156
Lowndes, John H.	Mary F. Griffith,	121
Ludden, Benj. M., M.D.	M.T.(Bassett)Corner,	24
Ludlow, James E.	Sarah J. Vosburgh,	141
Lum, Wm, H.	Margaretta B. Munn,	107
Lund, Chas. C., Esq.	g Lydia French,	72
Lyford, Joshua E. G.	Emma A. Judkins,	119
Lyman,Rev.Addison	g Catharine A. (Porter) Pitkin,	29
Ahira	Theresa Lyman	19
Albert H.	Catharine A. Sprague,	85
Ansel B.	Clara S. Nash,	60
Asa	Elizabeth P. Cutts,	79
Chas. E.	Emma C. Hall,	152
Edward E.	Rosina Willis,	64
John E.	Emily E. Brockway,	152
Rev. Josiah	Mary L. Bingham,	20
Moses,	Sarah H. Beebe,	109
Rev. Payson W.	g Caroline E. Root,	96
Theodore, M.D.	Elizabeth Scrugham,	31
Rev. Timothy,	Mary Saben,	130
Lynn, Charles F.	Mary A. Wright,	50
Lyon, Chas, L.	Caro Allen,	149
Emory, M.D.	Mary C. Burrage,	27
Lyons, Rev. W. L.	Elizabeth M. Hollister,	40
McAllister, J. G., M.D.	g Almeda N. Tirrell,	103
McAndrew, Geo. J.	Sylvia W. Hurlbert,	160
Macaulay, Richard,	Josephine A. Foster,	33
McBride, D. H.	Edith Penfield,	147
McBurney, Wm. A.	Kate Rollins,	122
McCabe, J. W.	E. N. (Belden) Taylor,	185
McCall, Henry S.	g Sara M. Miller,	51
Rev. Salmon	g Emily E. Whitney,	42
Thomas R.	Ella A. Fiske,	112
McCallom, John, M.D.	Susan Carter	90
McCauley, J. D., M.D.,	g Elizabeth G. Conkling,	85
McClean, A. S., M.D.	g Rebekah R. Browne,	20
McClellan, George B.	Mary E. Sanderson,	147
Robert H.	Clara Denison,	90
McClurg, James M.	Ardelia A. (Spencer) Burnside,	31
McCollum, Joel, Esq.	Augusta M. Greves,	53
McCoy,AlexanderEsq.	g Sarah J. Mathews,	48
Henry P.	g Clara A. Robie,	72
McCreary, R. J.	Emily E. Stanley,	111
McCutchen, Augustine	M. Adeline Dewey,	49
McCutcheon, John L.	Lenore H. Phillips,	160
McDonald, James Wm.	Rebecca A. Rogers,	54
McDowell, John T.	Mary E. Wilder,	82
Rev.Thos. R.	Sophie S. Pusey,	153
McElwain, Edwin	Caroline Church,	87
McEwen, Carlton J.	Mary E. Chapin,	115
McFarland, Chas.	Mary E. Thompson,	111
David M.	g Mary M. Rothrock,	92
McFee, Frank E.	Elizabeth R. Aiken,	149
M'Gear, John S.	Ellen E. Bateman,	55
McGeehan, Seldon E.	FrancesE.Hitchcock,	127
McGibbon, Jno.	Mary D. Dibblee,	153
McGiffert, Rev. J. N.	g Harriet W. Cushman,	41
McGonagle, Wm. A.	Sarah L. Sargent,	145
Macgowan, Rev. John	Jane S. Peet,	104
McGregor, Frank P.	Lucia Sanderson,	138
McGrew, Burton J.	Annie W. Pond,	133
McIlvene, John, Esq.	Grace E. Kilner,	132
McIntire,——	Lizzie Parish,	113
Harry H.	Caroline E. Cahoon,	140
Mack, Rev. Edward	Mary A. Kirby,	102
S. D.	g Sarah E. Dutton,	89
McKay, Wm. P.	g Mary S. Green,	32
McKee, Myron A.	g S. Elizabeth Rose,	96
McKelvey, Sidney A.	Hattie F. Hotchkiss,	140
Mackenzie, George M.	Anna K. Pierce,	110
W. D., M.D.	Lucy G. Norris,	107
McKim, Harry J.	Mary E. Chapman,	152
McKinley, James B.	Jane Sanford,	63
McKinney,A.M.,M.D.	g Almira Cutler,	51
McKinstry, Rev. J. A.	g Mary E. Morton,	20
MacLean, Rev. Geo. E.	Clara S. Taylor,	114
McLean, Rev. John K.	Sarah M. Hawley,	53
McLene, Jeremiah	Martha A. Bailey,	59
McLeod, Rev. John	Eliz.W.(Seaver)Frost,	28
McLouth, Geo. W.	Amanda Rush,	67
Macloy, Rev. Robert S.	Henrietta C. Sperry,	35
McMahan, John F.	Annie D. Meech,	143
McMahon, Rev.John T.	Sarah E. Douglas,	87
McMurtrie, Abraham	Almira M. Harris,	129
Geo. K.	Delphine M. Harris,	107
McNair, Wm. S.	Harriette L. Waldo,	35
Rev. Wm. W.	Jennette Shiland,	63
McNeill, Rev. Geo. N.	Margaretta M. Gilbert,	43
McNicol, John,	Adelia Arms,	39
McQueen, Rev. Geo.	g Georgiana M. Bliss,	38
McQuesten, C., M.D.	g E. R. E. Baldwin,	23
	Elizabeth Fuller,	18
John K.	Lucia Cutler,	73
Maddox, Joseph	Cornelia J. Belden,	39
Magill, William A.	g Matilda W. Smith,	76
Magoun, Rev. Geo. F.	g Elizabeth Earle,	82
Mahana, J. O.	Sarah H. Shaw,	85
Mallette, Stanley A.	Effie J. Norton,	170
Mallory, Henry L.	Mary L. Phillips,	130
Maltby, E. C.	Hannah S. Hoadley,	40
Manderson, C. F., Esq.	Rebecca S. Brown,	80
Manier, John	g Julia Sophia Smith,	100
Marchant, David S.	Elizabeth N. Dillingham,	59
J. G.	Susanna Fitch,	38
Marden, Rev. A. L.	Amelia D. Erdman,	70
Margarum, Theo. F.	g Isabelle Whitaker,	109
Marsh, Rev. Alfred F.	Martha L. Rawson,	104
Rev. Chas. A.	Emma L. Case,	126
Chas. H.	Annie B. Davison,	115
Frank W., Esq.	M. Elizabeth Clarke,	135
Rev. Geo. D.	g Ursula V. Clarke,	95
Henry F.	Jane F. Bagg,	32
Henry F.	g Elizabeth S. Frissell,	36
L. C.	Caroline B. Meeker,	56
Rev. L. G.	Sarah P. Harlow,	49
Marshall, Clifton G.	Fannie F. Worstell,	141
Edgar D.	Alida C. Van Duzer,	105
Rev. Henry G.	g Marietta Crosby,	89
J. Bryan	g Mary Hopkins,	32
William	Mary A. Burnham,	57

MARRIED NAMES.

		Page
Marshall, W. S., Esq.	g Katherine S. Montague,	86
Martin, Arthur P.	g Margaret J. Hadlock,	125
Benj. W.	I. Hoyland Taylor,	136
Rev. George W.	Sarah G. Lambert,	70
M. C.	g Eleanor L. Fuller,	131
Thomas	Jennie D. Burrall,	140
Marvin, Asa C.	Mary S. Adams,	30
George S.	g Augusta C. Pratt,	134
Lewis	g L. Vesta Beard,	79
Mason, Alverin A.	g Amelia R. Gere,	51
Lyman	Adaline M. Pratt,	110
Marcus M.	Edith H. Isham,	145
Orlando	{ Sarah J. Fifield,	46
	{ g Calista A. Streeter,	72
Mather, Frank C.	Angeline S. Bissell,	115
Matthews, H. M., M.D.	Martha S. Wheelock,	31
Stephen H.	g E. Louisa Gillett,	51
Matthewson, Joseph	Mary G. Cotton,	115
Matthies, Geo. E.	g Annie T. Wooster,	130
Maxwell, Samuel	Eliza A. Sellon,	26
May, A. C., Esq.	Eliza S. Reed,	44
Edward S.	Emeline Ferry,	16
Samuel P.	Mary J. Sears,	35
Mayhew, Joshua B.	Emily A. Bass,	83
Maynard, Edward	Elizabeth Dean,	172
Edward H.	Sarah A. Newton,	25
Rev. Eliphal	g Celestia A. Kirke,	42
Henry G.	Sophia W. Brooks,	77
James B.	Sarah McLean,	25
William A.	Emma E. Brown,	83
Mayo, Haskell F.	Lois S. Hastings,	34
J. Rhodes	g Elmira S. Bruce,	18
Mayou, Rev. Joseph	Margaret A. Schultz,	50
Mays, Cyrus V.	g Hannah L. Romig,	86
Mead, Rev. Geo. B.	g Anna M. Benedict,	166
Harry E.	Mariana P. Houk,	132
John G.	g Harriet N. Thompson,	20
John H. G.	Charlotte L. Robinson,	35
Martin L., M.D.	g Myra M. Jenkins,	96
Nehemiah	g Elizabeth Durham,	108
Stephen P.	Susan M. Barker,	24
Mears, Edwin M.	Nancy J. McCullough,	98
Leverett	Mary V. Brainerd,	135
Meeker, Fred. H.	Lizzie J. Duley,	154
Meigs, Capt. Timothy	Catharine W. Bridgman,	20
Rev. Matthew	Mary M. C. Gould,	20
Mellen, Geo. F.	Alice Hayes,	40
Mellish, D. B.	g Lucy M. Fitch,	75
Mello, Pedro de	Ella L. Crandall,	121
Meloy, David H.	Sarah P. Sherman,	31
Menaul, Rev. James A.	Sarah M. Foresman,	126
Menzies, James	Mary E. Voorhees,	158
Merrell, Edw'd T.	Mabel Waite,	168
Merriam, Charles F.	Caroline A. Boutelle,	87
H. H.	Fannie S. Guthrie,	84
Rev. James F.	g A. Maria Parrey,	72
Merrifield, Francis N.	g Lucy A. Brigham,	18
William T.	Maria C. Brigham,	27
Merrill, Charles	Catherine C. Sheldon,	78
Charles H.	g Elizabeth M. Farwell,	51

		Page
Merrill, David A., M.D.	Elsie A. Choate,	96
George W.	Mary L. Hitchcock,	147
Joseph	Ellen Hawes,	94
Melville C.	Leah M. Humphrey,	77
Rev. Selah	Frances L. Cooke,	93
Willard, Esq.	g Clara L. Dickinson,	64
Merriman, Chas. G.	g Martha L. White,	42
Frank E.	Ellen M. Fletcher,	87
Merritt, Abijah	g Celia L. Palmer,	125
Rev. E. W.	g Eliza J. Strong,	69
Samuel C., Esq.	Clara Browne,	37
Merwin, Joseph B.	g M. Agnes Beach,	108
Marcus E.	Anna A. Carter,	52
Meserve, John A., Esq.	Alice C. Kimball,	43
Messenger, Austin E.	g Harriet E. Reed,	96
William A.	Elizabeth Chaffee,	46
Messner, David	Marriette Wilson,	35
Metcalf, N. W.	Caroline Henshaw,	27
Meyer, Gustav A. F.	Lucy A. Shaw,	130
Michael, Rev. George	Sarah E. Tewksbury,	91
Mickles, N.	g Abbie M. Ainslie,	35
Mifflin, Chas. W.	g Mary B. Haire,	143
Mildner, Ernest I. W.	Abbie L. Billings,	109
Mildrum, Orrin S.	g Julia S. North,	76
Millard, John A.	Ellen C. Wheeler,	47
Miller, Charles	Harriet N. Fithian,	56
Edward D.	Harriet P. Caswell,	96
Elijah	M. Ella Dow,	121
Emory F.	Sarah J. Andruss,	96
Ezekiel L., Esq.	g Julia S. Trumbull,	26
Frank	Lucretia M. Randall,	35
Gaylord B., M.D.	g Caroline A. Watson,	52
Henry M.	Emily L. Holmes,	63
Prof. Homer R.	g Ellen D. M. Crane,	159
J. Edward	Delia S. Burnette,	129
James	g Frances Tower,	73
Rev. Joel D.	Maria L. Sanderson,	98
John	Nancy B. Miller,	28
Joseph G.	Adelle E. Schirmer,	63
Joseph W.	Helen M. Thompson,	19
Lester C., M. D.	g C. Idella Burgess,	166
Lewis A.	Lena S. Merriam,	160
Lewis W.	Susan A. Tilton,	95
Samuel F.	Charlotte Howe,	37
Silvanus	g Mary E. Graves,	29
T. L.	g Anna E. Hodges,	42
Theodore T.	Harriet Goodspeed,	46
William T., Esq.	Ursula G. Tufts,	75
Mills, Rev. Cyrus T.	g Susan L. Tolman,	33
Josiah A., Esq.	Mary A. Husted,	27
Miner, D. Worthington	Mary H. Warner,	23
Minot, Jonas	Electa F. Morton,	19
Mitchell, Asahel W.	g Frances S. Cogswell,	58
Daniel	Angeline Brigham,	37
F. B., Esq.	g Harriet A. Houston,	143
Heman C.	Orissa W. Converse,	132
J. W., M.D.	g Eliza J. Thompson,	36
John W.	Jane (Merrill (Henderson) De Rochefort,	53
Lester, C., M. D.	Marcia M. A. Hatch,	94
Neil R.	Agnes M. Lewis,	150

INDEX.

Mitchell, Samuel S.	Lucy M. Wright, 99	Morrow, M. L.	N. Helen Brainerd, 69
Winthrop D.	Hattie L. Morgan, 147	Morse,Rev.Andrew B.	g Mary J. Crofut, 51
Wm. L., Esq.	g Lucia L. Bass, 17	Anson D.	Margaret D. Ely, 126
Mix, H. A.	Mary Jacobs, 34	Rev. Chas. F.	g Eliza D. Winter, 65
John M.	Mary P. Barrett, 80	Chas. W.	g Mary S. Bennett, 120
Mixter, Madison	Adeline S. Barton, 83	Chas. W.	Annie G. Cross, 110
Moderwell, J. M.	g Martha A. Jones, 131	Edward M.	g Caroline Wentworth, 58
Molineux, Edward L.	Harriet D. Clark, 83	Frank L.	Hettie P. Carpenter, 185
Moneypenny, J., M.D.	Margaret McA. Hill, 59	Harmon N.	g Caroline A. Brooks, 120
Monie, Thos.	M. Ella Van Doren, 153	Rev. Morris W.	Laura Blasdale, 157
Monks, Richard J.	Mary A. Allen, 65	Orson P.	Eunice W. Bull, 100
Monroe, James	Virginia M. Martin, 44	Morton, Rev. Alpha	Laura E. Field, 77
Montague, Henry W.	g Achsah L. Burt, 89	Charles J., M.D.	Annie E. Coates, 73
George E.	g Carrie E. Jones, 148	Frank R.	Abbie J. Sharp, 104
Samuel E.	Allie M. Jones, 145	Moseley, James H.	Eliza Spencer, 19
Montgomery, Rev. G. L.	Susan N. Philbrook, 74	Mosher, George F.	M. Frances Stewart, 113
H. G.	Charlotte A. Francis, 84	Mosley, Arthur	Hattie E. King, 132
Montross, John T.	g Phebe E. Putnam, 61	Mott, James M.	g Ermina L. Thomas, 149
Moody, Charles E.	g Margaret P. Leavenworth, 142	Dr. O. H.	Minnie S. Newell, 155
John E.	Olive A. F. Gerrish, 104	Mousseau, Charles E.	Julia A. Crossman, 40
Henry	Luella M. Lyman, 155	Mower, Calvin R.	Annie F. Penfield, 124
Moore, A. J. P.	Grace G. Robbins, 136	Ephraim C.	g Philomela S. Greene, 39
J. B.	g Mary W. Plummer, 106	Mowry, Rev. A. F.	Adeliza E. Hadselle, 77
Charles W., Esq.	g L. Amanda Harthan, 65	E. L.	Harriet Price, 136
Davis G.	g Martha J. Hudson, 61	Mulligan, H. S.	ElizabethB.Haddock,118
Edward S.	g Jeannette Fisher, 79	Mumford, John K.	Carolyn C. Tanner, 155
Franklin	Emily S. Parmelee, 107	Mundon, Daniel	Ellen M. Clarke, 59
George D.	Mary J. French, 81	Mundy, Pierson	S. Augusta Strong, 88
Henry G.	g Myra E. Parsons, 117	Munn, Joseph L., Esq.	Elizabeth P. Randall,191
Hiram W.	Cora W. Howe, 127	Munroe, Rev. Egbert N.	Mary L. Farnar, 132
James, Esq.	Ann M. Smith, 71	Munson, Edward G.	Caroline S. Brewster, 66
Justin P.	Charlotte D. Bates, 100	Murdick, Clarence H.	Emma E. Pierce, 155
Robert	Mary S. McQuitty, 132	Murray, Chas. H.	g S. Grace Peckham, 106
Silas B.	Cornelia Landon, 57	Edward E.	Clara F. Merrill, 110
Wm. S.	Catharine A. Richmond, 104	Rev. Edwin W.	Abby H. Crocker, 52
Moors, James A.	Nettie M. Palmer, 140	Myers, Dudley H.	Cora J. Noyes, 167
More, William	Mary A. Cushman, 30	John J.	Mary B. W. Hewitt, 107
Mores, Lucius L.	Adaline Gowen, 62	Narramore, Gaius H.	Maria Critchlow, 66
Morey, Anzi H.	Eveline H. Pier, 34	Henry L.	Daphne S. Warriner, 71
Andrew J.	Sarah L. Harris, 81	Nash, A. J.	Hatty Jeudevine, 157
Louis	S. Frances Benner, 128	Abner P.	Rachel (Blanchard) Pool, 20
Morgan, Elisha	g Sarah E. Grant, 82	Lucius	Elizabeth S. Marsh, 21
E. Charles	Charlotte M. Ward, 82	Nasmith, Rev. Jared S.	Florence S. Wake, 141
Ralph	Martha A. Chase, 33	Naylor, Peter	g Ellen C. (Whitcomb) Haven, 52
Samuel	Mary C. Emmons, 84	Neadwell, Prof. A. M.	Sarah M. Hill, 152
Thomas J.	Madelia A. Patrick, 44	Neal, Edwin C.	Mary F. Plumer, 130
Morley, George W.	Eliza M. Hitchcock, 81	Samuel F.	Luella F. Hibbard, 91
T. M.	Lucy Martindale, 77	William J.	Barbara A. Werlein, 60
Morrell, D. Dighton	Sidney Reamy, 91	Neale, Stanley,	g Emma H. Humphrey,148
Morrill, Rev. Abner	g Ann M. Hussey, 61	Neeley, Frank	Mary E. Sessions, 78
Julius A.	g Sarah C. Bell, 99	Neill, G. W.	g Elizabeth W. Shepard,72
Rev. Stephen S.	Ellen B. F. Bachelder, 76	Nelson, A. J.	g Jennie B. Houston, 134
Morris, C. V. H., M.D.	g Caroline LeConte, 22	Elwyn C.	Elizabeth Brooks, 139
Charles B.	Mary J. Perry, 78	Robert	g WilhelminaT.Meader,117
Rev. Chas. D.	g Eliza B. Harrington, 72	T. L.	g Mary L. Moody, 61
Rev. Edward D.	g Mary B. Treat, 65	New, Tobias,	Lizzie A. Parmelee, 71
Ephraim	Almara M. Nickerson, 56	Newcomb, E. D.	J. Belle Smith, 133
Morrison, Frederick W.	Ann M. Sutherland, 17	Newell, Edward W.	g Lucia A. Chandler, 151
Solon D.	Henrietta M. Fay, 84	John W.	Selina Booth, 24
Morrow, Rev. Horatio	g OliveJ.Emerson,M.D. 39	Newhall, Daniel	g Roxena B. Tenny, 33

MARRIED NAMES. 211

Name	Spouse	Page
Newhall, George H.	Louise E. Page,	98
Rev. George H.	Harriet F. Lindsey,	53
Newkirk, Frank P.	Jennette C. James,	129
William	Elizabeth Ely,	27
Newland, H. N.	g Elizabeth D. Avery,	155
Newton, Ambrose	g Lucy Smith,	29
Arthur S.	Mary Rossiter,	141
Charles A.	g Emma J. (Ford) Piers,	96
Edward W.	Jennie M. Smith,	143
Geo. J., M.D.	Nancy B. Thomas,	28
Simeon	Clara S. Packard,	44
W. A.	Mary L. W. Bowlend,	27
Warren, Esq.	g Lydia A. Wheeler,	36
Nichols, Chas. B.,M.D.	Eliza B. Mattocks,	98
David F.	g Ella C. Marshall,	117
G. M., M.D.	Hannah C. Paine,	57
George W.	Elizabeth Clarke,	93
Rev. Howard S.	A. Elizabeth Morley,	94
Ira J.	g Mary M. (Foster) Bartlett,	68
Rev. John T.	g Anna C. Herrick,	134
Rev. W. A.	{ Bethia A. Miller,	17
	{ g Sarah A. Bonney,	26
Nicholson, James	F. Ella Ives,	124
Nickerson, Charles,	Ella M. Graves,	129
Rev. Charles S.	g Julia C. Dickinson,	143
W. T.	Charlotte A. Bishop,	109
Nightingale,Rev.Chas. S.	Caroline V. Thayer,108	
Niles, Addison C.	Elizabeth Caldwell,	73
Edward S.	g Elizabeth P. Wright,	112
Rev. H. E.	Jeannie E. Marsh,	40
John O., M.D.	Cornelia D. Norton,	34
William C.	Sarah M. S. Blinn,	27
Nimmo, Alexander A.	Anna M. Smith,	145
Nims, Marshall W.	Alice M. Whitcomb,	130
Noble Frank W.	Alice J. Fowler,	142
George	g Elizabeth M. Webb,	123
Nolton, Daniel	Angelina H. Fox,	18
Noone, Albert W.	Isabel P. Cutter,	110
Norcom, Fred B.,M.D.	Mary Mosher,	50
Norcross, C. O.	Cora L. Sawin,	119
Jacob	Emeline Taylor,	63
Norris, John C., M.D.	Emily P. Tupper,	60
North, L. Hoyt	g Martha C. Newton,	128
Northrop, George D.	g Ella K. Hoyt,	143
Linus O.	Margaret W. Holmes,	63
Norton, Arthur B.	Ethel A. Littlefield,	152
Charles E.	Mary J. Leonard,	67
E. C.	Fannie L. Rice,	130
Edward	Helen R. Hodges,	140
Henry F.	Gertrude H. Washburn,	92
Lemuel D.	g Mary E. Gass,	102
Nourse, ——	Amanda A. Hodgman,	185
Noyes, Chauncey	Mary J. Fowler,	62
Edmund	Mary S. Wells,	114
Edward W.	Adeline D. Josselyn	34
James	Annie M. Colley,	103
James	g Frances M. Leavitt,	51
John W.	{ Clara D. McFarland,	21
	{ Harriette S. Bouton,	45
Rev. Joseph T.	Elizabeth A. Smith,	41
Noyes, Luke B.	Frances C. Robinson,	98
Nute, John W.	Annie B. Laudach,	155
Nutting, Wm. S.	Mercy J. Fetch,	49
Nye, Charles B.	Artemesia E. Bradley,	55
Charles D.	g Emma C. Lowe,	61
Horace S.	Mary S. Nash,	19
Oakes, James L.	g Jane M. Wilson,	106
O'Bryan, S. D.	Lucy A. Lawrence,	84
Ogden, Rev. Joseph M.	Emeline Sweasey,	17
Ozier, John M.	Jennie McPherson,	138
O'Gorman, James	g Lucinda Hilborn,	89
Olcott, W. Harry	g Alice Hedrick,	141
Oldham, Rev. Wm. F.	Marie A. Oldham,	152
Olds,ChaunceyN.,Esq.	g Mary B. Williams,	39
Olmsted, H. K., M.D.	g Anna M. Olmsted,	32
Olney, Albert H.	Frances E. Olney,	78
Orbison, David W.	g Hannah D. G. Jones,	29
Orcutt, Wm. B.	Mary E. Kingsley,	110
Ord, Arthur B.	g Annie E. Childs,	121
Orear, B. F.	Margaret C. Bartlett,	49
Orr, Lyle W.	g Marian B. Miller,	164
Washington J.	Ella E. Deering,	126
William P.	Frances J. Meily,	136
Orwig, Thomas G.	Mary E. Sipp,	28
Osborn, Luke	Martha Luce,	47
Osborne, Charles K.	Anna Southmayd,	116
N., M.D.	Anna L. Randall,	91
Rockwell E.	g Louise L. Ober,	106
Osgood, C. H.	Annie E. Hart,	116
Edward S.	Etta Haley,	132
Capt. Henry	Harriet M. Hubbard,	101
Rev. H. P.	Mary A. Reed,	50
James H.	Jane T. (Sherman) Smith,	21
Osmond, Rev. S. M.	Harriet (Samson) Lane,	60
Osterstock, Joseph S.	Sarah A. Siegfried,	91
Otterson, Ira	Sarah E. Easton,	97
Oughtred, Allan R.	Elvira F. Webber,	136
Overstreet, R. S.	Mary C. Vannnys,	92
Packard, Henry C.	g C. Amelia (Whitney) Card,	69
William A.	Susan B. Gallagher,	40
Page, Benjamin,	Lucy Barnard,	16
Benj. F., M.D.	Caroline Farr,	93
Rev. B. G.	g Fanny M. Hidden,	80
E. Ransom	g Lucy A. Paige,	92
George, M.D.	Loraine H. Dike,	18
George H.	Eliza Button,	77
George M.	Edith Morrill,	122
James F.	Dora D. French,	154
J. L.	Ellen H. Lewis,	34
Joel	Mary A. Cushman,	59
Minor G.	Eliza A. Greene,	46
Phineas L., Esq.	{ Julia Putnam,	35
	{ g Lorie A. Eldridge,	61
Paine, H. M., M.D.	g Charlotte Mann,	48
Jeremiah W.	Harriet Dakin,	43
L. B.	Kathreen A. Sawyer,	94
Reuben	Abbey A. Bell,	76
Painter,Henry W.,M.D.	g Alice F. Lord,	131
Palmer, Albert A.	g Helen Humphrey,	18

INDEX.

		Page			Page
Palmer, Frank H.	Martha Cummings,	43	Pease, Edward L.	Marietta Piper,	119
Jacob P.	g Mary A. Kimball,	58	Fred N.	Delia M. Morris,	119
Ozias E.	Abby A. Cowdery,	33	Henry	g Ann E. Church,	38
Smith T.	g Margaret B. (Judd) Gaines,	102	L. Hoyt	Julia L. Sawyer,	122
Rev. Wm. R.	Clara Skeele,	54	Peck, Dr, A. F.	g Lizzie F. Bates,	151
William S.	g Marietta M. Williams,	80	Austin, La F.	Mary D. Hawks,	67
Pancroft,Prof.Stephen	g Lydia A. Gile,	167	Charles	Mary F. Davis,	49
Pancoast, William H.	g Anna M. Worrell,	106	Rev. J. Oramel	Susan R. Robinson,	81
Pardoe, Avern	Mary J. Sprague,	113	John F.	Cornelia Towne,	54
Park, Calvin	Fannie L. Fenton,	56	Martin M.	Harriet E. Wooster,	119
Charles H.	Lillie S. Stannard,	133	Robert C.	Elizabeth M. Dewell,	43
Rev. Charles W.	g Anna M. Ballantine,	102	William W.	Henrietta B. Taylor,	60
D. F.	g Lydia M. Carner,	89	Wyllis	Sarah J. Gillette,	62
John N.	Rebecca F. Titcomb,	78	Peckham, F. H., M.D.	Catherine D. Torrey,	17
Parker, Rev. ——	g Rosanna H. Cobine,	29	Pedley, Rev. Hilton	g Martha J. Clark,	156
Charles	Sarah C. Eno,	118	Peet, Rev. Lyman B.	g H. Louisa Plimpton,	42
Charles C.	Sarah J. Taylor,	23	Rev. Lyman P.	g Caroline Körner,	154
Charles E.	Ellen L. Perkins,	28	Rev. Stephen D.	g Olive W. Cutler,	92
Geo. W.	Annie M. Lyford,	157	Peirce, Charles F.	Harriot O. Putnam,	26
Rev. Lucino	Jane M. Skinner,	50	Rev. Charles H.	g Elizabeth W. Goffe,	64
William D.	Asenath B. Wood,	95	Pelton, Charles B.	A. Minnie Whitney,	145
Parks, James Wm.	{ Caroline Jewell,	34	F. W., Esq.	Mary R. Whitney,	89
	{ Maria Jewell,	34	Pendleton, Rev. H. G.	Emily Booth,	18
Parmalee, Lucius	Fidelia A. Wilder,	38	Penfield, John G.	Mary E. Crosby,	46
Parr, Richard C., M.D.	Almira P. White,	85	George M.	Cornelia A. Penfield,	71
Parsons, Benj. F.	Martha A. Bush,	24	Rev. Thornton B.	Charlotte E. Hubbard,	97
Enos, Esq.	Eliza H. Sears,	41	Pennell, Rev. Lewis	Mary C. Sherwood,	26
Isaac	Rachel C. Edwards,	34	Pennock, S. M.	g Caroline Eaton,	68
Jay F.	g Orra E. Miller,	86	Penny, Rev. Geo. B.	Harriette N. Love,	165
Josiah	Mary G. Alden,	16	Pepper, Rev. G. D. B.	g Annie Grassie,	72
Partch, Wm. H.	FlorenceJ.Hawthorne,145		Perkins, Abraham R.	{ Louise M. Fiske,	105
Partington,FrederickE.	ElizabethH.Bateman,121			{ g Mary A. Hart,	128
Partridge, A. C.	g Eliz. A. Philbrick,	42	Charles W., Esq.	Sophia V. W. Knowlton,	49
Alwyn H.	S. Elizabeth (Maltby) Winn,	50	Frederick	Ellen L. Blackler,	37
Frank J., M. D.	g Lucy C. Upham,	154	Frederic B.	g Frances B. Johnson,	51
Parvin, John A.	Mary L. Westcott,	35	James E.	g Margaret A. E. Heacock,	65
Patch, Geo H.	Loretta A. Ramsey,	130	John P., M.D.	g Achsah Wheeler,	36
Patrick, Rev. H. J.	g Martha A. Loomis,	51	Joseph L.	Flora H. Perry,	57
Joseph E.	Mary H. Lyman,	77	Justin B.	Mary L. McKeown,	140
Patten, Claudius B.	Mary D. Perkins,	57	Luther, Esq.	Lizzie H. White,	99
F. Jarvis	Hattie C. Bessé,	139	Perley, Charles A., Jr.	M. Ella Waite,	133
George M.	Emilie J. Pratt,	78	Chauncy C.	g Sarah T. Penniman,	79
Henry B.	Emily A. Allen,	137	Thomas A.	Mary A. Chaplin,	118
Patterson, Lucius	H. Jane Marshall,	28	Perrin, J. Q. A.	Elizabeth A. Talcott,	26
William M.	CorneliaS.Fehrmann,140		Simon A.	Selina A. Rice,	101
W. R.	Sarah A. Probasco,	141	Perry, Amos B.	ElizabethJ.Gilchrist,113
Patton, Desha	Susan Snowdon,	74	Rev. David	Sarah Platt,	17
Paul, Franc M.	g Amanda M. Cole,	41	H. Danforth	{ Elizabeth S.Howland,	40
Payne, Franklin	E. Elizabeth Wilcox,	148		{ g M. Elizabeth Childs,	68
Peabody, Rev. Charles	g Eliza A Hubbell,	29	Horace B.	Sarah A. Stewart,	17
David L.	Lucy D. Tolman,	44	Job T.	Catharine A. Bigelow,	33
Dean, Esq.	g Matilda F. Peabody,	42	Joseph S.	Lucy A. Day,	66
Pearce, Edgar P.	g Mary G. Ewart,	82	Oliver H.	Sarah E. Flagg,	34
Rev. George	g Lavinia Peabody,	109	Thomas W., M.D.	CarolineD.Grosvenor,	22
Pearson,Rev.CharlesH.	Emily C. Clemens,	16	Peterson, C. A., M.D.	g S. M. Jennings, M.D.	139
Henry L.	g Laura A. (Rice) Rice,	68	P. S.	Mary A. Gage,	90
Peart,W.L.,Esq.	g Virginia G. Sloan,	120	Samuel W.	Zeruah E. Egleston,	112
Pease, Claudius B.	g Mary W. Chapin,	26	Sidney,	Caroline Ford,	87
David H.	g Sarah A. Burton,	64	Petran, Rev. Henry J.	Mary A. Armstrong,	149
Earl M.	Eva L. May,	165	Pettee, S. E.	Fidelia T. Carpenter,	55

MARRIED NAMES.

		Page
Pettibone, A.W., Esq.	g Cordelia O. Wilson,	61
Phelps, Prof. Chas. S.	g Orra A. Parker,	161
David B.	g Lydia R. Baldwin,	32
Rev. Fred B.	Sarah T. Dickinson,	52
George M.	Abbie J. Case,	100
George S.	g Fannie E. Bissell,	128
Gurley A., M.D.	g Nancy P. Stoughton,	39
Henry	Cornelia P. Tarbox,	26
Phetteplace, Jay	g Lura E. Newhall,	96
Phillips, Elmer E.	g Ellen E. Carpenter,	99
Frank B., Esq.	Grace E. Longley,	119
Jay E.	Carrie P. West,	138
Stanley A.	g Martha E. Lamson,	128
William B.	g Adelaide E. Nichols,	86
William S.	Ellen A. Griswold,	34
Phipps, Rev. Geo. G.	g Kathleen M. Carruth,	92
Rev. Wm. H.	g Mary E. Williams,	118
Pickert, Corlis J.	Anna F. Hathaway,	116
Pickett, Aaron	Caroline M. Williams,	47
Edwin D.	Sarah C. Harrington,	59
Rev. Joseph W.	Mary J. Roberts,	78
Pierce, Albert J.	Jane M. Everett,	121
Henry A.	Mary P. Ely,	43
Henry H.	Maria D. Smith,	74
Homer E.	Catharine S. Chamberlain,	109
Horace T. N.	Sophia C. Dickinson,	27
John C.	Emma S. Boynton,	121
L. L.	Jane W. Smead,	98
Rev. L. M.	g Catharine E. Billings,	79
Rev. N. H.	Eliza M. Dewey,	43
William G.	H. Janette Towne,	57
Pierpont, Rev. James	Maria C. Dibble,	52
Piers, Gordon	g Emma J. Ford,	96
Pierson, D., M.D.	g Fanny Lathrop,	65
Eugene	Anna P. Sayre,	147
Rev. Isaac	g Sarah E. Dyer,	102
Pillsbury, Josiah W.	Elizabeth Dinsmore,	18
Pinckney, D. H.	Katherine A. Sharp,	133
Pinkham, James K.	Cornelia A. Fuller,	62
Pinney, Julius	Mary W. Grant,	101
William	g Mary T. Webb,	139
Piper, Myron H.	g Clara F. Allen,	120
Pitkin, Rev. F. H.	g Catherine A. Porter,	29
Rev. Paul H.	R. Ellen Pierce,	110
Pitman, Chas. F.	Grace A. Vaughn,	153
Pitts, Jesse G.	Helen R. Day,	52
Pixley, Rev. Stephen C.	Louisa Healy,	67
Plack, Rev. George W.	Margaret M. Coyle,	135
Platt, Rev. Edward F.	Agnes E. Barney,	66
George F., M.D.	Mary N. Montague,	67
L. Tudor	Rebecca C. Hurlburt,	101
Plimpton, Cassius E.	Aurelia A. Chapman,	124
Edward G.	Eames,	83
Louis F. S.	g Chiara A. Curtis,	95
Rev. Salem M.	Beulah M. Belknap,	42
Plumb, Francis E.	Ellen M. Powers.	113
Plumer, Rev. Alex. R.	g Lucy A. Gibbs,	79
David	Susan S. Ordway,	34
John M., M.D.	g Julia M. Coan,	51
Plummer, Rev. Fred.	Rachel Hathaway,	17
Pogue, Rev. John F.	Maria K. Whitney,	21

		Page
Pollard, Uriah A.	Elizabeth P. Moore,	25
Pomeroy, Charles	Marion H. Leonard,	28
C. G.	Maria A. Pomeroy,	63
E. Frank	g Jane E. Carpenter,	75
Isaac, Esq.	g Mary J. Taylor,	39
Julian	Charlotte Morgan,	70
Robert S.	S. Madora Breese,	83
S. C.	M. S. (Mann Harrington) Whiting,	37
Samuel	Caroline Fuller,	20
William	Frances Blackington,	39
Pond, Rev. J. Evarts	Lydia S. Hoadley,	40
James F.	Abbie B. Draper,	77
Orlando B.	Althea J. Buck,	90
Willis L.	Sarah M. Mills,	100
Pool, A. J.	S. Rebecca Wright,	26
Alfred C.	Lydia F. Burns,	30
Joseph	Rachel Blanchard,	20
Poor, Rev. David J.	Susan Thompson,	21
Pope, Willard S. Esq.	g Harriet L. Bissell,	38
	g Julia A. Bissell,	41
Porter, Edwin A.	Jane S. Warner,	95
Howard L.	g A. Rosalie Hammond,	141
Joseph W.	g Rhoda K. Perkins,	32
Rev. William	g Clementine M. Locke,	32
William P., Esq.	g Sarah A. C. Perry,	76
Post, George R.	Elizabeth L. Whaples,	41
Hiram H.	Amanda H. Blakslee,	112
Rev. Martin M.	g Eliza M. Breed,	18
Reuben L.	H. Louisa Mason,	28
William	Susanna Hazeltine,	25
Potter, ———, M.D.	Elizabeth L. Root,	19
Alden	Annie E. Goodwin,	110
Joseph S.	Sarah E. Adams,	29
Lewis	Anna Aldrich,	83
William R.	Cynthia Bowen,	30
Powers, Frank E.	Laura B. Lincoln,	140
Myron E.	Jessie H. Sheldon,	150
Wilbur H., Esq.	Emily Owen,	136
Powning, C. C.	Clara A. Poor,	127
Pratt, B. F.	Sarah P. Lyon,	50
Charles, A. B.	Helen A. Coggin,	77
Rev. Dwight M.	Martha A. Rood,	133
Edward W.	Cornelia M. Doane,	46
H. A.	Marietta Kingman,	43
Henry A.	Cornelia M. Long,	60
James H.	Mary Bates,	22
L. C.	Melaneia B. Wright,	41
O. H.	Caroline D. Gridley,	34
Rev. Stillman	Hannah Brigham,	16
Pray, O. M., M.D.	Meta L. Lawrence,	91
Prendergast, Francis E.	Mary A. Childs,	110
Prentice, Everett D.	Teresa L. House,	116
Prentiss, A. F.	g Sarah E. Foote,	32
Edward W.	g Martha A. Curtis,	51
Lory	g Lucy A. Stearns,	161
Pressy, Charles	Elizabeth Patten,	50
Preston, Francis W.	Emma A. Dimmick,	121
Prevear, Edward	Elizabeth M. Pranker,	60
Price, Wm. H., Esq.	Susan M. Swift,	21
William I.	Caroline B. Anderson,	52

INDEX.

		Page
Priest, Rev. J. Addison	Frances Walker,	44
Prime, Rev. E. D. G.	Abbie D. Goodell,	37
Procter, John R.	Julia L. Dobyns,	93
Prochl, Frederick R.	g Sarah L. Graves,	61
Proffit, Rev. Arthur H.	Katharine F. Pease,	158
Prosser, Levi	Harriet E. Wilcox,	28
Prouty, John W.	Isabelle H. Dewar,	137
Puetz, John C.	Mary N. Walker,	141
Pulling, B. W., Esq.	Emma D. Bouldrey,	137
Pulsifer, William H.	g Cornelia L. Boardman, M.D.	99
Purington,—	g M. Louise Chamberlain, M.D.,	95
D. V.	g Jane F. (Barnes) Crandall,	99
Rev. Lewis M.	g Mary A. Beard,	79
William A., Esq.	Eva E. Allen,	142
Purinton, Rev. Jesse M.	Nancy A. Lyon,	21
Putnam, Granville B.	Jane E. Hitchcock,	56
Horace	Lucy W. (Smith) Chamberlain,	28
John, M.D.	g Elizabeth S. (Hawks) Reed,	23
John S.	Caroline McCray,	31
Levi	Alicia Kendall,	47
Quested, Wm. M.	Althea M. Cooke,	160
Quick, H. Lansing	g Sarah F. Mott,	174
Quinn, William W.	Aurora M. Lee,	98
Quinton, Herbert T.	Anna W. Swift,	105
Rabb, David G.	g Rachael A. Fitch,	45
Ramsay, Rev. J. Ross	Mary L. Diament,	62
Rand, Albert H.	H. Catherine Hitchcock,	129
John P., M.D.	g Harriet M. Anderson,	158
N. W., M.D.	g Jenny Peek,	146
Randall, B. H., Esq.	Wilhelmina H. Langé,	43
Isaiah	g Emma A. Powis,	76
Randlett, Geo. W.	Hannah H. Willard,	71
Randolph, W. H. F., M.D.	Dorcas E. Butler,	96
Rankin, John C.	g Mary E. (Barber) Carpenter,	75
Ranney, Rev. J. A.	Phebe A. Hitchcock,	22
James W., M.D.	Deborah D. Gerould,	25
Ransom, John	g Emma Ransom,	137
Rathbun, J. Alden	Hannah A. Ashbey,	87
Rathburn, William P.	Catharine W. Daniel,	62
Ray, John H.	Genevieve S. Eldredge,	115
William R., M.D.	Susan E. Barker,	131
Raymond, Henry N.	Elizabeth A. Strong,	57
John B., Esq.	F. Evelyn Hunt,	88
Robert F.	g Mary E. Walker,	151
Samuel W., Jr.	Eliza H. Smith,	104
Raynolds, G. C., M.D.	g Martha W. Tinker,	80
Read, A. N., M.D.	Elizabeth Cook,	37
Henry G.	Frances L. Williams,	47
Lavant M., Esq.	Sarah A. Perkins,	113
Robert M., M.D.	Anne G. Lauriat,	121
Thomas B.	Mary J. Pratt,	23
Reardon, William	Marian H. Gardiner,	94

		Page
Redfield, G. H.	Mary McCord,	145
Reed, Andrew P.	Theresa M. Leonard,	88
Edward P.	Clara M. Winegar,	75
Fred	Mary E. Dodge,	124
Fred L.	Lizana E. Miller,	147
Horace R.	S. Elizabeth Hersey,	127
Hubbard W.	g Nellie C. Jewett,	117
John C.	Rachel Higgins,	74
J. V.	g Annie M. Griggs,	159
Rev. Orville D.	Caroline M. Byington,	137
William B., M.D.	g Elizabeth S. Hawks,	23
William K.	Sarah E. Converse,	77
William R.	g Carrie H. Twombly,	146
Reeder, S. A., M.D.	g Anna M. Harris,	99
Reeve, Felix A.	Wilhelmina D. Maynard,	98
Reeves, Walter	Marietta M. Cogswell,	103
Reilly, William, Esq.	Rachel M. Hoover,	113
Reineck, John T.	Olive E. Farnsworth,	87
Relyea, Albert, Esq.	Eleanor Wood,	158
Requa, George W.	Harriet I. Anable,	83
Resley, S. G., M.D.	g Elizabeth King,	32
Rew, Mellville W.	g Clara E. Whipple,	100
Reybold, Barney	Sophronia C. Hyde,	21
Reynolds, B. W.	Harriette D. Randall,	133
Henry F.	Anna T. Merritt,	70
J. J.	Emily C. Hawley,	40
Jesse, M.D.	Lucy A. Coleman,	88
William D.	Cornelia H. Smith,	71
William P.	Sarah E. French,	107
Rhea, Rev. Samuel A.	g Sarah J. Foster,	64
Rhinesmith, Charles	Minnie J. Rice,	143
Rhymus, Chas. W.	Flora Benedict,	109
Rice, Albert S., Esq.	Frances W. Baker,	69
Charles E.	Mary L. Ames,	24
Charles L.	Harriet E. Perry,	98
David, M.D.	Harriette Clapp,	24
Rev. E. J.	g Laura A. Rice,	68
Edward	F. Louisa Davis,	87
Franklin M.	Eliza J. Howard,	118
L. B.	Abbie L. White,	67
Oliver	Mary A. Caldwell,	16
R. Merrick	g Anne S. Wingate,	45
Reuben J.	Minnie E. Roberts,	162
Rev. T. O.	{ g Mary C. Washburn,	29
	{ g Margaret Mann,	23
William I.	J. Eliz. Edgerton,	100
Richards, Alfred T.	g Laura R. Johnson,	76
Chandler, Esq	g Adeline H. Willcox,	55
Charles H.	Ettie Harlow,	101
Josiah S., M.D.	Mary P. Egery,	16
Lucas F.	Martha D. Billings,	59
Solomon	g Frances A. Haskell,	80
Zalmon	g Mary F. Mather,	68
Richardson, A. N., M.D.	g Mary C. Gore,	117
Rev. Charles S.	Frances M. Weed,	105
Rev. Cyrus	g Annie Dearborn,	99
David	L. S. (Catlin) Bearden,	27
David M.	Eliza J. Holliday,	97
Edward A.	Clara E. Page,	152
George L.	Alice A. Giles,	118

MARRIED NAMES. 215

		Page
Richardson, Henry W.	Catharine S. Smith,	74
M. C.	F. C. (Catlin) Ticknor,	37
Robert M., Esq.	g Eveline A. Sherwood,	32
Walter J., M.D.	g Sarah Sagar,	151
Richmond, Charles	Sarah M. (Noble) Lord,	40
Henry J.	Emma J. Hermance,	145
Ricker, Earle J.	Annie C. Marshall,	122
Riddle, William E.	Ida B. Wheaton,	130
Rideout, Joseph	g Eliza E. Cowles,	92
Riegel, Albert J.	Julia Fritcher,	107
Riley, Charles S.	Ellen P. Furey,	110
Ring, George E.	Ada M. Fogg,	152
Ripley, Charles D.	Delia M. Montague,	88
Erastus L.	Emily J. Isbell,	47
Rittgers, M. D.	Mary E. Barton,	112
Robbins, Cyrus S.	Mary L. Rockwood,	74
Daniel J.	Elizabeth C. Ruggles,	47
Edwin H.	Caroline A. Barton,	109
Harrison	Charlotte B. Mead,	53
Samson M.	g Harriet S. Clark,	82
Roberts, George L., Esq.	Hinda Barnes,	69
Rev. John S.	Emma M. Hughes,	70
Rev. William C.	Mary L. Fuller,	70
Wm. T.	Helen A. Barnes,	149
Robertson, Cadmon D.	Emoretta M. Taft,	111
Charles H.	Dorothy L. Judd,	21
Frank	Mary W. Rawles,	158
Robins, Robert W.	g Ellen A. Parsons,	123
Robinson, E. F.	Abbie S. Redman,	98
Rev. E. W.	Sarah B. Adams,	16
Silas A., Esq.	Fannie E. Norton,	94
Theodore P.	Eliza M. Monroe,	104
Rev. U. B.	Eliza B. Cotes,	93
Robson, W. O.	Ellen Riggs,	78
Roby, Henry W.	Sallie Collier,	103
Roche, John F.	Hannah Freeman,	73
Rockfeller, C., Esq.	Lucinda Van Ness,	133
Rockwell, F. W., Esq.	g Mary G. Davis,	108
Rodman, Rev. J. T.	g Keturah Longstreet,	61
William W., M.D.	Jerusha Pomeroy,	17
Roessler, Paul	Sarah E. Lindsley,	56
Rogers, Charles W.	Joanna M. Coggeshall,	16
Edwin E.	Rebecca P. Van Deusen,	35
Rev. Edwin E.	Mary E. Hulbert,	140
Frank D.	Annie M. Lawrence,	138
George M.	Mary A. Hartwell,	43
Henry, V. D.	Elizabeth H. Slack,	119
Moses, M.D.	Elizabeth F. Lewis,	21
Rev. N. B.	g Lydia G. Bailey,	32
Richard T.	Olive M. Page,	57
Robert	Cornelia M. Dowling,	59
S. J. S., M.D.	g H. Augusta Belcher,	82
Rood, Rev. David	Alzina V. Pixley,	40
Root, Rev. Augustine	g Mary F. Stearns,	58
Moses	Mary A. Blanchard,	45
Russell S.	Marietta Cummings,	110
Solomon F.	Anna Smith,	41
Spencer B.	Mary R. Allyn,	30
Rosa, F. G.	g Jane Cahoon,	111
Rose, Alfred W.	Sarah E. Eaton,	20
Rev. Samuel	Grace M. Chamberlain,	157
Walter B.	g Electa M. Smith,	83

		Page
Rose, Walter C.	Frances W. Morey,	119
Ross, Edwin	Valina J. Woodward,	114
Marcus J.	Mary L. Coleman,	73
Samuel	Mary E. Chamberlain,	122
Wm. F.	Margaret J. Hearne,	152
Rossetter, Rev. G. R.	g Elizabeth P. Clark,	29
Rossman, Retine L.	Irena Casper,	129
Rounds, Charles B., Esq.	Harriet N. Chase,	73
Stephen	Minnie Briggs,	121
Rounsevel, Chas. S., M.D.	Flora M. Horton,	142
Rouse, Rev. Clarence W.	g Annie L. Greene,	164
Rev. T. H.	g Eliza Hallock.	18
Rowan, D. M.	Mary J. Burdett,	43
Rowe, H. J., M.D.	Helen I. Taylor,	136
William	Lizzie G. Baldwin,	128
Rowell, Rev. Geo. B.	g Malvina J. Chapin,	22
Joseph E.	Mary F. Rockwell,	98
Rowland, Samuel S.	g Emily C. Thorpe,	52
Rowley, Rev. Charles H.	Martha C. Brown,	115
Rowse, Rev. Fred H.	g Mary E. Brown,	128
Royce, Charles A.	S. Elizabeth Branning,	126
Julius H.	Harriette A. Wells,	38
Rubier, C. M., M.D.	Sarah E. Clarke,	33
Rugg, David F., M.D.	Julia A. Hager,	127
George H.	g Rachel Vaughn,	76
Ruhl, John L.	g Julia S. Walker,	144
Rupert, Frank E.	Bernice M. Budd,	172
Russell, Albert P.	Cordelia M. Ferry,	104
Elford C.	g Orilla D. Richardson,	128
Frank W.	Louise W. Hall,	116
Fred. W., M.D.	g Caroline E. Marvin,	106
J. A.	g Florence H. Alexander,	146
William A.	Nellie B. Jones,	119
Zeno	Charlotte M. Rice,	63
Ruthven, R. E.	g Sarah C. Goddard,	39
Ryder, Edward S., M.D.	Charlotte A. Huse,	30
Morgan L.	Ina Allen,	135
William	Bertha E. Pettee,	78
Saeger, Alfred G.	Ella E. Troxell,	85
Thomas W.	Florence A. Troxell,	125
Safford, Rev. Myron W.	g Lucretia P. Morton,	20
Ralph S.	Mary W. Howard,	63
St. John, Charles R.	g Catharine M. Porter,	55
Rev. I. I.	Sarah M. Foster,	66
Rev. Oliver S.	Elizabeth G. Bull,	20
Salisbury, Albert H.	Sabra A. Allen,	90
Salmon, Rev. Clark,	g Harriet C. Gates,	72
Sanborn, C. A., M. D.	g Mary B. Mudge,	144
Isaac N.	g Flora A. Sawyer,	72
Hugh M.	Adelaide C. Morrison,	78
John W.	Hannah H. Willard,	71
William	g Lucy B. Muzzy,	61
Sanders, George	Charlotte M. Clark,	20
William M.	Angeline M. Crosby,	112
Sanderson, Asahel W.	Lucy S. Sanders,	23
Dwight L.	Elvira Stearns,	41
Horace	Mary E. Bent,	128
P. M.	Mary L. Powers,	113
Sandusky, C.	g Ida L. Watson,	144
Sanford, Edson	g Elizabeth C. Gleason,	105
Horace N.	g Dora L. Kasson,	82
Loda V.	Emma L. Ecker,	97

INDEX.

				Page
Sanford, R. K.	g Lucy A. Carrier,	38	Seeley, Charles A.	g Caroline A. Boltwood, 82
Santon, Joseph	Mary L. Gilbert,	107	Hiram M.	Rachel A. Rowe, 119
Sargent, George W.	Jane A. Lord,	129	Seibert, William A.	g Rosa A. Werkeiser, 151
Savage, Albert R.	Ellen H. Hale,	116	Seip, Howard S.	Anna E. Anewalt, 154
Rev. Charles A.	g Mary F. Fiske,	117	Selby, Paul	g Mary J. (Smith) Hitch-
Francis	g Anna M. Lawrence,	103		cock, 58
Savery, William H.	K. Elizabeth Ferry,	154	Stephen F.	Alice C. Sanborn, 147
Sawyer, Charles	M. Ellen Mack,	116	Selfridge, J. M., M.D.	Eliz. C. Loveridge, 67
C. Burdette	Jessie D. Pope,	138	Sessions, J. D.	g Laura W. Walker, 90
Charles	Mary E. Mack,	119	Severance, Elmer D.	g Mary S. Graves, 141
E. W.	Antoinette M. Smith,	74	Rev. Milton L.	g Emily A. Spencer, 76
Edward A., M.D.	Minnie H. Pierce,	145	R. A., M.D.	Mary W. Smith, 186
Henry E.	Martha H. Rogers,	98	Sevin, George V.	Alice T. Crandall, 124
Joseph H.	Sarah W. Beekman,	96	Seward, L. J.	Mary F. Coe, 118
William B., M.D.	Emma J. Nichols,	143	Sexton, Joel B.	Sarah W. Lyman, 132
Saxe, Charles	Susan M. Baker,	24	Seymour, Rev. B. N.	g Emily Morse, 61
Saxton, Isaac A.	Louisa W. Pier,	34	Christopher, M.D.	Fanny A. Barrows, 90
William D.,M.D.	g Isabella G. Bierce,	51	Frederic W.	{ g Mary M. Curtis, 36
Saylor, David O.	Emma M. Saegar,	78		{ g Mary J. Smith, 69
Sayward, Charles A.	Henrietta Wilkins,	82	Rev. Henry	L. Arabella Fiske, 25
Schermerhorn, Henry			John D.	Abby Welles, 31
J. D.	g Jennie R. Cobb,	111	Lucien C.	Mary H. Mix, 47
Schlesinger, Auguste D.	Jerusha C. Pitkin,	44	Rufus P.	Mary J. Alford, 69
Schoonover, Jacob A.	Martha J. Wear,	108	Seys, Henry H., M.D.	Harriette H. Foote, 43
Schrader, Frank von	g A. Jean Freeman,	164	Shackelford, Baylor S.	Lucy S. (Cooley) Good-
O., Esq.	g Mary S. Webster,	65		sell, 73
Schreiner, H. B.	g M. Augusta Martin,	29	Shailer, Francis A.	Belle A. Rogers, 127
Henry	g Julia Esty,	79	Sharon, John M.	Mary Cunningham, 142
Jacob	Cornelia H. Martin,	37	Sharp, Edward	Louise S. Robinson, 116
Joseph F.	Lillian E. Stair,	170	Sharpe, Rev. Robert H.	Marion J. Sollen-
Schroeder, Bernhard C.	Frances L. Fitch,	148		berger, 173
Schryver, Israel G.	Mary H. Knapp,	67	Sharpless, P. O.	g Martha M. W. McIn-
Schuyler, William H.	Oella Brown,	66		tyre, 61
William R.	g Clarissa Eastman,	18	Shattuck, Charles C.	g Frances M. Swett, 93
Schwartzky, Otto H. L.	Mary J. Reese,	127	Fred R.	Phebe H. Hildreth, 70
Scott, Rev. Charles	Hannah J. Grant,	56	Shaw, Lieut. Chas. P.	Helen M. Simpson, 130
Charles E., M.D.	Mary E. Bradley,	27	G. J.	g Elvira W. Morton, 61
Edward H.	Jessie L. Hurlbut,	129	Edward	Mary C. Hurlbut, 116
Harry H.	Martha E. Roys,	85	Isaac	Salome P. Freeman, 73
J. Austin	Sarah S. Ranney,	26	Joseph A.	g E. Antoinette Thomp-
Rev. James L.	g Eliza J. Foster,	54		son, 93
Rufus	Dorcas W. Hapgood,	37	Joseph P.	Mary D. Perkins, 34
Walter E., M.D.	Isabel H. Harwood,	142	Sheardown, Samuel B.,	
William G.	g C. A. (Robie) McCoy,	72	M. D.	Mary A. Winton, 60
William H.	Mary Winans,	47	Sheldon, Martin	E. J. (Mowle) Wand, 81
Scoville, Irving J.	g Carrie E. French,	141	Shelmire, William H.	g Lucy Cope, 134
Scudder, Rev. Joseph	Sarah A. Chamberlain,52		Shepard, Edward D.	Ellen R. Newton, 124
S. Downer	g Sarah W. Scudder,	156	Fred D., M. D.	g F. P. Andrews, M. D.138
Seagrave, Charles S.	Watie A. Scott,	78	Henry M.	Clara Thayer, 111
Seaman, Geo. W.	Martha E. Amidon,	59	H. S.	Abbie F. Harlowe, 168
Seamans, William H.	C. C. (Sanford) Allen,	44	Isaac F.	Deborah E. N. Bates, 20
Searle, Frank P.	Ellen M. Edwards,	110	Josiah	Jane M. Yale, 114
Rev. Jairus C.	Emeline C. Youngs,	29	William N.	Mary A. Yale, 130
L. B.	g Susan Turner,	58	Shepley, Charles H.	Engelia M. Whitney, 108
Stephen T.	Gertrude G. Arms,	109	Sheppard, Isaac A.	Margaretta C. Little, 34
Searles, Charles E.	Harriet E. Forbes,	111	Joseph F.	Julia B. Cummins, 52
Francis G.	Abbie F. Willmarth,	75	Sherburn, Rev. J. O.	Ella R. Gridley, 121
Seaver, Lewis W.	Susan W. Dixon,	25	Sherman, A. Prescott	Julia C. Farrar, 110
Seccombe,Rev.Charles	{ Ann Maria Peabody,	37	Chas. S.	May F. Kirby, 160
	{ Harriet M. Tolman,	44	Edgar	Selinda T. L. Nichol-
Seccombe, Charles C.	g Annabell F. Crosby,	95		son, 25
Sedgwick, G. H.	Elizabeth J. Granger,129		William H.	Sarah W. Lawrence, 101

MARRIED NAMES. 217

		Page
Sherry, Arthur G.	Frances M. Scott,	138
Sherwood, A. C.	Cynthia E. Noyes,	78
Henry D.	Sarah W. Quick,	78
Joseph B.	Mary F. Rider,	47
Shew, A. Marvin, M.D.	g Elizabeth C. Palmer,	92
Shirk, Rev. M. S.	Eliz. S. Washburn,	21
Shoemaker, Harvey	g Laura M. Lane,	151
Owen	g Mary M. Jack,	151
Shotwell, Rev. N.	g Martha A. Abbott,	16
Stewart B., Jr.	g Caroline R. McIlvane,	151
Walter G., Esq.	g Flora B. McIlvaine,	146
Shupp, Irvin	Susan McGill,	135
Shurtleff, Giles W.	Mary E. Burton,	80
Shutter, Chas.	Susan E. Solomon,	54
Shuttleworth, Henry J.	Laura E. Wheeler,	38
Sibley, Edward	g Clara I. Thorndike,	106
Sickles, George H.	Almira Morehouse,	53
Sikes, Frank	Clara A. Dickinson,	140
Quartus	Hannah Jones,	43
Silkman, Henry O.	Frances E. Gardner,	90
Silver, Wm. S.	Eva T. Lacey,	147
Simmons, Edward,	g Agnes J. English,	148
Wm., M.D.	Ettie E. Pratt,	151
W. H.	g Aletta M. Bronson,	85
Simmonds, L. B.	Anna E. Tinkham,	19
Simonds Henry A.	g Elizabeth Goodnough,	146
Joseph W.	Adaline A. Pike,	98
Simons, David H.	Laurintha A. Eaton,	97
Simpson, William J., Jr.	Mary W. Dodd,	124
Sisson, Nahum S.	Phebe F. Bowen,	18
Skeele, Rev. Amos	Sarah W. Ide,	104
John H.	Clara M. Ellms,	59
Skillings, Allen S.	Mary H. Boynton,	126
James T.	Martha J. Norton,	116
Skinner, Lucius B.	Elizabeth A. Dole,	66
Sloo, William A.	Abbie M. Goss,	77
Small Augustus E.	Ida E. Norton,	147
B. F.	Lucetta G. Jackson,	94
Rev. Uriah W.	g Mary E. Gilman,	64
Smalley, Bryan D.	Marie E. Bell,	139
D. C.	Marionette A. Barnette,	76
Smith, ——	Katherine A. Sweetser,	114
A. A.	g M. Louise Pettibone,	96
Rev. Albert D.	g Ellen S. Taylor,	156
Benjamin W.	Lydia D. Hathaway,	30
Byron	Nancy M. Dwight,	37
Rev. C. S.	Lucy A. Maynard,	44
C. W. M., Esq.	Celia A. Gridley,	56
Carlos	Isabella G. Maltby,	56
Charles A.	Mary L. Mack,	135
Charles B.	Edith A. Church,	142
Charles Edward	Mary C. Johnson,	129
Charles K.	Mary Ellen Smith,	116
Chester F.	Elizabeth M. Washburn,	158
Rev. Clifford H.	g Martha L. Votey,	144
D. D.	Carrie A. Brackett,	96
Rev. Daniel J.	Anna M. Seavey,	71

		Page
Smith, Denison K., Esq.	Maria B. Follett,	55
Don C.	Catharine Norton,	70
Rev. E. P.	Hannah C. Bush,	43
E. S.	Eliza Holbrook,	37
Edward	Mary E. Howland,	27
Rev. Edward H.	Jane G. Woodward,	95
Edward L.	Adeline Magranis,	84
Edward M.	Laura E. Bartlett,	69
Edward P.	Charlotte J. Woods,	45
Edward P.	g Julia M. Church,	102
Edward W.	Sarah P. Ladd,	124
Elizur	Mary A. Smith,	51
Elmon D.	Sarah M. Waldo,	23
Erastus G.	g Elizabeth M. Mayher,134
Ernest N.	g Elizabeth A. Durant,	117
Francis B.	Clara Carpenter,	87
Frank K.	Emma M. Troxell,	92
Fred. M. D.	g Frances Gregg,	48
Fred M.	Jos. M. Gandolfo,	97
Frederick	Mary P. Sloan,	71
G. Frank	Emma E. Smith,	111
George B.	g Laura C. French,	105
George B.	g Mary A. Doty,	120
Geo. E.	Ada M. Ramsdell,	119
H. F. M., M. D.	Belle A. Arnold,	149
H. J. M., Esq.	Helen A. Henry,	19
Henry D.	g Jennette C. Higgins,	41
Henry G.	Harriet D. Flagg,	34
Henry J.	Anna J. Gustin,	104
Henry W.	Mary A. Hooker,	70
Hugh R.	Kate Hallock,	154
Rev. I. Perley,	g Clara R. Smith,	86
Isaac H.	A.W.(Bingham)Smith,57
J. Edward	Lucy A. Clark,	37
J. N., M.D.	S. Cornelia Bates,	39
J. Wylie	g Lydia W. Brackett,	71
Jacob W.	AmoretteW.Bingham,87
James L.	Julia M. Case,	24
James M.	Jane T. Sherman,	21
Rev. James R.	Mary L. Chase,	59
John, Esq.,	Emily Bridge,	186
Rev. John F.	g Sarah E. Sears,	112
Joseph A.	g Emily C. Dennison,	68
Le Grand B.	Margaret Harkness,	129
Lewis N.	g Elizabeth W. Wood,	93
Lucius D.	Estelle M. Blodgett,	120
Luther R., Esq.	g Adaline Ely,	99
M. Wilbur,	Emily E. Nash,	140
Rev. Moses	g Emily A. White,	76
N. Payson	Caroline P. Baker,	80
Oberlin	Charlotte E. Hill,	77
P. Herbert	g Ednah F. Beane,	120
Presley R.	g Mary T. Daniels,	54
R. Morrison	Mary J. Wright,	111
Richard B.	g Abbie W. Ellis,	54
Samuel D.	Frances L. Safford,	60
Samuel F., M.D.	g Alice S. Kimball,	131
Sidney A.	Delia E. Dowd,	90
Stephen S.	Margaret E. Brown,	83
Sumner I.	Mary Hayes,	34
Sumner T., M.D.	g Martha E. Lovell,	112
Walter A., M.D.	Mary P. Abbe,	135

INDEX.

Smith, Weston O., M.D.	Kate M. Roscoe, 166	Starr, Henry W., Esq.	*g* Eliza A. Merrill, 29
William	Keziah C. Kellogg, 37	Rev. Milton B.	*g* ElizabethG.Knowlton,29
William	Louisa M. Hill, 56	Stearns, F. W.	Emily W. Clark, 129
Wm. A.	Clara Harmon, 162	Rev. Geo. I.	*g* Amelia D. Jones, 45
William A. J.	*g* Lucretia Foster, 45	Rev. J. G. D.	Lucy Murdock, 19
William B.	Virginia T. Thrall, 75	Rev. Josiah M.	*g* Flora P. McIntyre, 32
William L.	*g* Ann M. Olcott, 58	Stebbins, George E.	Charlotte S. Hulbert, 119
William L.	*g* Catharine R. Moody, 78	John M., Esq.	*g* Harriette C. Halle, 41
Smyth, Rev. Geo. B.	*g* Alice B. Harris, 146	John W.	Louisa J. Osband, 40
Snell, Rev. M. Porter,	Mary C. Hallock, 91	Menzies R.	Adaline E. O'Farrell, 74
Snook, J. M., M.D.	*g* Julia F. Hitchcock, 105	Stedman, Henry S.	Laura McGlashan, 113
Snow, Rev. Benj. P.	Anna L. Chandler, 80	Rev. J. O.	Mary A. Hayden, 25
Charles I.	Juliet Harrison, 53	Steele, James,	*g* Catharine S. Farwell,102
Daniel	Harriot A. Slate, 41	William,	Abbie L. Wyman, 99
Edward L.	Elizabeth Lyman, 25	Steere, Warren H.	Adelaide S. Phillips, 145
Russell L.	Phebe Snow, 71	Stephens, Frank L.	Gertrude E. Bron-
William H.	*g* Anna B. Walker, 139		son, 159
Snowden, Thomas	Mary J. Parsons, 37	Rev. H. S.	Marietta Atkins, 42
Solier, George F.	Louise A. Willett, 145	James L.	Amy G. Whitmore, 171
Southworth, C. A.	Serena Field, 20	Stephenson, Adelbert H.	Mary G. Miller, 130
Rev. Francis,	Emma W. Farrington,84	Reuben	Charlotte P. Bayley, 24
Spafford, Wm.	*g* Mary O. Preston, 139	Rev. Thomas	Frances E. Holmes, 63
Spalding, Albert M.	*g* Sarah Pickit, 96	Sternbergh, James H.	Harriet M. May, 70
Edward H.	Emma Holt, 84	Stetson, William	Mary M. Swift, 21
Sparhawk, J. Will	*g* N. Louise Norwood, 144	Zerah	Elizabeth P. Atwood, 48
Sparks, Franklin	*g* Georgiana Haley, 72	Stevens, A. Beverly	*g* Gertrude E. Kelsey, 142
James H., Esq.	Abbie S. Butler, 62	Benjamin W.	Mary E. Staples, 136
Sparrow, James H.	Julia A. Bridges, 49	Briggs F.	Celestia Cheney, 77
Spaulding, Edward,	H. Ellen Platts. 94	C. Newcomb	Blanche Gibbons, 84
J. W., Esq.	*g* Mary J. Clark, 82	David	Hannah C. Baldwin, 59
Speakman, Edward,	Amelia J. Mussey, 91	Frank L.	Gertrude E. Bron-
Spear, Asa A.	Carrie A. Crocker, 97		son, 159
Spencer, Chas. S., Esq.,	S. Grace Scribner, 88	George, Esq.	*g* Elizabeth R. Kim-
Harvey D.	Margaret V. Brokaw, 52		ball, 39
Rev. Henry F.	Mary B. Weeks, 88	Henry M.	*g* Elizabeth King, 99
John C.	R. Alice Day, 49	James M.	Amy G. Whitmore, 171
R. C.	*g* E. A. (Whiton) King, 58	John L.	Maria T. Wells, 108
Robert T.	Abbie B. Blackman, 126	Manning W.	Julia A. Wadsworth, 50
Stephen O.	Caroline Adams, 80	Melville R.	Winifred Powers, 113
William S.	E. C. (Youngs) Searle, 29	S. S.	Emily G. Baldwin, 48
Sperry, Joseph H.	*g* Clara L. Kendall, 106	Stanley L.	Harriet L. Griswold, 81
Spiller, Levi	*g* Mary P. Boies, 48	Rev. William R.	Louisa F. Cook, 24
Spink, George A.	Edna M. Gilman, 97	Stevenson, Benj. F.	*g* Mary W. J. Roff, 26
Spitzli, Alfred	Abby H. Nash, 101	S. C.	Minerva A. Bosworth, 24
Spooner, Rev.ArthurW.	Hattie M. Clapp, 137	W. George, M.D.,	*g* H. Henrietta Baker, 85
Thomas	*g* Sarah A. Emmons, 58	William G., M.D.	Mary Hamilton, 94
Sprague, C. G.	*g* Mary A. Hall, 146	Stewart, Alexander	Eliza M. Becker, 69
C. L.	Mira A. Jefts, 113	David	Amelia S. Cooley, 27
Rev. Wm.	*g* Viette I. Brown, 117	Stickney, Edward W.	Annie G. Grassie, 160
Rev. William P.	Margaret S. Hen-	James M., M.D.	*g* Augusta S. Chase, 64
	derson, 124	Willett B., Esq.	Sarah C. Baldwin,
Squire, William L.	Lucy C. Butler, 55		M.D. 137
Stacey, Geo. E.	Abbie M. Douglass, 149	Stiles, Oliver J.	Ella R. Wright, 105
Stackpole, Geo. E.,M.D.	Henrietta M. Pease, 107	Stillman, Walter	Mary A. Whitmore, 38
Stafford, Cyrus G., Esq.	Cynthia M. Abram, 83	Stimis, Alvah	*g* Kate C. Pond, 126
Stanley, Oliver	Grace G. Robbins, 136	Stimpson, Thomas M.,	
Staples, Ernest L., Esq.	*g* Esther J. Penfield, 144	Esq.	Sarah E. Perkins, 133
Starbuck, Henry F.	Charlotte E. Noyes, 116	Stockbridge, Henry	
Stark, William L.	Rhoda D. Sisson, 88		*g* Helen M. Smith, 139
Starkey, Henry C.	Mary L. Richardson, 19	Sylvester L., Esq.	*g* Mary E. Beaman, 92
Starkweather, Alfred	Frances A. Loomis, 47	Stocking, Rev. W. R.	*g* Isabella C. Baker, 108
Starne, Alexander.	Elvira S. Potter, 25	Stoddard, Rev. D. T.	*g* Sophia D. Hazen, 22

MARRIED NAMES.

Name	Spouse	Page
Stoddard, William H.	*g* Helen (Humphrey) Palmer,	18
	g Sophia D. (Hazen) Stoddard,	22
Stolz, Louis H.	*g* Mary A. Rowell,	128
Stone, Burton D.	*g* Harriet L. Devereux,	143
Charles M.	*g* Sarah Fairbanks,	51
Harley	Kate H. White,	130
Rev. O. B.	*g* Julia A. King,	39
R. B.	Margaret S. Baldwin,	73
Rev. Samuel M.	Joann Allen,	20
Solon W.	Lauretta P. Richardson,	116
Rev. W. B.	Martha Robinson,	19
	Phebe W. Robinson,	19
Stoutenburgh, Rev. L. J.	Mary E. Voorhees,	57
Storm, Henry C.	Caroline G. Rogers,	104
Storrs, Chas. L.	*g* Harriet H. Cowles,	92
Edgar F.	Anna F. Gilbert,	137
Rev. Henry M.	*g* Catharine Hitchcock,	32
Story, Charles R.	Caroline P. Bayley,	48
James W.	*g* Elizabeth Benedict,	148
Walter H.	Lora E. Chells,	144
Stout, M.	*g* Ida P. Sylvester,	103
Stow, Rev. John M.	*g* Sarah D. Locke,	79
Marshall V.	Emma L. Pierce,	110
Stowell, Chas.	Abbie F. Hubbard,	70
Stranahan, J. S. T.	Clara C. Harrison,	46
Stratton, C., M.D.	Charlotte Kenfield,	27
Eben P.	Harriet M. Washburn,	21
Frank M., M.D.	Maria H. Wadsworth,	57
Streeper, John S.	*g* G. Gertrude M. Brundage,	151
Streeter, Harley H.	Helen L. Weeks,	122
Strickland, Horace L.	Ada L. Fletcher,	112
William P., Esq.	Mary A. Pelton,	71
Strode, Andrew C.	Agnes B. Wilson,	141
Strong, Rev. Charles B.	Ella M. Beach,	137
Edward, M.D.	*g* Harriet L. Hayes,	26
Henry	Eleonora H. Strong,	60
Rev. John C.	*g* Celia S. Wright,	36
Judson	Mary E. Freeman,	115
T. D., M.D.	*g* Lucy M. Ainsworth,	45
Strowbridge, Benj.	Olive D. Hathaway,	30
Sturges, Rev. Fred E.	Mary E. Inglee,	97
Sturtevant, Edmund D.	Eunice R. Filley,	97
Stuckley, Charles M.	Caroline M. Shaw,	143
Sudler, Joseph	Candace L. Pomeroy,	54
Suiter, Walter F., M.D.	Nancy F. Cooke,	62
Sullivan, Frank P.	Addie L. Gardner,	149
J. A.	*g* Julia F. Hammond,	123
John W.	Ann F. Greenough,	25
Sumner, E. G., M.D.	Mary S. Hinckley,	63
	Ellen M. Hinckley,	74
Sunderland, Rev. J. T.	*g* Eliza J. Read,	100
Supplee, Henry	Clarina B. Sturges,	60
Sutherland, Bliss	Martha L. (Harwood) Crafts,	43
Charles H.	Jemima L. Cox,	93
John	E. (Strong) Lewis,	67
Sutton, John E., M.D.	Lizzie P. Bruner,	132
Thomas	Mary S. Swan, M.D.	38
Suydam, Asa	Rachel Higgins Reed,	74
Swahn, George A.	Annie M. Hartwell,	66
Swan, John	Ellen M. Haven,	25
Roscoe W.	E. Helen Prentice,	147
Sweeny, H. L., M.D.	*g* Ellen J. Towle,	131
Sweezey, Herman E.	*g* Emma L. McKeown,	148
Swenarton, Seman A.	Mary E. Hastings,	94
Swift, Charles R.	*g* Mary E. Everett,	68
Rev. E. Y.	*g* Catharine S. Leach,	20
F. M.	*g* Jane E. Stone,	103
Swigart, J. R.	*g* Mary E. Farman,	131
Swing, James J.	C. Jane Sturdevant,	67
Sylvester, Rev. Charles.	Harriet Arms,	22
George F.	Mary A. Allen,	100
I. Waters	Ida E. Pond,	130
Taber, C. E.	Elizabeth H. Miller,	67
Cyrus H.	Annie A. Lowell,	145
Tabor, Harris, Esq.	*g* H. Jane Johnston,	123
Taft, Alphonso,	Louisa M. Torrey,	31
Calvin	Cornelia A. Brigham,	27
Henry C.	H. Sophia Parkman,	28
Horace D.	Winnie S. Thompson,	133
Taggart, John B.	Cornelia E. Belcher,	80
Talcott, Charles D.	Harriet McLean,	28
	g H. Maria Freeman,	92
Taplin, E. Tenny	Mary A. Smart,	60
Tarbet, Rev. Wm. L.	*g* Emma H. Calvert,	45
Tasker, Rev. Edwin	Grace C. Pitkin,	164
Tate, William	Virginia Potter,	25
Taylor Albert	E. M. Belden, M.D.	185
Ashman H.	Julia Spencer,	19
Blain W.	*g* May Jackson,	148
Rev. C. H.	Julia A. Edwards,	33
Charles A.	Julia M. Carter,	66
Rev. E. D.	F. E. (Daniels) Wells,	73
Elmer R.	S. Arabella Lyman,	135
Rev. Frederick C. E.	Louise Chamberlain,	168
Horace S.	Jessie M. Bell,	176
Horace W., Esq.	*g* Anna A. Robinson,	39
Rev. James F.	*g* Mary A. L. Porter,	61
John N.	A. Katherine Kittredge,	56
Leonard E.	Mary E. Metcalf,	132
Rev. T. E.	*g* Persis G. Thurston,	35
Rev. W. D.	*g* H. Sophia Hayes,	68
Wm. L.	Anna F. Salmon,	145
Teachout, Almond D., M.D.	Harriet A. Cooper,	37
Asher	Elizabeth A. Reid,	60
Temple, James,	*g* Jane A. Cook,	29
Rev. Josiah H.	Mary Belden,	24
Tenney, Rev. H. M., D.D.	Anna E. Parsons,	113
Rev. Leonard,	Malvina Baker,	22
Perley W.	Susan B. French,	46
Terry, Rev. Cassius M.	*g* Emily Hitchcock,	79
Frank T.	*g* Jennie L. Montague,	156
Willard S.	Cassie A. Reamer,	127
William, M. D.	Maria R. Slocomb,	38
Thacker, Alonzo B.	Sarah Bailey,	33
Thatcher, John W.	Morgianna E. Davis,	77
Thomas	*g* Ann Butterworth,	102
William	Mary Pasloan Smith,	71
Thayer, Addison P., Esq.	Lydia S. Partridge,	47

INDEX.

Name	Spouse	Page
Thayer, Alfred S.	g Julia M. Putnam,	48
Rev. Herbert E.	g Mary E. Barney,	155
John G.	Mary J. Houghton,	56
Thomas.—	Mary E. M. Bates,	20
Edward I.	Henrietta W. Briggs,	55
Frank W., M. D.	g Mary Lee,	137
Howard	g Ada I. Porter,	126
John B.	Elizabeth D. Harries,	84
John W.	Sarah Blanchard,	20
Rev. Ozro A.	Eliza Dimond,	53
R. J.	Nannie E. Stobaugh,	141
Walter S.	Isabella (Collins) Thomas,	101
Thompson, A. B.	Matilda K. Smith,	65
Rev. Amherst L.	Esther E. Munsell,	81
E. A.	Caroline Skavlem,	166
Edward H.	Mary A. Hopkins,	91
Edwin B., M.D.	Helen E. Osborne,	88
Eleazer,	Harriet N. Sanford.	44
George T.	Mary F. Peck,	78
H. W.	g Adelle H. Hall,	156
Jas. Willard	Paulina A. Leathe,	47
John H., M.D.	g Anna C. Ludlam,	86
Mark	Mary A. Parry,	57
Myron W.	Maria L.Babcock,	112
Nathan M.	Julia P. Ford,	93
Samuel	Elizabeth L. Berger,	83
Wm. H.	Emma Clapp,	157
Thomson, Rev. John	g Maria G. Burgess,	85
Thornton, Alfred E.	Myra A. Montague,	133
William H., M.D.	D. Eloise Taylor,	147
Thorp, James H.	Minnie E. Hurd,	104
Thrall, Frank B.	Amelia C. Dages,	147
Thresher, S. S., Esq.	Calista V. Potter,	88
Throop, Benj., M.D.	g Harriet E. Walker,	50
Thurman, O. A.	Elizabeth W. Mc-Naughton,	107
Sylvanus	g M. Abbie Pillsbury,	100
Thurston, Charles F.	Serina Bull,	24
Thwing, Rev. Edw. P.	g Susan M. Waite,	65
Tibbitts, B. L.	Alice B. Martin,	143
Ticknor, Almon P.	Frances C. Catlin,	37
Tidd, Charles Joseph E.	Rebecca W. B. Trask, Mary A. Bosworth,	17 129
Tiffany, F. Augustus	Frances J. Comstock,	46
Tifft, Rev. Charles B.	Henrietta C. Hill,	77
Tilden, George G.	g Lydia A. Cooper,	102
Tillinghast, G. G.	g Sarah B. Gallup,	100
Tillotson, Rev. G. H.	g Mary S. Wood,	29
Tilly, Rev. E. A.	Ella V. Porter,	147
Tilton, Benjamin B.	Mary Clark,	33
John W.	Sarah E. Page,	119
Timlow,Rev.Heman R.	Martha F. Bigelow,	33
Tinker, Edward L.	g Emeline F. Cross,	61
William L.	Nancy M. Taylor,	28
Tinkham, Francis M.	g Edith M. Ellis,	108
Tirrell, Albert Warren	Charlotte Blanchard, g Alice Tirrell,	16 151
Titus, Oliver C.	Emma Watson,	85
Tobey, Rev. Rufus B.	g M. Caroline Gifford,	128
Todd, Cyrus A.	Julia G. Marsh,	63
J. B.	g Mary C. Knowlton,	39
Todd, J. M., M.D.	g Nora Abbott,	155
O. A. G., Esq.	g Josephine G. Sturges,	90
Tolman, Lucius A.	g Julia M. Tolman,	42
Reuben	HannahL.B.Goodwin,	17
Tomblen, Rev. Chas. L.	Helen E. Bliss,	115
Tomkins, Silas P.	Anna Mersereau,	53
Tomlinson, Charles	Charlotte E. King,	53
Myron E.	Charlotte H. Ford,	97
Tomson, Truman	g Cora A. Welch,	80
Torrence, Rev. Geo. P.	Mary Ferguson,	129
Torrey, Rev. David	g Mary E. Humphrey,	32
Tower, Francis M.	Sarah A. Ransom,	38
Rev. Freeman P.	Julia A. Cleveland,	93
Towers, Rev. Lewis	Louisa F. Packard,	17
Towle, James H.	g Mary G. Spaulding,	61
Townsend, Calvin M.	Mary A. Button,	30
Henry J.	Sarah E. Marquand,	56
Toy, Frank	Mabel E. Schuyler,	145
Tracey, A. M., M.D.	Libbie M. Cadmon,	142
F. B.	g Ida Stone,	105
Rev. M. M.	g Ruth A. Kent,	109
Sidney	Fanny E. Ely,	37
Trask, Henry F.	Adelaide Hubbard,	119
Trainer, Abram	g Phebe T. Hall,	65
Treadwell, Levi P.	Caroline C. Rogers	101
Treat, Henry	Alice C. (Kimball) Meserve,	43
Theodore, M.D.	Eliza J. Newell,	44
Trimmer, Rev. J. A.	g Marion Shepperd,	159
Troup, Charles A. S.	g Clara E. Wheeler,	106
Troutman, George H.	Rosetta E. Crossett,	107
Trowbridge, Hoyt	g Julia A. Goodlue,	96
Trubee, Samuel C.	g Mary C. Terry,	103
Truesdell, Orran P. Ransom	g Amelia C.Woodward, Caroline A. Curtis,	76 77
William, Esq.	Martha A. Janes,	34
Trumbull, Dr.John	Flora E. Smith,	138
Tryon, Sylvester	Mary E. Merrill,	98
Tuck, Rev. J. W.	{ Irene M. Moody, g Ann R. Mowry,	22 24
Rev. Nathan F.	Harriet M. Warner,	19
Tucker, Frank W.	Helen M. Wilkins,	125
Tufts, Rev. James Thomas T.	Mary E. Warren, Henrietta Pool,	35 31
Tull, Thomas J.	Caroline E. Warner,	57
Tupper, Royal H.	g Martha Rogers,	24
Turnbull, Rev. Jas. S.	Abbie D. Haskins,	104
Turner, A. M.	Dorcas H. Johnston,	101
George Roscoe W.	Emma M. Coggswell, g Anna F. Curtis,	59 108
Tuthill, Henry E.	Lydia M. Butler,	115
Wm. H.	g P. Jane Downs,	102
Tuttle, Austin S.	Anna Perrin,	60
Joseph R.	g Marie I. Leonard,	123
Tuxbury, Dwight	Eusebia S. Williams,	99
Tweedy, John R.	Delia J. Fuller,	81
Twiss, Geo. H.	Susan H. Ransom,	60
Twitchell, Rev. J. E. M. H.	Allie R. Bentley, Henrietta N. Day,	73 97
Twombly, Roswell S.	g Ruth W. Thayer,	86
Tyler, A. W.	g Melissa Usher,	69

MARRIED NAMES.

Name	Spouse	Page
Tyler, Francis M.	g Delia M. Wells,	100
Howard	Phebe A. Cowles.	110
J. H., Esq.	Harriette M. Peck,	50
Rev. John E.	Caroline E. Goodrich,	53
Philo S.	Maria A. Arnold,	118
Philos B.	Margaretta B. Hunting,	40
Upham, Edward W.	Georgiana F. Lord,	74
Franklin H.	Florence E. Sturtevant,	153
Upton, George W., D.	g Lucy A. Latham,	89
Vaile, J. Fred, Esq.	Charlotte M. White,	122
Vaill, Charles B.	Emeline M. Steele,	31
Timothy D.	Isabella Brock,	62
Valentine, George H.	Julia C. Fidler,	107
William	Mary A. Barnes,	76
Van Allen, A. Oakley,	Anna B. Waples,	155
Van Bochove, B. J.	g Adela M. Wheaton,	65
Van Deren, A. C.	Mary S. Persons,	158
A. J.	g Mary W. Lloyd,	76
Van Deusen, James	g Elizabeth Cook,	102
Van De Water, Henry	Margaret E. Boyce,	55
Van Duyn, Gilbert A.	C. Louisa Wilcox,	75
Van Dyke, Henry N.	Annie V. Rogers,	130
John G.	Margaret G.VanDyke	28
Van Houten, Peter L.	Martha N. Howe,	27
Van Lennep, Rev. H. J.	Emma L. Bliss,	18
Van Millingen, Prof. Alex.	g Cora M. (Welch) Tomson,	80
Van Schaack, T. B.	Harriet L. Chapin,	80
Van Tassel, Nelson	Jane H. Sterling,	122
Van Vechten, George M.	Florilla H. Crofut,	33
Van Vorhes, A. I.	Elizabeth W. Hawkes,	30
Vance, S. C.	N.Amelia Harrington,	91
Vandenhoff, George	Mary E. M. (Bates) Thomas,	20
Vanderwater, Walter S.	O. Adelia Dickinson,	142
Vary, S. C., Esq.	S. E. (Thomas) Jones,	35
Vasey, Robert W.	Clara A. French,	110
Vaughn, Alfred N. H.	g Rena E. Sweet,	156
Roswell, C.	Nancy J. Bacon,	55
William	Cynthia Morehouse,	25
William E.	Susan E. Gurney,	84
Vent, Charles F.	g Emily Goodman,	86
Vermilye, Robert M.	Annie Hunter,	101
Ventres, Hubbard,	Mary E. Tyler,	19
Verner, William	Julia K. Ensign,	70
Verrill, Charles H.	Emma J. Shattuck,	98
Vittum, David S.	Amanda P. Hall,	46
Vollmer, Wm.	Gwenllian Hunt,	160
Voorhees,Abraham,Esq	Caroline C. Tufts,	54
J. Newton	g Laura J. Leach,	92
Vosburgh, Wm. R.	g Annie L. Jones,	143
Vose, George H.	Eliza F. Dixon,	33
Wade, I. C.	Theresa A. Hastings,	124
Wagner, Frederick	Emma Gund,	175
Wainwright, Loren B.	Frances M. Giles,	62
Wait, Hiram	Louise M. Palmer,	110
Horace	Mary Bridgman,	16
Robert J.	Carrie E. Warner,	125
Waite, George A.	Mary S. Batchelder,	27

Name	Spouse	Page
Waite, H. F., Esq.	g Jane E. Garfield,	35
J. E.	Ella L. Wight,	133
Wakeman, Alfred J.	Harriet P. Taylor,	153
Maurice	Mary C. Thorpe,	26
Walcott, W. S.	Emma A. Welch,	102
Waldo, C. C.	P. Jane Raymond,	38
Clarence A.	Abby W. Allen,	126
Edward H.	Mina K.Stockbridge,	168
Waldron, Leonard T., Esq.	Annie A. Wetzell,	171
Wales, Atherton	Elizabeth S. Tyler,	17
Walker, Rev. Augustus	Eliza M. Harding,	34
Edward E.	Rachael E. Palmer,	101
Rev. James	Julia M. Hitchcock,	60
Rev. William	g Prudence Richardson,	20
	g Zeviah L. Shumway,	20
Rev. William S.	Lillian E. Mateer,	138
Wallace, Andrew B.	Madora C. Vaille,	133
Ebenezer G.	g Sarah E. Greenfield,	51
Robert	Caroline B. Newton,	122
Rev. S. A.	g Mary F.Scarborough,	126
Thomas	Christiana Ferguson,	30
Walter, Benj. F.	Sophia M. Chollar,	93
Walton, J. Douglass	g Sophie P. Todd,	139
Walradt, Henry M.	g Elnora Freeman,	125
Wand, Marmaduke	E. Jane Mowle,	81
Wanning, Henry	Anna E. Bosworth,	16
Waples, Frank A.,M.D.	Cora Riggs,	162
Rufus, Jr.	g Christine A. Isham,	137
Ward, Rev. Earl J.	g Julia E. Batchelder,	85
	Helen A. Sabin,	111
Edwin F.,M.D.	Abbie L. Sweetser,	78
M. J.	Martha E. Lee,	101
S. B., M. D.	g Annah F. Fisher,	100
Samuel W.	Lizzie E. Hunt,	119
Sullivan L.	Mary F. Morgan,	34
William G.	Marietta J. Battles,	80
William H.	Sarah A. Stone,	88
William W.	g Cornelia Collins,	72
Wardwell, J. O., Esq.	Ella M. Eaton,	126
Ware, Howard B.	Ella P. Disbrow,	135
J. B., M. D.	Ellen E. (Bateman) M'Gear	55
Samuel W.	Mary A. Chandler,	18
William D.	Elizabeth W. Jones,	22
Warfield, Alexander,	Mary E. Adams,	45
Warner, Allen H.	Delisa T. Page,	130
Benjamin E.	Eliza (Paine) Weeks,	44
Charles D.	Anna E. Green,	87
Chas. W.	g Mary E.Loring,	146
DeWitt C., M. D.	g E. Josephine Ayer,	51
Edward R.	g Clara A. Dodge,	99
James	Eleanor L. Scrugham,	28
John	Amelia O. Paine,	31
John F.	Esther C. (Hayward) Warner,	91
Lewis H.	Esther C. Hayward,	91
Lucien	Delia Sylva,	54
Rev. Lyman	g Elizabeth S. Olmsted,	45
Rev. Warren W.	Anna G. Lewis,	56
William	g Frances S. Leach,	32
Warren, Charles C.	Anna Gray,	74

INDEX.

Name	Page	Name	Page	Name	Page
Warren, Dexter		Charlotte A. Green,	18	Wells, Edgar C.	
Francis E.		Helen M. Smith,	101	J. E.	g Rebecca M. Chase, 72
H. Winslow		Julia C. (Farrar) Sherman,	110	L. R.	Ellen M. Hart, 43
Henry K.		Lillian E. Hamilton,	145	Rev. Rufus P.	Chloe B. Belden, 18
Rev. Israel P.		Juliet M. Stanley,	91	Willard B.	g Ellen A. Hatch, 79
John J.		g Helen Gorham,	51	Welton, Bela A.	g Felicia A. (Frisbie) Holmes, 64
Washburn, Alfred		Cornelia A. Crane,	77	Werden, Leland B.	Minnie L. Cooke, 149
Julius F.		g Fanny M. Hunt,	82	Werlein, Philip P.	Margaret Halsey, 25
		g Sarah A. Hunt,	86	West, Abel K.	g Caroline E. Wood, 42
Washburne, Rev. F.Y.	g	Mary A. Pond,	32	E. S.	Sarah O. Youngblood, 08
Waterman, Rev. Alf. T.		Emily J. Stocking,	88		g Virginia A. Smith, 111
Frank		Mary W. Rice,	108	Westcott, William S.	g Emily A. Hills, 65
Waters, Rev. Simeon		Elizabeth D. Goodale,	46	Weston, Charles T.	Mary C. Crawford, 46
Watrous, Erastus		g Eva L. Chapman,	122	Geo. R.	Luette J. Morgan, 160
J. L.		Mary M. Samson,	81	W. H., M.D.	g Frances E. Pope, 123
Watson—		Amanda Conklin,	126	Wetherell, Eugene	Sarah E. Burdon, 122
J. W.		Clara E. Dickinson.	107	Wetmore, Abner C.	Margarett Merwin, 67
Henry L.		Amelia M. Brown,	106	Weutz, John L. W.	Anna S. Barber, 66
Winslow C., Esq.		Ella S. Barnes,	131	Wharton, Charles A.	Lenna I. Lyon, 127
Weaver, William		Adelia W. Sutton,	111	Whedon, Geo. D., M.D.	Ella M. Kellogg, 110
Rev. Willis		g Anna R. Kuhn,	112	Wheeler, Abijah R.	Adeline Jones, 21
Webb, Rev. Edward		g Nancy A. Foote,	29	Alonzo, Esq.	Sophia A. Poole, 81
John P.		Rhoda Kingsley,	31	Rev. Crosby H.	Susan A. Brookings, 55
Edmund R.		Sarah F. Woodhull,	47	E. Sterne	Elsie E. Lees, 138
Louis A.		Mattie S. Danforth,	149	Hiram, Esq.	g Cornelia S. Lapham, 76
Seth		Ariadne L. (Kimball) Bullock,	47	John	Susan R. Hammond, 11
Webber, Franklin T.		g Julia E. Hitchcock,	123	Jonathan W.	Sarah Chaffee, 40
Rev. Geo. N.		g Caroline K. Ladd,	102	Rev. M. G.	Frances C. Parkinson, 34
Ralph E.		g Harriet T. Van Valkenburgh,	120	Samuel P.	Catharine F. E. Goss, 77
Samuel C.		Frances A. Cook,	163	Thomas	Lydia B. Pomeroy, 31
Thomas C.		Annie M. Ordway,	122	Wheelock, Eugene A.	Sarah S. Taft, 105
Webster, B. G.		Helen M. Newell,	56	Whelden, Obed B.	Sarah B. Swift, 26
Cady		Maria T. Hancock,	25	Whipple, John A.	Elizabeth Mann, 17
David		Luella Webster,	85	Whitaker, Rev. Epher	g Hannah Maria Force, 48
Henry S., Esq.		g Mary C. Johnson,	109	Eugene E., M.D.	Clara E. Lane, 186
Lewis		Martha F. Dunbar,	49	Robert T.	Martha Thompson, 63
Lucius		Aurelia L. Linsley,	67	Whitcomb, Charles B.	g Mary J. Pratt, 148
Weed, Chas. T.		Alice P. Bronson,	149	Simeon L.	Harmony A. Noyes, 25
Walter A.		g Ellen B. Stowell,	69	White, Adoniram J.	Emma P. Childs, 118
Weeks, Alton R.		A. Louise Lambert,	162	Alfred B.	Harriet Fuller, 20
George H.		Martha A. Mattocks,	40	Alonzo J., Jr.	Alice J. McLellan, 132
John S.		Caroline L. Paige,	25	Charles T.	Mary E. S. Mendall, 130
N. S.		Eliza Paine,	14	Rev. Charles T.	Anna M. Child, 56
Weeter, John C.		Harriet B. Towne,	168	D. Sherman	Elizabeth D. Adams, 96
Weiss, John F.		Phebe H. Beers,	66	Edmund	g Sarah Beebe, 68
Welch, Archibald H.		Sarah E. (Coit) Barrows,	24	E. S., Esq.	g Alice E. Smith, 112 / g S. Adelaide Moody, 117
Henry L.		Jane C. French,	77	Elihu	Marian A. Mann, 21
George O.		g M. Eliz. Breed, M. D.	54	Rev. Geo. H.	Joanna Fisher, 70
John H., M. D.		g Elizabeth M. Bell,	38	Henry K.	Abbie A. Brown, 132
Weld, Charles P.		Mary A. Lambert,	49	Henry R., M.D.	Sarah B. Clark, 46
Welden, Edward		Catharine W. Plotts,	91	James E.	Anna M. Barnes, 80
Welles, Rev. T. Clayton	g	S. Jane Southworth,	106	James H.	Laura E. Cheseldine, 80
Wells, Albert S.		Caroline Booth,	33	John S.	g Georgiana Reed, 115
Alexander W.		Mary J. O'Dwyer,	44	M. P.	Susan P. Adams, 52
Byron		g Lucy C. Clark,	128	Rollin	Emily L. Bailey, 33
		g Mary A. Hemingway,	125	Samuel B., Esq.	Experience P. Wells, 26
Charles C.		J. Sophia Hill,	77	Samuel G., M.D.	Catharine M. Davidson, 49
David P.		Maria J. Foster,	115	Spencer A.	Sophronia M. Dickinson, 24
				Stephen,	g Lydia Bradstreet, 22

MARRIED NAMES.

Name	Spouse	Page
White, W. A., M.D.	Mary E. Gilbert,	97
W. A., M.D.	g Artemesia Sturges,	96
William	Amanda Preston,	47
William A.	Roxanna Dixon,	154
Whitehead, James	Louise M. Nash,	104
Whitehill, N. J.	Ellen L. Strobridge,	150
Whitehouse, Charles H.	Julia P. Snow,	67
John T.	Mary E. Walker,	108
Whiting, Charles B.	Sarah Hayes,	49
Jenison J.	{ Sarah J. Spaulding,	26
	{ g Mary Phelps,	68
Joseph J.	Martha S.(Mann) Harrington,	37
Samuel	Anna M. Mayo,	81
Whitmore, James D.	Ruth C. Morton,	63
John	g Fannie N. Smith,	156
Whitmoyer, M.	Hannah E. Waller,	82
Whitney, Daniel	Sarah S. Fiske,	25
Edmund	Mary E. Seaton,	81
George O.	Abigail T. Fitch,	25
Harrison G.	Eliza A. Solander,	31
Horace P.	g Mary Bishop,	79
J. Hamilton	g Sarah M. North,	61
Rev. Joel F.	g Louisa M. Bailey	108
Whiton, H. K., Esq.	g Mary F. Phinney,	55
Whittemore, ——	S. A. (Adams) Wilcox,	65
Charles,	Rebecca W. Taylor,	41
Thomas W.	g Atossa F. Stone,	30
Whittlesey, Rev. F.	Elizabeth K. Baldwin,	18
Wickham, Joseph A.	LucyO.Cunningham,	107
Oscar S.	Mary O. Doughty,	97
Wicks, Charles T.	g Mary E. Hall,	114
Wight, Arthur	Carrie L. Cowles,	152
Rev. Daniel	Lucy Flint,	25
Emerson	g Elizabeth N. Lewis,	65
John G.	Flora A. Stiles,	91
Stanley G.	Nancy A. Rice,	35
Wilber, Charles W.	Sarah A. Lyman,	67
Wilbur, Frank H.	g M. Evelyn Church,	158
Henry O.	Harriet C. Lawrence,	70
Wilcox, Benj. C.	g Clara S. Birge,	114
Frederic	Lucy S. Hodges,	101
George N.	Ellen H. Wheeler,	95
Henry E.	Esther C. Birdsey,	103
Henry L.	g Mary S. Rowland,	112
Moses S., Esq.	g Lydia G. Beard,	79
Rev. Philo B.	g Sophronia S. Fisher,	51
R. S.	g Eliza P. Knight,	29
S. J. Mills	Mary J. Dana,	33
Sextus	Sarah A. Adams,	65
Wild, Rev. Edward P.	Ruth S. Nichols,	88
Wilder, Charles T.	g Mary E. Ware,	55
John C., Jr.	g Harriet A. Hinman,	131
Rev. H. A.	Abby T. Linsley,	43
Rev. Royal G.	Eliza J. Smith,	31
Wilds, Charles M., Esq.	Frances A. Wright,	119
Wiles, Robert H.	Alice R. Bradford,	121
Wiley, David G.	Marie F. Holt,	138
John D.	Louise S. Safford,	136
Wilkes, Rev. A. B.	g Mary L. Warner,	139
Wilkins, Aaron M.	Mary F. Barber,	69
Wilkinson, Henry W.	Anna Reed,	67
Wilkinson, Thomas B.	Anna L. Lockwood,	140
William H.	g Jane Humphrey,	42
Willard, Chas. W., Esq.	Emily D. Reed,	44
Everett C.	g Charlotte E. Smith,	126
Jacob P.	Helen E. Stone,	50
Rev. John D.	Mina D. Beaman,	124
Myron G.	g Julia E. Nolton,	109
Willcox, Rev. Chas. H.,gMary C. Dudley,		136
W. C.	Sarah J. Beach,	49
Willey, Rev. Worcester	Annie S. Chase,	52
Williams, B. F.	Sarah F. Harrison,	59
B. H.	g Mary Williams,	109
Rev. Charles A.	g Susan F. Hawks,	23
Charles E., Esq.	Mary C. Dulmar,	100
Francis A., Esq.	g L. Jane Clarke,	79
George W.	Frances S. Child,	30
Harrison	Julia M. Tarr,	57
Horace D.	Elizabeth P. Gould,	59
James M., Esq.	L. Emeline Francis,	62
John A.	Ida E. Corwin,	147
John K.	g Abbie T. White,	83
Lewis K.	g Abbie D. Sabin,	100
Oliver E.	Jennie H. Dodge,	147
R.	Mary A. Baldwin,	66
Robert	g Gracia Marsh,	68
P. Smith	Mary H. Allen,	35
Rev. T. B.	Clara B. Clark,	129
Rev. Theodore C.	Velma C. Wright,	117
Thomas H.	Martha W. Wheeler,	35
Thomas J.	Louisa Rumiser,	91
William G.	g Sallie H. Gould,	146
Rev. W. F.	g Clara C. Pond,	72
Willis, John H.	Olympia Brown,	66
Williston, Lyman R.	g Ann E. S. Gale,	61
Wills, Chas. J.	Helen C. Emory,	157
Wilmarth, Alfred W.	g Theodora M. Kolb,	164
A. M.	g Ella J. Thompson,	109
Wilmer, Rev. Wm.	ElizabethK.Peabody,	186
Wilson, George T.	Charlotte E. Todd,	143
H. C.	g Abbie E. Baird,	35
Howard M.	g Fairene Stone,	161
I. N.	Clara Worthington,	68
James M.	g Grace F. Pettengill,	164
Rev. James D.	g Minerva M. Metzger,	76
Rev. Joseph K.	Lucy S. Taylor,	114
M.W., M. D.	Emily O. Pelton,	81
Samuel A., M. D.	Frances Benton,	59
T. P. Simmons	Ida G. Canfield,	109
Wiltsie, W. D.	g Charlotte Benton,	61
Windecker, Simeon	Helen J. Adams,	73
Windom, William, Esq.	Ellen T. Hatch,	46
Wing, James C.	Abbie M. Newton,	122
Winn, John A.	S. Elizabeth Maltby,	50
Thomas	Elizabeth D. Adams,	96
Winslow, William A.	Harriet C. Eames,	56
Winston,GeorgeT.LL.D,Caroline S. Taylor,		116
Winter, Jonas H.	Harriet N. Kellogg,	56
Wise, Henry G.	g Josephine J. Griggs,	114
Witherbee, Dr. Orville O.	Margaret A. Rhody,	160
Witherby, Edwin T.	g Mary F. Cleveland,	95
Withey, Rev. Edwin A.	Irene F. Adams,	109

INDEX.

		Page
Wolcott, Rev. Samuel	Harriet A. Pope,	19
Rev. William H.	g Rosabelle Whitney,	134
Wolfe, E. E.	Carrie M. Smock,	162
Wood, Austin H.	Mary S. Butler.	55
Alexander M.	Margaret C. Cox,	93
Enoch G.	Martha A. S. Gerrish,	25
Ezra F.	Mary I. Bucklin,	18
Frank W.	Clara W. Morton,	110
George H.	Calista S. Morse,	107
Rev. Glen	Philomela O. Bascom,	39
Henry W.	Mary E. Cogswell,	129
J. Llewellyn	g Laura J. Snow,	96
Rev. John	Laurinda M. Dimond,	18
John B.	Lucy M. Hadselle,	77
Judson I.	g Hannah M. Mead,	137
Rev. Morgan L.	Mary Wakeman,	60
O. M.	g Hortense Parker,	148
Rev. William	g Elizabeth W. Penny,	48
Woodbridge, Edwin S.	g Mary E. Forman,	36
Henry B.	Rosa Johnson,	37
Woodbury, J. P.	g Louisa A. Long,	58
L. P.	g Florence V. Ostrom,	146
William H.	g Louisa A. (Long) Woodbury,	58
Woodford, Rev. O.L.	{ g Paulina Avery,	48
	{ g Esther P. Butler,	58
Woodhull, Rev. G. S.	Elizabeth D. Martin,	67
Woodin, Rev. Simeon F.	Sarah L. Utley,	67
Woodman, Joseph	Emma C. Sawyer,	116
Woodruff, Charles G.	g Delia S. Pease,	51
Forbes B.	g Nellie C. Richards,	128
George H.	g Achsah (Wheeler) Perkins.	36
Henry E.	Almeria S. Hall,	43
Samuel	g Lucy E. Dutton,	38
Silas D.	Elizabeth M. Clark,	73
Woods, Harding	g Caroline W. Clarke,	79
Rev. Robert M.	g Anna Fairbank,	139
Rufus D.	g Isabella Smith,	36
Woodward, David	Helen E. Baldwin,	128
Luther T.	Elizabeth Hall,	46
O. Leroy	Mary E. Strong,	130
Oliver C.	Isabella G. Dana,	30
Woodworth, Cyrus S.	Sarah Buckingham,	62

		Page
Woodworth, Rev. W.	W. g Lydia A. Sessions,	68
Wm. F., M. D.	g Emily Tracy, M.D.,	96
Woolson, James B.	H. Gertrude Dayton,	165
Woolverton, A. N., M.D.	Caroline Udell,	28
Woolworth, Frank	Sarah E. Curtis,	33
Word, T. J.	g Mary A. Stearns,	42
Work, Rev. Wm. R.	Sarah R. Gould,	20
Worstell, John P.	Abbie M. Doane,	59
Worth, Hiram E.	Elizabeth J. Durell,	81
Worthen, Thomas W.D.	M. Louise Wilcox,	117
Wotkyns, George D.	Sabra A. Stevens,	26
Wright, Albert A.	g Mary L. Bedortha,	108
Charles H.	Emma L. Giffin,	132
Rev. Edward	Susan E. Arms,	18
Edward F.	Jane R. S. Fessenden,	77
Rev. Edwin S.	g Lucia E. Dutton,	36
Frank H.	Mary E. Dort,	140
Gilman J.	Harriet H. Hales,	84
Henry	J. Victoria Wilkes,	128
Ira B.	g Elizabeth S. Trask,	65
Rev. J. E.	Ellen M. Kerr,	94
Richmond L.	Maria E. Pease,	54
Wm. F.	Mabel E. Leach,	150
Wm. S.	Lucy S. Wheeler,	166
Wyman, Moses	Francena A. Whipple,	88
Yardley, Thomas	Helen F. Price,	41
Yeckley, Jonathan A.	Ellen J. Treadway,	78
Yeiser, Frederick	Frances S. Morris,	94
Youmans, Wm., Esq.	g Nancy H. Dickinson,	48
Young, B. U.	Lizzie V. MacMath,	132
Charles H.	Julia (Goodrich) Ferguson,	53
Rev. D. P.	g Lucretia W. Tomblin,	61
Daniel H.	Mary W. Harries,	84
Edward M.	Kate R. Anewalt,	154
Henry C.	Frances A. Hitchcock,	59
Henry J.	Charlotte H. Schradi,	141
Hiland H.	Eliza F. Cushman,	30
James H.	Maria H. Griffin,	104
James R.	Elizabeth T. Packard,	23
John	Martha A. Wright,	29
L. Monroe	L. Emily Hallock,	62
Rev. W. S.	g C. Adelle Nichols,	146

INDEX.—STUDENTS.

Names of graduates are indicated by the letter *g* prefixed. Non-graduates are classed in the last year of their connection with the Seminary or College.

Abbe
'77 Mary P............135

Abbot
'89 *g* Alice B............164
'94 *g* Fanny H..........176

Abbott
'59 Adelaide S........ 80
'54 Augusta E......... 62
'59 Chloe.............. 80
'82 Cora E............146
'50 Fannie O.......... 48
'46 *g* Lydia E. M....... 35
'48 Lydia R........... 42
'38 *g* Martha A......... 16
'86 *g* Nora..............155

Abell
'72 *g* Emeline P........120

Abram
'60 Cynthia M........ 83

Ackley
'48 *g* Mary E........... 41

Adams
'75 *g* Abbie A..........128
'59 Caroline.......... 80
'53 *g* Elizabeth......... 58
'64 Elizabeth D....... 96
'70 Ella M............115
'69 Emma..............112
'70 Emma M...........115
'93 *g* Florence I........174
'64 Helen A........... 96
'57 Helen J........... 73
'68 Irene F...........109
'38 Julia.............. 16
'95 Kate E............179
'87 *g* Kate L............158
'44 Mary E............ 29
'49 Mary E............ 45
'51 Mary H............ 52
'53 Mary S............ 59
'56 *g* Nancy L........... 68
'40 Sarah A........... 20
'55 Sarah A........... 65
'38 Sarah B........... 16
'44 Sarah E........... 29
'78 *g* Sarah W..........136
'57 Susan A........... 73
'51 Susan P........... 52

Agard
'95 Katherine M......179
'80 *g* Sarah J.......139, 141

Aiken
'83 Elizabeth R.......149

Ainslie
'46 *g* Abbie M........... 35
'46 Helen A........... 36

Ainsworth
'50 Emma L............ 48
'77 Eva V.............135
'49 *g* Lucy M..........7, 45
'77 *g* S. Elizabeth......133

Albee
'91 Ellen L...........170

Alcott
'94 Mary H...........177

Alden
'65 Eleanor P........100
'55 Emily G........... 65
'69 *g* Harriet E........111
'70 Mary C...........115
'38 Mary G............ 16

Aldrich
'74 Alice L...........126
'52 Angeline M....... 55
'60 Anna.............. 83
'65 *g* Eleanor W......... 99
'48 Juliana........... 42
'46 Laura............. 36
'95 Lena M...........179
'63 Mary A............ 93

Alexander
'56 *g* Ada J............. 68
'56 Ellen L........... 68
'82 *g* Florence H.......146
'79 *g* M. Jeanette......138

Alford
'73 *g* Clara J..........122
'56 Mary J............ 69

Alger
'90 *g* Florence H.......166

Allen
'44 Abby.............. 30
'74 Abby W...........126
'51 Alida............. 52
'50 Anna C............ 48
'64 *g* Anna W........... 95
'90 *g* Annie T..........166
'83 Caro G...........149
'92 Carrie M.........171
'72 *g* Clara F..........120
'82 Constance E......146
'50 Delinda J......... 48
'47 Elizabeth C....... 39
'88 *g* Elizabeth S......161
'94 Elsie A...........177
'38 Elvira P.......... 16

'56 E. Maria.......... 69
'78 Emily A..........137
'76 *g* Emma M..........130
'57 Emma T............ 73
'80 Eva E............142
'45 *g* Harriette......... 32
'77 Ina...............135
'40 Joan.............. 20
'75 Lizzie E.........128
'63 Lonisa P.......... 93
'95 Luella M.........179
'95 Mabel L..........179
'50 Maria............. 48
'69 Martha B.........112
'42 Martha D.......... 24
'55 Mary A............ 65
'65 Mary A...........100
'74 Mary E...........126
'45 Mary H............ 33
'90 *g* Mary L...........166
'55 Mary M............ 65
'95 May W............179
'43 Phebe H........... 26
'62 Sabra A........... 90
'66 Sarah A..........103
'51 Sophia............ 52
'47 *g* Susan A........... 38
'45 *g* Susan M........... 32
'80 *g* Zella B..........141

Allender
'58 Annie E........... 76

Alling
'43 Emeline S........ 26

Allis
'48 Mary E. W........ 42

Allyn
'94 *g* Eleanor..........176
'44 Mary R............ 30

Alter
'76 Josephine B......131

Alvord
'74 L. Hope..........126
'79 Susan G..........139

Ames
'89 Alice W..........165
'91 *g* Josephine S......169
'42 Mary I............ 24
'46 Semantha M....... 36

Amidon
'53 Martha E......... 59

Anable
'60 Harriet I......... 83

INDEX.

Anderson
'51 Caroline B......... 52
'57 g Harriet M.........158
'68 g Martha A.........108
'89 g Mary.............164
'90 g Mary E...........166
'71 g Mercy A..........117
'48 g Sarah J.......... 41
'70 g Susan E..........114

Andrea
'95 Elizabeth R.......179

Andrew
'73 Elva W............123

Andrews
'79 g Fanny P.........138
'95 Florence M........179
'68 Frances M.........109
'95 Harriet E.........179
'66 Harriet N.........103
'90 g Katherine.......166
'74 Lucy Caroline.....126

Andros
'45 Martha N.......... 33

Andruss
'67 Lizzie C..........106
'64 Sarah J........... 96

Anewalt
'85 Anna E............154
'85 Kate R............154

Angell
'71 g Helen J......... 117
'78 Metta E..........137

Annett
'93 g Sarah E.........174

Archbald
'92 Jessie............172

Archer
'45 Amanda M........ 33

Arey
'49 Annie E.......... 45
'49 Susan............. 45

Armington
'90 Alice H...........167

Arms
'47 Adelia............ 39
'61 Ella M............ 87
'51 Fanny............. 52
'68 Gertrude G.......109
'41 Harriet........... 22
'48 Maria P........... 42
'43 Mary W........... 27
'44 Sarah S.......... 30
'39 Susan E.......... 18
'38 Theresa T........ 16

Armstrong
'51 g Caroline P...... 51
'78 g Elizabeth I....136
'56 Lucy W........... 69
'83 Mary A..........149

Arnold
'71 Amelia D.........118

'83 Belle A...........149
'48 Cornelia B....... 42
'39 Harriet T........ 18
'71 Maria A..........118
'71 Mary J...........118
'41 Sophia........... 22

Arthurs
'83 Julia B..........149

Ashbey
'61 Hannah A........ 87

Ashby
'85 May S...........154

Ashley
'66 g Lydia L........102

Aten
'94 Edna B..........177

Atherton
'62 Sarah W. (Lyman) 90

Atkins
'56 Frances M....... 69
'90 Mabel M.........167
'48 Marietta......... 42

Atkinson
'40 Louisa M........ 20

Atwater
'78 g Lucy..........136
'81 Lucy F..........144

Atwood
'73 Amanda.........123
'57 g Anna J........ 71
'88 Annie I.........161
'50 Elizabeth P..... 48
'63 g Emma J....... 92
'39 g Frances M..... 12, 17
'51 g Hannah J...... 51
'44 Harriet P....... 30
'57 Mary F......... 73
'49 g Mary K....... 45

Augur
'71 Mary E.........118

Aumock
'84 g Carrie L......150

Austin
'52 g Eliza H....... 54
'77 g Flora L.......133

Averill
'74 g Helen W......125
'84 g Mary A.......150
'93 g Sarah........13, 174
'95 g Sarah........178

Avery
'48 Anne F......... 42
'80 Annie H........142
'45 g Caroline......13, 32
'55 Elizabeth...... 65
'48 Elizabeth A.... 42
'86 g Elizabeth D..155
'84 Jeannette M...152
'77 Jerusha P......135
'76 g Julia S......130
'39 Mary........... 18

'84 g Mary A.......150
'74 Mary E.........126
'50 g Paulina....... 7, 48

Ayer
'51 g E. Josephine.. 51
'80 Elizabeth M...142
'63 Emily D........ 93
'85 g Fy...........153
'54 g Laura W...... 7, 61
'86 Louise.........157
'82 Gertrude......146

Ayrault
'51 Jane............ 52

Ayres
'79 Elizabeth A....139
'94 g Frances C....176
'77 Keziah.........135

Babb
'95 Emily A........179

Babbitt
'76 Emma I........131
'53 Hettie W....... 59
'48 g Lydia H...... 41

Babcock
'88 Cara J.........161
'44 Jerusha........ 30
'69 Maria L........112

Bachelder
'72 g Annie A......120
'84 g Carrie W.....151
'58 Ellen B. F..... 76
'77 Grace D........135

Backus
'40 Harriet........ 20

Bacon
'66 g D. Antoinette...102
'78 g Imogene......136
'94 g Imogene......176
'52 Nancy J....... 55

Badger
'43 Emily D........ 27
'57 Sarah E........ 73

Badgley
'68 g Jane M.......108

Bagg
'45 g Jane F........ 32

Bailey
'50 Caroline P..... 48
'38 Charlotte...... 16
'44 Elizabeth G.... 30
'61 Ellen S........ 87
'45 Emily L........ 33
'39 g Hannah O..... 7, 17
'63 Isabel M....... 93
'68 g Louisa M....108
'62 Lucy L......... 90
'45 g Lydia G...... 8, 10, 32
'53 Martha A......12, 59
'84 g Mary E......151
'88 g Mary F......161
'93 sp Mary F.....176
'74 g Minnie F....125

STUDENTS.

'82 g Rebecca............146
'45 Sarah.............. 33
'44 g Sarah T........... 29

Baird
'45 Abbie E............ 33
'67 g Emily J...........105
'47 Esther C.......... 39

Baker
'68 Abbie W..........109
'84 Ada C.............152
'59 Caroline P......... 80
'56 Frances A......... 69
'56 Frances W........ 69
'90 g Grace B..........166
'51 g Hettie E............ 51
'61 g H. Henrietta...... 85
'68 g Isabella C.........108
'81 g L. Jennie..........143
'87 Lizzie M...........159
'86 Lucretia............157
'95 Lucy F............179
'88 Mabel L...........161
'41 Malvina............22
'51 g M. Antoinette...... 51
'78 Minnie F..........137
'95 sp S. Marinda......184
'42 Susan M.......... 24

Balch
'63 Alice M.......... 93
'60 H. Anna.......... 83
'62 g Laura A........... 89

Balcom
'62 g Ella L............. 89
'48 Mary A........... 42

Baldwin
'54 Abigail C.......... 62
'64 Adelaide........... 96
'52 Adelaide A........ 55
'73 Carrie............123
'84 Charlotte E........152
'39 Elizabeth K....... 18
'50 Emily G........... 48
'42 g Estimate R. E..... 23
'53 Hannah C......... 59
'75 Helen E...........128
'71 g H. Gertrude...... 117
'51 Jane M............ 52
'95 Jessie M..........180
'80 g Julia C..........141
'75 Lizzie G..........128
'45 g Lydia R.......... 32
'57 Margaret S........ 73
'60 Martha A......... 83
'53 Mary A........... 59
'55 Mary A........... 66
'42 Sarah A........... 24
'78 Sarah C..........137
'70 g Sarah D..........114

Balkam
'95 Susanne L.........180

Ball
'46 Semantha W...... 36

Ballantine
'66 Anna M............102
'57 g Elizabeth D......7, 71
'62 g Julia A........... 89

'55 g Mary............. 64

Ballard
'65 Alice G............100
'59 Elizabeth W....... 80
'84 g Winifred P........151

Bancroft
'48 Caroline T........ 42
'71 Mary N...........118

Banks
'91 g Annie C..........169
'88 g Lizzie C..........161

Banning
'69 Mary P........ 112

Bannister
'74 Ida C..............126

Barber
'55 Anna S............ 66
'66 Ella J............103
'74 Eva R............126
'66 Fanny A..........103
'68 Florence I........109
'94 g Harriet A. 176
'95 Harriet S..........180
'58 g Mary E.......... 75
'56 Mary T............ 69

Barbour
'76 g Amie L............130
'87 g Catharine H.......158
'95 g Catharine H......178

Bardwell
'66 g Elisabeth M.....7, 102
'79 g Emma C..........139
'43 Harriet W......... 27
'55 Mabel W.......... 66
'73 Maria H..........123

Barker
'65 Anna E...........100
'49 Catharine K....... 45
'46 g Mary E...........7, 36
'76 Susan E..........131
'42 Susan W.......... 24

Barkdoll
'83 Anna G............149

Barlow
'46 Lucy.............. 36

Barnard
'55 Alice L............ 66
'71 Ellen M...........118
'38 Lucy............. 16
'90 Rhoda F..........167
'51 Sarah A........... 52

Barnes
'59 Anna M........... 80
'76 Ella S............131
'83 Helen A...........149
'56 Hinda............. 69
'65 g Jane F............ 99
'56 Marilla............ 69
'47 Martha A......... 39
'58 Mary A........... 76
'82 Mary G...........146
'77 Mary L...........135

'77 Nellie H...........135

Barnette
'58 Marionette A...... 76

Barney
'55 Agnes E.......... 66
'90 Harriet E.........167
'86 g Mary E...........155

Barnum
'89 Grace E..........165
'83 g Mary F..........148
'82 Susan E..........146

Barr
'57 Ellen M.......... 73

Barrett
'71 Alice M..........118
'47 g Elizabeth G....... 38
'45 Ellen C........... 33
'51 g Lucy A........... 51
'59 Mary P........... 80
'88 g S. Eliza..........161

Barron
'68 Frances G.........109
'68 Olive M..........109
'93 Dorothy H.. 175

Barry
'68 Mary A..........109

Barrows
'76 Annie G..........131
'48 Caroline B........ 42
'56 g Cornelia C........ 68
'62 Fanny A......... 90
'58 g Harriet A......... 75
'62 Martha J.... 90
'57 Mary E.......... 73

Barstow
'90 g Mabel............166
'39 Margaret F....... 18
'71 Sallie C..........118

Bartholomew
'95 g Ellen E..........178

Bartlett
'62 Abby M........... 90
'62 Anna M........... 90
'88 Annie L...........161
'77 Cornelia S........135
'56 g Ellen C.......... 68
'83 Jennie H..........149
'56 Laura E.......... 69
'81 g Lizzie A..........143
'50 Margaret C....... 49

Barton
'90 Adeline S......... 83
'68 Caroline A.........109
'90 g Charlotte..........166
'75 g Frances H........128
'52 Josephine H...... 55
'69 Mary E..........112
'91 g Mellie W..........169

Bascom
'47 Philomela O....... 39

Bass
'60 Emily A.......... 83

INDEX.

'39 *g* Lucia L............ 17
'95 Mary E............180

Bassett
'42 Catharine A....... 24
'54 Elizabeth P........ 62
'92 Emily M..........172
'87 Grace I..........159
'61 Maria E.......... 87
'88 *g* Mary..............161
'41 Mary E........... 22
'42 Mary T.......... 24
'67 M. Louise........106
'87 Rebecca A........159

Batchelder
'74 Annie D..........126
'61 *g* Julia F............. 85
'43 Mary S........... 27

Batcheller
'40 Mary D.......... 20

Batcheler
'62 *g* Frances A......... 89

Bateman
'52 Ellen E.......... 55
'72 Elizabeth H.......121

Bates
'85 Alice E..........154
'65 Charlotte D......100
'40 Deborah E. N...12, 20
'60 *g* Elvira C.......... 82
'95 Emeline C 180
'73 Irene E..........123
'84 *g* Lizzie E..........151
'46 *g* Lydia 36
'61 M. Augusta........ 87
'40 Mary E. M........ 20
'41 Mary............. 22
'67 *g* Myra E...........105
'47 S. Cornelia........ 39
'45 *g* Susan F........... 32

Battelle
'66 Mary L...........103

Battis
'51 Harriet J......... 52

Battles
'59 Marietta J........ 80

Baxter
'59 Caroline E........ 80

Bayley
'42 Charlotte P....... 24
'72 *g* Sarah E..........120

Beach
'58 Anna A........... 76
'62 Anna I........... 90
'78 Anna I..........137
'59 *g* Aura J........... 79
'92 Dorothy B........172
'79 Ella C...........139
'78 Ella M...........137
'93 *g* Emily K..........174
'68 *g* M. Agnes..........108
'95 Martha...........180
'57 *g* Mary P........... 71
'50 Sarah J.......... 49

Beale
'56 Adelaide S........69

Beals
'75 L. Dora..........128
'65 Sarah A..........100

Beaman
'64 *g* Emma W.......... 95
'95 Harriet E........180
'46 *g* Mary A........... 36
'63 *g* Mary E........... 92
'72 Mina D...........121

Bean
'54 Lucretia A........ 62
'57 Mary E........... 73
'76 M. Ella..........131

Beane
'72 *g* Ednah F..........120
'78 *g* Flora S..........136

Beard
'59 *g* L. Vesta......... 79
'59 *g* Lydia G.......... 79
'59 *g* Mary A.......... 79
'51 Susan H.......... 52

Beardsley
'44 Mary............. 30
'85 Katharine A......154

Beare
'91 *g* Julia T..........169
'94 *g* Cornelia.........176

Bearse
'90 Lucy J.......... 167

Becker
'56 Eliza M.......... 69
'51 Helen............ 52

Beckley
'75 Annie J..........128

Beckwith
'82 *g* Emily H..........146
'83 Mary E..........149
'93 *g* Martha W........174

Bedortha
'68 *g* Mary L..........108

Beebe
'79 A. Adelaide......139
'67 Clara S..........106
'58 Elizabeth........ 76
'67 *g* Lucy J..........105
'56 *g* Sarah........... 68
'68 Sarah H.........109

Beecher
'72 Flora J..........121

Beede
'95 *g* Alice G..........178
'63 Eunice M......... 93

Beekman
'64 Sarah W.......... 96

Beeman
'93 Alberta L....... 175

Beers
'95 Florence E. 180
'55 Phebe H.......... 66

Belcher
'59 Cornelia E........ 80
'60 *g* H. Augusta......7, 82
'95 Ida M...........180
'63 Lucy G........... 93

Belden
'39 Chloe B.......... 18
'47 Cornelia J........ 39
'42 Mary............. 24
'65 Sarah E..........100

Belknap
'48 Beulah M......... 42
'45 Clara............ 38

Bell
'58 Abbey A.......... 76
'47 *g* Elizabeth M...... 38
'78 *g* Emma C..........136
'93 *sp* Jessie M........176
'64 Laura V 96
'79 Mary E..........139
'79 *g* S. Louise........139
'65 *g* Sarah C......... 99

Beman
'52 Orrel C.......... 55

Bement
'70 *g* Mary O......... ...114

Bemis
'93 *sp* Agnes T.......14, 176
'94 *g* Leigh J..........176
'61 *g* Seraph A......... 85

Benedict
'90 *g* Anna M..........166
'83 *g* Elizabeth........148
'73 Elizabeth M......123
'68 Flora............109
'45 Martha........... 33
'95 Mary............180
'91 Susan...........170
'81 *g* Ursula E........143

Benham
'81 Mary P...........144

Benner
'95 Caroline F........180
'75 S. Frances.......128

Bennett
'67 *g* Ellen L..........105
'74 *g* Gazella..........125
'72 Mary E..........121
'72 *g* Mary S..........120

Benson
'71 *g* Elizabeth R....... 117
'68 Frances H........109

Bent
'75 Mary E..........128

Benthall
'52 Mary L........... 55

STUDENTS.

Bentley
'57 Allie R............ 73
'52 Julia M........... 55
Benton
'52 g Anna E........... 54
'54 g Charlotte......... 61
'53 Frances........... 59
'45 Maria W.......... 33
Berger
'60 Elizabeth L........ 83
Berray
'59 Julia M........... 80
Berry
'53 Eliza A........... 59
'68 Ella A............109
'92 g Grace E...........171
'93 g Grace E..........174
'85 g Mary A........7, 153
'53 Phebe L.......... 59
Bertolet
'68 Elizabeth M.......109
Bessé
'79 Hattie C..........139
Best
'91 Nellie D.... 170
Betts
'66 g Harriet C........102
'39 Harriet M........ 18
'64 Mary A.......... 96
Bevier
'60 Alice D.......... 83
Bevin
'93 Pernella........ .175
Bickford
'83 Flora M..........149
'84 Mary M.........152
Bickmore
'73 Hattie A..........123
Bidwell
'95 Bertha C........180
'92 g Clara L..........171
'66 g Harriet A........102
'88 g Margaret..........161
'65 Mary E..........100
Bierce
'51 g Isabella G........ 51
'42 Lewey A.......... 24
Bigelow
'38 Abigail........... 16
'61 Ann Eliza........ 87
'75 Carrie E..........120
'45 Catharine A....... 33
'50 Chloe M.......... 49
'91 g Fannie L..........169
'48 g Frances F 41
'48 Isabel H.......... 42
'45 Martha F......... 33
'54 Mary J.......... 62
'51 g Sarah W.......... 51

Biggam
'67 g Carrie P...........105
Bilderbach
'80 M. Virginia...... 142
Billam
'95 Flora E..........180
Billings
'68 Abbie I..........109
'59 g Catharine E........ 79
'57 Cornelia F........ 73
'04 g H. Louisa......... 95
'67 Hattie E..........106
'54 Jane M.......... 62
'53 Martha D........ 59
'83 Mary A..........149
'53 Mary C........ 59
'57 g Mary F........... 71
Bills
'67 g Allie R..........105
Bingham
'61 Amorette W....... 87
'51 Elizabeth K....... 52
'53 g Martha M....... 58
'40 Mary L........... 20
Bird
'77 g Alice E..........133
'84 Emily F. J........152
'95 sp Mabel E..........184
Birdsey
'71 Alice A..........118
'66 Esther C........103
'65 Mary A..........100
Birge
'63 Anna A.......... 93
'59 Charlotte........ 80
'70 g Clara S..........114
Bisbee
'65 Clara L..........100
'77 Julia E..........135
'84 g Nettie M..... ...151
Bishop
'65 Alice L..........100
'64 g Anna M.......... 95
'86 Annette E........157
'68 Charlotte A........109
'48 Elizabeth.......... 42
'95 Elizabeth A......180
'48 Mary.......... 43
'59 g Mary.......... 79
'65 Nancy B..........100
'60 g Sarah L.......... 82
Bissell
'95 Alma W..........180
'70 Angeline S........115
'42 Arabella J...... 24
'64 g Cornelia H........ 95
'41 Elizabeth A....... 22
'50 g Emily......... 48
'81 Emily R..........144
'75 g Fannie E..........128
'47 g Harriet L......... 38
'79 Julia..........139
'48 g Julia A.......... 41

'48 Julia A............ 43
'72 g M. Louise. 120
'45 g Mary H........... 32
'63 Mary R. 93
Bixby
'38 Harriet.. 16
'50 Sarah E........... 49
Black
'71 g Frances B..........117
Blackington
'47 Frances........... 39
Blackler
'46 Ellen L.......... 37
Blackly
'50 Marion M.......... 49
Blackman
'74 Abbie B..........126
Blackstock
'95 Mary I.. 180
Blackwell
'43 Adaline.......... 27
'51 Sophie S........... 52
Blair
'41 Catharine L........ 22
'87 Grace R..........159
'50 Sarah E........... 49
Blaisdell
'69 Doll H..........112
'52 Harriet M......... 55
'52 Sarah............. 55
Blake
'94 g Clara L..........176
'66 g Ellen S..........102
'95 g Ethel W..........178
'69 Harriet F........ 112
Blakely
'84 g Annie G..........151
'93 g Bertha E..........174
'81 g Ellen M..........143
Blakeslee
'64 Jane M.......... 96
Blakslee
'69 Amanda H........112
Blanchard
'88 Ada L..........162
'38 Charlotte......... 16
'58 g Elizabeth........7, 75
'80 g Elizabeth D..........141
'77 Elizabeth G........135
'66 Emily E..........103
'74 Henrietta F......126
'62 g Louisa M........ 89
'64 Maria E.......... 96
'49 Mary A......... 45
'40 Rachel..........13, 20
'40 Sarah 20
Blanding
'43 g Juliet M.......... 26
Blasdale
'86 Laura M..........157

INDEX.

Blinn
'43 Sarah M. S........ 27

Bliss
'62 // Anna E............ 89
'54 Caroline F.... . 62
'55 Catharine L....... 66
'88 // Clara A............161
'39 Eliza E........... 18
'47 Eliza L............ 39
'39 Emma L............ 18
'63 // Flavia S.......... 92
'47 // Georgiana M....... 38
'70 Harriet M.........115
'52 Harriet S.......... 55
'70 Helen E...........115
'59 // Julia M............ 79
'91 // Lulu F............109
'95sp Lulu F............176
'95 M. Alice..........180
'61 Mary A............ 87
'49 Mary S............ 45
'50 Mary W............ 49
'92 // Maria W..........171
'95 // Seraph A..........178

Blocher
'86 // Flora B............155

Blodgett
'59 Adeline M......... 80
'88 // Emma M............161
'75 Estelle M..........129
'70 // Mary E..........7, 114
'56 Parthena H..,..... 69
'67 Susan G...........106

Blood
'71 Nellie E..........118

Bloomfield
'92 // E. Evangeline.....171
'93 // E. Evangeline......174

Blunt
'95 Florence T... 180
'79 Kate.............139
'95 // Kate M 178

Boardman
'88 // Alice I............161
'65 // Cornelia L......... 99
'95sp Elizabeth W.......184

Boas
'55 Sarah J............ 66

Bockée
'92 // Anna B............ 171

Bodge
'50 // Caroline A......... 48

Bodman
'45 Elizabeth B........ 33

Bodurtha
'81 Fannie M..........144

Bogardus
'47 Ruth 39

Bogue
'52 Adelaide J......... 55
'45 Catharine.......... 33

Boice
'56 Eliza E............ 69
'84 // Josephine..........151
'87 May 159

Boies
'42 Caroline E......... 24
'44 Elizabeth T........ 30
'42 Jane L............ 24
'50 // Mary P............ 48
'53 // Rebecca D......... 58
'49 Sarah E........... 45

Bolles
'59 Elizabeth P........ 80
'52 // Jane L., see
 Judson, Jane L. B.. 54

Boltwood
'60 // Caroline A......... 82

Bonar
'87 Mabel S..........159

Bond
'83 // Mary E...........148
'95 // Violet R...........178

Bonney
'43 // Sarah A........... 26

Boomhour
'73 // Clara A...........122

Boone
'47 Julia M.... 39

Booth
'48 Alma............ 43
'45 Caroline E........ 33
'39 Emily............ 18
'70 Harriet E.........115
'42 Selina............ 24

Borden
'40 Mary............. 20
'93 Sallie.............175

Bosworth
'38 Abby M.......... 16
'38 Anna E........... 16
'75 Mary A...........129
'42 Minerva A........ 24
'52 Nancy C......... 55

Bottum
'74 // Caroline E.........125
'77 Mary L...........135

Boudinot
'44 Elinor S.......... 30

Boudinott
'48 Mary H.... 43

Boughton
'89 Ellsworth A.......105

Bouldrey
'78 Emma D...........137

Bourne
'53 Celia M........... 59

Boutelle
'61 Caroline A........ 87

Bouton
'49 Harriette S........ 45
'44 Laura A.......... 30
'77 // Sarah M...........133

Boutwell
'90 // Sarah K............166

Bowdoin
'47 Abby W. A........ 39
'49 // Emily W. S... 7, 12,45
'38 Laura G........... 16

Bowen
'43 Annette L......... 27
'44 Cynthia........... 30
'51 Ellen M........... 52
'44 Emily J........... 30
'85 // Frances C..........153
'39 Phebe F.......... 18
'64 // Sarah........... 7, 95
'64 // Susan........... 7, 95

Bowers
'58 // Ellen P.......... 7, 75
'70 M. Lizzie......115

Bowlend
'43 Mary L. W....... 27

Bowles
'71 Kate E............118
'52 Mary Amelia...... 55

Boyce
'52 Margaret E....... 55

Boyd
'86 // Annie M...........155
'68 Caroline B........109
'51 Ellen W.......... 52
'61 Sarah M.......... 87

Boyden
'75 Cornelia F........129

Boyer
'88 Emily M..........162

Boynton
'56 Caroline.......... 69
'58 Eliza... 77
'72 Emma S..........121
'74 Mary H..........126
'79 // S. Ella...........139
'42 Sarah............ 24
'51 // Susan P.......... 51

Bracket
'64 Carrie A.......... 96

Brackett
'64 Emily A.......... 96
'57 // Lydia W.......... 71

Bradbury
'56 Anna R........... 69
'95 Emilie G.... 180

Braddock
'52 Emily A.......... 55

Bradford
'72 Alice R...........121
'54 // Celestia.......... 61
'73 Edith W..........123

STUDENTS. 231

	Page
'90 Elfleda J	167
'81 Elizabeth J	144
'93 Flora I	175
'69 *g* Martha E. E	7, 111
'85 Mary A	154
'71 *g* Mary C	7, 117

Bradley
'47 Ann E.............. 39
'52 Artemisia E....... 55
'42 Cornelia.......... 24
'81 Florence L........144
'52 M. Ophelia........ 55
'43 Mary E........... 27
'69 *g* Sarah E..........111

Bradstreet
'41 *g* Lydia............. 22

Bragaw
'90 Annie.............167

Bragg
'91 *g* Louise H..........169

Brainard
'54 Lucy A........... 62
'93 Nellie J..........175

Brainerd
'87 *g* Helen E..........158
'61 Julia D............87
'47 *g* Mary C........... 38
'62 Mary J............ 90
'77 Mary V............135
'56 N. Helen.......... 69

Branning
'74 S. Elizabeth.......126

Branscomb
'56 Josephine E....... 69

Brastow
'89 *g* Frances C..........164

Bray
'85 Alice P............154
'83 *g* Ella T........7, 13, 148
'93 Mary C............175

Breck
'54 Isabella........... 62
'53 Sarah B........... 59

Breed
'39 *g* Eliza M........... 18
'42 Eunice............ 24
'52 *g* M. Elizabeth...... 54

Breese
'60 S. Madora........ 83

Brewster
'55 Caroline S........ 66
'62 *g* Ellen D............ 89

Bricket
'52 Louisa A.......... 55

Bridges
'50 Julia A........... 49
'43 Lucy M........... 27

Bridgman
'40 Catharine W...... 20
'63 Emma A.......... 63

	Page
'77 Hannah C	135
'38 Mary	16
'74 Mary S	126
'86 *g* Minnie H	155
'45 Rebecca A	33

Brierley
'94 *g* Addie O..........176
'94 *g* Ella T............176

Briggs
'59 Elizabeth.......... 80
'95 *g* Ella M............178
'52 Henrietta W...... 55
'55 Mary B........... 66
'72 Minnie...........121
'49 Sarah A.......... 45

Brigham
'46 Angeline.......... 37
'43 Cornelia A........ 27
'67 Elizabeth M.......106
'38 Hannah.......... 16
'65 Helen F...........100
'68 Henrietta M 109
'39 *g* Lucy A........... 18
'46 *g* Lucy H........... 36
'43 Maria C.......... 27
'50 Mary A..........7, 49
'52 Mary H........... 55
'38 *g* Sarah..........8, 16

Brink
'71 *g* M. Josephine......117

Brinsmade
'46 *g* Mary M........... 36

Briscoe
'87 Alice.............159

Broaders
'52 Rebecca H........ 55

Brockway
'87 *g* Alice C...........158
'84 Emily E..........152
'83 *g* Martha S..........148

Brokaw
'51 Margaret V....... 52

Bronson
'61 *g* Aletta M.......... 85
'83 Alice P...........149
'84 Carrie M.........152
'87 Gertrude E.......159
'58 *g* Mary P.........8, 75

Brookings
'52 Susan A.......... 55

Brooks
'39 Almira........... 18
'72 *g* Caroline A........120
'79 Elizabeth.........139
'58 *g* Julia E............ 75
'51 M. Augusta....... 52
'58 Sophia W........ 77

Broughton
'76 Fannie H.........131
'77 Grace A..........135

Brown
'76 Abbie A..........132

	Page
'49 *g* Abigail M	45
'64 Ada B	96
'70 *g* Adelia M	114
'95 Adeline S	180
'94 Alice E	177
'95 *g* Alice W	178
'92 *g* Annie L	171
'67 Amelia M	106
'45 Caroline O	33
'68 C. Ida	109
'81 Clara	144
'89 *g* Clara L	161
'74 Cora I	126
'45 Eliza C. H	33
'52 Emeline F	55
'63 Emma E	93
'66 Emma G	103
'75 Esther M	129
'72 *g* Ethie E	120
'49 Harriet	45
'93 Helen C	175
'61 Jane H	87
'67 Jane S	106
'70 Julia A	83
'61 L. Maria	87
'66 *g* Love L	102
'78 *g* Louisa M	136
'72 Lucia S	121
'69 M. Agnes	112
'60 Margaret E	83
'44 *g* Marie F	8, 29
'70 Martha C	115
'75 *g* Mary E	128
'61 Mary E	87
'45 Mary J	33
'49 *g* Mary Q	8, 45
'82 Mary S	146
'88 *g* Nellie E	161
'55 Oella	66
'55 Olympia	66
'59 Rebecca S	80
'79 *g* Stella C	139
'51 *g* Susan N	8, 51
'80 *g* Sybel G	141
'71 *g* Viette I	117

Brownback
'79 *g* E. Louise..........139

Browne
'41 Anna A........... 22
'46 Clara............. 37
'82 Emily B..........146
'46 Frances L........ 37
'42 Lucia W.......... 24
'41 Malvina.......... 22
'40 *g* Maria J. B........ 20
'56 Mary E........... 69
'40 *g* Rebekah R....... 20
'40 *g* Sarah H.......... 20

Brownell
'59 Julia F........... 80

Browning
'55 Mary I........... 66

Bruce
'39 *g* Elmira S.......... 18
'87 *g* Harriet L..........158
'94 Sara S............177

Bruen
'58 *g* Evaline........... 75

INDEX.

Brundage
'84 *g* Gertrude M........151
Bruner
'76   Lizzie P...........132
Bryant
'95 *g* Florence M........178
'72   Lucy E............121
Buchanan
'62   Martha A.......... 90
'55   N. Amanda........ 66
Buck
'62   Althea J........... 90
'75   Eliza H...........129
'46   Mary E........... 37
'69   Mary H...........112
'88   Mary H...........162
Buckingham
'79   Agnes M..........140
'62 *g* Elizabeth H........ 89
'67 *g* Ella J............105
'56   Emma W.......... 69
'59 *g* Helen............. 79
'56   Julia............. 69
'73 *g* Laura A.........8, 122
'54   Sarah............. 62
Buckland
'87   Sarah M..........159
Bucklen
'38   Elizabeth.......... 16
Bucklin
'39   Mary I............ 18
Budd
'87 *g* Avarene I..........158
'92   Bernice M.........172
'95   Mary W...........180
'94 *g* Sarah R...........176
Buel
'47   Lucy H............ 39
'53   Mary A........... 59
Buell
'67   Florence A....... 106
'67 *g* Louise M..........105
Buffum
'73   Jennie G..........124
'72 *g* Mary E...........120
'74   Louise A..........126
Bull
'93 *g* Caroline A. G......174
'40   Elizabeth G....... 20
'65   Eunice W.........100
'42   Serina............ 24
'40   Susan T........... 20
'38   Ursula............ 16
Bullard
'66 *g* Caroline..........102
'67   Harriet M.........105
'67   Lucy A...........106
Bumstead
'77   N. Viola..........135

Bunker
'72   M. Amanda....... 121
Bunnell
'94 *g* Elizabeth H....... 176
Burchard
'49   Harriet M........ 46
Burdett
'48   Mary J............ 43
Burdic
'75   Louise A..........129
Burdon
'73 *g* Sarah E...........122
Burgess
'69 *g* Abbie L...........111
'52   Caroline R........ 55
'90 *g* C. Idella..........166
'79   Cora J............140
'61 *g* Georgiana M...... 85
'61 *g* Maria G.......... 85
'69 *g* Mary P........12, 111
Burke
'61   Margaret.......... 87
Burkett
'57   Ellen I............ 73
Burleigh
'95   Nettie C..........180
Burlingame
'80   Esther A..........142
Burnap
'62   Jane E............ 90
Burnett
'66 *g* Mary A...........102
Burnette
'83 *g* Annie J...........148
'75   Della S...........129
'76   Mary E...........132
Burnham
'90   Emma J..........168
'51 *g* Martha L.......... 51
'46   Mary A........... 37
'42   Sarah J........... 24
Burns
'44   Lydia F........... 30
Burr
'41 *g* Caroline.......... 22
'66   Eliza G...........103
'38   Elmina............ 16
'93   Jean M...........175
'42 *g* Mary............. 23
Burrage
'43   Mary C........... 27
Burrall
'79   Jennie D..........140
Burrell
'77   Ellen I...........135
Burrill
'50   Martha J.......... 49

'75 *g* M. Letitia..........128
Burritt
'47   Anna E............ 39
'92*sp* Jessie M..........173
Burroughs
'89   Alice.............165
'95   Grace.............180
'77 *g* Mary H...........134
Burt
'45   Abbey A.......... 33
'62 *g* Achsah L.......... 89
'60 *g* Caroline.......... 82
'50 *g* Delia B........... 48
'51 *g* Elizabeth........8, 51
'61   Eudora H......... 87
'92 *g* Grace M..........171
'93 *g* Grace M..........174
'56   Mary A........13, 69
'65   Mary F...........100
Burton
'59   Mary E........... 80
'55 *g* Sarah A.......... 64
Burtt
'95   Gertrude A........180
Bush
'48   Hannah C......... 43
'42   Martha A......... 24
'60 *g* Mary T........... 82
Bushée
'91 *g* Alice H.......169, 170
'74   Clara F...........126
Bushnell
'87   Anna I............159
'61 *g* Ellen W.......... 85
'51   Lavinia A......... 52
'92 *g* Lottie............171
Butler
'73 *g* Abbie J...........122
'54   Abbie S........... 62
'50   Agnes M.......... 49
'87 *g* Alice.............158
'73   Alice M...........124
'58   Angeline.......... 77
'90   Annie............168
'72 *g* Cora E...........120
'64   Dorcas E.......... 96
'63 *g* Emily A.......... 92
'53 *g* Esther P.......... 58
'50   Helen A.......... 49
'52   Lucy C........... 55
'70   Lydia M..........115
'95   Mabel I...........180
'47   Mary C........... 40
'52   Mary S........... 55
Butters
'75   Mary A...........129
Butterworth
'66 *g* Ann..............102
Button
'58   Eliza............. 77
'44   Mary A........... 30
'58 *g* Mary J........... 75

STUDENTS.

Buttrick
- '42 H. Maria.......... 24

Butts
- '55 Elizabeth K....... 66

Buxton
- '44 Eliza J............ 30
- '58 g Elizabeth M...... 75
- '79 g Elizabeth N......139

Byington
- '78 Caroline M........137
- '51 Lucy R............ 52
- '95 Martha D..........180
- '85 S. Lillian.........154

Byorth
- '82 Emily C...........146

Cadmon
- '80 Libbie M..........142

Cady
- '40 Mary W............ 20

Cahill
- '72 g Anna M...........120

Cahoon
- '79 Caroline E........140
- '69 g Jane.............111

Cain
- '56 A. Elizabeth...... 69

Cairns
- '79 g Mary F...........139
- '77 g Susan H..........134

Calder
- '95 Helen B...........180
- '95 Matilda S..........180

Caldwell
- '74 Alice.............126
- '57 Elizabeth.......... 73
- '38 Mary A............ 16

Callahan
- '67 Amelia............106

Calvert
- '49 g Emma H........... 45

Cambell
- '38 Eliza............. 16

Camp
- '51 g Nancy E.......... 51

Campbell
- '90 Emily B...........168
- '95 Francena L........180
- '95 Harriet...........180
- '61 Joanna M.......... 87
- '74 Lillie............126
- '75 g Mary A...........128
- '95 Mary F............180
- '68 Mary J............109
- '83 g Nellie E.........148
- '60 Sarah E........... 83
- '69 g Theresa M........111

Candler
- '91 g Eleanor S........169

Canfield
- '68 Ida G.............109

Cantrell
- '57 g Anna C........... 71

Capen
- '41 Miranda W......... 22

Capron
- '49 Caroline L........ 46
- '91sp Jessie C.........171
- '58 g Laura A. W...... 75

Carey
- '55 Sarah J........... 66

Cargill
- '53 Clarissa.......... 59

Carleton
- '64 g Sarah L.......... 95

Carner
- '62 g Lydia M.......... 89

Carpenter
- '59 g Anna E........... 79
- '61 Clara............. 87
- '65 g Ellen E.......... 90
- '52 Fidelia T........ 55
- '84 g Frances A........151
- '67 Frances A........ 107
- '55 g Helen E.......... 64
- '95 Jane B............180
- '58 g Jane E........... 75
- '73 Kate I...........124
- '75 Lilla A..........129
- '49 Mary F........... 46
- '70 g Mary L..........114
- '48 Sylvira A........ 43

Carr
- '95 Bertha G..........180
- '70 Florence A....... 115

Carrier
- '72 Emma.............121
- '92 g Florence L.......171
- '47 g Lucy A........... 38

Carrington
- '68 g E. Justine.......108
- '68 g H. Josephine.....108

Carruth
- '64 Ellen M.......... 96
- '63 g Kathleen M....... 92

Carson
- '85 g Julia A. M.......153

Carter
- '87 g Alice.........8, 158
- '51 Anna A........... 52
- '90 Annie............168
- '90 g Emily A..........166
- '95 Emma D...........180
- '90 Julia........167, 168
- '55 Julia M.......... 66
- '71 Mary S...........118
- '62 Susan 90

Carver
- '45 Lydia A.......... 33

Cary
- '38 Amelia........... 16
- '55 Lucretia......... 66
- '51 g Mary A.......... 51

Case
- '65 Abbie J..........100
- '70 Elizabeth J......115
- '74 Emma L,..........126
- '61 Emorette......... 87
- '42 Julia M.......... 24
- '67 Lucy I..........107
- '61 Malvina R........ 87

Caskey
- '92 Mary A...........172
- '95 g M. Olivia........178

Casper
- '75 Irena............129

Caswell
- '64 Harriet P........ 96
- '65 Helena A.........100

Catlin
- '53 Ada I............ 59
- '48 Cornelia I....... 43
- '46 Frances C........ 37
- '43 Laura S.......... 27

Cavan
- '78 Ellen............137

Chaffee
- '49 Elizabeth........ 46
- '76 Mary S...........132
- '47 Sarah............ 40

Challen
- '81 Winona...........144

Chamberlain
- '70 Alla S...........115
- '86 Carrie B.........157
- '90 E. Louise........168
- '39 Emma............. 18
- '86 Grace M..........157
- '58 g Helen M.......... 75
- '52 g Jane E........... 54
- '68 Katharine S......109
- '76 g Laura M..........130
- '52 Maria J.......... 56
- '53 g Martha A. J..... 58
- '50 g Mary E.......... 48
- '75 Mary E..........129
- '64 g M. Louise........ 95
- '51 Sarah A.......... 52

Chambers
- '50 Laura A.......... 49
- '95 sp Martha.........184

Chandler
- '39 Abby A........... 18
- '59 Anna L........... 80
- '39 Clarissa C....... 18
- '62 g Emma R.......... 89
- '66 Josephine E......103
- '84 g Lucia A..........151
- '39 Mary A........... 18
- '57 Mary E........... 73
- '88 g Sadie K..........161

INDEX.

Chapell
'83 Evalena............175
'88 g Harriet............161

Chapin
'82 Charlotte I........146
'52 Clarissa M.........56
'76 g Delia L............131
'43 Elizabeth..........27
'57 g Elizabeth L.......72
'52 Eunice M..........56
'83 Florence E.......175
'59 Harriet L.........80
'44 Jane..............30
'43 Jane E............27
'45 Julia A...........33
'47 Julia A...........40
'48 M. Augusta........43
'41 g Malvina J.........22
'42 g Martha R........8, 23
'43 Mary..............27
'44 g Mary B............29
'70 Mary E............115
'43 g Mary W.......6, 8, 26
'54 g R. Emily..........61
'54 g S. Elizabeth....8, 61

Chaplin
'71 Mary A............118

Chapman
'70 Alice B...........115
'45 Ann E.............33
'73 Aurelia A.........124
'82 Elva M............146
'68 Emeline E.........109
'84 Ethel.............152
'73 g Eva L.............122
'88 Harriet C.........162
'44 Julia A............30
'84 Mary E............152
'78 Minerva J.........137
'66 S. Frances........103

Chappell
'63 g Mary E............92

Charevoy
'39 Elizabeth..........18

Charles
'61 Lavan A............87

Charlton
'46 g Jane E.............36

Chase
'57 g Ada H..............72
'81 Alice M...........144
'51 Annie S............52
'55 g Augusta S.........64
'51 Charlotte..........52
'67 Eleanor F.........107
'55 g Emily..............64
'62 Eveline P..........90
'57 Harriet N..........73
'79 Lillian E.........140
'45 Lydia P............33
'61 Marion S...........87
'45 Martha A...........33
'58 Mary A.............16
'54 Mary C.............62
'78 Mary D............137

'53 Mary I.............59
'57 g Rebecca M.........72

Chasmar
'81 Coralie E.........144

Chatterton
'88 Almyra S..........162
'94 Gertrude M........177
'90 Minnie............168

Cheesman
'53 g Elizabeth..........58
'53 Jane P.............59

Cheever
'89 g Bertha A..........164

Chellis
'81 Lora E............144
'85 g Marcia B..........153
'83 May Belle.........149

Chenery
'41 g Zillah D...........22

Cheney
'95 Alice M...........180
'58 Celestia...........77
'74 Ellen E...........126

Cheseldine
'59 Laura E............80

Chesley
'47 Justina............40

Chick
'48 Harriet N..........43

Chidsey
'60 Helen L............83

Child
'52 Anna M.............56
'44 Frances S..........30
'47 Myra B.............40
'69 Sarah A...........112

Childs
'77 g Annie E...........134
'71 Emma P............118
'90 g Frances M........166
'61 Julia E............87
'68 Mary A............110
'60 Mary E.............83
'56 g M. Elizabeth....8, 68

Chilson
'57 Caroline...........73

Chisholm
'68 Margaret E........110

Chittenden
'74 Sara W............126

Choate
'64 g Alice D............95
'64 Elsie A.............96

Chollar
'90 Marion D..........168
'03 Sophia M...........93

Church
'47 g Ann E..............38

'58 Anna I.............77
'64 g Annie V............95
'61 Caroline...........87
'80 Edith A...........142
'85 Edith T...........154
'53 g Fanny..............58
'88 Isadore I.........162
'66 g Julia M...........102
'59 Laura L............80
'85 Lena R............154
'64 g Mary E.............95
'87 g M. Evelyn........158

Claggett
'64 Rebecca B..........97

Clancy
'49 Mary L.............46

Clapp
'90 g Carrie T..........167
'71 g Cornelia M.....8, 117
'75 Ellen L...........129
'81 g Emily M..........143
'86 Emma L............157
'73 Harriet...........124
'82 g Harriet E........146
'42 Harriette..........24
'78 Hattie M..........137
'61 Jane B.............87
'76 Laura H...........132
'88 g Lena L............161
'79 Mary E............140
'55 Sarah E............66
'38 Sophia A...........16
'55 g Virginia...........64

Clapsadel
'92 Katherine E.......172

Clark
'52 Abigail M..........56
'69 Alice E...........112
'87 Alice H...........159
'53 Ann E..............59
'76 Anna B............132
'64 Aurora B...........97
'83 Blanche M.........149
'82 g Carrie A.........146
'58 g Catharine B.......75
'49 Catharine L........46
'40 Charlotte M........20
'75 Clara B...........129
'80 g Clara P..........141
'68 g Cornelia D.......108
'88 Edith.............162
'88 Eliza S.......13, 162
'95 Elizabeth.........180
'88 Elizabeth C.......162
'43 Elizabeth E........27
'57 Elizabeth M........73
'44 g Elizabeth P.......29
'79 Elizabeth R.......140
'84 g Ellen K...........151
'65 g Emily A............99
'75 Emily W...........129
'95 Florence R........180
'95 sp Grace L.........184
'60 Harriet D..........83
'72 Harriet R.........121
'60 g Harriet S..........82
'90 Jennie G..........168

STUDENTS. 235

'74 Lilian E.......... 126
'39 Lovisa........... 18
'79 Louisa M 140
'61 g Lucia F......... 85
'46 Lucy A.......... 37
'67 Lucy A..........107
'75 g Lucy C..........128
'59 g Lucy W.......... 79
'59 g Lurissa A......... 79
'90 g Marion W........167
'78 Martha A. W......137
'86 g Martha J.......8, 156
'39 Mary............ 18
'45 Mary............ 33
'81 g Mary A..........143
'76 Mary C..........132
'65 g Mary F.......... 99
'60 g Mary J.......... 82
'77 Mary L..........135
'95 g Mary L......... 178
'83 Mary R..........149
'44 Mary S.......... 30
'79 g Sarah A..........139
'49 Sarah B.......... 46
'79 S. Lizzie..........110
'63 Susan E.......... 93

Clarke
'64 g Anna F.......... 95
'41 Anne M.......... 22
'59 g Caroline W......8,79
'63 Elizabeth......... 93
'54 g Elizabeth A........ 61
'68 Elizabeth M........110
'53 Ellen M......... 59
'41 Helen M......... 22
'44 g Josephine......... 29
'59 g L. Jane.......... 79
'40 g Lucy H.......... 20
'66 Mary A..........103
'68 Mary L..........110
'61 g Mary L.......... 85
'77 M. Elizabeth......135
'53 Mary P.......... 59
'45 g Sarah D......... 32
'38 Sarah E......... 16
'45 Sarah E......... 33
'66 Sarah E..........103
'64 g Sarah G......... 95
'55 Sarah J......... 66
'41 Sophia.......... 22
'64 g Ursula C......... 95
'45 Wealthy......... 33

Clarkson
'72 Virginia A........121

Clary
'95 Lusanna M........180
'62 Martha H......... 90
'63 g Susan M.......8, 92

Clauson
'95sp Jessie L.........184

Cleaveland
'67 Abbie D..........107

Clemence
'47 Ruth D.......... 40

Clemens
'38 Emily C.......... 16

Clement
'73 Mary E..........124

Clements
'62 Alice W.......... 90

Cleveland
'76 Dora P..........132
'63 Julia A.......... 93
'93 g Mary..........174
'60 Mary E.......... 83
'64 g Mary F.......... 95
'92sp Rose C..........173

Clifford
'43 Amanda E........ 27
'68 Ella P..........110

Cline
'55 Annie M......... 66

Clinton
'70 Imogene L........115

Clizbe
'42 Cecelia.......... 24

Close
'68 g Frances H........108

Clough
'64 g Mary E.......... 95
'76 Mary E..........132

Coan
'51 g Julia M......... 51
'42 Martha D......... 24

Coates
'57 Annie E......... 73

Cobb
'87 g Helen L.........158
'55 Lucia D......... 66

Cobbe
'69 g Jennie R.........111

Cobine
'44 g Rosanna H........ 29

Cobleigh
'94 Grace N..........177
'92 g Katrina A........171
'67 Lizzie..........107
'85 Nellie F.........154

Coburn
'64 g Sarah E......... 95

Cochran
'58 g Charlotte A........ 75

Cochrane
'68 g Elizabeth........108
'85 g Josephine G........153

Codding
'69 Thirza M.........112

Coe
'51 Adelaide E........ 52
'53 g Emily M........ 58
'91 g Gertrude W......160
'71 Mary Frances.....118
'90 Virginia M.......168

'71 Mary Frances......118

Coffin
'75 Chloe M..........129
'53 Lucy B.......... 59
'71 Mary C..........118
'68 g Sarah W..........108

Coggeshall
'38 Joanna M......... 16

Coggin
'58 Helen A......... 77

Cogswell
'59 Caroline S......... 80
'53 Emma M......... 59
'53 g Frances S......... 58
'66 Marietta M........103
'46 Martha P......... 37
'75 Mary E..........129

Cohn
'84 g Leah..........151, 152

Coit
'42 Sarah E......... 24

Colburn
'60 Ellen A......... 83

Colby
'75 Florence M........129
'73 Sarah M..........124

Cole
'48 g Amanda M........ 11
'88 g Anna M.........161
'94sp Clara S.........178
'80 E Viola.........142
'72 g Ella R..........120
'63 g Ellen S......... 92
'70 g Elvira..........114
'76 Lottie R.........132
'62 Mary F.......... 90
'79 Hattie E.........140

Colegrove
'95sp Lottie M.........184
'51 Sarah M......... 52

Coleman
'85 Anna M.........154
'83 Charlotte.........149
'91 Clatina..........170
'87 g Katharine D........158
'80 g Lucia A.........141
'57 Mary L......... 73
'86 Sarah W.........157

Coley
'85 g Carrie E.........153

Colley
'66 Annie M......... 103

Collier
'66 Sallie..........103

Collings
'92 Laura W.........172

Collins
'57 g Cornelia......... 72
'42 Cornelia W........ 24
'69 g Helen F.........111

INDEX.

'58 Mary J............ 77
'50 g M. Theresa........ 48
Colman
'42 Abbie P........... 24
'40 Emily P........... 20
Colt
'39 Sarah J............ 18
Colton
'53 g Clara R........... 58
'59 Elizabeth........ 80
'93 Elizabeth......... 175
'42 Marcia............. 24
'51 Nancy E.......... 52
'54 Susan............. 62
Colvocoresses
'70 Eva F............. 115
Comey
'54 Amanda A........ 62
'86 Annie F.......... 157
Comstock
'57 Bessie H.......... 73
'83 Carrie........... 140
'93 Elizabeth........ 175
'49 Frances J........ 46
'93 Jennie........... 175
'44 Mary J........... 30
'48 Mary L........... 43
'42 Sarah............. 24
Condit
'40 g Hannah M........ 36
'64 Sarah F........... 97
Cone
'70 Catie A......... 115
'70 g Mary C......... 114
'63 Sarah E.......... 93
Coney
'91 Harriette M...... 170
Conklin
'74 Amanda.......... 126
'61 g Elizabeth G..... 85
'77 Mary H......... 135
'79 g Stella.......... 139
Connell
'49 Mary............ 46
Conner
'68 g Olivia.......... 108
Connor
'67 S. Alice......... 107
Connolly
'63 Ada.............. 93
'62 Clara............ 90
Converse
'95 Anna B......... 180
'73 Charlotte B..... 124
'65 Elizabeth S..... 100
'76 Orissa W....... 132
'68 Rose S.......... 110
'61 Sarah A......... 87
'49 Sarah E......... 46
'58 Sarah E......... 77

Cook
'48 Caroline A....... 43
'66 g Elizabeth...... 102
'46 Elizabeth........ 37
'66 Frances A....... 103
'63 Frances L....... 93
'89 g Grace H....... 164
'45 g Harriet E...... 32
'89 Harriet S....... 165
'44 g Jane A........ 29
'92 Julia E......... 172
'42 Louisa F........ 24
'91 Mary A......... 170
'92 Margaret H..... 172
'75 Mary E......... 129
'62 Sarah C......... 90
Cooke
'43 Adah J......... 27
'87 Althea M....... 160
'84 Caroline G..... 152
'83 Frances A..... 149
'49 Harriet P...... 46
'83 Lillian R...... 149
'77 g Lydia M..... 134
'83 Minnie L...... 149
'69 M. Sophie..... 112
'54 Nancy F....... 62
'79 Rowena P.... 139, 140
'44 Sarah E........ 30
Cooley
'43 Amelia S....... 27
'55 Frances M..... 66
'53 g Harriet M..... 8, 58
'61 Harriet N...... 87
'44 g Julietta....... 29
'57 Lucy S......... 73
'86 Nellie D....... 157
'61 g Sarah J....... 85
'65 g S. Isabelle... 99
Coolidge
'56 Jane H......... 69
'95 Nettie E....... 180
'81 Sarah B....... 144
Coombs
'57 L. Jeannette.... 73
Cooper
'76 Annie F....... 132
'72 Ella M......... 121
'93 g Gertrude M... 174
'46 Harriet A...... 37
'53 Harriet S...... 59
'66 g Lydia A..... 102
'84 g Mary D..... 151
Cope
'77 g Lucy........ 134
Copeland
'95 Sara F........ 180
Corbin
'60 Elvira......... 83
'49 Laura M...... 46
'43 Sylvia........ 27
Cordley
'82 Annie M...... 146
Corey
'59 g Elizabeth S.. 79

'71 Susan E........ 118
Corle
'71 Frances E...... 118
Cornelison
'77 Elizabeth F..... 135
Corwin
'82 Euphemia K.... 147
'82 Ida E.......... 147
Coryell
'86 g Mary......... 156
Cotes
'63 Eliza B......... 93
Cotton
'95 Ethel H........ 180
'70 Mary G....... 115
Couch
'65 Sarah E........ 100
Coulter
'85 Anna L....... 154
'95 Bertha........ 180
Courtright
'58 g Ruth A...... 75
Covert
'53 Jane A......... 59
Cowdery
'45 Abby A........ 33
Cowles
'45 Abigail F...... 33
'84 Anna L....... 152
'84 Carrie L...... 152
'63 g Eliza E...... 92
'68 Elizabeth A... 110
'71 g Emma L..... 117
'63 g Harriet H... 92
'63 Jane E........ 93
'66 g Louise F.... 7, 8, 102
'82 Mary S....... 147
'68 Phebe A...... 110
'59 g R. Loretta... 79
Cowls
'85 Nellie G...... 154
'79 g S. Jeannette.. 139
Cox
'63 Jemima L..... 93
'63 Margaret C... 93
Coy
'56 Helen E....... 69
'69 g Sarah L..... 111
Coyle
'77 Margaret M... 135
Crafts
'95 Sue G......... 180
Craig
'92 sp Alice L..... 173
'65 Harriet M..... 100
Crandall
'73 Alice T....... 124
'72 Ella L........ 121

STUDENTS. 237

Crane
'58 Cornelia A........ 77
'54 *g* Eliza R........... 61
'87 *g* Ellen D. M......159
'74 *g* Flora M..........125
'47   Harriet........... 40
'87 *g* Mary P...........159
'43   Sarah M.......... 27

Crawford
'88   Clara E...........162
'53   Eleanor F........ 59
'59   Frances H........ 80
'50   Mary A........... 49
'49   Mary C........... 46
'55   Susan A.......... 66

Crie
'54   Jean L............ 62

Crissey
'60 *g* Olive F........... 82

Cristy
'70 *g* Anne.............114
'60 *g* Elizabeth H...... 82
'77 *g* Martha W........134

Critchlow
'55   Maria............ 66

Crocker
'51   Abby H........... 52
'64   Carrie A.......... 97
'73 *g* Sallie S...........122

Croft
'83 *g* Margaret.........148
'55 *g* Margaret......... 64

Crofut
'45   Florilla H........ 33
'51 *g* Mary J........... 51

Crookham
'83 *g* Elizabeth E......148
'91 *g* Sara..............169

Crosby
'69   Angeline M......112
'64 *g* Annabell F....... 95
'39   Elizabeth........ 18
'67   Elizabeth M.....107
'95   Georgina.........180
'58   Helen E.......... 77
'62 *g* Marietta.......... 89
'59 *g* Martha J......... 79
'49   Mary E........... 46
'42   Phebe H......... 24
'80 *g* Samuella.........141

Cross
'68   Annie G..........110
'51   Catharine C.... 52
'54 *g* Emeline F......... 61
'77   Esther H.........135
'72   Ulee P............121

Crossett
'53   Dora F............ 59
'67   Rosetta E........107

Crossman
'47   Julia A........... 40

Croswell
'61   Elizabeth B...... 87

Crouch
'66   Julia.............103

Crowell
'91   Annie L..........170
'41   Mary L........... 22
'89 *g* Mary W..........164

Crowther
'87 *g* Elizabeth........159

Crump
'71   Eliza R..........118

Cudworth
'61   Armenia.......... 87

Cumiskey
'84   Mary E..........152

Cummings
'83 *g* Anna M...142, 148, 149
'72   Layette E........121
'68   Marietta.........110
'48   Martha........... 43
'76 *g* Mary E...........131
'86 *g* Sarah R..........156

Cummins
'51   Julia B........... 52

Cunningham
'55   Catharine M.... 66
'55 *g* Jane N........... 64
'67   Lucy O..........107
'80   Mary............142

Currier
'44   Julia M........... 30

Curtis
'68 *g* Anna F...........108
'58   Caroline A...... 77
'57   Celia J........... 73
'64 *g* Cluara A......... 95
'52   Deborah H...... 56
'66 *g* Emily A.........102
'44 *g* Lucy M......8, 13, 29
'51 *g* Martha A........ 51
'46 *g* Mary M.......... 36
'45   Sarah E.......... 33

Curtiss
'95   Adele L..........180

Cushing
'49   Lucy E........... 46
'53   Mary A.......... 59
'48 *g* Sarah W......... 41
'49   Verona K........ 46

Cushman
'44   Eliza F........... 30
'64 *g* Harriet E........ 95
'48 *g* Harriet W........ 41
'44   Mary A.......... 30
'53   Mary A.......... 59
'66   Mary C..........103
'53   Mary M.......... 59

Cutler
'51 *g* Almira............ 51

'52   Charlotte M..... 56
'76   Helen E..........132
'86 *g* Louisa S.........156
'57   Lucia............. 73
'75 *g* Mary S........8, 128
'63 *g* Olive W.......... 92

Cutter
'61   Caroline E....... 87
'68   Isabel P..........110

Cutting
'81   Martha P........144

Cutts
'59 *g* Elizabeth P....... 79
'57   Emily C.......... 73

Dages
'82   Amelia C........147

Dailey
'84   Minnie M.......152

Dakin
'48   Harriet........... 43

Dame
'66 *g* Anna A..........102
'69 *g* Celia A..........111
'70 *g* Mary L. S......114

Damon
'49   Sarah J.......... 46

Dana
'59 *g* Clara B.......... 79
'44   Isabella G........ 30
'65   Mary A.........100
'45   Mary J........... 33
'82   Minnie L........147
'40   Persis C.......... 20
'44 *g* Rebecca H...... 29

Danforth
'42   Clarissa M...... 24
'56   Etta C............ 69
'61   Mary W.......... 87
'83   Mattie S.........149
'65   Rachel H........100

Daniel
'54   Catherine W.... 62

Daniels
'92   Caroline E......172
'57   Florence E...... 73
'42   Frances.......... 24
'67 *g* Mary E..........105
'52 *g* Mary T.......... 54

Danielson
'91   Caroline F.......170
'44   Charlotte T..... 30

Dann
'74   Mary Emma....126

Darling
'65   Margaret A.....100
'53 *g* Mary E.......... 58

Darrow
'77   Julia M..........135

INDEX.

Dart
 '73 *g* Jessie G............122
Davenport
 '53 Elizabeth A....... 59
Davidson
 '50 Catherine M....... 49
 '95 Eva F............180
 '78 Jane M............137
 '84 Isabella J........152
Davis
 '56 Abbie P........... 69
 '75 Ada C............129
 '76 *g* Alice M..........131
 '66 Amelia M.........103
 '67 Anna E...........107
 '73 Anna F...........124
 '74 *g* Anna Y...........125
 '95 Annie L..........180
 '52 Aurelia........... 56
 '50 Elizabeth......... 49
 '57 *g* Elizabeth A....... 72
 '66 *g* Elizabeth D.......102
 '90 Elizabeth W......168
 '89 Ella M...........165
 '95 *g* Evelyn H..........179
 '61 F. Louisa......... 87
 '86 *g* Florence J.........156
 '55 Henrietta......... 66
 '95 *sp* Isabella H........184
 '51 Julia A........... 52
 '67 M. Belle.........107
 '70 Maria L..........115
 '92 *g* Mary B...........171
 '74 Mary C...........126
 '59 Mary E............ 80
 '50 Mary F............ 49
 '08 Mary G...........108
 '85 Mary L...........154
 '58 Morgianna E...... 77
 '95 Myrtie I.........180
 '92 Neva O...........172
 '56 *g* N. Jane........... 68
 '04 Olive G........... 97
 '82 *g* Sallie M..........146
Davison
 '70 Annie B..........115
 '44 Elizabeth......... 30
Dawes
 '47 Clara............. 40
Day
 '95 Alice R..........180
 '38 Eliza M........... 16
 '60 Ellen H........... 83
 '47 Eunice B.......... 40
 '50 Harriet N......... 49
 '51 Helen R........... 52
 '04 Henrietta N...... 97
 '55 Lucy A............ 66
 '66 *g* Lydia D..........102
 '77 M. Stella........135
 '61 *g* Mary E............ 85
 '50 R. Alice.......... 49
Dayton
 '89 Clara E..........165
 '89 Gertrude H.......165

Deacon
 '95 Mamie E..........180
Dean
 '68 Anna L........... 110
 '92 Elizabeth........172
 '70 Emily K..........115
 '71 *g* Frances A........117
 '92 Margaret W.......172
Deane
 '59 Mary A........... 81
Deans
 '88 Harriet E........102
 '94 *g* Gertrude A........176
Dearborn
 '65 *g* Annie............8, 99
 '69 Elizabeth........112
Deering
 '74 Ella F...........126
 '55 *g* Mary............. 64
 '76 Myra F...........132
Delano
 '76 Alice L..........132
 '74 Maria W..........126
Demarest
 '77 S. Emma..........135
Deming
 '63 Louise M.......... 93
Demree
 '72 Almira V.........124
Denio
 '66 *g* Elizabeth H.......102
Denise
 '64 L. Anna........... 97
Denison
 '43 Augusta M........ 27
 '51 Caroline N....... 52
 '62 Clara............ 90
 '60 Jane A........... 83
 '61 Lucy............. 87
Dennison
 '56 *g* Emily C........... 68
Denniston
 '49 Annie............ 46
 '61 *g* Sarah E........... 85
Denny
 '47 Charlotte E...... 40
Derby
 '70 Ida E............115
 '84 *g* Mary E.......149, 151
Derrickson
 '82 *g* Elizabeth M.......146
Derrin
 '78 Lizzie C.........137
Deuel
 '94 *sp* Josephine........178
 '44 Mary M........... 30

Devereux
 '81 *g* Harriet L..........143
Dewar
 '78 *g* Isabelle H.........137
Dewell
 '48 Elizabeth M...... 43
Dewey
 '46 *g* Elizabeth......... 36
 '48 Eliza M.......... 43
 '50 M. Adeline....... 49
 '58 *g* Nancy M.......... 75
 '50 S. Jane.......... 49
Dewing
 '69 Caroline E.......112
 '44 Nancy A.......... 30
DeWitt
 '59 Harriet S........ 81
 '87 *g* Katharine.........159
DeWolf
 '56 Elizabeth P...... 69
 '61 *g* Sarah A........... 85
Dews
 '78 Nellie L.........137
Dexter
 '49 Eliza B.......... 46
 '83 Frances S........149
Deyo
 '94 Ella M...........177
Diament
 '54 Elizabeth........ 62
 '54 Mary L........... 62
 '54 Naomi............ 62
Dibble
 '72 *g* Ellen S..........120
 '51 Maria C.......... 52
Dibblee
 '85 *g* Mary D...........153
Dickerman
 '69 Alice A..........112
 '75 *g* Amelia S.........128
 '71 Emma E...........118
Dickerson
 '89 Frances M........165
Dickey
 '69 *g* Sarah A..........111
Dickinson
 '71 Amelia C.........000
 '44 *g* Amelia F......12, 29
 '42 Caroline......... 24
 '66 *g* Caroline E.......102
 '79 Clara A..........140
 '67 Clara E..........107
 '55 *g* Clara L........... 64
 '38 Cordelia......... 16
 '57 *g* Elizabeth M...... 72
 '95 Ella S...........180
 '45 Emeline H........ 33
 '48 Emily E.......... 43
 '67 *g* Emma E...........105
 '77 Emma L...........135

STUDENTS.

'78 Grace K..........137
'57 Helen E..........73
'62 Helen M..........90
'83 g H. Fanny.......148
'81 g Julia C........143
'63 g Julia E........92
'93 g Laura A........174
'94 g Laura A........176
'68 g L. Jane........108
'83 g Louise.........174
'57 g Louisa.........72
'44 g Louisa S.......29
'62 g M. Adelia......89
'50 Mary A..........49
'55 g Mary B.........64
'64 Mary M..........97
'83 Maud M..........149
'50 g Nancy H........48
'80 O. Adelia......142
'59 Sarah A.........81
'50 Sarah J.........49
'51 Sarah T.........52
'43 Sophia C........27
'42 Sophronia M.....24

Dickson
'56 Elizabeth W.....69
'56 Mary A. J......69
'70 Rebecca C......115

Dike
'39 Loraine H.......18

Dill
'92 Lenora A.......172
'57 Ruth C..........73

Dillenbeck
'91 g Eva............169

Dillingham
'53 Elizabeth N.....59

Dillon
'73 g Mary C........123

Dimmick
'72 Emma A.........121

Dimmock
'59 Caroline E......81

Dimond
'51 Eliza...........53
'39 Laurinda M......18

Dinsmore
'39 Elizabeth.......18

Disbrow
'77 Ella P.........135

Ditto
'61 g Margaret E.....85

Dixon
'45 Eliza F.........33
'85 Roxanna........154
'42 Susan W.........25

Doane
'41 Abby............22
'53 Abby M..........59
'49 Cornelia M......46
'41 Keziah S........22

Dobyns
'63 Julia L.........93

Dodd
'71 g Hettie M......117
'54 Maria C.........62
'73 Mary W.........124

Dodge
'89 Addie L........165
'65 g Clara A........99
'55 Helen A.........66
'82 Jennie H......147
'49 g Martha A.......45
'73 Mary E........124

Doland
'60 Emma............83

Dole
'74 g Amelia S......125
'55 Elizabeth A.....66
'41 g Martha C.....8, 22
'86 g Mary P........136
'89 g Mary P........164

Dolley
'95 Grace L........181

Dollinger
'93 g Anna W........174

Dolson
'60 Harriet I......83

Donaldson
'95 Jessie B......181

Doolittle
'55 Catharine E.....66
'82 g Jane E........146

Dorr
'58 g Sarah E........75

Dort
'79 Mary E........140

Doty
'90 Agnes J.......168
'76 g E. Marcia.....131
'72 g Mary A........120

Dougall
'70 Susan G........115

Dougherty
'46 Emma............37

Doughty
'64 Mary O..........97

Douglas
'67 g Emma..........105

Douglass
'83 Abbie M........149
'40 Elizabeth L.....20
'61 Sarah E.........87

Dow
'72 Isophene K....121
'72 M. Ella.......121

Dowd
'62 Delia E.........90
'86 Ella M........157
'65 Sarah E.......100

Dowe
'89 g Harriet H....164

Dowling
'53 Cornelia M......59
'64 Lilia R.........97

Downer
'81 g Mary E.......143

Downs
'66 g P. Jane......102

Dowse
'46 Deborah.........37
'43 Mary B..........27

Drake
'61 Cornelia A......87

Draper
'58 Abbie B........77

Dresser
'95 g Annie S......179
'86 g Eunice K..156, 157

Driver
'47 Helen E.........40
'67 Louise E......107
'65 g Mary E.......100
'67 g Susan S.....8, 105

DuBois
'95 Clara A........181

Dubuar
'65 Frances M......100
'65 Mary C........100

Dudley
'55 Ellen M.........66
'90 Gertrude G....168
'69 Katharine M...112
'78 Lillie........137
'75 Lizzie........129
'78 g Mary C.......136

Duff
'84 Susie T.......152

Duley
'85 Lizzie J......154

Dunbar
'50 Martha F........49

Duncan
'93 Elsie..........175
'76 Elizabeth C...132
'71 Harriet A. N..118
'84 g Leslie G.....151
'82 Margaretta....147

Dunham
'77 g Isabella B....134
'68 Jennie A......110
'68 Mary A........110
'76 S. Rosa.......132

INDEX.

Dunklee
'45 Ruth C............ 33

Dunlap
'87 Mary E............160
'41 Mary J............ 22

Dunnell
'59 Celia E............ 81

Dunning
'78 Annie K............137
'60 Antoinette......... 83
'77 g Clara C............134
'61 g Katherine A...... 85
'69 Mary O............112

Dunton
'72 Lillian W............121

Dupée
'86 June M............157

Durant
'71 g Elizabeth A........117

Durell
'59 Elizabeth J........ 81

Durgin
'94 g Cora A............176
'92 Martha L..........172

Durham
'68 g Elizabeth..........108
'68 g Sophia............108

Durkes
'82 g Ida E..............146

Dustan
'91 g Gertrude L........169

Dutcher
'45 Henrietta F........ 33
'56 Mary E............ 70

Dutton
'88 Charlotte R........162
'46 g Eliza P............ 36
'73 Ellen H............124
'91 g Emily H.... 169
'46 g Lucia E.......... 36
'47 g Lucy E.......... 38
'70 g Mary C............114
'56 Mary T............ 70
'62 g Sarah E.......... 89
'87 g Susie A............159

Dwight
'78 g Ada C............136
'64 Amelia L.......... 97
'47 g Anne E.......... 38
'39 Clara............ 18
'64 Clara L.......... 97
'60 Eliza R............ 83
'43 Ellen F............ 27
'46 Nancy M.......... 37
'61 Sophie E.......... 87

Dwinell
'72 g Alice H............120

Dyer
'91 g Alice G............169
'75 g Caroline F.........128
'63 Josephine L......... 93
'61 g Mary E............ 85
'66 g Sarah E..........102

Eager
'55 g Mary J............ 64
'58 M. Thane.......... 77

Eagley
'58 g Linda M.......... 75

Eaman
'61 g Mary A............ 85

Eames
'63 Emily W 93
'52 Harriet C.......... 56
'60 Julia C............ 83
'56 Martha M.......... 70
'56 Nancy............ 70

Earl
'84 Anna M............152

Earle
'60 g Elizabeth..........8, 82
'59 g Frances A........ 79

Eastman
'58 Abby M............ 77
'60 g Anna F.......... 82
'48 Caroline T........ 43
'39 g Clarissa 18
'44 Hannah 30
'55 Hannah D.......... 66
'59 g Julia.............. 79
'77 L. Carolyn........135
'94 Margaret..........177
'64 g Maria C.......... 95
'53 g Martha.......... 58
'50 Mary W.......... 49
'46 g Sarah M.......... 36
'61 g Sarah P.......... 86
'50 g Sarah S............ 48

Easton
'56 Mary Andelucia... 70
'64 Sarah E............ 97

Eaton
'53 Anna M............ 59
'50 Betsey S.......... 49
'56 g Caroline.......... 68
'78 Delia M............137
'45 Elizabeth.......... 33
'78 g Elizabeth W......136
'74 Ella M............126
'89 g Etta M............104
'87 g Grace M............159
'64 Lurinda A........ 97
'95 Mabel L............181
'47 Mary A............ 40
'76 g Mary S............131
'40 Sarah E.......... 20
'42 S. Rebecca 25

Ecker
'64 Emma L............ 97

Eddy
'59 g Cornelia.......... 79
'52 Elizabeth.......... 56
'45 Maria R............ 33

Edgerton
'65 J. Elizabeth.......100

Edmands
'75 Anna M.... 129
'48 g Lucy E.......... 41

Edson
'65 g Emily M........14, 99

Edwards
'59 g Anna C........7, 8, 79
'87 g Carrie M..... 159
'42 Elizabeth.......... 25
'68 Ellen M............110
'90 g Emily A..........167
'51 Esther............ 53
'56 Eunice M.......... 70
'45 Julia A............ 33
'87 g Julia M............159
'43 Lydia............ 27
'82 g Mary E..........146
'76 g Mary H..........131
'45 Rachel C.......... 34

Egery
'38 Mary P............ 16

Egleston
'69 Zeruah E..........112

Eglin
'60 S. Cornelia........ 83

Ela
'57 g Emily S............ 72

Eldred
'65 Helen E..........100

Eldredge
'70 Genevieve S.......115

Eldridge
'54 g Lorie A............ 61
'41 Sarah C............ 22

Ellinwood
'70 Eliza M............115

Elliot
'62 Almira F.......... 90
'43 Augusta C........ 27
'81 g Elizabeth M......143
'54 Mary A.......... 62

Elliott
'43 Mary M.......... 27

Ellis
'52 g Abby W.......... 54
'68 g Edith M..........108
'73 g Gertrude M........123
'76 Hattie L..........132
'83 Jennie M..........149
'62 g Lucy J..........8, 89
'67 g M. Abbie........107
'55 g Mary......... 7, 8, 64
'45 g Mary A............ 32

STUDENTS. 241

Ellison
 '95 Gertrude H........181
Ellms
 '53 Clara M........... 59
Ells
 '61 g Fanny........... 86
Ellsworth
 '92 Julia.............172
Elmer
 '48 Sarah E.......... 43
Elmore
 '87 Susan M..........160
Ely
 '65 g Adaline........... 99
 '64 Annie R........... 97
 '61 g Charlotte E........ 86
 '60 E. Carolyn........ 83
 '43 Elizabeth.......... 27
 '78 Elizabeth L........137
 '46 Fanny E........... 57
 '49. Harriet........... 46
 '71 Helen A..........118
 '86 Kittie M..........157
 '74 Margaret D........126
 '61 g Mary A. C......... 86
 '78 Mary B..........137
 '48 Mary P............43
 '38 P. Augusta........ 16
 '61 g Sarah E........... 86
 '73 Sarah M..........124
Emerson
 '91 Adaline...........170
 '54 Elizabeth F....... 62
 '67 Eunice E..........107
 '64 Henrietta C....... 97
 '74 Lizzie E..........126
 '70 g Margaret A........114
 '66 Mary S..........104
 '65 g Olive J..........12, 99
Emery
 '55 g H. Jane.......... 64
 '95 Mary L..........181
 '73 Priscilla..........124
Emmons
 '61 g Frances M......... 86
 '66 g Helen I..........102
 '63 Julia C........... 93
 '60 Mary C.......... 84
 '53 g Sarah A..........8, 58
Emory
 '86 Helen C..........157
Engelman
 '86 g Emma A..........156
England
 '74 Abbie H..........126
English
 '83 g Agnes J..........148
Eno
 '73 g Fannie A..........123
 '68 g H. Annette........108
 '71 Sarah C..........118

Ensign
 '56 Julia K............ 70
Epler
 '84 g Blanch N.........151
Erdman
 '56 Amelia D......... 70
Erickson
 '75 Carrie I..........129
Ermentrout
 '56 g Margaretta C...... 68
Essex
 '64 Grace............ 97
Estabrook
 '49 g Caroline J......... 45
 '47 Ellen A........... 40
 '95 Lula B..........181
 '71 g S. Adelle.........117
 '90 Susan I..........168
Esten
 '54 Sarah E.......... 62
Esty
 '59 g Julia............. 79
Eustis
 '49 Julia W.......... 46
Evans
 '78 g Elizabeth.........136
 '72 Elma.............121
 '91 Mary............170
 '60 g Mary A..........8, 82
Eveleth
 57 g Helen........... 72
Everett
 '69 g Eleanor M.........111
 '55 Eliza R........... 66
 '81 Ella A...........145
 '93 g Ida J............174
 '52 g Jane L........... 54
 '72 Jane M..........121
 '56 g Mary E.......... 68
 '53 Mary H.......... 59
 '38 Nancy S.......... 16
 '45 g Sarah E.......... 32
Everitt
 '85 N. Augusta........154
Everson
 '80 Lila D............142
Ewart
 '60 Harriet L......... 84
 '60 g Mary D........... 82
Faddis
 '86 Prudence P........157
Fairbank
 '79 g Anna............139
 '93 g Elizabeth.........174
 '85 Grace............154
 '77 Katie........... 135

Fairbanks
 '51 Emily............ 53
 '51 g Sarah............ 51
Fairchild
 '73 Eliza B..........124
Fairley
 '89 Annie L..........165
Fales
 '70 Ella E..........115
 '60 Marcia M......... 84
Fallows
 '94 Sarah H..........177
Fanning
 '82 Agnes M.........147
 '47 g Caroline E........ 38
 '43 Glorianna......... 27
 '91 g Helen J..........169
 '49 Julia............. 46
Farley
 '54 Mary E.......... 62
Farman
 '76 g Mary F..........131
Farmar
 '76 Mary L..........132
Farnham
 '67 Annette E........107
 '68 g Mary F..........108
Farnsworth
 '77 g Carrie P..........124
 '61 Olive E.......... 87
Farr
 '49 Andelusia........ 46
 '63 Caroline.......... 93
Farrar
 '74 Abbie C..........126
 '87 Anna H..........160
 '87 Grace...........160
 '74 Jennie..........126
 '68 Julia C..........110
 '73 g Lillian..........123
 '47 Louisa F......... 40
 '72 Mary B..........121
 '86 R. Dora..........157
 '49 Sarah E.......... 46
Farrington
 '47 Abigail A......... 40
 '60 Emma W......... 84
Farwell
 '60 Annie E.......... 84
 '66 g Catharine S.......102
 '62 g Clara M......... 89
 '51 g Elizabeth M....... 51
 '76 g Julia H..........131
Fassett
 '54 g S. Maria W........ 61
Faul
 '73 Frances I........124

INDEX.

Faunce
 '93 *g* Sara E............174

Faxon
 '73 Jeanette E........124
 '73 Laura W..........124

Fay
 '50 Henrietta M.......84
 '51 Zilpah E........... 53

Feen
 '64 Ellen J............97

Fehrmann
 '83 Cornelia S........149

Felch
 '50 Mercy J.......... 49

Felician
 '82 Anna..............147

Fellows
 '88 *g* Mary E............161
 '65 *g* Susan G........... 99

Felton
 '73 Susan W..........124

Fenn
 '90 *g* Isabelle H........167
 '64 *g* Mabel B........... 95
 '48 *g* Sarah G........... 41

Fenno
 '94 Amanda D........177

Fenton
 '52 Fanny L.......... 56

Ferguson
 '56 *g* Abbie P........... 68
 '44 Christiana......... 30
 '85 Margaret E.......154
 '75 Mary..............129
 '81 Mary..............145

Ferrin
 '92 Bertha L..........172
 '74 *g* Ella L.............125
 '94 *g* Ella L.............176
 '74 *g* Emma I............125

Ferris
 '83 *g* Charlotte E........148

Ferry
 '47 Amanda H........ 40
 '66 Cornelia M........104
 '38 Emeline........... 16
 '64 *g* Joan............... 95
 '85 K. Elizabeth......154
 '67 *g* Lucy E...........105

Fessenden
 '58 Jane R. S.......... 77

Feustel
 '95*sp* Mary E...........184
 '91 *g* Sarah E...........160

Fidler
 '67 Julia C............107

Field
 '55 *g* Anna.............. 64
 '43 Caroline.......... 27
 '59 Caroline F........ 81
 '47 *g* Caroline M........ 38
 '53 Ellen Z........... 59
 '47 *g* Elmira O.......... 38
 '58 Laura E........... 77
 '73 Lucie R...........124
 '43 Lucy A........,... 27
 '75 *g* Mary..............123
 '84 M. Elizabeth......152
 '40 Serena............ 20

Fifield
 '79 Emily W..........140
 '69 Sarah J........... 46

Filley
 '64 Eunice R.......... 97

Finch
 '90 Carolyn L........168
 '45 Tamson J......... 34

Fish
 '38 Elizabeth......... 16
 '63 *g* Ellen P............ 92

Fisher
 '68 *g* Annah F..........109
 '41 Elizabeth D....... 22
 '56 Eliza D........... 70
 '59 *g* Jeannette......... 79
 '56 Joanna............ 70
 '51 *g* Sophronia S....... 51

Fisherdick
 '86 *g* Anna L............156
 '92*sp* Anna L............173

Fisk
 '42 L. Arabella....... 25
 '42 Sarah S........... 25
 '67 Fidelia J..........107

Fiske
 '88 Alice B...........162
 '55 Caroline A........ 66
 '69 Ella A............112
 '42 *g* Fidelia........8, 23
 '68 Hattie A..........110
 '67 *g* Louise M.........105
 '41 Martha E......... 22
 '68 Mary E...........110
 '71 *g* Mary F...........117
 '88 *g* Mary P...........161
 '90 Mary P...........168
 '46 *g* Rebecca W......8, 36

Fitch
 '42 Abigail T......... 25
 '51 Ann E............ 53
 '81 *g* Clara M 143
 '59 Fanny C..........81
 '64 Florence E........ 97
 '64 Frances A......... 95
 '83 *g* Frances L..........148
 '84 Helen N..........152
 '58 *g* Lucy M........... 75
 '95 *sp* Mabel 1...........184
 '54 *g* Mary J............ 61
 '86 *g* Orianna P........156

Field (cont.)
 '49 *g* Rachel A.......... 45
 '47 *g* Susanna........... 38

Fithian
 '55 *g* Cornelia M........ 64
 '52 Harriet N......... 56
 '66 Martha R........104
 '44 Mary H........... 30

Flagg
 '45 Harriet D......... 34
 '45 Sarah E........... 34

Flagler
 '80 *g* Elizabeth R.......141

Fletcher
 '48 Abby R........... 43
 '69 Ada L............112
 '55 Annie B........... 66
 '61 Ellen M........... 87
 '66 Ellen W..........104
 '42 Lucy.............. 25
 '92 *g* Martha I.........171
 '43 Mary A........... 27
 '70 Mary W..........115
 '42 S. Maria.......... 25
 '49 Susan A.......... 46

Flint
 '71 Abby A..........118
 '80 *g* Helen C......8, 141, 144
 '91 *g* Helen C..........169
 '42 Lucy............. 25

Floyd
 '58 Sarah A........... 77

Fobes
 '78 *g* Mary A...........136

Fogg
 '84 Ada M......144, 152

Fogle
 '68 Mary L........... 110

Follett
 '51 Maria B.......... 53

Folwell
 '65 *g* Katherine L....... 99

Foot
 '58 Almira L.......... 77

Foote
 '43 Elizabeth J........ 27
 '48 Harriet H......... 43
 '47 *g* Mary M........8, 39
 '44 *g* Nancy A......8, 29
 '45 *g* Sarah E.......... 32

Forbes
 '38 Eliza S........... 16
 '71 Harriet E........118
 '66 Louise E.........104
 '65 *g* Mary J.......8, 99

Force
 '70 *g* Hannah M........ 48

Ford
 '58 Abbie C........... 77
 '61 Caroline.......... 87

STUDENTS. 243

'64 Charlotte H....... 97
'62 g Charlotte W.....12, 89
'63 g Elizabeth A....... 92
'64 g Emma J.......... 96
'82 Georgiana B..146, 147
'86 Inez H............157
'57 Julia B............ 73
'63 Julia P............ 93
'63 Martha............ 93
'67 Mary E...........107
'78 Sarah............137
'57 g S. Elizabeth....... 72

Forehand
'91 g Annie J...........169

Foreman
'54 Ermina N.......... 62

Foresman
'74 Sarah M..........126

Forman
'46 g Mary E.......... 36

Forsman
'79 Lucinda O........140

Fortesque
'79 Grace............140

Forward
'78 Elizabeth S........137

Foskett
'82 Clara G...........147
'55 Samantha.......... 66

Foster
'94 Annie G...........176
'57 Elizabeth L........ 73
'52 g Eliza J........... 54
'66 Ella L............104
'62 Ellen F............ 90
'64 Ellen F............ 97
'78 Etta M............137
'63 Josephine A........ 93
'70 Kate I............115
'56 Louise A......... 70
'49 g Lucretia........... 45
'70 Maria J...........115
'56 g Mary M......... 68
'55 g Sarah J........... 64
'55 Sarah M.......... 66

Fowler
'51 g A. Eugenia........ 51
'80 Alice J............142
'87 g Caroline D........159
'45 g Cynthia.......... 32
'94 g Elizabeth B.......177
'54 Frances A......... 62
'48 Harriet M........ 43
'54 Mary J........... 62
'51 Sarah F.......... 53
'45 g Susan H.........32

Fox
'30 Angelina H........ 18
'73 Flora W..........124
'42 Prudence V....... 25

Franchois
'94 Henrietta M.......177

Francis
'67 g Anna E..........105
'60 Charlotte A....... 84
'43 Elizabeth S...... 27
'42 Emily C.......... 25
'89 Jennie R.........165
'54 L. Emeline........ 62
'49 Mary A.......... 46
'63 g Nancy D......... 92
'60 g Sarah J........... 82

Franklin
'59 Adaline W........ 81
'45 Charlotte L........ 34

Fraser
'77 Frances..........135

Freeland
'86 g Marietta H.......156

Freeman
'89 g A. Jean..........164
'86 Annie H..........157
'91 g Catharine M......169
'58 Elizabeth.......... 77
'74 g Elnora F.........125
'67 g Georgiana B......105
'57 Hannah........... 73
'63 g H. Maria......... 92
'73 Kate A., see..... }
      Freyermuth...... } 124
'70 Mary E..........115
'57 Salome P......... 73
'46 Sarah H.......... 37
'50 Sarah W......... 49

French
'80 g Carrie E.........141
'58 Celia N........... 77
'68 Clara A..........110
'85 Dora D...........154
'57 g Ellen P.......... 72
'60 Frances E........ 84
'93 Frances W........175
'57 g Helen M.....7, 8, 72
'58 Jane C........... 77
'67 g Laura C.........105
'57 g Lydia............ 72
'60 Mary E.......... 84
'69 Mary Ella........112
'70 Mary F..........115
'59 Mary J........... 81
'74 Mary W..........127
'67 g Minnie P........105
'59 g R. Annie........ 79
'61 Sara E........... 87
'92 Sarah A.........172
'67 Sarah E......... 107
'70 Sarah N.........115
'49 Susan B.......... 46

Freyermuth
'73 Kate A...........124

Frisbie
'55 g Felicia A......... 64

Frissell
'46 g Elizabeth S....... 36
'69 g Seraph........12, 111

Fritcher
'57 g Ann Eliza........8, 72
'68 Ellen............110
'67 Julia............107

Frost
'94 g Caroline E.......177
'48 Hester A......... 43
'67 Maria A.........107
'68 Susan T.........110

Fuller
'40 Caroline.......... 20
'54 Cornelia A....... 62
'42 Chloe L.......... 25
'59 Delia J........... 81
'76 g Eleanor L........134
'59 Elizabeth........ 18
'65 Emma L......... 100
'92 sp Frances E.......173
'87 Genie C.........160
'40 Harriet.......... 20
'61 g Henrietta A...... 86
'83 M. Addie........149
'82 Marie L..........147
'58 Marian L........162
'56 Mary L.......... 70
'70 g S. Louise........114

Furey
'68 Ellen P..........110

Gabrielson
'81 g M. Christine.....143

Gage
'90 Alice M..........168
'90 Bessie M.........168
'65 J. Luella.........100
'62 Mary A.......... 90
'57 g Mary E......... 72

Galbraith
'75 Annie M.........129
'75 Lois C...........129

Gale
'54 g Ann E. S........ 61
'70 g Emma S.........114

Gallagher
'48 g Frances E....... 41
'49 Mary C.......... 46
'47 Susan B 40

Galloway
'89 g Ida G...........164
'95 Jennie G.........181
'59 Martha R........ 81
'59 g Mary A......... 79

Gallop
'89 g Annie C.........164
'68 Emily...........113
'86 Jennie B.........157
'68 g Sarah B.........109

Gambell
'54 Elizabeth......... 62

Gandolfo
'64 Josephine M...... 97

INDEX.

Gardiner
'86 Harriet C..........157
'58 g Jemima H.........75
'63 Marian H..........94

Gardner
'83 Addie L...........149
'62 Frances E..........90
'66 g Harriet L.........102
'52 Sarah..............56
'81 Seraphine L.......145
'87 Stella M...........160

Garfield
'46 g Jane E............36
'64 Jane M.............97

Garland
'72 Celia..............121
'08 Jane P.............110

Garratt
'57 Harriet L..........60

Garrigus
'81 Alice B............145

Gass
'66 g Mary E...........102

Gates
'77 g Adelia F.........134
'86 Alice V............157
'50 Anne N.............49
'77 Celia J............135
'59 Elizabeth S........18
'59 Frances F..........81
'83 g Grace E..........148
'57 g Harriet C.........72
'92 Sarah F...........172

Gay
'95 Maude C...........181

Gaylord
'94 Cassie E..........177
'61 g Elizabeth.........86
'69 Henrietta.........113
'61 g Martha R..........86
'79 g Marion I.........139

Geddes
'95 Margaret S........181

Genther
'93sp Nellie E.........176

Genung
'73 Adriana B.........124

George
'85 Clara D...........154
'86 Helen.............157
'84 Elizabeth W.......152

Gere
'51 g Amelia B..........51

Gerould
'42 Deborah D..........25
'81 Mary C............145
'59 g Sarah A...........79

Gerrish
'71 Adaline D.........118
'53 Martha.............59
'42 Martha A. (Smith) 25
'54 Mary...............62
'66 Olive A. F........104

Gerst
'68 Sophronia D.......110

Getty
'51 Anna M.............53

Gibbons
'60 Blanche............84
'95 Dora B............181
'95 Vernette L........181

Gibbs
'59 g Lucy A............79

Gibson
'80 g Emily J..........141
'60 Mary H.............81

Giddings
'84 Caroline L........152
'84 g Clara C..........151
'71 g Sophia C.........117

Giffin
'76 Emma L............132

Gifford
'94 g Grace............177
'48 Laura H............43
'75 g M. Caroline......128

Gilbert
'78 Anna F............137
'88 Bertha L..........162
'46 g Elizabeth H.......36
'63 Emily M............94
'50 Jane E.............49
'48 Margaretta M......43
'43 Mary A.............27
'87 Mary A............160
'64 Mary E.............97
'67 Mary I............107
'64 Matilda E..........97
'49 g Sarah A........8, 45

Gilchrist
'69 Elizabeth J.......113

Gile
'92 Almira H..........172
'90 g Lydia A..........167

Giles
'71 Alice A...........118
'72 Anna L............121
'55 Evelyn A...........66
'54 Frances M..........62
'71 g Helena F.......8, 117

Gilfillan
'55 g Catharine.........64
'55 g Helen.............58
'55 g Jane..............64

Gill
'76 Clara E...........132

Gillett
'51 g E. Louisa.........51
'38 Mary A.............16

Gillette
'76 Mary S............132
'54 Sarah J........13, 62

Gilman
'49 g Anna C.........8, 45
'64 Edna M.............97
'55 g Mary E............64

Gilmour
'70 M. Eleanor........115

Gilson
'68 g H. Juliette......109
'48 Samantha W........43

Gilt
'91sp Anna C..........171

Glazier
'95 Hattie E..........181

Gleason
'94sp Amy E...........178
'67 g Elizabeth C......105
'78 g Laura A..........137
'57 L. Maria...........73
'95 Margaret A........181
'53 g Mary E............58
'40 Weltby A...........20

Gleim
'72 Mary A............121

Glen
'94 g Catherine Y.....177
'94 Mary A............177

Glines
'82 Emma O............147

Glover
'73 g Clara F..........123
'91sp Ida M............178

Goddard
'95 Agnes L...........181
'70 Alice M...........115
'51 Elizabeth J........53
'47 g Sarah C...........39
'51 g Sarah L...........51

Godding
'57 g Isabella D........72

Godfrey
'64 Harriet E..........97

Goding
'87 g Sarah E..........159

Godman
'87 Inez A............160

Goffe
'55 g Elizabeth W.......64
'55 Hannah F...........66

Goldsbury
'47 Ann Maria..........40
'62 g Harriet...........89

STUDENTS.

Goldsmith
'64 Mary H............ 97

Goldthwait
'86 g Carrie M......... 156
'60 g Catharine......... 82
'75 g Elizabeth S....... 128
'84 g Martha C......8, 151
'66 Mary............ 104

Goodale
'49 Elizabeth D........ 46
'38 Elizabeth H........ 17
'82 Ellen C............ 147
'55 g Harriet W........ 65
'40 Lucy T............ 20
'73 Mary E............ 124
'50 Mary H............ 49
'94 g Sophia B......... 177

Goodell
'46 Abbie D........... 37
'46 Eliza............ 37

Goodenough
'91 g Helen E.......... 169
'86 g Mary A.......... 156

Goodhue
'64 g Julia A........8, 96
'79 Lettie W.......... 140

Gooding
'76 g Gertrude......... 131

Goodman
'60 Anne M........... 84
'61 g Emily........... 86

Goodnough
'82 g Elizabeth........ 146

Goodnow
'67 Martha........... 107

Goodrich
'61 Alice B........... 87
'51 Caroline E........ 53
'63 Harriet.......... 94
'51 Julia........... 53
'55 Martha C........ 66
'95 g Mary A......... 179
'67 g Mary E......... 105

Goodsell
'54 g Julia J.......... 61
'52 Mary E.......... 56

Goodspeed
'49 Harriet.......... 46

Goodwin
'71 Alice L.......... 118
'68 Annie E.......... 110
'76 Ellen R.......... 132
'38 Hannah L. B...... 17
'48 Helen S......... 43
'63 Julia A......... 94
'63 Lucy E......... 94

Gordon
'67 g Alice W......8, 105
'72 Anna A......... 121
'56 Annie V......... 70
'46 Elizabeth M...... 37

'70 Elizabeth P...... 116
'90 g Margaret........ 167
'94 g Mary........... 177

Gore
'71 g Mary C......... 117

Gorham
'56 Eliza B.......... 70
'50 Esther M........ 49
'51 g Helen......... 51
'79 Jennie L........ 140

Gorton
'57 Fanny........... 74
'46 Hannah G........ 37

Goss
'58 Abbie M......... 77
'81 g Adah.......... 143
'58 Catharine F. E.... 77
'61 Victoria M...... 87

Gossler
'94 Ella M.......... 177

Gottschalk
'76 g Mary Heron..... 131

Gould
'92 g Annie A....... 171
'53 Elizabeth P..... 59
'54 Emily.......... 62
'78 Frances D....... 137
'95 Hattie L........ 181
'38 Lydia.......... 17
'40 Mary M. C...... 20
'82 g Sallie H..... 146
'58 Sarah M........ 77
'40 Sarah R........ 20

Goulding
'55 g Abbie C. D.... 65
'50 Agnes S........ 49
'54 Cynthia K...... 62
'53 g Frances R.... 58

Gouldy
'66 Mary E......... 104

Gowdy
'64 g Julia A...... 96

Gowen
'54 Adaline........ 62
'54 g Amanda M. F.. 61

Grace
'75 Emma L........ 129

Grady
'95 Florence J..... 181

Graham
'86 Anna D........ 157
'48 g Laura....... 41
'93 g Mertie L.... 174

Granger
'39 Elizabeth H.... 18
'75 Elizabeth J... 129

Grant
'65 Abbie E....... 100
'71 Alice D....... 118
'95 Annie E....... 181

'72 Catharine...... 121
'93 Emelyn......... 175
'89 g Eva A........ 164
'52 Hannah J...... 56
'71 Huldah A...... 118
'90 Jean......167, 168
'44 Martha........ 30
'91 Mabel E....... 170
'65 Mary W........ 101
'60 g Sarah E..... 82

Grassie
'57 g Annie....... 72
'87 Annie G....... 160
'94 Effie D....... 178
'60 g Jessie D.... 82
'83 Jessie D...... 149
'92 g Mary K..... 171

Graves
'60 Caro A........ 84
'88 Clara I....... 162
'39 Cordelia M.... 18
'68 Ella M........ 110
'75 Ella M........ 129
'61 g Emily C..... 86
'44 Fanny......... 30
'39 Fanny A....... 18
'48 Harriet S..... 43
'51 Helen M....... 53
'49 Jennett L..... 46
'40 Maria......... 20
'44 g Mary E....9, 29
'86 Mary L....... 157
'80 g Mary S..... 141
'50 Myra R....... 49
'47 g Pamelia A.. 39
'54 g Sarah L.... 61
'64 g Sarah L.... 96

Gray
'57 Anna......... 74
'92 g Miriam..... 171

Greathead
'89 g Frances S.. 164

Greeley
'89 g Estelle E.. 164
'95 g Florence P. 179
'54 Sarah L..... 62

Green
'67 g Adaline E..9, 105
'61 Anna E....... 87
'39 Charlotte A.. 18
'49 Eliza A...... 46
'85 Eliza C..... 154
'45 g Hannah.... 32
'39 Harriet C... 18
'86 Jennie M.... 157
'78 Louise J.... 137
'51 g M. Augusta 51
'89 Mary E..... 165
'45 g Mary S... 32
'90 g Rachel... 167
'45 g Sarah E.. 32

Greene
'89 g Annie L.. 164
'89 g Caroline B.. 14, 164
'57 g Lucretia A.. 72

INDEX.

Greenfield
'86 Mary D..........157
'48 g Miranda D........ 41
'47 g Philomela S....... 39
'51 g Sarah E.......... 51

Greenhill
'61 g Adelaide......... 86

Greenleaf
'49 Elizabeth C....... 46

Greenough
'42 Ann F............ 25

Greenwood
'78 Gertrude I.......137

Gregg
'50 g Frances.......... 48
'89 Marietta.........165

Gregory
'89 Mary L..........165

Greves
'51 Augusta M....... 53

Gridley
'45 Caroline D....... 34
'52 Celia A.......... 56
'48 Eliza B.......... 43
'72 Ella R...........121

Grier
'93 sp Eva M..........176
'94 Jean B..........178

Griffin
'59 Lucy T........... 81
'66 Maria H..........104
'90 M. Louise.....167, 168

Griffeth
'93 Sara J..........175

Griffith
'91 g Lucy F..........169
'72 Mary F..........121

Griggs
'87 g Annie M.........159
'66 Catherine F.....104
'89 g Hattie A........164
'89 g Jennie E........164
'70 g Josephine J.....114
'84 g Nellie M........151
'80 Sarah B.........142

Griswold
'45 Ellen A.......... 34
'59 g Emily M......... 79
'87 g Fannie E........159
'91 g Florence E......169
'59 Harriet L........ 81

Grosvenor
'41 Caroline D....... 22
'92 Julia E..........172
'91 Mary M..........170

Grout
'66 Annie L..........104
'89 g Edith L. F......164
'56 R. Oriana........ 70
'38 Sarah H.......... 17

Grover
'54 Charlotte L...... 62
'66 Mary E..........104
'51 Helen M......... 53

Guernsey
'65 g Fannie O........ 99
'83 g Sarah E........148

Guild
'72 Clara V.........121
'76 g Fanny C........131
'46 Mary J.......... 37

Guilford
'47 g Lucinda T...... 39

Gulick
'74 Harriet M.......127

Gund
'93 Elizabeth.......175
'93 Emma...........175
'94 g Minnie C.......177

Gunn
'49 Sophia C........ 46

Gurney
'68 Mary P..........110
'60 Sarah M......... 84
'60 Susan E......... 84

Gustin
'66 Anna J..........104

Guthrie
'60 Fannie S........ 84

Haddock
'71 Elizabeth B.....118

Hadley
'56 Maria E......... 70

Hadlock
'74 g Margaret J.....125

Hadsell
'91 g Mary C.........169

Hadselle
'58 Adeliza E....... 77
'58 Lucy M.......... 77

Hager
'74 Julia A.........127
'74 Sarah E........127

Hague
'73 g Charlotte De W...123
'72 Gertrude M......121
(now Mary LeComte)

Haile
'48 g Harriette C..... 41

Haire
'80 Anna R..........142
'81 g Mary B........143

Halbert
'82 g Pauline W......146

Hale
'75 Annie M........129
'43 Eliza L......... 27
'70 Ellen H.........116
'83 Harriette I.....149
'76 g Jennie N.......131
'60 Lemoyne A...... 84
'76 Lucy E..........132
'51 g Mary E......... 51
'50 M. Elizabeth.... 49

Hales
'60 Harriet H....... 84

Haley
'62 Alice........... 90
'76 Etta...........132
'57 g Georgiana...... 72

Hall
'86 g Adelle H.......156
'89 Alice K.........165
'95 g Alice U........179
'48 Almeria S....... 43
'49 Amanda P....... 46
'95 Annie..........181
'95 sp Bessie M......184
'49 Elizabeth....... 46
'72 Ella A..........121
'84 Emma C........152
'61 g Emma L........ 86
'72 g Emma V........120
'54 Esther E........ 61
'45 Frances A...... 34
'42 Harriet A...... 25
'40 Harriet P...... 20
'74 g H. Frances M...125
'45 H. Rosamond.... 34
'91 Julia E.........170
'71 g Julia O........117
'40 Lois W.......... 20
'40 Louisa A....... 21
'70 Louise M.......116
'78 Lydia M........138
'92 g Mabel B.......171
'95 Margaret R.....181
'95 g Martha S......179
'82 g Mary A........146
'83 g Mary A........148
'63 g Mary E........ 92
'70 g Mary E........114
'89 Mary E.........165
'95 Mary E.........181
'56 g Mary P........ 68
'85 Mary..........154
'69 Matilda P......113
'86 g Phebe P.......156
'55 g Phebe T....... 65
'55 Seraph A....... 66

Hallett
'52 Octavia G....... 56

Hallock
'63 A. Adelaide..... 94

STUDENTS.

Hallowell
- '50 g Eliza........ 48
- '85 Effie V........154
- '50 g Fannie........ 48
- '92 Harriet P........172
- '85 Kate........154
- '54 L. Emily........ 62
- '57 g Margaret E........ 72
- '83 Margaret S........150
- '95 Mary E........181
- '62 Mary C........ 91

Hallowell
- '71 Ella M........118

Halsey
- '95 g Annie S........179
- '42 Margaret........ 25

Hamilton
- '63 g Anna........ 92
- '95 Christine H........181
- '81 Lillian E........145
- '63 Mary........ 94
- '52 Harriet B........ 56

Hamlen
- '51 Laura B........ 53

Hamman
- '89 Anna B........165

Hammond
- '80 g A. Rosalie........141
- '95 Ellen F........101
- '73 g Julia F........123
- '61 Mary L........ 87
- '62 Melinda........ 91
- '53 Susan R........ 59

Hancock
- '55 Annette........ 66
- '42 Maria T........ 25

Hand
- '48 J. Elizabeth........ 43

Hanmer
- '52 Elizabeth........ 56
- '48 g Mary........ 41

Hannahs
- '80 Mary E........142

Hannum
- '62 g Clara H........ 89

Hanor
- '79 Florence M........140

Hanson
- '91 Myra H........170

Hapgood
- '46 Dorcas W........ 37

Harback
- '52 Frances J........ 56

Harding
- '45 Eliza M........ 34
- '91 Mary B........170

Harkness
- '75 Margaret........129

Harlow
- '95 Ettie........101
- '94 Persis B........178
- '50 Sarah P........ 49

Harlowe
- '90 Abbie F........168

Harmon
- '41 Adeline B........ 22
- '95sp Aurelia P........184
- '88 Clara........162
- '77 g Harriet B........134
- '95 Winnifred L........181

Harmount
- '83 Isabel N........151

Harries
- '60 Elizabeth D........ 84
- '84 Imogen........152
- '60 Mary W........ 84

Harriman
- '66 g Harriet M........102
- '53 Sarah W........ 59

Harrington
- '57 g Eliza B........ 72
- '39 Eliza C........ 19
- '57 Mary P........ 74
- '62 N. Amelia........ 91
- '54 g Olive E........ 61
- '53 Sarah C........ 59
- '58 g S. Louise........ 75

Harris
- '70 Addie T........116
- '82 g Alice B........146
- '75 Almira M........129
- '95 g Anna M........ 99
- '96 Anna R........104
- '67 Delphine M........107
- '78 g Ellen E........137
- '52 Hannah O........ 56
- '81 Helen........145
- '84 H. Fronia........152
- '53 g Mary A........ 58
- '49 Mary C........ 46
- '72 g Mary J........120
- '45 Mary S........ 34
- '66 g Phebe E........102
- '59 Sarah L........ 81

Harrison
- '75 Anna W........129
- '49 Clara C........ 46
- '51 Juliet........ 53
- '56 Maria I........ 70
- '64 Mary A........ 97
- '52 Nancy J........ 56
- '53 Sarah F........ 59
- '75 Sarah F........129

Hart
- '70 Annie E........116
- '48 Ellen M........ 43
- '75 g Mary A........128

Harthan
- '55 g L. Amanda........ 65

Hartshorn
- '71 A. Agnes........118
- '72 g Eleanor A........120

Hartwell
- '55 Annie M........ 66
- '76 Emily S........132
- '48 Mary A........ 43
- '46 g Meliceut J........ 36

Harvey
- '74 g Anna M........125
- '84 g Julia B........151
- '46 Maria A........ 37
- '88 Nellie........162
- '71 Sarah E........118

Harwood
- '49 g Clara J........ 45
- '49 g Helen A........ 45
- '86 Helen L........157
- '80 Isabel H........142
- '61 Lemira M........ 87
- '47 Marion P........ 40
- '48 Martha L........ 43
- '47 g Mary E........ 39

Hasbrouck
- '50 Jane E........ 49

Haseltine
- '81 M. Edna........145

Haskell
- '52 g Clara W........ 54
- '56 g Eliza C........ 68
- '62 g Frances A........ 89
- '49 Harriet M........ 46
- '55 g Harriet N........ 65
- '38 Mary C........ 17
- '52 g Sarah J........ 54
- '42 Susan B........ 25

Haskins
- '86 Abbie D........104

Hastings
- '77 Alice D. W........135
- '60 Caroline E........ 84
- '45 Lois S........ 34
- '55 Mary E........ 65
- '63 Mary E........ 94
- '72 Theresa A........121

Hatch
- '40 Elizabeth B........ 21
- '50 g Ellen A........ 49
- '49 Ellen T........ 46
- '69 g Frances H........111
- '55 Lucy H........ 66
- '63 Marcia M. A........ 94
- '55 Mentoria V........ 66
- '47 Sarah H........ 40

Hathaway
- '46 Amy J........ 37
- '70 Annie F........116
- '95 Bertha F........181
- '44 Lydia D........ 30
- '69 g Martha N........111
- '70 Mary........116
- '44 Olive D........ 30
- '38 Rachel........ 17

Hatheway
- '85 Lissa I........154

INDEX.

Haven
- '40 Elizabeth B 21
- '42 Ellen M........... 25

Hawes
- '59 g A. Maria.......... 79
- '63 Ellen.............. 94
- '48 g Harriet.........12, 41

Hawkes
- '44 Elizabeth W....... 30
- '87 Mary E...........160
- '38 Philena N......... 17

Hawks
- '47 Adaline H......... 40
- '40 Adeline S.......... 21
- '42 g Elizabeth S........ 23
- '39 Harriet R......... 19
- '55 Julia E........... 66
- '42 g Marion A......... 23
- '55 Mary D........... 67
- '55 Sarah E........... 67
- '59 g Stella F......... 79
- '42 g Susan F........9, 23

Hawley
- '58 Emeline A........ 77
- '47 Emily C.......... 40
- '77 g Emily C.........134
- '56 Evelyn P.......... 70
- '41 Lucy A........... 22
- '58 g Lucy E.......... 75
- '51 Sarah M.......... 53

Hawthorne
- '81 Florence J.........145

Hay
- '95 Fannie A..........181
- '83 g Ida W..............148

Hayden
- '63 Catherine J......... 94
- '95 Celia M...........181
- '78 Gertrude E........138
- '67 Julia B...........107
- '42 Mary A............ 25

Hayes
- '50 g Adaline H........ 48
- '47 Alice............. 40
- '95 Alma L...........181
- '94 g Edith P.........177
- '66 Effie M..........104
- '43 g Harriet L.......... 26
- '89 Helen A..........165
- '66 g H. Sophia........ 68
- '45 g Julia A......... 32
- '45 Mary............. 34
- '39 Mary E........... 19
- '51 Mary E........... 53
- '56 Mary L........... 70
- '50 Sarah............ 49
- '62 Sophia W......... 91
- '83 Stella E.........150

Haynes
- '86 g Emma H........ ...156
- '95 g Frances E.........179
- '95 Harriet T.........181
- '83 g Helen E.......... 148

'64 g Mary............9, 96
'49 Olive E........... 46
'69 S. Elizabeth......113

Hayward
- '65 Clara A..........101
- '62 Esther C......... 91
- '92 Lena G..........172
- '58 g S. Jane.......... 75
- '62 g Sophia M......... 89

Hazard
'66 g Martha E.........102

Hazel
'93 Frances D.........175

Hazeltine
'42 Susanna.......... 25

Hazelton
'66 g Martha F.........102

Hazen
- '93 Ella M............175
- '75 g Frances A.........128
- '63 g Frances M........9, 92
- '95 Lucia W..........181
- '95 Martha M........181
- '77 g Mary S..........134
- '41 g Sophia D....7, 9, 11, 22

Heacock
'55 g Margaret A. E...... 65

Healy
'55 Louisa............ 67

Hearne
'84 Margaret J 152

Heath
'95 Adeline F..........181

Hebard
'50 Eliza S........... 49

Hedden
- '53 Catherine........ 59
- '51 g Emily............ 51
- '77 Harriet E........135

Hedges
'49 Mary E........... 46

Hedrick
'80 g Alice. 141

Heidenreich
'81 Katherine.........145

Hemenway
'76 Lizzie V..........132

Hemingway
'73 g Mary A..........123

Hendershott
'92 Delia A..........172

Henderson
- '52 Eliza J.......... 56
- '73 Margaret S.......124

Hendrie
'62 g Elizabeth F........ 89

Hendy
'81 Satie D..........145

Henney
'93 Christine.........175

Henry
- '56 Catharine S........ 70
- '39 Helen A.......... 19
- '60 Lucy J........... 84
- '62 g Mary H.......... 89

Henshaw
'43 Caroline........... 27

Herbert
'79 Georgiana E......140

Herendeen
'73 g Clara N..........123

Hermance
'81 Emma J..........145

Herrick
- '77 g Anna C..........134
- '46 g Eliza A.......... 36
- '78 Mary B..........138
- '95 g Minnie T........ 179

Herring
'89 Ida P..........165

Herron
'76 Anna B..........132

Hersey
- '71 g Martha E.........117
- '74 S. Elizabeth......127

Hettinger
- '93 Alice............175
- '87 Eva F...........160

Hetzel
'55 g Ellen R........... 65

Hewett
'56 Caroline.......... 70

Hewitt
- '77 Alice D..........135
- '81 g Emily H.........143
- '66 Lucy M..........104
- '67 Mary B. W........107
- '76 g Persis D........9, 131

Hibbard
- '57 Alice M.......... 74
- '58 Ellen M.......... 77
- '71 Kate T..........118
- '62 Luella F.......... 91

Hibbler
'62 S. Regina......... 91

Hicks
- '92 g Clara K..........171
- '62 Emma M.......... 91
- '93 Grace 175

Hidden
'62 g Fanny M........12, 89

STUDENTS. 249

Higgins
  '48 *g* Jennette C 41
  '48 *g* Laura A 42
  '54   Mary 62
  '57   Rachel 74
High
  '94   Anna P 178
Hilburn
  '76   Laura 132
  '62 *g* Lucinda 89
Hildreth
  '56   Phebe H 70
Hill
  '94*sp* Adella C 178
  '72   Alice 121
  '58   Charlotte E 77
  '66 *g* Cordelia M 102
  '87   Elizabeth C 160
  '85 *g* Elizabeth G 153
  '41 *g* Eliza B 22
  '91 *g* Grace L 169
  '58   Henrietta C 77
  '58   J. Sophia 77
  '61   Julia A. M 88
  '80   Laura J 142
  '61 *g* Laura P 86
  '52   Louisa M 56
  '73   M. Alice 124
  '53   Margaret McA 59
  '82 *g* Mary E 146
  '95   Myra A 181
  '58   Nancy M 77
  '95   Nellie I 181
  '90   Sarah E 168
  '84   Sarah M 152
Hillard
  '64   Emma S 97
Hillebrand
  '88 *g* Mary E 161
Hills
  '50   Amelia G 49
  '54   Ann E 62
  '55 *g* Emily A 65
  '62 *g* Julia L 89
  '57 *g* Laura 72
  '70   Lizzie G 116
  '60   Lucy G 84
  '50 *g* Mary E 48
  '58 *g* Mary J 75
  '88   Mary J 162
Hilton
  '87   Louise A 160
Hinchman
  '95 *g* Lesbia R 179
  '84   Marie I 152
Hinckley
  '57   Ellen M 74
  '54   Mary S 65
Hinds
  '44   Hannah 30
Hinks
  '75   Jennie I 129

Hinman
  '76 *g* Harriet A 131
  '72 *g* Lydia 120
  '47   Sarah C 40
Hinsdale
  '79   Anna P 140
  '44 *g* Aurelia B 29
  '44 *g* Harriet A 9, 29
  '52   Harriet M 56
  '47 *g* Sarah H 39
Hirst
  '95   Emma A 181
  '95   Sara J 181
Hitchcock
  '72 *g* Annette M 120
  '45 *g* Catherine 32
  '77   Caroline J 135
  '59   Eliza M 81
  '79 *g* Emily 79
  '41   Fannie W 22
  '53   Frances A 59
  '74   Frances E 127
  '39   Frances M 19
  '75   H. Catherine 129
  '52   Jane E 56
  '84   J. Elizabeth 152
  '53   Josephine L 60
  '73 *g* Julia E 123
  '67 *g* Julia F 105
  '53   Julia M 60
  '44   Laura S 30
  '64   Martha A 97
  '69   Martha J 113
  '42   Mary 25
  '69 *g* Mary E 111
  '82   Mary I 147
  '63   Mary O 94
  '41   Phebe A 22
  '52   Sarah A 56
Hittell
  '50 *g* Mary A 48
Hoadley
  '47   Hannah S 40
  '47   Lydia S 40
Hobart
  '44   Julia 30
Hobbs
  '89   Emily A 165
Hodgdon
  '71   Harriet A 118
  '69 *g* P. Elizabeth 9, 112
Hodge
  '60 *g* Lucinda D 12, 82
Hodges
  '79 *g* Amy M 139
  '48 *g* Anna E 42
  '65 *g* Caroline S 99
  '84 *g* Fanny L 151
  '79   Helen R 140
  '40   Lucy 21
  '65   Lucy S 101
  '81 *g* M. Louise 143
  '77 *g* Roxa J 134

Hodgkins
  '85 *g* Georgiana 9, 153
  '91 *g* I. Marion 169
Hoffman
  '63   Harriet N 94
Hoffses
  '55   Isabel M 67
Holbrook
  '83 *g* Annie M 148
  '94 *g* Bertha E 177
  '46   Eliza 37
  '78   Mary Anna 138
  '63 *g* Mary E 92
  '45   Rachel 34
Holcomb
  '66 *g* Hannah E 102
Hollands
  '89 *g* Edith 164
Holliday
  '64   Eliza J 97
Hollister
  '45 *g* Ann M 9, 32
  '47   Elizabeth M 40
  '40   Harriet B 21
  '40   Julia P 21
  '76 *g* Jane R 131
  '92 *sp* Mary A 173
  '67 *g* Mary G 105
  '47   Sarah H 40
Holman
  '53   Caroline E 60
  '47   Ellen D 40
  '57 *g* Myra M. F 72
Holmes
  '74   Abbie M 127
  '95 *g* Alice M 179
  '85   Edith M 155
  '50 *g* Eliza J 48
  '92 *g* Elizabeth W 171
  '93 *g* Elizabeth W 174
  '54   Emily L 63
  '77 *g* Emma F 134
  '71   Fanny J 118
  '54   Frances E 63
  '65   Harriet A 101
  '47   Harriet S 40
  '58 *g* Lucy J 9, 14, 76
  '54   Margaret W 63
  '56   Mary A 70
  '82   Mary G 147
  '49   Sarah 46
  '83   Susan B 150
Holt
  '76   Alice A 132
  '46   Elizabeth 37
  '60   Emma 84
  '71   Frances E. L 118
  '78   Marie F 138
Holton
  '95   Grace B 181
Homan
  '78   Agnes E 138

INDEX.

Homer
'71 Agnes M............118
'73 Harriet R............124

Hommel
'87 g Mina J........157, 159

Hood
'69 g Anna M.........9, 112
'72 Florence...........121

Hooker
'86 Annie J........ 157
'95 Bessie M..........181
'83 Eva F............150
'73 g Henrietta E.....9, 123
'45 g Mary............ 32
'56 Mary A........... 70
'46 Sarah D........... 37

Hoover
'77 Carrie C..........135
'70 g Jennie K.........114
'69 Rachel M..........113

Hopkins
'54 g Catharine......7, 9, 61
'51 Frances M......... 53
'57 Martha........... 74
'45 g Mary............ 32
'62 Mary A........... 91

Horton
'60 g Ellen M.......... 82
'80 Flora M..........142
'67 Lucy W...........107
'61 g Mary E.......... 86
'89 Luella............165
'87 g Nettie..........159
'63 Sarah W.......... 94

Hosack
'87 g Isabel...........159
'63 sp Isabel...........176

Hosmer
'49 Angelina......... 46
'63 Mary Frances..... 94
'88 Mary R...........162
'77 g Mary S.........134

Hotchkiss
'74 Emma I..........127
'79 Hattie F..........140

Hough
'43 Hannah J......... 27
'53 Sarah L. S........ 60

Houghton
'57 g Amanda I........ 72
'94 g Bertha R........177
'52 Eliza W........... 56
'46 g Marilla......... 36
'52 Mary J........... 56

Houk
'76 Mariana P.........132

House
'81 Annie I...........145
'70 Teresa I..........116

Houston
'81 g Harriet A........143
'77 g Jennie B........134
'89 g Martha A........164

Hovey
'80 Harriette R.......142
'79 Helen C...........140

Howard
'53 g Ada L..........9, 58
'59 g Alice............ 79
'71 Eliza J..........118
'66 Ella C...........104
'72 Ellen M..........121
'60 Julia A........... 84
'80 Marion M.........168
'72 Mary Alice.......121
'54 Mary W........... 63
'45 Nancy............ 34
'59 g Roxellana......... 79
'61 Sarah A.......... 88

Howe
'60 Annie M.......... 84
'68 Annie S..........110
'42 Caroline S........ 25
'46 Charlotte......... 37
'74 Cora W..........127
'94 g Grace B........177
'43 L. Eliza.......... 27
'38 Maria............ 17
'43 Martha N......... 27
'66 Melvina A........104
'46 Susan M.......... 37

Howell
'94 g Elizabeth M.....177
'71 Mary P..........118
'56 Phebe A.......... 70

Howes
'46 g Mary W......... 36

Howland
'76 g Abbie B........131
'49 Elizabeth........ 46
'47 Elizabeth S...... 40
'47 g Esther A........ 39
'43 Mary E.......... 27
'70 g Susan R........114

Hoxie
'64 Isabel I.......... 97

Hoxsey
'64 Margaret......... 97

Hoyt
'81 g E. Kate.........143
'95 Olive S..........181
'71 Sarah I..........118
'70 Theresa A........116

Hubbard
'56 Abbie F.......... 70
'71 Adelaide.........119
'92 Anna M..........172
'64 Charlotte B...... 97
'75 Frances I........129
'48 g Harriet A....... 42
'49 Harriet J........ 46
'65 Harriet M........101
'59 g Lucy M......... 79

'92 Lucy M..........172
'51 g Maria I......... 51
'89 g Marion E.......164
'89 g Mary L.........164
'88 g Nan K..........161
'59 Sarah R.......... 81

Hubbell
'44 g Eliza A......... 29

Hudson
'51 Almira C......... 53
'55 Margaret A....... 67
'54 g Martha J....... 61

Hufnagel
'50 g Julia M......... 48

Hughes
'56 Emma M......... 70
'86 g Mary A.........156

Hughitt
'73 Ella A..........124
'78 Emma M.........138

Hulbert
'71 Charlotte S......119
'79 Mary E..........140

Hulburd
'57 Delia S.......... 74

Hull
'73 g Caroline P......123
'70 Sarah E.........116

Hulse
'85 Susan...........155

Hulsizer
'89 g Rachel W.......164

Hume
'41 Lydia C.......... 22
'65 g Sarah J........ 99

Humiston
'48 Esther S......... 43

Humphrey
'83 g Emma H 148
'54 g Frances M...... 61
'39 g Helen........9, 18
'48 g Jane........... 42
'58 Leah M.......... 77
'74 g Maria B........125
'50 Martha.......... 49
'45 g Mary E........ 32
'43 g Mary H......9, 26
'90 g Mary H....167, 168
'58 Sophia C........ 77
'41 Sophia S........ 22

Humphreys
'48 g Sarah M........ 42

Hungerford
'82 g Antoinette I......146

Hunt
'86 g A. May........156
'86 g Anna J........156
'69 g Ariana L......112
'39 Charlotte....... 19
'54 g Ellen.........9, 61

STUDENTS. 251

'60 g Fanny M,............ 82
'61   F. Evelyn........... 88
'87   Gwenllian...........160
'58 g Hannah M........... 76
'71   Lizzie E............119
'45   Mary A............. 34
'55 g Mary I.............. 65
'57 g Mary M............. 72
'85 g May.................154
'61 g Sarah A............. 86

Hunter
'65   Annie..............101
'65   Jennie B...........101
'85   L. Annie...........155
'54   Mary H............. 63
'58   Mary J............. 77
'85   Sarah L............155

Hunting
'66   Mary A.............104

Huntington
'52   Amelia C........... 56
'44   Charlotte S........ 30
'70   E. Caroline........116
'75 g Eliza M.............128
'61 g Frances............. 86

Huntoon
'88   Bertha M...........162

Huntress
'60   Adeline E.......... 84

Huntting
'47   Margaretta B....... 40

Hurd
'54   Clara A............ 63
'45   Harriet C.......... 34
'60   Laura.............. 84
'42   Mary A............. 25
'59 g Mary A............. 79
'46   Minnie E...........104

Hurlbert
'87   Florence A.........160
'87   Sylvia W...........160

Hurlburt
'74   Mary L.............127
'65   Rebecca C..........101

Hurlbut
'75   Jessie L...........129
'89 g Marion E........9, 164
'70   Mary C.............116

Hurlbutt
'70 g Fannie I............114

Huse
'44   Charlotte A........ 30

Hussey
'54 g Ann M.............. 61
'89 g Clara A............164

Husted
'43   Mary A............. 27

Huston
'57   Esther J........... 74
'59   Loella E........... 81

Hutchings
'85   Harriet E..........155

Hutchins
'95   Mary L.............181
'52   Philenna R......... 56

Hutchinson
'90   Annie P............168
'91 g Harriet M..........169
'56   Josephine M........ 70
'89   Lucy M............. 19

Huxley
'48   Frances E.......... 43

Hyde
'42   Adeline............ 25
'62 g Augusta............ 89
'95   Bertha C...........181
'41   Charlotte A........ 22
'51   Eliza R............ 53
'95 g Elizabeth H........179
'95   Gertrude S.........181
'74   Hattie E...........127
'87 g Isabella...........159
'42 g Julia...........13, 23
'91 g Mary A.............169
'65   Mary P.............101
'47   M. Isabella........ 40
'92 g Sara G.............171
'40   Sophronia C........ 21
'88 g Susan C............161

Ide
'69   Hattie E...........113
'66   Sarah W............104

Ihling
'82 g Annie J............146

Ingalls
'80 g Ellen E............141
'94   Henrietta E........178

Ingham
'64   Diantha............ 97
'90 g Sarah.............. 82

Inglee
'64   Mary E............. 97

Ingraham
'75 g Carrie E...........128
'67 g Louise A...........106

Isbell
'49   Emily J............ 47

Isham
'78 g Christine A........137
'81   Edith H............145

Ives
'90   Bertha J...........167
'67 g Ella G.............106
'73   F. Ella............124
'93   Julia I............175
'43   Mary C............. 27
'69   Parnellie M........113
'52   Sara A............. 56
'95   Sue B..............181

Jack
'85   Anna C.............155
'84 g Mary M............151

Jackson
'81   Josephine A........145
'63   Luetta G........... 91
'73   Mary A.............124
'73   Mary E.............124
'83 g May................148
'84   Sarah E............152

Jacobs
'45   Mary.............. 34

James
'64   Annie S............ 97

Janes
'75   Jennette C.........129
'45   Martha A........... 34
'62 g Sarah P............ 89

Jansen
'90   Amelia P...........168
'87   Katherine E........160

Jaques
'76   Mary E.............132

Jay
'95   Carrie B...........181
'77 g Mary I.............134

Jayne
'51   Hannah J........... 53

Jefts
'68 g Mary P.............109
'69   Mira A.............113

Jenkins
'58   Marcia D........... 77
'74   Maria..............127
'76   Mary E.............132
'64 g Myra M.........9, 96

Jenks
'80   Ida M..............142

Jennings
'80 g C. Elizabeth.......141
'75 g Eleanor B..........128
'77 g Ellen M............134
'82   Hattie D...........147
'70   Isabella S.........116
'70 g Julia F............114
'47   Marcia A........... 40
'85   Mary R.............155
'43 g Sabrina.........9, 26
'79 g Susan M............139

Jennison
'74 g Abbie R............125
'74   Lucia N............127

Jerome
'43   Mary J............. 27

Jessup
'47 g Emily..........7, 9, 39

Jeudevine
'86   Hatty..............157

INDEX.

Jewell
- '45 Caroline 34
- '54 Charlotte A........ 63
- '43 g Maria............. 26
- '45 Maria............. 34
- '42 Sarah C........... 25

Jewett
- '86 Annie M........... 157
- '92 Bessie M.......... 172
- '89 Jessie E.......... 165
- '90 g Julia I......... 167
- '82 g Mary E......... 146
- '71 g Nellie C....... 117

Jobes
- '93 Anna B........... 175

Johnson
- '65 g Abby C......... 90
- '58 g Adeline N...... 76
- '90 Adeline S........ 168
- '69 Alice G.......... 113
- '79 Amelia G........ 140
- '67 g Anna M........ 106
- '93 g Annie A....... 174
- '69 Annie G........ 113
- '43 Charlotte E..... 27
- '95 Edina M........ 181
- '84 Eleanor A...... 152
- '51 g Frances B..... 51
- '64 Hannah A....... 97
- '75 g Hannah N..... 128
- '46 g Harriet...... 9, 36
- '64 Josephine C.... 97
- '58 Laura M........ 77
- '58 g Laura R...... 76
- '79 Lizzie L...... 140
- '95 Louise B....... 181
- '49 g Lucy T....... 45
- '67 Margery R..... 107
- '84 Martha E...... 152
- '75 Mary C........ 129
- '68 g Mary C...... 100
- '94 Maude A....... 178
- '86 g Nellie M.... 156
- '73 Nellie S...... 124
- '81 g Olive M..... 143
- '78 g Orpha E..... 137
- '51 Priscilla...... 53
- '46 Rosa........... 37
- '93 Ruth I........ 175
- '43 Selena L...... 27
- '69 Virginia II... 113

Johnston
- '65 Dorcas H...... 101
- '72 g Dorlissa E.. 120
- '53 Ellen R....... 60
- '73 g H. Jane.... 123
- '95 May J........ 181
- '56 Sarah E...... 70

Jones
- '80 g Adeline..... 21
- '81 Allie M..... 145
- '49 g Amelia D... 45
- '81 g Annie L.. 143
- '59 g Augusta L. 79
- '94 g Bessie L.. 177
- '83 g Carrie E. 148
- '95 g Cassina M.179

- '81 Edith S........... 145
- '41 Elizabeth W...... 22
- '87 Etta F.......... 160
- '48 Hannah.......... 43
- '44 g Hannah D. G..... 29
- '74 g Isabella L..... 125
- '59 g Maria E....... 79
- '56 g Margaret W.... 68
- '76 g Martha A..... 131
- '53 Mary A......... 60
- '72 Mary E........ 121
- '77 g Mary E...... 134
- '49 Mary H........ 47
- '65 Mary K....... 101
- '75 Mary R....... 129
- '39 Mary W........ 19
- '76 Mary W....... 132
- '71 Nellie B..... 119
- '93 Nellie I..... 175
- '57 g Sarah F..... 72

Josselyn
- '45 Adeline D....... 34

Joy
- '71 Harriet A..... 119
- '81 Ina A........ 145
- '95 Katherine D.. 181
- '81 Stella F..... 145

Judd
- '89 Annie B....... 165
- '40 Dorothy L..... 21
- '38 Eliza......... 17
- '72 Jeanette..... 121
- '66 g Margaret B. 102
- '80 g Mary I..... 9, 142
- '84 g Mirah L.... 151
- '40 Silence S..... 21

Judkins
- '71 Emma A....... 119
- '55 g Mary J..... 65

Judson
- '52 g Jane L. B... 54

Kajiro
- '95 Yoshi........ 181

Kane
- '94 g Elizabeth G. 177

Kanouse
- '65 Theodora C. P.. 101

Karch
- '72 Maria S...... 121

Kasson
- '60 g Dora M..... 82

Kathan
- '95 Florence A... 181

Keeler
- '80 g Jennet W... 82
- '79 Laura F..... 140
- '80 Lucy H..... 143

Keep
- '56 H. Eudora.... 70

Keese
- '72 g Julia E.... 120
- '74 Mary J...... 127

Keith
- '95 Cora F....... 181
- '84 Flora M. H.. 152
- '67 Gertrude A.. 107
- '92 g Lucy E.... 171
- '83 g Marcia A. 9, 148
- '92 g Mary H... 171
- '94 g Mary H.. 13, 177
- '95 g S. Emma.. 179

Kelley
- '77 g Julia A.... 134
- '75 Mary A..... 129
- '55 g Sarah A... 65

Kellogg
- '70 g Adelaide F. 114
- '93 g Cora H... 174
- '95 sp Cora H.. 184
- '95 g Effie L.. 179
- '68 Ella M..... 110
- '55 g Ellen E.. 65
- '52 Harriet N.. 56
- '54 Julia...... 63
- '46 Keziah C... 37
- '91 g Laura M.. 169
- '91 g Mary E.. 169
- '67 Mary S.... 107
- '46 g Nancy E.. 36
- '49 Sarah P... 47
- '45 Sarah W... 34

Kelsey
- '68 g Adaline D. H..12, 109
- '80 g Gertrude E. 142
- '79 g Ida B..... 139
- '86 M. Josephine.. 104

Kemble
- '77 Anna E..... 135

Kendall
- '74 Alice E.... 127
- '49 Alicia..... 47
- '56 Annie A... 70
- '81 g Agnes M. 144
- '67 g Clara L. 106
- '65 g Harriet E. 99
- '76 Leila..... 132
- '53 Mary E.... 60
- '60 Sarah W.. 84

Kenfield
- '43 Charlotte M.. 27

Keniston
- '61 g Dora D.... 86

Kennedy
- '79 Elizabeth C.. 140
- '64 Fannie E... 97
- '74 Fannie L.. 127

Kent
- '70 Florence... 116
- '55 g Frances L.. 65
- '68 g Ruth L... 109

Kenyon
- '95 Elizabeth W.. 181

Kerr
- '63 Ellen M..... 94

STUDENTS.

Kershaw
'59 *g* Mary B............ 79
Kevney
'51 Eleanor........13, 53
Keyes
'77 *g* Amy A...........134
'77 Ellen L............135
'62 Susan M...........91
Kibbe
'84 Julia E............152
Kidder
'49 Angeline H........ 47
'51 Tryphena......... 53
Kies
'86 Juliette...........157
'81 *g* Marietta........9, 144
'62 *g* Mary A............ 80
Kilbourne
'69 Elizabeth H. S....113
Kilburn
'44 Sarah A........... 30
Kilner
'76 Grace E..........132
'76 Jennie B. H......132
Kimball
'48 Alice C.......... 43
'76 *g* Alice S...........131
'77 *g* Anna J...........134
'49 Ariadne L......... 47
'47 *g* Elizabeth R...... 39
'73 Emma E.........124
'71 Emma F.........119
'77 Helen L..........135
'86 *g* Julia F...........156
'79 *g* Kate J...........139
'68 *g* Lucia E. F........ 92
'61 Lucy E........... 88
'68 Lucy J...........110
'54 Lucy S........... 63
'46 Margaret A........ 37
'93 Marian...........175
'53 *g* Mary A..........9, 58
'80 *g* Mary E..........142
'76 Mary W..........132
'90 *g* Mary W..........107
'53 *g* Sarah E.......... 58
King
'54 Abby P........... 63
'55 *g* Adelaide W....... 65
'64 Amelia T......... 97
'87 *g* Anna S 150
'51 Charlotte E....... 53
'45 *g* Elizabeth........ 32
'85 *g* Elizabeth......... 99
'82 Ella.............147
'76 Emilie F..........132
'67 Fanny A..........107
'76 Hattie E..........132
'55 *g* Jane M.......... 65
'47 *g* Julia A........... 39
'88 Margaret A......102
'61 Mary............ 88
'52 Sarah R.......... 56

Kingman
'75 *g* Ella..............128
'43 Jane J............ 28
'48 Marietta.......... 43
Kingsbury
'48 *g* Abby L........... 42
'49 Emily L 47
'61 Frances E.......132
'47 *g* Harriette N....... 39
'63 Julia E........... 91
'91 *g* Lucie E..........169
'59 Mary S.......... 81
'49 Sarah E......... 47
Kingsley
'93 *g* Charissa A.......174
'81 *g* Ella S............144
'65 Fidelia M........101
'64 Frances E........ 97
'57 *g* Josephine M...... 72
'84 Mabel D.........152
'68 Mary E..........110
'87 Nelly H..........160
'44 Rhoda............ 31
Kinney
'51 Happy T......... 53
'51 Mary N.......... 53
Kinsman
'67 M. Rosannah.....107
Kirby
'60 Josephine N....... 84
'88 Mary A..........162
'87 May P...........160
Kirk
'48 *g* Celestia A........ 42
'84 *g* Eleanor H........151
Kirke
'67 Annie M........107
Kittredge
'52 A. Katherine...... 56
'70 *g* Harriet D........114
'68 Maria A..........110
'77 Mary C..........135
Kleefisch
'82 Helena..........147
Knapp
'93 *g* Grace H..........174
'55 Mary H.......... 67
Kneeland
'63 Mary L.......... 94
'75 *g* Stella............128
Knight
'80 Camilla J........143
'47 Elizabeth........ 40
'50 Elizabeth........ 49
'44 *g* Eliza P.......... 29
'41 Eunice B........ 22
'67 *g* Mary H..........106
Knott
'95 A. Lois..........182
Knowles
'62 Caroline E....... 91

253

Knowlton
'61 Abby C.......... 88
'44 *g* Elizabeth G....... 29
'57 Evelyn C........ 74
'68 H. Orianna.......110
'47 *g* Mary C........... 39
'44 Sarah A......... 31
'50 Sarah T......... 49
'50 Sophia V. W..... 49
Koehler
'95 Margaret B........182
Kolb
'89 *g* Theodora M......164
Kops
'52 Gertrude de B....13, 56
Körner
'85 *g* Caroline..........154
Kosboth
'92 Kittie W..........172
Kuhn
'89 *g* Anna R...... 112
Lacey
'82 Eva T...........147
Ladd
'66 *g* Caroline K........102
'94 Grace E.........178
'50 Mary J.......... 49
'73 Sarah P.........124
Laird
'59 Marion.......... 81
Lake
'95 Margaret B... 182
'89 *g* Sadie M..........164
'92 *g* Sadie M..........171
Lamb
'61 *g* Mary C........... 86
'57 Sarah............ 74
Lambert
'88 A. Louise........162
'50 Mary A......... 49
'56 Sarah G......... 70
Lampman
'65 Catharine E......101
Lamprey
'91 *g* Luuette E........169
Lamson
'75 *g* Martha E........128
Lancaster
'51 Sarah S......... 53
Lancraft
'86 *g* Ettie A..........156

'70 Helen M.........114
'86 *g* Mary E..........156
'53 *g* Mary J........... 58
'94 *g* Ruth M..........177
'67 *g* Vina S..........106
'95 Wilhelmina C.....182

254 INDEX.

Land
'43 Margaret A....... 28
Landfear
'89 g Elizabeth M....... 164
'75 Mary Emma........129
'74 Sarah S............127
Landon
'46 Cornelia........... 37
'47 g Harriet............ 39
Lane
'81 Alice B...........145
'55 g A. Maria......... 65
'65 g Annie L..........100
'51 Harriet N......... 53
'49 Hittie P.......... 47
'62 g H. Louisa......... 89
'84 g Laura M..........151
'58 Martha........ 77
'45 g R. Augusta........ 32
Langé
'48 Wilhelmina H..... 43
Lantz
'87 g Augusta W........159
Lapham
'58 g Cornelia S........ 76
Larrabee
'77 Hannah M........135
Lasell
'95 Gail..............182
Laskey
'65 Ann E. M............101
Latham
'62 g Lucy A........... 89
Lathrop
'55 g Fanny............. 65
'41 Julia A........... 22
'79 Mary E..........139, 140
Latimer
'95 Anna C........... 182
Lauback
'85 Annie B..........159
'86 Jennie............157
Lauriat
'72 Anne G..........121
Laurie
'15 Annie............129
Law
'54 Annie M.......... 63
Lawrence
'66 g Anna M..........103
'78 Annie M..........138
'61 Clara M.......... 88
'49 Elizabeth G....... 47
'82 Eudora F. C......147
'57 Hannah P......... 74
'56 Harriet A......... 70
'56 H. Maria.......... 70
'60 Lucy A........... 84
'61 Mary A........... 88

'56 Mary F............ 70
'62 Meta L............ 91
'67 Mira B............107
'65 Sarah W..........101
'51 Susan F........... 53
Lawson
'50 g Catharine........ 48
'95 sp Susie M..........184
Lawton
'48 Catharine M...... 43
Leach
'40 g Catherine S...... 20
'71 Elizabeth S......119
'45 g Frances S........ 32
'63 g Laura J.......... 92
'83 Mabel E..........150
'39 g Martha A......13, 18
'80 g Mary F........9, 142
Learoyd
'70 Annie............116
Leathe
'49 Paulina A........ 47
Leavenworth
'80 g Margaret P......142
Leavitt
'92 Chloe M..........172
'95 Edith W..........182
'51 g Frances M........ 51
'95 g Marian F.........179
'42 Sophia S......... 25
LeConte
'41 g Caroline......... 22
Lee
'64 Aurora M......... 98
'74 g Caroline M......125
'54 g Catharine E...9, 12, 61
'91 sp Charlotte E....13, 170
'93 Charlotte E......175
'45 g Cornelia F. (changed
     from Diantha C.).. 32
'60 g Elizabeth J...... 82
'83 Fanny S..........150
'42 Julia............. 25
'65 Martha E.........101
'78 g Mary............137
'53 Sarah E.......... 60
Leeds
'86 Mary L...........157
Lees
'78 Elsie F..........138
Leffingwell
'59 g Caroline S....... 79
Lefler
'50 Jane C........... 49
Leh
'80 Sallie............143
Leland
'45 Adeliza........... 34
'45 Rhoda A.......... 34
'59 Susan A.......... 81

Le Maistre
'91 g Lida R........169, 170
Lemasseua
'57 g Jane E..........9, 72
Leman
'52 Susan H.......... 56
Leonard
'69 g Anna R..........112
'90 Bessie N.........168
'46 Ellen E.......... 98
'56 Emily J.......... 70
'63 Emma F........... 94
'51 g Hannah B........ 51
'75 Jane R...........129
'61 Lucy A........... 88
'73 g Marie I.........123
'43 Marion H......... 28
'88 Mary A..........162
'55 Mary J........... 67
'83 Mary M..........150
'61 Teresa M......... 88
Lester
'76 g Sarah J.........131
Lewis
'83 Agnes M..........150
'52 Anna G........... 56
'92 Carolyn M........172
'82 g Carrie E........146
'40 Elizabeth F...... 21
'55 g Elizabeth N..... 65
'45 Ellen H.......... 34
'72 Emma F..........122
'85 Gertrude E...... 155
'95 sp Grace............184
'48 Margaret B....... 43
Libbey
'72 g Isabelle H......120
Lillie
'39 Janett............ 19
Lincoln
'64 Elizabeth B...... 98
'44 Emeline.......... 31
'79 Laura B..........140
'71 Rebecca M........119
'44 Sarah A. B....... 31
Lindsey
'90 g Amy B...........167
'51 Harriet F........ 53
'54 Melissa A........ 63
Lindsley
'52 Alice M.......... 56
'74 Margaret V.......127
'73 Maria V..........124
'52 Sarah E.......... 56
Linsley
'48 Abby T........... 43
'55 Aurelia L........ 67
'55 Eunice F......... 67
'57 g Mary F.......... 72
'57 Mary F........... 74
'47 N. Ellen......... 40
Linville
'85 Florence M.......155

STUDENTS. 255

Lippincott
'88 Mary E...........162
Litchfield
'52 Adelia R...........56
Littell
'58 Kate............... 77
Little
'86 Alice M...........157
'45 Margaretta C...... 34
'58 *g* Priscilla........... 76
Littlefield
'84 Ethel A...........152
'76 *g* Helen E...........131
'53 *g* Martha............ 58
Livingston
'50 *g* Caroline A......... 48
'88 *g* Rebecca...........161
Lloyd
'52 *g* Juliet E........... 54
'58 *g* Mary W........... 76
Locke
'92 *g* Addie I............171
'45 *g* Clementine M..... 32
'60 Frances A......... 84
'93 *g* Marinda A........174
'57 Sarah A. J......... 74
'59 *g* Sarah D.......9,11, 79
'61 Susan C........... 88
Lockwood
'79 Anna L............140
'78 *g* Augusta H........137
Lombard
'94 Maud E...........178
Long
'72 Cornelia B........122
'53 Cornelia M........ 60
'53 *g* Louisa A........ 9, 58
'95 Sue G...........182
Longfellow
'86 Annie H...........157
Longley
'71 Grace E...........119
'45 Henrietta A........ 34
Longstreet
'54 *g* Keturah.......... 61
Loomis
'58 Collette........... 77
'49 Frances A......... 47
'46 Harriet........... 37
'51 *g* Martha A.......... 51
'88 *g* Mary S...........161
'49 Philomela A....... 47
'45 *g* Sarah 32
Lord
'76 *g* Alice F............131
'94 *sp* Anna B...........178
'81 Fannie A...........145
'57 Georgiana F....... 74
'41 Harriet W......... 22
'75 Jane A...........129

'41 Lavinia S......... 22
'48 Mary L........... 43
'90 *g* Nettie L..........167
'74 *g* Sarah A...........125
Loring
'82 *g* Mary E...........146
Lothrop
'40 *g* Almira W......... 20
Lougee
'91 Maud A...........170
Lourie
'62 Jeannie M......... 91
Love
'89 Harriette N.......165
Lovejoy
'95 Sara C...........182
Loveland
'76 *g* Elizabeth M.......131
'74 *g* Mary A...........125
'95 Mary H...........182
'70 Sarah J...........116
Lovell
'60 *g* Laura G......... 83
'69 *g* Martha E..........112
'56 Mary W........... 70
Loveridge
'55 Elizabeth C........ 67
Lovett
'63 Anna............... 94
Low
'95 Grace E...........182
Lowe
'54 *g* Emma C......... 61
Lowell
'81 Annie A...........145
'83 Mary C.......12, 150
Lucas
'74 Jennie M...........127
Luce
'49 Martha............ 47
Ludden
'79 Gertrude V........140
'85 Martha A...........155
Ludlam
'61 *g* Anna C........... 86
Lufkin
'93 Arizona...........175
'92 *g* Virginia...........171
Lupton
'49 Rhoda O......... 47
Lyford
'86 Annie M...........157
Lyle
'91 Hattie B 170
Lyman
'91 Alice S...........170

'95 Annie A...........182
'48 Climene C........ 43
'42 Elizabeth.......... 25
'89 Emma M...........165
'73 *g* Eunice A...........123
'85 Luella M...........155
'85 *g* Mary A 154
'58 Mary H........... 77
'77 S. Arabella.......135
'55 Sarah A........... 67
'42 Sarah C. (Hannum) 25
'78 Sarah F...........138
'74 Sarah G...........127
'65 Sarah M...........101
'76 Sarah W...........132
'39 Theresa 19
Lyon
'56 *g* Eliza A...........9, 68
'94 Florence...........178
'69 Ida C...........113
'95 Karleen S...........182
'74 Lenna I...........127
'40 *g* Lucy T.......9, 13, 20
'91 *g* Martha...........177
'67 *g* Mary E...........106
'54 Mary S........... 63
'40 Nancy A........... 21
'48 *g* Rosina 42
'50 Sarah P........... 50
Lytle
'53 Anna S............ 60
McAlpine
'65 Dana..............101
McArthur
'53 *g* Catharine.......... 58
McCabe
'48 Eliza M........... 43
McCaine
'93 *sp* Adelaide M........176
McCall
'70 Mary H 116
McCallister
'87 *g* Jean P...........159
'84 Nancy B...........152
McCampbell
'91 *g* Jennie..............169
McClelland
'83 Annie H...........150
'00 Mary C........... 84
McClenahan
'80 Nannie...........143
McClure
'42 Nancy H.......... 25
'94 *sp* Elizabeth M.......178
McConnel
'93 Jessie.............175
'91 *g* Lillian A...........169
'92 Mary E...........172
McCord
'81 Mary 145

INDEX.

McCray
'41 Caroline........... 31
McCullough
'64 Nancy J........... 98
McCurdy
'82 Elizabeth..........147
McCutcheon
'51 g Harriet N......... 51
McDanolds
'90 g Charlotte.........167
McDonald
'93 g Alice M............174
'64 Ella K.............. 98
McElwain
'89 Caroline M........166
'81 g Hattie A............144
McFarland
'40 Clara D........... 21
'75 Lizzie.............129
McGee
'57 g Rebecca A......... 72
McGill
'94 g Margaret..........177
'77 Susan..............135
McGlashan
'69 Laura.............113
McIlvaine
'82 g Flora B..........146
McIlvane
'84 g Carrie R..........151
McIntire
'54 Abbie E........... 63
McIntyre
'43 Eliza M.............28
'87 Elsie D............160
'45 g Flora P........... 32
'54 g Martha M. W...... 61
Mack
'42 Clarissa L......... 25
'75 g Isabella G........9, 128
'71 Mary E............119
'12 Mary H............ 25
'77 Mary L............135
'70 M. Ellen..........116
Mackie
'90 Ellen B...........168
McKean
'87 Eva C.... 160
'82 Fannie............147
McKennan
'79 g Effie..............139
McKenzie
'87 g Mary E.... 159
'53 Sarah............. 60
McKeown
'83 g E. Louise..........148
'79 Mary L............140

McKillip
'68 Margaret C........110
McKissick
'95 Elizabeth F........182
McLain
'86 Mary B... 157
McLane
'38 Eliza.............. 17
McLean
'87 g Hannah B... 106
'43 Harriet........... 28
'45 Hester............ 34
'52 g Mary............ 54
'42 Sarah............. 25
'74 Sarah P...........127
McLellan
'76 Alice J............132
MacLeod
'83 Martha A.....149, 150
M'Masters
'61 g Frances L......... 86
MacMath
'76 Elizabeth V....... 132
McMechan
'59 Sarah L.......... 81
McMillen
'51 Phebe............ 53
McMonagle
'43 Mary W........... 28
McNair
'58 Catharine......... 77
McNaughton
'67 Elizabeth W.......107
'70 g Mary E..........114
McNear
'65 Josephine G.......101
MacNulty
'83 g Gertrude A........174
McNutt
'72 Martha J. F......122
McPherson
'78 Jennie............138
McQueen
'77 Ella J............136
McQuitty
'76 Mary S...........132
McWilliams
'95 Martha E.........182
'90 Rose.............168
Magee
'82 g Harriet C........146
Magill
'74 Helen A..........127
'85 Maud H...........155

Magness
'83 g E. Frances........ 148
Magranis
'60 Adeline........... 84
Maitland
'51 Mary.............. 53
Major
'43 g Susanna........... 26
Makepeace
'80 Susie J............143
Makinster
'64 Augusta A......... 98
Mallery
'61 g Caroline J......... 86
Maltby
'52 Isabella G......... 56
'50 Margaret L. A..... 50
'89 Mary J............165
'50 S. Elizabeth....... 50
Man
'47 Caroline F........ 40
'47 Mary A........... 40
Manchester
'74 g Emily F...........125
Mann
'50 g Charlotte......... 48
'77 Elizabeth.........136
'38 Elizabeth......... 17
'70 Emily 116
'42 g Margaret. 9, 23
'46 Martha S......... 37
'40 Marian A......... 21
Manning
'46 Charlotte G....... 37
'57 Mary E........... 74
Mansfield
'63 Elizabeth A........ 94
'95 Mary P...........182
Manson
'83 Alice L...........150
Marble
'57 Susan A........... 74
Marchant
'89 g Agnes............164
Marcy
'62 g Ellen E........... 89
'88 Lucretia..........162
'58 M. M. K......... 77
Marean
'80 g Valetta C........142
Marks
'51 Arlina C. 53
Marquand
'52 Sarah E........... 56
Marr
'66 g Harriet A........103

STUDENTS. 257

Marsh
- '50 g Anna............... 48
- '55 Arabella........... 67
- '50 Caroline B......... 50
- '50 Elizabeth A....... 50
- '40 Elizabeth S....... 21
- '48 Elizabeth W....... 43
- '86 g Emily R..........156
- '89 Grace L...........165
- '56 g Gracia............ 68
- '47 Jeannie E.......... 40
- '54 Julia L............ 63
- '50 Lucy A 50
- '90 Lucy T........ 13, 168
- '49 Susan F........... 47

Marshall
- '72 Annie C...........122
- '50 Eliza A........... 50
- '71 g Ella C...........117
- '66 Helen R...........104
- '43 H. Jane........... 28
- '64 Jerusha A......... 98
- '72 Julia L...........122
- '51 Louisa............ 53
- '52 g Mary A........... 54

Martin
- '80 Alice B...........143
- '46 Cornelia H........ 37
- '55 Elizabeth D....... 67
- '44 g Emily A. G...... 29
- '70 Julia A...........116
- '78 g M. Alida........137
- '83 Mary L............150
- '44 g M. Augusta...... 29
- '48 Virginia M........ 44

Martindale
- '44 Jane M............ 31
- '48 Julia R........... 44
- '58 Lucy.............. 77
- '47 g Lucy A.......... 39
- '47 Minerva S......... 40

Marvin
- '67 g Caroline E......106
- '69 Julia S...........113
- '83 g Katherine M.....148

Mascroft
- '66 g Imogene W.......103

Mason
- '79 Alice M...........140
- '43 H. Louisa......... 28
- '57 g L. Jane......... 72
- '83 Mabel M...........150
- '49 g Maria E......9, 45
- '51 Mary J........... 53
- '53 Rebecca W........ 60
- '69 Teresa M.........113

Masta
- '71 Ida C............119

Masters
- '50 g Anna M. L....... 48

Mateer
- '78 Lillian E........138

Mather
- '38 Huldah............ 17

- '56 g Mary F.......... 68
- '38 Sarah A.......... 17
- '58 S. Jane.......... 77

Mathews
- '59 Julia E.......... 81
- '50 g Sarah J........ 48

Mathewson
- '62 g Elizabeth....... 89
- '62 Mary............. 91

Matson
- '38 H. Aurelia....... 17

Matthews
- '83 Mary L...........150

Matthewson
- '60 Mary............. 84

Mattison
- '78 M. Elizabeth.....138

Mattocks
- '64 Eliza B.......... 98
- '47 Martha A......... 40
- '47 g Martha (Porter)... 39

Mattoon
- '73 A. Lucy..........124

Maxwell
- '63 Elizabeth S...... 94
- '55 R. Annie......... 67
- '64 Victoria C....... 98

May
- '57 Ellen............. 74
- '89 g Eva L..........165
- '56 Harriet M........ 70
- '56 g Julia H........ 68
- '63 Sarah R.......... 94

Mayher
- '90 g Carrie B.......167
- '77 g Elizabeth M....134
- '77 Eleanor J........136
- '89 Mary S...........166

Maynard
- '51 g Frances E...... 51
- '51 Laura............ 53
- '48 Lucy A........... 44
- '53 g Mary E......... 58
- '38 Persis F......... 17
- '64 Wilhelmina D..... 98

Mayo
- '59 Anna M........... 81
- '54 g Ellen A........ 61

Mays
- '89 Edith R..........166

Meacham
- '55 g Cleantha M..... 65

Mead
- '51 Charlotte B...... 53
- '60 Charlotte M...... 84
- '85 Clara B..........182
- '60 Emily G.......... 84
- '78 g Hannah M.......137
- '51 g Maria E........ 51

- '89 Mary A...........166
- '56 Mary J........... 70
- '62 Myrtilla P....... 91

Meader
- '83 g Ellen L........148
- '71 g Wilhelmina T...117

Means
- '49 Emeline W........ 47
- '62 Lilla B.......... 91

Meech
- '80 Annie D..........143
- '80 Ann W............143
- '80 Susan B..........143

Meeker
- '52 Caroline B....... 56
- '43 Harriet E........ 28

Meigs
- '63 Mary G........... 94

Meily
- '77 Frances J.......136

Mckeel
- '95 sp Gertrude......184

Meldrum
- '61 Agnes I., see } 88
   Susan C.

Mellen
- '83 Emily K..........150

Mellish
- '87 g A. May.........159
- '75 Florence........130

Mellor
- '95 Eva T...........182

Melvin
- '56 g Harriette A.....9, 68
- '79 g Helen E......9, 139
- '65 Louise G........101
- '62 g Sarah H......9, 89

Mendall
- '75 Mary E. S.......130

Meredith
- '91 Charlotte R.....170

Merrell
- '58 g Susan.......... 76

Merriam
- '44 Eleanor M........ 31
- '85 Grace I.........182
- '95 Helen S.........182
- '87 Lena S..........160
- '57 Lucy A.......... 74
- '56 Lucy E.......... 70
- '65 Martha J........101

Merrick
- '49 g Caroline H....9, 13, 45
- '66 Catherine S.....104
- '41 Dorcas N......... 22
- '91 g Mabel E.......169

Merrifield
- '67 Orinda..........107

INDEX.

Merrill
 '51 Catharine........ 53
 '68 Clara F...........110
 '11 g Eliza A.......... 29
 '68 g Elizabeth F.......10.)
 '66 F. Gertrude........104
 '60 Ida................ 84
 '51 Jane............... 53
 '77 g L. Bell...........134
 '62 Lucy M............ 91
 '62 Mary E............ 91
 '64 Mary E............ 98
 '74 g Mary H..........125
 '95 May...............182
 '70 g Mina K..........114
 '45 Sarah P........... 34
 '59 Susan 81

Merriman
 '79 Eliza A...........140

Merritt
 '56 Anna T........... 70
 '90 Lucy S............168

Mersereau
 '51 Anna 53

Merwin
 '84 Agnes D..........152
 '62 g Lucy S.......... 89
 '55 Margarett......... 67

Meserve
 '95 g Elizabeth E.......179

Metcalf
 '72 g Dora L..........120
 '58 Ellen E........... 77
 '79 g Evelyn A 139
 '73 g Helen W........123
 '46 g Mary B......10, 36
 '76 Mary E..........132

Metzger
 '58 g Minerva M....... 76

Mildrum
 '95 Clara E..........182

Miles
 '81 Harriet J.........145
 '46 g Jane M......... 36
 '54 Myra E.......... 63

Millar
 63 Julia A........... 94

Millard
 '89 Edith H..........166
 '48 Hannah.......... 44
 '59 Mary L.......... 81
 '73 Phebe...........124

Miller
 '77 Addie E..........136
 '77 Adele S..........136
 '78 g Anna E..........137
 '90 Belle P...........168
 '82 Bertha A.........147
 '38 Bethiah C........ 17
 '85 g C. Irene........154
 '92 Carrie S..........172
 '90 g Edith R.........167

 '55 Elizabeth H....... 67
 '66 Elizabeth H......104
 '59 Emma J........... 81
 '50 Emma S.......... 50
 '61 Esther A......... 88
 '95 Frances..........182
 '82 H. Adele.........147
 '38 Hannah B........ 17
 '62 Henrietta D...... 91
 '57 Jane A........... 74
 '85 g Laura M........154
 '76 Lucy A..........132
 '82 Lizana F.........147
 '91 Mae.............170
 '45 Maria A.......... 34
 '89 g Marian R.......164
 '73 Martha P........124
 '79 Mary A..........140
 '75 Mary G..........130
 '70 Mary R. C.......116
 '43 Nancy B......... 28
 '61 g Orra E......... 86
 '51 g Sara M......... 51

Millett
 '51 g Laura G........ 51

Milliken
 '87 Carrie T.........160

Mills
 '72 Ada..............122
 '62 g Ellen Z......... 89
 '72 Elizabeth S......122
 '67 Frances C.......107
 '72 Helen C.........122
 '61 Helen S.......... 88
 '52 g Lucy C......12, 54
 '60 Martha A........ 84
 '58 g Sarah L........ 76
 '87 Sarah M........160

Minchew
 '95 Annie A.........182

Miner
 '58 Almira P........ 78
 '60 g Anna J........ 83
 '73 g Anna R........123
 '73 Eliza N.........123
 '76 Ellen M.........133
 '82 g Ellen R........146
 '91 g Fannie M......160
 '84 g Ida L..........151
 '51 Marion........... 53
 '40 Sarah B......... 21

Minor
 '80 g Emily T.......142
 '80 Mary R.........143

Mitchell
 '88 g Anna..........161
 '95 Bessie A........182
 '82 Caroline........147
 '61 g Julia P......... 86

Mix
 '49 Mary H......... 47

Miyagawa
 '93 g Toshi..........174

Mobley
 '45 Amanda......... 34
 '45 Martha.......... 34

Monilaws
 '64 Isabel............ 98

Monroe
 '66 Eliza R..........104
 '65 M. Augusta......101

Montague
 '62 Abbie L......... 91
 '68 Alice L..........110
 '87 g Aurelia L......159
 '44 g Clara S........ 29
 '61 Delia M......... 88
 '60 Emily B........ 84
 '45 Harriet.......... 34
 '86 Jennie A........158
 '86 g Jennie L.......156
 '61 g Katherine S.... 86
 '56 Laura M........ 70
 '89 Mary L.........166
 '55 Mary N......... 67
 '88 Mary N.........162
 '57 M. Eugenia..... 74
 '76 Myra M........133

Montgomery
 '70 Fannie..........116
 '95 sp May (Forbush)...184

Monyer
 '64 Mary A......... 98

Moody
 '51 g Anna W....... 51
 '58 Catharine R..... 78
 '42 Eliza P.......... 25
 '68 g Ellen L........109
 '41 Irene M........ 22
 '93 g Julia E........174
 '94 g Julia E........177
 '54 g Mary L....... 61
 '71 g S. Adelaide....117
 '78 Sarah M........138

Moore
 '38 g Abigail....7, 10, 13, 16
 '42 Elizabeth P..... 25
 '48 g Ellen E....... 42
 '57 g Julia.......... 72
 '71 Julia A.........119
 '39 Julia E......... 19
 '61 Martha......... 88
 '51 Martha M...... 53
 '58 Mary E......... 78
 '67 Melvina M......107
 '54 Rosa........... 63
 '75 Sarah A........130
 '54 Sarah M........ 63
 '90 Susan M........167

Morehouse
 '51 Almira.......... 53
 '42 Cynthia......... 25
 '77 g Jennie L.......134

Morey
 '71 Frances W......119

STUDENTS.

Morgan
 '51 Anna............... 54
 '49 Arabella C........ 47
 '56 Charlotte......12, 70
 '82 Hattie L...........147
 '87 Luette J...........160
 '45 Mary F............. 34
 '78 Mary J............138

Morley
 '63 A. Elizabeth...... 94

Morrill
 '61 g Charlotte......... 86
 '72 Edith.............122
 '55 Mary A............ 67
 '48 Sara.............. 44
 '70 Sarah M...........116
 '91 Thena.............170

Morris
 '70 Abby F............116
 '87 Alice A...........160
 '60 Caroline S........ 84
 '71 Delia M...........119
 '64 Elizabeth J....... 98
 '72 g Eliza.............120
 '58 Eliza K........... 78
 '63 Frances S......... 94
 '57 Harriet N......... 74
 '71 Jerusha...........119
 '54 Lois G............ 63
 '52 Lucy P............ 56
 '55 Marie A........... 67
 '86 Sarah L...........158

Morrison
 '58 Adelaide C........ 78
 '63 Helen F........... 94
 '80 Mary M............143
 '57 g Sarah P........... 72

Morrow
 '94 sp Margaret G........178
 '62 R. Sophia......... 91

Morse
 '57 Abbie C........... 74
 '86 Annie L...........158
 '67 Calista S.........107
 '80 g Carrie E..........142
 '47 Catharine S....... 40
 '49 Emeline. 47
 '54 g Emily............. 61
 '94 g Emma D...........177
 '88 g Etta L............161
 '69 Eunice N..........113
 '95 Kate N............182
 '68 Mary E............110

Morton
 '68 Clara W...........110
 '39 Electa F.......... 19
 '54 g Elvira W.......... 61
 '41 Harriet A......... 22
 '57 Judith W.......... 74
 '40 g Lucretia P........ 20
 '40 g Mary E............ 20
 '54 Ruth C............ 63

Moseley
 '71 Eveline J.........119

Mosher
 '50 Mary.............. 50
 '94 g Rhena E...........177

Mosman
 '74 Bessie G..........127
 '79 g Carrie L..........139
 '69 Emma C............113
 '64 Fannie E.......... 98

Mosser
 '85 Lucy E............155

Mott
 '64 Mary J............ 98
 '93 g Sarah F...........174

Moulton
 '50 Emma S............ 50
 '66 g Susan A...........103

Mowle
 '59 E. Jane........... 81

Mowry
 '42 g Ann R...........10, 24
 '55 Eliza R........... 67
 '95 Florence P........182

Mudge
 '68 g Clara H...........109
 '81 g Mary B............144
 '69 g Pamelia J.........112

Mulford
 '53 Maria B........... 60

Munger
 '71 Emma L............119
 '76 Isabel A..........133
 '73 Martha C..........124

Munn
 '67 Margaretta B......107

Munro
 '71 g Mary E............117

Munsell
 '59 Esther E.......11, 81
 '63 g Marion E.......... 86

Munson
 '87 Cora E............160
 '77 Lillian G.........136
 '48 g Mary A.......10, 13, 42
 '86 g Mary J............156
 '95 Maude E...........182

Murch
 '76 Margie J..........133

Murchison
 '50 Annie M........... 50

Murdock
 '78 g Carrie H..........137
 '39 Lucy.............. 19
 '50 g Mary J.........10, 48

Murphy
 '50 Rose H............ 50

Murray
 '92 Elizabeth R.......172

Musgrove
 '93 Carolyn G.........175

Mussey
 '62 Amelia J.......... 91

Muzzy
 '73 g Alice M. M........123
 '54 g Lucy B............ 61

Nash
 '65 Abby H............101
 '53 Clara S........... 60
 '66 Elizabeth C.......104
 '79 Emily E...........140
 '69 Helen M...........113
 '64 Isabella S........ 98
 '66 Louise M..........104
 '39 Mary S............ 19
 '45 Susan I........... 34

Neal
 '95 Lotta E...........182

Neale
 '82 Fanny C...........147
 '50 Jane E............ 50

Near
 '93 Grace.............175

Nearing
 '52 Ellen E........... 56

Nell
 '95 Cora..............182

Nelson
 '62 Anna J............ 91
 '39 Caroline E........ 19
 '71 Lucretia C........119
 '60 Mary E............ 84

Nettleton
 '95 Amy A.............182
 '74 Elnora C..........127
 '57 Martha D.......... 74

Newbury
 '43 Helen M........... 28

Newcomb
 '75 Elizabeth.........130
 '51 g Elizabeth M....... 51
 '48 g Martha L.......10, 42
 '50 Sophia W.......... 50

Newell
 '93 Annie M...........175
 '38 Elizabeth......... 17
 '48 Eliza J........... 44
 '52 Helen M........... 56
 '54 g Julia............. 61
 '63 Marion............ 94
 '85 Minnie S..........155
 '52 Rebecca E......... 56

Newhall
 '88 Anna B............162
 '81 g Edith F...........144
 '64 g Lura E.........10, 96

Newlin
 '79 Annie.............140

INDEX.

Newton
'72 Abby M........122
'41 Abby T.......... 23
'72 Caroline B.......122
'73 Ellen R...........124
'62 Harriet N........ 91
'75 g Martha C........128
'42 Sarah A.......... 25
'65 Sarah P..........101

Nichols
'61 g Adelaide E........ 86
'84 g A. Frances.......151
'82 g C. Adelle.......146
'56 Catharine W...... 70
'75 Charlotte C 130
'95 sp Edith 184
'48 g Eliza J.......... 42
'80 Emma J..........143
'91 Etta S............170
'50 Frances E........ 50
'51 Harriet S......... 54
'74 Jane E...........127
'57 g Laura A.......... 72
'56 g Laura B.......... 68
'57 g Martha W........ 72
'61 Ruth S............ 88
'94 Susie P..........178

Nicholson
'42 Selinda T. L....... 25

Nickerson
'52 Almira M 56
'45 Bethia S......... 34
'44 Eleanor.......... 31

Niles
'45 g Harriet S......... 32
'72 g Kate M..........120
'47 g Mary E.......... 39

Nims
'52 Abbie............. 57
'68 g Delia............109
'52 Esther........... 57

Noble
'46 Eliza R.......... 57
'57 Frances H........ 74
'58 g Hannah........10, 76
'66 Margaret E.......104
'47 Sarah M.......... 40

Nolton
'64 g Clara A......... 96
'08 g Julia E..........109

Nooney
'43 Abigail........... 28

Norcross
'48 g Emily L......... 42
'66 g Roseltha A......103

Norris
'67 Lucy G..........107

North
'95 g Eva M..........179
'51 g Harriet M........ 51
'51 Helen P......... 54
'58 g Julia S.......... 76

'65 g Mary A..........100
'54 g Sarah M......... 61

Northrop
'95 Evelyn H........182
'94 Helen............178

Norton
'63 Alice L.......... 94
'73 Annie B.........124
'81 g Belle M.........144
'56 Catharine 70
'77 g Cornelia A......134
'45 Cornelia D....... 34
'61 Deborah......... 88
'67 g Delia H.........106
'91 Effie J...........170
'83 Emma S.........150
'03 Fannie E........ 94
'63 g Frances A....... 92
'63 g Helen S........ 92
'82 Ida E...........147
'52 Louise C........ 57
'61 Lucy M.......... 88
'70 Martha J........116
'53 Mary Ellen....... 60
'50 Mary R.......... 50

Norwood
'63 Elizabeth........ 94
'81 g N. Louise......144

Nott
'63 g Mary P......... 92

Noyes
'59 Anna............ 81
'90 g Cora J..........167
'70 Charlotte E......116
'71 Clara M.........119
'58 Cynthia E....... 78
'62 g Elizabeth M..... 89
'72 g Ella M..........120
'54 Emily M........ 63
'95 sp Eva J..........184
'42 Harmony A...... 25
'72 g Mary E.........120
'95 Nellie M.........182
'59 g Zoe A. M....... 79

Nutt
'61 Mary L.......... 88

Nutter
'72 g Laura F.........120

Nutting
'87 g Mary H.........159
'52 g Mary O......10, 14, 54

Nye
'95 g Grace..........179
'87 Helen H.........190

Oakman
'68 J. Kate.........110

Ober
'67 g Louise L........106

O'Dwyer
'48 Mary J.......... 44

O'Farrell
'57 Adaline E........ 74

Olcott
'53 g Ann M.......... 58

Oldham
'84 Marie A. M......152

Olin
'92 g Jenny..........171
'61 Millicent A....... 88

Oliphant
'45 g Mary P......... 32

Olmstead
'84 g Caroline W......151
'70 Mary L..........116
'54 M. Cornelia..... 63
'54 Sarah F......... 63

Olmsted
'45 g Anna M........ 32
'49 g Elizabeth S..... 45

Olney
'58 Frances E........ 78

Orcutt
'41 Lucretia F....... 23
'95 Mary C..........182

Ordway
'72 Annie M........122
'40 g Hannah........ 20
'44 Lucy A.......... 31
'45 Susan S........ 34

Ormsby
'83 Helen M.........150

Orr
'80 Mary B.........143
'91 Matilda K.......170

Ortman
'95 sp A. Elizabeth...184

Orton
'64 Beulah C........ 98

Osband
'47 Louisa J........ 40

Osborn
'74 Alice M.........127
'69 Julia A.........113
'91 Mary E.........170

Osborne
'95 g Ella L..........179
'54 Frances M...... 63
'61 Helen E........ 88

Osgood
'45 Anna........... 34
'64 Daphne E....... 98
'73 g Ellen E........123
'47 g Julia H........ 39
'94 g Lucy R.........177
'60 Mary M........ 84
'45 g Sarah H........ 32

STUDENTS. 261

Ostrom
 '82 g Florence V........146
Otis
 '48 Eliza P............ 44
 '68 Luella A..........110
Ottman
 '89 Grace M..........166
Overlock
 '57 Delia A........... 74
 '57 E. Winnefred...... 74
Owen
 '51 Abby............. 54
 '48 g Clarissa........... 42
 '77 Emily............136
 '50 Lucia A........... 50
 '59 Minerva A........ 81
Packard
 '48 Clara S........... 44
 '95 Edith M..........182
 '41 Elizabeth T....... 23
 '40 Eliza L........... 21
 '38 Louisa F.......... 17
 '46 Lucinda J......... 37
 '46 g Sarah D........... 36
Packer
 '62 g Minerva E......... 89
Paden
 '88 g Lulu R............161
 '88 g M. Frances........161
Page
 '84 Clara F..........152
 '75 Delisa T..........130
 '67 Flora F...........107
 '73 g Josephine M 123
 '88 g Julia B............161
 '64 Louise E.......... 98
 '52 Mary F........... 57
 '70 g Mary L...........114
 '39 Nancy J........... 19
 '52 Olive M........... 57
 '71 Sarah E..........119
Paige
 '42 Caroline L........ 25
 '68 g Cordelia.. 109
 '63 g Lucy A............ 92
 '72 Mary C..........122
 '70 S. Elizabeth......116
Paine
 '44 Amelia O.......... 31
 '76 Dolly E..........133
 '40 Elizabeth......... 21
 '48 Eliza............. 44
 '86 g Emily F..........156
 '52 Hannah C........ 57
 '60 g Harriet M......... 83
 '75 g M. Evangeline....128
 '61 Mary E........... 88
 '56 Sarah L........... 70
 '41 g Sarah M.......13, 22
Painter
 '54 Elizabeth W...... 63
 '52 g Julia M........... 55

Palmer
 '86 Bertha...........158
 '41 Caroline.......... 23
 '74 g Celia L...........125
 '63 g Elizabeth C....... 92
 '68 Louise M.........110
 '41 Mary S........... 23
 '79 Nettie M.........140
 '63 Phebe............ 94
 '65 Rachel E.........101
Parce
 '56 g Sarah E........... 68
Pardee
 '59 Julia A........... 81
Parish
 '69 Lizzie...........113
 '52 Mary A........... 57
Park
 '41 Harriet S......... 23
 '95 Jennie A.........182
 '91 g Mary I...........169
 '93 g Mary I...........174
Parke
 '50 B. Jane R......... 50
Parker
 '72 Abbie M 122
 '57 g Anna E........... 72
 '53 g Fidella A......... 58
 '72 g Florence F........120
 '46 Henrietta......... 37
 '83 g Hortense.........148
 '74 g Ida F............125
 '54 Laura E.......... 63
 '47 g Lucy A........... 39
 '45 Margaret A....... 34
 '77 Mary E..........136
 '41 Mary J........... 23
 '82 N. Gertrude......147
 '88 g Orra A...........161
Parkhurst
 '47 Caroline M....... 40
 '46 Emily R.......... 37
 '63 Helen M. A....... 94
 '42 Sarah E.......... 25
Parkinson
 '45 Frances C........ 34
Parkman
 '43 H. Sophia........ 28
Parks
 '95 sp Greta.............184
 '49 Sarah E.......... 47
Parmelee
 '07 Emily S..........107
 '56 Lizzie A.......... 71
 '61 g Olive L.......10, 86
Parrey
 '57 g A. Maria.......... 72
Parry
 '52 Mary A........... 57
Parshley
 '58 Maria A.......... 78

Parsons
 '73 g Alice C...........123
 '95 g Angie E..........179
 '70 g Anna A......10, 115
 '69 Anna E..........113
 '83 Edith...........150
 '71 E. Lillie.........119
 '73 g Ellen A..........123
 '63 g Ellen C........10, 92
 '87 g Emma L.........159
 '66 Fanny S.........104
 '48 Harriet S........ 44
 '64 g Henrietta D...... 96
 '65 g Julia T..........100
 '80 g Katherine E......142
 '91 g Lillian G........169
 '66 Maria F.........104
 '45 g Mary E.......... 32
 '46 Mary J.......... 37
 '71 g Myra E..........117
 '41 g Roxana R......10, 22
 '66 g Sarah P.......10, 103
 '50 S. Elizabeth..... 50
Partric
 '91 Mary F..........170
Partridge
 '65 C. Adelaide......101
 '53 Eleanor A........ 60
 '55 Harriet H........ 67
 '49 Lydia S.......... 47
 '86 Mary L..........158
Patch
 '82 Martha A........147
 '83 g Mary H..........148
Patrick
 '92 g Augusta L........171
 '61 g Ellen M.......... 86
 '48 Madelia A....... 44
 '49 Maria L.......... 47
 '87 Mary L..........160
 '48 Mary R.......... 44
 '86 g Sarah L..........156
Pattangall
 '89 g Kate H..........164
 '94 g Kate H..........177
Patten
 '50 Elizabeth........ 50
 '91 g Lilian W.........169
 '91 g Marion T........169
 '85 Mary L..........155
Patterson
 '86 Mary S..........158
Paul
 '69 Sarah A.........113
Payn
 '79 Mary L..........140
Payne
 '63 g Etta.............. 92
 '76 Harriet B........133
Payson
 '45 Sarah E.......... 34

INDEX.

Peabody
- '70 Anna L............116
- '46 Ann Maria........37
- '79 Annie C.........140
- '48 g Helen..........10, 42
- '67 g Hontas A........106
- '68 g Lavinia........109
- '70 g Mary C........115
- '61 g Mary E........13, 86
- '48 g Matilda F......42
- '44 g Melissa........29

Pearce
- '75 Elizabeth........130

Pearson
- '95 Florence I......182
- '65 Grace............101
- '53 g Mary E.........58
- '60 Sarah............84

Pease
- '78 Annie............138
- '76 Clara A..........133
- '51 g Delia S........51
- '45 Elizabeth M......34
- '71 Eunice M........119
- '86 g Harriet R......156
- '67 Henrietta M.....107
- '95 Jennie E........182
- '86 Katharine F.....158
- '51 Maria E..........54
- '45 g Mary C.........32
- '82 g Mary E........146
- '58 g Mary J.........76

Peck
- '40 Abigail..........21
- '58 g Anna M.........76
- '76 g Elizabeth L...12, 131
- '66 Fannie M........104
- '50 Harriette M......50
- '82 g Jenny.........146
- '63 Juliet E.........94
- '95 Margaret........182
- '81 Marianna........145
- '58 Mary F...........78
- '62 Mary I...........91
- '52 Nancy G..........57
- '81 Sarah N.........145
- '76 Susan A.........133

Peckham
- '67 g Ella L. T.....106
- '61 g Catherine F....86
- '74 g Mary D........125
- '67 g S. Grace......106

Peet
- '83 g Ellen L.......148
- '71 g Frances R.....117
- '66 Jane S..........104

Pelkey
- '77 Mary L..........136

Pellet
- '47 Charlotte........40

Pelton
- '59 Emily O..........81
- '56 Mary A...........71

Pendleton
- '41 Lydia E..........23
- '41 Mary N...........23

Penfield
- '73 Annie F.........124
- '45 Catharine J......34
- '56 Cornelia A.......71
- '82 Edith...........147
- '39 Eleanor B........19
- '81 g Esther J......144
- '60 Frances E........84

Penniman
- '59 g Sarah T........79

Pennock
- '81 g Emma R........144

Penny
- '50 g Elizabeth W....48

Percival
- '95 Mary............182

Perkins
- '75 Blanche.........130
- '43 Ellen L..........28
- '90 Izzetta B.......168
- '59 Lucy M...........81
- '45 Mary D...........34
- '52 Mary D...........57
- '58 Mary F...........78
- '64 M. Isabella......98
- '45 g Rhoda K........32
- '69 Sarah A........113
- '76 Sarah E.........133

Perrin
- '53 Anna.............60
- '70 Emily F.........116

Perrine
- '96 sp Elizabeth S..184

Perry
- '77 Elizabeth H.....136
- '86 Esther M........158
- '69 Eunice L........113
- '52 Flora H..........57
- '64 Harriet E........98
- '79 M. Stella.......140
- '68 Marion E........110
- '66 g Martha........103
- '61 g Martha A.......86
- '43 Martha K.........28
- '58 Mary J...........78
- '88 Mary J..........162
- '66 g Mary M........103
- '54 Mary S...........63
- '78 Meta C..........138
- '60 g Nancy..........83
- '59 Phebe S..........81
- '58 g Sarah A. C.....76

Persons
- '86 Mary S..........158

Peters
- '78 M. Ella.........138

Petrie
- '50 Ellen A..........50
- '69 Kate M..........113

Pettee
- '81 g Adaline F.....144
- '58 Bertha E.........78
- '88 g Emma L........161
- '43 Harriet N........28
- '93 Julia L.........175

Pettengill
- '95 Agnes E.........182
- '84 Annie G.........152
- '85 Ellen S.........155
- '89 g Grace F.......164
- '95 Lillian.........182

Pettibone
- '85 g Emily F.......154
- '78 Mary C..........138
- '64 g M. Louise......96

Phelps
- '59 Alice D..........81
- '46 Anna C...........37
- '48 Emma M...........44
- '40 Fidelia..........21
- '83 Fidelia.........150
- '69 g Frances L.....112
- '78 Katherine L.....138
- '45 Martha...........34
- '56 g Mary...........68
- '77 g Mary A........134
- '84 g Mary E........151
- '48 Mary F...........44

Philbrick
- '69 Arianna S.......113
- '48 g Elizabeth A....42

Philbrook
- '57 Susan N..........74

Phillips
- '81 Adelaide S....13, 145
- '87 Elizabeth R.....160
- '47 g Elizabeth W....39
- '53 Jane Y...........
- '87 Lenore H........160
- '75 Mary L..........130
- '87 g Mary L........159
- '74 Mary O..........127
- '41 Sarah B..........23
- '85 g Zoe I.........154

Phinney
- '52 g Mary F......10, 55
- '60 Harriet N........84

Phipps
- '95 sp Harriet......184
- '62 Marion J.........91

Pickit
- '64 g Sarah..........96

Pier
- '43 Amelia S.........28
- '45 Eveline H........34
- '45 Louisa W.........34

Pierce
- '68 Anna K..........110
- '57 Augusta E........74
- '91 g Bertha A......169
- '64 Delia M..........98
- '85 Emma E..........155

STUDENTS. 263

'68 Emma L............110
'84 Helen A........... 152
'46 Julia C............ 37
'95 Marion............182
'81 Minnie H..........145
'68 R. Ellen...........110
Pierpont
'45 Mary J............ 35
'45 Susan S........... 35
Pierson
'90 g Eliza D...........167
'92 sp Fannie L.........173
'94 Harriet W......... 178
Pike
'64 Adaline A......... 98
'49 Harriet N......... 47
'67 g Sarah W..........106
Pilling
'86 Mary E.............158
Pillsbury
'60 Emma L........... 84
'65 g M. Abble.........100
Pilsbury
'94 Annie K...........178
Pingle
'82 Grace.............147
Pingrey
'86 Mary E............158
Pinkham
'92 Georgia A.........172
Piper
'71 Marietta..........119
Pitcher
'73 g Eliza M..........123
'57 Emma E........... 74
Pitkin
'45 g Elizabeth......... 32
'89 g Grace C..........164
'48 Jerusha C......... 44
Pitts
'59 g Helen............ 80
'59 g Jane W.......... 80
Pixley
'47 Alzina V.......... 40
'86 g Martha H.........156
Platt
'79 Ella M............140
80 Eva C.............143
'91 Jeannette E........170
'38 Sarah............. 17
Platts
'63 H. Ellen.......... 94
'76 Lizzie F..........133
Plimpton
'47 Catharine......... 41
'71 g C. Idella.........117
'48 g H. Louisa........ 42
Plotts
'62 Catharine W....... 91

Plowman
'73 Mary.............124
Plumb
'95 Mary L...........182
Plumer
'87 g Catharine M......159
'59 Elizabeth M...... 81
'75 Mary F...........130
Plummer
'51 Harriet M........ 54
'67 g Mary W 106
Poland
'62 g Mary F.......... 90
Pollard
'52 Mary A. B........ 57
Pomeroy
'95 Annie L..........182
'51 Candace L........ 54
'56 Emily............ 71
'52 g Harriet S........ 55
'88 g Hattie T.........161
'38 Jerusha........... 17
'44 g Lucinda.......... 29
'44 Lydia B.......... 31
'54 Maria E.......... 63
'42 Miranda.......... 25
'45 Phebe W......... 35
'46 S. Catharine...... 37
Pond
'76 Annie W..........133
'57 g Clara C.........10, 72
'75 Ida E.............130
'74 g Kate C...........126
'57 Lucy G.......... 74
'45 g Mary A.......... 32
Poole
'59 Caroline.......... 81
'44 Henrietta........ 31
'59 Sophia A......... 81
Poor
'06 g Annie L..........103
'74 Clara A..........127
'66 Rebecca J........104
Poore
'59 g Mary............ 80
Pope
'73 g Frances E........123
'39 Harriet A........ 19
'78 Jessie D..........138
Porter
'74 g Ada I............126
'72 Ada M 122
'65 g Alice............100
'08 g Augusta A........109
'44 g Catherine A....10, 29
'52 g Catharine M..... 55
'82 Ella V...........147
'62 g Hannah M........ 90
'79 Kittie H..........140
'54 g Mary A. L....... 61
'66 Matenah..........104

Post
'55 g Celestia L....... 65
'81 g Elizabeth F......144
'95 Estelle L........182
'74 Lucy E..........127
'95 g M. Agnes........179
Posten
'76 Mary M..........133
Potter
'61 Calista V........ 88
'42 Elvira S......... 25
'61 Maria E......... 88
'63 Mary J.......... 94
'42 Virginia......... 25
Potts
'63 g Amelia P........ 92
'61 Margaretta S..... 88
'61 Olivia A......... 88
Potwine
'65 Mary E..........101
Powell
'45 Harriet N........ 35
Powers
'69 Ellen M..........113
'68 g Harriet G........109
'65 Kate W..........101
'69 Mary L..........113
'69 Winifred K.......113
Powis
'58 g Emma A......... 76
Pranker
'53 Elizabeth M..... 60
Pratt
'68 Adaline M........110
'54 Anna A.......... 63
'77 g Augusta C........134
'60 Cornelia B...... 85
'51 Elizabeth A..... 54
'73 Emily F..........124
'58 Emily J.......... 78
'84 g Ettie E..........151
'52 Frances L........ 57
'76 Harriette J.......133
'74 g Helen M..........126
'59 g Jane L.......... 80
'48 g Jane W.......... 42
'56 g Julia L.......... 68
'88 Lizzie J.........162
'67 M. Ella..........107
'52 Martha A........ 57
'65 g Mary C..........100
'41 Mary J.......... 23
'83 g Mary J..........148
'58 Sarah M......... 78
Pray
'69 Ella P...........113
Preble
'49 Louisa........... 47
Prentice
'82 E. Helen.........147
'93 Helen............175

INDEX.

Prentiss
'62 *g* Elizabeth B.....10, 90
'92 *sp* Mary J............173
Prescott
'86 *g* Harriet B..........156
'67   Helen..............107
'72   Louise S...........122
'53 *g* Lucinda T........10, 58
Preston
'49   Amanda............ 47
'79   Ellen M............140
'46 *g* Frances O.......... 36
'49   Mary E............. 47
'79 *g* Mary O............139
Price
'77   Harriet............136
'47   Helen F............ 41
'70 *g* Martha E..........115
Prince
'58   Henriette M....... 78
Pritchard
'45   Elizabeth A....... 35
Pritchett
'88   Sadie B............162
Probasco
'79   Lydia C............141
'79   Sarah A............141
Procter
'70 *g* Ella L.............115
Proctor
'72   Clara E............122
'45   Edna Dean......... 35
Proseus
'59   Mary C............ 81
Proudfit
'60   Elizabeth L....... 85
Pulsifer
'95 *sp* Mary H............184
Purdy
'52   Anna E............ 57
Purington
'93   Emily.............175
'86 *g* Florence...... 10, 156
Purinton
'71   Mary L............119
Pusey
'84   Sophia S..........153
Putnam
'54   Ellen A........... 63
'69   Emma C...........113
'42   Harriot O.......... 26
'45   Julia.............. 35
'50 *g* Julia M............ 48
'46   Lucy P............ 38
'43   Mary P............ 28
'54 *g* Phebe E........... 61
'41   Sarah (Bradstreet) 23
Pyle
'89 *g* Belle H............165

Pyne
'79   Mary S............141
Quick
'91 *g* Leila C............169
'92 *g* Marian J..........171
'58   Sarah W.......... 78
Radford
'45   Elizabeth H....... 35
Ramsdell
'71   Ada E............119
'48   Hannah P......... 44
Ramsey
'80   Callie E...........143
'75   Loretta A.........130
Rand
'78   Ella A............138
Randall
'39   Amelia............ 19
'62   Anna L............ 91
'65   Elizabeth P.......101
'60   Elnora E.......... 85
'76   Harriette D.......133
'45   Lucretia M........ 35
'56   Sophia W......... 71
Randolph
'91 *g* Helen C. F........169
'72 *g* Louise F........10, 120
Rankin
'55   Lois A............ 67
'47 *g* Lucy A........... 39
'95 *sp* Mary H...........184
Ranlett
'61 *g* Elizabeth F....... 86
Ranney
'62   Martha C......... 91
'65   Phebe A..........101
'42   Sarah S.......... 26
'64   Stella E.......... 98
Ransom
'95   Caroline L........182
'78 *g* Emma............137
'46   Sarah A.......... 38
'53   Susan H.......... 60
Rathburn
'85   Maud E..........155
Rauch
'81 *g* Marion B..........144
Rawles
'86   Mary W..........158
Rawson
'66   Martha L........104
Ray
'81 *g* Amelia S..........144
Raymond
'46   Emma A.......... 38
'76   Fanny E..........133
'46   P. Jane........... 38
Rayner
'58 *g* Charlotte W..... 76

Raynolds
'71   Mary C...........119
Rea
'60 *g* E. A. Adelaide..... 83
'58   Harriette......... 78
Read
'65 *g* Eliza J............100
'70 *g* Georgiana........115
Reamer
'74   Cassie A.........127
Reamy
'62   Martha............ 91
'62   Sidney............ 91
Redington
'60   Sarah E.......... 85
Redman
'64   Abbie S.......... 98
'95   Edith.............182
'57   Jane.............. 74
Reed
'78 *g* Addie L..........137
'64   Amelia C......... 98
'55   Anna.............. 67
'74   Anna G..........127
'58   Anna P........... 78
'68   Anna S..........110
'95   Cora P...........182
'46   Cornelia A....... 38
'48   Eliza S........... 44
'93   Elizabeth F......176
'48   Emily D.......... 44
'68 *g* Emily W..........109
'66 *g* Emma L..........103
'60   Frances G........ 85
'64 *g* Harriet E......10, 96
'55 *g* Harriet S......... 65
'76 *g* Jane E...........131
'93   Kate L...........176
'50   Mary A........... 50
'40   Rhoda A.......... 21
'39 *g* Susan.......10, 13, 18
'47   Susan W......... 41
Reeve
'55   Maria............. 67
'55   Sarah M.......... 67
Reeves
'60 *g* Mary A........... 83
Reid
'87   Alice B...........160
'53   Elizabeth A...... 60
'67   Ellen E...........108
'93 *sp* Martha M........176
Reimer
'85   Fanny...........155
Relyea
'81 *g* Grace H..........144
Remington
'52   Sarah E.......... 57
Remsen
'62 *g* Eliza W........... 90

STUDENTS.   265

Renue
 '66 *g* Zelma H............103
Rex
 '57 Frances L........... 74
Rexford
 '81 *g* Mary E............144
Reynolds
 '95 Agnes R............182
 '90 *g* Edith M............167
Rhody
 '87 Margaret A....... 160
Rhyne
 '88 *g* Loula M............161
Rice
 '41 Abby C............. 23
 '67 *g* Anna E............106
 '71 Anne R.............119
 '93 *g* Caroline K........174
 '41 Charlotte.......... 23
 '54 Charlotte M....... 63
 '91 *g* Corinne L.......... 169
 '48 Elizabeth A........ 44
 '69 Ella M.............113
 '61 *g* Emily M............ 86
 '75 Fannie I...........130
 '61 *g* Feronia N......... 86
 '49 Frances M......... 47
 '48 *g* Hannah E......... 42
 '38 Harriet............ 17
 '88 *g* Harriet W.........161
 '56 *g* Laura A........... 68
 '45 *g* Lois W..........10, 32
 '49 Louisa J........... 47
 '43 Lucretia.......... 28
 '79 Mary A............141
 '46 *g* Mary S............ 36
 '67 Mary W............108
 '80 Minnie J...........143
 '45 Nancy M........... 35
 '56 Sarah............. 71
 '65 Selina A...........101
Rich
 '93 *g* Hattie S............174
 '65 Mary L.............101
Richard
 '95 Dorothy M........182
Richards
 '77 *g* Clara H............134
 '78 Emma W..........138
 '52 Helen C........... 57
 '52 Julia M 57
 '66 *g* Lydia............13, 103
 '95 Mae L.............182
 '92 *g* Mary A...........172
 '75 *g* Nellie C...........128
 '40 Sarah B........... 21
 '55 Sarah G........... 67
 '40 Sarah H........... 21
Richardson
 '93 *g* Abby M............174
 '95 *sp* Annie L......13, 184
 '70 Carrie V...........116
 '47 Emily O........... 41
 '93 Frances C.........176

Renne
 '77 *g* Harriet G..........134
 '70 Lauretta P........116
 '38 Louisa T........... 17
 '43 Martha A.......... 28
 '84 Mary E............153
 '39 Mary L............ 19
 '75 *g* Orrilla D..........128
 '46 *g* Prudence.......... 20
 '39 Sarah W........... 19
Richmond
 '93 Anna..............176
 '66 Catharine A......104
 '43 Frances T......... 28
 '43 Martha E.......... 28
Rider
 '88 *g* Addie M...........161
 '49 Mary F............ 47
Ridlon
 '95 Sarah E...........183
Rieman
 '50 Elizabeth G....... 50
Riggs
 '88 Cora I.............162
 '58 Ellen............. 78
 '88 Grace T..... 162
Ripley
 '72 Louisa W..... 122
Robb
 '85 *g* Julia I............154
Robbins
 '43 Anne E............ 28
 '77 *g* Anne M...........134
 '63 Annie E........... 94
 '87 Elizabeth M......160
 '84 *g* Gertrude..........151
 '77 Grace G...........136
 '46 Mary J............ 38
Robert
 '54 Martha A......... 63
Roberts
 '90 Ethel A...........168
 '53 *g* Jennette.......... 58
 '75 Mary C...........130
 '72 Mary E...........122
 '58 Mary J............ 78
 '88 Minnie E.........162
Robertson
 '48 Margaret M....... 44
 '47 *g* Mary R........... 39
Robie
 '57 *g* Clara A.......... 72
Robinson
 '95 *g* Alice M...........179
 '47 *g* Ama A............ 39
 '69 *g* Ann M............113
 '88 Anna G...........162
 '45 Charlotte L....... 35
 '62 *g* Emily S.......... 90
 '64 Frances C........ 98
 '48 J. A. Lucie......13, 44
 '70 Louise S..........116
 '65 *g* Lydia S...........100

 '95 Mabel S...........183
 '39 Martha............ 19
 '95 Mary B............183
 '91 *g* Mary D............169
 '69 *g* Mary J............112
 '51 Mary M........... 54
 '39 Phebe W.......... 19
 '88 Rosabel T.........162
 '58 *g* Sarah B.......... 76
 '59 Susan R........... 81
Rockwell
 '46 Chloe P........... 38
 '64 Mary F............ 98
 '43 *g* Olivia C.......... 26
Rockwood
 '57 Mary L............ 74
Rooth
 '95 Natalie S..........183
Rolf
 '43 *g* Mary W. (Judd)... 26
Rogers
 '83 Alice E...........150
 '48 Ann E............. 44
 '75 Annie V...........130
 '57 Augusta A........ 74
 '74 Belle A...........127
 '65 Caroline C........101
 '66 Caroline G........104
 '74 Celia A...........127
 '65 Charlotte E......101
 '39 Deidameia S...... 19
 '90 *g* Ella A............167
 '95 E. Gertrude......183
 '58 Harriet M........ 78
 '51 Lavinia J........ 54
 '76 Marcia P.........133
 '42 *g* Martha........... 24
 '64 Martha H........ 98
 '90 Mary..........167, 168
 '89 *g* Mary A...........165
 '66 Mary E........... 104
 '91 *g* Mary L...........169
 '78 Mary P...........138
 '86 May H............158
 '51 Rebecca A........ 54
Rolfe
 '77 Grace I...........136
Rollins
 '72 Caroline L........122
 '72 Kate..............122
 '92 Maud M..........172
Rolston
 '95 Martha B.........183
Romig
 '61 *g* Hannah L......... 86
Ronk
 '70 Letitia B..........116
Rood
 '76 Martha A........133
Root
 '46 Caroline A........ 38
 '64 *g* Caroline E........ 98
 '39 Elizabeth L....... 19

INDEX.

Ro
'64 Frances C..........98
'95 g Helena C..........179
'42 Lucy A............26
'67 Mary A......... 108
'76 g Susan B.........131

Roper
'61 g Ellen E............86
'74 Isabelle M.........127
'58 Jane S............78

Roscoe
'89 Kate M...........166

Rose
'66 Laura A........10, 104
'63 Margaretta........94
'64 g S. Elizabeth.......96

Ross
'64 Charlotte A........98
'54 Kate A............63
'84 Lillian A.........153
'89 g Mary E.........165

Rossiter
'56 Jane............71
'79 Mary............141

Rothrock
'63 g Mary M..........92

Rouillard
'92 Gertrude........172

Rounds
'87 Pauline..........160

Rousseau
'78 Mary L. H........138

Rowe
'59 E. Caroline........81
'59 Eleanor J........81
'70 g Ellen W........115
'71 Rachel A.........119
'40 Sarah E..........21

Rowell
'75 g Mary A........128

Rowland
'69 g Mary S........112
'93 g Tace F.........174

Rowley
'88 Clara..........162
'60 Mary J..........85

Royce
'64 Gertrude M......98
'63 Lillian M.......94

Roys
'60 Martha E........85
'42 Rhoda A..........26

Ruggles
'92 sp Eleanor M.....173
'49 Elizabeth C......47
'86 Ellen L.........158
'73 M. Theolotia...124

Rule
'68 Selina A........110

Rumiser
'62 Louisa..........91

Rumsey
'84 Emma V.........153

Rundall
'56 Sarah I..........71

Rundell
'75 Emma A........130

Runnette
'94 Grace..........178

Rush
'55 Amanda..........67

Russ
'44 Eliza P..........31

Russell
'43 Catherine........28
'61 Charlotte M......88
'65 Harriet H.......101
'89 Martha M.......166
'56 Mary M..........71
'64 Sarah N..........98
'46 Susan............38

Rust
'51 Elizabeth W......54
'54 Eliza A..........63

Ryder
'57 Annette E........74

Rymph
'67 Jane E.........108

Saben
'75 Mary..........130

Sabin
'65 g Abbie D.......100
'84 Emily O.........153
'68 Helen A.........111
'62 g Maria D........90

Saeger
'58 Emma W..........78

Safford
'84 Annette.......153
'53 Frances I........60
'44 Helen E.........31
'77 Louise S.......136

Sagar
'84 g Sarah.........151

Sage
'41 Elizabeth A......23
'88 L. Belle.......162

St. John
'92 Julia E........173
'58 g Mary C........76

Salmon
'81 Anna F........145

Salt
'73 g Elinor M.....123

Sampson
'69 Amelia J......113
'40 g Bessie S......167
'65 g Eliza J.......100

Samson
'53 Harriet........60
'59 Mary M.........81

Samuel
'80 g Elizabeth I...10, 142

Sanborn
'82 Alice C.......147
'88 Amy G........162
'88 Frances S...13, 162
'64 Mary E.........98
'69 g Mary A.....112
'49 Susan A........47

Sanders
'68 Ellen F.......111
'48 Frances C......44
'41 Lucy S.........23
'43 Mary J.........28

Sanderson
'78 Lucia..........138
'44 Lucy W.........31
'95 g Lydia E.....179
'64 Maria I........98
'82 Mary E........147

Sandford
'43 Sarah..........28

Sands
'44 Catharine.......31

Sanford
'48 Caroline U......44
'78 Elizabeth E...138
'92 g Emma D......172
'48 Emily..........44
'48 Harriet N......44
'54 Jane...........63
'87 g May E......159

Sanger
'95 Abbie M......183

Sargeant
'50 g Cordelia......48
'70 Ellen F......116
'47 Maria..........41

Sargent
'58 g Adeline......76
'67 Ellen H......108
'58 Cornelia.......78
'52 Frances M......57
'95 g Martha A...179
'85 Mary E......155
'81 Sarah L.....145

Saunders
'84 Lucy B.......153

Savage
'84 Charlotte E...153
'40 Harriet B.....21
'78 Harriet E....138
'68 g Helen M...10, 109
'45 Jane W........35

STUDENTS. 267

'42 g Maria................ 24
'94   Marietta I........178
'67   Ruth F............108
Sawin
'39   Catharine F........ 19
'71   Cora L............119
'73   Ella F............ 124
Sawyer
'49   Ann E.............. 47
'68 g Annie E..........109
'40   Catharine......... 21
'70   Emma C. 116
'57 sp Flora A....s...... 72
'72   Julia L............122
'63   Kathreen A........ 94
'63   Laura A........... 94
'39   Martha............ 19
'60   Martha M......... 85
'79 g Mary A..........139
'76 g Mary L..........131
'63 g Mary N.......... 92
'75   S. Emma 130
Saxton
'95   Mary L............183
Sayre
'82   Anna P........... 147
Scales
'44 g Sarah M........... 29
Scammell
'61   Amanda C........ 88
Scarborough
'74 g Mary F..........126
Schanck
'53   Eleanor H........ 60
Schirmer
'54   Adelle E.......... 63
von Schrader
'87 g Bertha...........159
'90 g Laura............167
'92 g Rosamund S..... 172
Schradi
'79   Charlotte H......141
Schultz
'50   Margaret A....... 50
Schumacher
'94 g Rosalie...........178
Schuyler
'45 g Julia W.......... 32
'81   Mabel E..........145
Schwartz
'87 g Jennie E........159
Schwendler
'95 g Sadie.............179
Scism
'93 sp Josephine..........176
Scofield
'86 g Jane..............156
'54   Louisa H......... 63

'53   Mary E............ 60
'86 g Sarah C..........156
Scott
'55   Caroline S........ 67
'52 g Emily A.........10, 55
'56   Emma............ 71
'78   Frances M........138
'48 g Hannah C......10, 42
'79 g Hettie E.........139
'45 g Martha C......10, 32
'72 g Mary H.........120
'91   Rachel T........170
'58   Watie A.......... 78
Scovell
'48   Julia R............ 44
Scoville
'85   Elizabeth W...... 155
Scribner
'63 g Abbie............. 93
'72 g Julia A. G........120
'54   Louisa J......... 63
'54 g Sarah E......... 61
'61   S. Grace......... 88
Scrogy
'75   Mary A..........130
Scrugham
'43   Eleanor L........ 28
'44   Elizabeth........ 31
Scudder
'60   Agnes H......... 85
'85   Harriet 155
'95 sp Isabelle..........184
'46   Jane M......... 38
'86 g Sarah W.........156
Seabury
'45   Caroline R....... 35
'49   Helen F......... 47
Seamans
85 g Ida E...........154
Searle
'95 g Clara P.........179
'76 g Minnie F........131
Sears
'92   Amelia N 173
'92 sp Bertha M.........173
'62   Eleanor W....... 91
'56   Elizabeth....... 71
'47   Eliza H......... 41
'90   Eugenia C.......168
'43   Harriet.......... 28
'43   Lucy A.......... 28
'45   Mary J......... 35
'54   M. Eliza......... 63
'69 g Sarah E.........112
Seaton
'59   Mary E......... 81
'59   S. Frances........ 81
Seaver
'45   Angeline T........ 35
'63   Anna M......... 94
'43   Elizabeth W...... 28
'56 g Ellen E......... 68

'44   Hannah P....... 31
'42   Sarah R......... 26
Seavey
'56   Anna M.......... 71
'56 g Ellen A... 68
'56   Mary J.......... 71
Sedgwick
'42   Elizabeth S....... 26
'91 g Mabel J..........169
'92 sp Mabel J..........173
Seely
'90 g Caroline M.. 167
'58   Louise M 78
Seelye
'47   Elizabeth B...... 41
Selden
'47   Cynthia M....... 41
Sellon
'42   Eliza A.......... 26
Serfass
'63   Maria J.......... 94
Sessions
'56 g Harriet E........10, 68
'60 g Laura R.......... 83
'56 g Lydia A........10, 68
'58   Mary E......... 78
'56 g Mary D......... 68
Severy
'86   Nellie M........158
Seward
'52   Fanny H......... 57
Seymour
'62   Amelia........... 91
'88   Charlotte M.....162
'44   Mary A......... 31
'55   Mary A......... 67
'77   Mary C.........136
'95   Mary C.........183
'85   Mary E.........155
'95   Mary F.........183
'88   May............162
'80 g M. Oretha.......142
'41   Susan S......... 23
Shackleton
'58   Lucy M.......... 78
Shafer
'82   Helen M.........147
Shank
'95   Jessie L..........183
Sharp
'66   Abby J..........104
'62 g Caroline B....... 90
'76   Katherine A......133
Shattuck
'64   Emma J........ 98
'70   Georgiana E......116
'74   Helen W........127
'74   Ida E...........127
'74   Loella V........127

INDEX.

Shaw
'51 *g* Lydia W..... ...10, 51
'61 Mary A........... 98
'57 *g* Alice T............ 72
'80 Caroline M........143
'47 Hannah L. 41
'60 Helen F........... 85
'83 Lucy A...........150
'93 M. Agnes..........176
'80 Mary J....:.......143
'63 Priscilla B........ 94
'60 Sarah H.......... 85

Shaylor
'76 Emma A..... 133

Shearer
'95 Elizabeth E.......183

Shedd
'89 Jessie............166

Sheffield
'65 Sarah F...........101

Sheldon
'58 Catharine C....... 78
'66 *g* Clara.............103
'69 Jennie M..........113
'83 Jessie H..........150
'95 Lena.............183
'46 Mary............. 38
'41 Nancy C......... 23
'80 Nellie D 166

Shepard
'57 *g* Elizabeth W .. 12, 72
'88 Ellen F...........162
'69 Susan N..........113
'38 Wealthy H....... 17

Shepperd
'87 *g* Marion...........159

Sherman
'95 Anna P...........183
'40 Jane T............ 21
'80 *g* Lillie L..... .10, 13, 142
'86 Marion L.........158
'89 Sara L...........166
'44 Sarah P.......... 31

Sherwood
'45 *g* Eveline A......... 32
'84 Harriet A.........153
'47 *g* Marietta........... 39
'60 Mary A........... 85
'42 Mary C 26

Shiland
'54 Jennette.......... 63

Shipman
'93 Helen E.......... 94

Shively
'81 Flora L.......141, 145

Shney
'88 Elizabeth M.......162

Shumway
'59 *g* Catharine A....... 80
'73 *g* Emma A..........123
'75 Leila S...........130

'61 *g* Mary E............ 86
'85 Mary F......... ..155
'39 Mary H........... 19
'40 *g* Zeviah L.......... 20

Sibley
'60 *g* Mary L............ 83
'59 Persis H......... 81
'39 Sarah A.......... 19

Sickels
'72 Emma C........122

Siegfried
'62 Sarah A.....:.... 91

Sigourney
'78 Myrtis S.........138

Silkman
'89 *g* Emille C.........165
'79 Katherine A......141

Sill
'56 Louisa P......... 71

Simes
'45 Sarah E. 35

Simmons
'65 *g* M. Elizabeth 100
'88 Mary E..........162

Simonton
'84 Martha S.........153

Simpson
'75 Helen L..........130
'78 L. Ida...........138
'91 *sp* Margaret F.......171
'66 Sarah E..........104

Sipp
'43 Mary E.......... 28

Sisson
'80 Phebe E..........143
'61 Rhoda D......... 88

Skavlem
'89 Caroline.... 166

Skeele
'51 Clara............. 54

Skerry
'58 *g* Mary J............ 76

Skinner
'57 Ellen M.......... 74
'65 Emily D..........101
'66 Helen W.........104
'70 Jane M.......... 50
'49 Sarah............. 47

Slack
'71 Elizabeth H......119

Slate
'47 Harriet A......... 41

Slayton
'77 Mary L..........136

Sleeper
'69 Emma C.........113
'64 Nancy T......... 98

Sloan
'76 *g* Emma J..........131
'53 Mary............. 60
'56 Mary P.......... 71
'72 *g* Virginia G........120

Slocum
'57 *g* Rachel........... 72

Slocumb
'46 Maria R......... 38

Small
'56 *g* Beulah............. 69
'95 Vivian B.........183

Smart
'53 Hannah K....... 60
'53 Mary A......... 60

Smead
'56 *g* A. Amelia......... 69
'64 Jane W.......... 98
'38 Martha A........ 17
'52 *g* Maria L........... 55
'61 *g* Sarah A........... 86

Smith
'91 *sp* Abbie M..........171
'73 *g* Abbie W..........123
'80 Ada K...........143
'77 Adelaide K. 136
'93 Adeline..........176
'69 *g* Alice E...........112
'84 *g* Alice T...........151
'73 Amelia A........124
'46 Anna............. 38
'47 Anna............ 41
'56 *g* Anna E... 69
'81 Anna M..........145
'44 Annie............ 31
'80 *g* Annis A..........142
'92 *g* Annis A..........172
'56 Ann M.......... 71
'57 Antoinette M..... 74
'90 *g* Arma A.....10, 167, 169
'59 Augusta A........ 81
'58 *g* Asenath L........ 76
'52 Caroline T....... 57
'81 *g* Carrie A..........144
'93 *g* Carrie L..........174
'57 Catharine S..... .. 74
'69 *g* Charlotte E.......112
'74 *g* Charlotte E.......126
'48 Charlotte M...... 44
'85 *g* Clara E...........154
'78 *g* Clara N..........137
'61 *g* Clara R........... 86
'56 Cornelia H.......71
'64 Eleanor F....... 98
'60 *g* Electa M......... 83
'51 *g* Eliza............10, 51
'66 Eliza H..........104
'44 Eliza J........... 31
'61 Eliza T.......... 88
'47 Elizabeth A.......41
'67 *g* Elizabeth A.......106
'39 Elizabeth P....... 19
'63 Ella G........... 94
'73 *g* Ellen A..........123
'95 *g* Elsie F...........179
'62 *g* Elvira........... 90
'46 Emily F.......... 38

STUDENTS. 269

		Page
'95	Emily L	183
'77 *y*	Emma C	134
'68	Emma E	111
'85	Emma M	155
'77	Esther R	136
'66	Eunice M	104
'95	Eva F	183
'92	Eva M	173
'86 *y*	Fannie N	156
'78	Flora E	138
'84	Florence N	153
'70 *y*	Frances A	115
'67 *y*	Frances E	106
'49	Francese	47
'44	Harriet A	31
'59 *y*	Harriet B	80
'68	Harriet E	111
'75	Harriet E	130
'64	Helen E	98
'65	Helen M	101
,79 *y*	Helen M	139
,80	Helena A	166
,74	Ida A	127
,83 *y*	Ida V	148
,46 *y*	Isabella	36
,44	Jane	31
'76	J. Belle	133
'84	Jennie A	153
'82	Jennie F	147
'80	Jennie M	143
'91 *y*	Jennie W	169
'91 *sp*	Josephine A	171
'74 *y*	Julia R	126
'68 *y*	Julia S	109
'57	Juliet B	74
'85	Kate L	155
'94 *y*	Kate W	177
'85	Kittie L	155
'86	K. Maude	158
'95	Laura E	183
'66	Laura P	104
'38	Lavinia S	17
'65	Lottie M	101
'44 *y*	Lucy	29
'59	Lucy M	82
'84 *y*	Lucy M	151
'43	Lucy W	28
'73	M. Anna	125
'86 *y*	M. Belle	156
'70	M. Elmina	116
'95	M. Helena	183
'94 *y*	Mabel E	177
'41	Margaret	23
'44	Margaret O	31
'52	Maria	57
'57	Maria D	74
'39	Maria H	19
'88	Marion S	162
'38	Martha	17
'66 *y*	Martha E	103
'59	Martha H	82
'62	Martha I	91
'71	Martha I	119
'56	Martha M	71
'45	Mary	35
'44	Mary A	31
'72	Mary A	122
'70	Mary B	116
'40	Mary C	21
'38	Mary E	17
'71 *y*	Mary E	117

		Page
'70	Mary E	116
'70	Mary E	116
'78	Mary E	138
'53 *y*	Mary J	58
'56	Mary J	71
'56 *y*	Mary J	69
'54	Matilda K	63
'58 *y*	Matilda W	10, 76
'93	Maud E	176
'91	May A	170
'54 *y*	Minerva	10, 61
'39	Miranda A	19
'64	Myra A	98
'85	Nellie L	155
'95	Nellie L	183
'54	Ophelia	63
'73 *y*	Rebecca F	123
'81 *y*	S. Bertha	144
'86 *y*	S. Effie	10, 156
'44 *y*	Sarah	29
'50	Sarah E	50
'88 *y*	Sarah M	161
'95	Stella E	183
'84	Stella R	153
'68	Virginia A	111
'91	Winnifred B	170

Smock
| '88 | Carrie M | 162 |

Smythe
| '87 | Anna M | 160 |

Snell
'92 *y*	Ada L	172
'56	Mary K	71
'66 *y*	Sabra C	103
'53	Sarah	60
'63 *y*	Tirzah S	93

Snow
'74	Carrie I	127
'58	Frances A	78
'55	Julia P	67
'64 *y*	Laura J	96
'56	Phebe	71

Snowdon
| '57 | Susan | 74 |

Solander
| '44 | Eliza A | 31 |

Sollenberger
| '92 | Marion J | 173 |

Solomon
| '51 | Susan E | 54 |

Somers
| '51 *y* | Anna M | 51 |
| '84 | Maude E | 153 |

Somes
| '89 | E. Gertrude | 166 |

Soule
| '86 | Mary C | 158 |
| '95 | Theresa H | 183 |

Southmayd
| '70 | Anna | 116 |

Southwick
| '50 | Sarah J | 50 |

Southworth
		Page
'67	Clara B	108
'56	Lucy M	71
'67 *y*	Sarah Jane	106

Spalding
'46 *y*	Caroline A	36
'81	Isabel	142, 144, 145
'45	Martha E	35
'54 *y*	Mary G	61

Sparhawk
| '73 *y* | Kate W | 123 |

Sparks
| '72 | Clara L | 122 |
| '88 *y* | Alice C | 161 |

Sparrow
| '45 | Sarah A | 35 |
| '50 | Susan | 50 |

Spaulding
'38	Abigail N	17
'74	Harriet L	127
'44	Harriet N	31
'71	Mary	119
'51 *y*	Mary L	52
'42	Sarah J	26

Spear
| '41 | Elizabeth | 23 |
| '59 | Julia S | 82 |

Speer
| '53 | Nancy J | 60 |

Spence
| '94 | Adele P | 178 |

Spencer
'47	Ann E	41
'44	Ardelia A	31
'39	Eliza	19
'58 *y*	Emily A	76
'39	Julia	19
'39	Lucy	19
'50	Susan B	50

Sperry
'49	Ann O	47
'45	Henrietta C	35
'75 *y*	Ruth T	128

Spier
| '62 | Sarah A | 91 |

Spilman
| '77 | Sallie | 136 |

Spofford
| '46 *y* | Sophia | 7, 10, 36 |

Spooner
| '66 *y* | Eliza D | 103 |
| '72 *y* | M. Ella | 10, 120 |

Sprague
'60	Catharine A	85
'42	Eunice	26
'44	Lucy D	31
'69	Mary J	113
'93 *y*	Olive A	174

INDEX.

Staats
'55 *g* Maria A. L. 65
'82 N. Louisa.. 147

Stair
'91 Lillian E. 170

Standish
'70 J. Ella. 116

Stanley
'68 Emily E. 111
'92 *g* Eva M. 172
'94 *g* Irene. 177
'62 Juliet M. 91

Stannard
'76 Lillie S. 133

Stanton
'52 Abby (Willard).... 57
'59 Edna E. 82
'49 *g* Malvina 45
'59 M. Annette........ 82

Staples
'77 Mary E. 136

Starkweather
'51 Elizabeth. 54
'41 Jane C. 23

Start
'52 *g* Sarah A. 11, 55

Stearns
'53 *g* Abbie S. 58
'42 Abby M. 26
'47 Elvira. 41
'70 Fannie E. 116
'69 Flora P. 113
'95 *sp* Harriet M. 184
'90 Ida A. 168
'88 *g* Lucy A. 161
'49 *g* Lucy E. 45
'74 Margaret E. 127
'48 *g* Mary A. 42
'53 *g* Mary F. 11, 58
'74 *g* Mary S. 126

Stebbins
'61 Ellen C. 88
'95 Jessie W. 183
'47 Laverna. 41

Stedman
'72 Hattie M. 122

Steele
'57 Angeline L. 74
'41 Emeline M. 31
'56 Joanna D. 71

Stephens
'60 Mary S. 85

Sterling
'63 Hannah M. L. 95
'72 Jane H. 122

Sterrett
'91 S. Lulu. 170

Stetson
'48 Almira B. 44
'79 Clara 141
'58 *g* Elizabeth T. 76

Stevens
'86 *g* Alice P. 11, 156
'93 *g* Alice P. 175
'55 Caroline A. 67
'95 Carolyn C. 183
'81 *g* Clara F. 11, 144
'46 Eleanor F. 38
'61 Elizabeth B. 88
'48 Elizabeth C. 44
'93 *g* Grace. 175
'45 *g* Helen M. G. 32
'86 *g* Julia W. 156
'95 Louise D. 183
'59 *g* Louise P. 11, 80
'95 Mary A. 183
'52 Mary L. 57
'42 Mary M. 11, 13, 26
'42 Sabra A. 26

Stevenson
'87 *g* Elizabeth E. 159
'92 Emily G. 173
'76 *g* Emma M. 131

Stewart
'57 Eveline. 74
'93 *g* Helen A. 175
'69 M. Frances....... 113
'38 Sarah A. 17
'67 *g* Sarah A. 106

Stickney
'95 Julia H. 183

Stiles
'66 Alice L. 104
'66 Emma B. 105
'62 Flora A. 91
'62 Helen E. 91

Stillman
'41 Jennette 23
'46 *g* Julia E. 36
'40 Lucia M. 21

Stilson
'72 Alice M. 122

Stimson
'80 *g* Juliet W. 142

St. John
(See after Sage.)

Stobaugh
'79 Lizzie M. 141
'79 Nannie E. 141

Stockbridge
'84 Anna. 153
'68 S. Estella. 111
'90 Mina K. 168

Stocking
'55 Harriet N. 67
'61 J. Emily. 88

Stockwell
'93 *g* Adeline R. 175

'81 *g* Emma 153
'89 Julia S. 166
'81 Lula. 153

Stoddard
'88 Alice J. 162
'46 Mary D. 38
'66 *g* Sarah T. 103

Stodder
'95 Elizabeth T. 183

Stoerlein
'95 *sp* Mary 184

Stokes
'89 *g* Jeanie W. 165
'89 *g* Mayne A. 165

Stone
'47 *g* Atossa F. 39
'89 *g* Cora A. 165
'69 Emma A. 113
'88 *g* Fairene M. 161
'90 *g* Florence G. 167
'73 *g* Harriet E. 123
'50 Helen E. 50
'95 Henrietta. 183
'89 *g* Ida. 165
'66 *g* Jane E. 103
'39 Lucy 19
'65 *g* Margarette D. 100
'65 Maria S. 101
'64 Mary B. 98
'50 *g* Mary E. 48
'61 Sarah A. 88

Storm
'72 Fannie A. 122

Storrs
'51 *g* Harriet M 52
'90 Mabel O. 168
'75 Sara A. 130

Stoughton
'67 *g* Anna E. 106
'47 *g* Nancy P. 39

Stout
'85 Anna R. 155
'83 *g* Bertha B. 148
'84 Calore V 153

Stow
'49 Elizabeth P 47

Stowe
'74 Harriette B. 127
'94 *g* Mabel E. 177
'95 Mary E. 183

Stowell
'95 Elizabeth D. 183
'56 *g* Ellen B. 69
'88 Ida G. 162

Stratton
'92 *g* Anna R. 172
'79 Nellie M. 141

Straughan
'77 *g* Caroline W. 134

STUDENTS.

Street
 '78 Luella A............138
Streeter
 '57 g Calista A........11, 72
Strickland
 '57 Ellen M............ 74
 '84 g Helen L..........151
 '59 Miranda E......... 82
Strobridge
 '83 Ellen L............150
Strong
 '41 Abby B............ 23
 '95 Carolyn A.........183
 '53 Elenora H......... 60
 '52 Elizabeth A....... 57
 '56 g Eliza J.......... 69
 '74 Ellen S............127
 '55 Emeline........... 67
 '87 Harriet M.........160
 '94 g Mabel D.........177
 '75 Mary E............130
 '56 Mary J............ 71
 '77 Mary K............136
 '89 Mary R............166
 '61 S. Augusta........ 88
Stryker
 '94 g Minnie..........177
Stuart
 '60 Mary.............. 85
 '90 Mary O...........168
Stubbs
 '95 Helen G...........183
 '49 Helen M........... 47
Studley
 '76 Elma L............133
Sturdevant
 '88 Bertha I..........162
 '55 C. Jane........... 67
Sturges
 '64 g Artemesia E..... 96
 '53 Clarina B......... 60
 '53 Lucretia M........ 60
Sturgess
 '62 g Josephine G..... 90
Sturtevant
 '84 Florence E........153
 '63 Rachel B.......... 95
Styles
 '70 Isabella E........116
Sumner
 '43 Mary H............ 28
Sutherland
 '38 Ann M............ 17
 '68 Ida E.............111
Sutphen
 '95 Minnie C..........183
Sutton
 '68 Adelia W..........111

Swain
 '77 Gabriella.........136
Swan
 '45 Angelina B........ 35
 '47 Ann B............. 41
 '46 Mary S............ 38
Swartz
 '95 g E. Pauline......179
Swasey
 '65 Annette F.........101
Sweasey
 '38 Emeline A........ 17
Sweeney
 '85 Florence D........155
Sweet
 '86 Clara A..........158
 '92 Nellie J..........173
 '86 g Rena E..........156
 '58 g Sadelia S....... 76
Sweetland
 '44 Anne............. 31
Sweetser
 '74 g Abbie L..11,78,126,134
 '58 Abby L........... 78
 '48 g Emily P........ 42
 '69 Katherine A......114
 '76 Martha Z.........133
 '60 g Sarah E 83
Swett
 '58 g Ellen............ 76
 '93 g Frances M...... 93
 '50 Lucy F........... 50
Swezey
 '73 Bertha...........125
 '89 May G............166
Swift
 '66 Anna W..........105
 '88 g Kate B..........161
 '40 Mary M.......... 21
 '95 Nellie H..........183
 '42 Sarah B.......... 26
 '40 Susan M......... 21
Swinerton
 '67 Alice............108
Switzer
 '84 Marie A..........153
Sykes
 '88 Anna G..........163
 '87 g Emily Louise...159
 '53 g Gertrude......11, 58
 '56 Jane S............ 71
 '61 Ruth A.......... 88
Sylva
 '51 Delia............ 54
Sylvester
 '66 g Ida P...........103
 '63 Mary............. 95

Syvret
 '95 Clara M..........183
 '95 g Florence........179
Taber
 '57 Sarah B......... 75
Taft
 '68 Emoretta M......111
 '66 Sarah S..........105
 '76 Theo.............133
Taggart
 '62 g Josephine L..... 90
Taintor
 '87 Ella E............160
Takahashi
 '94 sp Chika..........178
Talbot
 '86 Esther B.........158
Talcott
 '42 Elizabeth A...... 26
 '45 Elizabeth K...... 35
 '53 g Elizabeth O..... 58
 '57 Maria............ 75
 '66 g Martha R........103
 '46 Mary J.......... 38
 '55 g Sarah G........ 65
Tallman
 '82 Emily A.........147
Tandy
 '88 Mabel L.........163
Tanner
 '85 Carolyn C.......155
Taplin
 '50 Susan P......... 50
Tappan
 '40 Caroline G...... . 21
 '70 Lucia............116
Tarbell
 '46 Sarah A......... 38
Tarbet
 '86 Emma H..........158
Tarbox
 '42 Cornelia P....... 26
 '42 Laura........... 26
 '64 Mary M......... 98
Tarr
 '52 Julia M.......... 57
Tatlock
 '55 Jane............ 67
Taylor
 '74 Abbie W.........127
 '78 Ada M..........138
 '76 Agnes...........133
 '81 g Bessie R........144
 '70 g Caroline P......167
 '70 Caroline S.......116
 '69 Clara S..........114
 '82 D. Eloise........147

INDEX.

Thomas
- '86 g Ellen S.........156
- '15 Emeline.........63
- '45 g Emma L.........33
- '80 g Estelle.........142
- '73 g F. Lillian.........123
- '42 Frances H.........26
- '84 Harriet P.........153
- '77 Helen L.........136
- '53 Henrietta B.........60
- '77 I. Hoyland.........136
- '64 g Isabella W.........96
- '95 sp Jacobina W.........184
- '45 Jane.........35
- '89 Jennie M.........166
- '41 Lucinda.........23
- '69 Lucy S.........114
- '95 Martha J.........183
- '43 g Mary E.........26
- '89 Mary I.........166
- '47 g Mary J.........39
- '81 May E.........145
- '43 Nancy M.........28
- '47 Rebecca W.........41
- '45 Sarah A.........35
- '74 Sarah H.........127
- '41 Sarah J.........23
- '46 Susan H.........38

Telford
- '89 Caroline M.........166

Temple
- '83 g Anna O.........149
- '57 g Emily A.........73

Tenbrook
- '67 Ellen C.........108

Tenney
- '89 g Annie M.........165
- '94 g Charlotte L.........177

Tenny
- '45 g Roxena B.........33

Terrill
- '95 g Bertha M.........179

Terry
- '71 Annie M.........119
- '62 Ellen.........91
- '90 Elvira N.........168
- '55 g Hannah W.........65
- '57 g Jane M.........73
- '66 g Mary C.........103

Tew
- '54 Katie A.........63

Tewksbury
- '71 Mary A.........119
- '62 Sarah E.........91

Thayer
- '90 Caroline V.........168
- '68 Clara.........111
- '91 Elsie P.........171
- '86 g Emma S.........156
- '79 Harriet F.........141
- '58 Kalista W.........78
- '61 g Ruth W.........86
- '60 g Sarah A.........14, 83

Thomas
- '82 Blanche.........147
- '48 Clara E.........44
- '83 g Ermina L.........149
- '76 Georgia.........133
- '51 Hortensia M.........54
- '65 Isabella (Collins)..101
- '95 g Letitia E.........179
- '95 Lucinda C.........183
- '83 g Margarette B.........149
- '43 Nancy B.........28
- '45 Sarah E.........35
- '42 Susan A.........26

Thompson
- '76 Abbie H.........133
- '76 Anna A.........133
- '63 g E. Antoinette.........93
- '46 g Eliza J.........36
- '68 g Ella J.........109
- '91 g E. May.........170
- '48 Harriet.........44
- '49 Harriet.........47
- '62 Harriet D.........91
- '40 g Harriet N.........20
- '39 Helen M.........19
- '62 Josephine G.........92
- '59 g L. Hope.........80
- '54 Martha.........63
- '56 g Martha A.........69
- '68 Mary E.........111
- '71 g Mary E.........117
- '71 Mary E.........119
- '69 g Mary N.........112
- '45 g Mary P.........33
- '54 Polly C.........63
- '48 Sarah G.........44
- '39 Sarah M.........19
- '40 Susan.........21
- '51 Susan F.........54
- '76 Winnie S.........133

Thorndike
- '67 g Clara I.........106

Thorpe
- '51 g Emily C.........52
- '59 g Emily D.........80
- '42 Mary C.........26

Thrall
- '57 Virginia T.........75

Thresher
- '52 g Mary A.........55

Thurston
- '68 Arista.........111
- '48 Clara B.........44
- '53 Mary H.........60
- '45 g Persis G.........11, 33

Thwing
- '84 g Grace.........151

Tichenor
- '56 g Louise J.........69

Tidd
- '67 Esther M.........108

Tiffany
- '95 Jessie W.........183
- '68 Rachel A.........111

Tillotson
- '69 Elizabeth L.........114
- '79 Sarah M.........141

Tilton
- '41 Eunice A.........23
- '91 sp Mary B.........171
- '63 Susan A.........95
- '63 Theresa M.........95

Tincker
- '64 Helen.........98

Tingley
- '55 g Ellen D.........65

Tinker
- '59 g Martha W.........80

Tinkham
- '39 Anna Eddy.........19
- '64 Phebe H.........98

Tirrell
- '66 g Almeda N.........12, 103
- '38 Hannah.........17
- '84 g M. Alice.........151
- '75 Mary B.........130
- '73 Ruth E.........125
- '85 g Sarah B.........154

Tirrill
- '40 g Eliza A.........20

Titcomb
- '50 g Elizabeth.........11, 48
- '50 g Mary.........11, 48
- '58 Rebecca F.........78

Todd
- '80 Charlotte E.........143
- '74 g Helena L.........126
- '75 Julia A.........130
- '46 Lodema H.........38
- '63 g S. Amelia.........93
- '79 g Sophie P.........139

Tole
- '44 Nancy A.........31

Tolles
- '53 Frances J.........60

Tolman
- '45 Ann.........35
- '41 Elizabeth.........23
- '41 Emily N.........23
- '48 Harriet M.........44
- '51 g Jane C.........11, 52
- '48 g Julia M.........7, 11, 42
- '48 Lucy D.........44
- '78 Mary M.........138
- '41 Sarah D.........23
- '45 g Susan L.........11, 33

Tombes
- '95 Edyth H.........183

Tomblin
- '54 g Lucretia W.........61

Tomlinson
- '73 Elizabeth B.........125
- '73 Emmeline S.........125

STUDENTS. 273

Topping
 '90 Leila L..............168
 '39 Sophronia H........ 19
Torrance
 '46 Anna A............. 38
Torrey
 '54 Caroline........... 63
 '38 Catherine D....... 17
 '54 g Clara H........... 61
 '44 Della C............ 31
 '44 Louisa M.......... 31
 '52 Miranda........... 57
 '54 g M. Isabel......... 61
 '73 M. Louise.........125
 '39 g Sarah H........11, 18
Tower
 '55 Abbie L............ 67
 '57 g Frances E......... 73
 '55 Henrietta B........ 67
 '54 Jane S............. 64
 '50 Julia S............. 50
 '39 Mary E............. 19
 '65 Mary N............101
 '52 Pamelia C......... 57
Towle
 '76 g Ellen J............131
 '76 Lilla B............133
Towne
 '51 Cornelia........... 54
 '90 Harriet B..........168
 '52 H. Janette......... 57
Townley
 '83 Grace.............150
 '82 Mary B............147
Townsend
 '60 g Margaret J........ 83
 '62 g Mary C.........11, 90
 '62 g Susan M.......... 90
Tracy
 '64 g Emily............. 96
 '81 Hattie R..........145
 '68 Jane..............111
Trask
 '67 Abbie J......... ...108
 '95 sp Elizabeth.........184
 '55 g Elizabeth S........ 65
 '38 Rebecca W (Brooks)17
Travis
 '45 Henrietta.......... 35
 '83 Josephine E.......150
Treadway
 '70 Alice M............116
 '58 Ellen J............. 78
Treadwell
 '95 Alice............. 183
 '62 g Louise E.......... 90
Treat
 '88 Fanny P...........163
 '55 g Mary B............ 65
Tremper
 '91 g Edith.............170

Trevett
 '57 Susan T........... 75
Trow
 '75 Elizabeth F.......130
 '64 Lucy E............ 98
Troxell
 '60 Ella E............. 85
 '62 Emma M.......... 92
 '73 Florence A........125
 '85 Marion E..........155
Truair
 '66 g Harriet N..........103
 '63 Mary A............ 95
Trumbull
 '43 g Julia S............ 26
Trusler
 '83 N. Salome........150
Tryon
 '79 Anna P...........141
Tubbs
 '64 Ella E............. 98
Tuck
 '66 Anna M...........105
Tucker
 '95 Emma C..........183
 '52 g Julia N........... 55
Tuckerman
 '74 Corinne E........127
Tufts
 '51 Caroline C........ 54
 '60 g Ellen M........... 83
 '40 g Margaret.......... 20
 '74 g Mary C...........126
 '42 Sarah A. B 26
 '40 Sarah P........... 21
 '57 Ursula G.......... 75
Tupper
 '53 g Augusta L........ 58
 '53 Emily P........... 60
Turner
 '95 Abbie H..........183
 '92 g Bessie M..........172
 '58 g Frances V.......11, 76
 '64 Helen M.......... 98
 '74 Julia A...........127
 '91 Lillian M.........170
 '92 g Lillian M..........172
 '75 Mary S...........130
 '46 P. Jane........... 38
 '53 g Susan............ 58
Turrill
 '51 L. Maria.......... 54
Tuthill
 '50 g Sarah S........... 48
Tuttle
 '85 g Alice J...........154
 '56 Anna E... 71
 '86 Ellen J............158
 '77 g Eliza W..........134
 '64 Laura E........... 99

Tuttle
 '56 Lenora 71
 '84 g Lizzie E..........151
 '57 Lorena............ 75
 '71 g Mary C...........117
 '83 Theodora A.... ...150
Twining
 '54 g Pauline M......... 61
 '51 Sarah J........... 54
Twitchell
 '73 g Emma L..........123
Twombly
 '82 g Carrie H..........146
 '41 Mary L........... 23
 '52 g P. Jane........... 55
Twyman
 '64 g Harriet S. (Vivian) 96
Tyler
 '45 Elizabeth B. 35
 '38 Elizabeth S....... 17
 '50 Lucy I............ 50
 '39 g Mary E............ 19
Udell
 '43 Caroline.......... 28
Ufford
 '58 Elizabeth D....... 78
 '53 g Mary G........... 58
Ulrich
 '78 Mathilde..........137
Underhill
 '67 Anna F...........108
 '69 Georgiana T......114
Underwood
 '65 Ellen I...........102
Upham
 '64 Ellen P........... 99
 '56 Frances A......... 71
 '85 g Lucy C...........154
 '85 g Mary C...........154
 '65 Susan B..........102
Upson
 '73 g M. Fanny.........123
Upton
 '67 Dora L. V........108
 '69 Lilla F...........114
Usher
 '57 g Jessie...........11, 73
 '93 Jessie H..........176
 '95 Maude P..........183
 '56 g Melissa........... 69
Utley
 '57 Julia M........... 75
 '55 Sarah L........... 67
Vaill
 '40 Asenath C........ 21
Vaille
 '76 Madora C.........133
Van Deusen
 '51 Ellen M........... 54

INDEX.

'90 g Mary E............107
'45   Rebecca P..........35

Van Doren
'70 g Helen M..........115
'70   Kate T............116
'81   M. Ella...........153

Van Duzer
'66   Alida C...........105

Van Dyke
'43   Margaret G........28

Van Meter
'73 g Mary L...........123

Vann
'54   Delia A............64

Van Ness
'73 g Abby.............123
'72   Anna.............122
'76   Lucinda..........133

Van Nostrand
'95   Harriet L........183

Vannuys
'62   Mary C............92

Van Pelt
'73   Gertrude.........125

Van Sickle
'79   Anna.............141
'79   Eliza............141

Van Slyke
'52   Anna M............57

Van Valkenburgh
'61 g Catharine M.......86
'72 g Harriet T.........120

Van Vechten
'45   Catharine.........35

Van Voorhes
'76   Kate.............133

Van Wagenen
'88 g Loraine M. N.....161

Van Wie
'84   Margaret S.......153

Van Winkle
'94   Edna M...........178

Van Wyck
'60 g Mary..............83

Vaughn
'81   Grace A..........153
'58 g Rachel.............76

Vedder
'55   Elizabeth M.......67

Ventres
'56   Ellen J............71

Verrill
'95 sp Ina B............185

Vickery
'95   Myra F...........183

Vietz
'93 sp Clara B..........176

Vining
'84   F. Louise........153

Vinton
'61 g Sarah A............86

Voorhees
'95   Grace M..........183
'89   Helen G..........166
'52   Mary E............57
'86   Mary E...........158
'54   Sarah A...........64

Vosburgh
'79   Sarah J..........141

Vose
'55   Anna M............67

Votey
'81 g Martha L.........144

Waddingham
'90 g Nellie A.........167

Wadhams
'53 g Antoinette D......58

Wadsworth
'59 g Caroline S........80
'50   Julia A...........50
'80 g Kittie L.........142
'52   Maria H...........57
'61 g Mary L............86
'48   Mary M............44

Wait
'57   Elvira M..........75

Waite
'55   Lucy B............67
'90   Mabel............168
'77 g Mary F...........134
'76   M. Ella..........133
'71   Susan A..........119
'55 g Susan M.......11, 65

Wake
'79   Florence S.......141

Wakefield
'60   Alice.............85
'71   Jane M...........119

Wakely
'62   Electa J..........92

Wakeman
'57   Irena J...........75
'53   Mary..............60

Waldo
'43   Frances...........28
'72   Genevieve........122
'45   Harriette L.......35
'45   Margarette........35
'41   Sarah M...........23

Waldron
'92   Ada L............173

Wales
'76   Jennie E.........133
'82   W. Josephine.....147

Walker
'57   Abbie C...........75
'51 g Adelia C......11, 52
'76   Adelia S.........133
'95   Alice J..........183
'43   Almira G..........28
'79 g Anna B...........139
'50   Anne E............50
'50   Arabella..........50
'60   Elvira............85
'88   Fanny E..........103
'56   Flora M...........71
'48   Frances...........44
'70 g Harriet A........115
'47 g Harriet E.........39
'91 g Isabel F.........170
'50   Isabella..........50
'82   J. Maria.........148
'60   Josephine.........85
'81 g Julia S..........144
'49   Laura.............47
'83   Laura A..........150
'62 g Laura W...........90
'62 g Louise............90
'89   Lucretia H.......166
'40   Martha A..........21
'62   Mary..............92
'46   Mary A............38
'51 g Mary A............52
'67   Mary E...........108
'84 g Mary E...........151
'79   Mary N...........141
'93 sp Mary W..........176
'38   Sarah E...........17
'46   Sarah I...........44

Wall
'50   Helen L...........50

Wallace
'71   Emma W...........119
'92 sp Louise B.....11, 173
'77   Matilda G........136

Waller
'59   Hannah E..........82

Walsh
'61   Mary E............88

Walsworth
'82 g Mary A...........146

Walter
'83 g Helen............149
'93   Mary E...........176

Walton
'95 g Edith M..........179
'87 g Georgiana C......159
'84   Sarah............153

Walsworth
'93   Luella M.........176

Walworth
'80   Clara E..........143

Waples
'85   Anna R...........155

STUDENTS.

Ward
- '65 Celestia E..........102
- '59 Charlotte M........ 82
- '93 g E. Lena..........175
- '46 Eliza J............. 38
- '50 g Elizabeth D........ 48
- '54 Emily T............ 64
- '57 g Julia E........7, 11, 73
- '40 Lucy A............ 21
- '48 Lucy B............ 44
- '53 M. Caroline........ 60
- '56 g Marion M.......... 69
- '56 Mary A. H......... 71
- '95 Mary I............183
- '79 g Myra............. 80
- '84 Sarah E............153

Warden
- '95 sp Frances L..........185

Ware
- '58 g Alice M............ 76
- '67 Belle F............108
- '64 Ella M............. 99
- '66 Ellen L............105
- '52 g Louisa M.......... 55
- '52 g Mary E........... 55
- '57 g Sarah C............ 73

Warfel
- '74 Ila................127

Warner
- '86 g Adelaide S........156
- '69 g Anna E..........112
- '52 Caroline E......... 57
- '73 Carrie E..........125
- '74 g Delia H........11, 126
- '79 Elizabeth B........141
- '54 Ellen............. 64
- '69 Fannie L..........114
- '76 Fidelia C..........133
- '39 Harriet M......... 19
- '62 Jane G............ 92
- '63 Jane S............ 95
- '54 Lucilla B.......... 64
- '83 g Mary A..........149
- '41 Mary H............ 23
- '82 Mary J...........148
- '83 Mary M...........150
- '79 g Mary S..........139
- '88 Mary S...........163
- '89 g Mary W..........165
- '50 Rebecca........... 50

Warren
- '53 g Amanda E........ 58
- '49 Caroline A......... 47
- '66 g Clara J..........103
- '44 g Delia M.......... 29
- '75 Elizabeth H........130
- '43 Hannah L.......... 28
- '95 Harriet R..........183
- '76 Lizzie M..........133
- '60 g Mary C.......... 83
- '45 Mary E........... 35

Warriner
- '56 Daphne S.......... 71

Washburn
- '67 g Annette D........106
- '69 g Cassandra V......112

Washington
- '76 Mary A...........133

Waters
- '58 Marion G.......... 78
- '70 Martha O..........116
- '60 g Mary J.......... 83
- '92 Mary J...........173
- '59 Oraville H........ 82

Watkins
- '93 Ella M............176
- '88 Grace L...........163
- '90 Lucy B...........168

Watrous
- '91 g Harriet..........170

Watson
- '51 g Caroline A........ 52
- '52 Charlotte E........ 57
- '65 Ellen M...........102
- '60 Emma............ 85
- '95 Evelyn H..........183
- '81 g Ida L...........144
- '71 g Laura S..........117
- '95 Lena L...........183
- '95 Mabel A..........184
- '58 S. Augusta........ 76
- '67 g Susan C..........106

Watts
- '66 Alice M...........105
- '95 Faustina E........184

Way
- '76 Cornelia H........133
- '79 Lucy.............141

Wear
- '72 Abbie L..........122
- '67 Martha J..........108

Weare
- '47 Harriet S.......... 41

Weaver
- '44 Mary C........... 31

Webb
- '73 g Elizabeth M.......123
- '52 Emma F.......... 57
- '54 Josephine A....... 64
- '79 g Mary T..........139

Webber
- '77 Elvira F..........136

Webster
- '50 Anna C........... 50
- '42 g Ann R.........11, 24
- '40 Lucy D........... 21
- '90 Luella........... 85
- '64 Marietta E........ 99

Weed
- '66 Frances M........105

Weeden
- '78 Maria H..........178

Weeks
- '94 g Angelina L........177
- '61 g Amanda.......... 86
- '72 Helen L..........122
- '44 Maria E.......... 31
- '61 Mary B.......... 88
- '77 Mary E..........136
- '51 Mary J........... 54

Weigley
- '64 Anna I........... 99

Welch
- '59 g Cora A.......... 80
- '71 g Elizabeth B.......117
- '65 Emma A..........102
- '70 Mary E..........117

Weller
- '62 Elizabeth W........ 92

Welles
- '44 Abby............. 31
- '95 g Grayce S.........179
- '71 Mary E..........119

Wells
- '67 g Annie M.......11, 106
- '65 g Delia M.........100
- '68 Ella A...........111
- '42 Experience P...... 26
- '46 Harriette A........ 38
- '45 Helen............ 35
- '84 Julia E...........153
- '67 Maria T..........108
- '68 Marie E..........111
- '69 Mary S..........114
- '84 M. Bonita........153
- '63 Sabra M. S........ 95

Welsh
- '81 g Ida F..........144

Wemple
- '93 g Jeanne E.........175

Wendall
- '44 Kate............. 31

Wenner
- '92 sp Bertha E.........172

Wentworth
- '53 g Caroline........11, 58
- '86 g Caroline S........156

Werkheiser
- '84 g Rosa A..........151

Werlein
- '53 Barbara A......... 60

West
- '78 Carrie P..........138
- '83 g Fanny E.........149
- '81 g Harriet H........144

	Page		Page		Page
'86 Kate R..........	158	'75 Mary E..........	130	Whitman	
'43 Margaretta A.....	28	'43 Mary L...........	28	'83 Iola E..........	150
'73 Marian W.........	125	'43 Stella C.........	28	'39 g Mary C....6, 7, 11,	18
'61 g Thera...........	86	Whistler		'50 Rosina P.........	50
'89 Thera F..........	166	'82 Julia F..........	148	Whitmarsh	
Westcott		Whitaker		'70 Maria D.........	117
'89 g Maria P.........	165	'84 Cora............	153	Whitmore	
'45 Mary L...........	35	'83 Corinne.........	150	'91 Amy G...........	171
Westfall		'75 Frances I........	130	'50 Ellen R..........	50
'66 Mary G...........	105	'55 g Harriet A.......	58	'85 g Lucy M..........	154
Weston		'68 g Isabelle........	109	'46 Mary A...........	38
'55 Rebecca J........	67	'92 sp Jennie E.......	173	Whitney	
Wetmore		'79 g Martha..........	139	'81 A. Minnie........	145
'74 Frances M........	128	'76 g Sara............	134	'56 g C. Amelia.......	69
'58 Jane S...........	78	Whitcomb		'76 g Clara S.........	131
'83 Martha S.........	150	'75 Alice M..........	130	'63 g Elizabeth J.....	93
Wetzell		'51 g Ellen C.........	52	'48 g Emily E.........	42
'91 Annie A..........	171	'91 Gertrude F.......	171	'67 Eugelia M........	108
Wever		'88 Jessie...........	163	'40 Maria K......13,	21
'77 Mary C...........	136	'46 Sarah............	38	'58 Mary A...........	78
Whallon		'67 g Susan A.........	106	'61 Mary R...........	89
'74 Lillian M........	128	White		'77 g Rosabelle.......	134
Whaples		'55 Abbie L..........	67	Whiton	
'47 Elizabeth L......	41	'60 g Abbie T.........	83	'51 g Ann E...........	52
Wheaton		'60 Almira P.........	85	'53 g Ellen A.........	58
'55 g Adela M.........	65	'48 Ann A............	44	'58 Ellen J..........	78
'75 Ida B............	130	'91 Annie E..........	171	Whittemore	
Wheeler		'44 g Caroline A......	29	'47 Eliza............	41
'46 g Achsah..........	36	'64 g Caroline D......	96	'46 g Harriet L.......	36
'59 Adelaide M.......	82	'71 g Caroline I.....11,	118	'54 Laura............	64
'47 g Augusta.........	39	'94 g Caroline L......	177	Whittlesey	
'76 g Caroline L......	131	'72 Charlotte M......	122	'44 Cornelia.........	31
'55 Caroline R.......	67	'66 Dorcas...........	105	'49 Helen M..........	47
'58 Charlotte E......	78	'65 Ellen M..........	102	'67 Jane E...........	108
'67 g Clara E.........	106	'66 Ellen S..........	105	'43 Louisa D.........	28
'52 Cornelia E.......	57	'58 g Emily E.........	76	'85 Margaret B.......	155
'86 g Eleanor S.......	156	'72 g Florence M......	120	'64 Mary E...........	10
'49 Ellen C..........	47	'61 Harriet A........	89	'88 Maude............	163
'63 Ellen H..........	95	'48 Jeannette C......	44	Wiard	
'48 Emeline A........	44	'86 Jessie B.........	158	'95 Bertha L.........	184
'70 Emily C..........	117	'66 Julia S..........	105	Wicker	
'85 Hannah R.........	155	'75 Kate H...........	130	'64 Mary W...........	99
'38 Harriet..........	17	'64 Lizzie H.........	99	Wickham	
'46 Laura E..........	38	'95 Lucy M...........	184	'87 Julia M..........	160
'89 Lucy S...........	166	'57 g Lydia A.........	73	Widmer	
'46 g Lydia A.........	36	'90 g Mabel A.........	167	'81 Fannie...........	145
'44 Martha J.........	31	'47 Martha E.........	41	Wiesing	
'45 Martha W.........	35	'48 g Martha L........	42	'77 Bertha A.........	136
'64 Mary L...........	99	'74 Mary A...........	128	Wiggin	
'52 Mary S...........	57	'41 Mary C...........	23	'92 g Annie P.........	172
'57 g Mary W..........	73	'66 Mary R...........	105	'95 Mary P...........	184
'57 Phebe E..........	75	'90 Maud E...........	168	Wiggins	
Wheelock		'40 Sarah H..........	21	'68 F. Gertrude......	111
'44 Martha S.........	31	'71 g Victoria A......	118	Wight	
Wheldon		Whitehill		'76 Ella L...........	133
'95 Elizabeth K......	184	'82 Mary J...........	148	'54 Emily J..........	64
Whipple		Whithed		'84 Ruth E...........	153
'65 g Clara E.........	100	'44 Isabella.........	31	Wilbraham	
'55 Eliza B..........	75	Whiting		'85 g Josephine.......	154
'61 Francena A.......	88	'70 Abbie M..........	117		
'56 g Maria J.........	69	'56 g Amelia..........	69		
		'51 Cyrene E.........	54		
		'89 Ellen L..........	166		
		'56 g L. Amanda.......	69		
		'54 Mary E...........	64		
		'91 Sara.............	171		

STUDENTS.

Wilbur
'84 g Helena G............151

Wilcox
'94 g Alice M..............177
'66 Annie M.............105
'56 Catharine B........ 71
'57 C. Louisa........... 75
'82 E. Elizabeth.......148
'52 Fanny R............ 57
'43 Harriet E........... 28
'81 L. Augusta........145
'54 Laura O............ 64
'77 g Mary F.............134
'43 g Melissa R.......... 26
'70 M. Louise..........117
'67 Myrtie S...........108
'59 Sarah J............ 82

Wild
'88 Laura H...........163

Wilde
'53 g Amelia B........... 58
'54 Caroline E......... 64

Wilder
'63 Abbie P............ 95
'63 Abby A..........12, 95
'42 Elizabeth J........ 26
'52 Esther F........... 57
'46 Fidelia A.......... 38
'83 g Grace E............149
'69 Helen A...........114
'55 g Mary E............. 65
'59 Mary E............ 82
'52 Mary J............ 57
'64 g Sarah A............ 96

Wilkes
'75 g Ellen M............128
'74 J. Victoria........128
'71 Susan P 119

Wilkins
'64 Almira C........... 99
'58 Harriet A.......... 78
'73 Helen M...........125
'59 Henrietta.......... 82
'51 Mary A............ 54
'59 Mary C............ 82
'71 Mary E............119

Wilkinson
'90 g Elizabeth..........107
'52 g Ellen J............. 55

Willard
'56 Hannah H.......... 71
'79 Jennie J..........141
'73 Mary..............125

Willcox
'52 g Adeline H.......11, 55
'72 Ella G.............122

Willett
'64 g Emogene F........ 96
'81 Louise A..........145

Willey
'88 Rose M...........163

Williams
'52 g Adaline............ 57
'83 Alberta K.........150
'66 Alice A...........105
'67 Anna A...........108
'49 Caroline M........ 47
'43 Clara A........... 28
'84 Clara E...........153
'62 Clarissa 92
'59 Clarissa B........ 82
'72 g Cornelia P........120
'72 E. Isabel.........122
'46 Emily............. 38
'63 Emily A........... 95
'67 g Emily A..........106
'62 Emma B........... 92
'64 Eusebia S......... 99
'49 Frances L........ 47
'89 g Grace.............165
'43 Harriet H......... 28
'73 H. Blanche........125
'83 H. Louise.........150
'89 Jessica...........166
'79 Jessie 141
'87 Jessie M..........160
'67 g Julia S...........106
'88 Lena..............163
'48 Lucinda........... 45
'58 Maria L........... 78
'56 g Marietta M........ 69
'67 Margaret..........108
'68 g Mary..............109
'47 g Mary B............ 39
'48 Mary E............ 45
'71 g Mary E............118
'85 g Mary G............154
'92 Maud..............173
'73 Minnie A..........125
'53 Rebecca P......... 60
'68 g Sarah J............109
'48 Susan A........... 45
'61 Susan D........... 89
'43 g Tirzah M.......... 26
'95 Winifred M........184

Williamson
'88 Anna A...........163
'72 g Clara G............120
'54 Hadassa T......... 64
'58 Martha M......... 78
'89 g T. Gertrude........165

Willis
'71 Emilie C..........119
'71 g Ianthe............118
'73 Ida J.............125
'54 Rosina............ 64

Williston
'64 Clara B. S........ 99
'45 Harriet R......... 35

Willmarth
'57 Abbie F........... 75
'55 g Mary E............ 65

Wills
'87 g Mary E............159
'95 Rebekah B........184

Wilmarth
'69 Sarah J...........114

Wilson
'79 Agnes B...........141
'87 Anne B............160
'75 Annie S........12, 130
'95 Carolyn E.........184
'54 g Cordelia O........ 61
'89 g Elizabeth V.......165
'69 g Ellen L...........112
'61 g Emily S.........11, 86
'93 sp Emma W..........176
'78 Isabel............138
'64 Isabella H........ 99
'67 g Jane M............106
'66 g Josephine M......103
'61 g Lavinia A......... 88
'45 Mariette........... 35
'62 g Mary A............ 90
'62 g Mary A............ 90
'63 Mary A............ 95
'86 Mary C............158
'95 Mary F............184
'64 g Mary L. D........ 96
'77 Mary M...........136
'91 sp Minnie...........171

Winans
'49 Mary A............ 47
'53 Pamelia C......... 60

Winchell
'40 Amanda F......... 21

Winegar
'57 Clara M........... 75

Wing
'46 g Electa............. 36
'79 Electa M..........141
'40 Martha C.......... 21

Wingate
'49 g Ann S............. 45
'49 g Sarah A........... 45

Winn
'60 Elizabeth A....... 85

Winslow
'95 sp Clara F...........185

Winter
'62 Adelaide.......... 92
'55 g Eliza D............ 65
'78 Hattie K..........138
'77 H. Louise.........136

Winton
'53 Mary H............ 60

Wiswall
'88 g Sarah E...........161

Wiswell
'83 Lillian A.........150

Witherell
'64 Eliza J........... 99

Witter
'82 M. Agnes..........148

INDEX.

Wolcott
'45 Elizabeth E........ 35
'88 g Emily P............161
'48 g Harriet............ 42
'60 M. Antoinette...... 85

Wolverton
'81 Mary E.............145

Wood
'72 g Alice A...........120
'52 A. Maria W......... 57
'84 Amy C..............153
'50 Arabella M. G...... 70
'63 Asenath B.......... 95
'53 Betsey J........... 60
'78 C. Alice...........117
'59 Caroline A......... 82
'48 g Caroline E........ 42
'73 g Clara W........11,123
'95 Edith H............184
'86 Eleanor............158
'63 g Elizabeth W....... 93
'89 Fannie.............166
'67 Harriet S..........108
'44 g Mary S............ 29
'48 Olive W............ 45

Woodard
'78 Mary B.............138

Woodbridge
'43 g Nancy M........... 26

Woodbury
'68 Emma C.............111
'95 Mary H.............184

Woodford
'83 Abbie M............150
'61 Henrietta M........ 89
'72 Ida J..............122

Woodhull
'43 g Ann H............. 26
'51 g Josephine......... 52
'55 Phebe W............ 68
'49 Sarah F..........12, 47

Woodin
'53 Eliza J............ 60

Woodman
'78 g Elizabeth C.......137

Woodmansee
'90 Edith L............168

Woodruff
'55 g Cornelia K........ 65
'60 Isabella H.........114
'48 Jane T............. 45

Woods
'43 Amanda M........... 28
'48 Caroline M......... 45
'54 Catharine.......... 64
'43 Charlotte E........ 29
'48 Charlotte J........ 45

'92 g Edith B...........172
'48 Harriet E.......... 45
'86 Helen F............158
'54 Mary J............. 64
'38 g Persis C......11, 13, 16

Woodside
'95 sp Grace O..........185

Woodward
'64 g Abbie J........... 96
'84 Alice L............153
'95 Elizabeth W........184
'58 g Amelia C.......11, 76
'61 g Emma C............ 96
'81 g Helen M...........144
'63 Jane G............. 95
'45 Lydia M............ 35
'50 Mary W............. 50
'69 Valina J...........114

Woolsey
'56 Mary............... 71

Wooster
'71 Alice D............119
'87 g Annie T...........159
'83 Elizabeth D........154
'71 Harriet E..........119

Worcester
'57 S. Elizabeth....... 75
'50 g Sarah............. 48

Worden
'52 Harriet A.......... 57
'63 Harriet B.......... 95

Worrell
'67 g Anna M............106
'65 Maria E............102

Worstell
'79 Fannie F...........141

Worth
'93 Marion W...........176

Worthington
'55 Clara.............. 68

Worthley
'95 Evelyn M...........184

Wright
'94 g Alice C...........177
'76 g Alvinia S.........131
'92 Anne F.............173
'42 Augusta............ 26
'53 Augusta L.......... 60
'50 g Bessie F..........167
'42 g Catharine A....11, 24
'63 Catherine E........ 95
'52 Celia P............ 57
'46 g Celia S........... 36
'52 g Cynthia A......... 55
'69 g Elizabeth P.......112
'66 Ella R.............105
'71 Frances A..........119

'52 g Georgiana M....... 55
'38 Harriet............ 17
'54 Henrietta M........ 64
'90 Isabel S...........168
'83 g Laura B...........149
'42 g Laura E........... 24
'64 Lucy M............. 49
'54 Margaret P......... 64
'43 Martha A........... 29
'50 Mary A............. 50
'55 Mary A............. 68
'65 Mary C.............102
'95 g Mary H............179
'68 Mary J.............111
'95 Mary L.............184
'49 Mary M............. 47
'47 Melancia B......... 41
'50 Sarah E............ 50
'73 Sarah E............125
'42 S. Rebecca......... 26
'70 Velma C............117

Wurtz
'64 g Anna.............. 96

Wyckoff
'82 Gertrude A.........148
'95 Harriet J..........184
'95 Julia..............184

Wyman
'64 Abbie L............ 99
'46 g Lucy G............ 36
'75 Mary F.............130

Yale
'68 Caroline A.........111
'69 Jane M.............114
'81 Martha.............145
'48 g Martha R.......... 42
'75 Mary A.............130
'48 g Mary E.........11, 42

Yamawaki
'95 g Hana..............179

Yates
'51 g Caroline R.....11, 52
'78 Clementine R.......138
'86 Katharine Y........158

Yeomans
'86 Ellen L............158
'94 Edith M............178
'93 g Frances A.........175

Young
'82 F. Della...........148
'40 Lucina S........... 21

Youngblood
'55 Sarah O............ 68

Youngs
'45 Caroline E......... 35
'45 g Cornelia.......... 33
'43 Emeline C.......... 29
'62 g Harriet W......... 90

STATISTICS FROM ANNUAL CATALOGUES.
1837-1887.

CLASS.   CLASS.

Year.	Teachers.	Assistant Pupils.	Senior.	Middle.	Junior.	Whole No. Students.	Year.	Teachers.	Assistant Pupils.	Senior.	Senior Middle.	Junior Middle.	Junior.	Whole No. Students.
1838	4	3	4	34	78	116	1862	23	1	56	43	70	85	254
1839	5	3	12	31	60	103	1863	23	0	40	47	87	127	301
1840	6	4	17	40	62	119	1864	23	1	51	41	98	153	343
1841	5	3	10	27	70	113	1865	23	1	38	47	87	117	289
1842	8	3	15	50	107	172	1866	24	1	60	40	87	100	287
1843	13	2	16	50	118	184	1867	24	0	50	38	59	124	280
1844	12	1	34	66	106	206	1868	24	0	45	31	64	122	262
1845	18	2	51	72	123	246	1869	25	0	38	30	64	136	268
1846	16	1	42	69	71	182	1870	26	0	33	40	84	111	268
1847	13	2	44	59	85	188	1871	27	0	37	34	77	132	280
1848	12	2	47	62	126	235	1872	29	0	42	40	74	118	274
1849	13	2	23	58	138	219	1873	28	0	48	40	75	108	271
1850	16	0	34	69	121	224	1874	30	1	37	42	74	148	301
1851	13	2	60	55	129	244	1875	27	1	29	36	95	128	288
1852	16	2	31	59	162	252	1876	27	0	39	54	80	110	283
1853	16	1	46	49	163	258	1877	28	0	44	31	73	114	262
1854	17	2	43	55	180	278	1878	27	0	29	41	84	97	251
1855	19	1	57	73	162	292	1879	28	1	31	38	86	118	273
1856	19	2	49	70	156	275	1880	27	1	33	48	68	77	226
1857	18	0	59	68	139	266	1881	26	1	47	35	84	83	249
1858	20	1	57	71	147	275	1882	28	0	30	29	90	118	267
1859	19	1	56	70	150	276	1883	28	0	42	45	81	121	289
1860	22	1	42	70	148	260	1884	29	1	47	43	78	119	287
1861	22	1	66	65	157	288	1885	30	0	27	56	70	116	269
							1886	30	0	53	48	73	120	294
							1887	33	0	47	52	65	149	313
							1888	37	0	40	52	80	132	313

Before 1862 the course of study occupied three years; from that time, four years.

1888-1895.

COLLEGE.   SEMINARY.

Faculty.	Senior.	Junior.	Sophomore.	Freshman.	Special Students.	Whole No. Students in College.	Year.	Faculty.	Assistant Pupils.	Senior.	Senior Middle.	Junior Middle.	Junior.	Whole No. Students in College and Seminary.
37	2	1	0	8	0	11	1889	37	0	49	50	63	128	301*
37	1	5	11	25	0	42	1890	37	0	43	49	68	71	273
36	4	10	27	43	7	92	1891	36	0	50	43	24	60	269
34	10	35	41	59	22	167	1892	34	0	30	15	15	62	289
34	34	49	70	127	22	303	1893	34	0	8				311
37	48	57	86	87	22	300	1894	37						
38	50	82	70	84	43	328	1895	38						

*Two students are counted in both departments.

STATISTICS FROM

A TABLE SHOWING THE ATTENDANCE FROM DIFFERENT PLACES EACH YEAR.

United States and Territories.

Years.	Ala.	Ark.	Cal.	Col.	Conn.	Del.	D.C.	Fla.	Ga.	Idaho.	Ill.	Ind.	Ind. Ter.	Iowa.	Kan.	Ky.	La.	Me.	Md.	Mass.	Mich.	Minn.	Mo.	Miss.	Neb.	Nev.	N. H.	N. J.
1838					13															82							3	3
1839					13													1		64		1					6	2
1840					21															68			2				7	2
1841					18															64			1				11	1
1842					36	1														87	1		1				14	6
1843					31		2							1						89							13	7
1844					44							1		1						93							11	4
1845	1				45						1	4								100							18	3
1846					25									1					3	78							15	4
1847					32	1													3	71							14	5
1848					44					2	1	1		12		79		1					25	6
1849					32					1	2		1	12	1	75	2				25	8
1850					33					2	2		7			78	3				20	8
1851					49					6			1			73	4				22	8
1852					32		1	4	1	1		9		77	1		1		16	14
1853					45			1	2			5		77			1		22	20
1854					52	1		9	2	3			7		68	1		1		30	16
1855		2			42	1		6	5				15		91	3				24	9
1856					42			7	3		1		21		75		1	1		25	6
1857	1				35	1		1	5	1		1	1	23		75		1			30	13
1858					33			1	7	5	1	1		12		96	3				24	7
1859					39	1		1	9	1	1	1		14		91	2				22	3
1860					41	1	1	1	7	3	2			16		77	4		1		23	4
1861					40	1		1	2	1	1		15		98	4		1		21	9
1862					32	1		3	3	1	1		10		83	4			1		19	8
1863					32	2		5	3			3	17		101	5		1		25	14
1864					40			6	3	1	2		19		115	5	1	1		23	25
1865			2		41	1	1	9		1	11		88	5				16	21
1866		1			41	1		4	1		1		14		85	3				21	15
1867			3		37			6		1		14		100	1		1		20	12
1868	1			1	32	1		3		1		22	1	85		1	1		23	8
1869				1	44		1	1	1	3	1		15		90	1			2		20	12
1870				1	35	1		1	2	5		14		98	1		1	1		16	8
1871		1		1	43	1	1	2	1	1	1		13		102		1			18	7
1872		1	1		48	1	1	1	7				8		87	1	1	1		13	13
1873					46	1	1	3	2				11		95	3	1			11	9
1874					51	1		4	2	1	1		9	1	102	4	2			14	11
1875					65		2	3	2	1			9	1	101	1				14	12
1876					55	1	1	5	3			1	13	2	86	1	2			10	9
1877					46	2	2	7	2			1	5	1	74	1	3	4	1	1	13	8
1878					45	2		7		1			1	67	2	2	3	1		14	13
1879					56	1	2	7		3		5	2	73	3	1	1		16	13
1880					43	1	1	7		3		4		50	2	2	2		5	11
1881					42	1		9	3	3		6	1	62	3	3	1		12	10
1882			1		40	1		7	1	8		8	2	68	3	1		9	17
1883			1	1	46	2		5	11		6	1	73	7	1		8	14
1884			1		48	1	1	4	1	8		6	3	85	1	3	1		16	13
1885			1		51	2	1	7		7		9	3	86	3			13	14
1886			2		39	2		14	1	2		11	2	92	2	3	2		12	16
1887			1	1	46	1		17	12	3		16		87	3	2	2		9	11
1888			2	1	49	1	1	14	10	2		14	1	83	10	2	2		10	7
1889			2	1	50	2	1	10	9		14	1	94	1	2	1		8	8
1890				1	51	1	1	13	5		12	1	87	2	1		11	7
1891					37	1	1	12	3	1		9		70	1			13	9
1892					34	2	1	20	2	3	17		79				11	13
1893					38	1		19	2	4	1	21	1	69	1			15	14
1894					49	1		9	1	1	24	1	67	1	2	2		12	17
1895					59	1		10	1	2	3	25		91		2			15	14

This table includes resident graduates.

A TABLE SHOWING THE ATTENDANCE FROM DIFFERENT PLACES EACH YEAR.

	United States and Territories.																	Other Countries.																			
Years.	N. Y.	N. C.	Ohio.	Oregon.	Penn.	R. I.	S. C.	Tenn.	Texas.	Utah.	Vt.	Va.	Wash.	West Va.	Wis.	Canada.	N. B.	Nova Scotia.	Borneo.	Brazil.	Bulgaria.	Cape Colony.	China.	Hawaiian I.	Holland.	India.	Italy.	Japan.	Macedonia.	Natal.	Persia.	Roumelia.	Sweden.	Syria.	Turkey.	West Indies.	Total.
1838	3		1		1	3					7																										116
1839	8										8																										103
1840	3		2								11																										119
1841	10										8																										113
1842	16		1			1					6				1									1													172
1843	29		1			1					7	1			1	1																					184
1844	32		1		2						18	1												1											1		209
1845	42		4		1						19													1											1		246
1846	39		4		1						9					2																					182
1847	36		3		1						19					2		1																			188
1848	33		4		3	1					16	1			1	3		1																			235
1849	34		4		4	2					10	1			2	1		1						1													219
1850	36		2		5	1					18				6	1		1						1													224
1851	34		6		8	1					24				5									3													244
1852	44		6		7	1					26	2			1	1								6	1												252
1853	40	1	8		7	2					13	2			2	2								4		1											258
1854	44		9		6	2		1			20	1			2				1					1		1											278
1855	53		8		8	2		1			16				1			3								2											292
1856	53		4		10	3					12	1			3			5								1										1	275
1857	42		3		9	1					11				1			5								2										1	266
1858	40		12		11	4					17				1																						275
1859	44		16		6	3		1	1		15				2											2										1	276
1860	42		8		9	4		1			13				1			1																			2[illegible]0
1861	48		6		6	3					26				2		1	1													1						288
1862	39		5		16	2					19	1			1		1	2								1					1						254
1863	55		3		9	3		1			11				3	1		3								1					2				1		301
1864	56		4		10	3		1			19				4								1			2					1				1		343
1865	48		4		7	2					16			1	7								1			3									1		289
1866	40	1	11		11	4		1			14			1	9								2			2					1			1	1		287
1867	30	1	5		11	6					18				8	1	2	1					1											1			280
1868	44		4		7	1		1			17				3	1	2						1			1											262
1869	41		5		3	4		1			16				2	2	1						1			1								1			2[illegible]8
1870	35		2		10	4					25				1	1							1			4									1		2[illegible]8
1871	43		6		9	4					20					1		1					2			2											280
1872	34		2		11	7					29				1	1								1		4											274
1873	36		3		5	5	1				30				1	1		1						2							1				1		271
1874	35		2		7	5	1				34				1	2								2		1	1								1		301
1875	33		4		7	6					21				1	1								1		2											288
1876	36		9		10	5		1	1		24	1				1										2									1		282
1877	35		7		11	3					23				1	1	1							1		3									3		2[illegible]3
1878	40		6		11	2					14						1							1		1									1		247
1879	45		11		12	2			3		16				3									1		4											273
1880	37		12		9	1	1				15			1	5		1									1											225
1881	44		8		16	2	1		1		14	1		2	3		1									1											251
1882	39		10		21	1			1		19		1	3	3		2			1																	268
1883	44		9		21	1	1		1		22		1	3	1		2					1								1							289
1884	44		5		25		1		1		14		1	1			2					1				1				1							289
1885	42	3	4		24			1			10		2		1		1					1				1				1							270
1886	49	2	3		20	2		1	1		14		1											1		1				1					1		297
1887	52	2	7		22	1		1			11		1		2									1		1				1					2		315
1888	49	3	10		16	1	1	1			14				3	1	1				1			1								1			1		314
1889	48	3	4		16	1		1		1	7				5		3				2												1		1		300
1890	38	3	3		8	2		1		1	10				3		2				2			1		1											272
1891	43	6	9		13	2		1			13				6		2				2			1		1		1					1				267
1892	41	4	7		18	1					25	1			5		1				2			1		1		1	1				1				289
1893	46	3	9	1	20	4					23	1			4		1				1			1		1		2	1								311
1894	41	4	12		19	5			1		23	1	1		4													3	1								300
1895	49		15		9	3		1		1	19				3													2	1								328

This table includes resident graduates.

SUMMARIES, 1837-1895.

Year.	Graduates.			Non-Graduates.*			Whole Number.		
	No.	Married.	Deceased.	No.	Married.	Deceased.	No.	Married.	Deceased.
'38	4	4	3	74	53	51	78	57	54
'39	12	12	7	76	61	46	88	73	53
'40	15	10	10	76	61	49	91	71	59
'41	10	8	7	69	48	49	79	56	56
'42	15	14	6	109	94	63	124	108	69
'43	16	10	12	101	68	59	117	78	71
'44	34	27	17	87	57	38	121	84	55
'45	51	36	29	130	97	72	181	133	101
'46	42	30	21	81	58	38	123	88	59
'47	44	32	21	85	62	44	129	94	65
First ten years.	243	183	133	888	659	509	1,131	842	642
'48	47	36	25	116	80	55	163	116	80
'49	23	17	16	107	68	37	130	85	53
'50	34	25	12	103	70	38	137	95	50
'51	58	52	11	106	82	37	164	134	51
'52	32	18	14	121	86	44	153	104	58
'53	45	33	15	92	74	31	137	107	46
'54	43	31	19	108	71	39	151	102	58
'55	57	41	18	100	68	25	157	109	43
'56	48	30	9	112	80	29	160	110	38
'57	59	39	17	96	58	34	155	97	51
Second ten years.	446	322	156	1,061	737	369	1,507	1,059	528
'58	57	38	14	100	71	30	157	109	44
'59	57	38	16	91	71	25	148	109	41
'60	42	26	11	99	67	28	141	93	39
'61	66	38	13	91	57	27	157	95	40
'62	56	25	22	81	55	17	137	80	39
'63	39	24	9	96	63	25	135	87	34
'64	51	35	8	127	97	22	178	132	30
'65	37	22	6	87	52	21	124	74	27
'66	60	31	8	86	53	24	146	84	32
'67	57	32	12	83	52	17	140	84	29
Third ten years.	522	312	119	941	635	236	1,463	947	355
'68	45	30	8	93	60	15	138	90	23
'69	37	21	5	81	51	16	118	72	21
'70	33	14	6	94	55	16	130	69	22
'71	37	20	4	88	56	13	125	76	17
'72	41	25	9	81	52	11	122	77	20
'73	48	22	7	72	37	10	120	59	17
'74	35	20	1	88	61	12	123	81	16
'75	29	19	3	90	55	5	119	74	8
'76	38	17	5	95	61	9	133	78	14
'77	43	18	5	79	45	9	122	63	14
Fourth ten years.	389	206	56	861	533	116	1,250	739	172

*Non-graduates are counted only in the last year of their connection with the Institution.

SUMMARIES, 1837-1895.

Year.	Graduates.			Non-Graduates.			Whole Number.		
	No.	Married.	Deceased.	No.	Married.	Deceased.	No.	Married.	Deceased.
'78	27	12	2	72	39	11	99	51	13
'79	31	18	2	81	56	8	112	74	10
'80	33	15	2	43	26	4	76	41	6
'81	46	23	2	55	28	8	101	51	10
'82	30	20	2	66	40	5	96	60	7
'83	42	20	5	71	34	2	113	54	7
'84	46	25	4	76	25	5	122	50	9
'85	27	10	2	65	28	6	92	38	8
'86	53	21	7	76	15	3	129	36	10
'87	47	14	3	54	22	4	101	36	7
Fifth ten years.	382	178	31	659	313	56	1,041	491	87
'88	40	11	1	67	22	3	107	33	4
'89	50	11	0	57	20	1	107	31	1
'90	44	11	0	57	13	3	101	24	3
'91	54	4	1	45	6	2	99	10	3
'92	40	2	0	50	11	1	90	13	1
'93	44	2	0	64	6	0	108	8	0
'94	51	1	0	43	0	0	94	0	0
'95	50	0	0	271	1	0	321	1	0

GENERAL SUMMARY, 1837-1895.

Graduates	2,355
Non-graduates	5,073
Whole number students	7,428
Graduates from College Course (1889-1895)	149
Graduates married	1,243
Non-graduates married	2,946
Whole number married (reported 1837-1895)	4,189
Graduates deceased	500
Non-graduates deceased	1,296
Whole number deceased (reported 1837-1895)	1,796

ADDENDA.

ADDITIONS AND CORRECTIONS.

PAGE 5. Rev. Julius H. Seelye, D.D., LL.D., d. Amherst, '95.
9. Marietta Kies, Ph.D., not M.A..
10. M. Ella Spooner, B.L.
11. Caroline L. White, B.A.
14. Sarah A. Thayer, *g.* '60.
19. Elizabeth L. Root; m. Edward Potter, M.D.; d. Guilford, Ct., August 30, '45.
23. Marion A. Hawks; m. *C. P. Buckingham; *care Ulric Sloan, Hillsboro, O.*
24. Abby P. Colman; 3805 *Lake Ave., Park Ridge, Ill.*
Marcia Colton; name to be omitted, as she was never a Mt. Holyoke student.
29. Rosanna H. Cobine; m. Rev. H. I. Parker; d. Austin, Minn., '65.
Elizabeth G. Knowlton; m. *Rev. Milton B. Starr; *Dehesa, Cal.*
32. Susan H. Fowler; d. Philadelphia, Pa., '94.
33. Florilla Crofut; m. Geo. M. Van Vechten, not Vechtend.
37. Clara Browne; home on Staten Island.
37. Elizabeth Cook; 50 *W. Main St., Norwalk, O.*
39. Elizabeth W. Phillips; 6½ *Dearborn Place, San Francisco, Cal.*
41. Non-graduate '47. Antoinette Prosens, Valatie, N. Y.; m. *Alexander Ewing, '67; *Valatie, N. Y.* (Name not previously recorded.)
Eliza Whittemore, d. Fitzwilliam, N. H., '95.
49. Agnes M. Butler. *Galesburg, Ill.*
50. Margaret A. Schultz; m. Rev. Joseph Mayou, not Mayon; *Oskaloosa, Kan.*
52. Sophie S. Blackwell, 933 *Cooper St., Camden, N. J.*
52. Caroline N. Denison; m. * Geo. W. Higgins.
53. Laura B. Hamlen; m. Jas. C. (not O.) Bellman; 5041 *Shaw Ave., St. Louis, Mo.*
58. Ellen A. Whiton, 178 *Prospect Ave.* (not St.), *Milwaukee, Wis.*
59. Mary A. Cushing (not Cushman), *Box 203, Groton.*
60. Jane Y. Phillips; 10 *Hooker Ave., Poughkeepsie, N. Y.*
65. Sarah A. Kelley; m. D. J. (not I.) Gibson.
66. Mentoria V. Hatch; *Dayton, O.*
70. Evelyn P. Hawley; d. Homer, N. Y., '66 (not '86).
72. Flora A. Sawyer; *Box 951, Pomona, Cal.*
73. Florence E. Daniels; m. * Rev. E. D. Taylor.
73. Emily A. Temple; 204 *N. 8th St., Oskaloosa, Io.*
77. Ellen E. Metcalf; m. John Edmunds, not Edwards.
85. Cornelia B. Pratt; m. Richard W. Comstock, '74; 124 *Waterman St., Providence, R. I.*
89. Sarah H. Melvin; d. Mt. Holyoke College, S. Hadley, June 4, '95.
90. Almira F. Elliot; m. *Rev. Austin Hazen.
97. Ellen J. Fenn, not Feen.
101. Fanny S. Parsons; *St. James Place, Chicago, Ill.*

ADDENDA.

105. Allie R. Bills; *Oakland, Cal.*
127. Margaret E. Stearns; 3637 *Delmar St., St. Louis, Mo.*
129. Anna M. Galbraith, M.D.; 128 *W. 70th St., N. Y. City.*
131. Abbie B. Howland; *Demill College, Oshawa, Ont.*
  Sarah J. Lester; d. Brooklyn, N. Y., '95.
156. Florence J. Davis.; 917 *Nebraska St., Sioux City, Io.*
160. Bessie L. Leonard, Easthampton ; name omitted.
162. Fannie Clark, Worcester; m. Lawrence Bigelow, '89; *Worcester* (Name not previously recorded).
164. Grace C. Pitkin; m. Rev. Edwin Tasker, '95; 806 *Bridge St., Lowell.*

ADDENDA.

NOT HEARD FROM DURING THE YEAR 1894-1895.

'38 Lydia Gould.
    Elizabeth Lane.
    Huldah Mather.
    Persis T. Maynard.
    Abigail N. Spaulding.
'39 Elizabeth Charevoy.
    Elizabeth Fuller.
'40 Louisa A. Hall.
'42 Susan A. Thomas.
    Emily D. Badger.
    Adaline Blackwell.
'43 Harriet N. Pettee.
    Martha A. Richardson.
    Nancy M. Taylor.
'44 Elizabeth G. Bailey.
    Laura A. Bouton.
    Frances S. Child.
    Helen E. Safford.
    Catharine Sands.
'45 H. Rosamond Hall.
    Susan I. Nash.
'46 Abbie M. Ainslie.
    Clara Browne.
    Julia A. Pierce.
    Sarah A. Ransom.
    Susan Russell.
    Jane M. Scudder.
    Mary S. Swan, M.D.
'47 Elizabeth M. Hollister.
'48 Cornelia R. Arnold.
    Anne F. Avery.
    Elizabeth A. Avery.
    Mary A. Balcom.
    Mary J. Burdette.
    Sara Morrill.
'49 Mary L. Clancy.
    Sarah B. Clark.
    Andelusia Farr.
    Mary E. Hedges.
    Louisa Preble.
    Caroline A. Warren.
'50 Elizabeth D. Ward.
    Chloe M. Bigelow.
    Marion M. Blackly.
    Mary A. Crawford.
    Harriet N. Day.
    R. Alice Day.
    Anne E. Gates.
    Jane E. Hasbrouck.
    Eliza S. Hebard.

'50 Jane C. Lefler.
    Emma S. Miller.
    Emma S. Moulton.
    Jane E. Neale.
    Sophia W. Newcomb.
    Mary R. Norton.
    B. Jane R. Parke.
    Elizabeth G. Rieman.
    Sarah E. Smith.
    Anne E. Walker.
    Helen L. Wall.
    Arabella M. G. Wood.
'51 Martha L. Burnham.
    A. Eugenia Fowler.
    Jane M. Baldwin.
    Esther Edwards.
    Elizabeth J. Goddard.
    Eleanor Kevney.
    Anna Mersereau.
    Cornelia Towne.
'52 Emily A. Braddock.
    Henrietta W. Briggs.
    Rebecca H. Broaders.
    Mary S. Butler.
    Aurelia Davis.
    Eliza J. Henderson.
    Alice M. Lindsley.
    Anna E. Purdy.
    Mary L. Stevens.
    Cornelia E. Wheeler.
    A. Maria W. Wood.
53 Martha Littlefield.
    Martha A. Bailey.
    Harriet S. Cooper.
    Jane A. Covert.
    Frances A. Hitchcock.
    Eleanor H. Schanck.
    Mary E. Scofield.
'54 Julia J. Goodsell.
    Amanda M. F. Gowan.
    Lucretia A. Bean.
    Melissa A. Lindsey.
    Rose Moore.
    Kate A. Ross.
'55 Sarah A. Adams.
    Sarah A. Burton.
    Agnes E. Barney.
    Oella Brown.
    Maria Critchlow.
    Helen A. Dodge.

ADDENDA. 287

'55 Annette Hancock.
Aurelia L. Linsley.
Marie A. Morris.
Sarah M. Reeve.
'56 Lucy W. Armstrong.
Louise A. Foster.
Mary A. Holmes.
Phebe A. Howell.
Emma M. Hughes.
H. Maria Lawrence.
Mary F. Lawrence.
Sarah Rice.
Elizabeth Sears.
Louisa P. Sill.
Mary P. Sloan.
'57 Mary M. Hunt.
Annie E. Coates.
Juliet B. Smith.
Julia M. Utley.
Abbie C. Walker.
'58 Ruth A. Courtright.
Ellen Swett.
Sarah A. Floyd.
Emeline A. Hawley.
Mattie M. K. Marcy.
Almira P. Miner.
Harriet M. Rogers.
Ellen J. Treadway.
Mary A. Whitney.
'59 Chloe S. Abbott.
Elizabeth P. Bolles.
Lucy T. Griffin.
Emily O. Pelton.
'60 Harriet L. Dolson.
Sarah Pearson.
'61 Mary W. Danforth.
Ellen C. Stebbins.
Elizabeth B. Stevens.
Francena A. Whipple.
'62 Sophia W. Hayes.
Susan M. Keyes.
Sarah E. Tewksbury.
Elizabeth W. Weller.
'63 Elizabeth A. Ford.
Emma E. Brown.
A. Adelaide Hallock.
Elizabeth A. Mansfield.
Elizabeth S. Maxwell.
'64 Cornelia H. Bissell.
Adelaide Baldwin.
Laura V. Bell.

'64 Rebecca B. Claggett.
Emma L. Ecker.
Henrietta C. Emerson.
Grace Essex.
Matilda E. Gilbert.
Frances E. Kingsley.
Aurora M. Lee.
Helen E. Smith.
Helen Tincker.
Ella E. Tubbs.
'65 Alice L. Bishop.
J. Luella Gage.
Harriet A. Holmes.
Mary P. Hyde.
Dorcas H. Johnston.
Mary K. Jones.
Theodora C. P. Kanouse.
Dana McAlpine.
Josephine G. McNear.
Grace Pearson.
Sarah F. Sheffield.
Ellen M. White.
Maria E. Worrell.
'66 Mary M. Perry.
Mary L. Battelle.
Esther C. Birdsey.
Amelia M. Davis.
Ella L. Foster.
Effie M. Hayes.
Helen R. Marshall.
Jane S. Peet.
Mary E. Rogers.
Mary G. Westfall.
'67 Ellen L. Bennett.
Carrie P. Biggam.
Susan C. Watson.
Clara E. Wheeler.
M. Louise Bassett.
Eleanor F. Chase.
Abbie D. Cleaveland.
Anna E. Davis.
M. Belle Davis.
Julia C. Fidler.
Margery R. Johnson.
Gertrude A. Keith.
Fanny A. King.
Elizabeth W. McNaughton.
Frances C. Mills.
Ellen C. Tenbrook.
Esther M. Tidd.
'68 Charlotte A. Bishop.

ADDENDA.

'68 Katharine S. Chamberlain.
Mary A. Dunham.
Mary L. Fogle.
Clara A. French.
Ellen P. Furey.
Jane P. Garland.
Sophronia D. Gerst.
Margaret C. McKillip.
Adelia W. Sutton.
Arista Thurston.
'69 Charlotte E. Smith.
Amanda H. Blakslee.
M. Agnes Brown.
Mary O. Dunning.
Eunice L. Perry.
Kate M. Petrie.
Emma C. Putnam.
'70 Emma M. Adams.
Florence A. Carr.
Elizabeth J. Case.
Letitia B. Ronk.
Isabella E. Styles.
71 Mary E. Thompson.
Frances E. Corle.
Eliza R. Crump.
Mary E. Mack.
Mary E. Thompson.
72 Jeannette Judd.
'73 Kate W. Sparhawk.
Sarah M. Colby.
Eliza B. Fairchild.
Kate A. Freyermuth.
Mary Plowman.
H. Blanche Williams.
Minnie A. Williams.
'74 Eva R. Barber.
Emma A. Hotchkiss.
'75 Florence M. Colby.
'76 Laura Hilburn.
Mary E. Jaques.
Alice J. McLillan.
Harriette D. Randall.

'77 Eliza W. Tuttle.
Eva V. Ainsworth.
Keziah Ayres.
Mary L. Bottom.
N. Viola Bumstead.
Mary H. Conklin.
Anna E. Kemble.
Adelaide K. Smith.
Sallie Spilman.
Mary C. Wever.
'78 Metta E. Angell.
Marie F. Holt.
Annie M. Lawrence.
'79 Rowena P. Cooke.
Kate Blunt.
Louise M. Clark.
Mary L. Payn.
'80 Sarah B. Griggs.
Ida M. Jenks.
'81 Mabel E. Schuyler.
'82 Elizabeth Goodnough.
Mary G. Barnes.
Emily C. Byorth.
W. Josephine Wales.
'83 Julia B. Arthurs.
Maud M. Dickinson.
Corinne Whitaker.
Alberta K. Williams.
'84 Jeannette M. Avery.
Emily F. J. Bird.
Isabella J. Davidson.
Susie T. Duff.
Helen M. Fitch.
Florence N. Smith.
Marie A. Switzer.
'85 N. Augusta Everitt.
'86 Mary B. McLain.
Marion L. Sherman.
'88 Ada L. Blanchard.
'91 Anna C. Gill.
'92 Maud M. Rollins.
'93 Frances C. Richardson.

CONSTITUTION
OF THE MOUNT HOLYOKE ALUMNÆ ASSOCIATION.

Art. I. This Association shall be called the Mount Holyoke Alumnæ Association.

Art. II. All present or former pupils of the Seminary or College, including non graduates, may become members by the annual payment of one dollar.

Art. III. The object of this Association shall be to promote the prosperity of the College in recognition of its claim upon those who have received from it so "freely." This Association shall seek to incite all to increased devotion to the service of Christ.

Art. IV. The officers shall consist of a President, twelve or more Vice-Presidents, a Secretary, and a Treasurer. An Executive Committee shall also be chosen from among these officers.

Art. V. The President shall preside in all meetings, and, in case of a tie, shall have the casting vote. In case of the President's absence, her duties shall be performed by one of the Vice-Presidents.

Art. VI. The Secretary shall keep a record of the proceedings of each meeting, prepare for the annual meeting a report of the transactions of the year, and, under the direction of the President, shall give all necessary notices. She shall also preserve all important documents relating to the work or history of the Association.

Art. VII. The Treasurer shall keep an account of all receipts and expenditures, and shall disburse money only as directed by the President of the Society, the First Vice-President, and the President of the College. She shall present the condition of the Treasury at each meeting and prepare a full report for the annual meeting.

Art. VIII. The Secretary and the Treasurer shall be elected from the members of the Faculty resident at the College.

Art. IX. The officers shall be elected for a term of two years.

Art. X. The presence of twenty members at any regularly appointed meeting shall constitute a quorum for the transaction of business.

Art. XI. The Constitution may be amended at any regular meeting by a vote of two thirds of the members present and voting; a notice of its proposed amendments having been given at the previous meeting.

Art. XII. The annual meeting of this Association shall be held at Mount Holyoke College during Commencement week; another in connection with the annual meeting of the American Board, and other special meetings as the President shall direct.

Art. XIII. The President of each local Association shall be *ex officio* a Vice-President of the Mount Holyoke Association.

OFFICERS.
Elected June, 1894.

President, Mrs. Moses Smith.

Vice-Presidents.

1st Vice-Pres. Mrs. Wm. H. Fairchild,
" Susan Tolman Mills,
" Helen French Gulliver,
" Sarah Foster Rhea,
Miss Anna C. Edwards,
Mrs. Sarah Fairbanks Stone,
Miss Harriet E. Sessions,

Mrs. Harriet Bronson Merriam,
" Jane Carpenter Pomeroy,
" Caroline Clark Woods,
" Jeannette Fisher Moore,
" Orlando Mason,
" A. A. Smith,
" Charles C. Baldwin,

ADDENDA.

Mrs. Henry D. Hyde,
Miss Mary Evans,
Victoria White, M. D.,
Mrs. Sarah Tufts Dewey,
and *ex officio*, the Presidents of Local Associations.

Miss Charlotte Jewell,
Mrs. Wm. H. Gulick,
" Michael Burnham,
" Harriet Haile Stebbins,

SECRETARY. Miss Louise F. Cowles.
TREASURER. Miss Sarah H. Melvin.

LOCAL ASSOCIATIONS.

New Haven, formed Oct., 1871; Hon. President. Mrs. Wm. H. Fairchild; President, Miss Emma J. Sloan.
Of the Northwest. formed Nov., 1874; President, Mrs. Zella Allen Dixson.
Worcester and Vicinity, formed May, 1875; President, Mrs. Alonzo S. Kimball.
Hawaiian, formed March, 1879; President, Miss Martha Chamberlain.
Boston and Vicinity, formed Nov., 1882; President, Miss Laura S. Watson.
Philadelphia and Vicinity, formed Feb., 1886; President, Mrs. Henry O. Wilbur.
New York, Brooklyn and Vicinity, formed Feb., 1886; President, Mrs. Edwin Atwell.
Hartford and Vicinity, formed April, 1886, President, Mrs. Alfred T. Richards.
Franklin County, formed Nov., 1886; President, Mrs. John Cowan.
Pacific, formed April, 1887; President, Mrs. Susan Tolman Mills.
Hampden County, formed May, 1887; President, Mrs. Wm. A. Magill.
Eastern New York, formed March, 1888; President, Miss Mary S. Cutler.
Central and Western New York, formed Oct., 1888; President, Mrs. E. A. Huntington.
Hampden County, formed Feb., 1889; President, Mrs. H. W. Bosworth.
Utah and Rocky Mountain, formed Nov., 1889; President. Mrs. Lucius E. Hall.
Oriental, formed Oct., 1891; President. Mrs. Marcellus Bowen.
New Hampshire, formed Oct., 1892; President, Mrs. Isaac N. Blodgett.
Washington and Vicinity, formed Jan., 1893; President, Mrs. T. C. Dickinson.
Southern California, formed March, 1893; President, Miss Helen Peabody.
European, formed June, 1893; President, Mrs. Wm. H. Gulick.

www.ingramcontent.com/pod-product-compliance
Lightning Source LLC
Chambersburg PA
BHW032101230426
672CB00009B/1605